THE DIARIES OF

Charlotte Perkins Gilman

Midnight ——— Morning —

The clocks ring 12.

With no pride, with little hope, with uncertain occasional happiness, with no glad energy and living power; with no faith or nearly none, but still, thank God! with firm belief in what is right and wrong; I begin the new year.

Let me recognize fully that I do not look forward to happiness; that I have no decided hope of success.

So long must I live.

One does not die young who so desires it.

Perhaps it was not meant for me to work as I intended. Perhaps I am not to be of use to others.

I am weak.

I anticipate a future of failure and suffering. Children sickly and unhappy. Husband miserable because of my distress; and I —————— ! I

I think sometimes that it may be the other way; bright and happy; but this comes oftenest, holds longest. But this life is marked for me, I will not withdraw; and let me at least learn to be uncomplaining and unselfish. Let me do my work and not fling my pain on others.

THE DIARIES OF

Charlotte Perkins Gilman

Edited by Denise D. Knight

VOLUME I: 1879–87

University Press of Virginia / *Charlottesville and London*

THE UNIVERSITY PRESS OF VIRGINIA
Copyright © 1994 by the Rector and Visitors
  of the University of Virginia
First published 1994

Frontispieces: Diary entry of December 31, 1883–January 1, 1884,
and photograph of Charlotte Perkins Stetson, age twenty-three.
(Courtesy of the Schlesinger Library, Radcliffe College)

Library of Congress Cataloging-in-Publication Data
Gilman, Charlotte Perkins, 1860–1935.
    The diaries of Charlotte Perkins Gilman / edited by Denise D.
  Knight.
        p.   cm.
    Includes bibliographical references and index.
    Contents: v. 1. 1879–87 — v. 2. 1890–1935.
    ISBN 0-8139-1524-4
    1. Gilman, Charlotte Perkins, 1860–1935—Diaries.   2. Women
  authors, American—19th century—Diaries.   3. Women authors,
  American—20th century—Diaries.   4. Feminists—United States—
  Diaries.   I. Knight, Denise D., 1954–   .   II. Title.
  PS1744.G57Z465   1994
  818'.403—dc20
  [B]   94-4988
                                                                          CIP

Printed in the United States of America

CONTENTS

ACKNOWLEDGMENTS

I WISH TO express my sincere thanks to the staff at the Arthur and Elizabeth Schlesinger Library on the History of Women in America, and particularly to Eva S. Moseley, Curator of Manuscripts, for her generosity and kindness in answering numerous questions and for her support through the various stages of this project. I also wish to thank Patricia King, Director of the Schlesinger Library, for granting permission to publish this project and Marie-Hélène Gold, Photograph and Exhibit Coordinator at the Library, for her help in locating and preparing the photographs that I have included in this edition. The interlibrary loan departments at the State University of New York at Albany, where I began this project, and the State University of New York College at Cortland, where I completed it, also deserve thanks for their assistance during various stages of my research.

For financial support I wish to thank the following: the State University of New York (SUNY) College at Cortland Research Committee for awarding me a 1990–91 Faculty Research Program grant and Tom Bonn for his invaluable assistance with my grant proposal; the SUNY College at Cortland Alumni Association and Development Foundation for assisting my research with a travel grant; and the New York State United University Professions Professional Development and Quality of Working Life Committee for providing me a New Faculty Development Award. Without such support the undertaking of this project would have been extremely difficult.

The English Department at the State University of New York College at Cortland also deserves my gratitude for granting me a course reduction during the spring semester of 1992 so that I could devote more time to this project. Several of my colleagues, friends, and professional acquaintances have consistently offered support and encouragement. Lauren Stiles of Cortland College's Memorial Library deserves my sincere thanks for lending his expertise to the translation of passages written in French. I am also grateful to Cindy Pilok, who served as an undergraduate research assistant during the final stages of manuscript preparation.

Special appreciation goes to Cathie Brettschneider, Humanities Editor at the University Press of Virginia, for her good-natured and timely responses to the numerous questions I posed during the preparation of the manuscript. Cindy J. Hall's thoughtful suggestions were invaluable, as was her consistent interest in my work. Most of all, I am deeply indebted to my husband, Michael K. Barylski, for his unfailing support through every phase of this project: for bringing me countless cups of tea while I sat working at the computer, for reading and responding constructively to my manuscript, for cheerfully asking every evening, "So how is Charlotte coming?"—and for genuinely wanting to know. His sustained generosity has, in no small part, made this project possible.

INTRODUCTION

O N DECEMBER 25, 1875, Charlotte Anna Perkins's older brother, Thomas, gave to her a small leather-bound Excelsior diary as a Christmas present. Inside, he inscribed:

> Within this book, if *every day*
> You entry make of some import,
> On Christmas next, to you I say
> I'll give one dollar. *Naught if naught*.

> Each entry must *upon the day*
> *'Tis entered, entered be*.
> If this rule's broke and is not kept,
> Thou shalt get naught from me.

Fifteen year-old Charlotte enthusiastically accepted her brother's offer with "sincere thanks," and the next week she began a practice—the making of daily entries of "some import"—which would continue over much of the next twenty-eight years.

As part of the Charlotte Perkins Gilman Papers, owned by the Schlesinger Library on the History of Women in America at Radcliffe College, the extant diaries begin on January 1, 1876, with Thomas's gift and continue virtually uninterrupted (except for occasional omissions or infrequent breaks, most notably after the birth of Charlotte's daughter, Katharine Stetson) until April 19, 1887, the day before twenty-six-year-old Charlotte Stetson left for Dr. Silas Weir Mitchell's sanitarium to undergo the rest cure for nervous prostration. After a break of more than two and a half years, the diaries resume on January 1, 1890, and continue, with more frequent and more substantial breaks, until May 3, 1903, at which point they abruptly end. Thereafter, beginning in 1904, Charlotte Gilman preferred to keep engagement books rather than diaries.

Charlotte Perkins Gilman's biography has been well documented in numerous writings.[1] But even a brief overview of her life reveals a remarkable

woman who overcame incredible obstacles to become one of the most celebrated leaders of the turn-of-the-century women's movement. Charlotte Anna
Perkins was born on July 3, 1860, in Hartford, Connecticut, the great-niece
of author and abolitionist advocate Harriet Beecher Stowe. Her childhood
was characterized by loneliness, isolation, and poverty, particularly after her
father, a gifted but temperamental librarian and fiction writer, abandoned the
family when Charlotte was nine. Contributing to her emotional insecurity was
her mother's tendency to withhold affection, which left Charlotte exceedingly
wary of personal relationships. Moreover, the Perkinses' precarious economic
condition forced the family to move nineteen times in just eighteen years.[2]
The constant uprooting left Charlotte Perkins with only four years of formal
schooling, "among seven different schools," which ended when she was fifteen
(*Living*, p. 18). Her father's love of books, however, propelled her own intellectual curiosity, and Charlotte became largely self-educated as a result. She
frequented the public library and joined the Society for the Encouragement
of Studies at Home, through which she avidly read about ancient history and
civilizations. She also solicited advice from her estranged father about which
books might best prepare her to serve society.

The trials of Charlotte Perkins's childhood helped, in fact, to prepare her
for the life that lay ahead: they fostered an incredibly strong individual spirit,
an unwavering desire for independence, and an enduring devotion to hard
work. By the time she was twenty-one, Charlotte had decided the direction that her life would take: she would contribute something meaningful to
humanity. In her autobiography, *The Living of Charlotte Perkins Gilman*, most
of which was written at the age of sixty-five, she remembered it this way:
"From sixteen I had not wavered from that desire to help humanity which
underlay all my studies. Here was the world, visibly unhappy and as visibly
unnecessarily so; surely it called for the best efforts of all who could in the
least understand what was the matter, and had any rational improvements to
propose" (p. 70).

Healthy, productive, and secure in a loving relationship with her longtime
friend Martha Luther, Charlotte was set to conquer the world. In a letter
to Martha, she affirmed her desire to forgo the traditional roles of wife and
mother in favor of cultivating her intellect. In her mind the two were mutually
exclusive. "I am really glad not to marry," she wrote. "*I have decided.* I'm *not*
domestic and I don't want to be. Neither am I a genius in any special sense,
but a *strong-minded* woman I will be."[3] Martha satisfied Charlotte's craving
for intimacy and affection, and Charlotte believed that her relationship with
Martha would even "make up to me for husband and children and all that I
shall miss."[4] With Martha in her life, Charlotte seemed genuinely content.
Her autobiography offers a summary of the relationship that she and Martha

shared: "With Martha I knew perfect happiness. We used to say to each other that we should never have to reproach ourselves with not realizing this joy while we had it; we did, thoroughly. We were not only extremely fond of each other, but we had fun together, deliciously. . . . Four years of satisfying happiness with Martha, then she married and moved away" (*Living*, p. 80). Charlotte was devastated by Martha's decision to marry. "It was the keenest, the hardest, the most lasting pain I had yet known," she wrote (p. 80).

Then in January 1882, as Charlotte was still coming to terms with her loss of Martha, she was introduced to Charles Walter Stetson, a handsome young Rhode Island artist who promptly proposed marriage. Charlotte quickly declined, convinced that marriage would destroy her plans to contribute to the improvement of society. While holding the conviction that women should be able to combine marriage, motherhood, and career, she explained that the preservation of "self" was a key concern. In a letter to Stetson, Charlotte wrote, "My Individual Self, the Soul I hope you will meet when we are dead, is a thinking creature, and I hate to lose its cleareyed strength for even a moment."[5] Again and again, in letters to Stetson, Charlotte expressed the fear that marriage would bring an end to her independence. "My life is one of private aspiration and development, and of public service which only awaits to be asked. . . . I will give and give and give you *of* myself, but never give myself to you or any man," she wrote (*Endure*, pp. 29–30). Walter Stetson persisted for nearly two years, however, and finally, after he had suffered a "keen personal disappointment,"[6] Charlotte agreed to marry him, despite serious reservations. The marriage, predictably, was a failure.

The chronic depression that would plague Charlotte for most of her adult life had its origins in her engagement and subsequent marriage to Walter Stetson. While numerous entries in both her diaries and Stetson's reveal a marriage characterized by discord from the outset, Charlotte rather dubiously remarked in her autobiography, "We were really very happy together." And then, a qualifier: "There was nothing to prevent it but that increasing depression of mine" (*Living*, p. 87). The depression persisted, and within several weeks after the wedding, Charlotte discovered that she was pregnant.

"A lover more tender, a husband more devoted, woman could not ask," she wrote of Walter Stetson. Still, "a sort of gray fog drifted across my mind, a cloud that grew and darkened" (*Living*, pp. 87–88). More than two years before their marriage, Charlotte had informed Walter of her priorities and had clearly articulated the conflict she was now confronting: "As much as I love you I love *WORK* better, & I cannot make the two compatible. . . . It is no use, dear, no use. I am meant to be useful & strong, to help many and do my share in the world's work, but not to be loved" (*Endure*, p. 63). Despite Walter's best efforts to make Charlotte feel loved, her depression only deepened. If Charlotte had found marriage and work incompatible, impending motherhood, which would require the forfeiture of any remnants of freedom, was certain to produce disaster.

Katharine Beecher Stetson was born on March 23, 1885, just ten and a half months after Charlotte and Walter were married. The depression that Charlotte experienced continued to escalate following Katharine's birth, and over the next several months, Charlotte became dangerously despondent. A friend, fearing that Charlotte was going insane, funded her stay at a Philadelphia sanitarium where she underwent the rest cure, a new and experimental treatment for nervous prostration. During her six-week stay, the twenty-six-year-old Charlotte was fed, bathed, read to, massaged; in short, all responsibility (and hence, all power and control) was taken away. At the end of her stay, she was pronounced well, sent home, and told by Dr. Mitchell to: "Live as domestic a life as possible. Have your child with you all the time. . . . Lie down an hour after each meal. Have but two hours' intellectual life a day. And never touch pen, brush or pencil as long as you live" (*Living*, p. 96).

Charlotte Stetson returned home and attempted to follow the doctor's prescription; within weeks, she was on the verge of a nervous breakdown. Biographers have documented how the tremendous subjugation of her own desires—to work and to help humanity—in favor of fulfilling the socially prescribed roles of wife and mother resulted in her brush with total insanity. Fortunately, Charlotte was able to pull herself together, seek a separation from her husband, and move to California, where she began to thrive. For the first time, she would be free to answer her calling.

Although she had begun, tentatively, to develop her skills as a writer by producing a handful of poems and articles during the early years of her marriage, her career flourished after she arrived in California. In 1890 alone, the first year of her "freedom," Charlotte Stetson produced thirty-three articles and over twenty poems. She became interested in the Nationalist movement and began her work as a public speaker, lecturing to women's clubs and becoming active in the Pacific Coast Women's Press Association. For several months she edited *The Impress*, a small family weekly. In 1894, the year her divorce became final, Charlotte arranged to send her daughter to live with her ex-husband and his new wife (Charlotte's lifelong friend Grace Channing). Her continuing struggle with poverty and the demands placed upon her by her burgeoning but ill-paying career, made it increasingly difficult for her to provide adequately for Katharine. After her daughter's departure Charlotte Stetson spent much of the remainder of the 1890s on the lecture circuit, speaking on socialist issues and on women's rights throughout the United States and in England.

In 1898 Charlotte produced her groundbreaking work, *Women and Eco-*

nomics, which brought her international acclaim. In 1900 she married her first cousin George Houghton Gilman, and the marriage lasted for thirty-four happy years, until Houghton's sudden death from a massive cerebral hemorrhage. During the early years of their marriage, Katharine lived with Charlotte and Houghton much of the time and alternately with her father and stepmother, Grace.

Throughout the first part of the twentieth century, Charlotte Gilman's incredible prolificacy continued (see the Epilogue for further discussion of Charlotte's activities after 1900). She produced numerous books of sociological import, several novels, hundreds of short stories and poems, and her autobiography. Nearly all of her writing touched on human rights in one way or another. For seven years, from 1909 to 1916, she single-handedly wrote, edited, and published the *Forerunner*, a progressive monthly magazine of some 21,000 words per issue. In 1922 Charlotte and Houghton Gilman moved to Norwich, Connecticut, where she continued to write and to lecture occasionally. In 1932 Charlotte Gilman learned that she had inoperable breast cancer, and in 1935 she ended her life, citing among other reasons her diminished "power of service" to contribute meaningfully to society (*Living*, p. 333).[7]

Except for the early journals, the diaries that Charlotte Perkins Gilman kept throughout much of her life are not characterized by any kind of conscious literary style. She was not in the least concerned with producing a set of documents that could be lauded for their sophisticated eloquence or artistic effect. Rather, the diaries provide an often unpolished record of daily events. "My purpose in diary-keeping, since girlhood, was not at all to make revelations of feeling, though[t], or of incidents not readable by other people," she wrote in *The Living of Charlotte Perkins Gilman* (p. 244). That tendency to be "guarded" may well have been shaped by Thomas's teasing admonitions to Charlotte that he must read her diaries in order "to be sure that the entries [were] made" so that she could legitimately collect her $1 reward. "I must lookout," she remarked with mock alarm in that original diary.[8] At the same time, however, the pages of the diary for 1876 are full of declarations of unrestrained passion for one Willie Daboll, a young Providence actor with whom Charlotte was hopelessly infatuated, even though the two had never met. Certainly, much of the drama surrounding Charlotte's designs on young Willie was embellished for Thomas's benefit. Nevertheless (and despite disclaimers to the contrary), several of Charlotte's juvenile entries were recorded in shorthand for the very purpose of discouraging the prying eyes of Thomas and others.

Despite their failure to conform to standards of literary excellence, the diaries nevertheless offer a revealing look at the day-to-day activities of a woman who struggled against overwhelming odds to attain respect and popularity as an author and lecturer. At times confessional, at times startling, at times mundane, Charlotte's "old friend" or "beloved journal" offers a rare opportunity for the reader simultaneously to study nineteenth-century domestic life in general and to witness the consequences of one woman's rebellious rejection of the exclusionary limitations imposed by the "cult of domesticity" in particular. Indeed, the domestic scenes around which many of the entries are centered would likely be deemed too marginal for inclusion in a man's diary; for the nineteenth-century female diarist, however, such activities were considered noteworthy and invariably safe to record. But Charlotte supplements her record of domestic life in nineteenth-century America with a variety of unrestrained protests and spirited assertions. She damns those who oppose women's rights, castigates her young husband for attempting to "mould" her, sympathizes with another "victim" whose husband used his " 'marital rights' at her vital expense," reviles the drudgeries of housework, and derisively condemns feminine vanities on the pages of her diaries. From an early age it was apparent that Charlotte Perkins Gilman would not conform to societal expectations of appropriate roles and vocations.

On the whole Charlotte Gilman's diaries serve as a barometer of her state of mind: when she was feeling well, the entries are bright, animated, and often humorous; when she was experiencing her low "grey" periods, the entries are stark, eclipsed, sometimes cryptic. Except where she remarks on her dear friend Martha Luther and on Walter Stetson (and even then, infrequently), Charlotte's emotions as presented on the pages of her diaries are often understated. As she noted in *The Living of Charlotte Perkins Gilman*, the decision to withhold some of the most personal details of her interior world was a conscious one. In reviewing the diaries at the age of sixty-five, for example, during the process of writing her autobiography, Gilman was "amused by [the diaries'] paucity of material which might be eagerly looked for by—well, a newspaper-minded person" (p. 244). Although she was enormously affected by various events in her life—the deaths of loved ones, her decisions to marry, her long separations from Katharine—the diary entries depicting these turning points are frequently, and intentionally, guarded: they often consist of rather flat and factual reports that obscure the pain, the fear, the ambivalence that Charlotte actually experienced. There is, in fact, often a striking dichotomy between the living Charlotte and the voice that emerges on the pages of her journal.

The reality of Charlotte's life was that it was often complicated by intense emotional entanglements. The public persona that she cultivated from an early age, however, was strong, rational, and very much in control. Her exclusion from the diaries of the details of her intensely personal experiences, particularly after 1887, was deliberate: it was designed to protect the vulnerable part of herself that was at odds with the carefully constructed public image. Ever mindful of the imposing curiosity of the "newspaper-minded person," she preferred, instead, to capture on the journal pages "the living" in which she was engaged. Nevertheless, page after page of the diaries tells us much about the reality of her existence: the poverty, the hardships, the anxiety, the insecurity, the despair, the hysteria, the anger. But in addition to the many trials, we also witness the triumphs and strengths: the intellectual growth, the feisty spirit, the fierce determination, the drive to effect social change, the kindness, and the compassion.

Interestingly, Charlotte documented the majority of her most intimate thoughts not on the pages of her diaries—the traditional forum for confessional writing—but on odd scraps of paper that she kept in a folder marked "Thoughts & Figgerings" and in personal correspondence and poetry. Many of those writings have been collected in the appendixes in this edition, and they provide an extraordinary glimpse into the private Charlotte: often enormously insecure, suffering from emotional paralysis, self-reflective to a fault, a markedly different woman from the self-confident public persona. The striking dichotomy between the two selves—the public figure and the private woman—emerges on the pages of the appendixes. It is here that we see much of the sensuality, the passion, the desperate efforts to reclaim her health that contributed to the shaping of Charlotte's life.

Collectively, the diaries of Charlotte Perkins Gilman and the appendixes document a series of fascinating stories about the life and experiences of a brave and highly intelligent woman. The stories, however, are disjointed and fragmented; they are interwoven through the fabric of many years. While it is difficult to see a discernible pattern through a review of individual excerpts, the diaries become easier to "read" when entire selections, written over a long period of time, are examined. As in any life, some of the individual stories conclude; some intersect; occasionally some resurface after having been submerged and nearly forgotten. These analectic threads chronicle the experiences of nearly twenty years of Charlotte's life: her on-again, off-again romantic interest in the charming Brown University undergraduate Sam Simmons (and occasionally in his brother, Jim); her intense love of Martha Luther and the subsequent pain of losing her; her ominous premonition that her marriage to Charles Walter Stetson would prove a disaster; her unbridled contempt for Stetson as she left Philadelphia to undergo Dr. Mitchell's rest cure. They also tell the story of her mother's losing battle with cancer, her own struggle with chronic and often debilitating depression, her love for Adeline ("Delle") Knapp, her reacquaintance with her first cousin and future husband, Houghton Gilman, and, of course, the realization of her dream: to "find out what ailed society" and to improve it (*Living*, p. 182).

The early diaries included in this edition (1879–87) are somewhat different in content and mood from the later diaries (1890–1935), those written after her nervous breakdown. (No diaries exist for the two-and-a-half-year period immediately preceding, during, and following the breakdown in 1887.) The Charlotte of the early diaries tends to be somewhat more introspective, more methodical, and more playful, although certainly some of these characteristics are, at least in part, a function of age.

The sparse little diary for 1890, the first postbreakdown record and the least developed of all of the diaries, is a remarkable document; its understated entries paradoxically capture a rather dramatic transformation in Charlotte as she finally started to take control of her life. As the year progressed, the brief entries gradually reflected more confidence, more stamina, and certainly more output in her literary endeavors. In *The Living of Charlotte Perkins Gilman*, Charlotte commented on that "scrappy little . . . diary" (measuring only 2⅛ by 5⅜ inches) that she "tried to keep that first year [in California]" and particularly on the large gaps that exist. "The blanks were the drowned time, not even sense [enough] to make . . . scanty notes," she wrote (pp. 114–15). The diaries for the remainder of the 1890s, in contrast, show a woman still plagued by episodes of depression but generally calmer, more in control, more decisive, and far more independent. Together, the diaries document a life where periods of incredible productivity were juxtaposed with months of intellectual paralysis.

When Charlotte Stetson was preparing to travel to Philadelphia for treatment at Dr. Mitchell's sanitarium, she expressed regret that she would have to leave her diary behind: "I have kept a journal since I was fifteen, the only blanks being in these last years of sickness and pain. I have done it because it was useful. Now I am to go away for my health, and shall not try to take any responsibilites [*sic*] with me, even this old friend."[9]

Eventually, after she had achieved fame, Charlotte Perkins Gilman abandoned the practice of keeping diaries. "These diaries are a nuisance," she complained in the autobiography. She continued: "Page after page of those dismal 'downs' with the cheerfully welcomed 'ups.' Record of writing, record of lecturing, record of seeing people, record of housework. After 1903 I gave up the fat three by six kind, with two days to a page, and took to thinner ones, with seven days on a page . . . with the right hand page for cash account. These are big enough to set down engagements, train time, and such necessities" (p. 294). It is almost as if after having documented the climb, Charlotte Gilman no longer needed her "old friend." Besides, she had a new friend in the person of her second husband, George Houghton Gilman, and he acted as her advocate, her companion, her confidant, until his death in 1934.

But the diaries had served a useful purpose. They fulfilled Charlotte Gilman's need—indeed, her responsibility if we are to heed her word choice as she headed to Philadelphia—to document even the most trivial events as evidence of her "living." The living in which Charlotte Perkins Gilman engaged, and on which she based the title of her autobiography, is not exclusive to the work that she contributed to society; the living that she experienced was as much a result of her immersion in day-to-day activities as it was standing on a platform before a large crowd. The diaries are, above all, a validation of her life; they offer tangible evidence that it did, indeed, have value and meaning.

Charlotte Perkins seemed to sense, in fact, that she would someday be famous. In an extraordinary letter to her brother Thomas at the age of twenty-two (see Appendix B), she predicted the mark she would make on the world: "I have ideas and theories which time will develope. . . . Bye and bye when I know much more and hold such place in society as I will hold, perhaps I might write you letters that would be of some use. But now I am only acquiring knowledge, . . . and my 'ideas and theories' change and change as the years go by." She relied heavily on her diaries in documenting those changes as she wrote her autobiography some forty-two years later.

I was originally drawn to this project by reading diary excerpts in the various biographical writings about Charlotte Perkins Gilman; they picqued my interest, and I wanted to read more. I was, in fact, somewhat surprised that they had never been published, until I undertook the task myself. Editing the diaries has not been an easy project, but it has, unquestionably, been a rewarding one. My objective has been to make the diaries accessible to scholars, researchers, students, and general readers: to facilitate research, to broaden our knowledge of Charlotte Gilman's life, to continue to open up the field of personal writings to further inquiry and investigation. It is my earnest hope that the publication of these diaries will do just that.

NOTES

1. See, in particular, Mary A. Hill's biography, *Charlotte Perkins Gilman: The Making of a Radical Feminist, 1860–1896* (Philadelphia, 1980); Ann J. Lane's *To Herland and Beyond: The Life and Work of Charlotte Perkins Gilman* (New York, 1990); and Gary Scharnhorst's *Charlotte Perkins Gilman* (Boston, 1985).

2. Charlotte Perkins Gilman, *The Living of Charlotte Perkins Gilman* (1935; rpt. Madison, Wis., 1990), p. 8.

3. To Martha Luther, July 29, 1881, Gilman Papers, Arthur and Elizabeth Schlesinger Library, Radcliffe College, Cambridge, Mass. (hereafter CPG Papers).

4. To Martha Luther, July 20, 1881, ibid.

5. To Charles Walter Stetson, Jan. 29, 1882, quoted in Mary A. Hill, ed., *Endure: The Diaries of Charles Walter Stetson* (Philadelphia, 1985), p. 36. Stetson routinely re-

copied Charlotte's letters verbatim into his private journals to be "doubly sure" of their preservation.

6. See chap. 7 for further discussion of Charlotte's decision to marry Walter Stetson.

7. On the evening of Aug. 17, 1935, Charlotte Perkins Gilman ended her life by inhaling chloroform, preferring it, she said, to dying of cancer (*Living*, p. 334). Gilman's death mask, which was made by her daughter, Katharine Stetson Chamberlin, is part of the Charlotte Perkins Gilman collection at the Schlesinger Library. Although the cancer had caused her face to become emaciated, Gilman wore a determined and contented expression at the time of her death.

8. Diary entry, Jan. 1, 1876.

9. Diary entry, April 18, 1887.

A NOTE ON THE TEXT

THE PURPOSE of this edition is to make available to scholars, researchers, and students the personal diaries and journals of Charlotte Perkins
Gilman. Until now, the diaries have been available only through microfiche
copy or by personally viewing the original manuscripts—which is permitted
only in exceptional cases—at the Schlesinger Library at Radcliffe College in
Cambridge, Massachusetts.

Included in this edition are the complete extant diary texts written between
December 25, 1880, and January 1, 1900. There are no extant diaries for
1888, 1889, and 1895. I have chosen to focus in this edition on the nearly
twenty-year period (from the time when she was twenty to shortly before her
fortieth birthday) during which Charlotte Gilman first made her mark on the
world. These years best illustrate Gilman's development from a restless, high-
spirited, and rather opinionated young woman to a mature, internationally
known author and lecturer whose words and wisdom touched thousands of
lives as she attempted to effect social change. In addition, selections from
the juvenile diaries (those she wrote between the ages of fifteen and eighteen)
and the later diaries (those she wrote between 1900 and 1903, after she had
attained fame as a result of *Women and Economics*) have been included in the
Prologue and Epilogue, respectively; ellipses are used in these two sections
whenever I quote partial passages. In the complete diaries for 1880–1900, the
only material I have omitted, except where it seems particularly noteworthy, is
extraneous appointment information, account records, addresses, etc., which
Gilman occasionally included at the bottom of various entries; any ellipses in
these texts were placed there by Gilman.

Because the role of an editor is to be less interpretive than objective, I have
attempted, in the chapter introductions, to retain a fair degree of neutrality
while still providing as background an appropriate amount of historical and
biographical contextualization. Readers wishing to have a fuller psychological
profile of Charlotte Gilman should consult full-length biographies.

Texts for this edition were drawn originally from microfiche copy; the transcribed version was then verified against the original diaries housed at the
Schlesinger Library during the summer of 1991. In only one instance was it

impossible to verify the transcribed copy against the original text: the journal for 1880–81 has been missing from the Gilman collection for several years, according to the Curator of Manuscripts at the Schlesinger Library, Eva S. Moseley. Whether the diary was stolen or misfiled is unknown; efforts to locate it, however, have been unsuccessful. The 1880–81 journal transcription was, therefore, edited against the microfiche copy.

The Gilman Papers, including the diaries, were stored by Charlotte Gilman's daughter, Katharine Stetson Chamberlin, for nearly thirty-six years before they were acquired by the Schlesinger Library in 1970–71. During those years three of the extant diaries—those for 1891, 1892, and 1893—were badly damaged along the spine and appear to have been chewed by rodents or insects, most likely by mice or termites. On September 13, 1972, when she was negotiating the sale of her mother's papers to the Schlesinger Library, the eighty-seven-year-old Katharine Chamberlin wrote a letter to the library director at the time, Jeannette Cheek, indicating that some of the missing journals may have been "so eaten by termites that I destroyed them." It seems unlikely, however, that they were destroyed by Katharine since Gilman does not quote from diaries for the missing years—1888, 1889, and 1895—in *The Living of Charlotte Perkins Gilman*, although she quotes extensively from the other diaries. Moreover, the diary for 1890 is very clearly a "transitional" diary; it has all the signs of a writer attempting to reestablish a former habit which has not been practiced for some time.

The editorial method I used was a conservative one: my purpose has been to reproduce Gilman's original text insofar as typographical conventions allow. Gilman's spelling, capitalization, often erratic (and sometimes missing) punctuation, underlinings, indentations, and abbreviations have been preserved. In cases where parts of words are missing because of damaged or mutilated text in the extant diaries, I have attempted to reconstruct the passage based on the partial word. Where there is any question, however, as to the content of the text, I have indicated the missing text with *"msm"* (manuscript mutilated) in brackets. In cases where text is indecipherable, I have included a bracketed *illegible*. On rare occasions I have inserted missing punctuation within brackets to enhance readability. I have also occasionally inserted words within brackets for clarification of a particular passage. Any conjectural readings are indicated by a bracketed question mark. Only where something in the original may appear to be a printer's error have I included a bracketed *sic*. Gilman was a particularly poor speller; even the names of friends and/or acquaintances were frequently misspelled. She occasionally would even use variant spellings of a name within a single entry. On November 19, 1883, for example, Carrie Hazard's name is spelled both "Carrie" and "Carry." Particularly noteworthy is Gilman's frequent misspelling of her daughter Katharine's name (as "Katherine") in the months following her birth.

Charlotte Gilman not only had difficulty in spelling names; she occasionally had difficulty remembering people. "I haven't the faintest memory . . . of most of the names in the diary, but the record shows the kind of calls I had, from all kinds of people. . . . I do not, can not, hold in mind a fraction of the innumerable people I have met" (*Living*, pp. 134, 261). Her circle of friends and acquaintances was indeed wide; I have identified and annotated those people with whom Gilman shared a close relationship, those with whom she spent a substantial amount of time, and those who were well known enough to be included in *Webster's Biographical Dictionary*. A few people, however, remain unidentified, primarily those of whom there is infrequent or only brief mention.

In addition to having a wide circle of friends, Charlotte Gilman was an avid reader, and on the pages of her diaries she alludes to literally hundreds of works that she read. I have identified as many of the less-well-known works as possible, although at times it was impossible to locate obscure or incomplete titles. Annotation has not been provided for works that are widely recognized (e.g., Dickens's *A Tale of Two Cities*; Shakespeare's *All's Well That Ends Well*); historical works and biographies where the title conveys a strong sense of the content (e.g., *A History of Egypt*; *Carlyle*); works for which Gilman has included title and author (e.g., Rawlinson's *The Five Great Monarchies of the Ancient Eastern World*; Spencer's *Fairie Queen*; Austin Dobson's *Vignettes in Rhyme*); or works (primarily short fiction, poems, and essays) appearing in popular press magazines for which no index is available. As a rule I have not provided annotation for Charlotte Gilman's own works, except where publication information is particularly noteworthy. Readers wishing complete publication histories of Gilman's works are referred to Gary Scharnhorst's virtually complete listing, *Charlotte Perkins Gilman: A Bibliography* (Metuchen, N.J., 1985). His bibliography also lists information on published reports of Gilman's lectures.

Charlotte Gilman used numerous abbreviations in the diaries; I have expanded, with brackets, the first use of an abbreviation, left the abbreviation intact thereafter, and provided a list of those she most commonly used at the end of this section. Numbers at the beginning of an entry record the time that she arose that particular day. Dates have not been standardized; they have been reproduced as they appear in the original diary. Where Gilman included drawings and illustrations that were impossible to reproduce in the text, a note has been provided to that effect in a separate section entitled Textual Notes. Any of Gilman's own editorial emendations that were awkward to include in the text (particularly words that were written and subsequently crossed out) have also been documented in the Textual Notes. An asterisk in the text of the diary signals that there is a textual note; these notes have been arranged chronologically by year and date.

In addition to the Textual Notes, a full set of Explanatory Notes is included in a separate section. Except where they can be located in a standard dictionary, allusions to places, people, events, words, or objects that might be unfamiliar to the contemporary reader or that might benefit from clarification have been elucidated to make the text more accessible.

Also included in this edition are two appendixes. Contained in these appendixes are a variety of writings by Charlotte Gilman (and some by Walter Stetson), many of which are being published for the first time. They elucidate Gilman's life; in many cases, they enlarge upon what is only hinted at on the pages of the diaries. The enormous passion between Charlotte and Walter Stetson, for example, which is rather tempered in the diaries, is plainly apparent in the private writings appended to this edition. Appendix A contains selections from "Thoughts & Figgerings," a collection of miscellaneous perceptions or objectives that Gilman occasionally jotted onto little scraps of papers and eventually compiled into a folder. Appendix B contains verses, letters, and miscellaneous writings that are either tucked into the diaries or are alluded to in the text but located elsewhere (either in volumes 21 or 22 of the Gilman Papers or in an unprocessed addendum to the collection).

The diaries are arranged chronologically; the only substantive alteration I have made is to divide the text into thirty-four chapters (which tend to mark significant events, milestones, or other transitions in Charlotte Gilman's life) and to include titles and contextualizing commentary for each chapter, in addition to the Prologue and Epilogue.

COMMON ABBREVIATIONS IN THE DIARIES

Anc.:	Ancient
Art Ex.:	Art Exhibition
A.S.B.:	Alice Stone Blackwell
Ath.:	Athenaeum
Aunt C.:	Aunt Caroline
B.C.:	Boys' Club
C.A.H.:	Charlotte A. Hedge
C.W.:	Charles Walter [Stetson]
Dr. C.:	Dr. Channing
F.A.M. Club:	Friday Morning Club
F. in C.:	Friends in Council
G.O.V.:	George O. Virtue
gym. *or* gymn.:	gymnasium
H. *or* Ho.:	Houghton
h'k'f *or* h.d.k.f.;	
or han'ch'fs:	handkerchief(s)
Hist.:	History
K.F.W.:	*Kate Field's Washington*
Lit.:	Literature
M.:	Martha [Luther]
m.g.'s:	marigolds or morning glories
Mr. L.:	Mr. Lane
Mr. V.:	Mr. Virtue
N. N. Club:	New Nation Club
N.Y.K.:	New York Kitchen [restaurant]
Pas.:	Pasadena
P.L. *or* Pub. Lib.:	Public Library
Pop. Sci.:	*Popular Science* magazine
R.W. Park:	Roger Williams Park

S.F.:	San Francisco
Scrib.:	*Scribner's* magazine
sen.:	senior
S.H.:	Society for the Encouragement of Studies at Home
S. & M.:	Small & Maynard
S.P.S.:	Socialist Purity Society
S. S.:	Sunday School
sta.:	station
T.:	Thomas [Perkins]
U.C.W.:	Union for Christian Work
W.:	Walter [Stetson]
W.E.I.U.:	Women's Educational Industrial Union
W.J.:	*Woman's Journal*
W.S.:	Women's Suffrage
Xtian:	Christian

THE DIARIES OF

Charlotte Perkins Gilman

VOLUME 1: 1879–87

PROLOGUE

"Gentle reader, wouldst know me?"

WHEN Charlotte Perkins received her first diary from her brother Thomas at the age of fifteen, her entries were characteristic of what one might expect from any typical teenage girl: accounts of her love life, of her childish feuds with her brother, of her power struggles with her mother, Mary, and occasionally, of her ambivalent feelings toward her estranged father, Frederick Perkins. But it was the object of her infatuation, a young actor in a local theater company, William S. Daboll, who received much of the attention on the pages of Charlotte's diary for 1876, even though the two never met: "I saw him! I saw him! My own, dear, darling, lovely, handsome, tall, graceful, splendid, glorious, excruciating, gorgeous, Willie Daboll! Bless him! Bless him! Bless him! & he saw me! Hurrah!" [*] Charlotte also experienced the thrill of anticipation: "Willie has been in Worcester . . . & is coming here! In 'As You Like It'! And *I'm* going!!! Just think of it! It's too lovely to happen! To sit & see him for a whole evening! I can't believe it possible!" And over the next several days, a series of sightings: "Oh I wish I could get acquainted with him!" "Oh be joyful! I saw my darling 4 times. And he saw me! And I blushed! What should I do if I was introduced?" "Saw my darling . . . I love him more & more every day. I hope he will always be happy." Day after day the pages of Charlotte's first diary chronicle the hope, the ecstasy, and, inevitably, the profound disappointment of young love. "Oh Dear! is it never going to be anything more?" "W. S. D. has been seen walking with a lady on Westminster St. several times. Alas! poor Charlotte! T'is false! Prove it!" And then, toward the end of the year: "I went down St. & saw him! He visibly sneered! I am devoured with grief."

While the year 1877 brought an end to her heartache over the unrequited love of Willie Daboll, the diary entries remained strikingly similar, although

---

[*]Unless otherwise noted, all quotations in the chapter introductions are taken from entries within that chapter. Excerpts from letters are taken from unpublished correspondence in the collection of Gilman Papers at the Schlesinger Library, Radcliffe College.

somewhat less melodramatic, as Charlotte approached her eighteenth year in
Providence, Rhode Island. Cousin Arthur Hale, who was attending Harvard University, became Charlotte's primary romantic interest, and the two exchanged
frequent letters. During a visit to Boston in early 1877, the two cousins enjoyed
some cozy time together: "A[rthur]. & I go to see the 'Scarlet Letter.' Had a
nice time. Then lunched on gingerbread in the seclusion of the red parlor. The
friendly A. evidently likes his little cousin." But Charlotte's interest in Arthur
wasn't very serious, and there were plenty of other callers who were vying for her
attention during 1877 and 1878. Still, Charlotte grew impatient whenever Arthur
failed to keep in touch. In June, for example, Charlotte remarked in her diary:
"Guess Arthur is 'sick or in prison.' What can ail him?" The next day, her loneliness was apparent. "I wish I had a 'feller,' " she wrote. Finally, two days later,
she received a card from Arthur. "The dear boy sends me his photo. He *is* homely.
But so nice!" By the end of 1878, she had lost her interest in him altogether.
"I like him less and less unfortunately," she wrote on December 28. "He grows
homlier and homlier. . . . I wouldn't mind that if he would only dress well, and
was not so conceited."

While matters of the heart were prominent among Charlotte's confessions in
her juvenile diaries, so too was her tendency to exaggerate the most mundane
and trivial of events, particularly those which threatened her self-image as she
stood stranded on the shaky threshold between adolescence and womanhood. A
few days before her seventeenth birthday, for example, Charlotte was chagrined
by a comment made by a friend's father. "Mr. Carpenter mortally offends me by
thinking I was about 15! And I *seventeen* next Tuesday!" And later that summer,
"Twilight conversation with mother on all sorts of potent grave and reverend subjects. Verily I am grown exceeding old." And the next year: "Mother & I go to see
Mary Anderson in Romeo & Juliet. Very fine indeed, but alas. At eighteen I am
already losing my delight for the theatre. It is a pity."

But in addition to anxieties about age and identity, also embedded in the pages
of Charlotte's teen diaries are subtle allusions to the work ethic that was already
beginning to form and would influence so dramatically her future years. "Have
taken a fancy to work hard and be very smart," she wrote in March 1877. And in
August she chided herself for wasting precious time: "What a wasted day! I have
accomplished nothing. Neither learned anything, or grown any. Home and work
is best." In October, after a particularly hard wash day, the seventeen-year-old
Charlotte altered Benjamin Franklin's familiar maxim to fit her own burgeoning
feminism: "Go to bed at 7!! Early to bed, and early to rise, makes women healthy
contented and wise," she wrote cheerfully. While much of Charlotte's work during her adolescence was of the domestic kind—sewing, washing dishes, cleaning
house, and the like—she also tried her hand briefly at employment outside of the
home. In December 1877, for example, she worked as a cashier for a few days, and

in late 1878 she was employed for two weeks by a Mr. Tingley, of a marble works company, to help in the design of marble monuments.

In September 1878 a friend of her parents began encouraging Charlotte to attend the Rhode Island School of Design, which was to open in Providence that fall. Her father was unusually supportive. "Go to the School of Design by all means, and learn all you can. You could not do a better thing," he wrote to Charlotte. She promptly enrolled as a member of the day class for 1878–79. A few weeks after classes commenced, Charlotte herself began teaching art to others. At the age of eighteen, Charlotte Anna Perkins was already educating people: offering encouragement and teaching them how. It was a pattern which would last a lifetime.

The Prologue contains selections written by Charlotte Perkins between January 1, 1879, and December 24, 1880, after which I have included the complete, unabridged diaries dating from December 25, 1880, through January 1, 1900. At the beginning of 1879, Charlotte abandoned her commercial diary in favor of a journal, which would allow her unrestricted space for making entries. The year 1879 also marked the beginning of a subtle shift away from the juvenile nature of the diaries, as Charlotte began to grow—intellectually, socially, artistically. Still, we see both sides of the girl/woman. On the one hand, Charlotte was earnestly practicing a course of self-improvement, not unlike Benjamin Franklin's plan for moral perfection: she was trying to make herself less egotistical, attempting to outgrow laziness, and, most importantly, exercising control over her own life. On the other hand, she could still be incredibly childlike, writing some of her diary entries entirely in verse (see, for example, the entries dated January 9 and 10, 1879) or naively dismissing the gravity of the diptheria that she and Thomas both contracted early in the year. Still, 1879 was, in many ways, a turning point for Charlotte. It marked the beginning of her lifelong friendships with Martha Luther and Grace Channing, and late in the year a visit to her aunt Katie Gilman reacquainted Charlotte with her twelve-year-old cousin, Houghton, whom she would marry some twenty-one years later.

Charlotte's friendships continued to blossom in 1880 when Martha Luther introduced her to the brothers Jim and Sam Simmons, with whom she would share a long, if turbulent, friendship. But on-again, off-again relationships aside, Charlotte had more serious matters with which to contend, particularly the poverty against which she and her mother, Mary, were constantly struggling. Brother Thomas had moved to Nevada in the fall of 1879 to work as a surveyor (*Living*, p. 92), and father Frederick Perkins, who was living in Boston, rarely offered financial support to his estranged family. Charlotte attempted to contribute whatever monies she could to the household budget, but there were some lean times. After an entry noting the receipt of seventy cents, for example, Charlotte added simply, "It goeth to squench our hunger." Fortunately, in late 1880 Charlotte learned that an aunt had bequeathed $66 to her and Thomas. Though it was a small sum, it would carry the family through the current financial shortfall.

Jan. 1st. 1879.

Having kept a diary for three years, and not liking a set space, I herewith begin on a journal.[1]
It feels good.
Gentle reader, wouldst know me? Verily, here I am. 18 years old. 5 feet, 6½ in. high. Weigh some 120 lbs. or thereabouts. Looks, not bad. At times handsome. At others decidedly homely. Health, Perfect. Strength amazing. Character———. Ah! Gradually outgrowing laziness. Possessing great power over my self. *Not* sentimental. Rather sober and bleak as a general thing. At present I am not in love with anybody; I don't think I ever shall be.

I arose late this morning and was somewhat lazy. Am committing Macaulay[']s Horatius to memory. Skate all the afternoon with T[homas]. Fourth trial. (1st this year). Really progress. Thomas goes in the evening to a church-social-New-Years-party affair, but on account of an unpleasant eminence of a ruddy hue on my fair brow, and the unsuitableness of my one dress, and the necessity for early rising tomorrow, and lack of inclination to go, I stay at home. Fix things for school tomorrow, and christen my new inkstand and beloved Journal.
Cloudy all day. A little cold dredge of snow at dusk.

Jan. 3rd.

Windy and *very* cold. But with fresh air to feed the fire I carry a furnace inside which keeps me warm. Make a great step in drawing. i.e. learn to grasp the spirit of the thing and draw that. Really improved on my copy. Enter into a solemn contest with Miss Salisbury & Blanche Vaughn to which of us makes the best bread.

Jan. 4th. 1879.

. . . I have decided that I *will* get married. Whereas before, I thought it more likely that I should not. Purpose: Happy man and Noble Family. "Our Sis-tah! Oh! has spoken!"

Jan. 8th.

Skate on Roger Williams park with Mary Jackson. See many fair damsels & noble youths. Skate with a noble youth by the name of Mathewson. Learn much. Tea, & spend evening at Mary's. Very pleasant time. Play Buffalo. Walk 3 mile. Skate 2 h.

Jan. 9th.

All through the muggy morning we were snug and warm within, but the snow was drop, drop, dropping on the muffled roof of tin. And now through the long evening we still are snug within, but the rain is drip, drip, dripping on the sounding roof of tin. . . . I endeavor to poetize, with but indifferent success.

Friday. Jan. 10th.

The weather changed last night to cold, and I this morning did behold, as I unto my school did go, a dreary waste of ice and snow. I fear that skating now is fled, but sleighing cometh in its stead.

Tues. Jan. 14th. 1879.

. . . Am overtaken, greeted, and affably conversed with by Mrs. Putnam. Subject "Sydney." [2] Messieur Thompson denotes his arrival by an ambiguous card, and follows it by his noble prescence. . . . He is fair to average.

Jan. Wed. 15. 1879.

. . . (Private.) Mentally canvass young Thompson. Ans. Won't do.

Jan. Wednesday. 22. 1879.

. . . Fred Keach appeareth & asketh me to a sleighride. . . .

Jan. Saturday. 25th. 1879.

. . . Morning at Essay Club. Very pleasant. Quite distinguish myself in discussion. Saunter home in balmy sunshine, eating snowball. . . .

{Jan. 27th}

Behold a day is lost! in this wise. On Monday eve, at half past six, I departed with lord Keach to our unfortunate sleighing party. It rained. We rode in a moving wagon on runners. . . . Great fun in the sleigh. They put the lantern out! Oh-o-o! Stop at Ryder's house North Attleboro. Supper. then dance till one or after. I didn't dance but was besought thereto. . . . Rode home in pitch darkness, and damp warmness. "Lie still Miss Perkins"!!!! Potter home in the wet at 4.30 A.M.

Wednesday. Jan. 29. 1879.

. . . Thomas owns to sore throat.

Thursday. Jan. 30. 1879.

Annie Aborn calls at school and expresses great grief that I did not go last night. It is pleasant to be missed, but I do not regret it. See the overweening Mr. Ernst at Riders. He converses with affable condescension. Ride home in the car, laden with claret & oranges for Thomas. He is worse. We bring down the little bed into the dining room, and make it as cosy and comfortable as possible. Dr. B[arrows]. arrives in hack at about 7.45. Pronounces it a case of diptheria. "And gave him bitter medicine". Poor little boy.

Saturday. Feb. 1. 1879.

Am awakened at 6.30. by T. who bangs incessantly and will not be appeased. If I leave the room he plaintively cries "Hi!" til I reappear, and when I am out will not be consoled. . . .

Sunday. Feb. 2nd.

Patient better. Toil and moil. John Willie appears at door and inquires for patient. Aunt Caroline[3] appears at door and enquires for patient. Robert Brown call[s] and invites me to go to church with him. Refuse on account of patients and contagion. Spit of snow. Cold.

Tuesday. Feb. 4th.

. . . Doctor says T. is all right now. Begin to write valentine. Mother went out for the first time since T. was sick. Having after much toil arrived at a state where pain and pleasure are nearly immaterial to me I now resolve to practice Duty for a while. Without the slightest doubt that as I progress it will grow easier and pleasanter till I shall never be tempted to forsake it. Of course some slips are to be expected, but I long ago learned not to be discouraged by them. A steady struggle if never wilfully relaxed, is invincible in such matters. . . .

Friday 7th.

. . . As I put on a damp nightie last night, and then sat round in nothing else, I have a not sore, but lame throat today. My worthy family very scared, consign me to a knarly grave. But I work all the afternoon, take camphor on sugar, dress up in fine array, wear wool wadding round my neck, eat ice, sip beef tea, and promise to be all well tomorrow. Thomas goes out after oranges in the evening. . . . If it were not for mother I had just a [*sic*] lief "go out" as not. As a tired child drops asleep, I could lay down my arms, and stop the endless battle, in this world, without any feeling but calm content. but I won't, for her sake; and—I blush to own it, because I should be pointed out as an example of foolhardy recklessness.

Sat. 8.

Alack and welladay! I have succumbed! Doctor here this A.M. Got it bad. . . .

Monday 10.

O-ho! Almost gone. feel quite well. . . . Mrs. Smith . . . wants me to come and visit her as soon as I am well. (As if I was sick! Why I havn't had a pain enough to call one, *no sore throat*!; not sick in bed!!! Call that *Diptheria?*)

Wed. Feb. 12.

The worthy and venerable doctor did not arrive as usual. Natheless I subsist in peace without out [*sic*] him. and sip up all my toothsome draughts with infinite relish. . . . Am unnecessarily lazy.

Feb. Thursday. 13. 1879.

Last visit of ye ancient physician. . . .

Friday. Feb. 14. 1878. {sic}

No Valentines! No regrets. . . . Mother is scared and blue. Her throat *is* sore. I believe I have no heart.

Feb. Sat. 15. 1879.

Mother has got it now. . . . Doctor here. Aunt C[aroline]. calls, all in a bluster, wants us to have a nurse. Not so. . . . Work some for a convalesent.

Sunday. 16.

Thomas sat up all night. I slumbered ingloriously. But then I needed it as I am not strong yet, and have all the work to do. . . . By dint of obstinate sitting up, and no persuasion, I am gratified to see TAP [Thomas A. Perkins] take a nap. From 8 to 12. Then I wake him.

Mon. 17.

Catherine comes, and does all the work and more. . . . Mother is very cross and fretty. As for me, I weep.* Pretty business. She sends me to bed at 8.

Wednesday. 19th.

Catherine comes. Irons and chores in general. . . . My time is principally occupied about now, in playing Go-Bang and Parcheesi with mother. Egotism should be excused in a journal. . . . I am by no means satisfied with my present condition. *Not circumstances*.

Thursday. Feb. 20.

Perform in their appointed order the various menial offices belonging to my present condition. . . .

Saturday. 22.

Hurrah! Go to the Essay Club! Read my Valentine. Make the acquaintance of my double, Miss. Blake, and Miss. Carrie Hazard (E-r-mense!)[4] She assaulteth me and demandeth my residence with purpose to call. Aha! I shall diligently encourage the Hazards one and all. For why? They are agreeable. They are smart. i.e. intelligent. They are (two of them) noble youths. They have a country residence in Peacedale. They have (here we come to it) *Saddle Horses*!!!

Monday. 24. 1879

Return to school and greet them with "My gallant crew; good mor-o-r-ning"! Am received with great joy, or the semblance thereof. . . . As for cash account, it would be objectless just now. I possess precisely 8 cents. . . .

Wednesday. 26. 1879.

Sweep all around. Change our bed back again into our own room, and replace Thomases in the dining room. He is sick again. Dr. Barrows says it is a rheumatic affection of the lungs. Exposure before he was entirely strong; the cause. He can hardly move or breathe for the pain. Mother has gone to take a nap, and I am "watching" in state. He asks for nothing but water. . . .

Thursday. 27. 1879.

Thomas is worse this morning. A torturing cough sets in. A little easier at night. Dr. Barrows A.M. Son P.M. Write to father about it. . . .

Friday. Feb. 28. 1879.

Thomas a little easier. I Had about 5 hours sleep last night. . . . The doctor comes again P.M. Looks anxious. Tells Phelons lung fever! . . .

{March} 2nd.

. . . I write father telling Thomas was worse, and asking him to come and see him.

March. Monday. 3rd. 1879.

. . . Postman with letter from father saying he will come if it is necessary! . . .

Thursday. 6.

. . . I wish I had some one to fight with. Possessed of reason. How blind people are! Here I never had anything to complain of in mother with the exception of—modes of speech; and it seems to be all that she has against me, yet one would think I was the worst of criminals to here my accusations at times. And Thomas too! One would think he had enough to answer for without molesting me. I must really abolish all desire for comfort or any sort of happiness if I expect to have any peace. Things look black tonight. A person who has a good creed and does not follow it is a weak fool. . . .

Saturday. 8. 1879.

. . . I read "House and Brain"[5] to mother. We were both permeated with cold chills. I like it. The mere contact with such clear strong ideas, the even mythical possibilities of the human will, have roused me from my enervating course of novel reading during these sick times. I long for science again. That is a weak girlish expression, "but it will serve". Spring on the south, wild wicked wintry wind on north side of anything.

Wed. March. 26.

[*Charlotte was in Boston visiting friends and relatives, including her father. She arrived there on March 24.*]

Read Daisy Miller. . . . Go to tea at Aunt Es. Arthur appears, and escorts me to see Fechter[6] in The Howard Atheneaum. "Monte Cristo".

Sat. 29th.

No bells were rung, so we rose late, and I presided over a second breakfast, with W.[7] at the foot. Engage the lordly youth in a game of beanbags. Touching Farewells and he departs for Cambridge. Nellie calls, more touching farewells. Am blue, and weepse. Rather enjoy it. . . . Persuade papa to put me on the train. He does so, but does not contribute the ticket. Mildly attempt to flirt with gorgeous neighbor in cars, but perceiving his station from "Yes, Miss," congeal. Fred Keach meets me at the depot. . . . Bring home a heavy cold.

Friday 4th. April. 1879.

. . . Go over in high feather to teach the evening scholars. With the fair Miss. Angel as co-assistant. Grand success as teacheress. We escort each other to our respective cars. Thus have I disdained the festivities at the chapel, and entered on a life of toil.———

Mon. 7th.

Privy conference with Mr. Barry. Confidential. Proposition—Teach evening school next winter, (6 hours a week for 8 months), return; $75.00, Certificate of vast value, and the years tuition in Day School free! We consider it. . . . Write to father.

Mon. April 14. 1879

. . . Robert Brown calls. Has found another possible place for T. Makes an extravagant offer to pay my board next winter if there is no other way for me to accept Mr. Barry's proposal. I think I see myself! People do not give something for nothing. Generosity without reason, is as bad as anything else in like case. . . .

Tues. 15.

Accept Mr. Barry's offer, recklessly. . . .

Sat. April 26.

. . . Ned Ely, blessed cherub, brought me some arbutus out of the goodness of his heart when I was away! . . .

Mon. 28. April. 1879.

. . . Paint a card with a sprig of arbutus and "thank you" on it, for Ely. . . . Fred Keach arrives in great state and a phaeton buggy to take me to ride. Mother and T. appear, and I depart. A very pleasant ride. My first. . . .

Thurs. May. 1st. 1879.

. . . See Caleb Burbank. He walks home with me from Governor St. I like him. . . .

Sat. May 3rd. 1879.

. . . Stop in with Carrie Hazard and Ada Blake at the college Library. Wash dishes, dress, and go per invitation of morning to dine at the Hazards. Stop for Ada. The friendly Arthur was the attraction. It appears that that beloved seraph had brought a copy of Monte Christo, and come to the Boston depo to give it me and bid me good bye when I left Boston!! I wish he had been in time. I should have had a pleasanter journey. I am escorted to dinner by the noble Fred Hazard in great state. . . . The friendly Arthur desires to walk home with me, but F. Hazard supervenes. Come home, denude, re-dress, and make bread. . . .

Tuesday. May 13. 1879.

Mama has a headache, and I am a little debilitated, so I don't go to school. Play 21 games of chess with mother, of which she beat *one*!! (the 20th). Vainly adorn myself, & retire in rather a morose.
Hot & lurid.

Thurs. 15.

Ride to school in open car model. Mary Channing brings me two letters, one from her father, the other from Aunt Isabella Hooker. She wants us to go there, take their house, boarding them for rent, and enough others [*sic*] boarders to keep them all. Small chance of a fortune, but a comfortable home. It would be very nice in some ways. A large handsome, house and grounds, less of the unpleasant if more actual work. All our friends & people,—a change of air, scene, &c,—. On the other hand, here goes my school of Design arrangements, and all the friends and acquaintances I have just begun to form. Farewell to my well-loved Miss Salisbury, to the serene Hazards, Ada Blake, and the other Clubbists. To all our pleasing cousins, and—to—"Kellup"![8] But as more there than sufficient counteraction, behold the gentle Gillett. Aha! Aha! Hot.

Actually Rain! at 9 P.M.

Fri. {May} 16.

Rain. Vegetation joyous in consequence. Mother & I ride down together to see ye circus. There isn't any. Meet her after school. dine at Café. Get gloves for me & other things. Purchase tea rosebud to paint. But Martha Luther[9] arrives and I don't. She stays to tea. . . .

Thur. {May} 22.

. . . See Martha Luther. . . . Martha Luther and her mother call. Robert Brown came over at about 3 to take me to ride. "O no, I had to sew carpets". No, my friend, the length & breadth & the height of it are equal, and you won't do. . . .[10]

Wed. May. 28. 1879.

Iron. Paint. We all go to tea at Martha Luther's.

Thurs. 29.

. . . Call at Channings to enquire for Grace.[11] Better. See Mary. She exhibits picters to praising parents. May Diman has had an accident.[12] Horse fell on her. Not expected to live. Last day of school. . . . Grand farewell. . . .

Tues. June 3rd.

. . . I am blessed with a cold sore of such amazing size & hideous aspect as to strike terror to all beholders.

Oh it is grievous.*

Fri. June. 13. 1879.

Class day. I don't go to anything. Mother goes out. Marthar Luther comes and stays two or three hours. Robert Brown comes to take me to ride. Don't go. . . .

Thurs. 19. 1879.

Sew with startling rapidity all the morning, crawl into the last dress almost before it is done, and speed me away to Boston. Meet Caleb on my way down. Tell him of my coming glories. Arrive all right. Am met by papa who who [*sic*] will give me no definite hopes of another year of support; merely saying that he don't know what his affairs will be next fall. He bestows on me by request, a pair of white kids as a birthday gift; and see me into a Cambridge car. Received with much joy. . . .

Fri. June. 20. 1879.

. . . Whom do I see but the saintly Almy. I straightway address him with "Neighbor, neighor, how art thee?" to which the bright youth answers instantly "Very well as you may see". . . .

Wed. June 25. 1879.

. . . Almy knows more tricks & games than any person I ever saw. He can play one tune on the piano with one hand, another with the other, and a third with his nose(!) at the same time. And he and his twin brother play a duet with their noses!

Thurs. June. 26. 1879.

Pleasant morning call from Edward. He gives me his photograph; choice of 6. I calmly inform him that I like him better that [*sic*] A[rthur]. And he blandly replies that I "had better restrain my ardor", as in a year or two he will be just like him!

Fri. 27 June.'79.

. . . Arthur arrived; not having received my letter at all. We play one game of whist much to A's disgust, and then I converse pleasingly with him till 10.30. I tell him about my lovers and lovees, planting him as the second of the latter. Which confidence he reciprocates by telling me of his four, of whom I was the second also. And all before Miss C! It was truly absurd. but I gained my point; we understand each other now, and rest on a calm super-flitatious ground. Much comfort will ensue. Possibly reinstatement. He seemed to enjoy it immensely. . . .

Mon. 30. 1879.

. . . Arrange letters & sich. P.M. read some of A's, & do 'em up in blackedged paper, singing mournful ditties about the perfidy of mankind. He sent me his picture this A.M. acknowledged by next mail.

Tues. July 1st. 1879.

. . . Am immersed in gloom—natural consequence of my late festivities

Wed. July 2nd. 1879.

. . . Discuss the Arthur question with mother in full. Decision. To refrain. Written by moonlight. And faith.

Thurs. July 3. 1879.

My 19th birthday. No gifts but those beforehand. Celebrate by having teeth filled. Rather enjoy it. Stop at Browns. Stop at M[artha]. Luthers. Card from her. Thomas goes off on three days cruise. Mother & I play bezique by moonlight! (*Pain* is a sure cure for ——)

Sat. July 5. 1879.

More tooth filled. Martha L. over. We babble in the woods. See a horse run and neatly skip out of his harness, leaving the wagon against a tree. . . .

Sun. July 6. 1879.

. . . Odd coincidence. One Mr. Rider gave mother a pearl paper cutter philo-peana, in 1845. She gave it to T. though I always wanted it. T. lost it. Robert found it, and gave it to Me! tonight. So I have it at last.

Wed. July 16. 1879.

Letter from Marthar Luther. Answer it. Am blue. Very blue. Lively thunder storm.

Thurs. July 17.

. . . Letter from father & Nellie. Father chose the "stylish" photo. and says in effect that I had better learn to dance if I want to certainly, but he don't like it. Nellie says "when can we come?" Oh-ho! And Almy is to be there! Hi-yi! We go Sat. Mother & I call on May Diman. I am invited to tea tomorrow. . . . Oh I am filled with friskiness[.]

Sun. July 20.

[*Charlotte was visiting Matunuck, Rhode Island, on the beach.*]

. . . We go out, a lot of us one day, Nellie and Miss L. paint, the boys swim, and I trot off and go to sleep under a tree quite romantically. Am prosaically discovered by Edward who awakes me up with a "Hullo! here she is." I refer it to the toadstool we ate to see if it was or not. . . . Edward surrounds me so I don't care for the interloper. Nice boy, E. I like him in a grandmotherly sort of way.

Sun. {Aug.} 24.

Sleep till 11.30. Lizzie Brown over. Stays to tea. Robert subsequently. Go to walk with him. Pitch dark Grove. Attempts a mild embrace. *First time* from *any* man! Quench his advances with much coolness. Becomes respectful, even awestruck. Hot.

Monday Sept. 1.

. . . Hattie & I *Sleep on the roof*! Make up a sumptuous couch of comforters & things on the slant. *Very comfortable.* So nice to wake up and see the moon and the sky. And flitting mosquitoes between me and the moon.

Tues. 16. 1879.

. . . Begin to systematize the ideas on athletics I have held for years with the assistance of Blakies "How to get Strong".

Present measurements:

Chest.	31 in.	Upper arm.	10–11.
Waist.	27 in.	Fore arm.	9–10
Thigh.	14–19.	Calves.	13.
Weight.	——		

Thurs. Oct. 30. 1879.

Walk down with May. Stop at dentists, and walk up with Martha. I love the pussy. Horrid windy.

Fri. Oct. 31. 1879.

The friendly Caleb walketh down with me, and, strange to say, the friendly Caleb walketh up with me. Martha over P.M. till 8.30. Do some Hallow'een tricks.

Mon. Nov. 3. 1879.

Hurry & scurry to get Thomas off. Mother & he down st. buying at a great rate. Trunk, valise, soap, candles, watches, etc. He goeth about & calleth on relations. I drop in on Martha P.M. Snow this morning, 1 in. deep! little more at 10 P.M. I don flannel & rue it, but endure. Cold.

Sat. Nov. 8.

Letter from Aunt Kate Gilman.[13] Bessie *died* last Thursday morning! Of an affection of the heart. The dear little girl got my last letter, when to weak to read, and held it in her hand or kept it by her all day! I am so glad she did not have to fret for the absence of it. . . .

Mon. Nov. 10.

So hot that I doff flannel, catch no cold, & thereby explode an ancient fiction.

Sat. Nov. 15. 1879.

Stop for Martha and go down street. Telegraph yes to Aunt K[ate Gilman].

Mon. Nov. 17. 1879.

On New York boat. 10.40 P.M. Rise betimes. hie down to depot and start for Norwich. No one at station so travel by the aid of friendly stranger to Aunt Ks. She immediately arrays me in complete suit of Bessie's clothes.* To my amazement and surprise she hales me away to N. Y. Houghton & Francis very nice. Aunt K. delightful.

Mon. Dec. 1st. 1879.

. . . Letter from Thomas, Houghton, C. Hedge & Martha. Paint. Go to M's. Stay to tea.

Tues. Dec. 2nd. 1879.

. . . Aunt Katie Gilman is dead!

Thurs. Dec. 4th. 1879.

Letter from Houghton. . . .

Thurs. Dec. 18. 1879.

Go to school for anatomy. . . . Pleasant lesson. Meet mother & shop till 2. Meet Martha & shop till 5. I have got every single thing I wanted, & more beside!! Spent $11.00 today. I have earned, so far $40.00!!! Letter from T. . . .

Christmas. 1879.

A Glorious & entire success! The best Xmas I remember. Retired at 12.5 this morning & rose at 5.30. Sweep and toil. . . . Lizzie comes here at 6. and helps me dress. Entertainment opened at 7 P.M. all lovely. My costume charming. More presents all round than anyone expected. . . . All lovely. All pulled their crackers & wore their hats. All happy. Robert in an hour or so. O I am so tired!

Cambridge
Tues. Dec. 30. 1879.

Ride over from Brookline. On arriving here go and call on the Hollands. Stay to lunch. . . . Mr. Ivan Panin, a genuine Russian Refugee here afterward. He was at lunch at the Hollands. Father in Siberia. Poor as poverty—entered college with a ten dollar bill, borrowed of giver. A Nihilist. Set him talking. It didn't take much persuasion.

[1880]

Cambridge. 11. odd P.M. *Thurs. Jan 1st. 1880!*

. . . Come home at 11 or near it, regretting not having said goodbye to Greeley, and, can I believe my *senses*, find that identical youth artlessly happening by as we get out of the back!!! Am going to a museum with him tomorrow!———— I never was so courted and entertained and amused & done for in all my little life. It seems as if the memory of today would last me in solid comfort through all the ills that flesh is heir to. I thought nothing was needed to my happiness when I rode home, and then to find Lewis Greeley actually loitering about to see *Me*! I cannot understand it. Not that I mean him in especial, but the attention.——The—the—why to think of its being *me*!

Boston. Jan 2nd. 1880.

Mr. Greeley, whom I have really begun to wish was a blonde, arrived at 9.30 or thereabouts, and he & I traverse the zoological & archealogical museums. Very enjoyable. He rode in with me, as I did not return for more farewells, and sought to prevail on me to go to the opera with him Mon. Then capitulated to Sat. I left it uncertain and dashed his hopes by a note this P.M. Letter from Mother which induces me to arrange for return on Sat. 4. P.M. train. As I shall be accompanied by May Diman it will be pleasant. . . .

I wonder,——, if,——,——,. Time will show. O, I had a call from

Nellie. . . . Dear Nellie. I think I've had enough. Work will seem pleasant. And swainlessness? Guess I can stand it.

Tired, body and soul.

Providence.
Sat. Jan 3rd. 1880.

Note from the gentle Greeley, regretting failure of opera scheme. Very respectful gentlemanly note. "Miss Perkins". "Yours ever". . . . Find a gorgeous New Years card from "Henry Alford Short." Jacket, N.Y. Card, & his card. All in a box. Beuteous. And I never saw him but once! Truly, my cup runneth over. . . .

Friday January 23. 1880.

Refrained like a fool, from going to school,
As mamma with a headache appeared,
But was grieved to remain, for she suffered no pain
the moment the weather had cleared.
6 cents I did spend, on three pinks to the end
of enhancing L. G.'s valentine,
and the rest of the day, spent in painting the spray,
with effect most uncommonly fine.
Went round to see Ray, at two P.M. today,
to get means for our next months survival;
Had a letter from T. full of pleasure and glee,
announcing his boxes arrival.
Left the dishes to Belle, who delighteth full well
on some pretext to come in & stay,
And by Bolan the gifted our ashes were sifted
and the cellar cleaned up for small pay.

Saturday. January 24. 1880.

. . . Anna & Annie Westcott in. Martha too. Wants us to come down this evening. . . . Whist. One Simmons appears. James Simmons, friend of Marthas. . . . Smart youth.

Thurs. Jan. 29. 1880.

. . . Mother & I dress for calls. Letter from T. He has been sick. Quinsy. Mother wails. Call on Mrs. J. Carpenter, & Jessie. . . . Very blue when we return to our lonely domicile. I revive on principle.

Mon. Feb. 9th. 1880

. . . Sit peacably down to sew, when who should call but Jim Simmons, Samuel Simmons son! I feel quite set up, for we never asked him to call, except with Martha. Not that he amounts to much, but he's a caller! *

Sat. Feb. 14.th. 1880

Arise and diddle about in full expectation of Valentines. Get 4, and a P. O. card from Cassie to mail. 2 Pretty cards from the girls, A funny letter from George Bissell. . . . And a mysterious epistle in ardent verse from some unknown individual. Hazards suspected.

Call at Martha's. She is better, going to matineé this P. M., and was quite pleased with my valentine. Is innocent of the mysterious one. . . . Meet mother at car, and get home just in time to receive a most interesting telegram. From the pleasing Almy, who sends a three verse Valentine in answer to mine. And so bright! And so witty! And so delightfully immediate! And so complimentary to come by telegraph! I am more pleased than if I had had 40. . . . 9 P.M. A ring at the bell. I descend. I open the door. No one there. I see a letter on the step. I claw at it. No effect. I claw at it again. I surmise. I examine my lily fingers. Chalk! Not a circumstance! O I am so pleased! . . .

Tuesday. Feb. 17th. 1880.

. . . Mother & I make a calling tour. . . . Travel home with intent to retire but Jim Simmons, Samuel Simmons son appears, and stays till 11. Dont like him. . . .

Wed. Feb. 18th. 1880

. . . Call on Martha. Jim Simmons, Samuel Simmons' Son called in my absence, and invited me to go to a concert tonight! He's getting as frequent as the bat.

Thurs. March. 4th. 1880.

. . . Go to Cousin Mary's to tea. Robert B. calls there, and escorteth me home. Don't ask him in, on the score of proprieties. Rather tired.

Sunday. March. 14th. 1880.

Aunt C. to dinner. Veal. Go to hear father lecture at Beethoven Hall. On Voltaire. Very good[.] saw and conversed with him. Found Martha there and sat by her. . . .

Tuesday. March. 23rd. 1880.

My respected papa returns the rent bills mother sent him. . . .

Wednesday. March. 31st. 1880.

. . . Aunt C. in. Mutually read "Jolly" [14] all day, and make gawks of ourselves over the last of it. Weep and snivel consumedly. I break down, and mother reads and sobs while I stand by the stove drying my handkerchief. I don't see why it is any worse to cry over a book than to laugh over it. And bogus emotion is better than real, for it leaves no sting.

Tuesday. April. 6th. 1880

Loaf. Go shopping. . . . Simmons. I cannot abide him.

Sunday. April 11th. 1880

Am industrious from 7.30 till 2. Paint a little on poplar tassels. Aunt C. to dinner. Mutton. Martha arrives infested with Simmons, and we all take a miserable frozen walk out Swan Point way. Horrid day. Wash dishes & write to T.

Monday. April 12th. 1880

Red letter day. Mr. Peck in with 9 ½ doz. eggs. Letter from Thomas & invitation to the Junior Ex. from Edward W. Taft. Ah-ha! Ah-ha! Aunt C. to dinner. Go to Helens. Am presented with an "at home" from Mrs. Burney! Ah-ha! Ah-ha! Of a truth I am coming out. They are going to the J. X. & will take me. (As I privily desired.) And, furthermore, as the crowning glory of all my desires, I—Am—to—be—Invited to Oak Woods this summer!!! At the same time as May! "Joy! Joy! my task is done! The gates are passed and heaven is won!" Go to Ada's with Carrie. Essay Club. Nothing original. Mary Bushnell sings like a nightingale. I like her better. Carrie sang also. Tea & cake. Back with Carrie. Mrs. Hazard gives me a gown & hat as was Helens. All gorgeous. Outgrown. I do love her.

Wednesday. April 14th. 1880.

Arise betimes. Spry. 2nd invitation to Junior X. *"James D. Simmons"*. Oh yis! Oh yis! We got out a calling. . . . Very warm. Shed under-f[rock?]. For this occasion only.

Tuesday. April 20th. 1880

Being utterly overcome with "spring-feeling" in general & laziness in particular, I don't go to school, but loaf about all day. Aunt C. in. Read aloud & sew on T's neckties. Mr. Lamb brings T.'s clothes. "It" and I clear up at nightfall. . . . Write to Helen & Houghton.

Wednesday. May 12. 1880.

Am considerably under the weather. . . . Letter from father. Says "D.G." will appear in the N. E. J[ourna]'l of Ed'tn.[15] Very good. . . .

Saturday the 22nd of May. 1880.

. . . New England Journal of Education from father, with my first appearance in print therein. "To D xxx. G xxx."

Thursday. June 3rd. 1880.

. . . Martha and Samuel Simmons called. In vain.

Friday June 4th. 1880.

. . . Invitation to the big spread [Harvard] Classday. No card. Simmons (Sam) speedily repeats his call. I like him.

Wednesday. June 9th. 1880.

Invitation to Pudding spread from *Arthur*! Hi-yah! . . .

Friday June 25th. 1880

Harvard Class Day. Rise at six. Charlie Staples calls. Mr. Greeley, Senior calls. I go to Miss Holland's a moment. Mary Poor and a Miss Heath here to go. I sit in the theater between Emma Holland, and Mr. G. Sen[ior]. Amuse him. Home to dinner. then to the H. P. C. spread. Then to Gymnasium spread with Dr. Hedge. Back again. Then to Walter's room.[16] Then to the tree with girls & Mr. Staples. Then to Mr. Greeley's room & others. Then home, in car to tea. Then to the Gymnasium where we sit walk & dance till 11. Then home all four & Mr. G. Home tired. Saw Arthur, Walter, Almy, Willistons, Elder, Staples, Birney, Hazards, May & Retta, Mary Channing, Longfellow, & Lorde, of others. I had rather stay at home with the much maligned Simmonses, whom since the advent of Sam, I regard as friends—Oh hum! I'm tired.

Saturday June 26th. 1880.

A more pleasurable day than yester. . . . Carry Club books to Hollands, and get directions for the Willistons. Trot there and loaf agreeably for an hour. Mr. Greeley drops in. Alice W., Sam W., & I go to a swell Archery Party, at Mr. Lowells grounds. *Very* swell. Longfellow himself there, Arthur, Greeley, & many other swains & damsels. . . . On such a pleasant day. Start to arch, and hit the red at the 5th arrow. After that no more.

Monday. June 28th. 1880.

Am quite "feak & weeble", and so much indisposed that my kind host send for the Doctor. A stately and agreeable man. He leave meddi; and says to go to bed, but I don't. No picnic of course. Mr. Greeley drops in about nine to see about it.

Friday, July 2nd. 1880.

Mama arrives in the rain. Spends the day. Nap. Walter Smith to tea. Nice boy. He goes abroad Thursday. Behold I have a letter from Little Haskins! Wants to know my address! So as to call if his business should take him to Providence. Oh-ho-! Ah-ha! Prehaps [*sic*] he can make his business go where he pleases.

Saturday. July 3rd. 1880.

My twentieth birthday. Kisses a plenty. Eke a V [dollar bill]. Three for mother & two for me. I send my address to Mr. Haskins. Only that. We go to Lexington. Very pleasant place. Willie and Harry instantly at my feet. . . .

Monday. August 16th. 1880.

Up betimes and iron. . . . Make belt for bathing dress. Mother is a bothering me.

Tues. August. 17th. 1880.

. . . Who should call but the gentle Jim! Quite "feak and weeble". Were glad to see him.

Mon. Aug. 23rd. 1880

. . . Mr. S. Simmons calls. I learn of him many things. secridly.

Friday. August 27th. 1880.

> . . . I chanced upon the guileless Sam,
> and home with me he walked,
> He was as quiet as a clam,
> although I talked and talked.
> Invited him to Sunday's tea,
> he actually refused!
> But we'll have Jim, for really we
> not often are so used.

Wednesday. Sept. 22nd. 1880.

. . . Go to Martha's. Get much satisfaction. Discovering from her that the infant Samuel has made her a mother confessor in part, I abandon my scruples and "tell her all". It appears that Sam really considers himself insulted and forbidden the house. Insulted! And here I have refrained from telling my most intimate friend on account of his feelings forsooth! And the stealthy Jim has known the whole business all the while! I wash my hands of 'em. Just let me catch him alone—perhaps I may induce him to reconsider. . . .

Thursday. Sept. 23rd. 1880.

Joy to the brave! (And the bold faced.) All is well. . . . Do several errands, and guilelessly happening into that blessed Post Office meet the recreant Sam. Bow. Give chase. Easily overtake. Excuse myself, and request a few moments conversation. He gladsomely leaveth his office an hour too early, and walketh home with me. I give him a large piece of my mind. He is finally convinced; as who could help being? The thing is entirely cleared up, and I feel very comfortable in my mind. Ma chére mama however is mortally enraged, and loads me with opprobrium. I answer not a word, and she is comparatively benign by bedtime. . . .*

Friday Sept. 24th. 1880

Clean the parlor and diningroom windows. Martha over in the morning. Dear little chick. Grub and scrub, dress up and go to Ada's. Learn of handmaid that she is over here via George. Scurry home. Mother had met and kept her. She brought me 7 pair of four button *Gloves*. All shades dressed and undressed. I walk home with her and she furthermore bestows upon me a pair of black silk stockings & a silver headed comb; balls on top. Lovely. I admire, extol and gratitudinize in fine style. Stop at door and have a word with Martha. Come home ready to drop, and ravenously hungry. Nice hot dinner all a cooking. Very tired.

Tuesday. Sept. 28th.

. . . I go to M's for a few minutes. Then down st. Sam whisks out and joins me, ten words or so. I slip steathily home by Crawford st. bridge. If he wants to see me he can come and do it. . . . Sam must have been watching, for he hopped out infront of me, and then waited on the bridge in the most innocent way.

Sunday. Oct. 3rd. 1880

. . . Martha comes. After preliminary fuss we go to walk. . . . Go home with M. & meet Both Simmonses on Pitman St. Sam turns and comes home with me. I think I shall be unSamified before long. . . .

Wednesday. Oct 6th. 1880.

Martha's birthday. I give her a horse chestnut, a pear, an apple, a needlecase, a fetich in many wrappers, the pocket atlas which Sam gave her yesterday and left here last night, and the M. letter which unfortunately didn't come. I spent the day with her from 1 to 6. . . .

Wednesday. Oct. 13th. 1880.

Fly about somewhat. Martha over. Wants to go to walk. Stops for me at 11, and we go way out beyond the Hopkinses. . . . Get leaves, revel in gorgeous land & skyscrapes, and thoroughly enjoy ourselves. Three hours fast walking *ought* to be 9 or ten miles. But we will meekly say eight. Jim and Sam appear and ask me to go on the Pawtuxet. I discourage 'em. . . .

Thursday. Oct. 14th. 1880.

Letter from C. Hedge & from Thomas. He is actually run for office! Republican nominee for county surveyor! Stop at Martha's with a "yes"! for the Pawtuxet. . . .

Friday Oct. 15th. 1880

Bright sunrise but cloudy morning, to my infinite disgust. . . . I don my flannel and call for Martha. Jim cometh for us and we seek the Bridge. Sam joins us there, only to inform us that he wasn't going! He certainly invited me, and Martha thought he was going as much as I. I was wroth at first, but the first glimpse of blue water was enough, and I haven't enjoyed a day more this summer. Such flames of maple and sumach; such emptiness of blue above, and placidity of blue below; such warm glowing sunlight; the tumbling rapids, and cool shadows————O it was the perfection of autumn glory in sight sound and *feel*. And we thoroughly enjoyed it. Reached Soccanosset at about 3.10. and then down through all the loveliness with the great round white moon and Jupiter looking at us. A feast indeed. Home by 9.30. . . .

Thurs. Oct. 28th. 1880

. . . Robert comes, and we produce between us some designs for advertising cards. Soap business.[17]

Tuesday. Nov. 23rd. 1880.

. . . Mother wants to go and see the Rawsons, but I hang fire, and Lo! A call from Sam. I open on him in full force with a "triangular row". Rake over the whole business from beginning to end, and settle up with mutual satisfaction. He departs in friendly mood, and all is serene. Selah!

Wednesday, Dec. 8th. 1880.

Mother is afflicted all day with a sort of dizziness, hardly gets through school. . . .

Monday. December 13th. 1880.

Up betimes. Sweep parlor. Letters from Thomas. Mother goes a calling all by herself. Sketch for cards, & do Christmas card for Jim. That youth arrives at about 6 and wants me to go to a sterioptican thing at Howard Hall. Mother smiling I go, and enjoy it immensely. One continuous giggle. Jim very polite, suggests chocolate drops, and does the devoted in fine style. Nice boy, Jim.

Friday. Dec. 17th. 1880.

Up betimes. . . . Edward & Henrietta come over and play whist. I sew on doll things for Alice, & Jim calls so I am not lonesome. The Browns depart hilariously at 10.30 or so, and Jim and I beat "the old folks" 3 games straight. One whitewash. James ameliorates. "I've had a very pleasant time" quoth he as he tripped home at 11.30. He never used to make any such remarks. It is all owing to Aunt Caroline's beneficent influence I tell her.

Saturday. Dec. 18th. 1880

. . . Meet Martha at Watermans, gyrate ceaselessly for some three hours, and lose about 3 dollars. We met Jim going up, and I laid 5 cts. worth of gumdrops to as many cream almonds that he would walk home with us, and won the bet. For lo! the Martha smitten youth saileth up Hopkins St, gradually overtaketh us, and seeth us severally home, bundle laden. Comes in and has some hot gingerbread and sits a while. Nice boy, Jim. . . .

Thurs. Dec. 23rd. 1880

. . . Had a letter from George Bissell today. It appears that there was some bank stock of Aunt Nancy's left around somewhere, which has just come to light, and Thomas & I have some $66.00 coming. Good enough. Therefore will I spend Carrie's five for Christmas & sich, and be gay.——

Friday. Dec. 24th. 1880.

Up betimes . . . finish Ada's cards. Carry the card I fixed down to Marthas, the others to Ada, & then go a shopping for the last day this time. . . . Send off 5 cards, Sam, Sam, Sam, Jim, & Mrs. Henry Anthony. Do up all my Christmas things. . . .

ONE

"As lonely a heart as ever cried"

December 25, 1880–May 11, 1881

BY THE AGE of twenty, Charlotte Perkins was a popular young woman with a keen sense of humor and a restless spirit. She and her mother, Mary, were often at odds, and Mary's provincialism would frequently leave Charlotte irritable or sullen. Sometimes, however, her moodiness was fueled by the reality of the Perkinses' poverty: her inability to afford new shoes, for example, caused extreme physical discomfort, and in the cold, snowy month of January, she went barefoot in the house after her old, shabby shoes finally wore out. Even when she and Mary appeared to be getting ahead financially, their "prosperity" was invariably short-lived.

To help her mother pay the bills, Charlotte devised various strategies for earning an income. In addition to running a small day school with her mother, Charlotte found that her classes at the Rhode Island School of Design were paying off. Orders for her dainty, hand-painted stationery were a steady, though insubstantial, source of income; moreover, in collaboration with her cousin Robert Brown, Charlotte was successful in designing advertising cards for Soapine, a household cleaning product made by the Kendall Manufacturing Company of Providence. While the business was not particularly lucrative, it enabled Charlotte to contribute, at least nominally, to the family earnings. Private art lessons given by Charlotte also yielded some much-needed cash. At the same time that she was teaching others, however, Charlotte continued her own education by enrolling in classes, attending lectures, and spending countless hours at the public library and the local athenaeum reading and studying on her own.

During this period Charlotte's friendship with Martha Luther blossomed, and the two of them were often joined in their activities by Sam and Jim Simmons. The Simmons brothers were frequent guests at the Perkins house where they enjoyed whist parties and lively conversations. But although Charlotte's circle of friends was constantly enlarging, she still suffered from episodes of loneliness.

On Christmas night of 1880, Charlotte had a particularly hard time dealing with the holiday letdown, which seemed to amplify her sense of isolation. In a verse included in her December 25 entry, Charlotte's self-pity is apparent.

In reality Charlotte's life was not as bleak as she suggested that Christmas evening. While Martha and the Simmons brothers were welcome companions, Charlotte also enjoyed the company of some of Rhode Island's most prominent families. Among them were the Dimans, headed by Brown University history professor J. Lewis Diman, who died on February 3, 1881, after a short illness. Less than three months later, his daughter, May Diman, whom Charlotte described as the "most utterly charming" member of her circle of friends (*Living*, p. 49), was killed after being thrown from a horse. Her death occurred as the Perkinses were settling into a new, more spacious house, which understandably tempered Charlotte's enthusiasm for the "wholly advantageous" change that the move was intended to signal. Although Charlotte tried to "preserve the appearance of composure" at May Diman's funeral, the death of her friend left her sad and shaken.

Christmas Day.
Saturday December 25th. 1880.

Late and Lazy. Martha over A.M. She bringeth me a white fan, & two ties. I love her. The postman brings me many cards[;] one from Jim. Where's Sammy? We go around to Mary's at 1. Grand tree there for Alice *And* the family. All seemed happy but regret that Anna could not be there. I had a gorgeous fan from Ada, a very handsome book from Robert, and lots of splendor that I hadn't expected, A stamp box from Grandpapa Carpenter. My little bottle paid. Ten dollar check from Carrie Hazard. Droves of cards. See Xmas book. Mother goes up to Anna's to stay over Sunday, ye nurse going home for Xmas. I come home and find a card from Sam. Prettiest of all. Quiet evening making up accounts & enumerating presents. I have dispensed some 80 gifts to some 25 people, 40 to mother. I have had about 40 myself, cards inclusive. I am dreadfully tired.

Not quite such a success as last Xmas, but very jolly.

9 P.M.

Christmas night, and all alone!

> All alone in the quiet room
> With the lamplit space and the shadowy gloom
> In the distant corners. Overhead
> Aunt Caroline has gone to bed
> Tired out with the week before.
> Mother has gone to Anna's to stay

Over Sunday. Thomas away
in Nevada. Never a friend
Christmas night with me to spend.
It makes me cry. I've worked away
Getting ready for Christmas Day
Got up mornings and sat up nights
Lots of work and lots of fun
Getting presents for every one;
Had no end of presents myself——
And now at nine o'clock at night
To be all alone—it isn't right.
There's a dreary whirling wind outside
Over the common bare and wide;
And a snowy ground and a cloudy sky
And nothing but a clock that ticks
Till each vibration stabs & pricks.
A clock that ticks and a lamp that burns
With blinks & flickers and starts by turns.
And a little girl with her feet in a chair,
And tearstained cheeks and tumbled hair
And tired eyes like the soul inside
And as lonely a heart as ever cried.

Dec. Sunday 26th. 1880.

7.30 or more. Get breakfast. Mend carpet. Go down to Martha's P.M. A horrid windy snowy rainy disagreeable day. Sprinkle clo'. Robert over. Cards.

Monday 27th. 1880.

Sweep parlor. A big snowstorm last night. Mother returns from Anna's. Iron a bit. Get out some slate sketches for Robert. Go and call on Carrie & Helen and then come over with Martha. Robert later and Deutsh. A mush. Miss Mabel. Robert very blue.

Tues. 28th. 1880.

Up early. Sweep. Trot down st. Got dress pattern & facing. Peek at Martha. Darning & buttonholes. Draw a bit. Edward over. Then Sam. Whist. Edward & I 4. to Sam & Aunt C. 8.! He was pleased with his picters.

December.
Wednesday. 29th. 1880.

Up betimes. Draw on cards. Letter from C. A. Hedge. I am to go on in February. Answer her letter. Jim over. Whist. 9 to 4. Odds on our side. Snowed all day & snowing now at 11.30–12.

Thurs. Dec. 30th. 1880.

Snow very deep, and cold as Labrador. 6, 4, zero, as the day advances. Heavy snow, deep every where, & drifted besides. Our gas which was so deliciously unsatisfactory last night, won't go at all tonight. But we rejoice in a lamp. Write to Mary Poor and Carrie Bissell. So cold that I put on my red flannels & thickest hoses. Horrid cold. Turn the water off. Letter from T. Write to that youth. Robert over. cards. Annie Aborn & Will Fillinghast. Whist. 4 to 3. W. & I.

Fri. Dec. 31st.

Cold. Sit around all the morning getting warm. Mother goes down st. a shopping. I do up the work. Write to Thomas. Mrs. Luther calls. Jim comes and we go down there and play whist. Sam there. Jim & Martha beat us 4 to 3. Come home and play the old year out. 3 to 3. Henry Townsend called with dry goods from Grandma Anthony.

[1881.]

Saturday
January 1st. 1881.

Go down St. stopping at Martha's, Ada's, and the Hazards. Get gorgeous rubbers for 60 cts. and some agreeable slippers for 1.25. Get patterns for dress also. I think I must have that bête noir of my childhood, chillblains! My feet swell after walking, and are hot and achy. Can't get my shoes on hardly. Poor little me! Mrs. Mathewson comes in to see about mothers prospective vacation. We begin our year with a quiet solitary evening. Not bad for a change. I shall be very very glad to go to Boston and see some more people. Verily my soul weareth of the swains incumbent. I am tired. I am sleepy. I am *not* energetic. I do not progress. Not a bit. Oh dear———— .
The happiest time of day is————bedtime.

Sunday. Jan. 2nd. 1881.

A *little* warmer. Still frozen up. Boiled lamb. Martha over. Robert also. Cards. Mary in. Mother goes up to Annas and back, and is now to postpone for her vacation as Anna is still too sick to relinquish her nurse. Clarence down with mother. Cards.

Monday. Jan 3rd. 1881.

Up and work by lamplight. Finish cards. School. Julia Jastrum & Sophie Aborn call. I go down to the German but the German doesn't go. Mabel & Martha go to a Symphony Concert, some row or other. Jim was there and came home with me. Edward & Henrietta come over and play whist. He and Aunt C. beat mother & Henrietta 6 to 4. Then Edward and I beat a game.

Tuesday. Jan. 4th. 1881.

6.30. Iron a bit. Carry cards down to Robert. Call at Ada's. B. Hazard there, & a cousin of Ada's from New Haven—Arthur Osborne. Call on May. Call at Prof. Green's. Martha over. Lizzie B. & Mrs. Sheldon call. Ablute. Sam. Whist. 4 to 2. Mother introduces her new rule of stopping at 10, but I smile on, and he prolongs his call until 11. It is snowing heavily now. Splendid sleighing all this week last, and likely to be for some time. I like it.

Wednesday. Jan. 5th. 1881.

Up very betimes and swear over the kitchen fire for an hour or so. Never, never, never again will I attempt to cook a new fire out of an old one. Fresh snow four of {*sic*} five inches deep over the already drifted landscape. I go out and shovel, assisted by the genial though elderly "Pa Willey". Martha over on business. (To illustrate a parodiacal joke for her Aunt Sarah.) Sweep bedroom and kitch[en]. Apply snow to my miserable little toes, which were totally insensible to the cold thereof, and settle the question after the swelling went down. Corns, *not* chillblains. One on the outside and two between each little toe! Write to that disconsolate pensioner, Mary Peck.

Thurs. 6th.

Up early. Mother scalds her right wrist with boiling fat. A bad burn. Flour and hammemelis, as we had no plaster. Seems to get well. Snow again last night, very heavy. Thaws and mists all day. Go over to school. .75 [cents]. Get some cornplaster. Call at Ada's. Whit sick. Saw Mr. H. Call at Martha's for a minute. Home and fix up for Martha's Whist Party this evening. Mother wouldn't let me go without her, and wouldn't go herself on account of the nasty weather and walking. I have a good cry, and don't get over it yet awhile. Aunt Caroline an interested auditor.

Friday. Jan. 7th. 1881.

Snooze until 7. All serene by 12 or so. But mother has a bad headache. Martha over on that hymn business. I trot down St. & get some chloroform. Our water thaws. Quite a comfort. Jim over. 6 games, 3 apiece.

Saturday. Jan. 8th. 1880. {sic}

Rather late. Get breakfast & sprinkle clo[thes]. Do up all the work by ten. Trip on the board outdoors and saturate myself with hot water &—more water. And not a drop of hot water in the house! Take a shampoo under the faucet and go out to freeze my head. Lecture Club. Bishop Clarke holds forth on motion in etymology. Trot down st, and get salmon & orange & an account book. Stop at Ada's. Out. Stop at Martha's. She is not well. Stay to dinner. Roast beef. Home. Buttonholes. Dinner. Lizzie in. Partakes of our frugal meal. Whist. M[other]. & A[unt]. C[aroline]. 6 to our 3!

Sunday. Jan. 9. 1880. {sic}

Up, dressed, fires made, flats on, and writing to Thomas while it was yet starlight in the east. Do half the ironing and all the work and go to church at Dr. Behrends. Sat with the Salisburys. Don't Admire Dr. B. Take a nap, and then go down to Martha's. She and I go over to Anna's to see the baby, and so home. Uncle William here, but departs before dinner. Cousin Mary in a little while.

Monday. Jan. 10th. 1881.

Clean up draw[er] and table in kitchen. Iron a little. Sew a little. Read to mother out of Harper's "Mrs. Flint's married experience." A most edifying tale. Do up dinner dishes barefoot, as I have done before, for I can not stand up in any of my old shoes even. Ablute. Chrochet. Write to T. O we did want to play whist tonight.

Tuesday. Jan. 11th. 1881.

Up by 6. Sweep parlor & dining room & kitchen. Letters from Thomas. Mother goes off with Clarence to be gone for a fortnight. I finish off school, sew some, lunch and go after Martha. She only stays a bit. Maria over. Stays to tea. Henry Townsend calls for me to go coasting. Robert over. Warm—very.

Wednesday. January 12th. 1881.

Never stirred all night and didn't wake up until light. Do all the dishes and teach school. Card-letter from Allie Elder. Go up and see mother. Conclude not to go on the Brown-Field sleighing party with Edward. Sew. Do that hymn for Martha. John W. in a minute.

Thurs. Jan. 13th. 1881.

Up at 6. Sweep kitchen, black stove[1] & clean up generally. Biscuit & sich. Do all but the dishes, and am ready for school. Dismiss at 11 to go to Miss Bergs. Meet Martha & walk over together. 50 cents only. Meet M. again & back. Stop at Adas. Get that fur she gave me. Aunt C. returns early. French. Warmed up dinner. Aunt C. got some oranges. Didn't sew much. Sam calls. Stays until 25 minutes of twelve & then I have to look pointedly at the clock and remark "My interesting friend!" He went. All conversed. Fortunes, valentines, practical jokes, etc. I don't like him at all now, nothing startling, but a growing indifference.

Friday. Jan. 14th. 188. {sic}

Go up and see mother. Sew on dress. Crochet and [read] "The Confessions of a Frivolous Girl."[2] Jim calls. Argue as of old. *He* held my yarn.

Saturday Jan. 15 1880 {sic}

Up in broad bright starry moonlight and work thereby. Do all the housework, sweep kitchen, fill lamp and sich, and do the whole ironing before 10.15. Go down to Ada's. She don't go to the Lecture Club. I do. Saw Carrie & Helen there and am invited to their church. Call on Hattie Salisbury. Out. Trot for home, see Ada getting into a car and get in too, find it to be a govorner[3] and ride strait home Ada paying my fare. Foster Townsend to know if I would like to [go] coasting tonight if Henry would call for me. Call from Arny and Alice Payton with delinquent cash. "biled dinner." Go up to Anna's together, with a letter from Thomas. Make bread, dish wash, etc. Read aloud a bit. "Henry" comes for me, accompanied by Mr. Tolman. Cased in much flannel I go. Jolly time. Lots on the hill. Many doublers. Slide on Bowen St. from Prospect to Hope. They drag all us girls home. Very jolly time.

Sunday. January 16th. 1881.

Sleep and rest until nearly 7.30. Then "rise and shine" in lively style but fail to get down to Ada's to breakfast as I was invited. Join that damsel however on Williams St. and we all go over to Grace Church. Hot and sleepy, stick a friendly pin into myself as an exhilarator.[4] Ride back and stay to dinner. A little loving talk with Ada, and she and her happy swain, whom I begin to like, walk home with me.[5] They come in and stop a bit. Mother home for a little while. Our water has frozen again, although we turned it off yesterday. I do a little mending while Aunt C. finishes "The Confessions." I can't say I enjoyed the book much—yes, I think I did though; it seems singularly truthful and exact. Put me quite in a moralizing mood. Write to T.

9. We are not to be left alone it seems, Robert calls, and brings me two more sets of those soap cards. Very kind of him.

Monday. January 17th. 1881.

Up and going at 5. Sweep parlor, dining room and kitchen. All else as usual. Water still frigid, & it is growing colder tonight too. Start on archery cards but don't get far. Sew a little, and tucker away on my new gown. Ablute, pretense of crocheting, casino with Aunt C. and so to bed with a thankful heart. We havn't been so rich in a long time. Thomas has given Mother all his $62.00 even as I did, but instead of bills this will do some good. Then I have plenty of cards ahead, a large order from Ada, a dollar from Martha's Aunt Sarah, and what is the most surprising a dollar & a half clear after the market man was paid! Oh it does feel good.

Tuesday. January. 18th. 1881.

Not too early. All serene though. Go out after school. See Anna, Mother, Mary, Alice, & Charles all going sleighing in a gorgeous barouche & go too,

as far as Martha's. Meet Ada further on. (O, a dollar from M.) Shop much &
successfully. Walk home at 2 Samless. Call on Mrs. Anthony. The Browns,
our residents below stairs return at last. I got "Foxe's Book of Martyrs" & "A
Chance Acquaintance."[6] Aunt C. read the latter while I sew. Start out on some
white aprons.

Wednesday, January 19th. 1881.

I seem to have lost my early habits; [arising] after six. Venture on Johnny
cakes with dubious success. The water comes, rather too late to be of service
to the washerwoman. No one comes or calls, I paint & sew, and Aunt Caroline
finishes "A Chance Acquaintance" in the evening. A most enjoyable work,
especially coming after that last one.

Thurs. Jan. 20th. 1881.

7! Johnny cakes, a little better. School & school. No cent from Mrs. Berg.
Change "Foxe's Book of Martyrs" and "A Chance Acquaintance" for "Tunis &
Carthage." Call at Ada's. Carry ten cent C[harlotte]. Russe to Martha who is
better. Stay there about an hour or more. Home and get dinner. Who should
call but Edward Hale Jun[ior]! Ask him out to dine, which he does with
apparent enjoyment. Entertain him with letters from Thomas. Wash dishes
as usual. A new caller. Richard Hamlin yclept. A harmless youth with some
indefinable impediment in his not too ready speech. Does very well.

Friday. January. 21st. 1881.

7! Mes enfants only bring me a dollar. A wild northeast snowstorm sets in,
and I carry Jessie Budlong all the way home, from the corner of Waterman st.
With a big umbrella. Then I go up and see mother. All serene "thereaway".
Clarence thinks I'll never marry. Peut-être-pas.[7] Says they're afraid of me. I
hate a fool! Snow turns to rain, and we have a nasty night. I worked some on
the cards, but I can't seem to get hold of them at all this time. A pleasant
evening with "A Fair Barbarian".[8] In Scribner's.

Saturday, Jan. 22. 1881.

Up and dressed at 4. Ironing all done by 6.30. Then take a nap. Little fried
inguns for breakfast. Go the Lecture Club stopping for Ada, but she doesn't
go. Barclay there. Go down st. Order "The Snark."[9] Salmon and sich. Run
into Jim in front of the office, and he walks home with me via Martha's, whom
we take along. He says on W. st. at 1.30. Then he can't go in, must go to some
recitations this afternoon. Then he stops and waits for M. goes home with us,
comes in and stays till 3.45! Sewing, one word game, French, etc. Retire at 9.
in a state of abject sleepiness.

Sunday January 23rd. 1881.

7.! Don't even wash the dishes. Go to church with the Hazards. Hear Mr. Vose and like him better than any of 'em so far. Saw the stalwart James among the departing congregation. Walked home with the Hazards en masse. Stopped to see Carrie and show her my cards. Mr. & Mrs. Coats come in. Am introduced. Go to Ada's to dinner. A Mr. Rice there, her uncle-by-marriage. Very pleasant dinner whereof I most enjoyed the conversaion [*sic*]. All jeer at my cards much fun. Whisk in and out of Marthas. Home at 3.30. Turkey dinner. Trot up to Anna's with some of it. Clarence says I'll never marry. Peut-etre pas monsieur. Home and wash dishes. Robert over. Cards. Much.

Monday, January 24th. 1881.

Sweep parlor. School. Meet mother & go down st. Order coat. She lags in some necessaries. Lunch. Shop in general and come home. I trotted gaily through the sts. and bowed and smiled my fill, at Sammy on the horse-car bridge, and Jimmy on the hill. Joined by young Bogert on George, but not far. Call from Junie Keach. Read "Crusoe in New York".[10] Sew. Write to T.

Tuesday, January 25th. 1881.

7! Johnny cakes improve. On my way down st. am overtaken by Mr. Payton, sire of Alice, who gives me a sleighride all the way. Meet Aunt C. Get trimmings for dress, which garment I have carried in to a Miss Martin, our neighbor on the counter to be completed. Change books, pay Roots bill and otherwise disport myself. Am joined on Benefit St. by Margie Hazard, and walk home with her and on to Martha's. Then home and darn some clothes to put on. Ablute. finish Apron! Write to T. Robert over with proofs of the flower cards. Don't think much of 'em. He posts my letter, departing at 8.30 or nearly.

Wednesday. January. 26th. 1881.

6. Note about Kitchen Garden and letter from those superbly brassy Stevenses. Carry it up to M[other]. Anna very sick. Broken breast of the worst description. Dr. Mitchell there today to lance it. Mother called. Turkey soup. Trot to Mrs. Fillinghasts and Marthas. Mend and patch Slipper with wire and make sweeping cap. tired.

Thurs. January. 27th. 1881.

6 or near it. School out at 11 and trot to Mrs. B[erg].s.—$1.75. Go and have coat fitted. Go to Mrs. Lockwood's and tell her "yes" to the Kitchen Garden. Go to the Brown's, have some dinner and show two sketches to Robert. Go to Ada's and stay quite a spell. She gives me a striped satin and bunting party dress. White. Much lace. Go to Martha's. She'll kitchen garden too, if it is gratis. Home to second soup. Crochet. Sam comes. He has had peritoni-

tis. Don't care for meat and likes to spend money. Toast,—boiled milk—candy—Bah!——

Friday. January 28th. 1881.

6.30 or so. Nothing extra, except the buckwheats, which were. Martha over. Very pleasant afternoon. Note from C. A. Hedge. L[etter] from Miss Lockwood—Kitchen Garden postponed till next fall. No loss. Draw some on cards. Finish my shawl and start on Ada's thanks to Jim who holds yarn like an angel. Wrote to C. Hedge. Tired & cold.

Saturday. Jan. 29th. 1881.

7! Colder and colder. Scrabble. Shivering through the work, go and have dress fitted at Miss Martin's, catch a sleighride with Ray who drops me at Ada's, go to the Lecture Club, am introduced to the lecturer, Mr. Edward Hall of Worcester, talk to him concerning Thomas, go and do many errands, go and have coat fitted, and fetch up at the Browns at 1.40. A grand turkey dinner in my honor[;] crochet & chat in the afternoon, whist, oysters, and coffee in the evening. All at home, and a very pleasant time. Don't seem so jolly now, for I learn on returning that Sam and a friend of his, a Mr. Childs, came to play whist, and went away disconsolate. "Do it adain [*sic*].["]

Sunday, Jan. 30th. 1881.

7.30!! Do the ironing. Light snow. Darn things. Aunt C. after her daily trip Annawards reads "Sevenoaks" [11] quite persistently. Nice book. Robert over. Cards. Aunt C. goes to bed. I inform R. on his departure that I am "getting to like him ever so much." Wonder if he misunderstands?

Monday Jan. 31st. 1881.

6.30. Letter from Thomas. Mother down for two or three hours. I gad about and shut the school of for the present. General lamentation. "Sevenoaks", and make an apron for Mother. Ablute.

Tuesday. February 1st. 1881.

6.20. Long busy day of drawing. Get a lot of sketches done. Go to sleep bolt upright in my chair three times. Sleepy work. Chrochet and read for an hour or so when Jim and Sam arrive and we play whist. Sam and Aunt C. 4 to our three. He had several ingenious excuses for bringing his friend here t'other night. Said "he was a respectable bachelor, and as I was getting along——"! Said he dropped in on him, wanted to play whist, and as he hadn't anywhere else to bring him he brought him here! Very pretty, very pretty! Aunt C. delighted in him, and scorneth the Right Honorable James D.

Wednesday, Feburary 2nd. 1881.

6.30. I've had about enough of this weather. Below zero mornings and not much better all day. 40 above in our parlor this morning, forenoon rather. Send postal inviting Edward to come and play whist. Trot up to see mother for an hour or so. Annie Rawson snakes me in to her house as I am returning [to] paint a card. Martha over. Aunt C. goes up to Anna's in spite of the weather. Fresh fish for dinner of questionable character.

Thurs. Feb. 3rd. 1881.

6.30. I don't be warm in the night. Buckwheats. Run up to see mother. Anna has dipheretic sore throat. Stop for Martha, stop at Ada's, go to Atheneaum with her and leave the [*sic*] there and trot to school. Saw Sam sunning self south side store. 75 cts. "Stories of Roundheads & Caveliers," & "Manliness of Christ" at Lib. Stop to see Robert. Go to Ada's. Lunch. Quails. Sallie Vose. Cream candy. Chatter of bridesmaids & sich. Crochet. Home. Scarcely in when Jim calls. Brought me some lovely little fragile marguerites to paint. "Couldn't stop", but stayed to dinner & until after seven. My new coat comes home. $16.00. Mother's treat. My new dress comes home. $5.00. Mothers treat. Crochet.

(Later) Prof. J. Louis Diman died this afternoon.[12] Malignant ensephelus.

Friday. February 4th. 1881.

6.30—7. *Slept warm.* With my feet under 14 thicknesses of blanket. Warmer weather too. Paint marguerites with good success. Do a bit on cards. Aunt C. got along with a dinner out (being down st.) and I got along without a dinner. Manufacture an unsatisfactory rice pudding. It takes about 30 hours as I estimate it to make one of those shawls. I do 5 times across tonight, twenty minutes at time. Letter from C[harlotte]. A. H[edge]. Write to her.

Saturday. Feb. 5th. 1880 {sic}.

7. Actually *warm.* A most welcome thaw. Am left by Aunt C. prone on the lounge, with injunctions not to go out, but no sooner doth that good dame depart than I am up, re-dressed, and off. Don't go the L[ecture]. C[lub]. however, but stay at Martha's and crochet. Go down st. with that damsel later, and ride home, stopping to bestow on Henrietta Brown a soapshaker. Ada had been here, with two of those curtains to design. Aunt Caroline is very blue over Anna, who don't get better, but worse. We go stealthily to bed at 8 to escape possible Robert.

Sunday.
February 6th. 1881.

7. Do all the work and the ironing proper. Aunt C. goes up and mother comes down. That little woman is pretty well tired out. Anna is in a very

precarious condition, dying for want of the one thing that money can't buy her—an appetite. Martha over. A very pleasant time with her. We meet in lots of places. She has made me a lovely and most convenient little pincushion (by request.) Darn generally. Corn beef dinner, good. Aunt C. begins "The Guardian Angel" [13] while I piously crochet. Robert comes. Cards. I am tired.

Mon. Feb. 7th. 1881.

7! Bah! A lazy wasted miserable mispent day. Shall I never outgrow the fascination of a book! Here I started that "Angel" to myself, then let Aunt C. read it aloud because I knew she liked to, then go and read it all through today, wasting precious hours of work and now listen with hypocritical interest while that deluded lady goes all over it again. Paint less than one card. Mother has a letter from Hartford Clarke, Fort Leavenworth, Kansas. I take it up to her. He wants to correspond.

Tuesday, February 8th. 1881.

Up at 5. Work on Archery cards with some application, and finish 'em. Carry them up to Anna's. A letter from Thomas.
Trot over to Martha's, Ada's, and the Browns. R. isn't satisfied of course, so I needs lug my poor little cards back again. Then meet Martha, see her off in the train to Auburn, get some brown paper, and "My Wayward Partner", [14] and splash home. I haven't worn rubbers this winter, nor won't. Meet Aunt C. and stop in to Mary's. Hot corn & cold cornbeef. Write to T.

Wed. Feb. 9th. 1881.

7. O it is hotter than blazes! I draw all day more or less, design for curtains etc. Martha over for an hour or so. Aunt C. goes around to Mary's after dinner, I go after her, and we are overtaken by the Simmonses as we return. They stay uncomfortably until ten, and then go gladly away. Aunt C. wouldn't play whist on account of Anna; who has had another operation this week, and is low again. Those chaps are bad enough single, but dreadful together.

Thursday. February 10th. 1881.

5.40. Biscuit and omelette, my first and good. Start out at about ten. Call on May Diman. Poor little girl; she seems quite calm and quiet. Says she don't reallize it yet. Then to Martha's. Stop and leave bundles at Ada's and cards at the Brown's. Then to school. 75 cts. Then to Ada's to lunch. They bestow on me the "Snark" to my infinite delight. Then to Martha's, and with her way out on Camp St. to see a Miss Randolph who will give us an hour a week in German for nothing. Pleasant dame. Actually took the car home from M's. Diminutive warmed up dinner, and I sit around all the evening with a calico apron in lieu of a dress. Change in the weather? I should say so. 80 where it was 40 last week. I can't get cool.

Fri. Feb. 11th. 1881.

7. Sweep parlor and scrub and clean generally. Do Ada's curtains, one pair. Martha over. We giggle over "My Wayward Partner." Robert appears. Cards. I wish I could work faster for him. I have encompassed 13 oranges since last night's repast.

Saturday February 12th. 1881.

6.30. Black Stove. Sweep kitchen. Iron. General housework. Sweep bedroom. Mend promiscuously. Do a most gorgeous pen & ink Valentine for Ada. Nice little dinner of chops & sich. I am getting to be quite a cook. Mend some more, and crochet while Aunt C. finishes "My Wayward Partner". She retires at about 9.30, and after removing my dress, shoes & stockings, I Valentine a little more.

Sunday. Feb. 13th. 1881.

7. Biscuit and mackerel as usual. Clean up a bit. Cards. Mother appears. Fuss around for her. Martha arrives. She goes off with my wayward partner (mysterious phrase!) Send valentine to Ada, & a bit of a card to May. Beans and rice pudding. Robert. Cards. "Great heavens! Is it any harm to hug your cousin?" * Oui mon ami, il est. Quelquefois.[15]

Mon. Feb. 14th. 1881.
St. Valentine's Day.

6.30. Clean all up and start off by ten. Carry first pair of curtains to Ada. $3.00. Stop for Martha & trot down st. She went home at 12.40. Stay in Atheneaum till two, then get key for M. & carry it over to her. Music & French. Come home and draw a wee bit, get dinner, and sit quietly down to finish Ada's shawl while Aunt C. reads "Samantha at the Centennial" [16] which I procured for her today. But Martha, Sam, & Jim come to play whist and we disport ourselves therein till 10. 2 to our 3. I had two Valentines, one unknown, but Sam suspected, and one from Ned Taft unmistakeably! Jim was about as sociable as a Greek frieze.

Tuesday. Feb. 15th. 1881.

6.50. Draw. Ada's cards arrive. I go up to see mother & take lunch there. Draw. Veal cutlets. Crochet & Samantha. Robert. We were reading to him when Jim appears. Invites me to go to see the Pirates of Penzance, Boston Ideal Company, next Saturday. Will I? Of course I will. Whist two games apiece, and Aunt C. and Robert whitewash us once. No progress on cards tonight.

Wed. Feb. 16th. 1881.

6.30. Stay quietly at home and draw all day off and on. Finish Ada's shawl at 10 P.M. Aunt C. having retired at 9. worn out with helping up at Anna's.

Their girl has had to leave on account of health. I made a good beef stew and a custard today.

Thurs. February 17th. 1881.

6. Get the work all done by 9. Send half a dozen unbaked biscuit up to Anna by my peripatetic boarder. Paint little palette with name & love, tie it up with the shetland shawl with white satin ribbon & tote it down to Ada's. Helen there. Walk down st. with M. School. 75 cts. Shop. Get materials for a dark blue velvet opera bonnet; whole thing costs me just $2.03! Strings & all. Get likewise a pair of boots; similar to my present dilapidated pair. (Not similar in delapidation.) Feel very nice with my new purchases. Stop at Ada's and lunch. Stop at Martha's and get Snark & "Heredity". Home, paint, draw, rest, work on bonnet, & receive Robert as aforetime in the kitchen. Aunt C. retires. R. Brown seems to grow cousinly & affectionate in loneliness & proximity. "And I? And I? What shall I do? for all is vain. No book will rule, no frown deny, no words restrain. Nor any reason reach his mind to make him take his arm from me; or could they I should be inclined to let them be". I feel very dirty and ashamed of myself. He only had his arm on the back of my chair & me), and he's a cousin, but natheless it wasn't right in me to let him, and I won't any more!

Friday. February. 18th.

6.30. A blessed day of rest. No cards! Sweep parlor, Dining room, entry & stairs. Try on gloves. Martha over. Give her a pair that was too small for me. Make bonnet. A Grand Success.* Marie Stuart, plain & puckered, pink roses of last summer, all delicious. Trot up to show it to mother and wish I hadn't as she is discouraging and don't want me to wear the silver comb. Retire at 8.15.

Saturday. February 19th. 1881.

6. Iron. Carry bonnet for Ada's approval. Barclay there. Stay to dinner. Martha over. Mrs. Luther has sent me that lovely pink satin necktie I wanted, Funny. Hattie Salisbury calls. Lizzie over. Stays to dinner & till near 8.40. Make bread, ablute, adorn, and generally prink. Jim arrives in due time & we promenade over to see "The Pirates of Penzance". Boston Ideal Opera Company. Prov. Opera house. I christen my new coat and bonnet. Look well and feel well. Barker (Ben) sat right behind us. I was glad. Walk both ways. Jim carrys everything and is irreproachable. Nice boy, Jim. I haven't been to the theatre since a year ago New Year's night. Enjoyed it immensely.

Sunday. February 20th. 1881.

After 7. The first time that I have seen sunshine on my curtain before I was up, this year! Fix everything as clean and cosy as could be and go to church. Walked down with Mrs. Weeden, from Hope St. Sat with the Browns &

walked home with Martha. Stopped in to see her bonnet & then called on Mabel Hill who had been with us accompanied by Robert. He walked home with me. An afternoon of perfect happiness, of it's kind. A light lunch over a book, a leisurely attempt to alter the buttons on my new boots, a gradual droop on the sofa cushions and a good two hour's nap. O how I did enjoy it! Actually to be able to take a nap! Not to be in a hurry! Hop up and get dinner, "chops & tomato sauce". Wash dishes, more buttons, write to T. & so to my wellbeloved bed. I am very happy today. Probably a reflex action from last night's healthy enjoyment aided by quiet, warmth, & cleanliness. Seems rough on mother, don't it?

Monday. February 21st. 1881.

6.40 or so, put on flannel gown and arctics, and start up to Anna's in a snowstorm. Aunt C. goes around to Mary's to breakfast and tend baby while M. goes to the dressmakers. I cook, wash dishes and officiate generally up on the Avenue as their girl don't come till tomorrow—no Wed. morning. Fred Keach and Isabel Morse are engaged! (bide, Dr. Mitchel.) Return late P.M. in 6 or 8 inches of snow, and still snowing. Retire at 8.30. Aunt C. stayed up at A's, as mother is down with a headache. Letter from T.

Tuesday, February 22nd. 1881.

6.40 or so. Change buttons on new boots, write to T. and carry some tomatoes, senna syrup, clean aprons and headache medicine up to mother. Call on May Diman. Go over & tell Mrs. Berg I can't come Thursday, leave order to send those panels at Waterman's to Ada, get oranges & leave "Samantha" at Perrins. Call at Ada's. Out. Chace her up to Helen's. See Helen, Carry, Fred, & Barclay. Then to Ada's and see presents. Gives me a towel to design. Then to Martha's where I happily finish the afternoon. Home, sup, & dress up a bit. Jim comes for me to go & play whist at Martha's. Clarence stops to leave some clo' & say that Aunt C. won't be home tonight. Jim escorts me home also, what does ail that other thing! [17] 3 to 2. and the first 3 & a whitewash ours.

Wednesday, February 23rd. 1881.

Ere the sun. Letter from T. Do work, design on napkin for Ada, & trot. Meet Martha on Hope St. Go to Ada's. Not in. Leave towel. Go to Mrs. Luther's. Out. Go to School of Design. No school Weds. Go to Mrs. Berg's. Omit lesson this week. Call at Waterman's, & so to Ada's again. Out, but Helen & Mrs. Hazard visible. May Diman in heavy crape veil etc., & her cousin Grace DeWolf there also. Meet Martha & go home with her to dinner. Nice time. Come home and fix dress for tomorrow. Called at Mary's. Ada sends down that white ball dress, all remade & fixed up, & some flowers to wear with it. Aunt C. returns. Nice dinner for her. Try on clo'. Darn slipper & stockings & gloves. Henry Townsend calls. Aunt C. goes to bed, & I entertain him out of my top bookcase draw. I mended his gloves also, without exception the hardest pair of gloves to mend that I ever needled. He went away at ten. Invited me to go skating tomorrow P.M. & then (as I couldn't) on Friday. I elude him, & he jocosely puts it off to the 23rd of March. *I don't want to go a skating with him!*

Thursday. February. 24th. 1881.

6 to 6.20. Do up housework, array myself in purple and fine linen, & depart. Stop at exhibit at Mary's. Call for Martha & take a Brook St. car. Am ushered by Horace Burney. A very gorgeous affair. 8 bridesmaids & 8 ushers. Maids in creamy white bunting stuff, little straw hats, & flowers in pairs, wild roses, tulips, lilacs, & buttercups. Ushers in dark blue neckties. Ada in enough veil and orange flowers for ten, looked like a houri of course. Several miles of train. The Professor[18] gave her away. Trot back with M. petrifying Sam on the way, leave her to proceed homeward, & attend the reception. *Very* select. A gorgeous refection. See all the folk I please, & have plenty of time to kiss Ada & scowl at Another. Don't fancy any of the ushers. Hobnobbed with fair Coatses, was reasonably attended on, & chatted with the astute Marian for a season. Ada put on a meek travelling dress, and departed at about II amidst a shower of rice & an old shoe. I have a box of wedding cake. Leave among the last, & stop at M.'s on way home. Tired mother at Marys. Clarence was down this morning to get my already exhausted aunt, as mother's right arm has given out, strain or some such. I find her at Mary's. Come home & get good dinner, wash dishes, dress, sew a bit, and expect Sam. Didn't come. Drat him! Seems funny to have mother home again. I am no sort of good with invalids.

Friday. February 25th. 1881.

6.40. Don't do a thing but loaf around and tend mother. Rub her arm with liniment, which skinneth me. Go up to Anna's with eggs & do errands. Ride back with Clarences redhaired boy. Mother has another letter from Hartford Clark. Quite pathetic. J. Willey in, (by request.)

Sat. Feb. 26th. 1881.

6.40. Although up late I get the work & ironing done & go to the Lecture Club, stopping to call on Mrs. Anthony (Mr. Peck in with eggs.) Annie Morse introduced me to a Miss Blodgett, who blandly said, "How do you do Miss Hazard" with perfect assurance. Funny! Go and shop. Get infinitesimal C. Russe for mother. Home & start to finish up some morning glories for Thomas. Mrs. Sturgess Carpenter calls. Suggests that we take their house & board them, & others. Annie Rawson calls. Invites me to a party there Monday eve. Hartford Clark sends back those little duds of mothers. Boiled dinner. Write to Ada.

Sunday. Feb. 27th. 1881.

6.30. Meet Jessie Luther out on Gano St. & go to Grace Church with her. Not Mr. Greer [preaching] however. Mother goes up to Anna's with eggs. I try to paint but go to sleep in my chair. Henrietta over. Aunt C. comes home, quite exhausted. Robert drops in for a hour or so departing at 7.30. Write to T.

Monday. February 28th. 1881.

Rain fog & heat, a dreary tiresome day. Go to M's and down st. Note from Ada. Rejuvenate old slippers & go to the Rawson party. Slow affair, very. Nice Manchester girl, that was all. Jim & Sam come to play whist & do so in my absence with perfect contentment, Sam & Aunt C. 7 to others 2. Feel discontented generally.

Tuesday. March 1st 1881.

' "Late! late! So late!" ' half past seven or eight! Being in a season of moroseness & depression I laboriously grovel through the work and then help mother make an old dyed black silk for me. Pretty pretty. Hash. Write to C. A. H.

Wednesday. March 2nd. 1881.

Omitted on account of causeless weariness & total lack of events. Horrid weather.

Thursday. March 3rd. 1881.

Go down st. via Martha's, meet mother and see about Hamlin house. Baulked. Go to Pub. Lib. & read Pop[ular]. Sci[ence]. School. 75 cts. Get a comb, & a pair of capacious squaretoed 7.A. slippers. Home via Martha's. She comes back with me. (I went to Edward's office and invited him over to whist.) Lizzie calls & stays to dinner. Edward brings some gorgeous oysters. L. departs on his arrival. Oysters, chocolate, gingerbread & oranges at 10.30 or so. 9 games, & we beat the rubber.

Friday. March. 4th. 1881.

Arise morosely in our 6th consecutive day of all-pervading gloom. Wash the accumulated dishes of four meals. Mrs. Springer comes down after Aunt C.'s rent, and after some powow we all enthuse over taking her house root & branch. I especially am highly elate at the prospect.

Saturday. March 5th. 1881.

Up betimes, do the work and the ironing & whisk down to the Lecture Club. Mr. Edward Pearce holds forth on evolution illustrated in botany, assisted by an erratic individual with a steriopticon. Walk up to Waterman st. with Annie Morse; & then make a long call on Sophie Aborn. Demand refreshments and get 'em. She goes down st. with me, & we stop in to see her new neice. Shop. Call on Martha. Out. Call on May. Out. Call on Mary. Home weary & disgusted. Much dinner. Bread & dishes. Tired. Nearly gone to bed when Robert comes. Then Sam. Then Jim. (Unbeknownst to each other). R. & I cardify while the rest whist. Sam & Aunt C. 4 to 0. Then Jim & I 3 to 2. Glory. We made seven tricks one time!

Sunday. March. 6th. 1881.

7. It being cloudy, and mother having a headache, I don't go to church. Martha over. Mother & I trot around to Mary's for a few minutes. Clarence calls.

Monday. March. 7th. 1881.

6. Sweep parlor & dining room. Paint & draw on cards. Mother & Aunt C. call on Mrs. Maine. Mr. Stillwell calls. Whist. He & I one to one. Then Robert comes. Business. Whist again. Robert & Aunt C. 3 to our 2. They have started to paint this house. Blinds all off.

Tuesday. March. 8th. 1881.

6. Ubiquitous painters permeate our household. Work till after 2. Then don gala attire & call on May Diman, inquire after a house, go down St, get corset covers & s. silk, Meet Martha, go with her to Ath[enaeum]. & Pub. Lib, back with her & call on Helen Hazard. Home. Fritters & wine & sugar. Robert early & goes at 8.30. Retire with glee. Letter from T.

Wed. March 9th. 1881.

5 odd. Cloudy & rainy. Julia Jastram over, about the house behind her. Mother & I go down st. (I, via Martha's,) to see about it. No go. Sketch for R. Gorgeous and highly-objectionable-on-account-of-it dinner. Boiled fish with drawn butter & boild eggs, & Sunderland pudding with wine sauce. Robert over. Cards.

March. Thursday 10th. 1881.

Near seven. Rainy and detestable. Ride over to school. Draw for infants. 75 cts. Pub. Lib. "Hudibras" [19] and "Infidelity it's cause and cures." Horrid day.

Friday, March. 11th. 1881.

Clock stopped. Cloudy. Ere seven. Snow. Nasty today. Draw on cards. Martha over. (M[other]. & A[unt]. C[aroline]. went up to Anna's.) Verily I love the damsel. Robert. Cards & whist our 2 to their one.

Saturday. March. 12th. 1881.

6. Iron. Go to Lecture. Prof. Lincoln on Julius Cesar. Good. Walk to Butchers with Annie Morse & Miss Blodgett. Call on Martha. Call on Carrie Hazard. Out. Do errands. Pub. Lib. "The Common Frog." See Ned Ely. Call on May Diman. Call on Miss Manchester. Like her much. Call on Annie Rawson.

Sunday. March. 13th. 1881.

My laziness abashes my consience stricken soul, for save a pan of ashes & a single hod of coal, I've been an idle loafer through the livelong day, and on the bed & sofa have whiled the hours away. Clarence in.

Monday. March. 14th. 1881.

Draw. Painters "draw the windows" & paint the sink. I extract the closet window for one of 'em, who couldn't. Go down to Martha's, Atheneum, down st. & home in my new boots. Ow! Robert over. Cards. He and mother start out on a pie speculation, 15 cts. apiece.[20]

Tuesday. March. 15th. 1881.

6.30. Don't do much but draw. Scurry down to get them into the office before 12. Meet Robert there. Skip about. Meet Carrie & Helen Hazard in Butler Ex. Walk home with them. Then to Martha's. Dine there. Down St. with Martha. Shop. Toddle home in my horrid new boots, all tired out. Met mother Cor. Man. & Gov. She has been a calling on Mrs. Diman, Fillinghast, Budlong, Peck, & *Cyrus Taft*! O, Jimmy overtook & walked with me down st. a little way. In spite of painted steps, Robert comes and then Stillwell. Whist. Robert & mother 6 to our 1!

Wednesday. March. 16th. 1881.

6. Hire Mrs. Nolan to wash the dishes, and I go to painting. Do one card & a half. Letter from Thomas. Mother goes and gets Edward, inveigles him up the back stairs, and we play whist. But lo! As Eliza Simmons was married today, the gentle James, freed from his self-imposed embargo, comes for me to go to Martha's & play whist. I don't, of course, & he comes in & plays with mother. Edward & I 8 to their 2. Pie, rusk & oranges brought by E. Jim presented me with a rosebud from his lappel. I guess Martha has been gnashing her teeth this evening, Sam down there & Jim here.

Thurs. 17th. March. 1881.

6.20. Paint. Go to school via Martha's. We exult over mutual dissatisfaction of our adorers. 75 cts. Shop. Home, lunch, draw, doze, dine, wash dishes, loaf a wee bit, Clarence in, & draw from 8.30 to 11 under the supervision of Robert who arrives opportunely.

Friday. 18th. March 1881.

Up and painting by daylight. Do three cards. Martha over. Mother goes out; P.M. Maria calls. (Mrs. Springer was in A.M., no decision.) Carrie Hazard calls. Mary & Anna Westcott call. Robert of course. Dissatisfaction of *course*. Sam arrives. I leave him with the ladies & stay out and work with Robert. "Goodnight Aunt Caroline"! Drat little 2 by 4 anyway.

Sat. March 19th. 1881.

As above. Remake one card. Go down & post it ere 10.30. Saw Sam. Uncle Edward[21] lectures, very interesting indeed. On Deac (?) the Hungarian Statesman. Walk home with Carrie. Then Martha. Then home. Mother & I go and look at a cottage house on Camp St, call on Mrs. Daniels, & Mrs. Townsend. Get caught in the rain all in our good clo'. Ride home. Mrs. Springer down today. We are to have her house it appears. O, be joyful!

Sunday. March 20th. 1881.

6. Black stove, sweep kitchen, put away yesterday morning's dishes, wash yesterday's dinner dishes, do the ironing, wash dishes again scour the faucet & basins, and clean up all my paint things. Paint a pansie wrong side out. Lizzie calls. Eke Robert (A.M.) Write to T. & Ada. O! I broke the big kettle; dropped a flat iron in it.

Monday. March 21st. 1881.

Before 6. Sweep parlor & dining room. Draw & rip. Sit around in old apron & Jessie Luther calls. give her the pansie I painted yesterday. Junie Keach calls. Aunt C. goes up to Anna's to stay a week, that interesting invalid having betaken herself to Mama Carpenter's. Robert comes. Then Mr. Stillwell. "Is this what you call the piehouse?" "Yes," said I, "& there's a pie in it." Whist. They 4 to 3. Pie, oranges, etc. Started to write to T.

Tuesday. March 22nd. 1881.

6. Sketch in color for large "Soapine" show card. Mr. Peck in. Carry block to Robert. Meet Martha & call there on way home. Mother at Mary's. Stop there a bit. Home & dine. Take a nap to prepare for work, but am hurriedly waked up by the bell & go down in a dazed condition to let in Miss & Mr. Manchester. My wits were nowhere but they seemed to have a pleasant call.

Wednesday March 23rd. 1881.

With the sun. Sketch in color second big card. Red, blue, & black. Letter from Thomas. Aunt C. flits in and out again. Write to T, or start to. Robert over. "Perkins & Co. Designers"!

Thurs. March 24th. 1881.

5.50. Paint till 11. Met Martha on my way to school. Met by Lizzie afterwards & go to see Millie Cooley. Quite enjoyed myself. P. Lib. Home. Saw Sam. Paint. Mary & Alice call. Mrs. Springer also. The Pitchers have moved out today. Selah.

Friday March. 25th. 1881.

5.40. Paint & finish show card. Dinner at 1. Tote card down to the Browns. Satisfactory. Call on Helen. Then to Martha's. That maiden is somewhat ill.

Nothing serious, she sits up to tea however & afterwards Sam comes (having been here first) and we play whist. Mother & I beat Sam & M. 4 out of 6. Good.

Saturday. March. 26th. 1881.

5.20. Lace on necktie & patch glove. Stop at Martha's. Sick. Dr. Hedges lectures on "Spectrology." Go to the Browns. Shop. Back to Martha's. Congestion of the liver. Stay there an hour or so. Carried her some flowers from Butchers. Home. Nap. Mrs. Hazard & Helen call. Robert. Cards. Horrible March weather all along now.

Sunday. March 27th. 1881.

6. Black stove, sweep kitchen, usual chores, sweep bedroom, and wash dishes again after pies &c. Carry custard & tarts down to Martha. She is a little better. Call on Anna at Mrs. Sturgiss Carpenters. Two Florida oranges. Call on Mary. Home. dine. Nap. Am awaked by a call from Clarence. I sleep with preternatural heaviness, have done so all winter, don't seem to get near enough anyway. Am only too happy to go early to bed.

Monday. 28th. March. 1881.

before 6. Sweep. Miss Murphy comes, & does mother up generally. Call from May, who imbibes a soft custard & some tarts with much joy, and accompanies me as far as Prospect St. Carry some c. & t.s to Edward Brown. Carry my orange to Martha, who bites it with great glee. Dear little chick. I can't stand my feet much longer, went about a quarter of an inch into the epidermis without touching meat. Robert over. Cards.

Tues. March. 29th. 1881.

Ere the sun. Heavy nap after breakfast. Go up with Mrs. Springer & look at the house. good nice! Go down to Martha's with flowers from Kelly's & "Childrens Garland." [22] Jocose arbutilan in pot, 5 cts. Home & excavate in toe. Mrs. Fillinghast calls. Charlotte Hedge calls. I ride down st. with her, & walk home. Aunt Caroline returns. Sleepy.

Wednesday. March. 30th. 1881.

Unmentionably horrid weather. Regular nor'easter today, ending with hail & snow. Card from Sam. "Has she returned"? I answer in long-saved nasturtium card, "She has!" Go down in car & post it. Called on C. A. Hedge at Miss Addie Brown's. Out, but see her an instant in car. Home & draw. (Did up my toes in lemon last night, improvement.) Robert comes. He & I card while the other folk play whist with a dummy. Jim & dummy beat 3 games & then Robert & Aunt C. beat J. & 4 more. Pleasant evening.

Thursday. March. 31st. 1881.

Another day of nasty weather. Slop & drizzle. Do mats for Lizzie. Go over to school. Call on Millie Cooley. Refreshments. Call on Martha. Nice talk. She is better & sits up. Home. dinner. Nap. Draw. Sam calls. "Has she retired?" Whist. He and his lovely partner 5 to our 4. I made a revoke. Aunt C. led a heart. Mother trumped with a Jack, Sam with a queen, & I with the ace, and then led back a *heart*! No faintest shadow of an excuse. Knocked me all up, I couldn't feel worse to lose a fortune or half a dozen relations.

Friday. April 1st. 1881.

6. Draw. dishes etc. Draw. Mother & Aunt C. go shopping & get a lovely rug and cretonne. I go down to Martha's at about 3. Read her some "Phantasmagoria."[23] Solemn consultation apropos of cousinly caresses, wherein the chicken helps me to decide rightly. Glad to make her of some use. Come home & find mother with a headache. Get dinner, codfish. *Don't* dress up, in favor of good resolutions, and then Robert don't come after all, but Henry Townsend & Jim do. Jim was after my terms for painting lessons, but stayed natheless. Whist. Aunt C. & Jim 4 to our one. My third night of defeat.

Saturday. April 2nd. 1881.

5.20. Write to Ada. Chores. Go to Lecture Club via Martha's. Lottie Daly on "Palmistry." *Very* interesting. Dine at Martha's. Call on Mary. Louis DeWolf there. Call on Miss Manchester. Robert over. Cards. I carefully elude him, and make mild but conclusive remarks.

Sunday. April 3rd. 1881. *

5.42. Black stove, sweep kitchen, wash dishes, & write to Thomas before breakfast. Paint & draw all day. Mary & Alice over. Robert at 7, short call & departs with sketches.

Monday. April 4th. 1881.

5.40. Miss Murphy on my dress. Loaf around all day. Dress up & try on. Run down to Martha's. She has been out today. Henrietta to dinner. Then Edward. Whist. E. & I 2 to their two, & then he takes mother's hand & they beat us 4 to 3.

Tuesday. April. 5th. 1881.
Freezes now.

Near 6. Go down st. with mother and Mrs. Springer. Select lovely paper, get carpets, hassock, etc. Lunch at Café. Home at 5. Miss Manchester in the car. Mrs. Brown from below comes up with our newspaper & stays to dinner. The youth Manchester calls. Returns "Snark."

Wednesday. April. 6th. 1881.

6. Finish letter to Ada. Mother trots & retrots up to the house. Go down to Martha's and mark two pair of shoetrings [*sic*]. Glad of a muff. Maria calls to tell me of a bundle advertized for me. Adams Express. Uncle William saw it. On consulting the paper, we find that the ad. bundles are sold tomorrow, so I take a car with Maria, and we skip over and get it—35 cts. From the Gilmans and has been here since *Dec.'79*! 3 old hats, a halfmade dress, satin fan, pineapple h[an]'d'k[erchie]'f, ivory breastpin, parian statuette, & steel buttons. Show it to Browns, & walk home with it. Jim calls just as I return on the same errand. Don't stay. John Willey calls.

Thurs. April. 7th. 1881.

5.30. Wash dishes before breakfast. our first warm day this long-time. Go to school via Martha's, who walks down with me. Saw Sam. "I shall be over to see your aunt before long"! Drat him! 75 cts. Call on Milly. Custard and orange. Nice. Call on Helen, and borrow $100.00 from Mrs. Hazard on my "share". To be paid next Summer or fall. Hi-yah! Home at 4, footworn & intensely hungry. Aunt C. & mother go around to call on Mrs. Sayles. They return at 8 or so, and Edward calls. Stillwell arrives at about the same time. They just begin to smell pie, when Jim comes. He and I play chess in the dining room while the rest whist. Edward & Aunt C. beat 3 to 1. Then S. & J. beat E. & I 2 to 1. I beat Jim 3 at chess.

Fri. April. 8th. 1881.

6. Mrs. N. irons & washes dishes 65 cts. Mother, Mrs. Springer & I go down st. Get wallpaper, hardware, millenary, etc. Cash Mrs. Hazards check, and spend $15.00 of it outright. Meet Aunt C. in Café & home together. They go around to Mays & I trim bonnet. lovely. No callers! First night alone for 9 consecutive evenings.

Saturday. April 9th. 1881.

6. Scrabble two cards, do up work & go to Lecture Club via Martha's, who was out. An interminable bore named Ward droned for an *hour & a half*, and a more uneasy set of listeners a man never had. Maggie Farnum says she never will sit next [to] me again. Go to Art Club Ex[hibition]. with Annie Morse, & make A.s for her. Dine at the Browns. Go to call on May, but stop at Annie Aborn's & stay to tea, sending a note home. Played 4 games of chess with Mr. Fillinghast & beat the first three. 3 games of whist, lost 2. Sophie in, and she, Annie & Theo come howling home with me. Bah! Prescott Clarke called for the third fruitless attempt. I am glad of it, for its just as well he shouldn't see this house.

Sunday. April 10th. 1881.

6.30. Clarence in. Mother & Aunt C. go up to his house, & to Mary's. Wash dishes numberless. Young man to inquire about tenement. Martha over. She and I go to walk. About 5 miles. Awfully sleepy. Robert comes later, and wants big soapine card all done over, with yellow in it.

Monday. April 11th. 1881.

5.25. Sweep parlor, dining room, & kitchen, & black stove. Miss Murphy comes and tinkers for mother. Letter from father with $15.00. Draw a little. Grand dinner of roast veal & spinach. Mr. Stilwell calls. Mrs. Higgins in to see about the tenement. Afterwards Whist. Aunt C. & mother 3 our *one*! I haven't beaten at whist for 7 nights! Ichabod! Ichabod!

Tuesday April 12th. 1881.

5.25. Paint all day. Mother & Aunt C. go up to the house in the morning. Maria over P.M. Stays to dinner, and carries home the blue dress that was Bessie's. Survived all day.

Wednesday. April 13th. 1881.

Finish of card for Robert & mother takes it down st. Loaf all day on sofa. Jim. Whist. He & I 3 to 5. Northeast storm.

Thurs. April 14th. 1881.

Note from Martha. Meet her at Watermans. School. 75 cts. Go to see Millie. Nice time. Go to Miss Murphy's. Try on ad. lib. Go to Martha's and show her how to make buttonholes, trim hat, etc. Sam arrives. Whist. He and Aunt C. beat us 6 out of 9. That I ever should have been interested in him!

Friday April 15, 1881.

Wake up to find a raging northeast snowstorm. But steady wind and fits of sunshine have pretty much dribbled it all away. Take up tacks in three rooms. Empty drawers. Lizzie over. Edward later. Whist. He & I 2 to 4.

Saturday. April. 16. 1881.

Clear, bright, and beautiful at last. Do a lot of work. Mr. Bolan comes, and he and I lift the parlor stove with a fire in it. Carpets all up. Mother & Aunt C. go up to the house, and I take *everything* out of the front entry, and take up that and the stair carpet. Wash dishes. Start out to go to Miss Murphys. Carry socks over to Mrs. Keach. See Mrs. R. Keach. Drop in on Milly. Get satin, buttons, & salmon. Call on Helen & Carrie. Call at Martha's. Out. At May's. Out. At Miss Manchesters. Out. Home. dinner. Tired, very.

Sunday. April. 17th. 1881.

6. Pack books. 11 boxes, and all the big pamphlets up stairs yet. Delightful boiled dinner. Anna and Clarence stop a minute. Martha over in spring attire. I go to church with her, walk home with her, take tea with her, & so home. Write to T.

Monday. April 18th. 1881.

5.30. Don't do much but get ready and go down st. with mother. Go to Miss Murphy's. Get crettones, jute, etc. Mother calls at the Keaches, and I walk home. And joined on College St., & *mistaken for Annie Morse* by Mr. C. B. Dorrance, whom I have never seen save at the Art Ex. where I went with A. abovementioned. Call on Miss Ellie Bush. Meet Prof. Blake, and get that 75 cts. Call at Martha's. Out. Call and see Anna and the Babe. Stop for Martha at Hattie Kiltons, & she walks mostly home with me. Got some new boots, 7! B.'s! American kid, and so easy and capacious that I put them on in preference to my old ones, and amble about in ease & comfort.

Tuesday. April 19th. 1881.

5. Pack bookcase-drawer box. Mother goes down st. Rip old winter dress. Letter from Thomas. Trot down st. at 5.20. Get gimp tacks. Drop in on Milly. Go to Martha's at 6.20. Enjoy my big boots. Mr. Stillwell calls. Then Sam. Mr. S. & I beat 7 out of 8. Two with mother, & 5 to Sam's one. I exult. Pie, peach-&-apple, & Sam *actually eats a piece*! A very jolly evening.! Aunt C. over-weens. In the gladness of my heart she *invites* them to come again tomorrow night! I must protest! Sam *asks* for one of those cards of mine. I give him that lovely little wildbean. Glad *he's* got it.

Wednesday, April 20th. 1881.

5.30. Finish ripping. Pack woolen & dress goods trunks. Take a nap. Make buttonholes, trim bonnet, & assist mother to upholster lounge. Miss Murphy calls. Mrs. Springer calls. Jim comes. Robert comes. Whist. R. & Mother 3 to our 2. I fairly ached to say "Jim" tonight. Did once, sotto voce.

Thurs. April 21st. 1881.

5. Clean silver from 5.30 till two. Call for M. and go down st. Shop promiscuous. Go to Art Ex. Home with M. Trim bonnet.

Friday. April 22nd. 1881.

4.30. The dirtiest and hardest day's work yet, & the most done. All my duds and Thomas' duds, and all the bureau drawers. I work from before sunrise till 8 with about an hour & a half out for meals. *14 hours*! Am tired and concious of a back. Glad I've got one to be concious of. Edward over. Whist. 3 to 3.

Saturday. April. 23rd. 1881.

Moonlight. Clean silver. Dishes etc. & go out. Stop a [*sic*] Martha's. Out. Go to L. C. No go this week. Go down st. Meet Martha & mother. Get mother's. Go to Millie's. Autotypes at Waterman's. Walk up with M. Athenaeum. Lunch at the Hazard's. Good. Call for M. and we two call on Miss Manchester. Nice. home by 4.30. The two Miss Lymans and nephew come down from Boston to spend the day. We were all out. Mrs. Westcott calls.

Sunday. April 24th. 1881.

5. Set things in motion & then take a long nap before breakfast. Don't do much all day but wash dishes. Mother cleans out all the holes; etc. Aunt C. & M. go around to Mary's in the evening, Mary having just called here. So hot today that I have the windows open in every direction & they like it. Write to Thomas.

Monday. April 25th. 1881.

Up at 4 with mother. Hard day's work. Everything out of Thomas' room. Mrs. Thomas comes to look at the house. Miss Murphy calls. A Westcott infant comes for mother to go and see the genealogical relative. Can't. Pack all manner of Thomase's duds, old pamphlets, etc; glass and china. Mr. Bolan officiates all day, "hetherty-yender", cleaning, whitewashing & wheelbarrowing. Mr. Stillwell calls. Then Robert. ($7.50 for big Soapine card.) Then John evanescently. Whist. Mr. S. & I 4 to Mother & R. 3! Pie. Fun.

Tuesday. April 26. 1881.

5. Mother gads about with carpet men, & Mrs. Nolan & I clean & pack at home. Much done. Mrs. Thomas calls at the door. Helen comes in state, and brings some *wall paper*. (Widder Brown much impressed, stares after her over the gate.) I go up and gloat in the new house. (Sent Helen up there, great, awestruck.) Guess she found we had wallpaper enough. It is lovely up there. Spend half hour 8–8.30 glaring out of Thomas' window. Fruitless. no sneaks.

Wednesday, April. 27th. 1881.

5 or so. Pack and do up and arrange and continue. Go down st. at 12. Stop at Marthas, go way over to Mrs. Bergs, and up to Mr. Sheldons auction rooms, and do seven errands. Home at 1.40! Fuss around again, and snatch a needed nap. Mr. Bolan comes like a ministering angel, and carts off a lot of trash. I take a farewell shampoo and feel better. John Willey comes in and takes down curtain fixtures, and carrys Thomas'es little trunk and papers over to his house.

x   x   x   x

Last night in the little home where we have lived so contentedly for five changing years! Longer than I ever lived anywhere in my life. I am more glad than sorry for a thousand reasons. The step is wholly advantageous and the new house charming in every respect. So goodbye to ungraded "Coonville", and ho! for fresh fields and pastures new![24]

Thurs. April. 28th. 1881.

Wake at 4. Work swift and immeasurable. Mother goes up with the stove men, and I domineer over Mrs. Nolan and Katie to my hearts content. Then she comes back, the moving wagons arrive, and I go up, and, assisted by Aunt Caroline, and backed up by Mrs. Springer, see to the disposal of all our household truck. Never did we have so much furniture before, that hole below was vastly smaller than this, and not too crowded; but this spacious edifice fairly efferveces with upholstery and stuff. Oh but it's lovely! And oh but it's fine! Old Mr. Carpenter stopped here with Anna, and wandered about the house with evident delight. Mrs. Springer hirples up and down stairs, and revels in our comfort and splendor. Miss Murphy comes with my new dress, and is also impressed. Mary drops in later, and is as pleased as all of 'em are.

Oh! the dear beautiful little house! How did we ever live so long and contentedly in the "hole below"?

But I'm tired, tired, tired, and shall sleep the sleep of the righteous tonight. Nor I won't get up till morning!

Friday. April. 29th. 1881.

7.20. Get things much arranged, dishes in particular. Such a lot of 'em. Clarence called in. Also his mother. And in the evening about 8 o'clock, Mrs. Henry Carpenter was in to tell me that May Diman was thrown from her horse at about 7 P.M. and killed! I don't believe it yet for they said the same thing before, when she was thrown. But O, her mother!

Saturday, April 30th. 1881.

True. All true. Ben Barker was with her and got off scott free! Poor Man! Mrs. Diman herself said that he is the most to be pitied.

x   x   x   x

Miss Murphy here early, and finishes my dress. I put it on, and go to see Helen. Stop at M.'s. Out. Helen at home, red-eyed and sad. I walk out with her, but don't talk much. Go down st. and do a bit of errands. Prof. Poland joined and walked with me a bit. The dreadful accident is on every one's tongue, the city rings with it. Oh dear.

Mary & Alice in. Jim and Sam come over as requested and open all the book boxes. Put up most of 'em. 12 o'clock!

Sunday, May 1st. 1881.

Up betimes. Get breakfast and do everything else. Arrange furniture in my room. Ablute etc. Ray & Alice in A.M. Anna calls. Mary calls. Martha calls.

Clarence calls. Edward calls. Maria & Lizzie call. Robert calls with "soapine" proofs. Mrs. Springer calls. Am very tired. I can't write down much about May now, statements conflict too much.

Monday. May 2nd. 1881.

After 7. Mother no better. Lumbago. I do the work. Letter from father. Charlotte Hedge comes. I go with her to May's funeral. The dear girl looked as lovely as ever she did, in white silk and white roses. Great white casket and pedestals, (not trestles). For all it was so private the house was full to overflowing, and all were friends. The clergyman stood on the stair landing. Beautiful services, and a house full of tears. Poor Will Bogert sat right opposite me, and I think he must have loved her, for he covered his face with his hat all through the services, and shook with suppressed sobs. Fred Hazard came and sat by him, and laid a strong hand on his, for which I was grateful. As for me I found I couldn't stand the music, and took refuge in the "Sorrows of Amelia" and the "rivers and lakes of Mane". Which treatment enabled me to preserve the appearance of composure. Why should I sit and drivel to no purpose?

Dear May! I could have kissed her but for folk.[25] Edward Hale was down, and went home on the 2 o'clock train with Miss Charlotte. I walked down with her, and saw the post all strewn with sand to hide the blood stains, and the great hole in the fence where Barker's horse went through. People looking over. I get mother a porous plaster for her back. Walk swiftly home again. Nap. Dinner. Mr. Stillwell called. No whist.——

Tuesday. May 3rd. 1881.

Get breakfast etc. Work around up stairs. Go over to Martha's. She and I go down st. Stop at her grandmother's, who is failing fast, and not expected to live through the week. Home with M. and get some ginger as I am very cold. Home. Mrs. Springer was down with her work. Mother busy upholstering the chairs which have come, gorgeously well done, but much magnified as to price. Welcome dinner. I wash dishes. *Sam comes*! Whist. Mother & I three 1st and then he whitewashed us, and felt better.

Wednesday May 4th. 1881.

7 or so. Arrange bookcase drawers. Help mother put linen slips on all the parlor chairs. Arney & Alice Payton call in due form. (Mary & Alice in during the morning.) Henrietta and old Mrs. Henry Carpenter call. We have our first shad, and dame Springer dines with us in all humility and delight. For a wonder no one calls.

Thursday May 5th. 1881.

Do chores and go over to see Milly Cooley before school. Read her some of DeKay's poems. School. 75 cts. Meet mother at Waterman's and shop a bit.

Go to Dr. Gay's and have my broken tooth filled. It was composition and I chew it mostly out on a bit of cracker inside of half an hour. He should have forbidden mastication for some hours. Go to Martha's. She reads me her story. Send home. Send M. a card concerning her tale. Jim calls. He hangeth many pictures. Whist after 10. He & I beat the rubber.

Friday. May. 6th. 1881.

Hang more pictures. Quiddle about in my room. Mother finishes the chairs. Martha over. She plays for mother. Aunt C. gaddeth abroad incessantly. Delectable codfish dinner. Nobody comes. "early to bed and early to rise."

Saturday. May 7th. 1881.

Up very betimes. Fix everything below, and betake myself upstairs. Way up. Pick over chair seat of red flannel chopped. Go to M's. Go to Lec. Club. Shut up. Meet Blanche Vaughn. See Lizzie at the same time and am introduced by her to Mrs. Trian who boards with Mrs. Hamlin. Go shop. Go to Mrs. Shaw's. She is a bit better. Go to M's. Go to Atheneum, read, and lunch on three cookies. Martha stops there for me, and we go to divers dentists. I am refilled. Sam joins us on our way home and walks up as far as Benefit. I go home with M. Return at 3. Meet mother on George and home together. Delectable codfish dinner. Sophie Aborn called. I wash dishes, make bread, and write to T.

Sunday. May 8th. 1881.

Ere 6. Get my room inhabitable and inhabit tonight. Ray, Mary, Alice, & Clarence call A.M. Aunt C. goes to hear Mr. Staples farewell sermon. I go over to Millie's P.M. and read her two books of the "Light of Asia."[26] Call at the Brown's. Call at Anna's. Gorgeous baby. Walter Carpenter there. John Peck and Annie Aborn called this afternoon. O my dear little room!

Monday May 9th. 1881.

Upholster on my own account. Dinner at one an established fact. Trim mother's bonnet. She goes out. Anna's Ellen calls. Mr. Stillwell appears. Then Sam. Mr. Still. & I 3 out of 5, then Mr. Still & Aunt C. 2 out of 3. Bravo Mr. Stillwell! Then we examine mother's portrait; (Sam thinks I look very much like it,) have a little jig, and depart in peace.

Tuesday. May. 10th. 1881.

Up early, and engage in upholstery & miscellaneous chores. Get the chambers partially arranged. Letter from C. Hedge. Go down st. via Martha's, & accompanied by her. Sherbet. Lends me "The Story of Avis."[27] Home, rest, cool off and dress. Mr. & Mrs. Henry Carpenter call. Then Edward. Then Henry Townsend. Then Robert for a moment, with more work. Whist. Edward & I beat mother & Henry 2 to 1.

Wednesday. May. 11th. 1881.

7 or so. 2nd hot day. Finish my chair, read some & draw some. Martha over. Mr. Woodbury calls. I walk home with M. & stop to see the baby. All Mrs. Springers posterity here today. So hot we bash on the steps in the moonlight. Jim calls. Whist! bad luck to it. Mother and Aunt C. beat the rubber.

T W O

"The damsel Martha"

May 12, 1881–September 23, 1881

AFTER May Diman's death in 1881, the friendship between Charlotte and
Martha Luther continued to deepen. On the morning of Saturday, May 14,
the two went shopping together in downtown Providence and purchased "a pair of
lovely little bracelets" that they each vowed to wear as a "badge . . . of union"—
a symbolic acknowledgment of their mutual trust and affection. The rest of the
day they spent in "tranquil bliss," after Martha "surreptitiously" stole up to Charlotte's room where they passed a quiet afternoon. "With Martha I knew perfect
happiness," Charlotte reflected years later in *The Living of Charlotte Perkins Gilman*
(p. 78).

The "perfect happiness" that she shared with Martha compensated, in part,
for the lack of affection shown Charlotte by her mother, whose own disappoint-
ments in "early love" caused her to withhold "all expression of affection as far as
possible" (*Living*, p. 10). "Looking back on my uncuddled childhood it seems
to me a sad mistake of my heroic mother to withhold from me the petting I
so craved. . . . Denied that natural expression, my first memory of loving any
one . . . and immeasurably the dearest, was Martha. We were closely together, increasingly happy together, for four of those long years of girlhood. She was nearer
and dearer than any one up to that time," Charlotte wrote (p. 78).

Indeed, because love had been elusive all of her life, Charlotte's emotional in-
vestment in her relationship with Martha was enormous. Extant correspondence
reveals the extent of her trust in, and dependence upon, Martha. To Martha,
Charlotte could reveal vulnerabilities that to the rest of the world she would keep
concealed. "Fancy me strong and unassailable to all the world beside, and the
coming down and truckling to you like a half-fed amiable kitten," she wrote to
Martha on July 3, Charlotte's twenty-first birthday. The letter underscores the
striking dichotomy between Charlotte's public and private personas and reveals a
pattern which would characterize many of her adult relationships.

In addition to writing long letters to Martha, who was away for much of the summer, Charlotte assumed the bulk of the domestic responsibilities in the Perkins household, since her mother, Mary, was frequently debilitated by chronic headaches. But Charlotte also found time to cultivate her own interests, reading Emerson and Tennyson, studying Latin, painting cards for compensation, and learning to play the piano "to the dire distress of [her] friends." She also made substantial progress in convincing Dr. John P. Brooks that Providence needed a "Ladies Gymnasium." Thanks to her skills of persuasion and her tireless campaign to recruit potential members, the gymnasium project was soon under way.

Through all of her various experiences that summer, Charlotte's friendship with Martha remained her strongest tie. Still, she had no shortage of male companionship during the summer of 1881. Among her callers was Sidney Putnam, who would introduce Charlotte to Charles Walter Stetson in early 1882.

In general, Charlotte's spirits during the summer of 1881 were high; she felt strong, cheerful, and optimistic. "My circle widens," she noted in the middle of August. "Life may be happier than I thought." Just two days later, on August 15, Charlotte wrote Martha a letter reaffirming her love for her and apparently looking for reassurance that Martha felt the same way. "I think it highly probable (ahem) that you love me however I squirm, love the steady care around which I so variously revolve, love me and will love me—why in the name of heaven have we so confounded love with passion that it sounds to our century-tutored ears either wicked or absurd to name it between women? It is no longer friendship between us, it is love," she wrote. But Charlotte's dream of continuing to share mutual love and "perfect happiness" was shattered when Martha returned to Providence late that summer with the news that she had become enamoured of one Charles A. Lane of Hingham, Massachusetts.

Thursday. May 12th. 1881.

Whisk about and go down to walk to school with Martha, but miss her. Am joined by Sam though and accompanied across Exchange St. First time I've seen him to speak to [alone] since last fall. Drat her! Go to Millie's and read to her till 10.20. Then take an Elmwood car and ride over to Star St. and visit the damsel Martha while she teacheth the deafmutes. Then back, and to school. 50 cts only, as I was fleeing to catch a car. Home. Hot. Nice cool Salad for dinner. Allie & Maria call. Miss Manchester calls, and plays resplendantly. I walk home with her. Quiet evening of buttonhoes [*sic*] & book.

Friday. May. 13th. 1881.

Am awaked by my resonant bell. Go down St. Call on Allie. Call on Mrs. Anthony. Leave word for Miss Murphy. Home to dinner. Wash dishes, adorn, & sew. Anna & old Mr. C. stop in buggy. Aunt C. & Mother go out and return. I take my work and go over to Martha's. Stay to tea. They return with me, going ere eight. Robert over. Cards. Whist. Robert & I beat 3 out of 5. Wood fire at both ends of the day.

Saturday May 14th. 1881.*

Whisk through my work and go to Martha's. Go down st. and shop with 'em. Martha & I get a pair of lovely little red bracelets with gold acorns dependent theron, to be worn by us as a badge, ornament, bond of union, etc. 20 cts. And I superintend her shopping to great pecuniary advantage. Home to dinner. Martha comes surreptitious over P.M., I let her in unseen, she prowls up to my room, and we spend the afternoon in tranquil bliss. I trim her hat, and she hems my pillocase. She returns as invisibly as she came, at which I am exalted. Mr. Bolan here all day, and our yard takes on a most gorgeous appearance. No one here.

Sunday. May 15th. 1881.

Up betimes, make fire &c. before the ladies decend. darn shoes and draw. Dine & go over to Millie's. Read two more books. She goes to sleep under the infliction, but I kindly conclude that it was better for her than poetry and said nothing. Stopped at M's on way over. Rode back. Robert here. I get awfully cross over cards. I do *hate* waste, in work or anything else. And I get cross over mother's having invited Robert to go on the Pawtuxet! Robert Brown of all persons in the world to go with Helen Hazard, and now! *Yah*!

Monday. May. 16th. 1881.

Up betimes and very industrious before breakfast. Bind my carpet strips above stairs. We get a letter from Thomas. He has been sick, had a mountain fever, and wants to borrow two hundred dollars. I write to G. Bissell and trot down St. to post it. Met Jim. Trot back and write to T. Edward over. Whist. Mother & Aunt C. the rubber out of 5. He invites me to go and see Lotta, and the others are goin too.

Tuesday. May 17th. 1881.

Miss Murphy. I recline in my chambers all day mostly. Edward drops in about dinner time. Good seats procured. Robert over. Cards. Sam comes. I draw on Sam's envelopes. He plays dummy & beats the ladies 3 games. 28 points to 6, or 8. Then he and Robert play and beat the ladies the last three out of 4.

Wednesday. May 18th. 1881.

Get up in time to get the breakfast table, at least. Letter from G. Bissell. He won't let me have it, the pig![1] Says he has so many drains on his pocket book that he must stop somewhere! Good place to stop! Mother & Aunt C. go out and I snooze on the rug for two hours or more. Manage to draw a little. Martha over. Brings me a lovely little pink toilet cushion. Mrs. Springer comes down to keep company with Aunt C. while mother and I trudge down to the Carpenter's and see about that money. Mr. C. agrees to let us have it and is extremely kind. Also he walks home with us, and comes in awhile.

Thurs. May. 19th. 1881.

5th day of rain and clouds. Ride over, with Annie Rawson. She is engaged to Tom Vaughn. Hour at Millie's with "Samantha." (Posted letter to T. & certificate to G. Bissel.) School. [$]1.00. Buy bonnet frame & flour. Tooth filled. Ride home. Dine. Draw a bit. Mrs. H. Carpenter calls. Mother goes home with her, and returns with violets etc. Set 'em out. Mrs. Vaughn has a culinary conflagration up stairs. I loaf by the fire when suddenly Richie arrives. Then Robert. Then Mr. Putnam! He won't stop (owing to Robert I find) but will call again next week. Quite a crowd.

Friday. May. 20th. 1881.

Am aroused by mother at 5 or so, by reason of a sick-headache. Do everything, and also set out a lot of plants which Mr. Butcher arrives with. And Mr. Carpenter brings some lilies of the valley & more violets. Don't get to work till 12 or more. Carry some of the mock turtle up to Anna, and back in 7 minutes. Mrs. Springer comes down and partakes also. Paint. Miss Manchester & Helen Potter call. Very jolly. Paint. Start bonnet. Come down & endeavor to sup but Sam comes. Talk Pawtuxet. For a wonder! I get him to enter my den, and set him to cutting out cards, from which occupation there is no escape. And we talk. Queer, very. But I enjoy it. "Goodnight." *

Saturday. May 21st. 1881.

Up at 6. Make fire & then paint all day. Helen Hazard calls. Gas inserted in front hall. Mr. Peck in. Mr. Willey calls for his basket. Mr. Carpenter brings some air plants! Martha calls. I finish bonnet, dress in said attire, and we all four take the 7.20 car. Are duly joined by Edward, and we spend a delicious evening with Lotta the inimitable. Wish it was longer. The play was "Musette". Mrs. Springer enjoyed it as much as anyone. Edward comes home with us and we finish off the soup, with lobster & etc. I hope Sam went.

Letter from G. Bissell for mother, with power of att{orney}. business.

Sunday. May 22nd. 1881.

9! Paint. Mary comes & goes to church with Aunt C. I go over to Millie's P.M. 2 more books finished. Ride home. Robert here. This set to be increased to 12 & another similar set later. *And* the large sketch for F. L. Soap. *And* the Xmas cards not sketched yet. *And* the Easter cards to be done by the first of August! But profits will accrue. Hi yah!

Monday. May. 23rd. 1881.

Paint, paint, paint. Certain Mumfords calls on Aunt C. Miss Greene & Mrs. Dodge do likewise by me. And Martha and Mabel Hill appear a bit later and Mabel plays for us. I wire and beribbon a shade hat for mother. No calls.

Tuesday. May. 24th. 1881.

Up at 5.30. Cloudy and threatening, fog & northeast wind, but clears, and we all set out in high style. Sam meets us at the bridge, and we get to Pawtuxet at 11. Row up to the spring and lunch in comfort and luxury, straggle off in the woods with Sam, and enjoy ourselves generally. Go higher up, drift down, Get hoards of flowers, and home in the 6 o'clock car. Mary Brown & family in the car. Sam comes home with us, *Takes tea*! and plays a rubber of whist. Very pleasant day.

Wednesday. May 25th. 1881.

7 or so. Paint. Draw sinful jest on Death & Cupid for Sam. Mother & Aunt C. gad abroad all day more or less. Martha over. I go and see Mrs. Diman. She was in the summer house where May had "painted the roses as high as she could reach"! A moment at Miss Maria Kessler's, and a few more at Annie Rawson's. Clarence brought us some flour. Robert comes. John Willey over. Jim also, and last of all Mr. Stillwell. He & Aunt C. beat Jim & mother, & then, Robert going off with our Saturnine young friend, Mr. Stillwell and I play 2 to 2. He [Mr. Stillwell] brought me some lilacs (Stolen.)

Thurs. May 26th. 1881.

I find it agrees with me to get up just in time for breakfast. I buy my 5 cts. worth of almonds and send off my 26 ct. joke—signed, sealed, stamped, and registered in all directions. "Rev. F. S. Billings." Read to Millie, school, 75 cts, go and walk home with Martha, dine there, down st. with them, Dr. Gay a moment, errands divers, & home. Readorn, & go with Miss Manchester to see Martha. Sup and re-readorn. Sidney Putnam calls.

Friday. May 27th. 1881.

Paint & draw. Mother has a bad headache. Wash dishes. Class Day invit.[2] Promenade tickets from Jim, & note of ack. from Sam. Mary & Alice around. Julia Jastrum & Eddie call. Thunder shower. Robert. Cards. Hot Day. 91 etc.

May 28th. Saturday. 1881.

Get breakfast & wash dishes. Paint. do two cards. Early call from old Mr. Carpenter. Martha over.

Sunday. May 29th. 1881.

7.30! Go to church and sit with Martha. Hear the Rev. Slicer. Don't like him. Walk home with Martha attended by Robert. Home & dine. Richard Hamlin arrives at 3, promptly, and we sally forth in great state. Go to Hunt's Mills. Get lots of lovely flowers. Very pleasant time. Meet the Jastrum's, & Orville Fisher on Red Bridge. Home at 7. About 9 miles. Not a bit tired. Richie stays to supper & till 9 o'clock. Lizzie & Henrietta here also. And Richie asked me to a praise meeting in some church tonight, and to a game of ball tomorrow. Quite a rush——— .

Monday. May. 30th. 1881.

Paint two cards, draw one, sketch whale, alter last set, & paint four flower cards! Mother & Aunt C. go to the woman suffrage convention, and I go and invite Miss Manchester to spend the evening with me. Then I go to Martha's, meet her, & drag her over. Richie brings back my gloves & stays. Henry Townsend calls. Then Robert, with a poor show for work. Get along some though. Music. "Minister's Cat" etc. Very good time.

Tuesday. May 31st. 1881.

7 or so. Paint two cards & draw two & draw whale. Wash dinner dishes. Mother goes to some more Convention P. M. Robert over. John Willey in. Sam comes. Robert & Mother beat Sam and I 3 to 1. Bad luck to it. He never saw the bottom of that box till Sunday! And then his mother found 'em! Idiot. And he brought a quarter for his share of the boat, which we had a pentagonal row over of course.

Wednesday. June 1st. 1881.

Early for once, and sweep and garnish my room. Scrub up dressing case, and consecrate the same to cash, cologne, & candy. Paint all day. Mother & Aunt C. go out to Pawtucket to call on the Spencers. Annie Aborn comes to see me, & Junie Keach also. I run over to see Martha between 6 & 8. Write to C. Hedge, Class Day invitations from Fred Hazard.

Thurs. June 2nd. 1881.

Finish the 13 cards and post them ere ten. Go to Millies. School. 1.00. Lunch at Café, Salad, 25. Soda after. Get a 4 ct. comb. Tooth filled, I am getting really to like that operation. Call on Sophie. Home with my coffee & whisk off again. Mrs. Sayles & Miss Harris call here. Also W. Carpenter. I spend the afternoon with Miss Manchester, Miss Babcock calls there. Then I call on Helen Potter and stay to tea. Write to C. Hedge.

Friday June 3. 1881.

Hurrah! A day off! I do housework, and start to remodel and improve that checked linen thing of Ada's. I go not out & none come in.

Saturday. June 4th. 1881.

late and lazy. Help about house all the morning. Take work and trot over to Martha's at three, and stay till eight. Mrs. Henry Carpenter in. Jim calls. Very pleasant for once. We beat the rubber out of 5. Gives me a pink he had in his buttonhole, and I bestowed on him a tea rose, bit of forgetmenot, heliotrope, daisy, & pansie. Nice boy tonight. (Note from C. Hazard.).

Sunday. June 5th. 1881.

Miss Manchester cometh, and we go over to Martha's and here the Reverend Slicer. Better. Meet Robert outside and receive at his hands $37.50. 25 to mother, 2.50 to spend, and ten in my strong box. Go over to Millie's and finish Light of Asia. Home at 3.15 and dine. Uncle William calls. then Robert. Small progress.

Monday. June 6th. 1881.

Up early, black stove, make fire, etc. Go down st. at 9. Spend 7.50 diversely. Mercedes parasol, bonnet, mitts, necktie, & cir. Call at Millie's a minute. home, and am sent back straitway for strawberries, 75 cts. The Misses Spencer and their sister Mrs. Burlingame of Pawtucket spend the day with us. Lamb & lemon pies; salad, hot biscuit, poundcake, jellie cake & strawberries for tea, with choc. & coffee. Mr. B. comes to supper, and Cousin Mary. Miss Manchester called, ascended to my apartment, partook of refreshments from my casket, and played us the Chinese Serenade etc. Edward arrives, and we disport ourselves variously. They depart early and we have whist, losing the rubber, and a glorious "rere supper". Very pleasant day.

Tuesday. June 7th. 1881
cloudy and rainy.

6.30. Paint whale scene with good success. Mother & Aunt C. gad abroad all day. Clams for dinner. Richie calls. Whist. He & I beat 4 to 1. Invited me to the Promenade.

Wednesday June 8th. 1881

6.30. Finish whale mostly. Go over to M's for an hour or so. Home & dine. Invent Pawtuxet party, and scuttle over to Miss Manchester's. Out. Martha's again. She comes home with me. Sew, read, and eat candy. We two again assault Miss M. All arranged. Write three invitations, and post 'em before 8.30. Sam, Jim, & Robert. Clouds & rainy.

Thurs. June 9th. 1881.

5 or so. Mother has a headache. Do all the work, curse the weather, dress up in old clothes and go to Prof. Blakes's wedding. Very pleasant affair. Reception at Mr. Vernon's, bride's relation. All the junior Hazards. Delectable

lunch. Mr. Bradford of Cambridge there! I go home with the H's, then call on Martha, walk over together. She goes to Miss M's & I go to Mrs. Fillinghast's fair. Cloudy and cold, and rained a bit—dead failure I'm afraid. I sported with the babes and made myself generally useful. Robert over this P.M. and carried off the whale. Back again this evening & wants more whales, smaller and smallest, right off.

Friday. June 10th. 1881.

8! A cold driving northeast storm, 50° in the shade. I stay quietly at home and paint a small whale, as well as doing the housework. Call on Miss Manchester at 5. Mother went down to the Browns. Poor Mrs. F. didn't cover her expenses! Class Day is wisely postponed until tomorrow, but much I fear the weather will be still impropitious. I pity the young girls who are interested.
Beastly weather.

Saturday June 11th. 1881.

Another Class Day postponed, and another day of cold northeast wind and heavy clouds if no rain. But clears up at about 6, and shows a cloudless, moonlit night, (total eclipse!) to end the longest, coldest, abominablest, "June storm" that I ever saw. Mother still dolorous and ailing, we *must* get her off somewhere for a rest. Long letter from Thomas. Martha over & Mother & Aunt C. out. Paint and "fiddle." I can play on the painner!!! I can play the "Campbells are Coming"; and some of The White Cockade. Onehandedly. To the dire distress of my friends. Martha in again, & Cousin Mary calls. Write to T.

Sunday. June 12th 1881.

Sat up in a comforter and watched the total eclipse of a bright full moon. Dozed and woke alternately and saw it all. Worth seeing, too. Go over to Mr. Woodbury's and sit with Miss Manchester. Sermon on the Revised Edition. Miss Manchester stops in with me on returning and giveth me pansies. I go over to Millie's & read her Mrs. Browning. She fails. Stop at Martha's. Home by eight. Clarence & his father called. Eke Robert all P.M. Retire at 1. For the third time "tomorrow's Class Day".

Monday. June 13th. 1881.

Class Day at last. Cold, & rains; with wind N. E.! Up betimes, finish little whale and take 'em down to Robert ere 7.30. Home by way of Marthas. Go with her to morning ex. in all my old clothes. Walk over to Dr. Barkes with her. Home and dine luxuriously on beatified beefsteak, new potatoes, lobster salad, floating island, & delectable strawberries. Fiddle. Attire myself in pink muslin to the chilly horror of my family, stop for Martha, and go the afternoon business. Hot, hot, hot. Glaring sunshine and gasping crowd. Saw no end of folk I knew. Richie discovers us and sticketh closer than a brother. The gentle Jim in his tall hat cavorteth with Hattie Kiltons pretty cousin all day. Bad boy, Jim. Richie walks home with us as far as Martha's where I purposely elude him. Reappears in the evening, and as it has again clouded up he make a call instead of Promenading.

Tuesday. June 14th. 1881.

8–9. Note from Robert. Finish the three whales. Letter from Thomas. He has changed to Evaniston, Wyoming Ty. $100 per. month & expenses. Residency. Martha over. I condole with her with good effect. Sam calls. Edward. Whist. Aunt C. & Sam beat us 2 to 1 & then he & mother beat us 5 to 5. 12 o'clock!

Wednesday. June 15th. 1881.

Up betimes, and go to Commencement with Martha. Awful squeeze and rush, best seats possible, and jolly time. Catch the pink and blue cousin on the way out, and poison her. Home to lunch. Martha over. I go down st. with her, to get velvet frame for Jim's Class photo. Home & sup. Robert over with those everlasting whales to be fixed again. Sam calls with his friend Harold Childs. Whist. Mr. C. & I beat 2 to 1. Then he goes off to his class supper, & Sam & Aunt C. beats us 4 to 2. 1 game in one hand on our side.

Thurs. June 16th. 1881.

Really fair weather but still cool. Up bright & early and finally finish those whales. Get 'em down to Edwards by 9. Make him quite a call. Mr. Simmons Senior comes in. Ed. gives me a letter file & base ball guide. Get "Condensed Novels" and read to Millie. School. No pay. Ride home. Miss Briggs in car. She kindly lends me another h'k'f when I desecrate mine, my gloves, dress, car step, and the surrounding county. Home very wilted, and snooze continuously.

Friday June 17th. 1881.

Rise at 12. Paint pansies. Mother & Aunt C. gad. Card from Thomas. Mrs. Budlong calls. I disseminated icecream to the little "Budluns". Clarence calls. Jim & Robert. Sophie & Henry Townsend. Whales, whist, (even) muggins, candor, (exit S. & H.) whist. Robert & Aunt C. "weasle" us. Jim remarkably facetious.

Saturday June 18th. 1881.

Arise betimes & do the housework. Review the farming and paint whales. Martha calls & mother goes out. Miss Manchester & Helen Potter call. Very jolly. M. & I call on Miss M. later, and then I escort the damsel home. Write to T. Second step-sittable night this year.

Sunday. June 19th. 1881.

Miss Manchester to church, but I sit with Aunt C. & snooze under a dull English minister. Go over to Millie's in a dashing shower. She is sick in bed with an influenza. Call at Martha's and stay to tea. She comes home with me to cool off. Robert over. He is sick.

Monday June 20th 1881

Up very betimes, get breakfast and all the work done by 8.30. Finish whales, & take 'em down to Robert. He is worse, had a doctor. Martha went down with me, and we shopped. Spend my last half dime to fill the crypt. Mother goes down to the Brown's and comes back with a day lily, and Edward. Set out the one, and play whist with the other. Mother & Aunt C. 4 to 3. Weazled at that.

Tuesday. June 21st. 1881.

Sweep above stairs, and generally garnish. Explore the mysteries of the suttle, and discover a "bas-relief" angel's head, dirty old plaster, but pretty. Instate in in [*sic*] my room. Mend petticoats. Mrs. Putnam sent me some lovely Jaqueminots, and I vainly try to paint one. Trot over to Miss Manchester's a moment. Mother & Aunt C. go down to the Browns. Robert better.

Wednesday, June 22nd. 1881.

Late and lazy. Look in vain for my easter card sketches. Mother gaddeth abroad and brings me a birthday present of a cambric dress most lovely to behold. Start to make it. Go out and invite Sophie & Annie to my picnic. Rather discouraging. Home & sew. Martha over. Julia Jastrum calls. Junie calls. Mother & Aunt C. go around to the H. Carpenters. Robert over, gives me 18 dollars of which I take ten. For the three small whales. I give five to mother. Misses Manchester & Potter come around & back out of the San Souci.

Thurs. June 23rd. 1881.

Up early & do all the work. Call at Edwards, Millie's school, 1.25. Edward's, dinner with the Browns, Martha's, & home. Study of horseflesh & harness. Mother, Aunt C., Lizzie, Henrietta, Julia, Florrie, Edward, Ray, Pardon, Eddie, Richie, & I go to the Sans Souci to see "Billy Taylor".[3] Fairly amusing. R. persuades me to walk home.

Friday. June 24th. 1881.

Late—"All on account of Eliza." Fix whale, & sketch "Leader". Anna comes & spends the day. Mary, Alice, & the infant Charles also call. Mother & I go to ride with Anna. I call at Sophies, Annie's, and Martha's. Mostly out. Mrs. Carpenter & Florrie call. Robert over—Horse.[4] Jim calls. He & Robert fight over hames and harness. And especially legs. Whist. Our 4 to 2. 38 to 12 points.

Saturday June 25th. 1881.

Up very betimes. Paint on whale, & sketch horse and get them down to Edward's at 9 A.M. Call at the Browns. Call on Martha, shell peas, etc, revamp my old sunshade, and narrate "Heloise." Call at the Townsend's & invite them to the picnic. Call on Sophie a minute and arrange. Home & dine. Hot. Mother has a headache. Martha in, & we call on Miss M. a moment. I can play on the pianeer.

Sunday. June 26th. 1881.

7. Maternal headache & I do all the work, ablute & go to Miss M's church with Martha. Hot. Home & dine. Richie comes, peanut laden, to go to walk, but we soon return as it rains. He is to get bananas for the picnic & help us start. Robert over. $5.00 for big whale. Write to T.

Monday. June 24th. 1881.

Up early & wash dishes. Get breakfast. Ride down to Martha's with Mr. Carpenter, Sen. Jim went to Conanicut Sunday. I spend three & a half hours in the Atheneam drawing horses. Go to Roberts & dine there. Go down st. with Martha & Mabel Hill. Treat. Start to draw. *Mr. Stillwell* comes! Whist. They 4 to 3.

Tuesday. June 28th. 1881.

Draw horse. Martha over. We start for Rocky Point but back out on account of rain. Catch my "strawberry-roan" on Dyer St. & sketch him to my heart's content. Home with M. & draw. Call on Annie Aborn, Miss Manchester, & Annie Rawson. Miss M. & her mother call in the evening. Mrs. Springer returns.

Wednesday. June 29. 1881.

Wash dishes & draw horses with good success. Aunt C. & mother gad diversely. Mrs. Springer in and out. Miss Manchester in a moment. More flowers set out. I fiddle. Mr. Sturgiss Carpenter calls. Eke Edward. Hot.

Thurs. June 30th. 1881.

Up at 4! Finish horse, & take 'em down to Robert. To be altered of course. Carry Millie some waterlilies & "Rudder Grange".[5] Last lesson in Mrs. Berg's. 75 cts. Buy some scissors. 50 cts. Go up for Martha at the D.& D. school & walk down together. Home to dinner. Go over there P.M. with work, but "barberge" her instead. Call on Miss Manchester. Hot day rather. Our house is a [*sic*] cool as a grave.

Friday. July 1st. 1881.

Up at 4. Resketch horse, and carry it down by nine. Inhabit Edward's office, and am introduced to Mr. Samuel R. Simmons Senior. Unimpressive man.

Come home and sew. More thunderstorm. Clarence calls. Sophie & Theo. come over. Ray in on an errand.

Saturday July 2nd 1881.

Up at 4. Make cake and otherwise labor. We learn by John Arnold of Garfield's assassination.[6] He is not dead yet, I believe. Mother & Aunt C. gad incessantly, Mrs. Springer flitters in and out, and I go over to Martha's, (calling on Mabel Hill, out;) and stay to tea. Last day of minority.

Sunday July 3rd. 1881.

Up at 4. My 21st birthday. I am the richer by two white skirts from Aunt C. Some candy & strawberries from Frau Springer, a dress, two tin cups, five jars, a metalic hair brush, two speckled neck ruffles, twenty one cents, and a great bunch of hothouse flowers from Mother, and a lovely basket full of flowers from—Richie! Make sponge cake and labor generally. Hot.

July 4th. Monday. 1881.

Up before *light*. Compose innumerable sandwiches & pack spongecake, poundcake, & lemons etc. Martha over. Then Richie, and we haste away. We assemble on the bridge, Mother, Lizzie Brown, Annie Townsend, Sophie Aborn, Miss Manchester, Martha & I, Henry, Foster, Theo, Mr. Seagraves, Harry Manchester, Richie, & by great good luck Knight Richmond who was in the Pawtuxet car. I enjoyed him more than any of 'em. Delicious lunch, and very jolly time, save two showers, one tremendous, with the biggest hail stones I ever saw.* Martha, Knight, and I crouch under our umbrellas out on the meadow through the worst of it. Foster seems to take to Miss M. We try of the seven o'clock car, but refrain out of pure pity for the horses—& the imppossibility of getting in. Sophie, Annie, Seagraves & Theo walk to the park & take a car; Messrs. Hamlin, H. Townsent, & Manchester, Martha and I prance to Eddy St. & take one there. M. & N. go home via Point St., we others stop & get beer, soda, & candy, & so home, losing Mr. Manchester in our travels. He arrives later having vainly sought. Sophie comes back in gala attire with Theo, Henry drops in, the others all appear save Annie & Seagraves & Lizzie & Knight &c. & after departure we others play whist. Sophie & Henry beat Theo. an [*sic*] I 2 games. Tired, some.

Tuesday. July 5th. 1881.

Rise at ten. Birthday card from Helen. Call on Miss Manchester. All right. Call on Mrs. Diman. Do all the dishes today. Sew some. Martha over. I walk home with her at 8, and catch Robert leaving a horse car as I return. Talk horse. Cherries. Mrs. Sayles sent me a lot, and roses & honeysuckle. Mrs. Springer gave me a pretty cameo ring which I wear on my engagement finger & mystify all therewith.

Wednesday July 6th. 1881.

6. Hot at last. Gasp about. draw some. Martha over. I go down st., meet her at the boat, & we sail down to Rocky Point and back. Delicious. Snatch Foster Townsend from a hat store and we three go down to the New York boat to see Mrs. Springer off. But she went by train. Sails for Europe tomorrow. Go home with M. of course. Lizzie Brown and Hattie Batchelder call. Mr. Still-well comes, feasts upon cake and spends the evening. The elders retiring on account of coolness, we sit on the moonlit steps and talk of love & marriage. He's quite nice & sensible when you get at him.

Thurs. July 7th. 1881.

Cooler. 5. Paint horses. Blankets & spreads washed. Go over to Millie's P.M. & read "Rudder Grange." Home at 6.15 or so. Miss Manchester here. She goes down to the store & Miss Briggs with me & I go up with her and call at the Dimans. Stay to tea, and am gifted with cherries, roses, and a lovely bangle that was May's. A little curly silver snake. Home. Mrs. Thomas calls. Robert over. Sophie & Henry Townsend call and invite [me] out on the Pawtuxet Sat. night. *O* yes!

Friday July 8th. 1881.

7 or so. Paint horses. Call on Miss Man. They are going Sat. night and I must go with them. Go and refuse Sophie & Henry. They contemplate Martha in-stead. Get paper, return home & paint more horse. Old Mr. Carpenter brings us a blue-fish, and takes me to ride. Call on Jessie Luther. Stop at Martha's, and learn that she is here with the Simmonses. Come home & find Mr. & Miss Man. & Richie. Then come Martha, Jim, & Sam. Music. The Man.s invite all the rest of the company to join *their* rowing party. All accept but Sam.

I have made myself a gorgeous halo hat faced with brown velvet & trimmed with mull. Very pretty. Cost, $0.00. I have wanted one for six years.

Saturday, July 9th. 1881.

Up betimes and paint horse all day. Martha over P.M., Richie arrived, and we go down to the Seekonk. Jim was there, thank the gods. He rowed one boat with Miss Potter and Miss Man. & I row the others, Richie steering. He nearly spoiled the party by his incessant idiocy. We row nearly up to Pawtucket, hitch to a buoy, row down again, lunch in a lovely grove on the banks of the Ten Mile, Mr. M. & I get water from a crystal spring, Martha & I play "dumb orator" most effectively, and we row home in one of the loveliest moonlit nights I ever saw. Our only mishap was the loss of a lantern; which mysteri-ously disappeared. Jim goes home with Miss Potter, and then with Martha. He was the mainstay of the party, and won golden opinions all around. I *do like ca*pabi*l*ity. Richie waits for me to ask him in but I don't and he departs, all sorrowful. He wanted me to go to walk tomorrow P.M. but I extinguished him. What ever will I do with the man.

Sunday. July 10th. 1881.

Betimes. Paint. long nap. Ablute & call on Miss Man., in, Miss Potter, out, Miss Luther, out, Miss Hill, out, and Miss Abby Marian Maine, *in.* Edward, Robert, & Lizzie here to tea.

Monday. July 11. 1881.

Overslept. Finish off horses. Take 'em down, via Martha's. Call on T. C. Greene, and arrange the power document, go to Rider's & write the letter, take it up to Cousin Ray's and get him to sign and give me the certificate, and send it off by noon. Feels good to be of age. Ride home with Cousin Ray. Read and loaf. Start long F. L. Soap card. Cousin Mary calls. John Willey calls. Wrote to T.

Tuesday. July 12th 1881.

Rather betimes. Paint diligently. Run out to Miss. M.'s & M.'s A.M. Mother & Aunt C. go to Silver Spring & dine. I don't. Miss Man. calls at 3 or so. Then Martha arrives. Then Hattie Salisbury calls. I go home with Miss M. & so miss a ride with the Jastrums. They stop for me, but mother goes. Robert over. Horses again. Write to M.

Wed. July 13th. 1881.

Up betimes. Paint. Go to Marthas for an hour or so. Home & paint. Go to M's. again at dusk. Her mother calls here. I post a letter to Martha—No callers.

Thurs. July 14th. 1881.

Up betimes. Am decidedly overpowered by the huckleberry fiend. Natheless I don my pink muslin & go down to see Martha off. Mr. Stillwell in the car down. I hint at Hartford property, and he is evidently impressed. Miss Manchester, Gus Peirce, Winthrop Smith, etc. etc. All assist in bidding farewell to Martha. Then I go about with Miss M.—(O, saw Fred Hazard & Marian Whitney in the depot.) Call on T. C. Greene, out, & go up to Millies. Mr. Taylor calls there, & Lizzie Brown. Ride home. Mother gets in. Eat a good dinner, sleep all the afternoon, and am quite recovered. Jim calls. We go out to post letters, & take quite a walk. Very nice. Whist. We 2 to 1. Write to M.

Friday. July 15th. 1881.

About 5. Finish off all Kendall's things. Take 'em down to Edward's. Call on T. C. Greene. Am met by mother, cash check for $171.00, and proceed to pay bills. Called on Walter Paine. Handsome and delightful. Ride home. Call on Mrs. Diman. Go and get wild roses and paint 'em. Sam calls. I wouldn't give 2 cents for him one way or the other.

Saturday July 16th. 1881.

Paint on Easter cards. Sweep room. Loaf a much. Write to T. Miss Harris called. Card from Martha. And note from Harriet explaining her recusance in the Bristol Ferry expedition.

Sunday. July 17th. 1881.

Wash dishes and ablute. Go to Millie's and read her the whole of "Evangeline."[7] Saw Ellie Bush on way home. Called on Mrs. Anthony. Home at 6. Maria here. Anna had called to take me to ride, and Richie to take me to walk. Walter Paine Calls. Robert over. Tired.

Monday. July 18th. 1881.

Up betimes, and wash last night's dishes. Refinished the Kendall business cards, and carry 'em down to the Brown's. Shop a bit, and walk three or four miles. Rains P.M. Letter from Martha A.M. Miss Manchester over P.M. Very jolly time. I write a prim note breaking my engagement with Harry. Very prim and severe. Mr. Manchester, you must be aware that your unaccountable conduct in not calling on me since our engagement renders it impossible for that relation to continue. Hoping to see you at some future time. I remain your *friend* etc." Sophie calls after tea & stays till 8.30. I see her home, or nearly so. Warm tonight.

Tuesday. July 19th. 1881.

Early up, and paint intermittently all day. Letter from M., and note from Robert with reversible card to alter. He calls for it at about 11. Miss M. called. Cassie comes. Richie calls. Henrietta over with a bluefish. Richie, Cassie, & I walk down and induce the Jastrums to accompany us Thursday.

Wednesday. 20th. 1881.

Very betimes, wash dishes, get breakfast & paint. Aunt C. goes to Bristol Ferry. Cassie comes down at 10.30. Mother goes down st. I run around to Miss Manchester with tickets. Anna & Clarence call. Also Jim. Ark-arc discussion.

Thurs. July 21st. 1881.

V[ery]. B[etimes]. Paint all day. I'm as lame when I get up at night as if I'd walked ten miles. We all go to see "Boccacio" at Sans Souci. Us four, Cousin Mary, Miss M. & her mother (brother sick) Lizzie, Hen., & Maria, Edward, Julia & Pardon, Hattie Batchelder & Richie. "Reca Murilli["] as she calls herself, is as fine an actress & lovely a lady as I ever saw.

Friday. July 22nd. 1881.

Actually sleep till eight, having risen at my usual hour & fairly fallen back from dizziness. The other folks go down the river and I paint. Letter from

Harpers Bros for Martha refusing her story. Write to her. Clarence & Jessie Budlong in. The Jastrums stop a bit. Robert over.

Saturday July 23rd. 1881.

Letter from Martha. Paint lazily all day. Cassie down to breakfast! I dress up for her benefit in gorgeous attire. Miss Man. & her brother come over.

Sunday. July 24th. 1881.

Up early. Write to M. Sleep. Go out to walk with Cassie, Richie, and Robert. Short walk and long loaf. R. invited me to go to the Park Garden, "Mascotte", Monday, and then Cassie. Refused. Robert & Lizzie to tea.

Monday. July 25th. 1881.

to Breakfast. Paint. The rest spend the day at R{oger}. W{illiams}.'s Park.[8] Mrs. Daniels calls.. Mrs. Fillinghast & Mrs. Percy call. Cassie & I call on the Browns. Edward comes home & calls. Annie Aborn & Theo calls.

Tuesday. July 26th. 1881.

8.30! Morning thunderstorm. Paint a bit. Go down st. with Cassie via Prospect Terrace. Ride home & call on Miss M. Take our supper in a basket & go down to Red Bridge, via Waterman & Pitman sts.

Wednesday. July 27th. 1881.

to breakfast. Cassie off at ten. She bestows upon me a piece of dewdrop lace— ge—orgeous! Paint a much. Call on Clara Gladding & baby, & at Ray's. He has sprained his ancle. Letter from M. Write to her. Jim calls & I have him all to myself. Metaphysics.

Thurs. July 28th. 1881.

Ere five. Write to M. Paint. Go over to Millie's, carry her cream, shop a bit, & call on Mrs. Diman and Miss Manchester. I only weigh 113 lbs. A call from Sam. Mostly solus. Delightful talk. *He* says "Go ahead!" I'm going.

Fri. July 29th. 1881.

'Bout 6. Paint briskly, being reanimated with noble resolves since Sam's appreciation & approval. Not in the least degree *owing* to him, but merely more firmly fixed in my mind. Letter from M. Run down to Roberts & show cards, trot home & paint some more. Nap in chair. Got my two dollars of Miss Murphy. Henrietta to tea. Old Mr. Carpenter, Mr. Stillwell, & Edward call. Mrs. Dix has brutally chopped down all our m.g.s[9] on her place.

Saturday July 30th. 1881.

7, but was up till one last night. Work hard all day, and write to Thomas & father. *Cold*! Spend the evening with Miss Manchester, music & rest. Write to M.

Sunday July 31st. 1881.

Late. Putter about & wash dishes. Go to Millies. Wrote to M. Robert to tea and insufferable evening till 11.

Monday. August 1st. 1881.

Sew a bit before breakfast. Paint. Write to M., a bit. Paint. Dabble in Emerson & take a nap. Spencers call. Eke Richard.

Tuesday Aug. 2nd. 1881.

Sew a bit etc. Paint. Write to M. & Cassie. Paint. Jim called. Sort of row— results doubtful.

Wednesday Aug. 3rd. 1881.

5. Write a little note to Jim. Slept last night—without moving! Sew a bit. Letter from M. Write to her. Finish Easter cards. Sew some more. Call on Lu, and show the family my cards. Applause. Old Mr. C. stops in his buggy as we grace the steps. Write to Lu.

Thurs. Aug. 4th. 1881.

Ere five. Sew. letter from M. Finish my letter to her, 20 pages. Go gaily out. Leave Easter cards at Roberts. Shop a bit. Buy 50 ct. heliotype of "Daniel". Go to Hattie Salisbury's and dine. Go to Millie's & read. Try a bit of Bret Harte at Baugs Williams. Fall in with Mabel Hill; preach to her, go home with her, stay to tea with her. Home about 8. Robert stops a moment on that famous horse, attended by young Mr. Van Slyck, to whom I am duly introduced. Nice voice. Very pleasant day.

Friday Aug. 5th. 1881.

Up at 4. Out at 5. go down to see Lu off, wait around an hour, and miss her after all. Meet J. Willey on way home & give him flowers. Write to Lu. Write to Cassie. Mrs. Monroe comes & spends the day. I take a grand shampoo. Sewed a lot. Grandpa Carpenter came & took me to ride. Nice time. Hollyhocks.

Sat. Aug. 6th. 1881.

5. Sew. Wash dishes. Letters & papers from T. Hattie Farmer called. R. Hamlin's Pawtuxet party comes off—great success. Annie Townsend, Fosters, C. Hamlin & I. Just lunch enough, perfect weather, lovely moon, high water—everything nice. Walked up from the bridge. Very pleasant time. Old Mr. Carpenter in at breakfast time.

Sunday Aug. 7th. 1881.

Lay late for rest's sake. Wrote to Thomas. Wrote to M. Filed letters of two years back.

Monday. Aug. 8th. 1881.

5. Morning Glories. Aunt C. goes off to Bristol Ferry. General Greene calls. I go over to Millie's. Pub. Lib. & Athenaeum. Edward calls & brings me a kitten.

Tues. Aug. 9th. 1881.

Letter from Charlotte Hedge & Martha. Write to both. Make sweeping cap, out of seven pieces. Enjoy the cat. Go to Martha's "coop" and get a reference for her & borrow 3 books! Call on Mabel Hill. Out. Go to Atheneum. Pop. Sci. Call on Grandma Anthony. She gives me a great bag of sapun apples which I carry home—9¼ lbs. Harry Manchester calls. Annie & Mrs. Townsend call. H. & I walk home with them.

Wed. Aug. 10th. 1881.

5 or a bit later. Am taking my vacation at home—haven't painted a stroke for two days. Mother and I go to the Budlong baby's funeral. Fred Hedge & Lizzie Brown call. Mother goes out and I spend the afternoon at [*sic*] take tea at the Dimans. Retta Clark there. Nice talk with her, and jolly game of tennis. I like her. Old Mr. Carpenter stops as we sit on our steps—mother & I.

Thurs. Aug. 11th. 1881.

Continue to vacate, and don't get up before eight. Mother has a headache, and I wash dishes. Read Tennyson's "Queen Mary." Go over to Millie's & read "Lady of Shallott.["] [10] Buy some slippers—2.00. & a wee jar of olives for mother—28 cts. Stop at Ath. House empty. Call on Retta, Helen Potter, & Miss Greene—all out. Sit on steps with kitty when R. Hamlin appears. Invites me to go down to Bowser's & get some cream. Invites me to go to see the Mascot—Park Garden. Decline both. Bah! He gets unendurable. Fred. Hedge & Henrietta call. Pleasant evening. Wrote to Lu.

Friday Aug. 12th. 1881.

Late again. Arrange bathing dress. Write to Cassie. Go over & play tennis with Retta. Also talk.

Saturday Aug. 13th. 1881

Go to Squantum with Mary Carpenter. Carried my book & enjoyed the morning. Met the Sharps, and enjoyed the afternoon. Delicious dinners, bowling, environment, all serene. Got lost by my party and thereby gained more talk with Mary Sharp, and a ride up in Theo Fillinghasts buggy. Very pleasant. The most enjoyable day I've had for a long time. My circle widens. Martha, Cassie, Retta, Mary—life may be happier than I thought. Letter from Martha on return.

Sunday August 14th. 1881.

Go to church with Mary, and hear Dr. Hedge. Good. Walk home with Carrie Richmond, am invited in, and look at pictures. Fine old house. Hot day. Good dinner. Then a nap in pura naturabilis. Edward over to tea. "No" from Love.

Monday. August. 15th. 1881.

Ere the sun. Sew a bit. Letters from Martha & Lu. Write to L. Injudiciously bestow divers bread and butter upon an imposing little boy. Go down st. stopping at Retta's. Finish Rudder Grange to Millie. Buy boots 5.50, hkfs 40, envelopes 10. Book 6. Home & sup on watermelon, encumbered by cat. Who should call today but Clara Perry née Whitman, & her husband. Scene. Write to M.

Tuesday. August. 16th. 1881.

Ere the sun. Sew a bit. Letters from Martha & Cassie. Write to M. Go over there & get "Jacobi". Call on Mabel Hill. Get underflannels 3.90 & dress-pattern 25., and pay Calder's bill—2.71. Joined by Sam for a minute. Mary Sharp called while I was out, and invited me to spend a day there this week. Write a poetical note on barberry card. Robert calls.

Wed. Aug. 17th. 1881.

5.40! Colder than Greenland. Sew a bit. Mr. Carpenter with corn. Take tea at the Brown's with Caddy & her husband.

Thurs. Aug. 18th. 1881.

Late. Fire in the stove! Sew a bit. Go a shopping. Call on Millie. Call on Retta. Rousing talk.

Friday. Aug. 19th. 1881.

5.50 I guess. Letter from Lu, and card from Cassie. Begin thick dress. Go to P. O., and call on Retta. R. Hamlin.

Saturday Aug. 20th 1881.

Up betimes, took 9.50 train for Nayatt and spent the day at the Sharps. Very pleasant. Rode, walked, sung, and generally enjoyed ourselves. Good lunch & good dinner, Mr. Boget, Prescott Clark, Zack Chafee, & Mr. Homer appear at intervals. Home at 8. Lizzie here. Letter from Martha.

Sunday. Aug. 21st. 1881.

Go and hear Uncle Edward. Bring him home to dinner. Saw Retta. Clarence here. Uncle E. takes a nap and otherwise enjoys himself. Good dinner. takes some soap cards and departs. Robert over. Letterhead to do. Write to M. 40 pages.

Monday. Aug. 22nd. 1881.

Sunlight. Ablute. Sweep and garnish my room. Letters from Thomas, mine a blank, and card from M. wanting thread. I go down st. therefore. Call on Mabel Hill. Read to Millie. Beer & two cookies. Call on Ellie Bush, Sophie, Annie, & Retta. She comes home with me. I go home with her. Aunt C. returns. Anna in. Mary over. Mr. Budlong calls with some pears. Letter from father & card from Mabel Davis.

Tuesday. Aug. 23rd. 1881.

Sunrise. Paint more or less. Write to L. Call from Mabel Davis. She *can* talk. Write a bit to M. Mother & Aunt C. go down to the Brown's. Edward over. Whist. They three to our two.

Wednesday. Aug. 24th. 1881.

Ere five. Spend day with Mabel Davis. Very pleasant. Home by eight. Cassie here.

Thurs. Aug. 25th. 1881.

Late. Fly around and go down st. with Cassie. See Maria, and go to H. Townsend's to order tickets.[11] Read Mark Twain to Millie. Jolly. Go to Pub. Lib. & get a book on my new card. Saw Mr. Bogert there. Also made the acquaintance of a young youth of 13, puzzled over the catalogues. Mr. Peck to dinner. Nap. Write to M. & Carrie Hazard. Letter from M. Jim calls! Robert over. Do letterhead for R. & monogram for Jim.* A dime to be engraved. Results 50 cts. Pleasant evening.

Friday Aug. 26th. 1881.

Late. Am somewhat lazy. Write to Carrie Bissell, Carrie Hazard, father, and send letterhead to Robert. Nap. Read some in my book "Extraordinary Men" etc. by William Russel Esquire. A very good hash. Mother & Aunt C. went to the Park to tea with others. Retta called. John Willey called. Sleepy.

Saturday Aug. 27th. 1881.

About 6. Paint. Letter from M. Maria calls. I call on Retta & she gives me a dollar. Sorry she's gone. Stop at the Brown's, race over to H. Townsend's & get tickets, and back to leave them. Take fifty with me, and all twenty ere night. Miss Bush 2 & returns 1, Miss Murphy one, Miss Bogert 5, Mrs. Putnam 2, Mrs. Carpenter 4, Frank 2, Clarence 2, Mr. C. 2 & $1.00 beside. Write to Lu. Robert and Mr. Armstrong here when I was out.

Sunday. Aug. 28th. 1881.

Late. Heard Robert Collier—fine sermon. Saw Mabel Davis, and collected a quarter from her. Robert over to dinner and until 10 or so. Florrie called. R. & I went to walk.

Monday. Aug. 29th. 1881.

Betimes. Write to M. Go to Maybel Hill's. 6 tickets. Call for Maria. Go to Mrs. Bucklin's. Call on May Brown. Go to Jenk's. Call on Millie. Lizzie there. M. goes home. I meet the footman and get letter from Carrie Hazard with check for $10.00. Cash it. Meet Miss Austin & sell two tickets. Home at 3. Do letter head. dinner. Draw more. Note from Maria. Post that to Robert, note to Hattie Salisbury & Maria. Read Scribners.

Tuesday. Aug. 30th. 1881.

6.30. Note from Mrs. Augusta Hazard with $25.00! Mother sick all day, but goes off at 4.30. I saw her off, called on Lizzie Calder, got 50 cts. and offer of lanterns & bunting (*Beautiful* girl.) stopped at Maria's to tea. Home at 8. Mabel Hill called at noon. Jim over. More inscription. goes ere ten. I weigh 116 now.

Wednesday. Aug. 31st. 1881.

Up early, and do the work up briskly. Answer advertisement. Hot DAY. A little boy comes for flowers for a dead child. I go and see Mrs. Carpenter about Florrie. Prospective. Call on the Manchesters 20 cts. Call on Mrs. Perkins on George st. about tuition—no go. Call on Mrs. Higgins 20, Mary, Sarah Bullock 35, Mrs. Gurney 60, & Mrs. Sherman 35. Home and gormandize on graham bread & milk. Henry Townsend calls.

Thurs. Sept. 1st. 1881

HOT. A dry fog, sort of smoke, all day, and hot insufferable. And here a week or two ago my fingers were too numb to paint! Up at 5. Carry nasturtiums to Grandma Anthony. Sweet peas & cream to Millie. Read a bit of Twain to her. Watermelon. Stop at Ath. for half an hour or so. Letter from Martha with $1.00. Note from Mother. Start on Latin. Ellen calls. give her flowers. Robert over with pears & plums—4th installment of pears.

Fri. Sept. 2nd. 1881.

Rain at last. Letter from Lu. Mrs. Arnold for rent. I go to Maria's & get 25 more tickets. Mr. Rider gives me 50 cts. for one. Mrs. Ely, $2.00 for 5. Lu Peck, 2. Mother comes back. Good dinner & easily got. Finish my "Lives of Eminent Men". Write to Anna Ticknor. Go to Mr. Slicers induction services. Mr. Carpenter sees me home.

Saturday Sept. 3rd. 1881.

Ere 6. I undertake to do all the work. Letter from M. Mutton dinner. Call on Miss Sophie Fillinghast. $1.25. Theo 20. Called on Mrs. Diman. Mrs. Potter 30. Mr. Carpenter comes and we ride out to the Bliss'es. Write to Cassie. As cold as it was hot.

Sunday. Sept. 4th. 1881.

About 6. A difficult business to cook coffee, chocolate, milk, biscuit, sweet-corn, & frizzled beef on even three gas stoves. Mary comes over & we 3 go to church. Sat with Maria. Prescott Clarke walks home with me. Stop at Sophie's. Out. Invite P. C. in, and give him a posy for his buttonhole. Nice fellow. Write to Mary Sharpe. Aunt C. Mother & I go to "evenin' meetin'." Mr. Slicers first Sunday as pastor. I like his preaching. Ray saw us home.

Monday. Sept. 5th. 1881.

5.30. Sally forth at 9.12 See Sophie. P.O. Call for Maria. Go to the Bucklins. Go to Reginald's office. Go and order all our stuff at Fillinghasts. Pub. Lib. Call on Millie. Home in twenty minutes. Joined by Sam Bullock. Dine, wash dishes, & skip. "Do" the neighborhood. The Briggs 20, Mrs. Sayles 35, Miss Harris 25, Mrs. Aller 30, Pa Willey 50, Mrs. Rawson 50. Met the Gree-noughs there, and walked home with them. Call at Mabels. Hattie Salisbury called—$2.00 & offered cake. Begin "Historical Causes & Effects" by one Sullivan. Latin.

Tues. Sept. 6th. 1881.

The queerest day I ever saw. Heavy southerly fog in early morning. Haze with dim red sun. Then Increasing mist with result of a universal yellow glare that was positively distressing. So dark I had to light gas to wash dishes. Couldn't read away from a window. Gaslight as white as moonlight. So damp the clothes did not dry a bit. Theories of woods afire. Very funny. All the lights up down st. General uncertainty. Up by 5.30. Do chores. Piano tuned. Little Paytons call. Letter from M. Dine in lurid twilight. Go to Mrs. Fillinghast's. Annie 10 cts. Mr. Daniels 20. Mrs. Jackson 50. Mrs. Hope 25. Saw Mr. Goddard the new New Church minister in the car. Stop at the Browns. Sup. R.P.B. "sees me home". Richard calls. Mr. Stillwell calls with pears;—3 tickets. Latin.

Wed. Sept. 7th. 1881.

Hot! 98 in the shade. Up betimes. Do the chores. Letter from Cassie. Go & cash check at Union Bank. $25.00. Go to Millie's. Stop at Mrs. Bergs. Home and get dinner. Call at Briggs. Call at the Greenes—25 cts. Walk out to Mrs. Bliss'es. flowers & pears. Mr. Carpenter stops for me. Dahlia's at Briggs. Fix price lists etc. Jolly day. Didn't mind the heat.

Thursday. Sept. 8th. 1881.—

A Glorious Success! Perfect weather, everything pleasant, not one drawback. Up before light. Get sunflowers & hydrangea of Mrs. Budlong. Mabel comes over, & we go down in a hack. Stop at Mrs. Dimans. Pears & oakboughs. Get 50 2 ct. jars. 1 doz. boxes at Jenk's. Work till 1.30. Lunch at Mrs. Bucklin's. Gorgeous costume. White muslin, blue scarf & yellow h,k,f turban with blue hair pins. Mabel Hill, Lizzie Calder & I tend candy table assisted by Ned Ely & a Mr. Fidler—the latter was simply indispensable. Made about 10.00 at our table. The decorations were beautiful, lanterns lovely, headlights brilliant, and everything as perfect as if we had ordered it. I was most agreeably disappointed. Lots of people there that I never expected. Mr. Fidler comes home with me. No Latin today. Not a bit tired.

Friday Sept. 9th. 1881.

Up at 7. Letter from Miss Ticknor yesterday, one from M. today. Get over to May's by ten, and help the folk clear up the lot. Walk down with Maria, and pay Billings—7.75. We have *cleared* two hundred dollars! Stop at Ath. & see Ned Ely. Home and wash dishes & work generally. Aunt Mary Robinson comes. Don't like her much. Sam calls. Latin with Mother a la Uncle William.

Saturday Sept. 10th. 1881.

5.30–6. Mother gets breakfast, and I do all else. They all go down st. Help get dinner & wash the dishes. Go over and see Miss Manchester who returned last night & Jim called on her last night! Lizzie Brown over to tea. Introduce "le chat" into my study, and snooze together. The tiredest day I've had for a long time.

Sunday. Sept. 11th. 1881.

About 6. Leave dishes & go to church. Stopped at Mabel Hill's. Met Mr. Slicer on way home, & was introduced by Mr. Carpenter. I shall like that man. Home to set table & wash dishes. Wrote to M. Stop at Miss M.'s & go to church in the evening. Uncle William called P.M. & stayed to tea. Jim called. Old Mr. Carpenter "saw me home."

Monday. Sept. 12th. 1881.

Early, & wash supper dishes. Chores. Trim over bonnets. All go out. Miss Kimball & small fry called, but didn't get in. Miss Shaw called & recalled. (I was very undressed.) Postman also unable to enter. I go over to Millie's. Maria calls there. Two dentists, and 5 teeth out. Exerosis. Stop at Ath. Jim joins me at George, & insists on walking home with me in spite of boots & shoes. I do not sup. Edward calls.   x   x   x   If Aunt Mary has my lamp to play by, where does my studying come in? [12]

Tues. Sept. 13th. 1881.

5 or so. Work as usual. The family all go down the river. Fix flowers etc. hour of Latin, write to Mary Sharp, & go out. Engage Florrie Carpenter & Gracie Ross for school on Mon. 26th. Call at Mabels. Out. Call on Anna & walk to Mary's with her. Home & eat a bit, & set the teatable. Mr. Carpenter takes me over to May F. Browns for my baskets. Home & clear up and dress in linen gown. Cousin Mary, Miss & Mr. Manchester, Mabel Hill & Sam Simmons present

themselves, and were [*sic*] are regaled with much music. My first party. A success. Card from Sam & letter from Carrie Bissell with a [$]1. for Millie.

Wed. Sept. 14th. 1881.

6. Do chores. Write to M. Latin, dinner. Maria calls. Aunt M. & I go and call on two Mrs. Masons. Out, both. Saw the inside of the lovely house on Charles Field st. Mrs. Manchester calls. Robert over.

Thurs. Sept. 14th. {sic}* 1881.

5.30. Whisk through work and go down st. Stop at Miss Gardiners school to ask about books. Get drawing books at Calders. See Dr. Brooks about a Ladies Gymnasium and find him very much interested.[13] Shows me large room. I try the lift & reach 300 lbs. Met Mrs. Diman. First day of Mrs. Berg's lesson. No pay. Borrow 75 cts. of Mrs. Cooley! Left book at Calders so have to go after that. Renew it at Pub. Lib. Do some errands. Saw Sam. Call on Abbie Cooke, & engage her for art pupil this winter. Call on the Morses. Nice talk. Met Miss Bush. Home. Get tea. Read, study & sew. Retire at 9. because I *had* to.

Friday. Sept. 16th. 1881.

I wish I had a timepiece. To get up by. Letter from Martha. Home tonight. Paint on m.gs. All go out. I stop & talk with Mrs. Bogert on George st. Invites me to play tennis. Call on the Doyles. Out. Stop at Atheneum. Go to depot, Riders, depot, and meet the Luthers at about 6. Walk home with M. & stay to tea. Miss Ellen Shaw was there betimes and all was prepared. Home by eight. Latin & sew.

Saturday Sept. 17th. 1881.

Very betimes. Sacrifice my weekly sweep & my planning to a walk with Aunt Mary. To Swan Pt. with a pedometer—4½ m[ile]'s. Hastily dine & go to base ball with Edward. We beat the Chicagoes 3 to 1. E. says I am a mascot—they always beat when I'm there. Cousin Mary & Alice come to visit us, as Ray has gone to Philadelphia. Latin & book.

Sunday. Sept. 18th. 1881.

Betimes. First fire of the season. Go to Sunday School with Martha. She walks home my way. Wash dishes all the afternoon. Henrietta calls. She and I go to the Burnside Memorial Service. Crowded church & fine discourse. Richie lies in wait but I baulk him. Am escorted home by Edward first, & then by Mary Carpenter.

Monday. Sept. 19th. 1881.

Made the fire in scant attire. Chores. A bit of a nap! Paint a bit. More dishes. Paint a bit. We all go over to May Bell's (save Aunt C, Mary & Alice). The Manchesters, Martha, & Sam. Music. Sam [escorts me] home.

Tuesday, Sept. 20th. 1881.

6. Letter from Charlotte Hedge. Meet Martha and go to Miss Gardiner's & Miss Wayland's. But the last went to the first's so I didn't get there. Am grievously afflicted in the toe line—rashly molested waterblisters. Uncle William calls. We all spend the evening at Lu's. Mr. Gilson there.

Wed. Sept. 21st. 1881.

6. Aunt Mary departs at 10 A.M. Am rather lazy in a reactionary way. All out P.M. Annie Aborn & Martha call. If Annie *has* as many lovers as she *says*, why is she single? Heat little supper, for four. Little Latin, & "Warlock, O' Glen Warlock." [14]

Thurs. Sept. 22nd. 1881.

Ere the sun. Mother goes to Apponaug at 7 P.M. Little Paytons in. My two scholars call. I call on Mrs. Turney. Stop at M's School. .75 cts. Millie. Musk melon. Go home with Ruth Cushman to see about painting lessons. Ride down & get some paper at Riders. Order books. Meet M. at Ath. We call on Patty Doyle, "gym shun" Tea with M. Bible Class. Mr. Tingley [escorts me] home.

Friday. Sept. 23rd. 1881.

A little late. Mary & Alice go home before breakfast as Ray returned. Sweep my room. Florrie in. Martha over P.M. Arithmetic therewith. Lu & Harry spend the evening. Great fun. Aunt C. retired early. I finished "Warlock, O' Glen Warlock" MacDonald's latest. Hot. Thunder shower in the evening.

THREE

"She hath a ring. I have a pain"

September 24, 1881–January 10, 1882

DURING the early autumn of 1881, Martha's need for Charlotte continued to wane as her romantic involvement with Charles A. Lane of Hingham, Massachusetts, intensified. By the first of November, Martha was engaged to be married.

Charlotte was devastated, confiding to Sam Simmons that the loss of Martha was analogous to the amputation of a limb (see her letter dated November 14, 1881, in Appendix B). To her diary she confessed "lov[ing] the damsel," and several entries reflect the depth of her despair as a result of Martha's betrayal: "O my little girl! My little girl," she cried. The loneliness and pain as she "struggle[d] with [her] grief" was enormous. Charlotte tried to fight back, verbally "spar[ring] with the enemy," Charles Lane, but with little success. "Pleasant," she wrote bitterly, "to ring at the door where you've always been greeted with gladness; to be met by the smile that you value all others above—to see that smile flicker and vanish and change into sadness because she was met by *your* presence instead of her love."

As a way of coping with her grief, Charlotte immersed herself in work, establishing a lifelong pattern that would repeat whenever she was faced with loss or pain. She kept busy finalizing plans for the Providence Ladies Gymnasium and joined the Union for Christian Work where she spent her Saturday evenings. She also began confiding more in Jim and Sam Simmons and attempted to work through her sadness in letters and poems. Still, she would sometimes break down after seeing Martha home; at other times she would reduce Martha to tears by making her feel guilty. In a poignant poem (see Appendix B for complete text) that Charlotte wrote to Martha on the subject of their permanently altered friendship, she particularly mourns the loss of their former intimacy:

> Think dearest, while you yet can feel the touch
> Of hands that once could soothe your deepest pain;

Think of those days when we could hardly dare
Be seen abroad together lest our eyes
Should speak too loud. ** There is no danger now . . .

By Christmas Day, 1881, Charlotte seemed to feel somewhat better: "I am very tired, but not much hurt by the work & pain of the past two months, & begin to see light again." Charlotte ended the year lamenting the loss "of a perfect friendship," but she also celebrated the growth that had resulted from the pain. "I am stronger, wiser and better than last year, and am fairly 'satisfied,' as to the years work," she wrote. "I have learned much of self-control & consideration of others. . . . My memory begins to show the training it has had, I can get what I want when I want it, pretty generally. Most of all I have learned what pain is. Have learned the need of human sympathy by the unfilled want of it, and have gained the power to *give* it, which is worth while."

As to the new year, Charlotte looked forward, however uncertainly, to a fresh start. Less than two weeks later, she was introduced to Charles Walter Stetson, a man who would change her life forever.

Saturday. Sept. 24th. 1881.*

6 or so. M[artha]. spent the night. Retired at ten. Asleep ere 12. I plainly state my grounds, and we consent to divide if needs must. She went home before breakfast. Busy day. Black stove, sweep the five rooms more or less, fix flowers etc. beside usual chores. Harry brought back the waterproof & rubbers. School books sent up from Rider's. Study grammar. Mrs. Hayward & Julia Martin call. Henry Townsend calls, & helps me in Arithmetic. Brought me Jevon's Logic as I requested.

Sunday. Sept. 25th. 1881.

6 just. Bake & have all done by 9. Sunday School. Church. Mr. Lane of Hingham is interesting Martha now.[i] P.O. Clarke walks home with me. Forgot my key, so we frequent the yard & eat grapes. Dinner. Good. Mr. Stillwell calls with grapes & pears. Go to the Brown's with Aunt C. Church. Home with the Manchesters.

Monday. Sept. 26th. 1881.

President Garfield's funeral services. More black than there was for Lincoln.
x   x   x
Ere six. All work done by 8.40. Open school, and straitway close it again. Paint. Arithmetic. dinner etc. Paint. Arithmetic & Grammar. Mr. Hamlin calls. Invited me to go to walk. Anna, Clarence, & Florrie in. Martha & Mr. Lane stop for me and we infest the Manchester's. Mr. L[ane]. sings—well. Jolly time. Write to Cassie.

Tuesday. Sept. 27th. 1881.

6. School in earnest. Very good. Grace is every way ahead. Mother returns. Cut out & baste my work dress waist. Martha over. O very well Mr. Lane!, very well. Walk home with her. Arithmetic Latin etc.

Wed. Sept. 28th. 1881.

6. Settle into harness. Good progress. Hottest weather we've had. Paint a little. Nap. fit dress waist. Arithmetic. Edward over. I *hate* to spend an evening in enforced torpor. No exercise of any sort and yet no rest. No conversation worth the name, no ideas; and yet not even room for reverie. I'll have a house of my own yet, and choose my own society. Latin. *Hot.*

Thurs. Sept. 29th. 1881.

Ere the sun. Dismiss at 11.30. Mrs. Berg. 75 cts. Pub. Lib. Dont get any more books now. Ath. Dine on 5 cts. worth graham crackers. Martha there. Read. Tea at Brown's. Allie there. Stop with Lizzie at Mrs. Huston's. Bible Class. Large attendance & good talk. Escort Martha home, and come back alone. Mr. Stillwell & Mr. Tidler here. Whist. Mr. S. & mother 5 to o!

Friday. Sept. 30th. 1881.

6. All serene. School very pleasant. Paint. Sew. Call on the Manchesters. Grapes. Sew. Write. Letter from father, with $5.00 for reading etc.

Saturday. Oct. 1st. 1881.

6.30. Write to Mrs. Hazard returning her $100.00. & ask for it again. Write to Thomas. Write to Miss Ticknor enclosing $2.00. Paint. Go down st. Carry grapes and flowers to the Browns. Meet Martha. Meet Sam. Get *My Watch!* A neat delightful little nickelcase, black face, stem winder; and Mr. Luther only charged me $12.00, & that I can pay in installments! I am happy. Stop to see Dr. Brooks. All things in turn for the "Providence Ladies Gymnasium". Hurrah. Call on the Morses. Out. The Channings. In, & enthusiastic. The Maurans. In but faint. Mrs. Blake. In, but tired. Martha. In. Stay[s] to tea. Jim calls here. Arithmetic.

Sunday Oct. 2nd. 1881.

6 sharp, by My Watch! Chores. Meet Martha, & so to Sunday School and church. Nice time in Bible Class. A Mr. Barrows preaches. Poor stuff. Walk home with M. Home, dine, write to Nellie Sharpe & Helen Hazard on the "Gym[nasium]." finish (*nearly*) those morning glories and rest a bit. Sup. Call on Anna. Go to Martha's. She wont go to church, and I stay. Jim calls there. We discuss great things, and on the way home he touched my very soul. "There's something greater than Right & Justice". "Oh? And what's that?" "Love."

Robert was here, and brought some lettering for me to do. Rere supper.

Monday. Oct. 3rd. 1881.

6.5. Housework. School. Mother opens hers. That Harvard advocate arrives again! Dinner. Give my first lesson to the two little Cushman's, on Bridge-ham st. 1 hour—75 cts. Call on Ellee Darling, out, Mary Jackson, out, & Mrs. Downs, on Gym. business. No returns. Ride home in pouring rain. Sup. Dress—Latin, Lettering for R. Letter from Mrs. Hazard with $100.00.

Tues. Oct. 4th. 1881.

5.45. Letter from Ada! Letter from Thomas. Call on Mrs. Diman, Mrs. Fillinghast, Grace Channing, Annie Morse, & Cassie Richmond. Get coffee. Stop at the Browns. Stop & see Martha. Home & write & sew.

Fall of 47° in 24 hours!
Wednesday. Oct. 5th. 1881.

Ice! Up at 6, as cold as I ever want to be. Warm up with a bath, and do chores as usual. School. Take work (lettering) over to Martha's and do some. Home. Sup. John Peck calls. Paint some more. Robert over. Finish label, and John posts it. Latin, and a word to Ada. Awfully Cold.

Thurs. Oct. 6th. 1881.

6.5. *Just* one degree above freezing in my room. Mrs. Westcott called, one [*sic*] business, no results. Mr. Goddard called. Like him. Off at 11.47. Cash Mrs. Hazard's check, ten 10s. Reach Mrs. Bergs at 12. Call on Millie. On Lorraine Bucklin. On Hattie Salisbury. On Dr. Weaver. (She.) On Mabel Bridges. On Lizzie Calder. On the Voses. Encouraging results. Meet Martha down st. Ride home & tea with her. Bible Class. I enjoy playing escort. *Lovely* night. Call from Grace Channing & her cousin.

Friday. Oct. 7th. 1881.

6.5! Warmer. Letter from Miss Ticknor, Mary Jackson, Mary Sharpe, & Helen. No, yes, & yes. Cousin Caleb to dinner. Lamb. Call on Miss Palmer, Miss Anthony, Miss Taft, Miss Lockwood, Miss Bogert, Miss Bucklin, & Junie Keach. Small results, as most were out. Met Martha & Abbie Cooke, & home with M. Clara Pierce there. *Splendid* Moon. Mrs. Anthony & Mrs. G. Anthony called.*

Saturday. Oct. 8th. 1881.

6. Usual work, but slower. Sweep my room. Shampoo. Mother washes my thick dress. I call on Mrs. Carpenter, Miss Sherman, Miss Tucker, Miss Snow, Miss Rawson, Miss Briggs, Mrs. Wescott, Miss Greene, Miss Stillwell, Miss Potter, & Lu. Maria calls here. So sleepy that I ignominiously retire at 9.30!

Sunday. Oct. 9th. 1881.

7! Breakfast on the wing. Walk down with Mrs. Rawson and Arney. Martha's young man at church. Jim walks home with me. Keep him an hour in deep discussion. Wash dinner dishes instead of breakfast. The Arnolds come for rent. Robert over. Mrs. Fillinghast & Charlotte call. Write to Ada & Cassie & post. Church. Mr. Carpenter.

Monday. Oct. 10th. 1881.

6. Notes two or three. Walk a mile in 13'! Call at Miss Chace's school. See Harriet. Lesson at the Cushmans. 75 cts. Call at Mabel Bridges. She joins. Mrs. Anthony's. Lizzie Calders. Miss Tanners. See about frame to my picture at Watermans. Mr. Tilden says I may put it in their window. Meet the Sharpe's. Walk with them. Home by 6.40. Walked all of ten miles. Martha called. I was out. Jim comes over and helps me on my arithmetic. I am not tired, but those brains of mine are. Query. Weariness settled in the weakest place?

Tues. Oct. 11th. 1881.

6.10! Letter from Cassie. Martha over. We go "Gyming["] on Waterman St. (N.G.) I reason with her over the present "monsieur", with success. Paint "gutter-snipe" for Robert. Arithmetic. Sewing. Cool again.

Wed. Oct. 12th. 1881.

5.50. Good school day. F. Carpenter aetat *14* didn't know what *mutton* was, and neither of 'em could locate tallow! Aunt Ellen Payne & Lizzie called. Go to church meeting of ladies. Jolly time. Got acquainted with some good works and more settled in my way of life than ever. Down st. with Martha. We interview Dr. Brooks. Home with M. & stay to tea. Reason with her some more. Home & answer my "Society" letter. Arithmetic & buttonholes.

Thurs. Oct. 13th. 1881.

5.55. First letter from my "correspondent", & Lo! it is Miss Alden! Start on elecution in school. Go over to Mrs. B[erg]'s. 75 cts. Call on Millie. Go & see Martha off to Middleboro. Call at Miss Chace's school. Call on Dr. Webster. Didn't like her much. Pay 1.00 more on watch. Get Keary's "Dawn of History" at Pub. Lib. Ath. till 7.15. Bible Class. Jim at the door to walk home with me! Find Sam & Edward here playing whist. S. & mother 3 to 1. Sew contemporaneously.

Fri. Oct. 14th. 1881.

6. Letter from Carrie Hazard with offer of the loan of a piano from Prof. Blake. Wash dinner dishes. Cut out & fit sleeves to dress. Answer Carrie. Rearrange the Gym. papers sent by Dr. Brooks this morning. Grace Channing & Miss O'Connor call, & Mr. Channing comes for them. Pleasant evening.

Sat. Oct. 15th. 1881.

6. Look over and arrange the gym. papers. Fix things for mother. Aunt Ellen & Lizzie come to tea. Walter later.[2] Toothsome supper, & pleasant evening. Sewed, crocheted, & argued with W.

Sunday. Oct. 16th. 1881.

6.5. Busy day. Leave breakfast dishes. Walk down with Mrs. Rawson. Nice time in the Bible Class. Fair sermon. Chat with Martha. Jim reappears & requests "the pleasure." Comes in, criticizes Gym. circulars, *stays to dinner*, and, Martha arriving later, escorts us over the river. Pleasant walk, but Jim was unendurable. Acted like an infant fool! Robert over to tea. Guttersnipe to do over again. Escorts me down to church. *Jolly* sermon reviling Jacob among others. Mr. Tingley "sees"* me home. An escorting day altogether. What has got into Jim! Sunday, Monday, Thursday & Sunday—very attentive.

Monday. Oct. 17th. 1881.

6.20! Fly around. Ride over to the Cushmans. 75 cts. Walk back. Paid Mr. Luther another dollar. Call at Mrs. Blakes, Martha's, Mabels (50 cts) and Anna's. Home at 6.20 or so. Letter from Carrie Hazard—good. Answer the same.

Tues. Oct. 18th. 1881.

6. Call at Miss Diman's. Miss Alden sick. I tell stories to Louise, who has an ulcerated throat. Home & get work. Go to Martha's all alone. Stay till almost 8. Nice talk. ("*No!*") Draw letter for guttersnipe. Sew.

Wed. Oct. 19th. 1881.

6. Go to Mrs. Diman's to lunch. Carry my "snipe". Nice long talk with Miss Alden. Home. Finish snipe. Start to write. Mr. Stillwell comes with a big basket of pears & we play whist till nearly eleven. M[other]. & Aunt C. 7 to 0!

Thurs. Oct. 20th. 1881.

6.15! Note from Miss Vose on gym. Mrs. Berg. 75 cts. Pay Mr. Luther $1.00. $6.00 left to pay. Met Martha. Ath. together. Nice time. She went home. Mr. Slicer in later. Pleasant. Ellen Shaw, too. Read a lot. Went for Martha. Delightful evening. Go home with Julia Mauran—part way. Two slices of graham bread & some pears for meals.

Fri. Oct. 21st. 1881.

6.10! Miss Alden calls. Returns Robert Falconer[3] & Fireside Fairies. Borrows "At the Back of the North Wind." Mother & Aunt C. go a gadding. I luxuriate in a whole P.M. Sew on dress. Read, write, & study. Finish letter to C. A. Hedge. We have a grand new lamp. "They" rather.

Sat. Oct. 22nd. 1881.

6.30!! Grand transformation scene. Furniture moved about, & big stove put up. Scenery much improved. Alice spends the afternoon. A Miss Bachelder, Centreville schoolmistress, to dinner. Sew, read, & study. Jim comes. Theology. Direct disagreement on fundamental truths. I rebuke him for last Sunday's foolery.

Sun. Oct. 23rd. 1881.

6.30! Take Martha's [Sunday School] class. Hope they liked it. Walked home with Miss O'Connor. Lizzie & Henrietta over P.M. Write to Helen, Carrie Bissell & Abbie Cooke. Go to church with Lizzie. Home with Carpenters. Day of rest. Read Scrib[ner's].

Mon. Oct. 24th. 1881.

6.5. Health Primer from S. H. Cushman's. 75 [cents]. Pay Mr. Rider $3.00. Met Nellie Sharpe & called on Dr. Brooks. Progressing. Call on the Slicers. Stay to tea. Call on Martha. Old Mr. Carpenter there & sees me home. Lu & Harry here at whist. Letter from Carrie Hazard.

Tues. Oct. 25th. 1881.

6.20!—I must reform. Letter from Cassie & Helen. First lesson to Abbie Cooke—50 cts. Latin. Go over to Martha's. Mrs. L[uther]. goes out. Confidence. Home to study till my eyes give out. "Influenza!"

Wed. Oct. 26th. 1881.

6.10. Martha over. Mother has a new bonnet. I chace over to M's after tea for a bit of Arithmetic.

Thurs. Oct. 27th. 1881.

6. *Fire in parlor stove.* Horrid cold weather. School. Mrs. B[erg]. 75 [cents.] Millie. Pub. Lib. & renew Keary. Look at big hats and covet 'em. Pay Rider 38 cts. Ath. Martha there. We take walks & converse. Verily I love the damsel. Bible Class. Good. Julia Mauran & her young brother "see me home."

Fri. Oct. 28th. 1881.

6.20! Mary, Alice, & Miss Smith call. Martha over. I see her home. Read, sew, & study.

Saturday. Oct. 29th. 1881.

6.30 but then it's Sat. Loaf deliciously. Sweep room. Look over fire & flannels. Put pocket in coat & mend mitten. Darn hose. Study a bit. *Nap!* Go to M[artha]'s. Three Shaws & a Miss Miriam Earle there. Stay to a fine tea. Am closeted with Mrs. L[uther]. & change my views a bit. Tell M. to go ahead. Kiss her.[4]

Sunday. Oct. 30th. 1881.

7.30! (Blinds shut on account of rain) Mr. Woodbury preaches a sermon of which I heard little, being principally occupied in not crying. Walk home with M. Maria over P.M. Write to Sam asking help, & to Cassie. Call on Lu; & M. to show letter. Home & walk down with Maria. Rousing sermon by Mr. Slicer. Speak to M. a moment wishing her joy of her All Hallow'een. Old Mr. C. home. Jim here. O my little girl! My little girl.

Mon. Oct. 31st. 1881.

6.10. All as usual. Cushman's. 75 cts. History. Arith. Sam comes, and is good to me. We play whist and we beat the old folks 6 to 1. All Hallow E'en!

Tues. Nov. 1st. 1881.

7! No Abby owing to rain. Study and darn. Martha over. She hath a ring. I have a pain. Give her my blessing. Write to Sam and tell him all about it. Post the same. Note to Abigail. Sew.

Wed. Nov. 2nd. 1881.

6.30. Note from Dr. Brooks. Notes & Latin. Call for Mary Sharp, & go and dictate about tinting the Gym.⁵ Gorgeous. We call on Helen Hazard. She's an aunt. Call on Martha. Mother there this P.M. & was told of the engagement. History. Harpers Monthly a bit. Richard Hamlin calls. History.

Nov. 3rd. Thurs. 1881.

6.30. School. Mrs. Berg. No pay. Millie. Errands. Spent 38 cts. & lost 25. Ath. Read Ingersol—not bad. Bible class. Agree to join the Union for Christian Work, Boy's Room, Saturday nights. "That's my business!" I tell 'em. Ride home with Miss Mauran. Circulars come.

Fri. Nov. 4th. 1881.

6.30. School. Study. Sew. Study. Write. bed. End of a week's rain.

Sat. Nov. 5th. 1881.

6.45. Trim my hair. Letter from Ada. Sew. Go out & distribute circulars. Retta at the Dimans. Also a John De Wolf. Rather nice. "Call" broadcast Down st. & get stamps, tickets, envelopes, & flannel. Stop at the Hazard's and at Martha's. Saw Mr. Lane and congratulated him.

Pleasant, to ring at the door where you've always been greeted with gladness; to be met by the smile that you value all others above—to see that smile flicker and vanish and change into sadness because she was met by *your* presence instead of her love!

Sunday. Nov. 6th. 1881.

6.30. Walk down with Mrs. Rawson and the chicks. Marthas out with her new ring, but don't stay to church. See Mary Channing. Dinner, dishes, design. Call on Retta, and stay to tea. P. O. Clarke there. He starts for Europe Monday. John DeWolf escorts me to church. Jim escorts me home, and we walk way down to the Red Bridge talking of Martha. Anna and Clarence here. Bread and jelly. Much fuss.

Monday. Nov. 7th. 1881.

6! Walk down st. and cash Ada's order for $3.00. Ride up to the Cushman's. No pay. Ride down. Go to Gym. Mr. Burleigh in elevator down. Walk home with him, stopping at the Studio. Plans for sitting.[6] Consult Mrs. B. on the subject. O.K. Stop to say goodbye to Retta. Consult them on the subject. O.K. Stop to ask for Mr. Manchester. No better. Mother & Aunt C. go to first Stoddard Lecture. Study, and write to Sam. 16 pages.

Tuesday. Nov. 8th. 1881.

6.20. Only Grace. Out at 1. Dine. Call on Mary Channing. Lesson to Abbie. 50 cts. Meet & walk with the Morses. Call on Miss Russel. Like her. Call on Lu Doyle. Out. Saw Pattie. Tea at Marthas. Home. Go down & go with the Russels to The U[nion]. [for] C[hristian]. W[ork]. meeting. Splendid time. "Le Professeur" escorts me home. Teach him concerning Stonehenge & Carnac.

Wed. Nov. 9th. 1881.

6.20. No Florrie. Grace late. Letter from Sam. Kind but discouraging. Answer. Finish Keary & send off exam questions. Call at Lu's. Mr. M. no better. Sew a bit. Mr. Stillwell calls. Whist 5 to our 2. Am dully unhappy but can stand it.

Thurs. Nov. 10th. 1881.

6.30. Mrs. Berg. [$]1.50. Ruth Cushman. 75 cts. Millie's. Waterman's. Shop generally. Gym. All serene. Ath. Good read. Call for Miss Russel & we go to the Bible Class. Home alone.

Fri. Nov. 11th. 1881.

7! *Fly* around. Grace's cousin visits the school. Go with Aunt C. to sit for Mr. Burleigh. Good fun. 50 cts. Return Keary. Call at the Hazards. Nice talk. At Mrs. Luther's. Out. At the Carpenters. Home, sup & sew. Edward over. Jim also. Whist. E. & I 6 to 4. 11.40.

Sat. Nov. 12th. 1881.

7! Cut and baste Gym. Suit. Fine. Letter from Miss Alden, etc. Go to the Boy's Room, U. C. W. Good fun.

Sun. Nov. 13th. 1881.

6.45. Fun in the Bible Class. Walk over with the Russel girls, who call but won't dine. Darn hose. Wash dishes. Sam comes over and takes me for a short walk. Fall in with M[artha]. & Mr. L[ane]. They call. Lizzie over. Stays to tea. Write to Retta. Mr. Carpenter & I go home with Mrs. Luther. Spar with the enemy.

Mon. Nov. 14th. 1881.

5.50! Good days work. Florrie Absent. Walk to the Cushman's. 75 cts. Get ammonia. Stop a second at Dr. Brooks. Home at 6.10. Mr. Manchester no better. Study—O got Smith's Anc[ient]. Hist[ory]. of the East & Quackenbus' Hist. of Lit[erature]. at Pub. Li. Write to Sam.[7] Folks all out to the lecture.

Tues. Nov. 15th. 1881.

6.30. Abbie over. 75 cts. Nice girl. Darn a bit & study a *wee* bit. Spend an hour in the chilly twilight up at my window, and have my crucial struggle with my grief. Victory. Too utterly worn out to do anything in the evening but write down my "state o' mind." Bed at 9.

Wed. Nov. 16th. 1881.

6.5. Whisk down to the Burleighs only to find the engagement off. Explanatory note via the Slicers missing. It arrives by messenger at about 4 P.M. Study my new Books. Call on Lu, Mr. M[anchester]. worse. Mrs. Diman, & tea at Martha's. Walk the dark st.'s for an hour or so in dumb misery. Where is that victory? Sew. Sleepy. 10.

Thurs. Nov. 17th. 1881.

6.10. School. Mrs. B. 75 cts. Millie. Worse. Get Picture at W's & take it to Tilden's. Shop. Ath. Good time. B[ible]. Class. Good time. Am elected on a visiting comm[ittee]. with Martha. Home alone. Sam here. Whist. We 3 to 2. A word with him on the steps. Card from C. Hazard.

Fri. Nov. 18th. 1881.

6.45. School. Study. Call at Lu's. Worse. Call on Carrie H. Orders. Home in misty rain, darkness, & tears. Sup. Sew. Edward over. Jim. Whist. J. etc. 6 to E. & I 5.

Sat. Nov. 19th. 1881.

6.30. Design for Ada's. Go & "sit," stopping for Mrs. Burleigh. Capri Girl done. Read on Egypt at the Ath. Tea at the Burleigh's. Boy's Room. Good fun. Feel quite useful & happy.

Sun. Nov. 20th. 1881.

6.30. Martha not there. Take her class. Home alone. Write to Ada. Robert over. $1.00 for "snipe." He escorts me to church. A word with Mr. Slicer. Home alone. Clarence & Anna here.

Mon. Nov. 21st. 1881.

7! No bath! Letter from Retta & Cassie. Carrie Hazard comes down on me with an imperative order for 10 dinner cards before 6 P.M. Accept it, and drop the Cushman's in consequence. Go to the 3rd. Stoddard Lecture with Aunt C. & Mary. Horrid time, air detestable and people janglingly discordant. Pictures fine, but man highly unpleasant. Home to eat.

Tues. Nov. 22nd. 1881.

6.10. Abbie Cooke. 50 [cents]. Martha over. Mrs. Keach and Mrs. Greene call. Mrs. Budlong & younkits[8] call. Mother & Aunt C. go to see the Voke's Family. I wash dishes, dress, study, read Scrib. a bit, and retire ere ten.

Wed. Nov. 23rd. 1881.

6.40. *Cold.* Bathe in icewater. Only Grace at school. Good. Carrie Hazard in with $3.00 for cards. Hopkins & Pomeroy man duns us for the coal bill. Mother chaperons me at Mr. Burleighs. 50 cts. (Dutch girl in despair.) Go down st. in our first snow storm, (rain & drizzle), Send letter & stuff to Ada, buy another piece of linen for Carrie's design, & some things to paint on at Calder's. Ride home. Study, eat, and draw.

Thanksgiving Day.
Nov. 24th. 1881.

7 or so. Annie Aborn in & invites us all up there to dinner & tea. I call on Mr. Slicer. Out! (forgot another app.) Leave linen at Carries, all out. Call on Martha & Mr. Lane. Jolly. Home & go to the T's with mother. Theo. home. Grand dinner, crochet, fine tea, crochet, chess.

Fri. Nov. 25th. 1881.

6.50. Paint two cards for Carrie. Grand dinner, good again as yesterday's. Wash dishes. Go to see Lu. Her father died yesterday at 4 A.M. Go down to spend the evening at the Slicers. Talk with Mr. S. Mr. & Mrs. Toby call. Mr. S. goes home with me. We call on Mr. Tingley on our way.

Sat. Nov. 26th. 1881.

7 or so. Sew. Martha calls. Julia Jastrum, & babes calls. Edward Hale. Jim in to dinner. Martha & Mabel Bridges. Anna, Mary, & Alice call. Marie & Mrs. Andrews call. I go home with M. & sup. Boy's Room. Home with Mr. Crandall & alone. Jim here. Whist. 3 for our 7.

Sun. Nov. 27th. 1881.

7. Kindling wood, slow fire, late breakfast, eat little, go to S[unday]. S[chool]. with Florrie. Edward in church. Home with M. & get work. Home & wash breakfast dishes & fix up generally. Dinner at 2.30. Wash dinner dishes, call on Lu, call on Mrs. Slicer & weep, receiving kind attention & advice. Mr. Carpenter "sees me home". Anna & Clarence here.

Mon. Nov. 28th. 1881.

6.30. Read a bit of "Cape Cod Folks."[9] School. Walk over to the Cushman's as usual. 75 cts. Ride down. Stop & see Dr. Brooks. Call at the Hazards. Home. Study. Draw a bit. Folks go to the Lecture. Sam calls. Clear talk. Ladies return & we play whist. Sam & I beat 5 games. 44 to 15 pts.

Tues. Nov. 29th. 1881.

7.5. Late & lazy. Abbie. 50 cts. Finish Carrie's cards. Paint on Florrie's. Pennink Sam's. Dress & go over to Martha's. Myra, Lu, & Ed Brayton, Gus Pierce & Wintie Smith, Jim, & I. Whist & tricks. Jim funny. Gus comes home with me. Eddie Sheldon calls here for a bill of Aunt C.'s & escorts me over there.

Wed. Nov. 30th. 1881.

7. Card from Mr. Burleigh. Go down there with mother. Sit for a group. 50 cts. Spend it for box of cards. Meet Mabel Bridges & go to Dr. Brooks with her. Buy crackers & read Egypt in the Ath. Gus Pierce walks most way home with me. Sam & Mr. Childs call. H. C. & I 7 to Sam &c. 8. 12.30 when they go.

I have a "cold"! Vocal disturbance solely. (Surfeit of food & tears the cause.)

Thurs. Dec. 1st. 1881.

6.45. Mrs. Berg. 75 cts. Millie. Apple & orange. Ath. Good read. Bible Class. Martha not there. Gus Pierce [sees me] home.

Friday. Dec. 2nd. 1881.

6.45. Dutch girl on a mast at Mr. Burleigh's. Aunt C. as duenna. Annie Westcott arrives. Draw on Sam's cards. Mary calls. Anna & Clarence call. Edward calls. Whist. Less for us.

Sat. Dec. 3rd. 1881.

7. Annie Westcott departs. Finish Florrie's panel & one card for Sam. Prof. & Mrs. Blake call. Lu Manchester calls. See her home. Boy's room. Good time. Home afoot part way escorted by Mr. Crandall.

Sun. Dec. 4th. 1881.

7. Mother & Aunt C. have a headache, and I, with most unwilling piety stay at home and work. First of Mr. Slicer's sermons I have missed this season. Paint Sam's cards. Read Anc. Lit. Go to church. Mr. Tingley sees me home.

Mon. Dec. 5th. 1881.

6.30. Stop for my picture at Thurbers, & am requested to leave it. Meet Miss Chace & Mrs. Fielden, and Miss C. makes out a bill for me. Cushman's. 75 cts. Annie Anthony & nephew in there. Walk down. Stop at Waterman's & get order for small illuminatic. Get oatmeal. Call on Miss Russel. Out. On Mrs. Slicer. Home & sup. Mr. Stillwell comes. Then Jim & Sam, Sam bristling with orders. He gives me a gold half eagle for four cards & two panels. Work all the evening. Jim & Aunt C. beat 2 to 3. They go at 12.20!

Tues. Dec. 6th. 1881.

6.30. Abbie Cooke as soon as dinner is done. Wash a heap of dishes for mother. Draw. Mother goes to the last lecture. Sam over with panel to paint. Whist when M. returns. S. & I. 3 to their 2. 1.40 when he goes.

Wed. Dec. 7th. 1881.

7.40! Postpone the dishes. (Card from Miss Alden lately.) Rec'd. $20.35 for Grace's bill. Draw the Gladioli for Sam. Finish the next card. Crochet a bit.

Thurs. Dec. 8th. 1881.

7.15. Only Grace. Stop at Carrie Hazard's with cards. All out. Stop & see about pansies. Mrs. Berg. 75 cts. Millie. Waterman's. Calders. Get three panels. Hoggs. Oconnors & get pansies. Ath. Helen Kinne calls there. Eke Martha. See her home, weep, home & sup, & go to the B[oys]. C[lub]. with Lu & Harry. Good time. Gus Pierce comes home with me. Work a bit.

Fri. Dec. 9th. 1881.

6.30. Paint pansies for Sam. He calls at 6 or so. We go to "Lotta" with Edward. "Those who have known the pleasure of avoiding pleasure will never call the pleasure of pleasure pleasure." Lonesome. Oyster supper at home. Abed by one.

Sat. Dec. 10th. 1881.

7.15. Paint all day. Nearly finish gladiolus. Work till 6. Call on Lu a minute. Boy's room. Sam comes for me and stops to get a pound of gorgeous candy. Good talk with him till they come home & then whist. 3 to 2.

Sunday. Dec. 11th. 1881.

7.15. Sunday S. with Mrs. R. Go up to the Olney St. church & he [*sic*] Mr. Elder. Fair to middling. Home with Aunt C. & Mary. John Willey called. Anna & Clarence in. I read Anc. Lit. Go to church with Lu. Stop in at the Burleighs on way home. More Anc. Lit.

Monday. Dec. 12th. 1881.

7. Leave books at Pub. Lib. Cushman's. 75 cts. Stop at Gym. All serene. Get or[der?]. ver[ified?]. at Calder's. Take cards to Carrie. Highly satisfactory. $3.50. Stop at Martha's to supper. O my little girl! Home. Sam in for panel. Finish it up pretty much & let him have it. Mr. Stillwell calls. I work. Sam back with panel at 9. Mr. St[illwell]. runs home with his yeastcake & back. They play whist. I work. I play two games at last. Sam & mother 3 to 5. Carrie Hazard sent me four and Nellie Sharp two tickets to the Arion Club & Carrie

gave me a bottle of stuff for my hands & an order. Order from Martha. Order from Mr. Stillwell. Whew! [10]

Tues. Dec. 13th. 1881.

7.5 Finish Gladiolus. Do pansy. Abbie over. Martha calls. Mother & I go to the Arion Club concert. Martha on car home. —

Wed. Dec. 14th. 1881.

7.15. Paint Gentian for Sam & do a card or two for myself. Jim over with panel No. 2. Robert calls with a little job of *100* mailorder ink sketches to be done by Dec. 30th! Refuse. Jim says my picture is sold for $40.00!

Thurs. Dec. 15th. 1881.

7.15. Dr. Brooks sends tickets. Leave & send some. Mrs. Bergs. No pay. Millie's. Mr. Rein's exhibition. Dr. Sargent there. All serene. Like the instructors. Calder's & get cards etc. Tildens, & get $25.00 for my pic. Carrie Hazard bought it for 30 not 40. Get paper at Staples, and am weighed 23 [*sic*] lbs. coatless! Some of a gain for three months of the hardest work I ever knew and a deep pain thrown in. Call at Abbie Cooke's, Annie Morse's & Mary Channings with tickets. Ath. for an hour or two. Harry Manchester there for Lu, & we go to the B. C. He takes my basket & umbrella home. I go to Lecture at the Gym. Dic[?] Lewis not there. Good time. Home alone. Sam here. Whist. 3 to their 1. He takes away the Gladiolus. Was amazing pleased with the gentians.

Friday
Dec. 16th. 1881.

7.15. Jessie Carpenter calls at recess. Paint on pansies. Mother goes down st. & comes home dizzy & sick. I am very anxious about her. She sleeps all the evening & I muffle door bell. Edward over. Sam too. Letter his gentians, & he takes 'em off. Aunt C. retires, Edward goes, & I have a chance to moan to my one friend for a few minutes. Mother wakes up & he subsequently departs. He is kind & sympathetic but help-less. I see to mother & get her to bed.

Sat. Dec. 17th. 1881.

6.15. Slept in my clo' on the floor under the once open window in the front room. Mother unable to do anything. Paint from 9.30 to 4.30. Get some steak & cook it. Wash three meals dishes. Boy's room. Home with Mr. Crandall. Sam here. Discuss morning glories.

Sun. Dec. 18th. 1881.

7.20. Mother feeble again. Stay at home from church. Lucy in. Anna & Clarence with Charlie stop a bit. Make a thorough scrub with various implements. Lizzie appears. Mary & Alice in. I go to church with Lu. Jim comes home with me. We walk about talking, for an hour or so, and more when he comes in as they were all abed. He does not help me.

Mon. Dec. 19th. 1881.

7.25. Paint. The girls come and finish off their things. Go over the city, as usual. 75 cts. Spent 78 for Xmas duds. Call on the Slicers. Out. Call on the Blakes. Stay to tea & consume much meat. Give Whit a dear pig I bought. Home by eight. Sam here. I finish the m. g.s & he takes them away, & the pansies. $6.00. He is very jolly & comforting.

Tues. Dec. 20th. 1881.

7.20. Paint. Mrs. Nolan does the dishes. Finish all the little cards. Abbie over. 50 cts. She likes me. Mrs. Carpenter calls. Mrs. Luther calls. Martha calls. Read her my poem.[11] She weeps & wants it. Paint jolly little black & grey panels. Mr. Stillwell calls. Whist. He & I 4 to 3, & 3 weasels to 1!

Wed. Dec. 21st. 1881.

7. Paint two gentian panels, part of Carrie's, & some other stuff. Nap from 5 or so to 7.30. Richard calls. Then Sam. Whist. Sam & mother 5 to our 4, 2 weasels to our 1, 11 points ahead. Sam takes of all his cards & pays me 1.50 for Jim's. He's a comfort. Letter from Ada with check for $8.65.

Thurs. Dec. 22nd. 1881.

6.30. Do work. Paint. Carry panel to Martha, 50 cts. Cards to Carrie, $5.00. Got oxalis & flowers for mother. Cashed C.'s & Ada's checks. Got $8.00 music box for Millie. Mrs. B. $1.50. Millie. The poor child was all gone with joy & excitement. Well worth the money. Pay Waterman $8.00. Get Xmas things. Pay Calder $7.37. Gym. Walk home with many bundles in the rain. Get waterproof. Leave little dud for Grace. Call at Martha's. Out. Call on Carrie. Mrs. H. is sick. M.'s again. give her a dead letter which I sent her last Sept. & got here to me today. Stay to supper. O my little girl! Bible Class. Few there. Gus Peirce [sees me] home. Tired.

Fri. Dec. 23rd. 1881.

7. Paint all day. M.g. for Mr. Stillwell, Carrie's Card, card for Jim, etc. We receive a miraculous & unaccountable Xmas present. ½ bll. of flour, no end of sugar, heaps of coffee, piles of apples, a box of crackers, a box of raisins, six boxes of sardines, & 3 great jars of the best olives! Can't imagine the donor. Mr. Stillwell calls & gets his cards. $3.00. Work all the evening.

Sat. Dec. 24th. 1881.

6.20. Shirk the dishes. Finish my last order, Florrie's panel. Go & leave things for Martha, & cards for Carrie. Call at the Slicer's. Nice talk with Mr. S. Go down town & do my final shopping. Met Jim, & Sam. Get tintypes taken, 6 for a quarter. Home, bite, & paint a card for Mrs. Springer. Card from Retta Clarke & card & gay silk kerchief from Charlotte Hedge. Mother has ½ bbl flour & some candy from Clarence. Jim comes & brings me a pretty little carved thing to put my brushes in. He escorts me down to Martha's, & departs. Mr. Lane there. Go down & stop for the Slicers. Mrs. S. dont go, & trot by myself. Checkers & drawing with the youth Thomas Fisher. Nice boy. Mr. Slicer appears at 9, & reads parts of Scrooge to the boys. A success. Mr. Krantz "sees my [*sic*] home" with evident delight. Don't much like him. Mrs. Blake sent me ten dollars as an order for "something" pretty to be filled "when I have time." Yum yum. Middlin' good Xmas after all.

Sun. Dec. 25th. 1881.*

7. Stay at home. Grand turkey dinner. Martha & Mr. Lane, Mary & Alice in. Call at Lu's & leave duds. Call at M's. Church. Clarence [sees me] home.

Christmas Day.

7.20. Do up work. Do up duds. Go around to Mary's with a basketful. Clarence Anna & Charlie arrive. Tree & baby house. Very fine & jolly. Everybody surprised & delighted. I gave but little, & received in all:

1	Card & h'k'f from C. Hedge.	9	H'k'f's in box from Aunt C.
2	Martha's Photo.	10	Silver pin from Mag.
3	2 N. gowns from Aunt C.	11	Silver umbrella from Anna.
4	Red headed needles from Mother.	12	Carved leaf pencil holder from Jim.
5	Pocket book from Anna.	13	Grand card from Sam.
6	Card from Helen.	14	2 chemiloons from Mother.
7	$10.00 from Mrs. Blake.	15	Necktie from Ray.
8	Gold pencil from M.	16	Necktie from Lizzie.

Cake & coffee. Dead tired. Come home early & fix up the presents & room. Send note apropos of "orgie" to "Mr. James Samuel D. R. Simmons Jr." Shortly Sam arrives God bless him! and spends the evening. Whist. We beat 'em 8 games & they the 9th. So thoughtful and kind of him to come over. I owe all my good time this Christmas to him. Well, it's over. I have paid all the bills & have ten dollars odd in hand. I am very tired, but not much hurt by the work & pain of the past two months, & begin to see light again.

Tues. Dec. 27th. 1881.

7.25. Loaf deliciously. Go down St. Leave word for Edward, send other invitations. "Mrs. & Miss Perkins & the Boarder. At Home. Wed. & Thurs. 28th & 9th. From 8 to 5. Whist!" Get nuts & kisses. Call on Sophie. Out. On the Channings. Mr. Rein there. Lesson to Abbie. 50 cts. Home & change my wet clo. Henrietta here with little cakes for mother. Mother goes down with her. Jim over. Arithmetic. Prospective fun.

Wed. Dec. 28th. 1881.

Up at 7.20 or so. Clean silver & prepare in general. Get flowers at Kelly's. Nap. Dress up in fine style, lace, pearls, & nasturtiums. Mr. Stillwell arrives ere eight. Then Lizzie & Edward. Then Jim & Sam. Three clocks & five watches on the piano. No two alike. Sam & Aunt C. Edward & I, inhabit the back room, & play 24 games coming out even on games, ahead on points, & behind on a weasel. Jim & mother versus Lizzie & Stillwell, in the parlor. Jim ahead. Roast oysters & bread & butter & coffee at 12. Then whist. At four sardines & crackers, nuts & raisins, cake & coffee, olives & kisses. Retire at 5. A grand jolly unmitigated success. But it fills a mighty little place.

Thurs. Dec. 29th. 1881.

Slept from 5.15 to 7.15. Arise, get breakfast & loaf. Lizzie down at 9 or so. All loaf. She goes at 12. Dine & go to Millie's. Pub. Lib. & get Clarke's "Ten Great Religions." Att[end]. Bible Class. Driving storm & scant attendance. Go down with Lizzie and call there. Car home.

Friday. Dec. 30th. 1881.

7.50. Sew on Gym. suit. Carry lent books over to Martha's. Out. Leave 'em with inscription.

> "Some books & things for you dear, once kindly lent to me;
>   I have had pleasure from them all, & now with thanks for great & small
>   I bring them back to thee.
>   I'm rather glad you're out dear, I write without a sigh,
>   And miss the taste of bitter tears, the hopeless glimpse of dear lost years
>   I'd have if you were by" C. A. P.

Call at the Hazard's. Out. Go to party at the chapel, help about, and am drafted as a forlorn hope into the part of "Dinah" in a shadow pantomine. Mr. Burleigh as Parent, small boy Laurie Mauran as Villikens. Was useful & effective. Word with Martha. Home alone, by preference. Read Scrib. My heart aches and I am tired. What then? I can live and work.

Sat. Dec. 31st. 1881.

It is after midnight, but I write natheless the doings of the last day of the year. Up at 7.35. Cards from Hattie Salibury & Annie Morse. Read "Ten Great Religions." Call on Lu. Harry gives me a card. Call on Mrs. Diman. Engaged. Emily ill. Call on Annie Aborn. Out. Ath. Boy's Room. Mr. Krantz gives me a card and wants to go home with me. Elude him. Good drawing lesson, my boy has been practicing. Grand gift distribution. Jim awaits me. Home amicably. Whist, we beating one rubber. Aunt C. retires at 10.35. Mother "Patiences". I read Jim personal bits out of my Journal. Seems much amused. He goes at 12. And goes away with the old year.

A year of steady work. A quiet year, and a hard one. A year of surprising growth. A year internally dedicated to "discoveries and improvements.["] A year in which I knew the sweetness of a perfect friendship, and have lost it forever. A year of marked advance in many ways, and with nothing conspicuous to regret. I am stronger, wiser and better than last year, and am fairly "satisfied," as to the years work.

I have learned much of self-control & consideration of others. Often think before I speak, and can keep still on occasions. My memory begins to show the training it has had, I can get what I want when I want it, pretty generally.

Most of all I have learned what pain is. Have learned the need of human sympathy by the unfilled want of it, and have gained the power to *give* it, which is worth while.

This year I attained my majority—may I never loose [*sic*] it!

[1882]

[The following "resolution" immediately precedes the first diary entry for 1882.]

I have on my mind this year three cares. (So far.)

1. Others first.
2. *Correct & necessary* speech only.
3. Don't waste a minute!

If I can form the groundwork of these habits in a year, it will be well. Furthermore, I wish to form a habit of *writing* as much as I can.

12.50 A.M.!
Sunday, January 1st. 1882.
10.10 P.M.

Up at 7.35. Go to S. S. with Mrs. R. & Arney. Sleep through sermon. Home with Martha & get "Little Men." [12] Mutton & macaroni. Do dishes, read & snooze. Martha & Mrs. L. call. Go to church alone, and come back with Mrs. M. & Lu. A Howling drifting many-winded snow storm. Wrote to Retta. Retired at 10:30. Good day.

Monday. January 2nd. 1882.

Up at 6:15. Deep snow and drifted. Cold. Shovel and broom before light. Don't get the dishes done, first time I've left that to M. Start school again. All serene. Ride as far as Waterman's, reading "Ten G[reat]. R[eligions]." in car to save time. Take a bite of picture & walk up. [13] 75 cts. Walk down. Buy boots & blank book for accts. Ath. Sudy [*sic*] Egypt, Brugsch' book. Home ere seven. *Glorious* night. Cold, clear, full moon, universal snow. Enjoy it. Start to eat supper, but Martha & Mr. Lane arrive, and he sings to us. Funny & nice. Good day, with a few mistakes.

Tues. Jan 3rd. 1882.

6.35. Do the work. school. card from Abbie; some sick. Call to inquire for E. Diman. Better. Call on the Channings a bit, on Annie Morse, Ath., with Egypt. Called on the Slicers. Mr. Burleigh in, & goes to see Booth [14] in Richelieu with Mr. Slicer. Home. Tired.

Wed. Jan. 4th. 1882.

7.! Nap P.M., Anna called, Martha in. Two cups of *tea*! Mrs. Springer returns. Water pretty much frozen. Write to Cassie. Read.

Thurs. Jan 5th. 1882.

7.5! Cold. Water burst last evening, spoiled paper & ceiling in dining room. "Bloomber" here today. I go forth as usual. 50 cts. only. Milly. Get the music box to have fixed. Can't be fixed I find. Get bird's eye linen, blue hose & bit of blue flannel. Ath. with Mary Channing. Egypt & general browse. Home with the Mans, music, crackers & fun.

Fri. Jan. 6th. 1882.

7 or so. Watch stopped. Lazy day. Read "T. G. Re." Sew a bit. Eat lots. Anna & Clarence call. Richie appears & wants me to go to Julia Jastram's candy party. I wasn't going anyhow, & don't all the more. Where's Sam?

Sat. Jan 7th. 1882.

7.20! Actually sweep my room! Make necessary buttonholes & write Egyptian his[tory]. "Annie Henry" calls. Note from Mary Channing. Go to Boy's Room as usual. Drawing & noise. Mr. Krantz hangs around profusely, but Jim appears at the eleventh hour, and cuts him out. Whist. J. & I 5 to 0.

Sun. Jan. 8th. 1882.

6.50. Go to S.S. Go down and invite Edward to dinner. Am mistaken for Mary Sharpe by a Miss Keith. Good dinner. Write more Essay & copy it. Letter eke to Miss Alden. Annie Morse calls. Dear girl. Go around for Lu, miss 'em, wait under a lamppost & then scare them by stealthy pursuit. Sit with them. Jim appears and sees us all home. Give him a piece of my mind regarding his former attentions to Martha. He seems to think he did no harm. Write.

Mon. Jan. 9th. 1882.

Overslept. 7.40. Fly around. Ride over to the C's with Mr. Carpenter. 75 cts. Call at the Hazards. Hours Egypt at the Ath. Stop at the Blakes for my roll of paper. Home & Sup. Sam. Whist. 6 to 3. I wish I could see my friends by myself.

Tuesday. Jan. 10th. 1882.

7. Only Florrie. Paint jar. Abbie. 50 cts. Mrs. W. Greene, Annie G. and a Mrs. Wilbur call. Martha over. Mr. Putnam appears and invites me to go to Mr. Stetson's studio with him, and eke to an art thing tomorrow night.[15] Accept the latter. Read. Arithmetic. Mr. Stillwell. Whist. We 5 to 2, & a weasel apiece. Letter from Cassie.

FOUR

"A twilight tête-a-tête with Charles Walt"

January 11, 1882–June 28, 1882

O N JANUARY 11, 1882, Charlotte accompanied her friend Sidney Putnam to an evening lecture given by a handsome young Providence artist, Charles Walter Stetson. Still reeling from the loss of Martha, Charlotte was in a state of emotional vulnerability. Her reactions to meeting Stetson, however, were decidedly noncommittal. "I like him and his pictures," she wrote simply. And a couple of days later, "It's a new thing to me to be admired."

Stetson's feelings for Charlotte, in contrast, quickly turned serious: just two-and-a-half weeks after they met, he proposed marriage. Charlotte promptly declined. A few days later she composed "An Anchor to Windward," a narrative documenting her "Reasons for living single" (see Appendix B). Foremost among the reasons she cited was her desire for independence. "I am fonder of freedom than anything else. . . . I like to be *able* and *free* to help any and every one, as I never could be if my time and thoughts were taken up by that extended self—a family. If I were bound to a few[,] I should grow so fond of them, and so busied with them that I should have no room for the thousand and one helpful works which the world needs."

It is also quite likely, however, that Charlotte feared being hurt yet again. Her father had abandoned the family, her mother had not provided the love that she had craved, and Martha had committed her love to someone else. Denying herself a serious relationship was one way to avoid more pain. Throwing herself into work would be less risky, on an emotional level, and more rewarding, she felt, on a professional level.

Although she held the conviction that women should be able to combine marriage, motherhood, and career, Charlotte also recognized the personal cost should she decide to marry. "I felt strongly that for me [marriage] was not right, that the nature of the life before me forbade it, that I ought to forego the more intimate personal happiness for complete devotion to my work," she wrote in her autobiography (*Living*, p. 83). Undeterred by Charlotte's refusal of marriage, however, Walter Stetson remained a persistent suitor.

During the spring of 1882, Charlotte continued to assert her independence, by working out at the gym, by reading Mill's *Subjection of Women*, and by wistfully longing for a "home of [her] own." At the same time, however, and despite her best efforts to the contrary, she and Walter grew increasingly close. They exchanged letters, went for long, leisurely walks together, and wrote each other tender and passionate poems (see Appendix B). "There was the pleasure of association with a noble soul, with one who read and studied and cared for real things, of sharing high thought and purpose, of sympathy in many common deprivations and endurances," she wrote. "There was the natural force of sex-attraction between two lonely young people" (*Living*, p. 83).

Despite the mutual attraction Charlotte struggled with ambivalence when she recalled her earlier resolve to live single and to devote her life to public service. The extent of her emotional dilemma becomes pronounced when we read the love poems that Charlotte and Walter exchanged (see Appendix B). The passion the two shared is apparent; the problem was that it was incompatible with Charlotte's view of how she wanted her life to evolve. She constantly struggled between the pull of the two forces. Whenever the fear of commitment became too intense, Charlotte would enumerate for Walter the reasons that they should part company. She was invariably relieved, however, whenever a proposed separation failed to materialize.

Charlotte's ambivalence toward her relationship with Walter stemmed from a number of concerns. The pain of Martha's rejection, coupled with her mother's tendency to withhold maternal affection, left Charlotte understandably wary of emotional involvements. Also, her resistance toward the traditional roles of wife and mother was rooted in her genuine desire to serve humanity, a philosophy which was taking shape long before she was introduced to Walter Stetson. But that did not make her dilemma any easier. The depth of Charlotte's conflict is apparent in the letters written to Walter during the early weeks of their acquaintance: "You give me rich new happiness which bids fair to make up for the dear love, which I have lost," she wrote in late January (*Endure*, p. 37).

Clearly, one advantage that a relationship with Walter offered was that it helped to fill the void that had been left by Martha's departure. At the same time, however, Charlotte was terrified by the prospect of surrendering her "self" for love. "O my dear! my dear! the more I love you, and the more I grow accustomed to the heaven of your love, the less I wish for anything further. . . . You *must* believe that I love you. . . . But much as I love you I love *WORK* better, & I cannot make the two compatible," she lamented in late March (*Endure*, pp. 62–63). Within a day or two, however, she was wavering again, and by the middle of

April, Charlotte believed that she had grown "to understand . . . the full benefit of love" (p. 66).

On the whole, the spring months during which Charlotte and Walter Stetson spent time together were generally pleasant, and Charlotte reported passing several *"very* happy" evenings in his company. But the ambivalence remained. The magic of newfound love notwithstanding, she still looked forward with much anticipation to her summer vacation in Maine, when they would finally be apart.

Wed. Jan. 11th. 1882.

6.40 Snow on my face on waking. Shovel paths. Only Florrie. She stays to dinner. Lu over. Wash "heap" dishes. Go to store & Mabel Hills with Lu. Dress up, and go to a lecture on etching by Charles Walter Stetson, with "Sidney." *Rather* a waste of time. He brought me a piece of sugar cane. "S[tudy]. [at] H[ome]." letter.

Thurs. Jan. 12th. 1882.[1]

6.55. Frisk about. Only Florrie. Mrs. Berg. No pay. Millie. Carry back box. Get gingham for apron. 22 cts. Get pair of 4 button undressed black kids. 1.65. Meet Mr. Put[nam]. at Riders and go to Mr. Stetson's studio. I like him and his pictures. Ath. Forgot the etching Mr. S. gave me, & went back after it. He was out. Back to Ath. Lu comes there for me. Dear girl. Bible Class. Gus Pierce insists on seeing me home. Comes in and makes me a call, as the other was out.

Friday. Jan. 13th. 1882.

7. Only Florrie. Sew on suit. Edward over. 5 to 2. Write to Miss Alden and Cassie.

Sat. Jan. 14th. 1882.

6.45. Sew all the morning. Dine. Read a bit. Call on Mrs. Diman. Nice talk. Call at Mr. Stetson's for my proof. Sidney there. Miss Arnold comes in. All go, & I have a twilight tête-a-tête with Charles Walt. Like him. It's a new thing to me to be admired. Go to Pub. Lib. 4 cts. Walk down with Miss Murphy. Call for Mary Channing. Boy's Room. Draw. Lu comes. A recitation was given. See Lu home, and are joined by Jim just below. Unnecessary youth. He don't come in. Finish apron.

Sunday. Jan. 15th. 1882.

7.15. New purple apron, Katie lost mine. S. S. Martha no [*sic*] there. run class. Church. Home with Lu. Write to Cass. Copy it. Robert over. Wants a whale. He goes down to church with Lu, Mrs. M. & I. A young Potter home with us.

Mon. Jan. 16th. 1882.

6.55. Grace arrives. Letter from Retta. Go to Dr. Gay's. Pub. Lib. Cushman's. 75 cts. P. L. again. Get Rawlinson's Herodotus & Leoftie's Ride in Egypt. Stop at Gym. No go. order boots. Ath. for a bit. Home. Sup. finish copying 20 page letter to Cass. Read some E. bed.

Tues. Jan. 17th. 1882.

7.5. Mother makes johnny cakes. good ones. Card from Robert. Draw whale & send it. Lu in. No Abbie. Mr. Putnam calls, and asks me to a concert in Ametur Dramatic Hall. One McDougal's affair. I go, and quite enjoy it. Saw Mr. Stetson. Run and frisk with Mr. P. as it was cold. Jim here. Poor day.

Wed. Jan 18th. 1882.

7.5 Sew on suit. Call on Lu. Out. Call on Jessie Carpenter. Go to Martha's to supper. Carry bundle from Jessie to Mrs. Henry C. Read a bit. Sam. A chance to talk.

Thurs. Jan. 19th. 1882.

7.5. Note from Robert with $2.00. Get drawing book. Call at Gym. Pay for shoes—$2.90. Mrs. Berg. $1.00. Millie. Dr. Gay. Put cotton in for the present. Get lamp chimney. Copy book for Florrie. 10 cts. Ath. Good lunch, meat in it. Good read too. B. C. Home alone. Read sup & write.

Fri. Jan. 20th. 1882.

6.53. Only Grace. Anna over. Sew on suit. Martha over. Nice talk with her. Am rather blue & lonely. Sup in unison. Write. Read. Jim calls for me to go to Abbie's. Don't go. Mr. Putnam & Mr. Aborn call. Very pleasant time. Aunt C. & mother come in later. Go at 9:30.

Sat. Jan. 21st. 1882.

6.50. Leave dishes and go down to the Gym. to be weighed, measured and *not* found wanting. Watch the girls perform. Am moved to go and buy some more flannel & have a suit made like theirs. 4.38 for stuff—3½ yds. Ride home, as it rains. Arrange old letters. Letter from Mr. Stetson with invitation to a concert next Wed. (Shall go.) Henrietta calls. Sup. Call for Grace Channing. Am introduced to Mr. Saunders—Mary's fiancée. Like him. Go to Boy's Room with G. drawing & squabbling as usual. Ride home in the wet. Bed by 12.

*Sun. Jan. 22nd. 1882.**

Woke at 4, and lay spinning a fable about a music box. Up at 6.40. Church alone. Teach Miss Evans class—girls. They highly enjoyed it. Home alone. Anna & Clarence in. Write to Mr. Stetson. Write fable. Mr. Stetson calls. We are left alone, and have a nice talk. I introduce myself as fully as possible, and he does the same. We shake hands on it, and are in a fair way to be good friends. Go after Lu. She couldn't go. Church alone. The coldest night I've seen, with a raging wind. Mr. Putnam in church. Richie sees me home. Sleepy.

Mon. Jan 23rd. 1881. {sic}

6.45. Coldest yet. My pitcher freezes solid, and cracks in every direction. Letter from Ada. Take little jug over to the Cushmans to paint. Drop & break it on my way home. Stop and have Gym. suit fitted. Call on the Slicers. Out. Stop at the Ath. & read Egypt for an hour. Gus Pierce goes as far as Thayer St. with me home. Find a letter from my new friend. It's worth while to wait for some things. Good hot supper. Read Scrib. Answer letter. 12.

Tues. Jan. 24th. 1881. {sic}

7. Colder still. All things freeze. No Abbie. No halfdollar! Go out to post letter to C.W.S. & call on Martha. Out. Read Herodotus & Scrib. Co-o-o-ld!

Wed. Jan. 25th. 1882.

7.10. Warmer. Lazy day. Wash all the dishes. Loaf a bit. Dress up and go to concert at the Art Club with Herodotus.[2] Snows. The youth advances. Home by ten. Sam here. I value him.

Thurs. Jan. 26th 1882.

7.15! Warm & wet. Mrs. B. $1.50. Millie. Dr. Gay. Get Gym. Suit & pay 3.00 towards it. Ath. Met Miss Russel. Martha appears. Lu stops for me. Get soda. B. C. Home with Lu & Harry. Letter from Thomas. Mumps.

Fri. Jan. 27th. 1881 {sic}.

7.20! Letter from Herodotus. Paint on plaque for Flo. Lizzie with Bessie & Ethel call. Maria calls. Wash dishes. Mother not very well. Read Herodotus. Anna, Clarence, & Florrie call. Anna's Maria comes with telegram for Clarence—suspense—"6 inch pine etc"; not from Thomas. Sam & Richie call. Edward calls. Mr., Mrs., & Hattie Sheldon call. Grand levee. Sam cajoles Florrie, & goes home with her. Happy infant as ever I saw. Others go at 9.30 or so & E. & I beat Sam & Richie 2 to 1. & the rubber a weasel! Houp la!

Sat. Jan. 28th. 1882.

7. Can't go to the Gymn. as mother is sick & aunt C. out. Paint plaque. Cassie calls. Dear girl! Get dinner. Ride down with Cass, and begin my proud career at the Gym. Walk rapidly home, and find mother to sick & feeble to have me leave her. So I stay.

Sun. Jan. 29th. 1882.

7.15. Stay at home & get diner. Mother a bit better. Charles Walt. appears. Mary in. Go to church alone. Jim sees me home.

I have this day been asked the one question in a womans life, and have refused.[3]

Monday Jan. 30th. 1882

6.50. Card from Abbie. School. dinner. Walk down st. with Mrs. Allen. Stop at Dr. Gay's. Cushman's. 75 cts. Errands. Ath. & Egypt. Home & sup. Mother's better. brought her a ten ct. russe. Write a 12 pager to Herodotus.

Tues. Jan. 31st. 1882.[4]

7. Letter from Charles Walt. Grace late—10.45. Snows. Go to Hattie Sheldon's & Abbie's. 50 cts. Call on the Morses. Home in a great snowstorm. Read Herodotus, & snooze.

Wed. Feb. 1st. 1882

7. Heaviest snowstorm of the season. Clear & fine. Shovel manfully. Only Florrie. Wash dishes and grind coffee. Herodotus & nap. Go to the Payton's, & to Lu Manchesters to tea. Lu was here. Annie Morse called while I was out with invitation for me to read with her. Mr. Stillwell called. Whist. 5 to our 0.

Thurs. Feb. 2nd. 1882

6.45. Letter from Herodotus. Stop at Miss Waterman's & tell her I'll come. Mrs. Bergs. No pay. Millie. Poor thing! Pub. Lib. 12 cts. fine. Café on errand. Gym. Class of 15. great fun. Get boots. 3.50. Get things at Calders. Ath. B.C. Mr. Manchester has the class. Dull. Sit with Nellie Peck, & see her home. Lu & Harry stop in a bit. Card from Annie Morse.

Friday February 3rd. 1882.

6.45. Only Grace. Go to Dr. Gay's. No filling today. Get new watch-guard & ruffle. Meet Abbie Cooke & Margie Calder. Am to have the last named for a pupil. Walk home with Abbie & call on Annie Morse. A Miss George there. Nice girl. Hour at the Ath. Home. Sup. Dress. Go to the Morse's & so to the Reading Club at Miss Waterman's. Am "Mrs. Rogers" in "Esmeralda". Quite a gathering of big bugs. Am introduced to divers. A Mr. Waterman & Harry Farnum quite devoted. Especially the last. Cover myself with glory by my performance. Am inordinately complimented by all hands. Asked to call. Ride home in state in big hack sleigh with a basket of goodies for mother. Really enjoyed myself. Sam & his sister called. Too bad I was out.

Sat. Feb. 4th. 1882.

6.50. Cold. Go to Gym. & perform ad. Lib. That's going to be a grand success. See Carrie Hazard there, & she drives me over to Martha's. Stay there to dinner, & have a nice talk with M. Home in a rapidly increasing snow storm.

Sup, "hilt my kirtle above my knee", and go to the Boy's Room regardless of family obloquy. Splendid storm. Mr. Krantz very polite.

Martha says that if she dies I must bring up her children. Somewhat of a compliment.

Sunday. February 5th. 1882.

7.5. A tremendous snowstorm! I dig through drifts waist deep. No cars at all, but a snowplough with *14* horses and another thing with 8 at 2.15. 30 men or so with 'em. *Tremendous* snowstorm. Charles Walt arrived about 4. Stays to tea, and seems to enjoy himself.

Monday. Feb. 6th. 1882.

7. Waste first 15′ awake, & am that much late about my work. Card from Mabel Bridges. Dine. Walk over to the Cushman's. Tremendous drifts everywhere. High as my eyes on College St. The river full of it where they are dumping in. Jolly walk. 75 cts. Stop at Dr. Gays & get another dab of chemical cotton in my tooth. Meet Margie Calder, & tell her what to get for her drawing lessons. Spend 13 cts. on oatmeal etc. Home, bite, wash dinner dishes, bite, mind muff etc, bite. Write & "cipher" a little, take nap almost perforce, & write to Herodotus.

Tues. Feb. 7th. 1882.

5! Mother sick with a violent headache. Mrs. Springer goes down after cloroform. Letter from Herodotus. Very. School. Dine, go to Hattie's. $5.85. Materials & 2 lessons. Go to Abbie & Margie. 50 cts. Call on Annie Morse. Lu here to tea. Dear girl.

Wednesday. Feb. 8th. 1882.

6.52. All as usual. Mother still feeble. Paint on plaque. Dinner at 6 & wash dishes & make bread. Start to write to Cassie. Herodotus calls. Sam calls. Herod. & I betake ourselves to the back room and enjoy ourselves. He goes first. Have a bit of talk with Sam in the hall. He is much to me.

Thurs. Feb. 9th. 1882.

6.35 or so. Mrs. Berg. No pay. 20 cts for drawing book. Millie nice time. Pub. Lib. Gym. Helen there. Very nice time. Exhilerating talk with Miss Hill. Ath. Good read. B. C. Few there. Home in *slop*. Jim here. Arithmetic.

Fri. Feb. 10th. 1882.

6.55. Housework. School. (Letter from Herodotus.) Lesson to Hattie Sheldon. 50 cts. Half hour at the Gym. Grand. Walk home with Miss Hill. Like her. Hour (50′) at the Ath. Home, sup, Make 6 buttonholes for mother, write to Cassie, scribble, & retire.

Sat. Feb. 11th. 1882.

6.25. Black stove. Leave dishes. Call at Martha's a moment. Leave basket & plate at Miss Waterman's. Gymn. fun 9.40 to 2.30 or so. Stop at Calder's & pay for Hattie Sheldons things. Pay Mrs. Geer 2.50 more for suit. Pub. Lib. Get "Narda" & "Historical Characters.["] Call at the Slicer's. Out. Home. Read a bit. Lu over. Stays to tea. Wash dishes and mix bread. Home with Lu. Go to the Boy's Room with Miss Russel & sister. Mr. Crandell home.

Sunday. February 12. 1882.

6.55. Go to S. S. with Florrie. B.C. & C. Mr. Slicer observed at 12, "Now be restless about that clock, I'm not through for some time yet!" Home with Lu. Dine & wash dishes. Mr. Stetson arrives. Eke Lizzie. We two go to walk to avoid the crowd. Annie Westcott, Mary, Ray, and Alice call. Then Mrs. Aborn & Annie. Then Mrs. Fillinghast & Charlotte. Then Edward. Then Robert. Then Lu, & we go to church. Mr. S. read Jean Ingelow's "Brother & Alderman."[5] Fine. Anna & Clarence call. Wash the supper dishes. Write poem over for C. W. S.

Mon. Feb. 13th. 1882.

6.45. Go to have tooth filled, and don't have it; as I had not time enough. Utilize the half hour in reading, at the dentist's, a 30-page-letter from Mr. Stetson. Autobiographical, and interesting. Go to the Cushmans. Two fairy stories. $2.78. Ride down as it rained, and I was umbrellaless. Do errands. Go to Ath. for an hour. Go to the Brown's to tea. Grand turkey supper. All the family there, Elders inclusive. Horrid noisy quarrelsome gay boisterous nonsensical time. Hot and close physically and morally.

Tuesday. Feb. 14th. 1882.

6.45 Two Valentines, one a beauty, unknown; and the othe [*sic*] " 'Greek Goddes's" sketch with "Familiar *Quotations*". Sammy did that. Lesson to Hattie. 50. Lesson to Abbie & Margie. 65 from A. & 1.00 from M. Go to Ath. & read Egypt. Home by 7. Met Annie Aborn & saw her home. Sup. & read Narda. Write.

Wed. Feb. 15th. 1882.

6.45. As usual. Paint P.M. Annie Westcott, Mary, Anna & Clarence to tea. Muffins, cold corn beef, preserved pear, coffee, jelly & custard, & cake. Edward and Sam call later. Whist. E. & I against Sam & Annie 3 to 2. Sam & I to E. & Mother 2 to 1. Write a bit.

Thurs. Feb. 16th. 1882.

6.36. Labor at the dishes. Have to leave most of 'em. Letter—*sonnet*, from Herodotus. Mrs. B.—no pay. Nice talk with Millie. Got 4 pair of stockings.

$1.00. Gym. Lu comes to see the fur and is much impressed. Ath. E. History an hour. Then promiscuous. Lu stops for me. Bible Class. Good. Covenant of a church—"In the love of the Truth & the Spirit of Jesus Christ, we join for the worship of God, and the Service of Man." Good. Lu home. Martha & Mr. Lane called this P.M. Mr. Putnam brought back my fan and invites me to go somewhere. Glad I was out.

Fri. Feb. 17th. 1882.

7.4. Lesson to Hattie. 50. Tooth filled. $1.50. Call for Mrs. Hill & see her home. Call at Mrs. Dimans. At dinner so retire. Home. Sup. Run around to Mary's for opera glass. Mother & Aunt C. go to see Maggie Mitchell in "Fanchon."⁶

Wash dinner dishes. Read a bit. Sam comes. Real good talk. Most astonishing revelations on his part. He helps me—a little.

Sat. Feb. 18th. 1882.

6.30. Gym. from 9.35 to 12.20. Carrie Hazard takes me home. We stopped to call on Mr. Stetson, but he was out. She bestowed on me certain oranges, shaddocks, & figs "for our Sunday's dinner". Paint gentian card for Sam. Anna calls. Mr. Slicer calls. Lu calls. Wash dishes. Call for Grace Channing. Boy's Room. The youthful Fisher grows fond of me, and shakes hands with a cordial pressure that is very pleasant. Mr. Crandall [sees me] home. Sup. Read. Write. Am blue.

Sun. Feb. 19th. 1882.

6.35. S. S. with Mrs. R & Arney. Take the class. Jim & Lu home. He makes a detour with Sophie Aborn, and rejoins us. Comes in, talks Easter card, and shows me some arithmetic. Clarence calls, both to dinner. Jim stays (I urged him), and at 4.30 or so Mr. Stetson arrives. Very unhappy to find me engaged, and won't stay to tea. Gives me his photo. Fine. Martha & Mr. L. arrive at 5.40 about. Jim goes around for Lu. Gay tea party. Broiled chickens, cup custards, & cake. etc. etc. Then a pious sing. Jim was the life and soul of the party, and helped mother a lot. M. & Mr. L. go early, & Jim & Lu at 9.20. Wash dishes. Tired. Why can't they all be friends like the Simmonses?

Mon. Feb. 20th. 1882.

6.50. (Blinds shut.) Lesson at the Cushmans. 75 cts. Call on a Mrs. Mason, and make arrangements to teach her little girl twice a week. Hurrah! Ride home. Amuse a Miss Tucker on the way. Sup. Read & write.

Tues. Feb. 21st. 1882.

6.30. Letter from Cassie. Lesson to Hattie. 50. Gym. Walk home with Miss Hill. She reinvigorates me, for I can do her good. Go to Pub. Lib. & get Narda

11. Stop to tea at Prof. Blakes. A horrid day; rain, snow, sleet, freeze, and thunder & lightening. Write & read.

Wed. Feb. 22nd. 1882.

6.40 Shovel abortively. No school! Paint Sam's gentians. Lu in a minute. Go down st. & get drawing materials for Mabel Mason. Give her first lesson with good success. 6 cts. for carfare. Home at 4. Mother sort of sick. Write a bit, read a bit, dress a bit, and go to Lu's to tea. Sam calls later, and sees me home. 1.50

Thurs. Feb. 23rd. 1882.

6.35. Mrs. Berg's. No pay. Millie. Gym. Pay the last 53 cts. of Mrs. Geer's bill. Ath. B.C. Home alone. Edward & Henrietta here. Whist. Bah!——

Fri. Feb. 24th. 1882.

6.45 Only Grace. Lesson to Hattie. 50. Lesson to Abbie & Margie. $1.00. Pub. Lib. & get "The Subjection of Women." J. S. Mill.[7] Mrs. Sheldon gave me an old summer silk. Mr. Tingley walked up the hill with me. Call on Grandma Anthony. Mother & Aunt go to anti-Morman Lecture.

Sat. Feb. 25th. 1882.

6.45. Grand time at the Gym. Martha, Abbie, & Margie among the spectators. Home with M. to dinner, and then she comes home with me. Paint, talk, & knit. Mrs. Luther calls. Lu was in while I was out. Mary Channing goes to the Boy's Room with me. Was sleepy, but amused divers youths. Went home with Jennie Bucklin, partially attended by Mr. Crandall.

Sun. Feb. 26th. 1882.

6.50. S. S. with Mrs. Rawson & Arney. Take Miss Evans' class with much success. Home with Mrs. Henry Carpenter. Gorgeous boiled mutton dinner with canned peas. Herodotus arrives at 4 or so. Nice talk. Robert calls. Mr. S. stays to tea. I go to church with the Manchesters. Jim & Sam maliciously go home with us. Jim comes in, and outstays Mr. S. That youth enjoys the nonsense book, even as I. Haven't enjoyed anything so much in a long time. Pure fun. J. wants another card. 12 o'clock!

Mon. Feb. 27th. 1882.

6.30. Mother has letter from Thomas. Grace brings her $20.00. Go to the Cushmans via Calders. 75 cts. Mabel Masons. 4.82 for bill, and 50 for Wed's lesson. Ride down, 6 cts. Hour of Egypt at the Ath. Meet Abbie Cooke there, & give her one of my "Arion" tickets sent by Helen. Home tired. 13 hours steady work. Nap. Sup. Read a bit. Retire at 10!

Tues. Feb. 28th. 1882.

6.25. Letter from Herodotus. Went calmly through all the lessons till recess before reading. Miss Murphy comes. Lesson to Hattie. 50 cts. Hour at the Gymn. Home with Miss Hill. Hour at the Ath. Solid study too. Home gaily ater [*sic*] 12 hours work. Herodotus here. He had invitation to the Hazards "tea" Thurs. & want to inquire concerning the same. Bit of talk, but he has to go. Read an atom, sup, *Sam* called, so that I could not write! Whist till 10.20. Then he stayed till 11. Helped me in my arithemetic though. Tired, which I was *not* a bit when on my way home after 12 hours work.

Wed. March 1st. 1882.

6.30. Only Grace. Go to Mabel Masons in the rain. No Pay. Ath, & read E. & miscellaneous, for an hour or so. Home in rain. Read a bit, write a bit, knit some.

Thurs. March. 2nd. 1882.

7.05! (Blinds shut) Ride over to Mrs. Bergs. $3.75. Millie. Get 1/2 yd. ruffling. 10 cts. Gym. Home, change dress, & go to the Hazards tea party. Very grand. Stupid sort of time. Mr. Stetson was invited, but declined. Home alone. Mr. Stetson called at a little past 8.30. Some talk. *He understands*.

Fri. March. 3rd. 1882.

6.30. Florrie paid her bill. $20.00. Mr. Shldon [*sic*] sick so no lesson to Hattie. Abbie & Margie 1.00. Get some azalias & primroses at Hoggs. 20 cts. Hour at Ath. from 2.30 to 3.30. Met Martha, & had a bit of a ride with old Mr. Carpenter. Home at 6 or so, sup, read, draw, sew. Mr. Stillwell called. Then Edward. Then Jim about cards. Begged off, & retired at 10.

Sat. March. 4th. 1882.

6! Paint before fire. Paint after breakfast. Gym. Grand time. Collision with Miss Aylesworth. Lunch with Miss Hill. Shop a bit. Home & paint. Directoryman called. Lu in. Go to the Y.W.C.T.A. with Lucy Carpenter. Shall resign. Ath. Channings. No go, so take Miss Russel to the Boy's. Home alone.

Sun. March. 5th. 1882.

6.20. S.S. alone. "Church membership" up in the B.C. Home with the Mans. Anna & Clarence to dinner. J. Willey called. Uncle William called. Herodotus arrives. We go to walk, over the bridge, and sat awhile on a piney bluff. All serene. Home by six. Tea. Lu calls for me. Church with her. Home ere 9. More nonsense book. He leaves at 10.20.

Mon. March. 6th. 1882.

6.20. Wash dishes. Pay Mason bill at Calders, & get brush. Cushman's, 75 cts. Mason's, 1.50. Walk back. Stop at Millie's. Get Journal. Home, read, sup, write to Miss Alden. Finished John Stuart Mill's "Subjection of Women.["]

Tues. March. 7th. 1882.

6. Painted. Miss Murphy here. Hattie's. Father better. 50 cts. Go to "Friends in Council." Nice time. Martha goes down st. with me. get tidy cotton . 10 cts. Pub. Lib. & get "Ten Great Religions" over again. Home & sup. Mr. Putnam had been here, and called again to see if I would go to a Cecilia concert with him. Wouldn't. John Diman comes down & brings me his pedometer. Don't stay long. Letter from Herodotus P.M. Answer three sheets with five.

Wed. March. 8th. 1882.

5.55. Paint. Mrs. Payton visits mother's school. Mrs. Budlong calls. Go to Mabel Masons (2 fares). 50 cts. Buy dress, $7.50, buttons, .51, Hat, 85, trimmings etc. $1.07. Take dress to Mrs. Geer and arrange thereabout. Home via Martha's. Mr. Stetson here. Mother invites him to come & stay with me as she & Aunt C. go out. He does so, bringing Rossetti's poems (P.M. call). Sam calls, but goes ere long. Queer sort of evening—unsatisfactory.

Thurs. March. 9th. 1882.

6.4 (Six hours sleep.) Write to Herodotus. Mrs. Springer got locked out upstairs, & I went down to Pope's & got a man for her. Went in 12′!⁸ Had him here in 25 or so. Mother got breakfast. Mrs. Berg. No pay. Millie. Nice time. Gym. Very jolly. Buy two underwaists, $1.00. Ath, miscellaneous. B.C. Very pleasant. Home in the wet. Sup. Write to He. again.

Fri. March. 10th. 1882.

7.3. Letter from Cassie, & two from Herodotus, one long & unpleasant, the other short & amply reparatory. Lesson to Hattie. 50 cts. Lesson to Abbie & Margie. 1.00. Change underwaists, + 30 cts. Go to Mrs. Geer to to [*sic*] have dress fitted. Home & sup. Read a bit, knit a bit. Edward over. Whist. Jim calls for card. 50 cts. Retire at 10.15.

Sat. March. 11th. 1882.

6. Black stove, & discuss finances with Mother. No appreciable results. Gym. No end of visitors. Outdo myself. Do errand for Miss Hill & get pair of slippers for self—$1.80. Home to dinner. Miss Murphy here. Have blue silk waists fitted. Paint some. Letter from He. Go & measure fence on George St. for pedometric purposes. My step is 26–28 in. Stop for Mary Channing & Miss Russel. Good time with Tom Fisher and others. See Miss Russel home, and pursue my lone path contentedly.

Sun. March. 12th. 1882.

6.30. Martha absent from S. S. Kept awake in church! Home with Lu. Mutton dinner. Read some Rossetti. Washed dishes. Herodotus calls. Goes home perforce, but returns at 8.15. Anna & Clarence over. Arithmetic & chat.

Mon. March. 13th. 1882.

5.55. Paint a bit. Only Grace. Start out with pedometer, and walk 4¼ m. this afternoon. Cushman's 75. Mason. 50. Ride down. Stop at Mrs. Geer's a moment. Stop at Ath. No go, history out. Home & write to He. Read a bit.

Tues. March. 14th. 1882.

6. Arithmetic versus art. Letter from Herodotus. Miss Murphy here. Lesson to Hattie S. 50 cts. Gym. Mrs. Geer. Get tidy cotton & oatmeal. 8 cts. each. Home, sup, write note to He. to thank him for good store of fine stationery he sent me today. Sidney does not appear, but Herodotus does, just for a moment, to ask me if he might bring his friend MacDougal[9] to see me on Friday. *Course!* Read an hour or so.

Wed. March 15th. 1882.

6. Easy day. School as usual. Pea soup dinner. Go to Mabel's. Got letter from He. on my way. 50 cts. Walked down st. Got Sharp's & Birch's History of Egypt, changed ball of knitting cotton, and bought a dozen triple tulle ruffles for 55 cts. Stopped for Miss Hill & saw her home, called on Mrs. Diman, and stayed to dinner. Louis DeWolf there. John home. 6 miles today. Write to Cass. Read.

Thurs. March. 16th. 1882.

6.10. Helen calls with invitation to dine. Send note to He. suggesting "party call." Mrs. Berg. $7.50. Millie. Mr. Hazeltine, the violinist He. sent, appears. Leave him there, fiddling. Gym. fine time. Call a second at Mrs. Geer's, & the Ath. Go to the Hazards. Only we four girls, a veritable "dove party." Good dinner, & good time. Home at 9.50 in a belated snowstorm.

Friday March. 17th. 1882.

6. Letter from He. Lesson to Hattie. .50. Lesson to Abbie & Margie. $1.10. 1½ hours at Mrs. Geer's. Home, sup, & dress. Annie & Clarence over. Mr. Stetson & Mr. MacDougal call. Like the latter amazingly. Gay sort of time.

Sat. March. 18th. 1882.

6. Start out at 8.40, stopping for Miss Hill. Get half an hours exercise, and then, in stepping on a chair, to mount the piano, to set the clock, at Miss Hill's request, I clumsily fall, and give myself a violent bruise and profusely bleeding cut just in the "middle". Sit 'round a while, with cold wet towels in abundance; get advice from Dr. Brooks, and ride home serenely, in a horse

car. Am blest with an entire holiday till Thurs.! Houp la! Trim hat, nap, write, etc. Letter from He. Mr. Mac. was well pleased with me. Send 40-2 ct. stamps. Delicate attention!

Sun. March. 19th. 1882.

Rise at 12.30 or so. Bathe & dress up. Sit around serenely. Lu calls. Martha & Mr. Lane call. Herod. calls. Mrs. Rawson & Mrs. Payton call. He. gives me Rossetti & certain moneys in an envelope to "keep for him." Is much concerned.

Monday. March. 20th. 1882.

9 or so. Painted, read, knit, dozed, received call. Helen & Carrie with roses. 10 red bananas & two boxes of strawberries from Herodotus. Kitty Nathan & Josie Arnold call. Mary & Alice. Mrs. Alice Perry & Bell. Mrs. Henry Carpenter. Anna (after Alice & Mary) Herodotus calls. (The Hazards were out.) Sam calls. Queer evening. O' and Robert called with order for two cards.

Tuesday. March. 21st. 1882.

7.30. Write to He. Paint a *little*. Dr. Tyney calls. Examination highly favorable, two dollars. Says she would have sewed it if she had seen it Sat. Diet embargo removed. Carrie calls. Lizzie comes at 3 or so & stays till 9. Martha over. Hattie Chace calls. Herodotus stops in for a few moments. I give him a letter recommending departure. He goes. Jim calls. He. returns, has a few moments talk with me, and things slide on once more. But it was a long hour between 7.30 & 8.30, when I thought he had gone, and gone to stay. I could have stood it though for I thought it right—if *he* did.

Wed. March. 22nd. 1882.

9.30. Paint quite a bit. Annie Rawson calls. Knit, read, & sleep. The worst cold I have had since I can *remember*!

Thurs. March. 23rd. 1882.

7.25. Write to He. Henrietta calls. Eke Annie Rawson with jelly. Hen. gave me a quarter for car fares. Good idea. I go to Mrs. Bergs. 75. Millie. Gym, confining myself to *arm* exercises. Mrs. Geer's & have dress fitted. Home, in car. Got 20 tickets, & spent 3. Lu & Helen Potter had called. Maria Brown & Arthur Perry called. Miss Murphy here. Florrie calls. I feel better. Letter from He.

Fri. 24th.

9.30 or so. Knit & draw. Carrie & Helen call. I go to Hattie's, & Abbie's, $1.50 in, & 4 car-fares out. Home by 6. Lizzie, & the Jastrums to tea. Mr. Tingley calls. Jim & Sam later. Whist ad libitum. We beat the rubber of seven, Sam & J. J. to Mr. J. & I. Mr. Stillwell drops in at 11.

Sat. March. 25th. 1882.

9 or so. Go to the Gym. & feel much better. Leave my four cards at Miss McGary's. Lunch with Miss Hill & see her off to Boston. Home in car. Eat. Read. Letter from He. Aunt C., Mother, & I go to Mr. Stetson's Studio. Mr. Putnam & Miss Cutter there. Nice time. I call on Mrs. Bailey. Like her. Ath, *nice* time. Boy's Room. *Nice time!*

Sunday. March. 26th. 1882.

11.40! Last day of delicious idleness. Write to C. A. Hedge. Dine. Wash dishes. Herodotus arrives. Real nice time. In honor of his 24th birthday yestreen. Anna & Clarence over. Mrs. Manchester, Lu, & certain cousins stop to take Aunt C. to church. Mr. Stetson & I compare colds. His ahead.

Monday. March. 27th. 1882.

Up at 5.50. Do the work as usual. School. Write to He. before school. Ride over to the Cushman's & back, reading E. History both way. .75 cts. Find letter from He. at home, and write a 20 pager in answer. Horrid cough but feel well.

Tuesday. March. 28th. 1882.

6.30. Letter from He. No scholars. Answer letter, & paint whales. Robert calls for, but don't get 'em. *Walk* to Hattie's. 50 cts. Go with her to the Bible Class. Martha walks home with me. Jessie Carpenter calls. I met Harold Childs. Dress up. He and Sam call. Then Sidney. Then Mr. McDougal & Herodotus. A horribly incongruous evening. Whist & Biblical criticism in the same small room. Mr. M. plays. Mr. Stetson is sick—faint, & goes out to lie down. He might not have come over. Threatened pneumonia. O when shall I have a home of my own! 12.20

Wed. March. 29th. 1882.

5.50. Two letters from He. Grace goes early. Clam-chowder. Paint Whale & "Leader". Sup copiously. Mrs. Budlong called. Mrs. Luther & Martha come & stay an hour or so. Edward over. Letter from He. P.M.

Thurs. March 30th. 1882.

5.50. Paint on cards. Ride over to Mrs. B's. 75 cts. Am left to dismiss school. Tell 'em stories. Millie's. She grows weaker. Pub. Lib. Gym. Am the first to do the flying rings. 4 or 5 times. Mrs. Geer. Ath. B.C. Home in the moonlight. Hot chowder, "Romance of the 19th Century," [10] & write to He.

Fri. March. 31st. 1882.

5.30. Only Grace. Letter from He. Write him a bit at 5.45. Walk to Hattie's. 50 cts. Walk to Abbie's. 50. No Margie. Connie Pitman there. Walk to Pub. Lib. (ordered Easter lily at Hoggs.) Met Miss Alice Budlong at Pub., & vouchsafed an oration. Got Gould's "Good English." Rode home. Finish Mallock. Write to He.

Sat. April 1st. 1882.

Up at 5.25. Write to He. Stop for Miss Hill & go to Gym. Good time. Stay & lunch. Home & take nap. Call at Mrs. Geer's for suit, & pay her $8.00. Bill 11.70. Boy's room last night. Ride home. Easter lily—60 cts.

(Mrs. Rawson's 44th birthday.)

Sunday, April 2nd. 1882.

5.40. Paint lily. Go to S. S. Take class. Church. Home with Aunt C. Boy with note from Herodotus, who is really ill—slow fever etc. Send answer. Wash dishes. Christen new dress. Anna & Clarence call. Write to He. and get Clarence to post it.

Monday. April. 3rd. 1882.

5.20. Write to He. Sketch lily. School. Mother spends the day with Mrs. Sayles. Take lily to Herodotus. Brief call. Cushman's. 75 cts. Mabel Masons. Engaged. Car down. Call on the Hazards, & Martha. Home, sup, write to He., and go out & post it ere 8.30. Jim over. Whist.

Tuesday. April. 4th. 1881. {sic}

5.20. Write to He. Only Grace. Two letters from He. & one from Robert with $4.00 for those 2 cards. Ride over to Calders & get glass, stamp & card boxes, panel & disc. Ride down st. Go to Hattie's .50. Gym. Call on Abbie. Home. Write to He. Finish "The fate of Madame La Tour." [11] *Slee*-py.

Wed. April 5th. 1882.

5.25. Paint Easter card. Only Grace. Letter from He. Go to Mabel Masons. Hour between at Ath. Walk home. Joined by Foster Townsend. Mother sick—"dizzy spell." Write to He. Wash dishes. Get mother to bed. Write to Miss Alden.

Thurs. April 6th. 1882

5.20. Write to He. Paint. Florrie arrives, had a bad cold. Letter from He. Walk to Mrs. Bergs. No pay. Millie worse. Gymn. Fine time. Miss Helen Gammel meditates calling on me. Ath. Call on the Slicer's, being turned out of the Ath. at 7. B. C. Home & sup.

Fri. April 7th. 1882.

5.30. Write to He. Letter from Ada & He. Go to Hattie's, no pay. Home and finish Easter card for Jim. Mr. Stetson calls. Glad to see him out again. Stays to tea. Edward comes. He. goes. Jim calls a moment, for his card. $1.50. Mr. & Mrs. Jastram call. Whist. I retire at 10.

Sat. April. 8th. 1882.

5.45. Black stove. Stop for Miss Hill, gone, go and pay Mrs. Geer $4.00, & get receipted bill. Gym. Splendid time. Stay and lunch with Miss Hill. Gave Luise Mauran another watch guard for her shoe-string, and bought another. Home, rest a bit, paint a bit, shampoo myself (chilly,) sup, & write to Ada B. Hazard. Letter from He. this P.M.

Sun. April 9th. 1882.

5.55. S. S. & Church. New suit. Cloudy day. Call on Lu, who has been ill. Herodotus here to dinner. Sat around while I washed dishes. Read to him. Miss Murphy calls. Martha over with an Easter egg from Abbie, and my last summer's letters. I go to church with Mrs. Manchester. Aunt C. has a bad cold.

Monday. April 10th. 1882.

5.35. Write to He. Mother has a new scholar—Annie Peck by name. Cushman's. 75 cts. Mabel's. No pay. Ride down, get books at Pub. Lib. & call on Lu. Stay to tea, and have a good time till nearly 8.30. Harry sees me home. Read some Rawlinson. Have got his 4th & 5th Monarchy, & Barring-Gould's "Curious Myths of the Middle Ages.["]

Tuesday. April 11th. 1882.

5.25. Ablute. Go to Hattie's, $1.00. F[riends] in C[ouncil].s. Abbie's. $1.00. Home & find letter from He. Read & sup. Sam calls. Gobang & nice talk & buttonholes.

Wed. April. 12th. 1882.

5.30. Write to Ada. Go to Mabel's. no pay. Home, take knitting & call at the Manchesters. Lu out, Harry sick. Home, read at [*sic*] bit, write to Ada, & buttonholes.

Thurs. April. 13th. 1882.

5.30. *Cold!* Ablute. Write to He. Myra Durfree, a young friend of my pupils, visits school. Letter from He. Mrs. Berg. 75 cts. Millie. Gym. Fine time. Upset the water jar. Ath. Call at the Blake's but don't stop as they were dining, go for Martha, & escort her to & from the Bible Class. Home by 9.30. Letter from He. Sup. bed.

Fri. April 14th. 1882.

5.30. Write to He. School. Hurried chowder. Hattie. 50 cts. Stop at Mr. Stetson's studio, & invite him over this evening. Abbie & Margie $1.00. Home, sup, & wash dishes. Mother & Aunt C. go to J. Jastrum's to tea. Glad I didn't. Herodotus arrives early. And then—Richie! Anna & Clarence in for a few moments. Mr. S. has to go first, but lurks nearby, and returns after R. Hamlin departs. Good as a play. Mother & Aunt C. arrive with Edward, & Mr. Stetson departs thereafter. Queer evening.

Sat. April. 15th. 1882.

5.30. Write to He. *Sweep my room*! Go to Gym. Grand show day, seven Dr.s present. Dr. Sargent one of 'em. All went well. Saw Martha there, and others. Home & paint a bit. Hattie Salisbury calls. Retire ere nine. Letter from Cassie.

Sunday. April. 16th. 1882.

5.45. S.S. with class, Church, fine sermon, home alone, dine, dishes, & Herodotus. Take a delightful walk. Home to supper, & read to him afterwards. Pleasant day.

Monday. April 17th. 1882.

5.30. Card from Miss Alden. Herodotus calls at 12.10 or so with "Quackenbos' Hist. Anc. Lit. etc." Don't stop. Go to Mrs. Geer's with stuff for morning sack. Postman gave me a letter from He. Stop at Dr. Gay's and Calders. Cushman's. 75 cts. Mabel's. No pay. Ride down. Call on Jennie Bucklin on way home. Good. Sup, study half an hour, Sam, Anna & Clarence, Stillwell, cribbage, buttonholes, chat, irksomeness. retire at ten.

Tues. April. 18th. 1882.

5.10. Memory notes & write to He. Hot and dusty again. Go to Hattie's. 50 cts. First posted letter and met Sam in P.o, & he walked up with me to cor. George & Magee. Gym. Home, with Margie Hazard part way, & Clara Rawson all. Arthur Perry calls. Sup. Anc. Lit. Sidney calls, & Jim. Talk.

Wed. April. 19th. 1882.

5.10. Notes. Arthur arrives. Letter from He. Paint birthday card for Arthur. 50 cts. Write to He. in my room at 10–11.

Thurs. April. 20th. 1882.

5.50. Mrs. Berg. $1.50. Millie. Get another yd. of dress goods., 75 cts. Gym. Walk to Ath. with Mary Sharpe, who treats on Soda. Good. Ath. New Pop. Sci. Go to the Browns to meet Aunt C. & with her to the B. C. Home with her, Lu, & Gus Pierce.

Friday April 21st. 1882.

5. Memory notes. Only Grace. Read her Mrs. Browning etc. Go to Hattie's. 50 cts. Abbies. 1.00. Sam calls there. 2 letters from He. one with another sheet of stamps. Mother & Aunt C. go to cousin Julia's in the evening. Martha & her mother call. Mrs. L. retires, M. stays with me awhile, & I see her home ere 9. Write to He. Read some.

Sat. April. 22nd. 1882.

5. Write to He. Mem. notes after breakfast. Letter from He. Stop at M's on way down st. Call at Mrs. Geer's. No go. Gym. Fine time. Lunched with Miss Hill & saw her off in the train. Home & paint. Miss Russell calls. Read & study. Bed ere 9.

Sun. April. 23rd. 1882.

5.10. S.S., B. C., C., home with Lu who gives me tickets and programmes for Chopin Club business. Start to foot up accounts from old journal. Dinner, dishes, finish letter to Carrie, Herodotus calls, we go out and walk 5 ½ miles— Nice talk. He does not stay to tea, as mother refuses to invite him and I won't. Bite of supper, & spend the evening with Lu who didn't want to go to church. Anna & Clarence here.

Monday. April. 24th. 1882.

5. Notes. Write to He. Paint. Card & Arion tickets from Carrie Hazard. Cushmans. 50. Mabel's. 2.50. Ride down. Pub. Lib. Renew "Curious Myths" etc, & leave Rawlinson. Walk home with Fannie Chace. Sup. Read. Write to He. Edward over.

Tues. April. 25th. 1882.

4.50. Write to He. Mem. notes. School. dinner. Met postman, got letter from He. & posted mine, Hattie, 50. Called on Miss Russel & gave her my Arion tickets, went with her to F. in C., went with Martha to the Art Club Ex. (25 cts. out!) Saw Abbie & Margie there, home by George st. Met Bessie & Minnie Peck. Sup. Read & Studied. Mother & Aunt C. went to Reginald's to spend the evening. No one in. Feel a little blank. At nearly 9, Sidney Putnam & a Mr. Bumpus arrived. Good time, like him.

Wed. April. 26th. 1882.

5.5. Nellie Benson comes to school. (Mem. notes as usual.) All out but me P.M. Finish gentian and do one side of stamp box. Letter from He. Write to him. Some time lost today.

Thurs. April 27th. 1882—

5.5. Only Florrie. Nice time with her. Forget it was Mrs. Berg's vacation. More time with Millie. Lunch with Miss Hill at gym. Jolly time there. Ath. Call at the Slicer's. Mrs. S. sick. Look at L'Art & enjoy it. B. C. Gus Pierce home.

Fri. April. 28th. 1882.

5.5. Write to He. Letter from He. & card from Abbie. Go to Hattie's. 50. Abbie's, buying pansies on the way. 50. Met Miss Hill and went home with her. Home & supt and studied and wrote to He. Mr. Stillwell. Whist! "O had I the wings of a dove!"

Sat. April 29th. 1882.

5.15. Write to He. Gym. Go home with Miss Hill. Go to the May festival at U. of C. W. rooms. Serve at apron table with Mrs. Bridges & am useful. Kate Bucklin gives me my supper and it was *good.* I haven't been so hungry for years. Am presented with an apron by subscription. Go home with Lu at 10.10. Letter from He. Tired.

Sunday. April 30th. 1882—

5.15. See to S.S. lesson as it is my class now. Church and doze. Home with the Manchester's sans Lu. Write to Carrie Hazard. Herodotus over, and we walk around Hunt's Mills. Lovely day. Home at 7, sup heartily, reat [*sic*] "The Emperor," [12] study & retire at 9, praise the gods.

Monday. May 1st. 1882.

Because t'is Spring I needs must sing
My joy I cannot smother,
The grass is green, the sky is blue,
And I am I and you are you
And we have found each other!
Then what care we for Fate's decree
It *must* be one or t'other,
And if we live or if we die
Still you are you and I am I
And still we have each other!

Up at 4.10. Notes. Write to He. School. Dine. Get letter of postman. Send Chopin Club tickets to Mabel Bridges, & knit band to Dr. Tyney. (& letter to He.) Cushmans. 75 cts. Mabel's. No pay. ride down. Pub. Lib. a moment. Try on hats on way down st. Stop and dine at Prof. Blakes. Margie there. Whist thereafter. Home & study. & sup.

Tues. May 2nd. 1882.

4.52. Write to He. Notes. Only Florrie. To Hattie. 50 cts. Gym. Mrs. Geer. Walk up with Hattie Gammell. She teases me to come in. Call on Martha. Send note to He. Home & sup. Letter from He. Study. Anna & Clarence. Retire at 9.10.

Wed. May. 3rd. 1882.

4.55. Only Grace. Invitation from the S. to E. S. at H. Mother & Aunt C. go to see "The Colonel". Letter from He. Helen Gammell calls. Write to He. Finish ["]the Emperor." Robert over with more whales.

Thurs. May. 4th. 1882.

5.30! Letter from He. Stop at his Studio to leave him mine. Mrs. Berg. 75 cts. Millie. Gym. Ride to the Ath. with Helen Gammell. Read. Joined there by Walter, & we take an extended walk and then spend the evening at Martha's. Very pleasant, *very*. Home ere ten. Sup.

Fri. May 5th. 1882.

5.30.! Card from Robert. School. Card from Dr. Tyney. Go to Mrs. Geer's. Out. Gym. Abbie. Paint Hepatica's. Go to tea at the Channing's. Splendid time. Mr. Saunders there, and a most enjoyable talk in the dim-lighted parlor. Mr. C. comes home with me. A bite, & bed.

Sat. May. 6th. 1882.

4.30. Paint anemones. Mrs. Geer. (Letter from He.) Gym. Home, dine, paint whale. Sidney is haled in by mother & stays 1 ½ hours. Lu calls and fiddles. Look over my S. S. lesson & retire ere 9.

Sun. May 7th. 1882.

4.25. Notes, and finish whale. S. S. with the Rawsons, successful lesson. Home with Lu. Notes. dinner, a much. Jim calls, and goes to Anna's with mother. Dishes. Herodotus. Lizzie, Allie, Eddie, Marian, Tudy, & Pardon call. He. & I walk ten miles or so and come home blooming. Sup. Notes.

Monday. 8th. 1882.

4.30. Write to He. Card from Robert. Cushmans. 75 [cents]. (Finished notes & posted 'em). Mabel's. No pay. Ride down. Leave book at Pub. Lib. Get cardboard at Calders. Walk home. Write to He. Edward over. Then Sam. Beat S[am]. at Gobang, and he me at whist. Bed by 10.20–30.

Tuesday. May 9th. 1882.

4.30. Write to He. Paint one violet. Only Grace. Walter Smith is dead— April 8th.—poor mother! Hattie's. 50 [cents]. F. in C.'s. Doze at first. Get a plain answer to a plain question from Mr. Slicer! Call on Allie's baby. Pretty. Home and write to He. Sup. Study a bit.

Wed. May. 10th.

4.40. Paint bloodroot, fire brush, card for Grace, & Whale all the afternoon. Letter from He. Go around to Lu's at 6.30 & stay an hour or two. The Chaces here when I return. More whale.

Thurs. May 11th. 1882.

4.40. Finish whales & send them to Robert with versified note. Letter from He. Only Florrie. Mrs. B. No pay. Gym. Get waist of Mrs. Geer. [$]1.00. Ath. Sam in. Little fuss with Miss Angell. Miss Kate Bucklin lingered long for the sake of walking home with me. Little Mr. Bailey accompanied her. The [*sic*] came in and made a call. He is coming to play chess. I like him. Robert over. Fix Whales and retire at 9.25.

Friday May 12th. 1882.

4.30. Write to He. School. Letter from He. P.M. Go to Hattie's. .50. Abbie's. 1.00. Call on Mrs. Putnam. Home, read letter, sup, write & study. "May Storm"

Sat. May 13th. 1882.

5.10. Notes. Paint. Gym. Home. Dine. Paint, darn silk stockings. Call on Mrs. Diman. Go to Anna's to tea. Home at 8.40.

Sun. May 14th. 1882.

4.45. Mend clothes. Fix papers & things. To S. S. with Mrs. R., but home to help mother get dinner. Allie, Lizzie, Edward, & Bessie Brown over to dinner. He. afterwards, & stays to tea. 10.20 car. Sleepy.

Mon. May 15th. 1882.

4.45. Studied, read, arranged draw. Letter from Ada with order for $12.00 & letter from Miss Alden, very pleasing. Cushman's, (stopping at Brown's for my waterproof; and to cash notes) 75 cts. Mabel's, $1.00, ride to Snow [St.], & walk home. Write to Ada, Sam calls. Gobang. C.A.P. 26 to SRS. 6!

Tues. May. 16th. 1882.

4.50. Paint clover leaves. Letter from C. A. Hedge. School & paint pansy Grace brought. Hattie's. .50 cts. Gym. Order laced boots, leave gym. tickets for Lizzie Brown, call on Helen Gammel (she was ready and opened the door for me) and stop at Martha's. Home, sup, finish Ada's letter, & write to He.

Wed. May 17th. 1882.

4.20. Paint myrtles & afterward pansie Grace brought. Letter from He. Paint. read a bit. Write to He. Henrietta calls. Call on Lu. Out. See Clarence & ride down to Martha's. Home & find Lu. Home with her. Harry returns with me.

Thurs. May 18th. 1882.

4.50. Notes. School. Mrs. Berg. Millie. Gymn. Ath. Home in car. Note & violets from Sidney. Letter from He. Answer the latter. Jim calls & Robert. Gobang with J. 20 to 4. Bed at 10.30.

Fri. May. 19th. 1882.

4.50. Finish letter to He. School. Letter from He. Go to Hattie—no lesson; to Abbie's, 50 cts & a good talk. Home & paint violets. Read Mary Marston. Write to Cassie.

Sat. May. 20th. 1882.

5. Read Mary Marston. Practice as pedicure [*sic*]. Gymn. with great enjoyment & success. Lizzie, Abbie, and Eddie there. Ride both ways. Left "Mary" with Miss Hill to take to Boston with her. Home to clean loveliness which I enjoy. Dine, sleep & paint violets. Read a bit in new Century. Write for S. S. class & to Carrie Hazard.

Sun. May. 21st. 1882.

5. Read Scrib. Lecture on glass in S. S. Church & keep awake! Home with Lu. Fix straw hat & put on flannel suit. Our first summer day. Martha & Mr. Lane call. Herodotus arrives. We walk about ten miles, & get a lot of flowers. He goes home in the 7.45 car. Sup. Write to C. A. Hedge.

Mon. May. 22nd. 1882.

4. Paint violets and bell wort. School. Letter from Carrie Hazard with check for $10.00 for my summer vacation. I seem likely to have one. Dinner. Letter from He. Get stamps. Cushman's. 75 cts. Mabel's. Ride to Snow, and stop a bit at Watermans. Home, sup, loaf a bit, write to Carrie & He.

Tues. May. 23rd. 1882.

5. Write to He. Only Grace. Call on Miss Hill at gym. Go to Pub. Lib. with her & get her a book. Go to the F. in C.'s. Home, sup, read, Sam, gobang, 13 to 7!

Wed. May. 24th. 1882.

4.30. Nap & read. Letter from He. Paint Columbine P.M. Martha over. Good time. Do up my hair & go with Charles Walt to see Lu. Home by 10 or so.

Thurs. May. 25th. 1882.

5.50!! Paint a bit. Only Grace. Notes from Carrie & Abbie. Mrs. Berg. No pay. Millie. Gym. Miss Hill not there, [her] mother dying. We girls go on by ourselves. A fine big fire over in Ex. Place—some patent extinguisher. Ride home. Go up to Mrs. Dimans to dinner & see Carrie & Helen. Helen called at the Gym. Edward here. Letter from He.

Fri. May. 26th. 1882—

4.30. Write to He. School. Lesson to Hattie. .50 [cents]. Call at Mrs. Haskell's & Mrs. Torrey's to see Lu Hill. She don't feel able however. Call on the Channings & Annie Morse. Meet Mrs. Alden, walk home with her, stay to tea, and until 8 or after. Home & find Sam. Mother & Aunt C. go out to see Mrs. Budlong, & Sam talks to me as I wish he had six or eight weeks ago. He is a friend worth having.

Sat. May. 27th. 1882—

5.30. Black stove etc. Delectable griddlecakes. Letter from He. Loaf a bit!
Go to Gym. Louise Mauran leads; lots of spectators. Home, dine, paint, loaf,
cook, wash dishes, & write. Had a letter from Thomas! Dear boy! He is going
to be married. Write him, & send best wishes & violets to the dame. S. S.
lesson.

Sun. May. 28th. 1882.

5. Put letters in order, & write for S. S. Make rusk. S. S. General speechifying.
Church. Home with Lu, Harry, & Mabel Hill. They stop in. Lovely & cool in-
side. Comb hair, dine, dishes, Herodotus. Queer time. He goes at 6.20. Sup.
Go to hear Dr. Hedge with Lu & her mother. Carry flowers to Mrs. Potter.
Anna & Clarence here. Prospective scholar in Kate Bucklin.

Mon. May. 29th. 1882.

5.50! Card from the Cushmans. School. Letter from He. Answer. Note to
Kate Bucklin. Go to Mabels'. No pay. Home via Ath. Charles Walt called and
missed me. Write to him & post ere 8.30. Tickets $1.00, stamps 8 cts.

Tues. May. 30th. 1882.

5.30. No school. Thoroughly sweep & fix room. Rearrange work basket &
start waists. Letter from He. Dine. Miss Murphy with Aunt C's silk. Go to
Abbie's leaving love for Lu Hill. 50 cts. Stop at Charles Walt's door a moment.
Get 15 ct. cream for Millie. Did her good. Told her my yesterday's book—"A
strange Disappearance." [13] Did her good too. Call on the Slicers. Out. Leave
note. Call at Mrs. Diman's after Miss Alden. Not come. Home, sup, sew—
Bed.

Wed. May. 31st. 1882.

5.30. Write to Carrie & father. Poem from He. Sew. Dine. Kate Bucklin
calls & we make arrangements for lessons. Paint pink heart flower. Call at the
Dimans. Miss A. there. Home, sup, write

Thurs. June 1st. 1882.

4.15. Note to He. & Lizzie Brown. Do all the work but breakfast. Call for
Miss Alden. Sick & can't go. Send telegram for her, and take 8.30 train. Get to
the meeting early and enjoy it much. Reports, essays, remarks by Mr. Gilman,
(the Annex Man) Mr. Lyman, & Mr. Eliot, and poem by Oliver W. Holmes.
Then go up to Aunt Emilie's. She says nothing about dinner so I don't.
Grandma there. Nice talk with Aunt E. Then to the Hedges, via many horse-
cars. Dr. Furness here. Splendid dinner much enjoyed—11 hours fast with
no ill consequence. Quiet evening with the old men's anecdotes, & bit of talk
with Miss C[harlotte]. when I go to bed.

Fri. June 2nd. 1882.

7.35! Breakfast. Loaf & doze & talk to Dr. Furness. Dine. Loaf & doze & talk to Dr. Furness & the rest. Sup. Loaf & talk to Miss C. read a little. Cinder in my eye. Retire at 9.10. Sent postal to mother. (Parlor fire let out!)

Sat. June 3rd. 1882.

6.45. Learn "Dover Beach." Loaf. Talk with Dr. Furness. Lunch. Call at the Holland's. Ride on, Leave bag at Depot. Call on Mrs. Smith. She has moved to 286 Marlborough St. Poor woman! She is much worn. A beautiful house. 6.30 train for home. Catch Gov. St. horsecar, & get home by 8.20 or so. Sup, talk, write to C.A.H.

Sun. June. 4th. 1882.

5.45. Work as usual. S.S. City life vs. country. Poor sermon. Sat with Lu. Home, fix hair, dine, wash dishes, Herodotus. Stays till 10. Clarence in.

Mon. June. 5th. 1882.

5.30. School again. Send note to Kate Bucklin, & Tom Fisher. Look up science for K. B. Call on Lu. Out. See Miss Alden a few moments. Meet Mrs. Mason. No Mabel today. Call on Mrs. Luther. On K. B. Out. On Fanny Bogert. Out. Saw Mrs. & Hattie Sheldon. Met Miss Bogert & was introduced to Mrs. Called on the Slicers. Out. Met Miss Daly & walked a bit with her. Met mother and called on Josie Arnold & the Keaches. Rode home with mother. Met Walter & Sidney Paine on the bridge. Home & fix up a bit. Herodotus makes parting call & leaves me his keys. Supper.

Tues. June 6th. 1882.

5.30. Read a bit. Arrange drawer. School. Bolt some dinner and just catch 2.10 car. Lesson to Mabel. $2.00. Ride down. Stop at Kate Bucklin's. Go to F. in C.s. Stop for Miss B. & we come home together. Teach her a lot of natural philosophy and such like. Sup. Write to He.

Wed. June 7th. 1882.

5.15. Read a little Nat. Philosophy. Letter from He. School. Go to the Pawtuxet with Lizzie, Carrie Richmond, & Mr. & Mrs. Slicer. Splendid time. Literally splendid, with azalia, lupine, etc. Home by 8.15 car, stop with the S.'s, go down with Lizzie, & ride home. Anna & Clarence here.

Thurs. June 8th. 1882—

5.30. Hot. School. Mrs. Maine and her baby spend the day. Mrs. Berg. No pay. Millie too weak to see me! Lunch with Lu Hill, & take her 15 ct. cream. Nice time with the girls at the Gymn. Get shoes & boots, $6.75; Mitts, 75 [cents], & soda .05. Ath. Back to gym. after my watch. Home. Letter from He. Sup in luxurious loneliness as mother & aunt C. go out. Write to Mrs. Smith.

Fri. June 9th. 1882.

6! Card from Abbie. No lesson with her. Jim came after I had retired. Came down and beat him at gobang—72 to 22————! Felt better. Bed at 12!

Sat. June 10th. 1882.

6.10. Paint arethusas, and make a failure of it. Dust "a wee" in my room. Carry boots to be nailed. Nice time at the Gymn. Walk home with Lu Hill. Home. Dine frugally. Nap. Paint rough sketch. Mother and Aunt C. out. Anna calls. Go 'round to Lu's. Out. Home. sup. Arrange for S. S. lesson. Am dismally blue.

Sun. June 11th. 1882.

6.10. Read "Prudence Palfrey." Amusing. S. S. as usual. Slept at church. Home, read, dine, dishes, write to Thomas. Lu calls. Edward, Lizzie, & Eddie Jastram to tea. Tell stories to Eddie. Write to He.

Mon. June 12th. 1882.

4.45. Write to He. Fire etc. School etc. Letter from He. & Thomas. Write to F. Letter from He. noon mail. Go down st. Met Abbie Cooke & Margie Calder. Called at the Slicers. Am invited to another Pawtuxet party next Monday. Car to Mabel's. 50 cts—Call for Lu Hill, but she had had to go. Call at Martha's and enjoy it. Home & find mother sick with the worst headache she has had in a long long time. See to her and put her to bed as best I can. Write to He & T. Feel lots happier than for some time.
Perfect day.

Tues. June 13th. 1882.

4.55. Wash yestd'ys dishes. Letter from He. School. Am reading Gulliver's Travels to the girls. Martha over P. M. Stop for Lu. Out. Go with M. to Friends in Council. last meeting. Miss Bogert stopped me on way home. Just got here as Miss Bucklin did, Jews, Zuni Indians, Toltecs, Aztecs, Anc. History in brief, & monkeys; for own discourse. Sup, play with kittens, write to Cassie.

Wed. June 14th. 1882.

4.50. Write to Cassie. School. Call on Fannie Bogert, pupil prospective. Go with mother & call on Mrs. Jackson, Hope, Goddard, & Daboll. Home, write a word to He, sup, and "fix" a bit. Delightful call from Ben Wells. Like him much. Anna & Clarence in. They all leave us the parlor. Write to He.

Thurs. June. 15th. 1882.

5.5 Sew till 6.30. Strange cat yowling all night; find, feed & disperse. Bed slats descended rather hastily. Letter from He. Mrs. Berg. No pay. Millie. Lunch at Gym. Good time at the Ath. Home, sut [*sic*], write to Mrs. Smith.

Fri. June 16th. 1882.

5.30. Write to He. School. Paint heads on little mirror. Miss Bucklin. Hear Lu is ill & spend the evening with her. Mother quite sick—

Sat. June 17th. 1882.

5. Sweep my room. Wash b. dishes & help Sarah a bit, as mother is unable. Mr. Peck in. Nice time at the Gym. Home with Jessie Taylor. Nice girl. Cook steak for Sarah. Dine on cracker & milk. Paint a yellow lily—or begin to. Doze. Mother comes home from down st. very weak and tired. Read "Stillwater Tragedy" [14] to her. Make bread. Hot day.

Sun. June 18th. 1882—

5. Make fire. Aunt C. and I are so anxious to have some of *"mother's* sponge-cake" for tea, that we make it ourselves! Inside of ten minutes too. Start the dinner, wash dishes etc. (Aunt C. wiped.) Last day of S. school. Home & get dinner & finish "S. Tragedy" to mother. Mutton dinner. Wash dishes, scour bread board, fix salt cellars, & dress up with my hair in *just* the right place—and then friend Wells doesn't come! Nor send word. Robert in to order another whale! Bed early. Wrote to C. A. Hedge & finished letter to Cassie.

Mon. June 19th. 1882.

4.45. Start to write to father—letter from him Sat. Only Florrie, & Grace in for her books. Get dinner, dress, & go with Mr. & Mrs. Slicer to the Pawtuxet. Perfect time, very jolly & gay. A little rain while we were under a bridge. Home at 8.15. Stopped & got soda.

Tues. June 20th. 1882—

4.50. Whale. Only Florrie. Whale. Dine. Letter from He. Whale. Maria calls. Miss Bucklin. She invites [me] to go to Maine with them & stay a week. Mrs. H. Carpenter calls. Mrs. Manchester calls. Mr. Wells calls. Walter Paine calls. Pleasant evening—very.

Wed. June 21st. 1882.

5.15. Whale. Florrie. Whale. Dine. Carry whale to Robert. Cash Carrie's check for ten dollars. Call on Lu Hill. Lesson to Mabel. 50 cts. Engaged me for next fall. Stop for Lu. & she comes home with me. Seemed to enjoy herself. Walked home with her. Will Bogert walked part way back with me. Home, sup, write to He.

Thurs. June 22nd. 1882.

5.35. Last day of school. Grace calls & pays her bill $8.00. Mrs. Berg. No pay. Millie. Too sick to see me. Lunch with Lu Hill, & exercise. Ath. Call on the Slicers. Home. Miss Murphy here. Sup. Read Century.

Fri. June 23rd. 1882—

5.20 or so. I'm tired of washing a whole days dishes at a time. Mothers school out. Do some Arithmetic. Snooze. Get dinner. Mother, other mothers, & the fry go out to R. W.'s Park. Lu spends the afternoon. Nice time. Miss Bucklin. Wrote to father.

Sat. June 24th. 1882.

4.50. Arithmetic & snooze. Strawberry shortcake for breakfast. Do dishes & go to gymn. Don't exercise but read to Lu. Bring home a pint of coffee cream. 20 cts! Good dinner. Help get the parlor in order. Write to Mrs. Smith. Mrs. Rawson in. (Letter from He.) Mrs. Putnam & another woman called, Sam. Gobang 36 to 15. Hot.

Sun. June 25th. 1882.

6.50. *Hot*. Loaf all day. Good Shampoo. Read & doze P.M. Mr. Stetson comes back from Phil. & spends the evening. Misses Russel call. Hot! Hot! Hot!

Mon. June 26th. 1882.

5.30. Wrote note to He. Got one from Carrie Hazard inviting me down to spend the 4th, & He. to pass a day & go home with me. Whitneys to be there. Pity I can't. Mother starts to remodel my bunting for best dress. I darn chemiloon. Last lesson to Mabel. 50 cts. (Called on way at Lu Hill's, & gave her knit belt.) Got catnip 3 cts, s. silk 10, toothbrush 21, H'k'f, 25, Stamps 30. Called at Martha's; out. Mabel Hill's—out. Home, ablute, dress, sup, read Scrib on steps, He. appears, nice time till lo! Edward, & then Jim, who wouldn't come up the steps at all, but stayed down below and argued on instinct vs. reason. He. gets a little mad at sophism & pigheadedness. I'm too used to it to mind. He attempts a little explanation with mother but in vain. Needs some practice to get along with her—or a Simmons.

Tues. June 27th. 1882.

Mother gets tickets to a New Church Garden Party at Mrs. Jacksons. Remodel grey petticoat. Note from He. Wrote to Cassie A.M. & trimmed little brown bonnet. Dine. Sewed & fixed P.M. Anna over. Kate Bucklin, extends her invitation to *two* weeks! Go to see Lu & enjoy it. Uncle William called while I was out I joy to say. Mother has a headache.

Wed. June 28th. 1882.

6. Slept *all* the morning. Sew generally P.M. Robert in; brought me $2.82 for whale.

FIVE

"Even Heaven looks misty & grey"

June 29, 1882–October 3, 1882

CHARLOTTE left Providence for a vacation in Ogunquit, Maine, on July 1, 1882. There she enjoyed long, lazy days—loafing, sketching, watching the sun set, and corresponding with Martha, Walter, and various friends. A few days after her return to Providence on July 24, Charlotte spent a "pleasant evening" with Walter, and despite her increasingly frequent expressions of ambivalence, she was overjoyed to see him. On August 14 she left again, this time for twelve days at Martha's Vineyard.

Her happiest moments of the trip seemed to occur in the six days during which Martha Luther joined her at the Vineyard. Indeed, she seemed elated to have Martha to herself: "Meet Martha on the wharf at 12.45 or so. . . . Long pleasant ride, so glad to see her. Dinner, lots, & then we make tracks for & on the beach. I swim & disport myself as usual—catch a fish! She seems to like it. 'A bite' on return & bed. Bless her!"

When the vacation finally ended, Charlotte enjoyed another "pleasant ride" back to the wharf, with Martha seated securely upon her lap. By the time she returned to Providence on August 26, the summer was nearly over, and she and Walter had spent more time apart than together.

Over the next several weeks, however, she and Walter were together often. Walter began painting Charlotte's portrait, but he was unhappy with the result (see "The Painting of *The Portrait*" in Appendix B). Walter was frustrated by his failure to capture Charlotte's beauty adequately; nevertheless, he and Charlotte clearly enjoyed their time together in his studio. And although time must have been at a premium as her wedding day approached, Martha accompanied Charlotte to nearly every studio sitting.

In an attempt, perhaps, to deflect the pain she felt over being spurned by Martha in favor of Charles A. Lane, Charlotte used the quiet moments in the studio to boast about her own future plans of a life with Walter. According to Walter, "She talked . . . to Miss Martha about *our* lives, about what *we* had before us," he reported in his diary (*Endure*, p. 98). "She said it all in a way which showed how decided she was that it all would be," he continued. By focusing on her own future, which was actually still very much in limbo, Charlotte was better able to cope with the imminent loss of Martha. In truth, Charlotte was still vacillating on whether she could—or even wanted to—conform to the traditional roles of wife and mother. Bantering about it with Martha, however, helped to diminish her pain. At the same time that she braced herself for Martha's wedding, Charlotte valiantly tried to be supportive, escorting Martha to the dressmaker's shop and often dropping in at her home to share a cup of tea or a few stolen moments before Martha would finally, and irrevocably, belong to another.

Thurs. June 29th. 1882.

6-30. Go down to Lu Hills & stay an hour. Call at Mrs. Berg's for bill. Gone, left note referring me to Janitor. Millie, nice call. Shop a bit, sketch book & rubber, staylaces, pins, silicia, ammonia, etc. Meet Lu H., go with her a-shopping, & dine at Gym. with her on seafoam crackers and lemonade. Home with her, & call on Mrs. Diman. Get a lot of roses. Home, sup, and dress up in tissue skirt, bunting overthing, lace, pearls, silver stars, bracelets & rose. A party for one. Charles Walt. appears, & enjoys it. He says goodbye at 10.45. I love him.

Friday June 30th. 1882.

6.10. Shirk dishes & go down st. after cash. Can't find janitor, so borrow dollar of Mrs. Cooley & get gloves .60 [cents], thread 5 [cents], paper 15 [cents]. Stop at gymn. & get suit, & carry home. Mary Parson's. Stop at He.'s but he was out. Call on Martha & am comforted. Lamb & peas. Pack. Miss Bucklin. $8.00. Anna & Clarence in.

Saturday July 1st.

5.5 Pack. P.P.C. from Lu Manchester. Hack at 8.45 & off. Met party at depot, surrendered all care of trunk to Jennie Bucklin, and we set off for Boston, Kate Bucklin, Jennie B., Mary Gladding, Julia Mauran & her brother, a Lizzie Brown (as far as Boston), & a Miss Pratt whom we pick up at Pawtucket. Cut across Boston, stopping at King George's Chapel, & lunch at the Maine depot. Some of 'em shopped a bit. Reached Wells late & tired, no one to meet us. Engaged a sort of Black Maria & rode 9 miles or so up and down to Augunquit. Big bare boarding house, close to the rocks and surf. Hot supper, eat little, snooze and talk & recite & tell stories till trunks come at 10. *Bed.*

Sunday. July 2nd. 1882.

11. Fix up room etc. & dine at 1. Write letters to mother only. Go with the rest to spouting rock P.M. Supper. Talk to Emily Pratt. Like her. bed at 9.40 or so.

Monday. July 3rd. 1882.

4.30, but retire again. 6.45. Go fishing after breakfast. Catch two. Write to He. Dine on lamb killed today! Sleep two hours on the rocks P.M. & sketch in pencil a very little. Go sit on rocks with all of 'em till nearly 9. Tell stories to Willie Mauran. Come in when it rains, & have a little music in the keroseney parlor. See a dull moon rise. bed at 10 or so. Have left my flannel sack outsomewhere. Coldsores. 22 years old! Good!

'Tues. July 4th. 1882.

7. No signs of celebration save a few subdued firecrackers. Paint my first out door sketch. Pretty good. Icecream for dinner, & both fish & chicken! Play six games of chess with Miss Pratt. She beats the first & the last, & I the rest with one stale. Write to Mrs. Smith, & this:

> I sit at my ease & gaze on the seas
> Three things before me lie;
> The rock where I sit, the sea under it,
> And the overarching sky.
> The rocks iron brow is the life I have now;
> Too hard for peaceful rest;
> Too warm in the sun, too cold when there's none
> Uncomfortable at best.
> The wide ocean comes next; now quiet, now vext;
> It wants me, to hold & to keep;
> It looks pleasant & warm—but there might come a storm—
> And the ocean is pathless & deep.
> And above hangs the dome of our dear future home
> To be ours if we work through the day:
> But these rocks hide the sun, the azure is gone—
> Even Heaven looks misty & grey.

Came back under the cliff, supper, & evening on the rocks, enlivened with firecrackers. (Found flannel sack.)

Wed. July 5th. 1882.

6.50. Write to Lu Manchester. Go out to see it rage & foam (a driving northeaster) under the cliff, & pulpit. Dinner. All go over to Pebbly Beach. *Grand* surf. The worst storm for July known here for years & years. All do light gymnastics for warmth. Supper. How I do eat! Read & hear Lowell's poetry, argue, & play one-word game with Willie Mauran. Write to He.

Thurs. July 6th. 1882.

7. Wrote to Mother (card) & Martha. Rocks, & talk to Kate B. P.M. nap on grass, & rocks with K. B. After supper we go down the road a little way. Lean on haycock behind a deserted house & watch a gorgeous sunset. Happy. Letter from mother.

Friday. July 7th. 1882.

7. Help Willie Mauran mark out tennis courts. Mend dress, cavort on rocks, & start sketch of flume. Dinner. Rocks again, & write to mother. Paint a little panel. Tennis after supper. Bed early to the dismay of the others, who came up from rocks & couldn't find me.

Sat. July 8th. 1882.

Out by six, walk two or three miles & get a lot of flowers, roses, orchids, & sich. Write to He. & paint in gorge. Pretty good. Read George Eliot's poems P.M. & play chess with Will. 1st I. Then queen off, he 2 I 1. Tennis. Beat Mrs. Prat 1 game of chess, write more to He. & bed.

Sunday. July 9th. 1882.

6.30 or so. Wrote to He. Went to my seat in the Chasm, & wrote to Lu Manchester. Dropped ink-box & paper down the crack & had to go in for 'em. Precarious. *Hot.* Came up, undressed, took a nap. Dinner. Read Hunts "Talks on Art" which Miss Kate gave me, bless her. All go to ride after tea & post 17 letters! Hot!

Monday. July 10th. 1882.

7 or so. Patch two pair of pants for Will, & help a little on a bathing suit Devized by Miss Mauran for Kate. Write to He. Dinner. Read Sartor Resartus,[1] write to He. & play chess with Will till supper. Start to race up & I drop journal & letters into the chasm. He scrabbles down & rescues them, all safe, with lots of yelling & fun. Some visotors [*sic*] stand and watch us. Get letters from mother, Lu Man[chester]., & Martha. Go to walk with some of 'em, & explore old house. Very heavy shower later. Miss Pratt & Miss Mauran afraid.

Tues. July 11th. 1882.

7 or so. Slept all the morning. Dinner. Loaf & talk to Miss Kate who gives me Spencer's "Data of Ethic", & then to the rocks with her. Supper. Loaf, & more rocks. Letters from mother, Thomas, & Mrs. Smith. Bed.

Wed. July 12th. 1882—

6.40 or so. Write to He. A morning ride to York & York Beach. Crazy for a bath, but have to be content with a run on the beach. Late to dinner, &

write to Martha & Mrs. Smith all P.M. Fairly forget supper time. Emerson or Swedenborg after supper, watch sunset & talk to Mrs. Weir till the mail comes. Letter from He. forwarded by mother. Bed.

Thurs. July 13th. 1882.

3.15 or so, and am loaded with roses wild & tame at 4. Arrang tame ones for breakfast, & paint bud & a harebell. Read a little after break[fast]., & take a nap. Will swarms up the roof & sits outside my window while I paint an abortive sunset for his edification. Dinner. Rocks with Kate, she leaves at 4, & I finish Mrs. Smith's letter. Supper, the rest go off diversely, & I play chess with Will, he beating a game without odds, & then read & watch the sunset. Letter from Mother with one from Father inside.

Fri. July 14th. 1882.

7.10. Paint the other end of the split, or begin to. Am joined by Miss Kate & read a bit. Go up to house & read Tronde's Carlyle aloud to her. Lots of visitors today. dinner. Rocks, read in Adam Bede,[2] & write to He. Go to walk after tea with others, & call on "Sarah" & "Almira". (Rathburn) Very pleasant people. bed quite late, after some talk with Miss Kate.

Saturday July 15th. 1882.

7. Draw but cannot paint for lack of sun, & read aloud to Miss Kate. Down to see them bathe & wade. Dinner. Go to the rocks with the crowd, Jennie drones over Whites "18 Christian Centuries" & the others snooze. Buzz some soporific poems to them. At 6 arrive Miss Augusta Gladding & Miss Lizzie Brown, Miss Hoppin & Miss Cutter, & Louise Richardson. More rocks "en masse".

Sunday. July 16. 1882.

7. Quite enjoy my new room. A little Adam Bede, & read aloud to Miss Kate. Write to mother & Carrie Hazard. Dinner. More Carlyle, & some Adam Bede. Finish letter to Carrie, & write to Thomas. Supper, Adam, bed.

Monday. July 17th. 1882.

4.50 or so. Am at Captain Staples, whistling on the doorstep at 5.30, with roses for self & Miss Sarah. We take a nice little walk together, & I stay to a delicious breakfast. Quaint old home. She & Miss Almira walk back with me along the shore & we have a lovely footbath in cool inlet & warm pools. Back by 11.30. read till dinner. Mr. Daniel Beckwith, & Miss Mauran's "Aunt Julia" arrive to grace that meal. Rock now infested by scores of meandering females. Read to Miss B. & self. Letter from He. & mother. Evening on piazza with Adam Bede & talk.

Tues. July 18th. 1882.

7. Paint "rudechia". Read on the rocks. A large party of "transients," delightful people from Cambridge & New Haven arrive. They sing & are delightful. Dinner. Listen to the singers, covertly. Read to Miss Kate & self. Sup. Letter from He. & Mother. "Adam" & talk & recite.

Wed. July 19th. 1882.

6 or so. See off Miss Lippit & Mr. Beckwith. Second day's fog. Read to self, dance "Patience" to my heart's content, read a bit to Miss A. Gladding, & beat Miss Pratt 4 games of chess. Rocks, in spite of fog. Finish Adam Bede.

Thurs. July 20th. 1882.

7.10. Paint a bit. Walk over with Kate, scrambling in rocks, and spend the day at the Rathbone's. Splendid dinner. Ride home, Miss Gladding driving. Nice talk with her after supper (Whist *one* of these evenings.)

Fri. July 21st. 1882.

7. Get a few flowers for Miss Gladding. Paint. Read. Sketch in charcoal P.M. & go to ride with the others. Evening with Miss G. as usual.

Sat. 21st. July 1882.

Kate, Miss Pratt, & I slept out doors on a juniper bush. Enjoyed it. Paint. Read to Miss G. dinner. Miss Cutter makes herself known as a friend. I do not greatly reciprocate. More Miss G. Miss S. Rathbone comes over & we see her home after ten, I supporting Miss Orne. Hear of my gold pen. My luck!

Sunday. July 23rd. 1882.

7. Draw & paint Alba doobadees[3] for Miss Hoppin to give her crippled cousin Olly Alsop. Was much with Miss Gladding. Slept out, K., J., Louise, & I. Fun.

Mon. July 24th. 1882.

Awake at 3.30, in at 4, got hat etc., crawled down over roof & pillar, & took a walk with Kate. Saw the sun rise & got a lot of gorgeous flowers. Roses & daisies for Miss G. Back to house, fix flowers, bathe, & pack. Last visit to rocks with Kate. Breakfast. Off at 8 or so, amidst general bewailment. Hot ride to station, & hot ride to Boston, diversified by amusing children. Transfer trunk for 25 cts, and ride over to Prov. station in horse car. Meet Retta Clarke. Clean up, dine at depot café, & call on Mrs. Smith. Show her about painting a bit, & talk. Nearly miss 4 o'c. train. Pleasant ride home with Retta, & walk up Angell st. Hot & wilty atmosphere after Maine seawinds. Exhibit & talk. Lu & her mother over. Sleepy.

Tues. July 25th. 1882.

Nearly 8. Loaf & write to Kate & Thomas. Letter from T. & card from He. Mother and Aunt C. go down the river with Mary. Read "Moondyne."[4] Retire early. Write to He. Washed dishes.

Wed. July 26th. 1882.

8 or so. Put on cheesecloth renewed, and ride down st. Saw Sam and joined him. Nice boy. Got stamps[,] sent letter to He, got watch, 1.50, & called on Edward. Out. returned mothers book and carried 15 ct. cream to Millie. No better, but a bit brighter I think. The [*sic*] to Edward's again, and write letter to Love.[5] Posted same, bought tickets, 50 cts. got soda, & walked home. Dined. Went with mother to Mrs. Stimpson's funeral. Called on Lu who was not well, and stayed to tea. One word game with Harry. Bed at 9.

Thurs. July 27th. 1882.

8 nearly. Breakfast. Talk with mother over coal &c. Write to George Bissel, Aunt Emily, & Martha. Am persuaded to accompany Mother & Aunt C. to R.W.'s Park, to see a *tub race*! Carry "Data of Ethics" & matronize the party. 10 ct. cream for mother. Hot. Home, ablute & re-dress, sup, & inhabit front steps. Found letter from He. at Port Hastings. Sam called. He & mother went around to Marys. He came back. Aunt C. had gone up stairs, & we enjoyed ourselves. When mother returned she went to reading in the back room, & Sam and I sat & talked till 11.20. I'm very fond of Sam. He's a good friend for any girl.

Friday. July 28th. 1882.

8 or so. Wash dishes, all out. Letter from He. to know when I'm at home. Answer. Read & loaf. Paint in oils on plaque. Carry some books of Grace Ross'es home. See Mrs. R. Call on Jastrams. Evening on steps.

Sat. July 29th. 1882.

7.30. Help mother & Belle clean kitchen closet. Hot. Arrange flowers. Read Harpers Mag. Write to Cassie. Good dinner, steak & corn. Bathe and dress. Mr. Stetson returns. Glad to see him. Pleasant evening on steps.

Sun. July 30th. 1882.

7.45. Church in pink muslin. Dine, wash dishes & loaf, reading "Data" and "An Echo of Passion."[6] Mr. Stetson arrives, and we have a pleasant evening until Jim comes, & then Anna & Clarence. Sup at 11 or so.

Mon. July 31st. 1882.

8.10. Letter from He. Go to see Miss Augusta Gladding & stay till 3 nearly. She gives me a lunch, and plays for me. I love her. Buy soap—25 cts. Home &

redress. Mary, Alice, & Cousin Eva Webster to tea. I like Eva much. Edward over. Met Mr. Stetson twice. (& bowed!)

Tues. August 1st. 1882.

6.30. Breakfast, wash all the dishes. Fix cheesecloth a little & go down st. with Eva. Get cotton—10., & pay Calder [$]4.00 on acct. Gave E. a watercolor block. Rode home. Note from He. this A.M. He's had some teeth out. Wrote to him. Read "Data", nap, finish letter to Cassie. Paint on plaque. Mrs.es Anthony calls, Josephine & Grandma. All out but I. Supper. Read some Anc[ient] Lit. Write to He. again.

Wed. Aug. 2nd. 1882.

6.30. Letter from He. Trim bonnet for Mrs. Springer, & she gives me 25 cts. & 25 more for Millie. Sew on bathing suit. Dine. Letter from He. Paint less than little, knit, read, arithmetic & write to He. Grace Ross calls & brings back "Golden Deeds." As I finish He's letter, he arrives, and a nice time we have of it. He tears up his—the bad thing! unwarrantedly. We look over "Talks on Art", & I read him "The Well Bred Girl."

Thurs. Aug. 3rd. 1882.

6.20. I go over to Miss Augusta's, intending also to take in Millie & the Ath., but am persuaded to stay to dinner, where I meet her uncle, Zephiniah Brown; and she brings me home in a carriage. We go over Red Bridge, but it's dusty. The drought grows severe. Go to Martha's & have a very pleasant talk. Much of Dr. Keller of Boston. I am glad such women live.

Fri. Aug. 4th. 1882.

6. Arrange and sweep room. Spend 2½ hours doing charcoal sketch of self. Failure in point of resemblance, but I must do something. Good dinner, mutton hash, bread & butter & huckleberry pudding. Sew and knit, reading "Data" while knitting all P.M. Come down at 5.30, & write to He. Post letter, read a bit, & bed ere 9.

Sat. Aug. 5th. 1882.

6. Sew before breakfast. Dress & go out. Call on Abbie Cooke & walk down st. with her. Get fixatif, squirter, brushes & a whitewood palette at Calders. Go and see Millie. Go to Ath. & find it just closing—from 1 to 3. Louise Richardson was there & invited me home to dinner with her. Very good, brownbread in especial. Met her mother & brother "Jim." Then to Ath. & read till 7. Then call on the Bogert's, and stay an hour or so. Invited to dinner tomorrow. Home & find two letters from He. & Maria. Eat some nutmeg melon & see M. to the car, talking gardenparty.

Sunday. Aug. 6th. 1882.

6.30? Wrote to He. A.M. Dinner. Dishes. Bathe, dress, & go to the Bogert's to dinner. Pleasant time. See Mr. Bogert, a "club man." Mr. Stetson comes for me at 8.45 or so. See embroideries over again. He & I walk home by divers ways. He stops awhile, & has some crackers.

Mon. Aug. 7th. 1882.

? Paint on plaque A.M. Write to Kate & doze P.M.

Tues. Aug. 8th. 1882.

6.30. Letter from He. & Cassie. Make sealskin cloth cap out of *12* pieces! Gold pin on one side, very pretty. Draw in charcoal P.M., read, doze, call from Fannie Bogert. Robert calls & brings French L. Soap card. Very fine. *Rain at night*!

Wed. Aug. 9th. 1882

5.45. Paint sweet pea. Dress & go to Millie's, borrow knitting needle, go to Miss Gladdings to spend the day. She was away (I half knew it) & I go to Martha's. Mr. L[ane]. there, so I don't stay to dinner, but go to see Annie Aborn. Nice dinner alone with her, & spend the afternoon knitting sewing & reading aloud. Mr. Thurston there part of the time. Home & find C[harles]. W[alter]. He brought me a Salon catalogue. We take a little walk. Sam calls. They both go at 9. Supper & bed.

Thurs. Aug. 10th. 1882.

6.5. Paint sweet peas. Notes from Cassie & Aunt Emily. Wash dishes. Write notes & letters. Sew a bit, dine. Call at Martha's. Take 1.30 boat for Bristol. Lizzie Brown (Aborn St.) on boat, & Charlie Greene who is polite. Met by Cassie & trot about on errands. Get cream & cake—30 cts. A Mr. Crocker & Julian Herreshoff call. Go in swimming with Cass, Lena, & Mr. H. at about 10 P.M. Phosphorescent & lovely. Home & dress, undress rather. Sleep with Cass up garret. Glad to see her.

Fri. Aug. 11th. 1882.

6. Dress, grate corn for Cass. go swimming with Lena, breakfast, call from little Anna Taft, Mr. Julian comes, go in swimming again minus Lena & plus Frank Brownell. Sit under a tree & play one word game. Both come home with me, & Mr. B. stays till the dinner bell rings. Go out with Cass & get eggs afterwards & are joined by Mr. B. again, who comes home with us & stays till I go. Mr. Herreshoff calls again, has to go, but joins us at his gate & walks to the station with us, as does Mr. B. Take 4 P.M. train. Am introduced to Prof. Appleton who is coming up, and have a *very* pleasant time with him. Walk with him up Brook to Waterman. Home, sup, & to bed. Enjoyed my visit much.

Sat. Aug. 12th. 1882—

5. Paint cardinal flower sent by Abbie. Loaf. Letter from Kate with $12.00 for Millie & one from Love. Can't come till *next* Monday—21st. Much family disturbance. Finally decide to go with Mother & Aunt to Oak Bluff for the odd week. Because mother won't go without & I know she needs it. Sublime self-sacrifice! Go to Martha's to tea, carrying C.W.'s Art Catalogue thing. They liked it. Called at Lu's—she's in Seaconnet. Edward calls & we make all arrangements.

Sunday Aug. 13th. 1882—

6.45 or so. Get clothes & things all ready. Finish cardinal & write letters to Love, Cassie, Kate, & Mrs. Weir. Dress. Robert over to tea. Gives mother $2.00 for the vineyard,[7] good of him. C. W. later, we go out to post letter, & take quite a walk. A pleasant evening, I'm really getting fond of him. He gives me a stylograf.

Mon. Aug. 14th. 1882.

4.30. Pack & fix. Good breakfast & off with Aunt C. in 7.5 car. Mother comes later in a hack. Edward meets us at depot, & gives me my ticket, good of him. 8 o'clock train, reach New Bedford at 10 or so, & get to the Vineyard by a little after 12. May meets us, & a Miss Hoxie, who, with her mother, boards here. I spend afternoon in the hammock & arranging things. Go out with May after supper & stalk around army cottages & hotels, stores & people. A fine rink. We go into the Sea View. May gets candy & peanuts. We stand outside & hear the Jubilee singer in the Methodist Chapel. Some little girls on chairs are friendly & we see as well as hear. Home by ten, & sleep in the cupola on a canvas cot, thus realizing one of my early ambitions. Write to Martha.

[*Charlotte also wrote the following separate account of this day and the next (August 15) in a notebook purchased for the purpose of using the new pen that Walter had given her the previous evening.*]

Trip to Martha's Vineyard.
Mon. Aug. 14th. 1882.

Up at 4.25, and finish packing. Comfortable breakfast, and off with Aunt C. on the 7.5 car. Fell in with a defunct mouse in Butler's Exchange, and cast it into the street. Somebody might'a stepped on it. Arrive in the depot at 7.30. Leave Aunt C. with the bundles & purchase a notebook whereon to use my new pen. Am weighed at Staples, 21 ½ lbs. Edward sees us off, & gives me my ticket. "En train" 11.30.

On the boat. Clear breezy day, and all serene. Sit in a comfortable cor[ner] forward, and enjoy myself. Sketch a little, to the amusement of my neighbors. Eat a sandwich & some dried beef from home & seize on a cookie of mother's. Feel chipper.

15th.

Were met by May. Board with the twain at Mrs. Field's & lodge in the cupola. Enjoy it amazingly. Saw Jophanus this morning. Like him.

Tues. Aug. 15th. 1882.

6 or so. Slept in the cupola on a canvas cot. Like it *amazingly*. Always wanted to sleep in a cupola. Am pursued by the children who adore me straitway. All go to the beach, & I have a fine swim with May. Go up in the tower & view the country round. Saw Jophanus this morning. Like him. Dinner, & write to Thomas. Go down & dress, to please mother. Read a little Leslie literature, a little Spencer, write notes & journal & then go down to amuse the fry. Swing 'em in hammock, sing & tell stories. Go with May to P.O. & circulate among the cottages in general. Go to the hotel & watch them dance, go & have a cream, stop and hear music at one of the cottages. Home by 10, & gladly retire.

Wed. Aug. 16th. 1882.

6. Rained in. Had to wipe out my shoes. Saw Jophanus. Letter from Love. Can come tomorrow. Write to Martha & Miss Gladding. Nap. Come down, amuse Bess. Go to ride with Aunt C. Mother, May, Bess & Ethel in horse cars; & walk on the Bluffs. Carry little ones when tired. Go with May to fancy dress affair at the rink—quite enjoyed it. Bed by 10.30 I guess.

Thurs. Aug. 17th. 1882.

5. Go to beach & have a nice bath, diving off raft, etc. Out by 6. Home with suit, breakfast, snooze in hammock, amuse Bess, pack, bit of cake for lunch, & am off with Jophanus at 1.30 or so. Pleasant ride of about 8 miles. Arrive, get acquainted with Love, & start for the beach. Supper at 5.30 to 6, & go & watch sunset from the shores of oyster pond. Like the place—much.

Fri. Aug. 18th. 1882—

6. Breakfast at 7. Arrange room & off for beach. Wear bathing suit under dress, take off latter & sport diversely. Take a bit of a swim in Pagner Pond. Some gunners come along. Don't mind 'em a bit. Paint view of distant house & bit of pond. Dinner. Finish sketch. Swim in Oyster Pond. One gunner returns. Converse with him. He leaves & re-returns, making quite a call. Sketch him afar off. He asks for it—in vain. Get decidedly burned as to arms & legs. Got letters at dinner time—mother, Thomas, Geo. Bissell, Mrs. Weare, & Martha. Can vault fences. Supper. Wrote to Mother. Bed.

Sat. Aug. 19th. 1882.

6. Read "Bella".[8] Paint in orchard. Perambulate on shores of Oyster Pond. P.M. Sketch sheep a bit. Eat lots as usual, & bed. Wrote to Carrie Hazard.

Sun. Aug. 20th. 1882.

6. Read in orchard all day. An elderly caller there, who asked questions. Finished "Bella", & read a book on beauty, some Mosses from an Old Manse, a little of Sesame & Lilies, & some old Littells.⁹ Card from Martha.

Mon. Aug. 21st. 1882.

7. Breakfast. Ride in with Jophanus & go over his route with him. Stop at the Fields & have another breakfast. Beguile the infants as usual & talk to sundry people. A Miss Hawkins, rather nice; & a Mrs. Bacon of Hartford. Nap in the hammock when they go bathing. Meet Martha on the wharf at 12.45 or so & walk back with her & Miss H. Jophanus waiting for us, she writes a postal, and we set off. Long pleasant ride, so glad to see her. Dinner, lots, & then we make tracks for & on the beach. I swim & disport myself as usual—catch a fish! She seems to like it. "A bite" on return & bed. Bless her!

Tues. Aug. 22nd. 1882.

7. Finish sketch in orchard. Go to beach & bathe alternately. Two callers—gunners, middleaged & uninteresting. Home hungry. Afternoon in orchard, nap, letters, &c. Read a bit of Coleridge after supper.

Wed. Aug. 23rd. 1882.

7. Spend morning on the beach. No calls. I mend my shoes. Good dinner well-appreciated. Nap in parlor. Read to M. & one word game. Supper. More read. A big fire in the west. Watch it from pasture & roof. Not asleep before *10*!

Thurs. Aug. 24th. 1882.

Rainy day. Paint tiger lily; draw on doylies for M. read & amuse ourselves. Call on the beach after dark. "An Awful but a pleasing treat." Invent new game, ballad form of one word.

Fri. Aug. 25th. 1882.

5.30. Paint tiger lily. More ballad "The Hermit & Fair Rosalind.["] Beach, dig hole house, lie around & enjoy the surf. Paint house after dinner & give it to 'em. Go with Miss S. to see their old house & call on Mrs. Allen Norton. Home late, supper & pack.

Sat. Aug. 26th. 1882.

3.50. Finish packing. Pay bill—$8.00. Breakfast. Off to the Bluffs with M. on my lap. Pleasant ride. Mr. S. carries us to the wharf. Was sorry to go. Jolly time all the way up. See M. on car, & spend day at Miss Gladdings. Gave me a lace tie & yellow ribbon. I weigh 125 lbs. Home. Supper. Lizzie Brown calls. I'm skimming beautifully—fun.

Sun. Aug. 27th. 1882.

5.30. Wrote to the Smith's. Painted on plaque. Fixed my bureau drawers. J. Peck called. He's a conductor now. Washed hair & abluted generally. Still peeling. Mr. Stetson arrived at about 8. Long pleasant evening. bed by 11.30

Mon. Aug. 28th. 1882.

6. Sew. Get splendid letter from Thomas. Sit down and answer it—32 pages. Mr. Peck & Mary to dinner. Letter from He.; a good one. Answer. Call on Mrs. Diman. Miss Alden there. On Annie Aborn. Out. On Fannie Bogert, out, but see her mother. On Martha. Stay to tea & go with her to call on Miss Alden. Home with her, in fits over a ballad. Home here & find Sidney (I had stopped & saw his mother in her yard, & met him at the gate.) A pleasant call, I talking in great style. He seems pleased.

Tues. Aug. 29th. 1882.

6.15. Finish corset waist. Finish little mirror for Mrs. Blake. Work in old green dress 4½ hours P.M. Read Scrib. Call on Lu. She's just home. Edward & Henrietta call.

Wed. Aug. 30th. 1882.

5.40. Paint morning glories. Run over to Martha's & back. Sew. Finish. Century. Hour's arithmetic. Sew from 3 to 6.30. Sup. Read a little poetry. Copy ballads. Unexpected call from Charles.

Thurs. Aug. 31st. 1882—

6.3. Paint purple m[orning] g[lories]. Loaf about talking to mother. Meet Miss Gladding at wharf & take 11 o'c[lock] boat for Silver Spring. Splendid dinner & very good time in general. Home in 4.10 boat. Stop at Ath. till near 7. Home & sup. Write ballads. Harry Manchester calls.

Fri. September 1st. 1882.

5.5. Paint m. g.s. Letter from Carrie Hazard. Stop for Martha & give 1st sitting at Walter's studio. Very pleasant time indeed. Stop at Ath. & stay there till near one. Home. House empty, enjoy it, dine, paint barn window arrangement. Sew. Cassie calls, bless her. Show her everything possible, dresses, ballads, paintings, etc. Goes at 5.45. Sew, sup, write ballads (copy) & start essay on "The Fire Demon of Firth.["] Jim calls 8.45–10.45. In bed by 11.

Sat. September 2nd. 1882.

5. Paint m. g.s. Sew till dinner, & after till Lu M. calls. She comes up & looks at things, & then I show her picters down stairs. We write a lovely ballad, and she stays to tea. Harry calls for her in hot haste, Dick Aldrich being there to see her. See her home & then read Harpers. Picture of Baldhead Cliff in it, same view as one of mine. Bed by 10.

Sun. September 3rd—

5. Paint m. g.s in water & oil. Fix flowers for mother. Church. Walk home with the Channings—Home, change dress. Dinner. Ray in with opportune watermelon. Wash dishes. Write essay. Dress myself with great care hair high & ruffles to match. Grey dress with pleating put on square neck.* Silver comb. Pretty. Sam calls for a few moments. Mr. S. arrives at near 8. Show him things & we read some Lamb.

Mon. September 4th.

5. Arithmetic. Out by 8.45. Call on Annie Aborn. Out. Go to Ath. till 10. Saw Mr. Slicer. Call on Fannie Bogert & make arrangements to give her 6 lessons. Post letter. Go to the Gym., see Dr. Brooks & have a little talk; buy basting thread silicia & cambric, & home in car as it rained a bit. Dine, read story in Harpers, Sew from 2 to 6–30 or so. Sup. Start ere 7 and call on the Channings. Carry note & ballad book, and we have a very pleasant evening. Start & 9, home, & bed. We're going to write a novel!

Tues. Sept. 5th.

5. Paint on plaque. Call at Lu's for ballad, stop for Martha, & so to the studio. Sit till 11.15, & then meet Grace at Gymn. stopping at Calders for soda & amm. Walk up with Grace & call on Millie. Home, rest a minute, dinner, & off to Mabel Masons. $1.00. Call on Annie Aborn. Out. Home. Sup & write. Sam calls.

Wed. Sept. 6th. 1882.

5.10–15. Paint plaque. Wash dishes for mother. Give old bonnet & a bit of dirty lace to a girl who came for cold pieces. Also some peaches & talk to her. Call on Mrs. H. Carpenter, Mrs. Perkins, Grace Ross, Mrs. Luther, Mrs. Wilcox, & Mrs. Blake. Sidney walks home with me. Dine, do a little figuring, sew from 2.30. to 6. Sup. Begin our novel. Retire at 9.

Thurs. Sept. 7th. 1882.

5.35. Plaque. Stop for Martha, out, meet her at Rider's, & then to studio. Have to wait half an hour for Charles. Stay till 12.15. Discuss Malagawatch project.[10] Dine with M. She gives me clock scarf to paint. Home & sew till after 6. Mother & Aunt C. spent the day at Fruit Hill—enjoyed themselves. Write novel. Go to Lu's. Other Manchesters there. Enter unabashed and play at Ballads. Fun. Harry home.

Fri. Sept. 8th. 1882.

5.35. Sew—make little white skirt. Fly about briskly & get to the Channings at 9. Go with Grace to the Gym. & we are measured. I am much improved since last year. Almost perfectly symmetrical. Exercise. Go to Calders & get outfit for Fanny Bogert. Lunch at Miss Gladdings. $5.00 from M. Car to Mabels. $1.00. To Fannie's. $4.50 in advance. Home. Letter from He. Florrie in. Sup. Sidney calls. Nice talk. Then Ben Wells appears. Glad to see him. A prospective order.

Sat. Sept. 9th. 1882.
A long day's dressmaking. Dinner late & good. Write a little, read Morris, sketch m.g.s for Martha's scarf & paint them on in the white. [To bed at] 10 or so.

Sun. Sept. 10th. 1882.
5. Paint on scarf. Church. Home with Lu. Half dollar for Millie. Home, write on novel, dine, Clarence in with watermelon, wash dishes, write, Mary, Ray, & Alice call, Maria calls, Annie Aborn calls, supper, change dress, write, Charles Walter appears. He brings his old daguerreotypes & photos from babyhood, (at my request,) and I enjoy it. Also he brings a review of a poem of his by Macdougall—very funny. I read him my novel, and Ingelows "Four Bridges." A very happy evening all round. Goes at 10.

Mon. Sept. 11th. 1882.
6.30! Finish chap. of novel. Call on Mrs. Carpen[ter]. .30 [cents], Peggie Tucker, .50, Miss F. Chace, .50. Miss Harris .25, Mrs. Gurney .10. Home to dinner & sew an hour. Go to Gym, (met postman, note from Miss Gladding,) Mary Channing there, good time, walk up with her, call on Abbie Cooke, .50, on Annie Morse, on the Channings, .75. Help Mary about certain plans & designs of hers. Carried my novel to 'em.

Tues. Sept. 12th. 1882.
5.30–6. Looked over old journal accts. Wrote note to He. & one to Sam. First drawing lesson to the children. Go to Grace's. She's coming anyway. Call on a Mrs. Studly to see about her daughter, on Mrs. S. Carpenter, eat some cookies & peaches, on Mrs. Durfree—Myra coming to school; on Mrs. Fillinghast, $2.00, Annie .25 & a bonnet for myself. To P.O., post letter, & one from He. & Kate Bucklin; & one for mother from Thomas. Read mine in Perrins. Ride to Mabels. John Peck on car. Didn't notice it till I got off. No pay, but very good time, Drew map of house. Ride down & get to Fannie's at 4.30. Paint a m.g., bud, closed one & a leaf or two in ten minutes! She copies it. Go to Mrs. Luthers to tea. Call on the Carpenter's again & Mr. C. gives me $5.00. Home, Edward over. Whist. 2 x 2.

Wed. Sept. 13th. 1882.
5.30. Cold. Run around to Lu's & Florries. Lesson to the little folks, & off. Call on Mrs. Lyman, $1.00, on Sophie Aborn after. Mrs. Birney & Mrs. Poland—

out both. On the Slicers. Ath. Maria, stay to dinner. Go with Maria to get headlights &c. Order $30.00 worth of candy of Ardoene. Go with Lizzie to Calders. Get outfit for Annie. Ride home. Letter from He. bless him! Sup. Dress. Evening with Lady Augusta. She plays for us, and we enjoy it intensely. Walk home. He sent me up a lot of paper today & some stamps.

Thurs. Sept. 14th. 1882.

5.30 or so. A cold dismal day. Garden Party postponed till Monday. Paint tamborine for Lizzie. Nasturtium, in oil. Florrie in & stays all the morning. Nap. Dine. Sew, finish green polonaise, etc. Do little stampbox in neutral tint, very pretty. Sew. Bed by 9.

Fri. Sept. 15th. 1882.

6 or so. Finish tamborine. Take it & box down to Lizzie. She was delighted; gave me 1.00. Stop for Martha. Go to Studio. Nice time. He. walks up with me to Miss Gladding's. Nice lunch. A Miss Hoppin in. Car to Mabels. $1.00 & lot of flowers. Car down. Stop & get braid & silk, .17 [cents]. (Car tickets [$]1.00) Left boxes for Lizzie again, met mother, & rode home with her. She went on to the Payton's. Ellen & little Annie Jarvis called. Sarah Bullock in. Fix flowers, sup. Go to Lu's & stay till 9. Anna & Clarence here.

Sat. Sept. 16th. 1882.

6. Fix white dress & letter drawers. Call on Mrs Kimball about Laura. Doubtful. Stop for Martha, (returning my last summer's letters) & go to Studio. Get a good deal done. He had a letter for me. M[artha]. & I call on Miss Gladding. Out. We stop at Calders, she cars home & I call on Millie. Walk home. Dine. Go to Annie's with paint things. Out. Ath. S.S. Teacher's meeting. Few there. Tudie Mauran very lively. Walk home with her & to "grotto". Home. Sup. Ben Wells calls. Whist.

Sun. Sept. 17th. 1882.

6. Write to Thomas. Church. Good sermon. Rode home with Julia Mauran. Paint little dinner cards in India ink. Read a little. Go up stairs & sew. (Blue skirt *finished*.) Abbie Cooke calls. Is very enthusiastic. Dress, & am not down to open the door for my lover. A happy evening, conversing on paper.

Mon. Sept. 18th. 1882.

5.30. Paint on scarf. Call on Lu & Florrie. Carry scales & candelabra down to the Brown's, & go to May's. No carpenter [11] there, so I trot down to Rays, & he takes me in the buggy in search. Meet old Mr. Carpenter with *the* carpenter, and go back. Fix red drapery etc. Ray takes me home & brings me back again, I dressing & dining between times. Arrange shawls & things around my table on clothes horses, borrow dishes, assort candies, & am ready before anyone else. Wore white bunting, yellow ribbons & turban, & all the gold things reachable—very gorgeous. Abbie & Lu to help me—Sold over $25.00 worth, Much can be taken back. C. W. arrives at about 11, & helps me clean up. We walk home & get here by 12.15. A little tired.

Hot!
Tues. Sept. 19th. 1882.
7. Arrange top drawer. Stop for Martha, gone, meet her at Rider's, go to studio, Walter has an "off day", and don't work much. Lunch at Miss Gladding's, Mrs. Kimball there, & Mr. Zeph. Brown. Car to Mabels—no pay. Stop at the Brown's, get spice for mother, buy "Press" with account of our Lawn party. Stop at Martha's & go to see Mrs. Durfree about Myra. All right. Back to Martha's. Gus Pierce & Charlie Sheldon call. Home. *B e d.*

Wed. Sept. 20th. 1882.
5.50. Jim called last night, glad I'd retired. Paint on scarf before breakfast. Letter from He. Answer it. Ray brings me a splendid variegated pink gladiolus. Paint it all day with lively interest & pleasure. Annie Aborn calls to say I needn't come over there P.M. Heartily glad. She takes my letter. Mrs. Henry Carpenter calls. I leave off at 5.30 or sooner, dress, & go to Martha's. A very hot close day with showers. Home ere 9 & bed.

Thurs. Sept. 21st. 1882.
6.15. Finish gladiolus & dress-make. Martha stops in coupe with cards. Letters from T. & He. Dine. Call at Martha's & Mrs. Blakes. Stop at Studio & leave word we can't come. Walk up & meet He. Get porcelain plaque & carmine tube at Calders. Gym. Call on Miss McCary & she takes me in to see Sellinger. Am delighted with a little "Venus"—(planet). Get spool blk. thread. Stop in at Tildens. Ath. See Mr. Bailey. The Blakes to tea, whist, & Whit[ney Blake] home with me.

Fri. Sept. 22nd. 1882.
6. Write to Thomas. Little opening with mother to the effect that things I thought mine were not. Surrender claim to the large mirror, mother's portrait, gold bracelets, locket, & divers other things. A very mean business. Brief call from Annie Aborn. Meet Martha at Clarke's, studio till 11.45, then teach Annie & Charlie Fillinghast till 2, dine there, Mabel's from 3 to 5. $3.00, ride to bridge & home. Trim bonnet Annie gave me with unused necktie & oriole Miss Gladding gave me. Pretty. Finish letter to Thomas. Sew.

Sat. Sept. 23rd. 1882.[12]
6.5 Paint on scarf. Stop at Annie's for my waterproof & umbrella. Leave bloodstone pin at Osborne's. Gymn. Get pin .10. Meet Martha at Raymore's, &

go to studio. Walter walks up to Calder's with me. Leave little whistles & see about panel for M. Change twist—take one spool in exchange for two & *pay for it*! Home, rest a bit & read letter from Walter, dinner (a big one) & paint pansies on porcelain plaque for Thomas. Annie & Charlie call. Write.

> O God! My God! I thank thee For a day well spent!
> I thank thee for the happiness Which thou has sent!
> I thank thee & I pray thee To help me so to live
> As to deserve the blessing Thou didst give

Sun. Sept. 24th. 1882.

6. Paint on pansies. Church. Sermon merely a summary of the Saratoga proceedings. Home alone. Read the Century. Write to Miss Alden and Charlotte Hedge. Dress in green gown & white lace kerchief. Mr. & Mrs. Angell of Fruit Hill call, with their Lucy. Walter arrives. Sam calls and Robert. Mother tells Robert of Thomas'es approaching wedding. I keep Walter till 10.40 or so because of interruption.

Mon. Sept. 25th. 1882.

6.15. Sew a little, paint a little. Mrs. Sturgiss Carpenter calls in default of pupils, and finally Florrinda appears. A very good opening, she is wide awake and excited enough. Begin Oliver Twist, and take a scattered review of all her studies. Finish pansie plaque P. M. Florrie comes over after her arithmetic. Write to Cassie. & to He.

Tues. Sept. 26th. 1882.

6.35 or so! Scour gold buttons & sew 'em on. Florrie. Another good day with drawing lesson thrown in. The child grows. Dine, call at Martha's; walk down st. with her & her mother, leave Mrs. L[uther]., stop & studio & leave note, meet Channings, take Grace into studio to fix garters, walk up with her, meet Walter, get glass at Calder's, Mabel $1.00, back, stamps 30 cts. Call on Annie Aborn & stay to tea, home, letter from He., work on mirror. Harry Fillinghast saw me home. Wore sack!

Wed. Sept. 27th. 1882.

6.30. Arrange & fit dress. Breakfast. Paint on mirror. Good day with F. Begin Natural Philosophy. Letter & papers from Miss Alden. Martha comes for me P. M. Studio. Go with her to her dressmaker's & dentist's. Buy nails for mother. Walk most home with M. Met Doyle girls, Pattie & Bessie. Home. Dress. Sup. Walter comes. Brings some of Sidney Putnam's letters to read what he said of me. Anna & Clarence in. Goes at 10.20–30, bed ere 11.

Thurs. Sept. 28th. 1882.

5. Sew a trifle, paint on scarf. Begin elocution again with Florinda. Nice child. Ray comes to pack box for Thomas. Mary & Alice in to look at the things. I write note to Thomas. Go to Annie's. Good lesson. Talk with Annie & show her how to do her hair like mine.* Ath. for an hour. Home, sup, read a bit, write to Annie.

Fri. Sept. 29th. 1882.

5.45. Sew. Letter from He. Start Florrie on transposition. Dine. Give a brown skirt to melancholy woman with baskets. Meet mother at Arcade, (stopped at Mr. Slicer's on way down) and order coal of Hopkins & Pomeroy. To be paid in January & April—$52.00! Mabel's. No pay. Pub. Lib. & get "Stanley's History of Palestine" & Judas Maccabeus.[13] Go to tea at the Slicer's. A young New Yorker there, Will Halstead, very fine looking. Whist, Mr. S. & I two games. Walk home serenely. Sam here. Do clowns head for him—good copy.

Sat. Sept. 30th. 1882.

6.40! Begin Stanley. Call on the Channings & see Jean O'Connor. Poor thing! she looks weak enough. Call on Abbie. Get foolscap, 15 [cents], yeastcake, 2 [cents], braid 6 [cents]. Go to Gym. Good time. Go into Tildens. Saw Mrs. Alfred Stone & Mrs. Keach there. Home. Work on Mirror. Go to S.S. meeting. Nothing done. Down st. with Tudie Mauran & home with her. She stops in & looks at things. Sup. Mend clo', write in Jour[nal]. Mr. Wells calls. We discuss and alter the mirror thing. He does some good talking on the Catholic question, and stays till 10.45 nearly.

Sun. October 1st. 1882.

7! Read Stanley. Run around to Mary's & get nasturtium for mother. Open S[unday]. school, full class with a new one—Max Mauran. No time do [*sic*] do anything, Mr. Slicer talks, and an engraving is presented, from Miss Addie Brown. Hot in church, not much of a sermon. See Russells, call on Mrs. Bosworth (at Mrs. Putnams request) out I guess, stop and see Martha & Charles. Home, dine, write to Miss Alden & Julia, notes, read, put braid on skirt, Robert over, Lizzie & May. My boy later. Aunt C. retires, mother sits where she can see us and evinces disapproval.

Mon. Oct. 2nd. 1882.

5.30. Finish braid, paint, call on Annie Aborn who gives me an answer to my letter, Florrie, Martha in a minute, dine, meet Martha at Ath., studio all the afternoon. Last time. Home with M. She gives me some lace. Go down to see Mrs. Sullivan for her. Maria here. Send postal to Martha. Sup. Write & read. (Florrie & I consume some old peanut candy—am aware of it.) Anna & Clarence call. Retire soon after 9.

Tues. Oct. 3rd. 1882.

5.45. Notes. Finish clock scarf. Letter from Lady Augusta. Go with mother to see Mr. Greenough about a globe. Mabel. $2.00. (Got cork soles . 10 [cents]) Called on Millie. Lizzie, May, & Lorraine Bucklin called also. Walk home. Letter from He. Answer. Judas Maccabeus.

SIX

"Hot tears and self-abasement"

October 4, 1882–May 14, 1883

ON OCTOBER 5, 1882, Martha Luther married Charles Lane. Despite her insistence that she enjoyed the wedding, Charlotte's discomfort with the traditional wedding day rituals was apparent. She helped Martha with last-minute preparations, stood next to her during the "grand and solemn" ceremony, held her bouquet, and then kissed Martha as "Mr. Lane" stood by. When she and another wedding guest, Mabel Bridges, simultaneously caught Martha's bouquet, Charlotte relinquished it without hesitation, since Mabel, she reported, "cared more [for the bouquet] than I." Since Charlotte's brother, Thomas (who was living out west), had also gotten married the previous evening, Charlotte was undoubtedly anxious to reaffirm her autonomy. Work, and not marriage, despite her occasional disclaimers to the contrary, remained her first priority.

Within a month, however, Charlotte had once again changed her mind. She loved Walter, but she was terrified of commitment. She wanted to be free, yet she enjoyed their time together. She desperately wanted to work, but she feared that within the confines of marriage, Walter would not allow it.

On December 31, 1882, Charlotte reflected on the year just passed: "My last act in the old year was to kneel at my bedside in shame & repentance, with hot tears and self-abasement." Charlotte clearly felt that she had failed by wavering in her resolve to contribute meaningfully to the "world's work," as she had vowed to do in "An Anchor to Windward," written in early 1882. She therefore renewed her resolve to work. Yet by early February a wedding seemed inevitable as Mary Perkins suggested that Charlotte and Walter board in the downstairs tenement of her house. Money, however, was a valid concern. Walter's income from the sale of artwork was negligible and sporadic, and Charlotte earned little from her various self-employments. Predictably, there was an escalation in tensions and tears. Charlotte needed to affirm her independence, and Walter resisted it every step of the way. The simmering conflict finally erupted. Just three days after Charlotte had refused to accept a friend's gift of Whitman's *Leaves of Grass* because she had promised Walter that she would not read it (he felt that Whitman's sexual allusions were vile), the two parted company for a period that lasted five weeks.

Charlotte's sadness during this separation was intensified by the death of one of her young day school pupils, Isabel Jackson. A few days after Isabel's death, Charlotte experienced profound emotional pain, a culmination of her grief at Isabel's death, the lingering emptiness left by Martha's departure, and her sadness over her estrangement from Walter. "The least line of kindred thought in poetry brings all the ache and tears," she confided to her diary, "but by myself I wont think about it." She did think about it, however, and after reading some Rossetti poems on April 7, she cried "a great deal." By the end of April, although she was managing to pass some pleasant evenings, she still felt devastated by the loss of Walter. The feeling was mutual, and on May 14, 1883, the two reconciled.

Wed. Oct. 4th. 1882

2.30! Down stairs & out doors to look for comet. Not risen. Nap on lounge & wake at 4.30 or so. Up then, and a beauty. Wake the other folks to see it. General admiration. Bed afterward and don't rise till near seven. Notes & read. Get my gold pen in safety, neatly packed in a wooden cylinder. Call on Martha & take the scarf. Go to Annie's. Fanny Bogert comes & studies with them. Home, sup, work on mirror. Mother goes around to Ray's to spend evening, Mr. Bailey calls, & Mrs. Manchester & Harry. Thomas married tonight.[1]

Thurs. Oct. 5th. 1882.

6.30. Dressmake. Read Stanley. Dress in white bunting and get to Martha's by 12. Put on her flowers for her, and otherwise assist, Mrs. Sullivan doing the "maid" to perfection. I stand by her during the ceremony, hold her bouquet and kiss her next to Mr. Lane. Mr. Slicer was perfect;—very grand and solemn. Introduced to Mr. & Mrs. Lincoln of Hingham. A satisfactory refection, furnished by Ardoene. Really enjoyed myself. Help Martha change her dress, hand around the rice, carry home wedding cake, preserve one of her rosebuds, catch her bouquet, (as also did Mabel Bridges, and I let her have it, I had the bud & she cared more than I,) and throw the slipper (one of my own old ones, small & pretty) so that it lights airily on top of the carriage, and stays there till they all disappear in the distance. Go home with Lu, (run for a car for Mabel Bridges,) & dressmake till dark. Read & write.

Fri. Oct. 6th. 1882.

6 or so. Notes & read. Florinda. Do little whale. Mabels. Go to Mrs. Lindsey's to tea. Met by Charles outside. Mr. & Mrs. Stetson there. A pleasant evening. Very good supper. Hope they liked me. Home by 10.15. Jim here.

Sat. Oct. 7th. 1882.

6. Look over old shoes. Two pair good. Eat grapes. Notes & read. Take work & start for gym. Call on Mrs. Bosworth at Mrs. Putnam's. Take her with me to the gym. Very nice time there, a lot of the girls back again. Threelegged races and much jollification. Up to Perrins with Mrs. B. & then I spend the rest of the day at Miss Gladdings. I finish mirror & she sews some for me. Home by 6.15 or so. Lu & Harry call. Jolly ballad. Mr. Wells arrives and joins in, grand success. Mother & Aunt C. come in later, Aunt going to bed.

Sun. Oct. 8th. 1882.

6.3 or so. Paint little wooden palette for Mrs. Lindsey. S. S. with Mrs. Rawson. Read the boys about the Red Sea crossing. Very good sermon. Teachers meeting afterwards. Really something accomplished. Home. Dine. Finish pallette. Read Judas. Spend an hour or more in dressing—fuss over hair. Anna & Clarence in

Mon. Oct. 9th. 1882.

5.50. Read. Finish frigate bird. Good day with Florinda, introducing written "word game." Write note to C. W., & sew all P.M. Lu over. Go to see Retta & have very pleasant evening alone with her. Bring her over here to see Charles' pictures, & take her home again. Cookies & apples ere returning as no supper.

Tues. Oct. 10th. 1882.

5.55. Wrote & read. Paint dinner cards. Letter from C. & note from "S. H." Florinda brings candles to paint. Maria calls. Note to C. after dinner. Go to Mabel's. $2.00. Call on Mrs. Stetson. Walk down Cranston St. & wait about hoping to see Charles. don't. Walk home at speed. Sup, read & study. Edward over, Bed at 9.45.

Wed. Oct. 11th. 1882.

6. Sew. Letters from Charles, & Martha. The little girl is happy. Florinda. Dine. Letters from Miss Gladding & Cassie. Go to Annie's. She not feeling well. Stay & try to comfort her a little. Goodbye call on Retta. Home. Sew. Write to C. W. & post it. Sup, reading, sew some more. Write to Martha.

Thurs. Oct. 12th. 1882.

7. Wasted 45′ in bed. Write notes. Sew. Florinda. Go to Mabel's. (Met Prof. Blake & Whit. *Ada is here!!*) Ride down & go to Pub. Lib. Change Judas for Baldwins "Ancient America", & renew Stanley. Charles calls for me, & we walk to Olneyville & all around in that direction till 7. Ride down st. (he paid therefore) & go to Bible Class. Very nice. Old Miss Nightingale very conversational, seems to like me. Gus Pierce walks home with me without leave or license. Find Mr. Wells here. I don't quite like him yet.

Fri. Oct. 13th. 1882.

6. Journal. Notes. Paint candles for Florinda. Letter from He. P.M. Paint medallion palette. Go to see Ada. Call on Miss Bogert. Out. Go to Ath. till 7. Spend evening with the Channings. Jean better. Home, sup, read, bed, ere ten

Sat. Oct 14th. 1882.

6. Compose beginning of "My View." Notes. Call on Ada. Call on Charles Walter & stay a little over an hour. I went to see about Ada's business—had to as it were. Gym. Nice time. Walk up with Pussy Rawson & she treats me to chocolate, rolls, maccaroons, & ladyfingers. Stop at Calders. Go to Miss Gladdings & stay there till 6. Stop at Ada's on way back. Home by seven. Finish little white skirt. Bed ere 9.

Sun. Oct. 15th. 1882.

7. Read for S.S. Walk down with Mrs. Rawson. New boy in my class, Geo. E. Wran. Start on Abraham. Long scientific sermon from a Mr. Carpenter, an Englishman. Sam in our pew. Home with Lu. Read Stanley. Sew all P.M. C. W. gets here by 7. Long pleasant evening. Brought me some corresponding cards he didn't want.

Mon. Oct. 16th. 1882.

6.15. Feel happy. Write to Walter. Florinda doesn't come. Sew. Finish "My View." Copy it and send to the Journal. Go to Mabel's. $2.00. Go to Miss Gladdings. Meet Walter at Pub. Lib. & go home to supper with him. Then we call at the Blakes to see Ada. Very long call of about an hour. Then home in Ada's ulster & a happy half hour here. This stylograph was his! Now *that* is giving!

Tues. Oct. 17th. 1882.

6.10. Mother quite ill so I make fire & get breakfast. Mem[ory] Notes. Note from Aunt Emily inviting me there to spend Thanksgiving. Florinda writes a genuine composition, good too. Paint on medallion palette. Whisk down st. stopping at Ada's with ulster. Meet Miss Gladding in coach & go to Studio. Lo! Mother is there! An unpleasant call, with the poor picture severely criti- cized.[2] Then Miss G. takes me up to Annie's. A misunderstanding, and I am to come Friday. Call on Retta. Call on Lu for a minute. Home just in time to find Kate Bucklin. She makes a long call and engages the palette. Talk with mother. She thinks we'd better marry & come here to board. (I don't). Write to Walter and post it. Study.

Wed. Oct. 18th. 1882.

? Notes school etc. Paint "butter'n'eggs". Mother & Aunt C. being out, Mrs. J. Westcott, Miss Turry, Henrietta, Mrs. Namkin, & Retta Clarke call. bed early.

Thurs. Oct. 19th. 1882.

6.? Sketch two rosebuds in vase in oils; pretty good. Letter from Walter. Florinda also sketches in oils. Go to Mabels. Sup on three crackers in Pub. Lib. Walter joins me there, & we walk to Prospect St. its whole length almost & back, George, Thayer, William, & Benefit [streets]. & he with no supper! Buy Prof. Toy's Manual, "Hist[ory] of Religion of Israel" (.50), and enjoy the Bible Class. The Burleighs there. Home happily alone, sup & write little poem to W[alter].

Fri. Oct. 20th. 1882.[3]

6.50. Answer Aunt Emilys note. Get a superfluous one from Miss Loring of the S.H. Paint backgrounds on palette for Florrie, & two elliptical plaques. Two Miss Spencers call. I go to Mrs. Sayles after Mother & Aunt C. They brought apples & quinces. I go to Mrs. Diman's to dinner. Play one word game with Retta & Louise. Home, read & write mem[ory]. notes.

Sat. Oct. 21st. 1882.

7! Call on Retta, Call on Ada, (too ill with a cold to be seen) back for Retta & she goes with me to see the Whitaker-Stetson exhibition at Waterman's. Like it. We go the Gym. Mrs. Diman & small fry later. I perform generally. Get palette for mother at Calders. (Borrow clubs at Gym. for Florrie). Afternoon with Miss G. Seckel pears, cream walnuts, etc. Do three dinner cards— pretty. Hour at Ath. Mr. Wells calls. Lowell.

Sunday Oct. 22nd. 1882.

6.30. Prepare S.S. lesson. Read "Through One Administration,"[4] and otherwise look at Scrib. Walk down with Miss Rawson. P. O. Clarke appears & takes charge as Sec. & Treas. Glad to see him. Get as far as Jacob's leaving Laban. Pretty good sermon on Bible study. Home with Lu & her mother. Peaceable family discussion, all serene and smiling. Begin rosebud on palette for Florrie. Anna Clarence & Charlie call. Lizzie calls. Sup on a bit of bread & cheese & an apple. Dress, with yellow kerchief. Walter at about 7. Three happy hours. Family all serene.

Mon. Oct. 23rd. 1882.

6.15–20. Invent underclothes. Paint on Florrie's palette. She christens the clubs. Stop at Fannie Bogerts a moment—Mabels. $2.00. Stop to get ruffles & elastic at Boston Store. 10 cts. Call to inquire for Ada. Better. Home sup. Write a little, sew, read. Bed by ten as usual.

Tues. Oct. 24th. 1882.

7. Notes. Letter from Walter & from G. Bissell. No go about the [H]artford property unless Mrs. Wellman will sell. Florrie begins Dickens' Child's Hist. of England. Dine. Mend Maria's silk stockings. Notes. Go to Fanny Bogert's & leave her my study of rosebuds to copy. Call on Ada. Better. Home. Kate over. A little Carlyle & much talk on Anc. Hist. Dress, with white illusion. Walter comes at 7.35 or so, & stays three hours. A little business talk.

Wed. Oct. 25th. 1882.

6 sharp. Study during morning. Finish silk hose. Annie comes in & wants to postpone lesson till Sat. Run down to see Carrie Hazard. Not there but stop ten minutes with Ada. Go for Lu to spend the afternoon with me. She can't. Go for Retta. She can't. Home & paint gentians. Pretty. Retta calls at 1.15. We take a brisk walk across Red Bridge & back. Stay there to dinner. Home, write to Walter, study.

Thurs. Oct. 26th. 1882.

6 sharp. Paint all morning. Finish gentians. Letter from Walter. Call at Brown's leaving hose for Maria. Order stoves at Roots. Go to Mabels. Car fares 1.00. Change Stanley for Hereward,[5] no other book. Call on Miss Gladding. Out. Get 5 cts. worth of cookies & sup at the Ath. Mr. Bailey there. He goes out to supper, comes pursuasively back & we take a bit of a walk before Bible Class. Nice time there. Go home with Miss. Russel. Home by 9.25. Write to Walter.

Fri. Oct. 27th. 1882.

6. Read Hebrew Lit. Run around to the Manchesters on errand for mother. Write to Cassie. Lesson to Miss Bogert. Go to Ath. Kate meets me there. Home & read Couture's "Conversations in Art," Wordsworth & Shelley to her. Sup & write to He. Go to see Rebecca from 7.30 to 10. The rest went to bed, and we read Coleridge & Shelley, talked, and were happy. Wrote "Reserved."[6]

Sat. Oct. 28th. 1882.

6. Sweep my room thoroughly. (Dirty!) Copy "Reserved" & take it to Retta. (Letter from Walter). Go & see the man in Pierces about Xmas cards. Stop in at gym. & forget my pocketbook there. Take 10.10 car for Pawtuxet with Mr. & Mrs. Slicer & Lizzie & Mrs. Burleigh. Row for two hours, pleasant time. 1.04 car back, stop at arcade, run up & get pocketbook at gym. & rejoin party on College Hill. Home by 2.15, bathe, redress, dine, Annie Aborn from 3.10 to 5. Buy 48 cts. worth of stamps. Meet mother at Worcester depot & take 5.30 train for Pawtucket. Tea at Mr. Gideon Spencers. Delightful old-fashioned house. Large grounds & lots of fruit. Home in the 9.3 train. Found card on door—Sam & Richie.

And there was Ben Wells I never thought of! Write note of apology.

Sun. Oct. 29th. 1882.

6.3. Prepare S.S. lessons—Weeden boys absent! Church, sleepy again. Home with old Mr. Carpenter & then Mrs. Manchester & Harry. Write to Walter, Thomas & Julia. Bed ere ten.

Mon. Oct. 30th. 1882.

6. Wrote to Walter, read, & worked on dinner cards. Begin "Hereward" to Florrie. Dine. Letter from W. Go to Mabels. $2.00 & a big bunch of chrysanthemums. Give 'em mostly to Mrs. Cooley. Nice talk with Milly. Home, finish letter to W. & set out to post. Meet Mr. Wells at the gate. He goes to the box with me, comes back & in, and we play two games of chess, I beating both. Then he reads Shelley to me. Mother gets sleepy & steals to bed.

Tues. Oct. 31st. 1882.

6. Write to W. & Martha. Letter from latter. Finish mine, answering. Card from Phil. postmaster demanding more stamps for withheld matter. Send the due 2 cts. Go & post same in office. Call on Miss Bush. She is very kind, asks me to lunch & lectures &c. Last lesson to Miss Bogert. Meet Miss Esther Chapin there. Ath. for a few moments. Home. Kate comes, & brings Wordsworth & Browning, which I read aloud in to our mutual delight. Write to W. Sup. Post letter. Draw plan of house for mother. Write to Lena Muster about S. H.

Wednesday. Nov. 1st. 1882.

6.10. Owing to fog & shut blinds. A hot beautiful day, with m.g.s and bachelor's b[uttons]., nasturtiums, etc. all blooming. Arrange almost all my drawers of papers. Letter from Walter, & notice from the Y.W.C.T.U. Dine. Begin letter to T. (painted on Florrie's palette.) Lesson to Annie & Charlie. Home, find notice from Adams Ex. Co., trot down there & get little package which proves to be amber bead bracelet from Walter. A lovely thing. Bless him! Dress, sup, finish letter, go over to Annie's & read. Borrowed two Arnolds & Mrs. [Elizabeth Barrett] Browning from Mrs. Diman, and carried them & Shelley to read to A[nnie]. Pleasant evening, no one else there. Home in carriage by 9.30 or so, & find Sam playing cribbage with Mother. He orders divers Xmas cards (Old Mr. Carpenter called)

Thurs. Nov. 2nd. 1882.

6 I guess. Paint Arethusa, not very good. Letter from He. Go to Mabel's. Maude took her horns as Mabel wasn't well. Mrs. Mason up again, glad to see her. Am to give Maude lessons. Stop at Calder's & get tamborines for them & panels. Call at Miss Gladding's. Out. Call at Florrie's on errand. Run home & write to Walter. Sam comes with hepatica leaf. I sup piecemeal. He went out to post letter with me, we had a little poetry & much chess, he beating over one game with much triumph.

Fri. Nov. 3rd. 1882.

6.30. Write to Walter. Letter from him & Ill. Art. Cat. Write more. Have to go to Mrs. Budlong's & telephone to Lizzie about her rye getting. She & Walter Carpenter stop on their way home. Nice day with F., divers experiments, & do a new exercise—talking. Finish letter to W., paint hepatica leaf, & tea rose. Kate comes. Brings me a grand edition of Robert Browning—uncut! I am *pleased*. She stays to tea, mother & Aunt go to Marys, & we have a pleasant evening. I have to stop altogether in reading "A Blot on the 'Scutcheon,"[7] for crying! Home with Kate.

Sat. Nov. 4th. 1882.

7, more shame to me! Study map for S. H. Letter from W, & a long one from Mrs. Smith. Return books to Mrs. Diman & call on Annie to change lesson day. Stop at T. C. Greene's office. Gym. Lot of folks in, Miss Almira Rathbone among 'em. Reform with great glee. Give Miss Bush a lesson between 11 & 12. A light lunch there. .75 cts, too. Call on Millie. Meet mother at Rider's. We go to T. C. Greene's again, & make arrangements about Hartford business. Go to Miss Gladdings till 6.15 or so. An old Dr. Fuller there. I had a bite of *guava*—didn't think much of it. Miss G. is disappointed in me because I want to marry as I do! I feel a little blue—very.

Sun. Nov. 5th. 1882.

6.50. Bathe dress, prepare S. S. lesson, breakfast & to church with Mrs. R. & Arney. A full class, 8, & .28 cts! Ask them individually to come to the Harvest Festival in the afternoon, for my sake as it were. Home with Lu, who stops in & read to her a bit. Fill out map, & answer exam questions for S. H. The Angells from fruit hill arrive, with Lucy. Aunt C. & I go to the festival. All my class there but Harry Bliss. & I had two of a teacherless class beside. Good showing. A pleasant sort of service, Eddy Jastrum recited, doing splendidly, & another little boy & girl beside. Walk home with the Weeden boys & Lena, talking on theology &c. Nice boys. Write to W. & post. Sup. More S. H.

Mon. Nov. 6th. 1882—

6.15. Read Couture. Mend skirt. Paint Columbines. Letter from Martha. Sent of S. H. papers. Meet Maude Mason on Westminster St. She fairly ran to meet me. Ride out together. Carry 'em their tamborines. Ride down, stop at Root's. Walk home. Meet Mr. Slicer & go back with him. Then home, a bite, write to W. post it, sup with Couture, note to Ben Wells, look over accounts, & mend pillow case. (Card from Mr. Crandall as to Boy's Room.)

Tues. Nov. 7th. 1882.

6.50. Start to put new sleeves in dress. Florrie has a headache & we digress into physiognomy &c. Chicken soup. Letter from Walter, violets again. Bless him! Sew all P.M. Kate at 5. Read Carlyle. Write to W. Sup. Call for Kate & Miss Russell & go to Boy's Room. Business meeting. Mr. Burleigh comes home with all three of us. Show him a lot of things. Sam had been here. Posted my letter in P.O. Sam at 10.

Wed. Nov. 8th. 1882.

6? Finish sleeves & put 'em in. Run around to Lu's to see about her playing for the poor boys. Letter from Walter. Go to Maude Mason. Roses on a tamborine. Good beginning. Home strait, write to W. and post. Mother & Aunt C. out. John Willy calls. Sup. Mend clothes. Read a little. Bed.

Thurs. Nov. 9th. 1882.

6.30. Alter sleeves. Letter from Walter. Florrie ailing again. Another letter. Go to Mabel. Am now to teach her painting, geography, arithmetic & spelling. Enjoy it. Call on Mrs. Lindsey. Out. On Mrs. Stetson & there find Mrs. L. Pay Calder 1.35 for tamborines. Renew Hereward & get "Sinai & Palestine" at Pub. Lib. Go to Ath. See Mr. Bumpus there, & take bit of a walk with him. Bible Class. Great fun, a lively discussion; Slicer, Colwell & Parkhurst. Mrs. Mason. $3.00.

Fri. Nov. 10th. 1882.

S. H. Papers. Good report. Good day with Florrie. Note from Annie saying don't come. Dont, with much joy, but paint on blue plaque. Kate Carlyle three or four pages, conversation till 7.15. Go home with her a little way. John Willy comes to help look over Thomas'es things. Help him bring down box & trunk. Ben Wells calls. Then Jim. Then Sam and Richie. Dreadful evening, ameliorated by Mr. Wells politeness and fun. Jim orders cards. Bed about 11.

Sat. Nov. 11th. 1882

Paint on columbine card. Letter from Walter. Get 9 cts. worth of checkerberries for Millie & read Shelley to her for half an hour. Then to Miss Gladdings & to the Gym with her. Then ride up to Hoggs on Broadway with her, get some pansies, leave Miss G. at the door, ride home reading Stanley, & paint pansies P.M. Pretty too. Call on Carrie Hazard & leave there the dinner cards, (She gave me a lovely hat.) Stop for Miss Russell and go to the Boy's room. A good many there. Home with the others to Magee & then alone. read a bit & bed.

Sun. Nov. 12th. 1882—

6.30. Paint & prepare lesson. An "honorary member", (friend of Eddy Sheldon), & three "casual visitors", (teacherless scholars from the next class) swell my class to 11. We contemplate having a room down stairs. The boys are beginning to feel proud of their big class, and come regularly. Mr. Woodbury preached & I didn't stay to hear him. Called on Lu Manchester & borrowed Harry's "Percy Anecdotes" to look up The Man in the Iron Mask [8] for my class. Clarence, Frank & little Charlie here. Paint pansies all P.M. Write long letter to Walter. Read some Browning & Stanley. Ray over to see mother. Bed early.

Monday. Nov. 13th. 1882.

5.55. Read about early Quakers in the Harper's. Mend petticoat. Paint. Letter from Walter. Miss Murphy to dinner. Haste down st. Get stamps 15 cts. Call on T. C. Greene. Stop at Riders & read "Vica Versa" [9] till car time. Met Mrs. Cooke, Abbie sick. Read Stanley as usual in car. Mabel has a sore finger. Comfort her. Home happy & write to Walter. Found a letter from him. Note to Ben Wells rhyme. Clarence comes home with Mother. Read & sup. Write to Lizzie.

Tues. Nov. 14th. 1882.

5.50. Write poem to Walter. Read Sinai. Letter from W., P.M. Paint violet card. Cassie Thurston comes & makes long call. Kate at 5 or so. Write last letter to Walter & post it. Sup. Edward calls. Sam stops in a moment on way to Lu's. John Willey in a few moments. Sam back again. Whist. Mother & Sam 6 to E. & I 4. Bed at 11.

Wed. Nov. 15th. 1882.

6.45. Alter facing on blue skirt. Letter from Walter. Finish violet panel. Take 2.30 car for Maude, & read a bit more "Vica Versa" while waiting for it. Moralize to her a little. Ride down, stop at Hogg's, call on Abby Cooke, better, call on the Channing's, Jean better again. Stop to leave word for Annie Aborn, & find Will Fillinghast at home! He walks down with me, we are much pleased to see him. Mother & Aunt go to steriopticon lecture. Sup, read poem of Brownings, write welcome to Walter, from whom I had another letter this P.M.

Thurs. Nov. 16th. 1882.

6.50. Mabel's. $3.00. (Stopped at Hoggs on way down, & got 10 cts. worth of double sweet violets and jessamine, & left same in Walter's studio in little phial.) "Visa Versa" at Rider's. Ath. Ben Wells there. Mr. Bailey home with me. Sup. Ben Wells calls & we each beat a game of chess.

1st Snow—
Fri. Nov. 17th. 1882.

7. Stanley. Letter from Walter & Lizzie Brown. Not coming home till Sat! (waste of violets.) Lesson to Annie. Call on Mrs. Diman. Kate over, stays to tea and enjoys herself. I walk home with her and stay to Bible Class. Mr. Slicer reads part of an old address of his on "Cain & Abel." Home in the draggled

chilliness of our first snowstorm. Ray & John Willey here packing box for Thomas. Write a welcome for Walter.

Sat. Nov. 18th. 1882.

7. Shovel paths. Of by 8.40 or so. Stop at studio and leave little poem. Stop and enquire for stylograph at horsecar depot. No use. Call on Mr. Greene. Out. Stop at Pierces & show cards. All right. Get "Harold"[10] at Greg. & Whites to read to Florrie about the battle of Hastings. Gym for an hour. Call at T. Greene's again. Out. "Visa Versa" at Rider's. T. Greene's again. All right. Miss Bush. Sister there. 75 cts. Annie Aborn gives me a ride towards home. Miss Bush gave me a hat. Sew all P.M. & press dress. Call on Lu Manchester. Call for Miss. Russell and go to Boy's Room. Read "Percy Anecdotes["] to an interested audience of one. Home serenely. Cold.

Sun. Nov. 19th. 1882.

7.10. Prepare lesson. S.S. with Mrs. Rawson. Max Mauran absent owing to underclothes. More stories than lesson. Church. Mr. Slicer repeats, by request, one of his best sermons. Home, with Lu, who stops in a minute. Mary in & gets a pie. Anna calls, and then Clarence & Charlie. Then Mary & Alice for a moment & all go. Paint hepatica for Sam. Bathe and dress. Walter comes at 6.30. Glad, *glad* to see him. Sam stops & takes hepatica & others. Robert calls but is relegated to back room with the ladies. Long happy evening with Walter who stays till 11.

Mon. Nov. 20th. 1882.

6.35, bright & lively. Mend dress & nightgown. Read about Morman endowment house in paper Thomas sent. Paint on Gentians & do palette for mother. Florrie don't come. A Mrs. Stafford in to see about adding another scholar to mother's school. Mabel. Walter joins me on Main st. & walks home with me. Mother asks him to stay to tea & go down with me. He does. Reads me a letter of Mrs. Cressons. I love him. Henrietta here to tea. Walter walks down to Kate's with me. Go with Kate, Jennie, Tudie, & Miss Rathbone to se [*sic*] Sabrini. *Grand*! home in carrieage with 3. & I. John Willey here.

Tues. Nov. 21st. 1882.

6.30. Paint. Florrie. Paint. Mrs. Fillinghast 1 hour (Annie painted too.) Home, read Century, Kate and Carlyle, sup, read Stanley, put binding on felt skirt. John Willey comes to mark box, Sam & Jim call, Jim staying, and give more orders. I must fly.

Wed. Nov. 22nd. 1882.

6.35. Paint. Florrie. Carrie Hazard calls to see if I'll go to see Miss Wheeler this P.M. Go to Maude. 1.00 for carfares. Mabel has her arithmetic out also.

Meet Carrie at Miss W's door, and make a candle-lit call. Home with C. in carriage. Sup, dress, read Stanley, go with Walter to High Tea at the Art Club. Lu played. Saw lots of folks I knew, Annie Morse among 'em. Home by 10.40. He. stayed till 11.05.

Thurs. Nov. 23rd.

6.30. Paint. Finish Sam's cards, do little one for Jim. Mabel's. $3.00. Pub. Lib. Change & renew "Hereward" & "Sinai". Make appointment with Dr. Gay. Ath. Bible Class. Am requested to make short report on state of Egypt at time of Hebrew immigration. Miss Randolph to perform similarly. Walter came in my absence, & brought me two volumes of Shelley— imported—very nice. Note to Abbie & Carrie Hazard. letter mothers palette.

Fri. Nov. 24th. 1882.

6.45 Paint. Letter from Charlotte Hedge & Walter. Write to George Bissell, Carrie Bissell, & Walter. Paint P.M. Lent Florrie "A Double Story" and "House on Wheels." [11] Sew on dress. Annie Aborn stopped to decline lesson. Kate over. Lends me trip ticket to Boston. She has some pie & a cold bannock for tea, & stays till 9.30. I see her home. Ben Wells called, & eke Sam.

Sat. Nov. 25th. 1882.

6.30 or so. Sew. Start down town. Meet Kate & walk up with her. Meet Walter & he walks up with us. Kate leaves. He goes with me to see Millie. I walk down with him. Stamps, $.51. Ammonia $.06. Gym. Louise Mauran back again & glad to see me. I make remarks to Dr. Brooks on the window question. Book at Gregory & Whites, $.10. Look for ribbon for Mabel. Go to Miss Gladdings. Sew all P.M. Go to Ath. & read a bit. Walter stops for me and we walk over to Red Bridge & back. Stop for Miss Russell. She don't go. Go to Boy's Room, Two little bits o' girls play with great applause. & then Lu Manchester & Miss Torrey perform. The boys sing & enjoy it amazingly. Home in car with the girls. Meet friend of Lu's, a Miss Farrell.

Sun. Nov. 26th. 1882.

6.35. Sew. Down with Mrs. Rawson. Good sermon. Call on Ada. Asleep. Home, sew, dine, sew. Henrietta calls. Dress. Old Mr. Carpenter makes farewell call. Walter at 7. Pleasant evening. He has some cold chicken. Goes at 10.55.

Mon. Nov. 27th. 1882.

6? Sew. Note from Carrie Hazard & Abbie Cooke. Go to Dr. Gay's & have two teeth filled. See Mr. Slicer. Post madiera bulbs to Lizzie. Call on Ada. She has a bonnet for me! Call on Mabel Hill. Home & sew. Go to Mabel's, $2.00 in advance. Make pincases for Mabel to paint. Stop at bridge 5' in hopes to see

Walter from whom I had a letter this noon. Stop at Ath. with same idea & to warm my feet. Home. Sew. Walter comes over with some errand for mother, and stays till 10. Jim & Sam come in but don't stay. I have a "cold in my 'ed."

Tues. Nov. 28th. 1882.

7.5 Sew busily. Go to Mrs. Fillinghast's. Home & sew. Annie & Will T. stop in & give me [$]3.00. Kate. Takes my standard palette & pays me $2.00. Gave mother [$]10. for board. Then $5.00 more. Walter calls for me & we call on Carrie Hazard. Sew till 1.30 on suit.

Wed. Nov. 29th. 1882.

7-10. Fly around, & nearly miss my 8.30 train. Walter joins me and we ride to Boston in a dismal N. E. snowstorm. He sends off my bag & leaves me at Mrs. Smith's. A nice time with her, & lunch; then he comes for me in a Herdic, & we look at pictures in Wms. & Everetts for an hour or so. Then Martha stops for me, we bid adieu to C. W. & take a car to the vicinity of her mothers. Pleasant call there, & then take two cars to Aunt Emilie's. Houghton & Francis [12] there. Quiet evening, games with the boys, Edward arrives late. Bed between 9 & 10.

Thurs. Nov. 30th. 1882.

7.10. Church A.M. & a good sermon, very. Home & "dressup". I was a military gentleman, so was Houghton; Edward Queen Elizabeth, Bertie a fair damsel, Phil & Robbie Orientals, Aunt Susie a Zuni Indian. Uncle E. a judge, & Aunt E, a fine lady. Splendid dinner. Then sit around till six, & then some other people come, Rogers, & Bissells, &c. & we masqueraders a act ballads & things. Virginia Reel & all kinds of fun. A Morton Mitchell & Alice M. arrive later. I've outgrown this kind of fun.

Fri.

Dec. 1st. 1882.

7. Pack up. Goodbye all round, & off to call on Retta, escorted by Robbie & Houghton. Call there & then to Mrs. Smith's. More talk (She don't like it, nor him much) more lunch, & to the Hedges. No one at home but the Doctor. Wait long enough to see Mrs. H. & then back to the depot to wait, 45 minutes & so home. Walter to meet me, and home together. Ben Wells & Maria here. He goes when she does, at 9. Walter at 10. Sup, write this & bed at 11.10.

Sat. Dec. 2nd. 1882.

6.45 Paint. Gym. Miss Bush. .75 cts. Maude Mason. Mrs. Fillinghast. She gives me a lunch. Home. Mrs. Brown of Ogden calls here. Draw on cards. Start for Boy's room. Sam joins and walks down with me to Brown St. Stop for Miss Russell. Nice time at the room with some big boys I knew last year. Tom

Fisher there too,. Read a little & talk a good deal. Home in the fog & slop. Bed at 10.30.

Sun. Dec. 3rd. 1882.

7.15. Paint hepaticas. S. S. with Miss R. 05. Good sermon. Home with Aunt C. Paint. Dine. Paint. Sam in about cards. Goes off with three hepaticas & the two big pansies which I letter for him. Walter arrives. I'm not quite right with him somehow.

Mon. Dec. 4th. 1882.

Sunrise. Mend dress & put it on. Paint, finish another hep. & arethusa & nearly gentians. Florinda. Tickets for the Arion from Helen Hazard. Go to Mabels. Get box of cards. .50. Postal cards 13. Home, write, draw, & sew. Jim in to see about cards. Mr. Macdougall calls. Pleasant.

Tues. Dec. 5th 1882—

7.5 Paint. Nice day with Florrie. Miss Murphy here. Mrs. Fillinghast one hour. Home & paint. Kate at 5 or so. Kate pays me [$]13.50. Give mother 15. Carlyle. Supper & walk down with Kate. Go to meeting at the chapel to see about Xmas festivities. Prescott Clark home with me and comes in. Read him some poetry &c. Mother lends him "Happy Thoughts." [13]

Wed. 6th. 1882. Dec.

7.10. Sent answer to Walter. Go to Maude's. Call on Millie. (Got things for Maude on my way over, & went to Leavitts exhibition. Very fine, shouldn't want 'em). Go to Miss Gladdings, lunch, Walter calls a moment. Go to Arion Concert with Miss G. Walk home with Prescott Clarke. I asked him to come along.

Thurs. Dec. 7th. 1882.

7.5–10–15. Mabel's. No pay. Walter meets me on the square & we walk a little, but it's cold, so he leaves me at the Ath. See Mr. Slicer there, & proceed to get up my report for the B.C. Sup on half a hardtack. Miss Randolf had some notes on the hill, very good. So was mine; they all seemed to like it. Home and found long letter from Walter—27 pages. Edward & Robert here playing whist.

Fri. Dec. 8th. 1882.

7.15? Mabel Hill in. Sketch of head & rosebud from Walter. Paint, go to Abbie Cookes. .75 cts. Home by 5.1. Kate here. Read Carlyle. Aunt C's 6oth birthday, Mother gets her some white grapes, cards etc. Have a nice hot supper & Kate stays. Sam in & takes cards. Pays me $2.00. I go home with Kate at 9.

Sat. Dec. 9th. 1882.

Sunrise. Paint. Stop at Annie's. Cards 25 cts, blotting paper, 20. Pub. Lib. Get II Stanley. Go to Gym. Am faint, dizzy & vomit. (owing to unusual mixture inside, too much running & *closed windows in Gym!*) Ath, lunch (4 cts) draw & read, Abbie Cooke, teach & paint till 5. Pussy Rawson calls, she & Abbie walk down with me, go with Pussy to Employment store, tea at the Slicer's. Boy's Room. Read to six boys in little down stairs room. Some people there who play & sing.

Sun. Dec. 10th. 1882.

7.45! Go to S. S. 5 cents contribution. Walk back with Mabel Hill part way, & call on Lu. Mutton dinner. Paint on Jims cards. Clarence comes & takes mother over there to dinner. Walter at near 8! Desire him to read over his last letter to me. Then I discuss it with him with good effect. Happy half hour thereafter.

Mon. Dec. 11th. 1882.

7.10 Paint for Jim. Florrie. Finish Oliver Twist. Snow storm. Go to Maude in rubber boots. She gets me some shoes. Walk from there to High St. & finally get Governor St. car. Harry Manchester in, & then Knight Richmond. Sup. Write to Martha. Ben Wells comes. Buys card. 50 cts. Jim calls.

Tues. Dec. 12th. 1882

6.45 Paint. Slow bad sort of day. Actually don't feel like teaching! Mrs. Fillinghasts to lunch & then teach her and Annie an hour. Home & paint till dark. Call on Mrs. Sturgiss Carpenter. Go to the Hazards. See Helen, Carrie, Margie & Roland. Cup of tea! Carrie orders cards. Home. Draw & paint scribble poems for Xmas.

Wed. Dec. 13th. 1882.

7.10. Paint. Letter from Walter. Bless him! Go to Maude's. She joins me on the bridge & we ride out together. 5.38. Buy book for Willie. .10, pin for Julia, .50, & stop at Ath. to get blotters Kate left there. Home in deep slop. A heavy all day's rain on a heavy day's sleighing. Decorate blotter for Thomas, write inscriptions. Write to He.

Thurs. Dec. 14th. 1882.

7. Paint. Mary Poor's wedding invitation. Last day of Florrie. Go to Maude's. Call for Abbie Cooke & ride with her and Miss Calder to Louise Peck's kettle dinner. Annie & Sophie also receive. A good supper and very nice time with Knight Richmond in attendance. Go to Bible Class. Home. Sam & his mother were here.

Fri. Dec. 15th. 1882.

7.15. Pa-a-a-a-int! Letter from Lizzie. Carry arethusas down to Carrie Hazard's. Maria brings me a tamborine to paint & stays to tea. Paint & draw. Robert in wants labels done. Jim & Sam. Sam pays up, $1.90. Gives me another card to do. Jim takes his last, & pays 4.15. Draw.

Sat. Dec. 16th. 1882.

7.15. Paint. Call on Mrs. Burleigh. Go to Abbie's after pattern. Go to Mr. Burleigh's exhibition. Go to Calder's & get tamborine for Florrie & cards. Get 8 yds. Lonsdale cambric [$]1.06. 10 ct. toothpick slipper. Go to the Bush'es. 75 cts. Mrs. Fillinghast's. Stay to lunch. Home & paint. Carrie Hazard had been here with orders for 6 more cards for Mrs. Coates. & check for $5.00.

Sun. Dec. 17th. 1882.

7? Paint. S. S. 5 cts. Long dull sermon. Home. Edward to dinner. Paint. Dress myself. Walter at 7.15. Happy evening.

Mon. Dec. 18th. 1882.

7.10. Paint. Florrie in. Miss Murphy here. Letter from Martha. Carry cards to man in Peirce's. $3.00. Cash Carrie's check for $5.00. Get three cards at Calder's & pay him 5.00. Go to Maude's. $2.00. Home early. Stopped at Ada's. Paint all the evening.

Tues. Dec. 19th. 1882.

7.15–20. Paint five cards for Mrs. Coates. Ada sends tub of splendid Vermont butter; Xmas gift. Annie Aborn in to paint. Kate comes. Nice supper with scalloped oysters. Mother goes around to Mary's. Paint. Sam calls. Read "Princess & Curdie." [14] (Mrs. Sheldon brought $2.00[)]

Wed. Dec. 20th. 1882.

7. Paint. Letters from Cassie & Walter. Paint. Carry cards to Carrie & Mrs. Coates. Ada & Barclay there. Home. (Sam in P.M.) For a wonder Walter comes, & we have a pleasant evening together. I show him picters and he likes 'em. Give him the panel I made for a Xmas gift. Likes it much. Read to him out of Curdie. Likes it. Goes at 11.

Thurs. Dec. 21st. 1882.

7.45! Paint. Do Sam's last three cards. Miss Murphy here. Paint. Note from Mrs. Coates with $2.00. Write to Cassie & paint. Sam calls for his three little ones, and arranges about the big one. Write poems for Xmas. [$]1.00 from Sam. Give mother [$]15.00.

Fri. Dec. 22nd. 1882.

7.20. Finish Maria's & Florrie's tamborine. Card from Martha. Annie Aborn over. Brings me $5.00. I finish off her tamborine. Walter calls for just a moment. Brings me a watercolor block—"not a Xmas present"! Miss Murphy here. Kate comes. Supper. Kate goes to the Bible Class with me. Home read aloud, & a bit to myself. Write & do up things.

Sat. Dec. 23rd. 1882.

7.20 or so. Paint a bit. Start out with big packet tied on under my waterproof. Carry tamborine to Maria, 75 cts. Get 2 cts. stamps 26 cts. vase & mustard cup, 20 cts, gilt ball 10, pay for shoes, 1.15, doll's plaque for Alice, 10, dog for Charlie, 10, dish & dolls 5., cat 15, tooth pick slipper 10, box, sugar plums, hat, leaves & boot 25. Got brushes & panels at Calders, called on Miss Gladding & left card & got present in envelope, stopped at Slicer's, Home to paint P.M. Go to Boys Room, lend "[20,000] Leagues under the Sea," Verne, to a boy; stopped and left things for Sam, stopped at Pierces to see about plaque, stopped at Calders & got it, then Boy's & played checkers, home with Mr. Crandall, part way. Do up bundles & work on cards.

Sun. Dec. 24th. 1882.

7.40! Bath, work, breakfast, S.S. with Mrs. Rawson. Good sermon. Home, paint, Robert to dinner, Anna, Clarence, & Charlie in; Julia Jastram brings me a piece of cake. Paint, dress. Walter comes. Gives me two books & some fine linen & cambric & card. Give him a little vase. Sam in, highly pleased, brings candy.

Christmas Day.
Mon. Dec. 25th. 1882

5 A.M. Up, and busy doing up bundles, Retire at 1. Rise at 7.35. Have a surprise at breakfast; a silk umbrella, head of Savonarola & "Romola" [15] from Kate Bucklin, & two nightdresses from mother & some pretty cards. Harry Manchester stops & leaves me a ridiculous paintbox & some verses & a real pretty card. I breakfast under my umbrella, a gorgeous black silk one with a stick handle. Paint on Sam's card. Go to Mary's at 1.45. Annie Westcott there and the Carpenters. A very jolly time, my poetry proving very acceptable. Mother gave me Don Quixote, Robinson Crusoe, AEsops Fables, Alice through the Looking Glass, & The Princess & Curdie! Anna & Clarence an Emerson Calendar & Birthday Book, Mary a tidy, Ray a pretty wooden Box, Robert Brown little extension gold pen, Aunt C. splendid travelling bag & little fan in a stick. Card from Harold Childs. Came home, met Robert, Jim called & brought me a lovely little corner bracket, Japanese. Pack. Very pleasant Xmas. Walter comes & we take a walk in the dim moonlight. Goes at 10.

Tues. Dec. 26th. 1882.

7.30 I guess. Paint. All get cards from Thos. Answer Harry Manchester. Paint. Pack bag. Call on Lu. Call on Mrs. Blake. Call on Kate, out. Go to depot & send expressman for trunk. Get ticket. Go to Riders & read. Back to depot, see John Diman, & off, Eat lunch surreptitiously till we start. Boston by 3.15. Get transfer check for trunk & walk over to O.C. station. More lunch. Hingham by 4.30. Martha to meet me. Nice child. Trunk all right. Am very comfortable.

Wed. Dec. 27th. 1882.

7. Long pleasant day. Paint on plaques, learn some of Jacobi & read aloud & am read to. Mr. Collier the minister here to tea. Don't wholly like him. Good supper. A word

puzzle afterward.	CAP	These letters given in a mixed
state, & to be	OIL	thus arranged so as to make 8
words in four	DRY	directions. In bed by ten.

Thurs. Dec. 28th. 1882.

Called on Miss Alden & on Mr. Collier. Made his fire for him, and suggestions. Don't like him any better. Paint, read, talk, learn Jacobi, sew a little. Like being here.

Fri. Dec. 29th. 1882.

Mr. Lane has the pleasure of calling me to breakfast, and enjoys it. Martha not very well, so I wait on her and really make myself useful. Read her "A Blot on the 'Scutcheon" till we are both sobbing, and she won't hear any more. She sleeps nearly all the afternoon till I prevail on her to take a little walk. Then I call on Miss Austin and take a little walk with her. Mrs. Lincoln calls to see me. I like her in a way. Bed early.

Sat. Dec. 30th.

Up early. Write in journal & to Walter. Pack & balladize with Martha. Miss Alden calls, & begs for "Seven Sisters, or the Tale of Torrey." Dine. 1 P.M. train. Buy Stylograf at Ward & Gay's, Xmas present from Martha. Go to station & leave bag. Call on Mary Channing that was. Out. Go to Mrs. Smiths. Callers. Have some hot soup & meat & bread & an apple. 5.30. train home. Met by Walter. Go to Boy's Room. Left plaque at Pierces. Home, talk a bit, & to bed. Found note from Retta, note & card from Cassie, & letter from Walter.

Sunday Dec. 31st. 1882.

7.30. S. S. Church. Nap. Home with Lu & stop to see her cards. Dine. Go to Mabel's. Robert comes & we rehearse. A Mr. Vose calls. Home & dress. Walter early. Long happy evening. Goes in 10.25 car.

Called at Ada's P.M. to see about borrowing a dress for tomorrow.

My last act in the old year was to kneel at my bedside in shame & repentance, with hot tears and self-abasement. From which I rose resolved to pray no more for a season but to work again.

And so to sleep at eleven or so.

[1883!]

Monday.
January 1st. 1883.

6. Clean brush & combs, & write notes to Mrs. Mason & Carrie Hazard. Breakfast. Paint chimney & sign. Note to Kate & Walter with New Year's wishes. Go to Mabel's & to chapel with Lena, carrying curtain & books. To Mr. Slicer for [*illegible*], & then conclude to take the Crandall's, which do: in & wait for Mary. Lena goes home & back, I go to P.O. & back. Mary appears at 12.30 or so. Talk a little & then home with her. In a bit & then home, dine. Arrange things and start for Mabel's again. Mrs. Burbank & daughter there. Make breakfast cap & put pink bows on slippers. Home after chimney & found it gone. Back, & to chapel with M. & Mrs. B. Make myself generally useful, get good supper, help 'em dress, &c., act successfully & home early with Jim & Mrs. Manchester. Then Jim calls to see about some painting. Goes at 10. Folks home from Lotta. Eat some supper, & bed. Tired.

Tues. Jan. 2nd. 1883.

7? Florrie don't come. Write to Rebecca, put workbasket in order, & do a lot of little things. Go ahead with chemiloon. A little Jackson girl called to see about painting lessons in the morning, and I go down and see her mother about. Am to have her twice a week. Call on Mrs. Chace née Cutter. Stop and inquire for Willie Weeden. Go to Mr. Brier to get money for plaque, and he sends me to the "friend" who ordered it, one Mr. Williams of Hartwell & Richards. Pays me therefor and orders another just like it. Mr. Brier took my address. Go to Dr. Gay's. Not in. Go to Ada's. She gives me a bonnet, (pretty & nice) some handsome ribbon, and an order. Home just in time for Kate. Carlyle. Supper. Dress myself in fine array, & go to see "Iolanthe" with Walter. Enjoy it. Like it. Like to go with him. Home serenely, and he stops and has some supper as he had no time for one before. Writes letter to advertisement for mother. Bed by 12.

Wed. Jan. 3rd. 1883.

7.30. Florinda appears, and starts in bravely. Calder's bill—[$]10.69. Go to Maude's. Pay Calder & get outfits for the Bushes & the little Jackson girl. Get plaque for Mr. Williams & tamborine & brush for self. Get Stanley at Pub.

Lib. Call on Miss Gladding & have a piece of cake. Stop at Bush'es & leave things. Home, sup, write to Martha. Sew.

Thurs. Jan. 4th. 1883.

7.30. Note from Annie Morse, $5.00 from Tiffany, N. Y. card & note from Walter. Paint on plaque P.M. & write to Walter. Go to Lu Manchesters from 6 to 9. Ballads & fun. Home all abed, sew.

Fri. Jan. 5th. 1883.

Am aroused by mother at 6.45. She has a cold & headache. Come down, don working dress, and start the fire & breakfast. Make short biscuit. Card from Miss Bush P.M. postponing lesson. Kate. Carlyle. Supper. Call at Mrs. Diman's to see Miss Alden. Back & go nearly home with Kate. Mr. Wells calls. Read him "Seven Sisters or the Tale of Torrey." Off ere 9. Sew.

Sat. Jan 6th. 1883.

7–10. First lesson to Isabel Jackson. Ride over to Calders, pay for two outfits & get another for Florrie. Go to Gym. Mary Sharpe there. Glad to see her. Kate stops for me & we walk down together. Then to Brown St. with Mary. Home, dine, finish plaque. Amuse Mrs. Springer who gives me filberts. Read, sup, Boys Room in rubber boots. Very good time, with puzzles, etc. Home alone, sup, read, bed.

Sun. Jan. 7th. 1883.

7.40. S. S. alone. Start on Washburn's Handbook of Religious Instruction. Home part way with Amy Sharp & Theo Fillinghast. Read & eat snowcream, dine, Write to Grandpa Carpenter, & design on screen cover for Ada. Bathe & dress, mend clothes a little. Walter at about 7. Happy evening.

Mon. Jan. 8th. 1883.

7.30. Sew. Florrie christens her new paints. Go to Mabels, leaving shoes to be mended at Mrs. Meyer's. Stop at Dr. Gay's. Call on Millie. Get shoes, 65 cts. Call on Ada. Wants little plaque. Home, sup, sew. Robert & Edward. Whist R & mother 4 to 3.

Tues. Jan. 9th. 1883.

7.30. Sew. Letter from Walter* P.M. Answer a line. Go to Isabel Jackson's. Stop at Kelly's to get heath for mother. Hadn't any. Stop at Mary's a moment. Home. Kate. Carlyle. Sup. Sew. Sam for a moment. Shows me letter from receiver of the gorgeous card. High praise for me. Mr. & Mrs. Henry Carpenter spend the evening. dreary. Write to Walter some more. Mr. C. $5.00 for paints.

Wed. Jan. 10th. 1883.

7.10. Great snowstorm. Florrie absent. Paint m.g.s on tamborine. Mother had three scholars, Erma, Jessie B. & Caddey. Mrs. Springer lends (afterward gives) me leggings. Go to Maude $4.00. Walk all the way home to get warm, as their room was cold. Oatmeal porridge. Walter comes. Draws me a man for the "Health Bringer." Mr. Bolan comes & shovels us out at 9 or so. Clear at 10.30.

Thurs. Jan. 11th. 1883

7.15–30. Paint Health Bringer man. Grand success. No Florrie. Carry pattern to Ada. Take plaque to M. Wms. He wants another he thinks. Mabels, tell stories to her & Maude. Bring home her Xmas present to me, box of note paper, terra cotta & blue! Call on Mrs. Lindsey. Then on Mrs. Stetson & stay to tea. Walter walks to the chapel with me. Good time in Bible Class. Home, sew, bed.

Fri. Jan. 12th. 1883.

7.10. Mend work dress. No Florrie. Paint m[ari].g[old]. tamborine. Dine. Call at Ada's with pattern. .50 cts. Go to Dr. Gay's. Both wisdom teeth all hollow. Get calendula at Clarkes for mother. Meet Mr. Slicer there & he gives me 25 cts. worth of chocolates to get the flavor of creosote & varnish out of my mouth. Home. Kate. Write a little to Walter. Sew & talk with mother. Jim comes with a queer order.

Sat. Jan. 13th. 1883.

7.30. Off to the Jacksons. Lend Bella "The Princess & Goblin." [16] They take me down st. in gorgeous sleigh. Order stoveling at Roots & go to gym. Mrs. Neelan quite confidential as to her failure to please & the dismal prospect. I take hold, lead the marches, & give lots of vim to it. Go to the Bushes. Good lesson, the first in colors. Joined by Jim. Go to Coleman's & sketch camera & things. Go to Miss Gladdings & stay to dinner. Boy's Room. Read Little Pilgrim. Bed.

January thaw.   Aunt C. back again.
Sun. Jan. 14th. 1883.

6.50. Lilly being departed, I make fires &c. S. S. alone. Mr. DeNormandy preached. Good sermon. Home. Go around to Mary's on errand. Write to Lu Hill. Dine. Finish letter to Lu. & write to Eva Webster. Dress. Katy comes for clothes. Clarence calls. Walter comes. Read "Little Pilgrim" to him. Happy.

Mon. Jan. 15th. 1883.

6.35. Mrs. Springer washes dishes. Mother goes over to Mary's. Aunt C. sick. I teach mother's school. Lively time, all of 'em there. Dine on hulled corn & milk. Carry Health Bringer to Robert. Get stamps 50 cts. Go to Mabels.

Home strait. Sew. Write to George Macdonald. Jim. Discuss his order. Sam
sent his $3.00. Goes ere ten. Sleepy.

Tues. Jan. 16th. 1883.

6.30. Work all done and ready for Florrie by 8.55. She don't come. Paint on
Jim's thing. Card from Lu Hill. Note from Miss Gladding inviting me to go
to the Oratorio. Call to see how Mrs. Carpenter is. Stop 3 minutes at Lu's.
(Sent to Lippincott's for Macdonald's address.) Lesson at the Jackson's. Bring
home the "Princess." Kate. Read her one of the Arabian nights—partly. She
sketches me.

Wed. Jan. 17th. 1883.

6.30 or less. Florrie not to be here till Monday, so I enjoy my self. Work
on Jim's order. Got note from Walter—he was sick last night. Letter from
G. Bissel offering Mrs. Wellman $2000 in cash for her quarter. Carry it to
T. C. Greene, leave rubber boots to be mended, call to see Mr. Wms. Out. Go
to Maude's. Draw. Call on Milly. Ride home. Knight Richmond in car. I like
him. Snow & rain. Finish 2 vol. Stanley, & my chemiloon.

Thurs. Jan. 18th. 1883.

6.45. New girl—"Angy" tall, not as "nice" as Lilly. Finish Jim's card thing.
Aunt C. has Doctor Wilcox. Meet postman, no letter, go to see if Walter is
down town, meet Mr. Burleigh who says he has been, go to gym. & work,
only two beside me. Get vol. 3 of Stanley at Pub. Lib. Get Ada's plaque at
Calders. Call on Carrie Hazard. Mrs. Roland 2nd gives me a rose. Home. Sup
& read. Jim comes, is well pleased, fastens it together with eyelets etc. & pays
me $2.50. Ray & Clarence call to see how grandma is. At 9.10 or so, a call
from Walter, Bless Him! Wrote to Lizzie A.M.

Fri. Jan. 19th. 1883.

6.45. Dress & sit down to sew. Miss Angy doesn't come so I do work with
mother. She comes later, to say she isn't coming; can't bring up coal! Sew
all morning. Letter from Walter & G. Macdonald's address from Lippincott.
Lunch at the Hazard's with Carrie & Mary. See "the boy". Am presented with
the said boy's picture, the prettiest child picture I ever saw. Go to Gay's. Call
on the Slicer's. Stop for Kate. Home & read to her. She stays to tea & goes to
Bible Class with me. Home & sew. Snow over lots of ice—fell three times!

Sat. Jan. 20th. 1883.

6.30. Fly around & do the work. Go to *Isabel* Jackson's. (not Mabel). Sleighride down again. Get some of the girls excited over the prospective loss. Kate
calls for me with a bag of apples. Takes 'em home for me, & also my mended
rubber boots—50 cts. Afternoon at Miss Gladdings, sewing. Boy's Room.

Tell 'em stories, very much interested. A girl who play's & a young man who recites. Home in car as it rains—tired.

Sun. Jan. 21st. 1883.

7.30! Never work till this incredible hour, & then *flew*. Find myself attacked with the prevailing complaint, but resist the enemy, & so far successfully. S.S. alone. Part of the class are beguiled by a picture paper, & I lead the rest over to some other seats. Very effective. George Mason brings a new contribution box, made it himself, very pretty. Lu stops for me & I sit with her. Sketch. Home with Lu. Dinner, wash dishes, talk, & loaf. Dress. Clarence calls. Walter. Happy evening.

Mon. Jan. 22nd. 1883.

5.50. All ready for 9 or a trifle after. Florrie comes, much elated over her successful nursing, and her newly acquired physiological knowledge. Card from the church people—meet at chapel parlors—important business. Mabel's. Maude rides down with me. Call on the Slicers to see what the "business" is. Out. Call on Jennie Bucklin, nice little talk with her. Call at the Slicer's again. Mr. Burleigh there, walk up with him. Home. Read Stanley & sup. Just get ready to paint & Harry Manchester comes & stays till 10.10 about. Ballads & other nonsense.

Tues. Jan. 23rd. 1883.

6.15. Ready by 9.05 A.M. Florrie paints. Dine, sew. Go to Isabel's, see a Mrs. Vaugn & little boy Wheaton by name, lend Isabel "The Princess & Curdie". Call on Helen. Home, read & eat apple. Kate. Finish the Arabian night story. Paint night street scene. Mr. Wells calls shaven & shorn & with sealskin cap—just as I first saw him years ago. New poetry game. Goes at 10.30.

Wed. Jan. 24th. 1883.

6.15. Ready by 9. "Ghent to Air" in geography. Chowder for dinner, no time for it; cold lunch & off. Mabel in extra good behavior. Amuse her with the electric qualities of her amber necklace. Home straight. Sup, air out rooms, write to Walter. Sew.

Thurs. Jan. 25th. 1883.

6.45. Mother sick but manages to teach. Mrs. Springer & Aunt C. help a little about dishes. Annie Aborn calls, pays me $1.50 that was left over Xmas-time, & returns book & copy I lent them. Get dinner, clear off & go to gym. Nice time. Meet Kate cor. College & Main, & she walks home with me. Get some supper, wash dishes, & go to Bible Class with Kate. Home in lovely moonlight. Sew.

Fri. Jan. 26th. 1883.

6.25. No Florrie. Letter from Walter & card from Mrs. Wms. Sew. Set & clear table & dine. Go to Dr. Gay's, walking up with Miss Carter. Get thread, tape, & bottons, 38 cts. Post note to Miss Gladding & letter to MacDonald. Stop for Kate. We go to café & have a little spree. Meet Walter. Says he's coming over. Home via Waterman. Sketch tree. Apple slump for supper; wash dishes. Walter comes. Sam calls. He goes home with Kate. Half hour with Walter.

Sat. Jan. 27th. 1883.

6.30. Leave dishes. Bella's. Ride down st. reading Stanley; [$]1.00's worth tickets. Gym. Polka race with Connie Pitman. Nice time. Kate comes & goes up with me. Bushes. 75 cts. Home, dine, paint on tamborine for Lizzie. Julia Drowne calls. Sew. Boy's Room. Stop for Miss Russel. Tell stories. May Bell Hill there & plays. 3rd wet warm Sat. night. Doesn't rain though.

Sun. Jan. 28th. 1883.

6.30. Black stove. S. S. (.05) Remarks in S. S. & sermon by Prof. Kovacs of Hungary. Very interesting. Home with Mrs. Manchester & Robert, who comes to dinner. Good dinner, very. Robert suggests that I stay here this summer & paint for a winter sale. Good idea. Offers to lend me capital. Wash dishes. Mend chemiloon. Dress. Read Stanley & Bible aloud a little. Walter. Writes me a sonnet.[17] Late supper.

Mon. Jan. 29th. 1883.

6.10. Ready by 9. Finish Lizzie's tamborine, dine in hot haste & trot down street therewith. Get box at Gladding's, do it up at Tibbits & Randall's get Jennie Bucklin to post while I catch car. Lesson to Maude. Mrs. Mason appears & pays me $4.00. Get blank book for mother. $.10. She owes me 60 [cents] now. Ride home. Write to Cassie. Mr. Bumpus calls. Cocoon & Judean History. Jim with order for little whirligig.

Tues. Jan. 30th. 1883.

7! Breakfast on table at 7.45! No Florrie. Do Jim's thing in ink. Paint on Ada's pansies. Dine. Letter from Walter. Go to Jackson's. Drawing lesson. Aunt C. goes to Anna's. Stop & see Lu a minute. Kate. Jim. Takes thing. $.50. Walter comes rather late & stays here instead of calling as intended.

Wed. Jan. 31st. 1883—

6.45. Florrie, long lecture on health & morals. Dine with Stanley & go to Maude's. Walk down in tearing rain; streets wetter than I ever saw them. [$]2.00. Carrie Hazard sees me on Benefit St. & takes me home. Write Valentines for Lizzie. Paint on Easter cards.

Thurs. Feb. 1st. 1883.

6 1.15 [*sic*]. Florinda has nosebleed. Aunt C. calls. Go to gym. Call on Mrs. Selinger. Renew book at Pub. Lib. Get things for Bella Jackson at Calders, & cake of B[urnt]. Sienna [paint]. Walk down & meet Kate on the Bridge. Go up to café with her & she stops at Robert's on way down & gets some candy—some for me of course. Go to the Slicers to tea. Church meeting instead of Bible Class, so I stay there alone & sew & read the Century.

Fri. Feb. 2nd. 1883.

6.30. No Florrie. Finish bloodroot card & paint on plaque. Dine early & go to Dr. Gay's. Pay him $6.00. Go with mother to hear Dr. Keller lecture. Stop with Kate & see the dear woman & she goes to the café with us & we have some supper. Walk about, see Arcade & Tilden's, where she buys a paper knife. See her off. Gave her my Easter card. Home with Kate. Griddle cakes & valentines. Ben Wells calls. Both see Kate home.

Sat. Feb. 3rd. 1883.

6.40. Leave dishes. Lesson to Bella. Wants me to stay 2 hrs. Mrs. J. takes me down st. Gym. Kate & I the only ones there. Mrs. Gladding's & sew on chemiloon. Dinner. Sew. Oranges. Sew. Boy's Room. Jennie late. Few boys & few people. Home in half frozen slush—everything crusted.

Sun. Feb. 4th. 1883.

6.30. Very slippery. S.S. $.05. Home. Finish pansies. Wash oil brushes. Dine. Wash dishes. Talk with mother. Dress, wear lace bertha arrangement— old point d'Alencon. Very pretty. Walter. Read Edwin Arnold's "Indian Song of Songs" to him. Nice little supper. Goes at 10.45.

Mon. Feb. 5th. 1883.

6.30. Sweep kitchen. Florrie. Paint on E[aster]. card. Dine. Letter from Walter. Go to Mabel. Call on Millie. Home, sup, and fall to on Jewish Hist. Walter comes, wants supper, gets it, and goes at 8—some Art Club business. Dear boy. Miss Bullock & George Burroughs call. Entertain 'em. Write to George Bissell. More J[ewish]. H[istory].

Tues. Feb. 6th. 1883—

6.30. Letter from Cassie. Begin answer. Florrie. Dine. Lu calls. Carry pansies to show Mrs. Bullock. Card from Mr. Cushman, his motherinlaw wants lessons. Go to Bella's. Home, find Lu again, & tell ballads. Finish marguerite E[aster]. card. Kate. Carlyle. supper. Finish sketch of J[ewish]. Hist[ory]. Jim. Sketch him for silhouette. He goes home with Kate. Write more to Cassie.

Wed. Feb. 7th. 1883.

6.30. More snow & rain last night. The worst walking I ever saw. Florrie.
Compose Valentine for Miss Farrell. Dine. Mrs. Springer & Katie to dinner.
Stop at Miss Bullocks for placque. Leave silhouette (finished this morning) at
Jim's. Just catch car & go to Maude's. She being late Mrs. M[ason]. utilizes
my spare moments by having me help Mabel with her maps. Economical
dame. Call at the Cushman's & see Mrs. Gilman about lessons. Ride down.
Get 50 cts. worth off stamps & post Essay to Miss Alden. Leave placque at
Ada's. [$]3.05. Home. Letter from Walter, bless him! Sup. Alter the morn-
ings valentine & send it, with two other little things to the Century. Write
Val[entine] for Helen Gammell.

Thurs. Feb. 8th. 1883.

6.30. Florrie learns what Venice is. Letter from G[eorge]. Bissell recommending partition. Fl[orrie]. stays to dinner. Post letter to "Century" & Cassie. See
T. C. Greene about the business. Conclude to let it rest. Gymnasium. First
lesson to Mrs. Gilman. .75 cts. Go to Walters to supper. He walks to chapel
with me. Bible Class. Mr. Tingly home. Mother went to hear a Mormon
schoolteacher. Write to Walter. Letter from Sturgiss Carpenter.

Fri. Feb. 9th 1883.

6.30. Abbreviate & hasten dinner. Go to Dr. Gay. He fills his last hole, gold,
& I pay him 4.50. All square now. Go to Calders & get colors & brushes for
Mrs. Gilman. She has enough of the latter. Also sell her some of the cards
I had. .23 [for the cards] .75 for lesson. Walk straight home. Letter from
Walter, blue & discouraged. Kate. Carlyle. Scalloped oysters. Robert in with
new label to do, Jenkin's prepared flour! Home with Kate. Write.

Sat. Feb. 10th. 1883.

6.30. Scant breakfast, leave dishes, Bella's at 8.30 to 10. Emma Vaughn called
for to go to Gym. with me, & Mrs. Jackson carries us both down in sleigh.
Gym. Miss Gladding there with friends. Kate, & walks up with me. Emma
rode home in car. Miss Bush. 75 cts. Get cardboard at Calders & pay him
5.00—4.15 of it Mrs. G[ilman]'s. Go to her & give 1½ hour lesson. $1.12
cts. Pub. Lib. & read Pop. Sci. till Walter comes. Leave books & cardboard at
U. for C. work room & go to Ada's "Tea." Stop for Miss Russel, gone with the
Burleighs, go to boy's room alone Walter having left me at the R's. Read, do
puzzles, draw. Very successful. Home, tired. Letter from T. C. Greene, with
Bissell's & Wellman's.

Sun. Feb. 11th. 1883.

6.40. More snow. Small S. S. Mr. Woodbury. Nap. Theo. Fillinghast walks
part way home with me. Dine. Mend white skirt. Clean some paths. Dress.
Robert over to see about flour label; goes soon. Wait a bit, & then Walter.

Mother proposes a grand new arrangement to which we joyfully accede. We take the house & things, downstairs tenement that is, & live here for the present while she goes out west.

Mon. Feb. 12th. 1883.

6.30. Work on label. Mother pays me a dollar. Mr. Peck in & I buy 4 doz. eggs of him $1.45 cts. Aunt C. home to change her clothes while mother is with Anna. To Mabels. Miss home car. Call on Carrie Hazard who goes to Aiken S. C. on Wed. She gives me $5.00 to *buy things for Walter.* I love her much. She is a noble & beautiful woman. Home, wrote a little to Walter. Sup. Clarence calls, just home from Maine backwoods. Buys 2 doz. eggs. Mr. Wells calls. Poor ballad. Recite "Husband! husband!" to him. He enjoys it, goes at 10. Fix fires and retire.

Tues. Feb. 13th. 1883.

6.40. No Florrie. Work on Jenkins Flour. Nap P.M. Kate. Sam. Edward. Work more. Bed at 11.

Wed. Feb. 14th. 1883.

6.40. Mother up at five to wash last night's dishes. No Florrie. Finish label & take it to Robert. Wrote to George Bissell declining his advice. Sent ballads to St. Nicholas. Go to Maude's. $4.00. Leave Stanley at Pub. Lib. & get placque for Mrs. Gilman. Home. Sup. Dress a bit. Walter comes for me to go to Art Club but concludes to stay here. Sew button on his overcoat.

Thurs. Feb. 15th. 1883.

6.40. Hear from Florrie that she is not coming till Monday. Carrie Hazard sends me a manual on flowerpainting. Paint Easter cards. Go to gym. Lesson to Mrs. Gilman. Go to the Channing's, get some supper & have a nice little talk with Grace & the Dr. Bible Class. Home, sup again,*

Fri. Feb. 16th. 1883.

6.30. News of reception of letter by St. Nicholas. Get two little vases at Calder's. Last lesson to Mrs. Gilman. Get placque for Anna. Leave three Easter cards at Tibbetts & Randall's. (Met Walter on way up, gave me a letter.) Home, read letter, dine, paint easter eggs, Kate, Carlyle, supper, sew a trifle, Harry Manchester calls. Ballad, & story. Much laughter. Kate went early.

Sat. Feb. 17th. 1883.

6.30. Lesson to Bella. Ride down in car. Gym. Leave arbutus eggs at Tibbitts. Miss Gladdings. She sews for me & I read Rudder Grange to her. Good dinner. Boy's Room. See Mrs. Burleigh home.

Warm as summer. Two day's thaw. Get Rawlinson's Five Great Monarchies, Vol. I.

Sun. Feb. 18th. 1883.

6.35. Leisurely breakfast. S. S. Only the Weedens & John Kelly. Saw Mr. Hureshoff. Fine sermon. Harry Manchester walks home with me. Dine. Wash dishes. Mrs. Nolan called. Katie has a son—Thursday P.M. Write to Mrs. Smith. Anna & Clarence call. Dress. Read Rawlinson. Walter. Seems well & happy. Goes at 10.20. Sup & read Rawlinson.

Mon. Feb. 19th. 1883.

6.20. Black stove. No Florrie. Letter from Martha. Paint arbutus & m.g. Dine. Go to Mabel's. Bought braid, 7 cts. Call on Mrs. Stetson for a moment. Stop at Mrs. Cushman's & get $1.87 cts. Ride home reading Chaldea. Paint. Boys throw snowballs at the window. Go out & patrol but can't catch 'em. Jim calls & pays me 50 cts. for silhouette.

Tues. Feb. 20th. 1883.

6:35–40. Paint rosebud, m.g. & Easter Lily. No Florrie, no Bella, no Kate. Paint all day. Go to Lu's & spend evening. Pleasant time. Harry home with me, & orders arbutus. Read Chaldea.

Wed. Feb. 21st. 1883.

6.30. Paint in oils. Take cards to Miss Bogert & she orders one. Go to Maude. Read "The Talisman"[18] to her. Call on Millie. Mrs. Downs & Emma there. Get things at Calders. Car fares .12 cts. Home. Fine for Edwin Arnolds poems at U. C. W., .08 [cents]. Letter from Walter. He and his parents call in state, & they stay while he & I go & see the Hayden exhibition of etchings. Stop at the studio in the glorious moonlight. Then home & he stays till 10.30.

Thurs. Feb. 22nd. 1883.

6.35. Paint arbutus. Give lesson to Bella from 9 to 10. Wash dinner dishes. Gymnasium. Nice time. Walk up hill with Louise Mauran. Bought jasmine. Go to see Jean O'Connor but can't. stop to dine & see Grace. Home at 9.30, & finish this number's "Through One Administration."

Fri. 23rd.

6.30. Paint Jasmine & arbutus. Read a bit. Good letter from Walter. Kate. Carlyle. Gorgeous supper—tongue omelet, milk toast & cut up oranges. Edward calls. Sew. He sees Kate home.

Sat. Feb. 24th. 1883.

6.30. Black stove in fine style. Go to Bellas. Ride down to gym. Run a good deal. Leave more cards at Tibbits—lily, m.g., cross egg, & circle. Lesson to Misses Bush. .75 [cents]. Get things at Calders. Stop at Miss Gladdings. Go and read "The Blot on the 'Scutcheon["] to Millie. Likes it. Dine with Miss G. Read some to her. Go to Pub. Lib. & read Punch & Pop. Sci. Boy's Room.

Several drunk & noisy. Home with Mrs. Burleigh, stop in at the Slicers a moment. Home, squash pie & walnuts, bed!

Sun. Feb. 25th. 1883.

6.40. Leisurely breakfast. S. S. 8th consecutive stormy Sunday! Only 35 there. 5 of my class though. Leila Weeden as "Transient Visitor.["] Some very good remarks from a Rev. Crawford Nightingale. Pretty good sermon. Edward comes home to dinner. Wash dishes. Talk & loaf a little. Dress. Write invitation for Whist Party to Abbie Cooke. Walter. Happy evening. Goes at 10.30. Sup. Bed.

Mon. Feb. 26th. 1883.

6.30. Glorious sunrise. Florrie returns. Good morning. Dine. Go to Mabels. Feast my eyes in Tildens window while waiting for cars nowadays. Straight home. Maria here. Draw sabbatia for Sam. Supper. Harry Manchester calls & gets his arbutus [$]1.00. Tell a story & read him divers funny things. Goes at 9.30.

Tues. Feb. 27th. 1883.

6.30. No Florrie. Paint m.g. for Miss Bogert, & two sabbatia cards for Sam. Mrs. Jackson sends word not to come. Kate. Carlyle. Sup. Write to Mrs. Charles Howden Smith, née Farrell. Home with Kate, and enjoy the walk a much.

Wed. Feb 28th. 1883.

6.15. Wash last night's dishes. Florrie. Paint arbutus. Dine. Go to Maude. $2.00. Met Sam. Letter from Walter. Stop & get card at Tibbitt's and carry it to Ada. Quite a call there. Home. Sup. dress. Walter comes and we call on Anna at last. Pleasant time. Home & he stays till 10.30

Thurs. March 1st. 1883— [19]

6.20. No Florrie. Paint arbutus & letter. E[aster]. card for Ada. Dine. Leave card for Miss Bogert, who doesn't pay me. Another for Ada, who does— $1.50. Mrs. Blake wants one. Go to Gym. Run 50 laps—38 to the mile. Shower bath, walk up with Miss Pitman. (Connie.) Go to Mrs. Fillinghast's to dinner and have a nice talk with Annie, who is just engaged to Will. A Mr. Sampson calls during the evening. Not interesting. Theo sees us home.

Friday, March 2nd. 1883.

6.20. No Florrie. Paint on placque & vase. Dine. Wash a lot of dishes. Clean silver in company with Sarah. Ada calls. Dear girl! Help set table. Dress. Edward at 7; then Robert, then Abbie Cooke, then Jim, then Sam at 8. Whist till 11. E. & I beat the rubber, but they weaseled us. Roast oyster supper with pies, tarts, nuts, oranges, raisins, coffee, cake, etc. I get to bed by 1.30!

Sat. March 3rd. 1883.

6.30. Black stove & clean up generally. Letter from Walter. Isabel's, carry her paper & brush, 04 & 25 cts. Ride down reading Chaldea. Gym. bath. Get shoestrings 10 cts. Get Rudder Grange for Miss G. Get things at Calders. Miss G. Read to her while she sews for me. Dine. Bit of a nap. Return R[udder]. G[range]. Boy's Room. Home with Fannie Manchester.

Sunday. March 4th. 1883.

6.30. Leisurely breakfast. S. school. *Pleasant morning*! but a touch of snow as we come out. Home alone mostly. Dine. loaf. Write to Miss Alden. Wash few dishes. Mend little petticoat & put new braid on skirt. Dress. Read Rawlinson & sup. Walter at 7.30. He catches a little of the anagram fever, has some peach pie & "anise brod" at 10, and does some measuring in our room that is to be. Goes at 10.45.

Mon. March. 5th. 1883.

6.30. Florrie. Mabel Mason. $4.00. Call on Ada. Stay to dinner. Mr. Peace Vernon there. Whit sees me home, revelling in the One Word game.

Tues. March. 6th. 1883—

6.35. Things go a little wrong, bread don't rise, fire don't go, &c. Note from Miss Gladding inviting Walter. Florrie. Paint little landscape on E[aster]. card. Dine. Card from Martha and letter from Walter announcing the fact that he is not to have the sale he expected. Doll & Richards advise having the pictures worked off privately instead. Walter is sad enough. Write long letter to comfort him. Eat nuts. Kate, through all the snowstorm. The morning's biscuit for supper, & codfish & cream. Read Carlyle. Write Chaldea. Home nearly with Kate. More Chaldea. Snow turned to rain.

Wed. March 7th. 1883.

6.30. Florrie. Met Postman & got letter from Walter. Met himself on Main St. Maude's. Read "Talisman". Elmwood car down. Met Mr. Lane on Benefit St. Goodbye call on Ada. Go to our Church Fair & take supper with Kate & Miss Comstock. At Kate's expense of course. Willie Weeden's table. Stop at the Crandalls & call on Martha. (Saw Mrs. Luther at the fair—very glad to see me.) Home & sit around a little. Walter comes at 8.30. & stays two hours.

Thurs. March. 8th. 1883.

6.30. Florrie. Leisurely dinner. Gymnasium. Connie Pitman invites me to tea. Bath and general rearrangement. Pub. Lib. & enjoy Punch & Pop. Sci. for an hour & a half. Walter stops for me. Go to Miss Gladdings to tea. Mrs. & Mr. John Mason & Lizzie Brown there. Delicious supper & music in the evening. Home at 10.10 or so. Walter stays a while. Write after he's gone. Bed before 12.

Fri. March 9th. 1883.

6.35. Florrie. Good codfish dinner. Readorn old slippers. Wish I had some more. Read Assyria. Kate don't come. A moments call on Lu. Go to Connie Pitman's to tea. Abbie Cooke & Margie Calder there. Very nice supper— almost too much. Play little games, tell stories, do puzzles. The others go home with their fathers, and I have a bit of talk with Connie in her room. She says she likes me. I'm glad of it. Home by 10.15.

Sat. March. 10th. 1883.

6.35. Black stove. Go to Isabell's. Ride down reading Chaldea. Gym. Go away up the rope. The Bushes $.75. Stay there to lunch. Stop at U. C. W. to get book for Millie. Shut. Go to Pub. Lib. Take Edwin Arnold's Poems & read some of 'em to Millie. Change chrome yellow for white for Bella. Pub. Lib. till 6.10. Stop in Perrins a bit. Boy's Room. Read 'em some from Felix Oswald's "Physical Culture," talk, & draw. Walk home with Fanny Manchester. Good supper. bed. Heavy rain at noon, & clear now.

Sun. March. 11th. 1883—

6.35–40. S.S. we take up $1.17 in our class—all there—8. And take the corner seats. Church. Keep awake. Harry Manchester home. Stops in. Edward to dinner & Bessie Brown. Stay till 5.30. Sophie Aborn calls & I have a good talk with her. Dress. Walter. I don't feel very well. Bed by 11.

Mon. March. 12th. 1883.

6.40. No Florrie. Finish Mrs. Blake's card, & paint on Anna's placque. Go to see Lu. Out. Call on Mrs. Diman. Edward Hale Jr. there. He sees me home & goes elsewhere. Sam calls. Whist. Pleasant evening.

Tues. March. 13th. 1883.

6.30. Am late for school & caught thereat by Florrie. Good lessons. Knit her a garter. Dine. Letter from Walter, & Mrs. Charles Howden Smith. Wash dinner dishes for 15 cts. Dust & fix a little in my room. Kate. Carlyle. Whips for supper. Read more. (Bit of a rest, & help wash dishes first). Clarence stops in. Give him a whip. He goes. Ben Wells calls. Give him a whip. (Mother went with Mrs. Budlong to a Utah lecture). Jim calls. Mr. Wells is to be married in July & settle in Leipsix[?] *or* Providence. Seems to enjoy his evening. Jim home with Kate. Mrs. B. stops in & gets whip & pie after the lecture.

Wed. March. 14th. 1883.

6.30. Late again. I must eat less breakfast. Good day with Florrie. Dine. Leave card at Mrs. Blakes. $1.50. Leave "Hereward" at Ath. $.02. Go to Maude. Design in white on bottles, placque, & begin banner. Divers young fry come in and remain, rapt. (Met Walter before taking car.) Home. Read Atlantic.

Sup. Dress. Anagram a little. More Atlantic. Walter comes and we go to Art Exhibition. Home ere ten. Goes at 10.30. Bed.

Thurs. March. 15th. 1883.

6.15. Ready in time. Paint Florrie's faded roses. Dine. Gym. Bath with Connie. Call on Mrs. Slicer, who has sprained her ancle. Go to the Browns to supper. Good. Mother & Aunt C. come there. Go to Bible Class. Stop & [*sic*] the Simmonses for mother & Aunt, & play whist. Mother & Jim 3 to 1 with Sam & I. Then talk a bit, and home. Get to playing again by 10.10 & Sam & I leave off 12 to 10 in all. Bed by 2:15 A.M. Haven't enjoyed whist so much in a long long time. The boys enjoyed it. How very nice & pleasant & good and wise & kind they are!

Fri. March. 16th. 1883.

6.30–40. Florrie still interested. Dinner late. Take sewing & call on Lu. Out. On Mrs. Diman. Out. On Annie Aborn. Out. Home. Write letters. Abbie Cooke calls. Kate. Carlyle. Griddle cakes. Jim stops on business, a card for Arnold & McGowan. He goes home with Kate. She pays me $15.00. Give it to mother.

Sat. March. 17th. 1883.

6.10. Black stove. Talk with Jim on Mrs. Budlong's telephone. Paint sabbatias on card for him. Go to Tibbitts & Shaws & meet Jim. He walks up to the gym. with me. Perform successfully. Go to Public Library & transfer Rawlinson to mother's card. "Doors, Windows," etc. etc. Sew a little. Miss Clara Hoppin calls, & Mrs. Kimball. Dinner. Go to U. C. W. Library & look [at] material for tomorrow's lesson. Boys room. Successfully entertain two particularly detestable little imps. Home in car with Jennie Bucklin who was going to Tudies. Half a dozen oranges. Journal. Bed.———

Sun. March. 18th. 1883.

6.40. Prepare S. S. lesson. Walk down with Mrs. Rawson & Arney. Practice Easter songs in the church. Walk around the square with some of the boys, giving perapatetic instruction. A Mr. Haywood drones in Mr. Slicers place. Jim walks home with me. Lu stops in. Jim to dinner, & stays till 6.30! Anna & Clarence and Charlie call. Do nothing but wash the dishes & talk with Jim, partly on business. Dress, not down to let Walter in. Find him with an anagram. Spend an hour in that divertisement & then talk till 10.45 in the parlor. Tears.[20] Bed by 11.30.

Mon. March. 19th. 1883.

6.10. Read some Assyria before breakfast! Florrie with $33.00 of her bill. Pay mother $30.00. Dine with Rawlinson. Letter from Walter & card from Miss Gladding. Mabel's. Maude rehearses gymnasium compliments. Home.

Answer Miss G's note & finish letter to Martha. Take 'em round to Lu's, & get 2 ct. stamps of Harry, who posts the letters for me. Stay till 8 o'clock, and draw for a little girl there. Home. Mother out! Oranges. Write a bit. Bed.

Tuesday.
March 20th. 1883.

6.25–30. Mother has a headache. Get breakfast. Florrie. Emma Vaughn is a noble child, and will make a real woman strong and grand, I think. Dine. Letter from Walter. (He has begun his picture of the young Greek girl asleep on the bench, from a fair Miss Foster as model.) Paint arbutus on card for Miss G[ladding].'s Lizzie Brown. Kate. Carlyle. Supper. I frisk. Write to Carrie Hazard. Mr. Maine calls.

Wed. March. 21st. 1880 {sic}

6:-5. Wash dishes, get breakfast & get work all done by 8.45. Florrie. Dine. I am eating lightly just now, and feeling unusually well. Walk over to Calder's & get paint for the Masons, started at 2 and had finished my errand by 2.25. Carry Scot's poems to Maude & read her the "Fire King" etc. Mason pays me $3.57, the last for the paints. Maude asks to correspond after she leaves for Kansas City. Merhaps [*sic*]. Ride down & straight home in vigorous frame of mind & body. Read the end of "Through One Administration" Sup. Write to Carrie Hazard. Walter comes, and we call on Mary & Ray. They are glad to see us, and ever so kind. Oranges. Home by 9.30. Talk till 10.40. Bed.

Thurs. March. 22nd. 1883.

6.25. Florrie. Dine. Carry card to Miss Lizzie Brown on Aborn st. $1.00. Go to gym. Mother comes there for me. Ran a mile. Meet Aunt Caroline below and we ride out to Gilmore and call on Mrs. Stetson. Pleasant time. The grandson Charles there. We purchase yeastcake & creamcake & doughnuts, and ride home together. Read Assyria, wash all the dishes, write in Journal & acct. book & to Carrie Hazard.

Fri. March. 23rd. 1883—

6. Faucet froze in the closet—window open. Bread unrisen, breakfast late, leave dishes till after school. Florrie. Helen Wayland brings an orange apiece for mother and I, emulating Emma. Arney brings a box of shells for me, also emulating Emma. Emma herself brings nothing but love this morning. Lunch. Note from Miss Gladding. Wash dishes. Go to hear Julia Ward Howe on Maternity. Not new, but good. Stop on errand to Jennie Bucklin. Out, call on Mrs. Taylor for a moment—she saw & stopped me. Knock at Miss Rathbone's door, no reply. Home. No Kate. Paint. Set table. good supper. Clear table & fix things in general. Sew & read.

Sat. March. 24th. 1883.

6. Black stove. Read story in Century. Little Jackson boy to say his sister is sick. Finish Miss Gladding's cards. Buy stamps—60 cts. Get chloroform for mother .50 [cents]. Gym. Run a mile. Lesson to the Bushes. 75 cts. Change Rawlinson for 2nd vol. at Pub. Lib. Miss G.—Strokes gathers & I sew the yoke on to my chemiloon. Dinner. She plays & I sew. Boy's Room. Same little ruffians I had last time come and *ask* for more books! Show 'em animals & "Uncivilized Races." [21] Home with Fanny Manchester. Glorious night. Letter from Walter. Bless him. Write in Journal & acct. book. Oranges. bed.

Sun. March. 25th. 1883.

6. Easter Sunday. Clear March weather. S. S. mostly singing. Church. Home with Harry Manchester. Read novel & think about next chap. Dine. Dishes. George Earnest Mann (Gave me 6 gorgeous cards today;) calls for me, and we walk down together to the Easter Service. Very pleasant, the most enjoyable S. S. service I ever heard. Home with Max Mauran. Dress. Supper.

Mon. March. 26th. 1883.

6. Encourage cheerfulness by singing. Florrie. Sew. Miss Murphy to dinner. Go to Mabel's, stopping at Tibbetts & Shaw & reading about alcoholic effects. Delight Mabel with a spirited boy & crocodile scene. Stop at Millie's & read Browning to her. Home. Sup on seven oranges, reading Assyria as at all times. Write in J[ournal]. & novel.

Tues. March. 27th. 1883.

6. No Florrie. Paint on Anna's placque. Dine. Sew. Lu Manchester calls. Kate. Carlyle. Supper. Write to Walter. Kate goes early. Jim calls with "joke" to fix. Sam later and we play whist till 10.30. S & I 6 to 1!

Wed. March. 28th. 1883.

Ere 6. Read before breakfast. Florrie. Good talk with her. Lunch. Lace boots give out past mending. Get old buttoned ones. Maude. $2.00. Chase car & catch it. Stop at Tibbitts & Shaw & get cards that were left. $3.00. Buy two blocks—40 cts. Christ. Mayer declines making my boots & I order some at Pierces. He lets me take his placque home to retouch. Home. Henrietta here. Hot supper. Clear table & write. Am feeling unusually well & strong.

Thurs. March. 29th. 1883.

5.45. Read. Florrie. Letter from Walter. Dine. Call for Florrie & we go to the gym. Run mile. Call on Lu Hill at the Torrey's. Out. Go to Grace Channings & stay to dinner. See her uncle Mr. O'Connor and have inspiriting talk with him. Bible Class. Home. Walter here. Bed 11.30.

Fri. March. 30th. 1883.

6. Florrie is growing. Read, dine, sew, draw little rose, brush off front steps (snowed all day mostly) review my calendar, Kate, Carlyle, finish him. Supper extra good—"dig". Sew, read, Assyria. Home with Kate. bed 10.10

Sat. March. 31st. 1883.

5.45. Most glorious morning. Rose out in the parlor. Black stove. Wash dishes. Paint on Jim's thing. Stop at Florrie's for book. Call for Connie Pitman & go down with her. Run 50 laps, and do lots of other work—Louise Mauran there. Grace Channing came in—partly to see me perform. Wait on steps for Miss Gladding. See Walter a moment. Miss G. & I call on Mrs. Colonel Brown. A beautiful home. I call on Lu Hill. Out. Shop with Miss G. Get tidy cotton—10 cts. Home with Miss G. She gives me violets, ribbon, & 3.50 to buy slippers. Go to the Boy's Room for last time. Home alone leaving others at café. Find Walter had been here with a lot of violets for me.

Sunday, April 1st. 1883—

5.45. Fair bright and cold. S. S. Desultory lecture on justifiable homicide. I must reform. Church. Good sermon, starting good thoughts. Home alone, briskly. Write part of a poem. Edward, Mary & Alice. Anna. Wash dishes. Read. Jim. Dress. Read. Walter. We are happier.

Mon. April 2nd. 1883.

5.45. Mend dress & stocking and write in this before breakfast. We have changed our rooms about—since Sat. Take 1.45 car to Beane's, and get my long desired red slippers. [$]3.50. Buy pair of black hose—lisle thread— 87 cts. Go & show 'em to Miss Gladding, who was calling at the Brown's on Aborn st. Meet Tudie Mauran & walk about with her and leave her at Jennie's. Home. Exhibit footwear with but little appreciation, sup, write.

Tues. April. 3rd. 1883—

5.30. Paint on Anna's placque. Maria to tea. Sew. Dress. Go with Walter to see Janauschek in "Marie Stuart." [22] She fine, support poor. Bed by 11.30.

Wed. April. 4th. 1883—

6. The letter we sent to George MacDonald returns, thanks to mother's address, after manifold wanderings. Go to Maude's. [$]2.00. Walk to #3 Sutton St. & call on Lu Hill. Dear Girl! Am very glad to see her. Walk to her aunt's on Meeting st. with her. Stop for a moment at Connie Pitman's on way home; (she knocked for me.) Sup on 9 oranges & a little beside. Sew, finishing 3rd chemiloon. Trimmed a bit.

Thurs. April. 5th. 1883—

5.30. Study Assyria. No Florrie. Finish chap. in our novel, make apron, study. Dine, read a bit in the 19th Century Walter lent me, Go to Gym. Run mile. Buy Sapolis for Mrs. Springer, water crackers, 2 cents, and go to Grace Channing's. Mr. O'Connor had left for me a beautiful new copy of "Leaves of Grass." Walt. Whitman is an intimate friend of his. I am obliged to decline, as I had promised Walter I would not read it. Bible Class. Home. Jim & Sam here playing whist. Retire at 10.

Fri. April. 6th. 1883.

5.30. Note to Mr. O'Connor. Letter from Robert with job. Florrie. Mrs. Diman & children call. Fix hat, sack & parasol. Write part of essay. Read. Kate. Arabian Nights. Supper. Mr. & Mrs. Jastrum. Whist. I finish white skirt, read & knit & then play. Bed by 11 or so.

Sat. April 7th. 1883—

5.30. Black stove. Write in essay. Thoroughly clean out my room, sweeping twice & then wiping over with damp cloth. Wash china things & some paint, shake bedclothes, &c. &c. Dress. Walk from here to Pub. Lib. & back to gym. in half an hour. Run mile &c. Leave books at Ath. .02, lesson to the Bushes .75. Home. Dine, reading. Nap for an hour. Read a little Rossetti. Write essay. Supper. Finish essay & write to Miss Alden. Note to Eva Webster.

Sun. April 8th. 1883.

5.30. Mend petticoat & write most of a sermon for the boys. Was off in good season, had on spring suit & waterproof, felt unusually clean and nice in every way, and met a female who confidently remarked, "I presume you're a livin'-out girl, aren't you?" Such is human vanity. Home alone. Arrange top drawer a little & make beds. Dinner. Anna, C. & C., Mary, R. & A. all in. Dishes. Play with children. Bit of a nap, read some, draw on Robert's card, read Rossetti. Dress. Walter. We have the back room & wood fire. He is not coming any more.[23] Went at 11.15. (Simply to anticipate the parting & save pain.) Dear Love! Shall I come back?

Mon. April. 9th. 1883—

5.30. Fix some popcorn for tooth exercise. Florrie bright & early. Letter from St. Nicholas, very kindly declining things I sent 'em. Off betimes, buy lisle thread, gloves, 4 buttons, 48 cts. Go to Mabel's. Goodbye call on Lu Hill at the Torrey's. I like that girl much. Home. Letter from Martha. Answer it. Sup & read. Sew on the chemiloon. Jim. Sew. Knit. Talk. Go to bed at 10.15. Not a wasted moment.

Tues. April. 10th. 1883.

5.30. Read before breakfast. Card from Kate—her sister-in-law dead & she off to N.Y. Florrie. Dine. Run around, and leave word for Lu to come over. Alone all P.M. & paint on Soapine card. Wash dinner dishes. Sew. (My pain & sorrow is all behind & underneath as yet. The least line of kindred thought in poetry brings all the ache and tears, but by myself I wont* think about it.) Sam calls, and then Ben Wells. Whist. Wearisome.

Wed. April 11th. 1883.

5.20. Read. Breakfast at 7. Florrie. We jump. Dine. Go to Maude's, stopping at Calders. [$]2.25. Stop to see Millie. Mrs. Cooley gives me a chicken! Home. Sup. Write to Uncle Edward about a place. Edward Brown calls. Whist. He & I beat of course. Leave them at 10.15.

Thurs. April 12th. 1883—

5.45. Read. S. H. letter, good report. Florrie. Letter from Eva with catalogue. Call at Mrs. Diman's. Stop for Connie Pitman but she doesn't go. Gym. Only one there. Run mile etc. Not much work. Talk with Mrs. Neylan. Get boots at Pierce's; good calf ones, $5.00. Go to the Slicer's to supper. Very pleasant time. B. C. Home in the wet. (Thunder & lightening). Folks out. Eat oranges, write herein and accts. & bed.

Fri. April 13th. 1883—

5.30–35. Read. Am having a pleasant little fit of mending loose ends just now. The beginning of the clearance preparatory to departure. No Florrie. Another S. H. letter with map & ex[am]. q[uestion]s. Sew on skirt & finish & trim 4th chemiloon. Learn Rossetti's "Soothsay", & read a few others. Dine. Finish Soapine card, mend, arrange in top draw, Kate. Begin Carlyle's "French Revolution"; A grand pleasure. Supper. Read a little more. Kate goes ere 8. Write & read.

Sat. April 14th. 1883—

5.30. Wash yestdy's dinner & supper dishes, (black stove) wash dishes, sweep kitchen very thoroughly beside regular work. Go to gym, buying a box of Pears Glycerine Soap—60 cts. Run mile &c. Leave boots to have heels fixed. Buy stationery 70 cts. Lacing, elastic, pins, 14 cts. Pub. Lib. Read Punch, Pop. Sci., & gather facts on adulteration. Go to Millie's & read her Rossetti. Mr. Slicer called there. Ride home. Mother sick today—pain in her chest. Mix bread. Sup. Ben Wells calls. I sew. Goes at 10.15 about. A little tired.

Sun. April 15th. 1883.

5.45 Mother still sick. Breakfast & dishes. S.S. Talk about lying. Church. Fought with sleep. Home with Lu, *and* her mother & May Bel Hill. Cross.

Home. Help serve dinner. Start to write to Cassie, doze half an hour perhaps.
Wash dishes, and revive mother with a little percussion. Call on Miss Glad-
ding at Mrs. Masons above here. Harold Mason a dear baby, kissed me. Home.
Sup on crackers, cheese, milk, & Media. Go up stairs and write 4 sheets to
Walter. Read a little Rossetti. Cry a good deal. Bed before 11.

April 16th. 1883.

5.30. Get breakfast. Florrie. Finish 2nd white skirt. Dine. Go to Mabel's.
Stop & get brown paper for Louise Diman. Stop for boots. Not done. Get 3 big
envelopes at Tibbitts & Shaws. $.02. Call on Grandma Anthony. Stop to see
if Prof. Blake has Ancient atlas. Hasn't. Home quickstep. "Percuss" mother,
Sup, write

Tues. April. 17th. 1883.

5.30. This day died at 3.20 A.M. Isabel Jackson. Her mother sends me a note
at breakfast time, enclosing a gold pen I left there, and a cuff-pin I let Bella
wear one day. Answer in time for the postman. Florrie. Write a little poem to
Mrs. Jackson.[24] Dine lightly alone. Mother goes to ride with Mrs. Vaughn. I
give my first lesson to Louise & and Emily Diman. $.75 therefor. Beg a few
snowdrops which I take to Mrs. Jackson with my verses. The little brother
comes to the door. O I am grieved to lose her!

Wed. April. 18th. 1883.

5.30. Send letter to Cassie. Florrie & I measure feet, draw outline of boot sole
& then stand on it in stocking feet. Our *feet* are the same size. She is much
impressed. Dine alone. Leave knit belt for Connie. Go to Maude. Mrs. Mason
in the car out. Confides to me Maude's failings. I retouch some spots on her
wallpaper. $2.00. Get boots. $.25 for heels. Call on Mrs. Blodgett—Minnie Torrey that was. Home. sup. Evening watching Belinda,[25] who became a
happy mother at 10.30. Again at 11 or so, and again, I don't know when, as I
went to bed and to sleep with the furry family snugly ensconced at the foot of
the bed. Read a little.

Thurs. April 19th. 1883.

5.15. No Florrie. Spend morning in my room looking over closet and drawers.
More clothes than I thought I had. Go to Gymn. Skin my hands again on
rope. Look at Art. Ex. in Tilden's. Stop at Tibbitts & Shaw's and buy 10 ct.
book "Diseases of Modern Life," Richardson. Go to the Brown's to supper.
Maria gives me a pair of L[ea]th[er]. gloves. Discussion on gossip. Bible Class,
last meeting. I borrow April "Modern Review" of Mr. Slicer. Home. Jim
here. Argue, fruitlessly. Stays late. Bed at 11. Found note from Dr. Jackson
thanking me, and asking me to come and see them about painting a boquet.

Fri. April. 20th. 1883.

5.45–50. Call at Florrie's, not coming; call at the Jackson's, and bring home magnificent big cluster of roses to paint for them. Am to do it on black satin. Give me [$]2.00 to get it with. I post down to Gladdings & get 1¼ yds. = [$]2.81. Go to Calder's get 5 brushes, & pay him $5.00 on acct. Walk home from Mathewson st. in 20′. Rest a little & eat (orange breakfast,) shut myself up in little room, and paint about 5 hours. Tired. Put things up at 4.30 & read a little. Set table, sup, read more, write in this & finish letter to Ada. In bed at 10.

Sat. April 21st. 1883.

5. Black stove & sweep kitchen. Read. Do dishes etc. Read. Transfer book at Pub. Lib. (Received letter from Uncle Edward & answered it.) Gym. Nice girl there—Miss Richards—father the minister at St. Johns. Like her. Lesson to the Bushes. Not a good one, they didn't feel like it. .75 cts. Home. Dine. Nap til 3.15. Carry my things up stairs and paint on the roses from 3.30 til 6.30. Clean up, come down to supper, mix bread. Write in Jour[nal]. & Acct. & sermon on Justifiable Lying for my boys.

Sun. April. 22nd. 1883.

5. Work all done ere 8, and paint an hour. S. S. & read a sermon on Justifiable Lying. Against it. Dr. Hedge preaches. Home. Paint half an hour. Dine & wash dishes. Paint 2 hours in the cold till a southerly rain made me shut blinds & stop. Down stairs, rest a bit, look over Century, write to C. A. Hedge, because the Dr. said she had been ill. Sup. Upstairs & write to Walter. Sleepy.

Mon. April 23rd. 1883.

6! about. Blinds shut & watch stopped. Florrie. Spend most of the morning in talking to her about life and progress. Dine. Mabel's. $2.00. Leave shoes at Pierces to be stretched lengthways. Call at Sheldon's Auction rooms for mother. See a big mirror I'd like to own. Call on Connie Pitman & have a good talk with her; on Will mostly. Home. Sup. Write sketch of Media. Bed.

Tues. April 24th. 1883.

5.40. Letter from Cassie, & Mrs. C. Howden Smith. Florrie. Copy "Domicile erected by John" for Mrs. S. & answer her letter. Flo. stays to dinner. Lesson to the Diman's. [$]1.00. Home. Write letter. Kate. Carlyle. Supper. (Took notes of Aunt C. & Kate's conversation). Write. Cleared snow paths this morning*! ! !*

April. 25th. 1883—

5.45. Write note to Lu Hill. Florrie stays to paint and dinner. Go to Maude's. She tells me her side of her troubles & I advise her as best I can. Stop and get boots. Home. Paint till 6.30. nearly. Sup. Read Babylonia & then the Century. Full day, not unhappy. (Johnny Rounds froze his hand driving this morning!)

Thurs. April 26th 1883.

5.15 or 10. Get breakfast mostly. Florrie. Much interested in a study of felt skirt she is making. Dine. Stop on Florrie, & we go to Gym. Met Minnie Eddy at door, and she and F. watch the performances with much delight. Go up to Wolf's with Miss Richards, Louise Diman, Ellie Congdon, & Annie Vernon; and walk home with the same as far as Cooke & Manning. Two leaving by the way. Read Babylon before the fire. Mrs. Sturgiss Carpenter calls. Mend gloves. Arrange dress & go to and see Tudie Mauran. Take knitting & stay till 9.15. Max, though somewhat ill, will come down to see me. Pleasant evening. Home in car, at mother's request & provision. Find that Walter has been here, expecting to find me out, and left note, & sonnets. Answer. Not in bed before 11.35 or so.

Fri. April. 27th. 1883—

5.45. Mother up early by mistake. Florrie, very wide-eyed. Dinner a little late, & pepper soup at that. Paint on roses. Mrs. Manchester calls, and I, being alone, have to entertain her. Do so amiably & successfully. Paint. Sup on dates. Finish this 2nd vol. of Rawlinson & write. Have begun to practice knitting & reading as a special endeavor.

Sat. April. 28th. 1883.

5.30. Black stove. Wash dishes. Sweep my room. Gym. Buy 4 pair hose, $1.00. Go to Pub. Lib. & get 3rd vol. Raw[linson's]. "5 G[rea]t. Mon-[archies]. etc." Read to Millie. Miss Gladdings to dinner. Get shoe brush & blacking at Pierces. 50 cts. for brush, b. nothing. Change braid at Gladding's. Ride home as it rains. Black shoes. Write part of sermon on "Habits". Ben Wells calls. Read it to him & he criticizes. I enjoy it. Sam comes, but goes in the other room. Only wanted to know if I could paint a jacqueminot rose. Tell him no. Goes. Mr. W. reads "Pomona's Daughter["] to us all, and then Bab Ballads to me. Goes at 10.10. Mother tries to talk to me about Mr. Stetson, & blames him somewhat. I refuse to give any information.

Sunday April 29th. 1883.

5.30 or so. Get breakfast. Finish sermon. S. S. in snowstorm. 3 boys, &, later, 4. Read them sermon. on "Habits." Church. Home with Edward to dinner. *In snowstorm.* Read in Babylonia. Dinner. Clarence calls. Wash dishes. Go to see Lu, and stay to tea. Home by 7.30. E. still here. Go upstairs and write to Walter, not to send, he does not wish it. Bed, ere ten.

Mon. April 30th. 1883.

5.30. Refasten buttons on my dress. So clear cool and bright a morning that I prepare a walk & Florrie & I take one forthwith. Fully 6 miles I should say, for we were gone 2½ hours or more. She then does a little arithmetic, & writes an account of our walk. Well done too. Paint on roses from 3 to 6.30. Sup, Mother goes to cousin Julia Jastrum's to play whist. Aunt C. retires at 9; and I very contentedly finish "Babylon", keeping myself awake with knitting. Bed ere

Tues. May Day 1883—

Just before 5. Mend dress, and roll out cookies. Note from Mrs. Jackson, crape edged. Florrie. Write inquiring note to Boston Ad. Dine. Lesson to the Diman's; they wish it was two hours. 50 cts. Home. Cousin Julia, Eddie & little Julia call. Make friends with the latter. Kate, riding with her brother George. Carlyle. Tea. Walk down with Kate, get licorice drops for mother, post letters, and stop at the Brown's for cream. Home. settle up accounts.

Wed. May. 2nd. 1883.

5.15. Get breakfast. Mother sick; can't talk, "dumb!", dismiss her scholars. Florrie stays with her while I go for Dr. Wilcox & post letters. Note from Mrs. Jackson, & Edward Brown with enclosed gift of $5.00! Stay with mother some P.M. Paint some. Went after Fannie Manchester, & she comes over afterwards, and is to take charge tomorrow. Get mother some toast, &c. &c. get her to bed. Wrote to Edward, Cassie, and painted card for Will Mauran to whose birthday supper I am invited tomorrow night.

Thurs. May. 3rd. 1883—

5. Mother still sick. Get breakfast etc. Florrie. Fannie Manchester helps mother teach. Get dinner and clear away. Go down town and do errands. Stamps 50 cts. Gym. Mrs. Neylan interferes with me for the first time; prohibiting my doing the travelling rings with Annie Wilkinson. Walk up with Annie. Call on Sophie Aborn—out—going out west soon. Home. See to mother, make bread &c. &c., dress, & go to Willie Mauran's birthday supper. He was much pleased with his card and its inscription. A rich and palatuble [*sic*] feast. Patience step, games, and good time. I am solicited to repeat something, give 'em "The Domicile Erected by John", and start on "Keenan's Charge" but forget it. Read "The Hermit and Rosalind." Banana icecream, homemade, luxurious. Home with Will. Bed by 11. Pleasant evening.

Fri. May 4th. 1883.

5.40. No Florrie. Paint pansies as I did yesterday. Fannie Manchester again. Aunt C. goes to Anna's for 24 hours. Make beeftea for mother. Finish pansies. Very pretty. Kate. Supper. Sarah Bullock calls.

Sat. May 5th. 1883.

5 just before. Do all the usual work, and sweep mother's room and the kitchen upstairs. Go to the gym. Nice time, lots of work. An exhibition is proposed by some of us, and Mrs. Neylan gladly accedes. Erands for mother, and call on Mrs. Dr. Wilcox to show her some of my work. She admires it. See the Dr. and tell him more about mother. Gives me some more medicine for her. Home. Aunt C. back again. Rest a little bit, get dinner, eat heartily, sleep from 3 to 4.30 nearly. Begin essay on Babylonia, and write sermon on "Accuracy." Wait on mother of course.

Sun. May. 6th. 1883.

5.40. All the work and dishes. S.S. Not a successful sermon, and two "casual visitors" at that. Mrs. Bliss said she thought I had the most flourishing class in S. S! Church. See Mrs. Mauran on way out. Harry Manchester home from church and down to Red Bridge with me. Soup for dinner. Mary and Alice call. Wash dishes. Arrange second drawer, hose, &c. Sam calls and brings me some black birch tassells. Stays about two hours. Talk of "waiting," and hotels. Supper. Edward calls. I retire, finish drawer & write to Walter. I am missing him.

Mon. May 7th. 1883—

Just before 5. Write on essay. Do housework. S.H. letter. No Florrie. Finish essay & write note to Miss Alden. Mend dress. Paint. Arrange for a bit of gymnasium in my room, just to lift myself. Get dinner & clear away. Go to Mabel's, reading Babylonia. Stop at Mrs. Blake's to see Carrie Hazard who arrives at about 6. Nice talk with her, tell her about things. Home. Sup. Henrietta. Sew braid on felt skirt and read Socrates, a nice little translation given me by Mrs. Blake.

Tues. May. 8th. 1883.

5:15–20. Dressed by 8.30. Florrie. Get dinner—soup, & clear away. A *little* waste time & then to the Diman's 75 cts. Home & rip Carrie Bissell's dress, reading Persia. Mother goes to ride with Mrs. Fillinghast & feels better. Kate late. Griddlecakes for supper. Do not read it is so hot. Play "everlasting" with mother, knit & read Socrates.

Wed. May. 9th. 1883.

5.15–20. Wash dishes. Thomase's 24th birthday. Florrie. Read her some of my selfmade rules & stimuli & write her some. Dinner & clear it away. Go to Maude's. Get N.Y. Herald. Call on Jessie Taylor, long talk, like her. Overtake Mrs. Dexter on way home & stop to see her pink magnolia. Home. Sup. make bread. Answer an ad. from the Herald.

Thurs. May 10th. 1883.

About 5. Rip. House work. S. H. letter. Florrie, draggy. Aunt C. out; dine on biscuit and molasses. Letter from Ada. Gym. Interview the present owner, Mr. Smith, as to the prospects. Work a good deal, doing ladders & rings with Annie Wilkinson. Kate stops for me, we have some soda, are joined by Miss Wheeler, and call on Sarah Eddy together. She paints. I particularly admired some dandelion ghosts and "Pseuisis", her kitten. "P s e u i s i s s". Indian name. Home, sup, begin Socrates & knitting when Sam calls & afterward Edward. Whist. E. & S. bet a creamcake, then creamcakes, then bananas, & then candy on the play; and Edward lost every time. I retired at 10 or a bit after. Sorry I countenanced the betting.

Fri. May. 11th. 1883.

5:20–30. Make fire, etc. Murder a kitten with chloroform & bury it in the back yard.[26] No Florrie. Read Persia. Paint on roses. Get dinner. Letter from Mrs. Smith. Clear away things. Cut out corset covers P.M. Down stairs at 5 or so & write till Kate comes. Carlyle. Get supper, frying little mashed potato cakes. Lu Manchester calls. Kate goes early. I see Lu home. Back again, slippers, clear away again, read Socrates and knit. Bed! Mother gave me a dollar.

Sat. May. 12th. 1883.

5.15–20. Black stove, wash dishes etc. Sweep my room. (Letter with circular answering my answer to ad. in Herald. Blank sheet from Walter.) Gym. early, interviewing Dr. Brooks on subject of report. Good work. Read to Millie, "Pearls of the Faith."[27] Go to Miss Gladdings, sew on waists. Dine; sew. Pub. Lib. & look up Sokrates for S. S. class. Renew Persia. Home. Mix bread. Start to write on S. but am too tired & sleepy. Read a bit in Science.

Sun. May. 13th. 1883—

5. (almost) 7½ hours sleep! Write a little on S. & read him while getting breakfast. Wash dishes. S. S. with Knight Richmond. I like him. The boys enjoy Sokrates very much. Church. Good Pentecostal sermon, but too long. Home briskly alone. A Glorious Day! Set table & help take up things. Dinner. Talk a good deal before washing dishes, not through before four. Finish Ada's letter, short one to Harry Manchester, & begin one to Thomas. Nap between somewhere. Mrs. Jarvis calls. See her few moments. Write note to Walter and some lines to keep.

Mon. May. 14th. 1883.

Before 5. Write letter to Y.W.C.A. in N.Y. Florrie. Personal expenses for arithmetic. (Card from Carrie Hazard.) Dine & clear away somewhat. Mabel's.

Walked down with Mr. Burroughs & missed car. Read in Tibbitt's while waiting. "Mable" draws heads, draws them well. Call on Connie Pitman, & learn
much about the *horror* of modern society. I knew it before, but this was face
to face. Go to see Mrs. Jackson about lessons to Eddie. Poor little woman!
Home. Sup. Mix bread. Walter calls! O I was *glad* to see him! Jim comes with
an order. I excuse myself and stay with Walter. Goes at 10.30. Jim a bit late.
Bed without bath or journal and get 6½ hours sleep. Heavy rain in the night.

≈

SEVEN

"A despicable boy"

May 15, 1883–October 5, 1883

WITHIN a few weeks after Isabel Jackson's death, Mrs. Jackson approached Charlotte to propose that she serve as governess to Isabel's young brother, Eddie. When the plans were finalized in late May for Charlotte to commence work in July, she could hardly contain her excitement. The position seemed to offer precisely the kind of independence that she had been seeking. Charlotte ran "gaily home" to trumpet the news, but her mother and Aunt Caroline received it "with disapprobation." Undeterred by their disapproval, however, Charlotte maintained her high spirits all through the following week. "Felt particularly happy in the still warm moonrise. Awake early, still thankful and glad." And just a few days earlier, she had agreed—very suddenly—to marry Walter. The May 20 allusion to her decision is brief and matter-of-fact, betraying the ambivalence that Charlotte was undoubtedly working hard to suppress: "Walter. I have promised to marry him. (Robert called.) Happy." Whatever romantic notions she may have entertained about her impending employment and her subsequent marriage, they carried her happily through the next several weeks.

In her autobiography Charlotte remains vague about her sudden decision to marry Walter Stetson: "At one time when he had met a keen personal disappointment, I agreed to marry him. After that, in spite of reactions and misgivings, I kept my word, but the period of courtship was by no means a happy one," she wrote (p. 83). Walter, however, was more candid about the "keen personal disappointment" that he had suffered. He confides to his journal his decision to solicit from a friend, American art editor and author Charles de Kay, an opinion about the quality of the sonnets that he frequently wrote during spare moments (*Endure*, pp. 187–90). Walter apparently fancied himself a serious poet, and he was devastated by de Kay's assessment that his verse was mediocre at best, that it should be considered a source of "amusement of vacant hours, not a serious matter for publication" (p. 187). A passionate man, Walter poured onto the pages of his journal his humiliation over his fatuous blindness in believing that the sonnets had aesthetic merit. His depression, undoubtedly exacerbated by mounting debts as he struggled to survive on an emerging artist's salary, lasted for days. He wrote an impassioned plea to Charlotte, imploring her to burn the sonnets that he had previously sent. So tortured was Walter by his friend's criticism, and so shaken was his confidence, that he began to doubt the value of all of his artistic endeavours, even burning his old journal, consisting of "939 pages of foolscap" (p. 189). When Walter went to visit Charlotte later that evening, she was so affected by his emotional state that she vowed to marry him. (A couple of days later, she pleaded with Walter that he not force her to burn his sonnets, and he agreed; many of those that survive appear in Appendix B).

A few days later, before leaving Providence for a week's visit to Martha Lane and other friends in Massachusetts, Charlotte and Grace Channing, with whom she was spending more and more time since Martha's departure, paid a visit to Walter at his studio. "Dress and go for Grace Channing, and we call on Walter. She was much pleased with him and his work. Which pleased me much, as I value her, & any favorable criticism is an agreeable change." Years later, Grace would become the new Mrs. Stetson after his divorce from Charlotte.

On June 30 Charlotte left Providence again, this time for a two-week visit to Ogunquit, Maine. She passed her time reading, sketching, napping on the rocks, and spending a good deal of time with her friend Conway Brown, who would die from a self-inflicted gunshot wound less than six months later. Charlotte's diary reported that during a walk on July 9, young Conway had allowed her to "try his revolver," and she was pleased to have hit "4 shots out of 10." She also spent time with Conway counseling him and comforting him as he confided to her his suicidal impulses. (Charlotte's grief upon learning of his death is reflected in her diary entry of January 1, 1884. Later that summer, Charlotte learned that Sidney Putnam, who had introduced her to Walter, had drowned. Walter speculated that Putnam's death may have been a suicide; see *Endure*, pp. 221–22.)

After returning to Providence, Charlotte began work as Eddie Jackson's governess on July 16. She proudly remarked on her new arrangement in her diary. "Become a hireling as I phrase it for the admiration of my friends, at 5.35 [p.m.]," she wrote contentedly. She and Eddie seemed to hit it off immediately, and they spent hours playing billiards, baseball, and battledore. Charlotte also taught him sewing, reading, math, and drawing, and she was obviously pleased with the relationship that she and Eddie shared. But by early August, during which time she accompanied the Jackson family to Moosehead Lake, Maine, her patience with Eddie was wearing thin. "His mother *says* he must go to bed at 8, but lets him play come-as-you-come & sit up & sit up till almost nine!" Two days later she commented disparagingly, "Can't say I love these folk." By August 29 the honeymoon was clearly over, and by September 9 Charlotte wanted out of the arrangement. "Eddie rather ruder than usual to me. Can I stand it all winter?

'M-m-m!" As it turned out, Mrs. Jackson announced a few days later that she planned to enroll Eddie in school that winter, which meant that Charlotte would be out of a job. Charlotte was overjoyed; the ten weeks with Eddie, "a despicable boy," had seemed like an eternity. As she drolly remarked in her autobiography over forty years later, she "learned more about the servant question in that time than most of us ever find out" (p. 69).

On October 2 Charlotte returned to Providence. "Leave bundles [in the depot] & go straight to Walter. A happy morning," she wrote. But almost inevitably, the happiness only postponed the pain.

Tues. May 15th. 1883.

5.40 or so. Florrie. Suggest girls club to oppose "fastners". Dine. Write note to Walter. Am unhappy. Lesson to the Dimans. .75 [cents]. Lesson 1st to Eddie Jackson. Prospect of being his governess. No Kate. Mend Emma Vaughan's doll. Read Persia & knit a little. Supper. Beat mother two games of chess. Ben Wells calls. Talk to him about real things and enjoy it—somewhat. I can think well of him and be in some ways sorry for him; but I do not "like" or revere him. Note from Robert with dollar, due on card. (In) bed by 10.40. The first night I have cried because I couldn't help it. That is couldn't help *wanting* to.

Wed.
May. 16th. 1883.

5.33 or so. Work. Florrie. Talk to her, as I often do late. Letter from Cassie. Dine. Go to Maude's. Stop at Calders & get paper for Mable & cards for self. Home. (Persia with me of course.) Maria here. Set table. Start Jim's sabbatias. Write agonized letter to Walter. Post it. Edward calls. Retire, & write. Gym. sketch, report, what d'you-call-it. Bed by

Thurs. May. 17th. 1883.

5. Note to Walter. Florrie. Letter from Harry Manchester. Dine. Go to gym. Run 15 laps; lazy, all of us. Wait ten minutes for Florrie, and then straight home. Finish Sabbatia card for Jim. Sup. Arrange dress a little. Sew. Walter comes, bless his heart! Happy evening. Goes at 10.30—45.

Fri. May 18th. 1883.

5.45 or 50! All through by 8.30. Letter from Walter, & one from Y.W.C.A., N.Y. And "Science" from Harry Man[chester] etc. Florrie. She does improve. Dine & clear away. Write to Walter. Paint on Anna's plaque. Kate. No one at home but I. Take her up to my room which she likes. Sup. Mother comes back from a raid on Cal Swamps, tired. Walk part way with Kate & stupidly forget to post letter till on way back! Write gym. thing.

Sat. May. 19th. 1883.

5. Black stove. Copy article on gym. Take it to Journal office. Mr. Danielson, (edtr.) not in. (Give it to Dr. Brooks & he don't want to offer it. Send it to Carrie Hazard to put in if she will.) Gym. & work well. Maria Brown comes to see me. So do Marry Saunders & Grace Channing, the latter with advice from her uncle to try for a Washington clerkship. I will not, on principle. Talk with Dr. Brooks & with Mr. Smith against Mrs. Neylan as teacher. Go to Pub. Lib. & write about Mohammed. Get Koran to show my boys. Call for a moment on Miss Gladding. Conditionally buy crimson Jersey. Home. Walter had been here and left me some heliotrope. Mrs. John Mason calls. Emma Vaughn brings me violets. Go to Connie Pitman's to dinner. Evening with her and good talk. Home by 10.20.

Sun. May. 20th. 1883.

5.40. Sweep kitchen. Do not feel well! and avoid washing dishes. S. S. with Mrs. Rawson. Mohammed well received. Church. Mr. Collier of Hingham preaches—the grandest preaching I remember to have heard. Grand! and his prayers were *prayers*. Speak to Annie Aborn afterward & am—*jangled* by her inappreciation. Home with Harry Manchester. Dine. Koran. Dishes. Mary, Anna, Clarence, Charlie, Parson, Eddie, & little Julia call. Read part of Century. Nap. Retta calls for a few minutes, but can't see her to speak to. Sup. Dress. Walter. I have promised to marry him. (Robert called.) Happy.

Parlor fire out!
Monday. May 21st. 1883.

6!, meant to; but find mother up and getting breakfast. Parlor goes out & we let it! No Florrie. Mark hose & finish Anna'a placque. Write little letter to Walter. dine. Go to Mabel's. She draws leaves. Get oatmeal. Call on Retta & stay to tea. Good talk with her. She does me *good*. Prescott Clark calls. Nice little talk & home by 8.40. Bed.

Tues. May. 22nd. 1883.

Near 6. No Florrie. File all Walter's letters, and write to him. Jessie Kimball stays to dinner as it *rains*. Lesson to Eddie Jackson. Call at Anna's. Mother there. Home with her, calling to see Florrie & her mother. Home. Sup & read Century. Beat mother two games of chess, the last a good one. Read Cen[tury]. and knit. Up stairs by 8.50.

Wed. May 23rd. 1883

Down by 6. My article on Prov. Ladies Gym. comes out in the Journal. Note from Carrie Hazard saying she had sent it. Florrie. Dine. Go to Maude's. $5.00. Pub. Li. & change Koran for Persia again. Ath. & change "Pearls of the Faith" for "Daughters of an Egyptian King."[1] Home. Read. Sup. dress.

Wait. Walter comes, bless him; happy evening. My watch stopped at 10.20 & he stayed till 10.45 by reason thereof. Dear boy! Mrs. Jackson called & wants me to come and see them about the governess plan.

Thurs. May. 24th. 1883.

Down by 6. Again arrange to meet Florrie & get Pub. Li. card. Go to Gym. Full class, much fun. Wait for F[lorrie]. Does not come. Leave word at Root's to remove stove. Home. Write note to Carrie Hazard, and a little to Walter. Help mother with whips, table, etc. Go and see the Jacksons. Am engaged as governess for Eddie to begin in July. Run gaily home to tell. Sam here. News received with disapprobation by mother and Aunt. Edward with "banquet". We have salad & whips etc. Whist. Bed by 11.30. Mrs. Fillinghast gave me silk skirt & waist, & thin white overdress.

Fri. May. 25th. 1883.

Down by 6. Last of Florrie's term. Letter from Walter. Lesson to the Diman's. Mrs. D. is delighted with my teaching. Home & read W[alter]'s letter and answer and post. Try on Mrs. F[illinghast]'s gift, very pretty. Read "E. Princess". Kate. Read "Light of Asia["] to her and mother. Mr. & Mrs. Jastram to tea. Old Mr. Carpenter calls. Home today from the west. Has seen father & Thomas. Kate goes. He goes. Whist. Gave mother 5 more dollars on board— 15 since March 22nd. 1 from her for housework.

Sat. May 26th. 1883.

5. Bed last night at a little after 11. Felt particularly happy in the still warm moonrise. Awake early, still thankful and glad. Wash dishes and go to the first Annual exhibition of Prov. Ladies Gymnasium. Aunt C. went with Julia Jastram. A crowd of ladies to see us. All do well. Mrs. Neylan some fine club swinging. Lesson to Miss Ellie Bush between 1 & 2. Dine at Mr. Slicers, and start to prepare lesson there, but am reminded of its being a memorial Sunday. Home reading "D[aughters]. of an E[gyptian]. K[ing]." Nap. Read a little to wake up. Come down & set table. Read more. Sup. read. Go and spend night at Fannie Manchester's.

Sun. May. 27th. 1883.

5.30. Home by 6. Read. S. S., addresses of a memorial character by Mr. Shaw, Mr. Slicer, & Mr. Parkhurst. 05. Church. Very hard time to keep awake, fail perforce, but not from giving in. Home. Read. Dine. Wash dishes. Finish "D[aughters]. of an E[gyptian]. K[ing]." Finish Mrs. Jackson's roses. Sup. Dress. Walter. Goes by 10.45.

Mon. May 28th. 1883.

5–10. Note from Miss Gladding. Paint cards for mother. Dine. Mabel Mason, paints violets. Call on Millie & on Grace Channing. Stay to dinner there, and nice talk with Grace. Invest $1.00 in "The Alpha" a physiological paper. Home ere 8.30. Go to Fannie M[anchester].'s. Jim calls for me, home & see about card, $.50 & back again & to bed!

Tues. May. 29th. 1883—

5.35 about. Home by 6. Draw & paint on Jims beautiful card. Florrie in with bill, $30.00. Dine. (Letter from Charlotte Hedge A.M.) Lesson to the Diman's. 2 weeks unpaid. Home & get roses on satin & take them down to Mrs. Jackson. Lesson to Eddie. Home. No Kate. Write to Mrs. Jackson asking for pay—[$]22.62. Note to Walter. Sleep at Fannies.

Wed. May 30th. 1883—

Home by 6. Paint all day mostly. Fix silk skirt Mrs. Sheldon gave me. Read a little. Letter from Charlotte Hedge. Anna & Clarence call. Ben Wells calls. Jim calls, & likes pansies. Mr. W. escorts me around to Fannies. Read 1st chapter of James's "Confidence" to her. Mrs. Jackson sent me my bill—$22.63, and I have paid mother all my board bill! Hallelujah! Up to June 1st.!!!

Thurs. May 31st.

Stupidly overslept after waking—6 & after! First time in ever so long. Finish cards for mother & pansies. Read a little. Stop for Florrie & we do go to the Public Library & she gets card and "How to Do it".[2] Errands, Jersey .25 more, cambric .24, braid .07 tooth brush .20, mull 50. F[lorrie]. rides home. Call on Kate & on Jessie Taylor. Stay to tea and walk over with Jennie. *Black* gymnasium shoes! (brought home suit today.) Slept at home.

Fri. June 1st. 1883.

5.30. Paint nearly all day. Finish Jim's card at dusk. Read some in between. Letter from Walter. Last day of mother's school. Four mothers here. Great joy among the children, distribution of mother's "remembrances;" speaking of pieces, etc. Kate at 5 or so. Carlyle. Supper. Mr. Stillwell calls. Leave him at 9 & go to Fannie's. Read a little & bed at 10-15. Kate paid me $18.00

Sat. June 2nd. 1883

4.30. Home by 5. Room swept by 6. Black stove, do usual work, wash dishes, face & braid skirt, finish Persian history, shampoo hair, dine, dress, and off ere 3. Stop at Carrie Richmond's & beg lilies of the valley for Millie & get them. Kate joins me & we walk up together. get soda, (Kate), a man came in and ordered vichy & *ammonia*! & drank it too! Second one I've seen. Call on Millie. Call on Miss Gladding. Pub. Lib. & look at Punch. Kate stops for me & we go down together. Get blue veil .29 [cents], silk braid shoestrings. 09 [cents]. Kate gave me a lovely neckerchief, white with pink edge & spots. Had boots fixed, got oatmeal & yeast cake. (Left books at P. L.) Home. Jim comes for card. $3.00. He was well pleased. Goes to Fannie's with me but Harry had come, so I returned.

Sun. June 3rd. 1883—

5.20. Press dress & sundry neck ties, etc. S. S. with Mrs. Rawson. Tell about Buddha & read parts of "Light of Asia" to my boys. They are averse to the idea of losing me. Say they will have no one else—I *must* come. Pleasant. Walk home with Grace Channing. We are joined by Sarah Russel & she walks with us, more's the pity; & we discuss Rousseau, Balsac, Montaigne, Rabelais, etc. etc. Miss R. strongly conventional and against all such. Stop in and see Grace a moment. She gives me some chocolates. Home. Dine. Fix nails in bootheels to my satisfaction. Wash dishes. Go up in my room & arrange for tomorrow's journey. Anna & Charley down stairs, and some more I should judge by sound. Partly pack bed. Dress. Walter comes. Brings me two sketch books. He finds it very hard to wait. Bed after 11.

Monday. June 4th. 1883—

4.30. Pack. Do usual housework all but dishes. Off before 8. Carry her umbrella & some "Sciences" to Fannie Manchester. Car down st. Take 8.30 train & doze all the way. Arrange toilet in station (Boston) and eat chocolates & banana, & read. Walk up to Dr. Keller's. Wait over an hour contentedly. Good talk with her, personally & professionally. She drives me down to get my bag, then to notify Mr. Smith, & then out to her beautiful home in Jamaica Plain. A delicious lunch, and then I am operated upon by Dr. Betts, who "depilates" me & otherwise attends to my complexion. Then drive about with Dr. Keller, dear woman, and join Mr. Smith in the train at 4.55. Come to West Dedham, drive through lovely scenery to Mrs. Lockes, and after tea and a letter to Walter & card to mother and talk with Mrs. Smith go quietly to bed. Still warm and sweet, with the soft June air blowing through my room, and the low country sounds outside.

Tues. June 5th. 1883.

Up at 6.15–30. Breakfast, card to Rebecca Clarke, ride to the station with the Smith's & back, go to see a lovely little school with Mrs. S. Home. Nap, dinner. Sew & talk. Go to see more school. New ideas. Home. Fine views drive. Read "Homo Sum" till supper. Talk with Mrs. S. & enjoy "Vivian" & "Guinnevere", Tennyson—Doré.

Wed. June 6th. 1883.

6. Pack bag. Breakfast. Down to the station with Mr. S. then drive about slowly with Mrs. then put the team in a stable and visit Avery school. Am pleased interested and instructed. Then we drive to the station & I start for Boston. Mrs. Smith gave me $5.00 for travelling expenses. Stop on sudden thought at Jamaica Plain and call on Dr. Keller. She is a little ill. I ask for her picture and get it. Then I induce her to lie down and tell her some quiet poems. Off in the 12.50 train. Arriving in Boston I make a leisurely toilet and a leisurely dinner at the station, then visit the Art Museum & sketch Venus; then by divers cars to Rebeccas. She is out, not expecting me until tea time, but I am well received and given icewater and Pilgrims Progress. Go to her room and dress, she comes, and we have pleasant talk. Supper. Upstairs to open windows & we have more talk. George comes up, and Helen, and I repeat poetry and we talk. Very pleasant evening. Sleep with Retta, going to sleep while she was waiting for sage remarks. A woman I love & trust. Strength Purity & Courage.

Thurs. June 7th. 1883.

7.30. More talk with Retta. Pack bag. Off by ten. Ride to Kneeland st. & start for Old Colony station, but am ensnared by the Boston and Albany and leave my things there, also getting my ticket for Hingham—as I thought. Traverse the city, buying two fans and some soda—.25—.15—.10, stop at Mr. Smiths & get my old pink fan I had left at Dedham, & go the S. H. meeting. See Miss Alden. Find Eliza Mauran is a member! Talk to several strangers in kindly wise. A dreary address, too long, too slow, & too deep, from President Walker of the Tech. Inst., and one somewhat better from Dr. Bowditch. Go with Miss A. to Fera's and have dinner. An errand or two with her, & then to the cars. Discover that my Hingham ticket was a Needham one, get bag and cloak and we go to the Old Colony station and so to Hingham. Glad to see Martha and she to see me. Rest and dress, she giving me a white sack to replace my hot & dusty dress. Kind & thoughtful. Letter from Walter. Dear heart! Ballad with Martha. Mr. Lane comes. Also glad to see me. Supper. Talk. Martha & I read in "Tale of Two Cities" to him. Bed ere 11.

Fri. June 8th. 1883—

6.5 or so. Note to Walter & card to C. A. Hedge. Write up Journal & accts. Miss Alden calls. Dine. Shampoo Martha. Take "barge" at 3.15 or so. Buy lovely forgetmenots of boy .10 [cents]. Ticket .30 [cents]. Write to Dr. Keller on the way. Car to Temple Pl. Stop at Gas Office & get brush and comb I had left at Dedham. Walk to Cambridge st. Interview numerous horse-cars & finally take one promising to transfer me to Concord Ave. Amd [*sic*] dropped, and wait my transfer, placidly reading Homo Sum. Take next car and am left

near Concord Ave. Inquire at store and readily reach No. 9, Concord Ave. An
ordinary middleaged house, says "Darling" on door. Inquire in same store.
Doesn't know any Mr. Saunders. Directs me across the way to a Mr. Porter.
Coal office. He shows me directory. No Saunders that I want. Suddenly inquires if I do not mean in *Cambridge*! I look at him. Am in *Somerville*! More
directions—Walk to cor. Cambridge & Prospect sts. Wait & wait. Soda $.05.
Finally take car at random, inquiring after C. Ave. Am dropped within easy
walking distance and reach Mary's pretty house a little after 7. Cool supper and
pleasant talk, amusing them much with account of my adventures & journey-
ings with my heavy bag, sack, waterproof, umbrella, two books, three fans,
a package, and a bunch of flowers. A pleasant home and beautiful, and two
happy young people. I have a delightful room. Sent letter to Walter.

Sat. June 9th. 1883—

7-10. A luxurious night's rest, and a beautiful place to wake up in. Look over
a lovely book of "Cradle Songs", national, folk-lore-ish: Learn "Eve's C. S."
Breakfast. Mr. Saunders goes in town, (send letter to Dr. Keller, bless her!)
Mary does her work while I read & write, and then we sew and talk together.
Go to see Miss Charlotte at 12.20, and stay to dinner. They were all glad to see
me, and I to see them. Miss C. is as ever delightful. Mrs. H. gives me a five
dollar bill! Back to Mary's, pack, talk, and of by 5.10. See Mrs. Manchester
and her hostess while waiting car. Ride coolly in to the station, get ticket,
$1.00, write to Mrs. Smith, take train at 6.30. Walter meets me, is on board
before she stops; and we walk up together. He does not come in owing to the
family. Little have I to say to them, and retire by 9. Bed ere 10.

Sun. June 10th. 1883—

6. Delightful to have no fire. Darn grandmother's muslin. S. S. Finish Buddha. Weeden boys out for the season, hope to see me in the fall. Church. Walk
with Grace Channing. Home. Sew. Dine. Sew. Lu Manchester calls. Has had
a gay time in N. Y. Sup. Dress myself in grandmother's muslin, with rich lace
and amber bracelet, Deutsia & grass blossoms, & little white flowers in my
hair. Walter admires it even more than I do, I think. Happy evening. In bed
ere 11.30.

Mon. June 11th. 1883.

5.30. Sew & arrange for future sewing. A lady arrives with fan to be painted,
gorgeous, white satin & mother of pearl. Morning glories, to be done tomorrow! Take it and fall to. Bit of a nap also. Very pretty. Miss Murphy here for
mother. Dine copiously. Go to Mabel & have Maude. Her western lover has
married. Poor girl! And *I*! Get mitts .50 [cents]. Get Dr. Keller's prescription
put up $.25 [cents], Brush, .05, soda .05. Home. Clothes off mostly. Paint.

Supper. Chat with folks a bit. Write in Jour[nal]. In bed at 9. Am waked by Mrs. Springer at about 10.

Tues. June 12th. 1883.

5. Wash yesterdays d[inner]. & s[upper]. dishes. Finish fan. Trim Marie Stuart light straw with strip of Mull & put on cambric dress. Stop a few moments at Walters studio, to show him fan and ask way. He does not know, so I ask a policeman on the bridge. Carry fan to Miss Eleanora Mumford 39 Francis st. Stop at P.O. and get letter from Walter. Go to Annie Aborns to lunch, hem (run) Mull tie, and enlighten her benighted mind on various matters of sexual physiology. Give lesson to Emily Diman, Louise not in. Home, read letter, arrange rags and pieces. Begin "Wenderholme." [3] No Kate. Bed at 9.30. Paid mother $1.00 for washing

Wed. June 13th. 1883—

5 or 5:30 or so. Arrange pieces, baste piece-bag & mother stitches it for me. Re-baste blue plaid skirt and mother stitches that, I reading "Wenderholme" the whilst. Stock piece-bag proudly. Get xenophon at Ath., leaving "Homo Sum". Go to a A. S. teacher's Conference affair at the chapel. "Speak in meeting" for the first time, and enjoy it. Meet Walter down st. Stop at Gladding's & get black 5. silk, oz. spool, $.80, white $.10, braid $.07, & elastic. 03. $1.00 in all. Get to Maudes at 4. Am paid up, $4.00. Am to give no more lessons until "next fall"! I explain my engagement as governess. Am wanted Monday "if it's cool". Am not sorry to leave them. Home reading "W." sup, clear away, dress, read a little more, Walter comes at 8.15 about. Goes just before XI.

Thurs. June 14th. 1883

5.31: Get the breakfast to make up for last nights lateness. Wash dishes of course. Dress and go for Grace Channing, and we call on Walter. She was much pleased with him and his work. Which pleased me much, as I value her, & any favorable criticism is an agreeable change. Go with her on errands and I leave pin to be mended at Osbornes. Go home with Grace to dinner, and sew & talk with her afterwards. Leave at 5.45. Call on Kate. Out, but find Mrs. Taylor alone, stop to leave note, fall a-talking and stay. Mrs. T. goes to see a caller & Miss George comes in to lie down. Talk to her, and recite a little. Kate comes, stay to tea and she walks home with me and stays awhile. Go back with her and leave note for Mrs. Slicer under her door. Gave mother for board and washing through June ten more dollars. $11.00 in all.

Friday. June 15.th. 1883

5 or 5.30. Help mother about housecleaning and sew. Arrange my top drawer things and wash laces, etc. Take 5.10 car for Pawtuxet. Walter gets in at G. C.

Cemetary, and we row on the river from 6 to 9. Have to pull hard and run for our car at the last. Beautiful night. Home. *Sup.* Bed 11.30

Saturday. June 16th. 1883.

5.30. Look for rose quotations for the S. S. classes. More housecleaning. Dine. Call on the Slicers. Get more quo[tations]. from Mrs. S[licer]. Call on Millie and read her "John Ploughmans Talk".[4] Stop to see if Miss Gladding is at home yet. She is not. Call on Annie Morse and have a comforting talk with her. She believes in Walter. Call on Abbie Cooke and get studies. Lovely twilight walk, and call on Tudie Mauran. Home. Sup. Bed by 10

Sun. June 17th. 1883.

5.30 or so. Copy rose verses & write one or two more. S. S. with Mrs. R & Arney. Distribute verses to the teachers. Church. Mr. Barrows of Boston preaches. Tame and commonplace. John Diman, Edward Hale, & George Clarke in church. They essay to walk home with me, but Lu is waiting for me, and I flee away. I'm clumsy about such matters. Home. Write to Mrs. Smith and Retta. Dine. Wash dishes. Edward and George call, and we take a pleasant walk. In the B. Asylum grounds and otherwhere. Stop at the Dimans a little and G. comes home with me. Maria here. Set table & sup. Dress. Walter. Happy evening. Bed ere 11.30.

Mon. June 18th. 1883.

5.40. Sew on blue skirt. Meet Jennie Bucklin & Tudie Mauran at Brecks, and buy a trunk. $14.00. Jennie advises. Get oatmeal & gnassia cup for mother, call on Miss Bogert, and home. Sew. Dine. Give Mable Mason her last lesson. $1.00 due on some drawing paper $.25. Spent for car tickets $1.00. Net proceeds $.25. Home. Sew. Supper. Finish Retta's letter. Read Xenophon's Cyropaedia.

Tues. June 19th. 1883—

5.45 I think. Sew. Wash a lot of dishes. Sew. Dine. Mothers birthday. Thomas sent her two Mormon books. Read in one of them. Letter from Walter. May he be happy! Lesson to the Dimans on physiognomy. Ellen Clarke there. Very pleasant. [$]3.00. Go to Jackson's but find Eddie wants no more lessons now. A little talk with Mrs. Jackson, & she shows me my room. Large, third floor, double window, like it much. Call on the Manchesters. Home. Read more Mormon. Supper. Kate. Mother & Aunt C. go out. (My trunk arrived P.M.) Carry it up to my room, Kate with the tray. Mrs. Springer returns, shows Kate her rooms, and has supper. I go nearly home with Kate. Return. Mormons. Bed.

Wed. June 20th. 1883.

? Finish blue plaid skirt. Get trunks out and begin to arrange. Cut and baste a sort of Mother Hubbard waist out of flannel like my boat dress. Sup. dress. Walter. Had little banquet for him, 6 big strawberries on little glass plate with currant leaves, white clover, grass blossoms & one buttercup. (Letter from him & from Miss G[ladding]. P.M. Happy evening.

Thurs. June 21st. 1883—

6. Sewed, ripped, brushed, basted, tryed on, examined and arranged all day. Wrote letter to Walter & Dr. Keller. Last call from Dr. Wells. He is to be married on my birthday. Bed by 9.45.

Fri. June 22nd. 1883—

6.30. Letter from Walter. Arrange drawers of drawings etc. Read Century. Nap. Sew some. Read Mormon book, Mrs. Stenhouses, very good. Dress in Jersey etc. for Kate. Read a little with her. promiscuous. Home. Bed early.

Sat. June 23rd. 1883.

6. Ripped. Letter from Walter & Ellen Shaw. Answer the latter. Start out in cambric. Stop at carpenter's shop on George st. & ask prices of made boxes. Too much. Stop to see Kate about train. Out. Stop and look at paper in Rider's, put down what train for Miss Shaw, and send note. Get rubber cloth. $.12. Box at Pierces for $.15. Mr. Burgess takes it home for me very kindly. Piece—36 yds., blk. braid, $.75. ½ lb. camphor gum, $.18. Cambric $.12. Silk & twist. $.13. Fan $.21 with lilies .05. Go to Miss Gladdings. Sew. Dine. Call on Millie and leave "John Ploughman's Talk" for her mother to read to her. Walk down. Meet Walter. Stop and get basting thread .05 [cents]. Walk about with W[alter]. & ride home. 2 letters from him. Sup & read. Read more in Mormon book. Bed.

Sun. 24th June. 1883.

6.30. Ripped. Rose Sunday & last day of church & S. S. 3 of my boys out of town & one didn't come. Others there. Mr. Slicer gravely recommended the children to "look up" their quotations—the ones I wrote myself! Guess they wont find them. Church. Home, calling on Mrs. Sturgiss Carpenter and getting the $8.00 for Anne's placque. Sew. Dine. Sew. Dress. Walter. Talk a good deal, and come much nearer to each other. Goes at 11.

Mon. June 25th. 1883.

6.30. Sew on flannel jacket. Dine. Arrange letters & things. Letter from Walter. Emily Diman comes for me to give a lesson to her mother! Go at 5 & do it. Stay to tea. Call on Lu Hill & have a delightful talk with her. Home ere 10. Bed.

Tues. June 26th. 1883.

? Letter from Walter. Answer & take it to him at studio. Leave Xenophon at Ath. Get shawlstrap at Brecks [$]1.00. Shawl at Gladdings [$]7.00. Envelopes .50 (a box, 10 bunches, .10 a bunch, 25 in a bunch, $.01 apiece!) Ecru lace [$]1.00. Thread, pins, pins, [*sic*] $.18. Toilet paper. 15. Stuff for skirt $.45. Paint box (on acct.) 1.12 or 1.07. Stamps .57. Home. Dine. Lesson to Mrs. Diman & the little Dimans. Cherries. Home. Kate. read her old ballads. Supper. Kate goes early. Sew on sack. Bed.

Wed. June 27th. 1883

5.30. *Finish* sack. Make soft hat out of blue plaid like skirt. A success, took four hours. Pack. Lesson to Mrs. Diman. Pay, in advance for Friday, 3.75. Stop & see Lu, & get some lovely white roses. Home. Sup. Bathe & dress, rose adorned. Walter comes. Happy evening. Goes ere 11. I love him.

Thurs. June 28th. 1883.

6.30. Pack serenely all day, and read "Wenderholme", & enjoy it. Letter from Walter P.M. Bless him! Mr. Putnam calls. Talks with enthusiasm. Goes at 10.20.

Fri. June 29th. 1883.

6.40. Pack serenely. Read Wenderholme. Wash dinner dishes while mother goes down st. for me and gets nightdress [$]1.25, pin .10, & orders hack. She gives me Jane Carlyle's Letters[5] for a birthday present. I return it with $2.00 for a sun umbrella. Lesson to Mrs. Diman. Home. Sup. pack. Come down stairs for a while. retire at 8.30 or so.

Sat. June 30th. 1883.

5. Pack. Write to Walter. Hack 8.45 Off in 9.20 train. Same party as last year, even to Willie Mauran. He & I enjoy our trip, he gives me some soda & a box of chessman $.50. Make board out of 15 ct. chromo & play two games on Maine R. R. He beat the 1st. Lunch at B & M depot. Ogunquit ere 6. Supper. Rocks. Write to Walter. Bed. Glad to be here.

Sun. July 1st. 1883.

6.30. Arrange things somewhat. Converse with the two little Littles around the airtight. Breakfast. Write to Walter, Lucille Hill, & mother, on the rocks. Sketch a trifle in little book. Paint checkerboard P.M. And walk to Pebbly Beach & back with Kate, Mary, Emily, & the l[ittle]. Littles who already adore me. Back again, supper, and down on rocks with Willie Mauran. Talk to him earnestly. Retire at 9.

Mon. July 2nd. 1883.

7.30 or 40. Sit in Jennie's room and talk. Paint little bunch of flowers and take nap. Dine. Ride for mail with Miss Pratt, Miss Gladding, and Mr. Sturgus the deaf elderly stout boarder. Do errands. Drive back. Write a little to Walter. Sketch Mary Gladding. Watch waves. Sup. Play two games of chess with Will, one apiece. He plays a good game. Rocks with Kate & Mary. Talk a little over counter in the hall & draw cow's head in the book. Bed.

Tues. July 3rd. 1883.

7.10. I am 23. Paint cliff from hole. Draw Will's head. Pretty good. Dine. Talk. Nap on rocks. Read part of King John. Am sketched. Write to Cassie a little. Letter from Walter. Supper. Read letter on rocks. Talk to the new-comers, Mr., Mrs., & Conway Brown. And Will later. Retire at 8.15 or so, & write to Walter.

Wed. July 4th. 1883.

6 or so. Finish letter to Cassie. Paint from 9 till 12, finishing view of cliff. Spend afternoon on rocks toward Pebbly Beach. A thunder shower. Get wet and enjoy it. The first storm I ever was so out in. Come up & change dress and shoes. Sketch and am sketched after supper. More thunder shower. Am reading slections [*sic*] from the thoughts of Marcus Aurelius Antoninus.[6] That is the kind of man I admire. Retire at 9.

Thurs. July 5th. 1883.

7. Sit around a [*sic*] talk to Mr. Brown. Go to Pebbly Beach and fix the little spring, enjoying it like a child. Wash feet and hands and face in cold sea water. Dine. Nap on the rocks. Another thunder shower. Come up to the house and find three letters from Walter & a card from Lu Hill. Not coming. Read them in my room while it pours and lightens outside. (It does now somewhat.) Go down and entertain the little Littles until supper. Will and Conway have been out in a boat all day and only just missed the shower. Home late, and eat thin supper like dinnerless boys as they are. Some of them fish, I read Marcus etc. and watch sunset, cloud, & mist effects. Music later, dancing of Patience, and general gymnastics. I feel hilarious as they do. Retire at ere 9. (I think) Write to Walter.

Fri. July 6th. 1883—

6.30 or so. Begin grey petticoat. Walk down to Ogunquit with Will, and row nearly all the way back. First time I ever rowed on salt water. Like it. Paint two signs for Mrs. Weare, "PRIVATE ROOM". Talk with the boys. Dine[;] sketch the boys as they play chess, talk & sing a little and try hammock. Go down on the rocks and talk with Cora. Come up and talk with Conway after a little season of Marcus Aurelius. Sup. Then Conway and I take a bit of a walk and have some genuine talk. It does me good to feel that I do some good. Fireworks under the cliff of Tudie's construction. Fine effects. Come up all of us, and I recite "Keenan's Charge" to them. Retire by 9.30. Kate gives me a piece of chocolate.

Sat. July 7th. 1883.

Up at 5. Go down to Pulpit and write to Walter. After breakfast go to a chasm in the rocks beyond Pebbly Beach (Rose Cove), paint draw and write. And climb. Home just before dinner, try hammock & M[arcus]. Aurelius. Dine. Read M. A., nap on rocks, hammock & Conway, go to ride at 4 with J., K., M., E., & Tudie. Trouble in getting the mail & home late. Sup. Hammock, M. A., & Conway. Best thunder storm we've had yet. *Enjoy* it! M. A. Talk a bit with Mr. Brown. Retire ere 10.

Sun. July 8th. 1883.

About 6. Write to Walter. Breakfast. Draw in book. Have Bible Class on the rocks with the boys. They like it. Conway goes off to have his arm fixed, and I paint wild convolulus in my room with Will as interested spectator. Dine. Finish Convolulus with both boys in for a little while. Then more book, and more Bible Class and other talk. Sup. I begin letter to Miss Gladding. Splendid sunset & double rainbow. Am pleasant with the little folks, talk with Cora & Lucy, and sit long with Kate looking at the clear west. Stay there till 9.30 & then retire. The boys brought me a great bunch of wildflowers today and arranged them beautifully in my room while I was out. Wrote some— *thoughts*, for Conway.

Mon. July 9th. 1883

5.30. Two games of chess with Will before breakfast. He and Miss Pratt start for home at 8, Conway & I go with 'em, and ride back happily conversing. Sit on the rocks with him, and write more to Miss Gladding. Dine. Then he and I take a walk. He lets me try his revolver, and I hit with 4 shots out of 10. First experience too. Then we both have a nap on a sunny moss-&-grass-grown rock. Talk & recite poetry. Back, supper, and then watch the others fish and talk. Give him what I wrote, and he takes it *rightly*. Letter from Walter. A Miss Porter arrives.

Tues. July 10th. 1883.

5. Write to Walter on rocks as usual. Breakfast. Walk with Miss Porter, who is botanical, dressed as she should be, and can climb. See spouting rock. Are joined by Conway. He goes, then she goes, and I stay and finish a wild rose, and Marcus Aurelius. Dine. Sketch Mr. & Mrs. Brown, & talk to Conway. Nap on rocks. Then a tearing scramble down to pebbly beach and back, stopping to sketch rock, tree, & house. Supper. Two letters from Walter, & my chessmen, sent back by Miss Pratt. Read letters on rocks. Go to old house with Miss Porter[,] see sunset & get flower. Talk with Kate on piazza, & then talk & walk with Conway till 9.40.

Wed. July 11th. 1883.

5.30. Write to Walter. Breakfast. Loaf a little & then paint a red lily with Miss Marsh (Cousin of the Browns, arrived yestreen.) Success. Then loaf a little more more [*sic*] and sketch Miss Porter; good one. Dine. Sew industriously till tea-time on grey petticoat. Also had a nap. Some more new people, don't know 'em. Go to walk with Miss Porter and Mrs. Brown. Go over Captain Staple's new house, & up single beam stairs. On way down I lay boards for Mrs. B. Very funny. Home warm, & mosquito-ey. Cool off, walk & talk with Conway till 9.45 & then retire. Contemplate sleeping out.

July 12th. 1883. Thursday.

6.30. (Slept from 11.30 or so till about 4 on juniper bush, and the rest of the time on the rocks.) Write to Walter. Go down on the rocks with Miss Porter & sew. Then come up and sew; and rock Conway in the hammock with great vigor and endurance. Dine. Sew a little, and then get that poor Miss Hunter to go down on the rocks. She likes it. Introduce her to divers of us. Up, find letter, read it, and try hammock till supper. Sit around a bit & then spend about an hour by the little old cedar on the edge of the cliff. Then come up and climb the piazza to where Miss Porter & Miss March were sitting. Drop my shawl on Conway, & afterwards am sorry & ashamed & tell him so. Retire ere 9, & Kate comes in to see me awhile.

Fri. July 13th. 1883.

A little after 6. Write to Walter & card to mother. Sew in Miss Porter's room after breakfast, after an hour alone on the rocks. Miss P. learns double knitting & finishes my belt, which I give to Kate. Dine. Sew more. (Take a walk with Conway but are driven in by rain). Sew in my room, & Conway calls upon me therein. Read him some things & talk & write. Dress in Jersey & yellow silk kerchief for supper. Rocks, rain, promenade with divers, especially C[onway]. Retire at 9.15 or so.

Sat. July 14th. 1883.

5. Pack in a leisurely and masterful manner. Promenade on the piazza with Norton, & sing to him. He gets me a few wild roses, wherewith I adorn myself. Breakfast, Miss Porter down first and the rest of the party gradually appearing. Start at 8 or so, with general handshaking. Ride to Wells with Ed Weare. Wait about there for the belated train, & then doze and rest till we get to Boston. Transfer trunk $.25, (Kate gave me a dollar beside both tickets.) and take horsecar for Providence Station. Toilet there and then car to Mrs. Smith's. She is asleep, so I wait. Mr. Smith comes in, and orders lunch for me. A Miss Mansfield calls, cousin of Mrs. S. & we converse. In view of the lunch I take she asks if I was ever called a Colorado beetle! A little talk with

Mrs. S. and then back to station. Get three of Kate's six desired novels, 5.30 train home. Walter to meet me, and laboriously carries both bag & bundle all the way home. Stops just a moment. Talk with Mother, nice supper, trunk at about 9, and then a bath, & my own cool little bed.

Sun. July 15th. 1883.

7.30. Write rhymed letter to Kate. Dine. Harry Manchester calls. Walter stops to leave me a letter. Mother goes out, Harry goes, and Walter stops again for a few moments. Maria calls. Josiah Westcott calls. (His brother Henry dropped dead yesterday in Marblehead.) Mother returns. M[aria]. stays to tea. Dress. Walter from 7.30 to 11.30. Bed.

Mon. July 16th. 1883.

7.30 or so. Go down to Mrs. Jackson's for a few moments. Call on Mrs. Mauran. Out. Car down town & leave boots to be mended. Am weighed, and find, *according to Mr. Staple's scales* that I have lost 2 ¼ lbs! Fault of Ogunquit scales I guess; I don't believe it. Call on Miss Gladding & Millie. Ride home. Mr. Weeden in the car. The Hales all at home & Nellie well. Dine. Pack. Man comes at 3 or a little after instead of 5. Ready for him. He takes my big trunk, mother's little trunk, a box bag bundle & bookshelves, $.50. Sit around a bit and set out at 4.30 or thereabouts. Call on Anna. Call on Mrs. Mauran again and find her. Become a hireling as I phrase it for the admiration of my friends, at 5.35. Mrs. J[ackson]'s sister here. Arrange things in my room somewhat. Supper. Sit and talk with the family on the piazza. Retire at 9.40 & bed.

9Tues. July 17th. 1883.

6.30. Arrange more. Breakfast at about 8. Open & partly unpack box to Eddie's great interest & amusement. Sew a little. Go out and see his garden, play battledore with him, & ball. Mend one of his balls, & give him a button, which *he* sews on his shirt. Dine. Talk a little with Mrs. J[ackson]., write a short letter to Walter, and Miss Goslee, (Mrs. J's sister) Eddie, & I, go down town. Christen my lovely silk purse; as does she one of hers. A nice little woman. Ride home in car. Supper. Look over Youth's Companion and read Miss G. the story of Micah. Then billards with Eddie till 9.30 or so. I made 11 the first game, & 19 the second, leading in that for some time. He was tired before the end of the third, & we left it. Bed.

Wed. July 18th. 1883.

6.30. Sew. An hour with Eddy after breakfast, drawing, reading & arithmetic. Sew. Write to Walter. Early dinner, & then Miss Goslee, Eddie, & I go to see "Plunging Bucker," and "Wild Life in the West" in general. Real Indians, real bison, real Buffalo Bill. Splendid horses and racing. Fine shooting, and the "Attack on the Deadwood Coach" magnificent. "Concert" afterwards. War-dance by young braves, worthseeing; then a variety show the last of which was abominable—married people—drink & quarrelling. I sketched. home by 6.30 of after. Change dress. Supper. Letter from Walter & Maude Mason. Billiards with Eddie. Mr. J. joins us & lets E[ddie]. and I beat him to E's infinite delight.

Thurs. July 19th. 1883.

6.30 or so. Arrange things more. Breakfast. Hour with Eddie. Then sew, write to Maude Mason & poem to Walter, and take a nap. Dinner. Finish brown skirt all but pocket. Make polo cap of same stuff, pretty. Supper. Go and post letters & card for Miss Goslee, & then stop and see mother. Miss Murphy there. Have some blackberries. Bring home clean clothes and a dust cloth. Sit with Mrs. Jackson awhile, (—dear pretty little woman, she isn't at all well to my mind) play battledore & ball a few moments with tooth-tormented Eddie, and am in bed by 9.40.

Fri. July 20th. 1883.

5. Put pocket in skirt. Go down by 6.10 to dust parlor & can't get there. (Mrs. J. asked me to do that, in answer to repeated requests for more work) Write a little to Walter, and then dust successfully. Begin History of Scandinavian Races by Paul C. Sinding. Breakfast. Eddie goes to Pawtuxet for all day, fishing, with friends. I make a pincushion for Mrs. Jackson. Show Miss Goslee my flower studies, & she likes them much. Dine. Sew. Write to Walter & Kate. Nap on floor. A man fixes the scuttle & screws up my bookcase and bracket. Post letters with Miss G[oslee]. Sup. Piazza, reading "Tropical & Polar Worlds". A Mr. Frank Green calls. Go upstairs & read more. Bed by 10.10.

Sat. July 21st. 1883.

? Write to Walter. Lesson with Eddie, assisted by "Mauranny" his youthful friend. Letter from Walter. Go down st. with Miss Goslee. Got boots, $1.35, linen th[rea]'d, elastic, darning cotton & beeswax, .25 [cents]. Stamps. 12. Am weighed. I have gained two lbs. this week! Home. Dine. Assist in entertaining Eddie's playmates. "Eddie says you're such a good catcher he's going to have you on his baseball nine!" And E. told me one of them wished I was *his* governess! Good thing. Read Scandinavia & knit. Play billiards with E. & Willie Mauran. bed by 10.40. Mrs. J[ackson]. paid me $4.00.

Sun. July 22nd. 1883.

6.35 or so. Do a little washing. Breakfast at 9. Play billiards & battledore & tell stories all the morning. Sew a very little & set Eddie to painting, his mother having found a bit of an old palette & some black & naples yellow in the cellar. Go to see mother & lend her $4.00. Call on the Manchesters.

Home. Bathe. Dress in thin white. Sit on piazza. Walter arrives late—8.40 I should say. Stays till 10.10. Write a sheet to him before bed. Enter that sanctuary at 11.5 or less.

Mon. July 23rd. 1883.

6.20. Dust. Read Scandinavia. Lessons with two extras. Scandinavia. Get partly acquainted with another bookcase. Paint on red satin (P.M.) a pincushion, Mrs. J's order. Read to Eddie & 3 others out of "Bruin" etc. and tell stories. Note from Walter. Battledore in the evening. (Got sewing from home).

Tues. July 24rd. {sic} 1883.

6.30 or so. Dust. Lessons. Go to Dr. Gay at 10.35 & have two teeth filled. Get drawing materials for Eddie. Call on Millie. Get Bazaar & shuttlecock for Mrs. J. Get stamps $.30. Call on Mrs. Diman. Home. Read & write, beginning "Weighed & Wanting"—MacDonald, bless him! Dine out with Miss Goslee, shop a trifle, Park, & bring Dr. J. Home. Sit on fence with Eddie & watch baseball game. Battledore, & read Bruin to him. He grows interested. Bed by 10.30.

Wed. July 25th. 1883.

6.30 or so. Dust. Breakfast. Lessons alone. Eddie & I go to the Park & stay all day, rowing, riding, swinging, eating, and generally improving the occasion. (Expenses $1.69.) Home by 6. Supper. Read. Battledore. bed by 9.30. Two letters from Walter.

Thurs. July 26th. 1883.

5.30. Write to Walter. Dust. Write. Breakfast. Write. Letter from Walter. Lessons, alone. Read MacDonald. Turn & baste tucks for Miss Goslee for about 4 hours. Read. Read to Eddie. He gets more interested. Supper. Go to box with Miss G. Meet mother there. Talk to Miss G. Read. Battledore with Eddie. 60 the highest. Retire at 9—bed 9.30.

Fri. July 27th. 1883.

6 or so. Write. Dust. Write. Breakfast. Read. Letter from W. Lessons alone. He improves. The others go down town. Finish painting cushion for Mrs. J. *Finish* brown skirt, with buttonholes & pocket facing. Read. Miss Susie Philips to dinner. Read. Go down anxious to do something & they suggest fairystories. So I tell them the story of Maroof with great success. Read. Write to Walter. Had card from Mrs. Crandall asking me to paint bamboo splasher for her. Answer that I've no time now for outwork. Supper. Post letter & card. Read. Bed by 9.55.

Sat. July 28th. 1883.

Up at 4 with a touch of summer complaint. Eat lightly & do not drink until night, when it vanishes. Write to Walter A.M. & give it to the postman. Letter from him P.M. Thoroughly sweep my room with the pretty new Dustpan & Brush Mrs. J[ackson]. has provided for me. Start on winter dress—C. Bissells. Begin to read Mr. Isaacs to Mrs. J. Misses Susie & Lily Phillips come over to tea. Dress, bring down serving & help entertain, as requested. Eddie returns from the visit he began yesterday. Change dress & play battledore with him. 105! with a drop on top of the bookcase at 92 that we did not count for I could have hit it. Read another chapter of Mr. Isaacs to them all. Loto & puzzles of various sorts. They start to go and Eddie begins certain gymnastics in which I join him so successfully that he begs me to join his circus! Bed by 10.30 I think.

Sun. July 29th. 1883—

7.20 I think. Dust. Write to Kate. Breakfast. Battledore & billiards with Eddie. Dr. Jackson arranges his fishing and hunting gear. The handsomest rod I ever saw, & a beautiful doublebarrelled breechloading shotgun. Revolver & all manner of things. Write more. Dinner. Then go to ride & go to see mother. Look at Century. Home. Dress in same white muslin & blue skirt. Supper. Read in T. & P. worlds. Walter at 8.15–20. Goes at 10.30. Retire. Write to him. Bed by 11.20.

Mon. July 30th. 1883.

6. Write to Walter. Dust. Write. Breakfast. Sew. Lessons. Sew on dress. Mrs. Jackson helps me about fitting. Dine. Sew. Nap. Practice billiards. Sew. Read to Eddie. Read T. & P. W. Supper. Read Mr. Isaacs to Mrs. J. Read more to Eddie & "Mauranny". Battledore[;] bed ere 9.17.

Tues. July 31st. 1883.

5.45. Write. Dust. Write. Breakfast. Letter from Walter. Lessons. Read to Mrs. J. till dinner. Paint a picture illustrating "Mr. Isaacs". Supper. Go to see mother. Out. Come back. T. & P. Read bear to Eddie, & then battledore. 207 & 201 in succession! Bed by 9.25.

Wed. Aug. 1st. 1883.

6.10 Write. Dust. Write. Breakfast. Letter from Walter. Mrs. J. postpones lessons as she wants to go down st. with Eddie; and I go down st. also, and when Walter comes to his studio at 9.40 or so, he finds me in possession. Stay about an hour & a half. Then pay Mr. Breck for mending little trunk— $1.25. Buy thread & twist, .10 [cents] & tidy cotton .08. Stop at mothers & leave her $3.00[;] home, knit & read till dinner. Then draw monogram for Mrs. J[ackson], lessons, & paint another picture, not so successful. Eddie goes to "Mauranny's" to tea, so I put on linen dress. Show Dr. J[ackson]. puzzles, knit & tell stories till 9. bed by 9.30 or 40.

Thurs. Aug. 2nd. 1883.

5.35. Write. Dust. Write. Breakfast. Lessons. 3 letters from Walter. Go fishing with Eddie & five other small boys. Go to railroad pond, & have a very very good time. I sketch. Home. Dinner. Letter from Walter. Dress. All go to Mrs. Phillips to tea. Knit. Games & stories & supper, & music & reading—I read them Howells "Sleeping Car.", and battledore with Eddie & gymnastics more or less; & we don't get home till after 11. Find prose Homer note & card from Walter. Bed a little after 12.

Friday. Aug. 3rd. 1883.

6.6 about. Wake Nora as I had offered last night. W.D.W.B.L. Go down & carry letter to Walter. Stay there an hour & a bit more. Stop at Mother's & get gymsuit. Home & put it on to the edification of Mrs. J. & her sister. Dine. Read aloud. Mother calls & brings some more things I wanted. Ride down town with Miss G. Bring home Dr. J. Supper. Knit & read, finishing Mr. Isaacs. Bed by 10.45 certainly.

Sat. Aug. 4th. 1883—

6.40. Go shopping with Mrs. J. & get tennis-cloth skirt 2.55. Home. Lessons. Make arrow for Eddie. After dinner we two, with "Mauranny" & the little Allens go "hunting" with bow & arrows. No game secured. But we dig clams in the Seekonk; at least they do, while I keep guard & sketch; and then have a real bake, and eat thereof. Good too. I read aloud from the "bear book". Stop and explore the Narragensett boat house with same party to see a few fireworks given as salute to a Pawtucket excursion. Letter from Walter P.M. & one from Maude Mason.

Sun. Aug. 5th. 1883.

6.05. Paint sumach leaves. Breakfast. Games & make arrows with Eddie. Dinner. More Eddie. All drive from 4.40 to 7. Sup. Dress. Walter from 8 to 10. I am *Happy*. Bed by 11.

Mon. Aug. 6th. 1883.

6–6.30. W. D. Breakfast. Lessons. Start on "Ran away to Sea", having finished "Bruin" etc. Go in carriage to a pond in Rumford; where Eddie, Mauranny, & Willie Allen fish, & I paint & sketch. Took a boat & rowed up the pond. W. A. lost a rowlock & I paddled back. Hard, but glad of the chance for some work. Carriage at 4.20 or so. Home. dress. Sup. Read & knit. Battledore. Bed by 9.20.

Tues. Aug. 7th. 1883.

6.20. Dust. Baste facing on skirt. Breakfast. Lessons. Dine down town with Miss G[oslee]. Leave that old gold kerchief at Miss Gladdings who is away. Buy rowlock 20 [cents], & give it to Rumford stage driver, 10 [cents]. Call on Millie. Buy blk. hose $.62. Call on Walter. Mr. Dorrance there. Hear that Sidney Putnam is drowned.[7] His poor mother! Stay nearly two hours. Call at Mrs. Diman's. Away. Home. Dinner. Battledore. Go with Eddie to Dr. Fillinghast's, where he has two teeth filled & never murmurs. Home in Surrey, .50 [cents] (of theirs), & find mother has been here for me. Go around there. Back to supper. Knit, take bit of a walk with Mrs. J[ackson]., Battledore with Eddie & "Ran away to Sea". He begs for more! Bed by 9.40.

Wed. Aug. 8th. 1883

5.40 or so. Write in jour[nal]. & acct. bk. Dust. buttonholes for Mrs. J. Breakfast. 3 letters from Walter & one from Mr. Lane, Martha has a 9 ¼ [lb.] boy, born at 10 A.M. Aug. 6th. Lessons. Change dress & write to Walter. 11.20 car to the dentist's. Miss Goslee has a tooth out with gas, & Eddie one filled. Soda .03 with 2 of the J[ackson]'s. Home. Buttonhole's, dinner, buttonholes. Miss G., Eddie, Mauranny & I go to see Butler Hospital, and are treated with surly indifference. Leave the boys & go down st. Miss G. & I. Drive a bit, & bring home the Dr. Hem skirt. Supper. Knit & read, show Miss G. about multiplication of fractions. Knit. Read to Eddie. Bed by 9.40 or less.

Thurs. Aug. 9th. 1883.

6.30. Dust. Write. Breakfast. Lessons. Go fishing with E. & M[auranny]., are joined by the little Allen's. Start at Red Bridge, & then go on to Ten Mile River Bridge, where E. catches two baby bluefish. Home to dinner & then E. & M. & I go again; the Allens being forbidden by Mrs. Jackson. & Eddie leaves me to tell them of it, too. E. catches 6 in the afternoon and, after "Mau-ranny" had gone home, had the coolness to get me to take them off the hook because forsooth he didn't like the dirty work! Manly, that! He wont come home either till I leave him, and as punishment is allowed no battledore nor billiards nor reading in the evening. And his mother *says* he must go to bed at 8, but lets him play come-as-you-come & sit up till almost nine! I sewed in the evening. Bed by 9.35.

Friday. Aug. 10th. 1883.

6.6. Dust. Write. Lost my stylograph through the bridge yesterday! Break-fast. Lessons. Go to dentist's with Eddie, & then to Southwick's & then to P[ublic]. L[ibrary]. & look at pictures. Home in car. Take work to mother's P.M., Go down st. get two pair blk. Hose, $1.24 & pay Dr. Gay $2.50. Then to Walter. Mr. Dorrance there, more's the pity. Get to mother's again at 6 or a bit after, & stay to supper & sew. Aunt C. returns. Back here before 8. Battledore & book.

Sat. Aug. 11th. 1883.

5.30, & swept my room thoroughly. No lessons. Drive to the Park, stopping for a Frank Williams, and stay there from 10 A.M. to 5 P.M! Carry lunch. Row swing, etc. See a miserable semi-furless cat, skinny, bare-legged, and am instrumental in having the poor beast slain. Sketch during concert, thereby attracting considerable attention. Should think they had never seen a pencil used before. A fire in a muck heap, engines, etc. Attend in person, but have to leave, with my reluctant charge, and take 5.10 car home. Read Mrs. Carlyle's letters at intervals all day. Supper, shuttlecock with tennis rackets, (as Miss Goslee has a severe headache), book, & bed by ten. Left Mr. J[ackson]. reading "Ran Away to Sea" with every appearance of interest. Can't say I love these folk.

Sun. Aug. 12th. 1883.

7.20! Dust. Mend. Write. Breakfast. Battledore, billiards, hide-&-seek, & "Ran Away to Sea". Dine. A man named Sloper here, P.M. Nasly [sic] type. More Battledore & billiards. Come within *one* of beating Eddie! Find time to finish letter, to C. A. Hedge, post it & two more of Miss G[oslee]'s, & call on mother. Back. Battledore. (We play altogether with the new tennis rackets now.) Dress. Supper. Read. Prose Odyssey while the "gentlemen" play billiards above stairs. Walter from a little before 8 to a little after ten. We are Happy. Stop and talk to Miss G. a bit till the b. balls stop. Then to bed. Write a bit to Walter. Bed ere 11.25.

Mon. Aug. 13th. 1883—

6.25–30. Dust. Sew. Breakfast. Lessons between 10.30 & 11.30. Then impromptu tennis over a string in the yard, wherein he wins. A niece, Miss Edith Jackson, here. Ordinary, in appearance. Dine. Finish tennis skirt. Write rhymes for Eddie, two stanzas. Begin letter to Mrs. Smith. Sup. Finish knit belt and give it to Miss Goslee. Battledore or rather shuttlecock with rackets, billiards, & read to Eddie. He gets much excited, and I hear him teasing for the book, after I go out. Bed by 9.30 I think.

Tues. Aug. 14th. 1883.

6.10–15. Dust. Write. Breakfast. Lessons. Went with Miss Goslee for flowers. Make bird trap for Eddie. Sew. Dine. Arrange flowers. Letter from Walter. Dress. Sit around. Miss Susie & Lillie Phillips & a cousin Miss May Green of Chicago arrive; later Mrs. P. & Annie, later Mr. P. Talk, supper, games, music, general drag. Miss G[reen]. Highly Unpleasant on first impression. Bed by 12.30. (Letter with three dollars for that painted fan.)

Wed. Aug. 15th. 1883—

6.30–35. Dust. Write. Breakfast. Lessons from 10.30 till 11.30 as Eddie was not up earlier. Early dinner too & then drive down town. Dentist with Eddie for half an hour. Buy 10 cts. worth of drawing paper for him, & a 5 ct. dish-mop for Miss G[oslee]. Lend E. 10 cts. & he returns 1. Return 10 cts. to little Frank Williams. Car home. Tennis. Letter from Walter & Answer. Post it with Miss G. Are waylaid by the fair Phillipses, & return for her after having read to Eddie.

Thurs. Aug. 16th. 1883.

6.10. Sew. Dust. Sew. Breakfast. Lessons. Dine down town with Miss G. Get 2 doz. buttonmoulds at Murray's. .10 cts. 2 corset covers. 50 cts. each. ½ ream of letter paper, 75 cts. Am weighed. 120 lbs. Go to Walter and stay till 12.45 or so. Call at the Slicer's. Not at home yet. Miss Nightingale ill, neuralgia. Stop to see mother; gone, but see Aunt C. & Mrs. Springer. Home[;] billiards with Eddie & Willie. Dinner. Mrs. & to [*sic*] Miss Jacksons here—sister-in-law & neices. Stuff pincushion for Mrs. J. Write to mother. Play billiards with Eddie & Willie. W. & I. beat E. one game. Finish Ran away to Sea to E. Supper. (Last of last chapter after.) Then shuttlecock, hopping about, hide the handkerchief &c. &c. Teach E. the "I think of something that rhymes with" game; he likes it. Retire at 9 or a little later. Write. Bed by 10.30.

Fri. Aug. 17th. 1883.

6.10–15. Sew a bit. Dust. Write. Lessons. Cover red satin cushion. Dinner. Go fishing with Eddie & Frank W[illiams]., who returns me five cents! Lose it. Fish at the T.M.R. bridge as before, & E. catches 40 in three hours. Baby bluefish, & very good eating. Back at 6.30. Letter from Walter. Call on Eva Webster at Ray's, Dear girl! Back at 8.33. or so. Billiards with Eddie, he beating. Write letter to Walter.

Sat. Aug. 18th. 1883.

6.? Eddie goes to Silver Spring with the Maurans. Eva calls. Finish pincushion successfully. Sew P.M. & call for Eva to go to Walters Studio with me, but she can't as Cousin George Greene & his wife have come to see her. Call there awhile, & then go to see Lu. Manchester, See Harry for a moment. Back before 6. Billiards with E. I name the balls, mine "Little Jane,'['] etc. which makes it very funny. Bed by 10.

Sun. Aug. 19th. 1883.

7. Dust. Billiards. Breakfast. Games, chocolate drops, etc. till dinner. Go to walk with Eddie P.M., around the reservoir. See frogs & fish. Back again. Dress. Supper. Homer. Walter. Goes at 10 as usual. Write a word to him.

Mon. Aug. 20th. 1883.

6.10–15. Dust. Write. Breakfast. Lessons. Go walk with Miss Goslee to Silver Spring, stopping first at the Phillips's, and visiting the College Library with them. A long day, mostly wasted. See Aunt Caroline there, & call on Florrie Carpenter, who is glad to see me. Watch the welldressed darkies dance. Back at 6.30 or so. Eddie has "Mauranny" in the evening, and attempts his magic lantern.

Tues. Aug. 21st. 1883.

6.15 or less. Dust. Write. Breakfast. Lessons. Go seine(!) fishing with Eddie at Red Bridge. *HOT*. Back. Dine. Pick & tie colored worsted all P.M. Dress. Write again. Sup. Billiards with Eddie & then out. Call on Mrs. Mauran. Away. On Lutie Manchester. She is still feeble after Seaconnet larks. See Harry and he sees me home. Letter from Walter & mother.

Wed. Aug. 22nd. 1883.

6.30 nearly. Sew. Dust. Sew. Breakfast. Dentist. Lessons abandoned on account of heat! Sew & read and play billiards with E[ddie]. Dine. Go with E[ddie]. to the Base Ball grounds. Prov. 8 to Phila. 2. Stop down st. & he gets "eclairs" & book. Edward Brown at the game; glad to see him. Walk back, from Prospect St. to here in 2000 steps & 17 minutes. Letter from Walter. Sup, Arrange flowers for Mrs. J[ackson]. Billiards. Read aloud to Eddie & Willie Mauran. Retire at 9.5 or so. Write to Walter.

Thurs. Aug. 23rd. 1883.

5.40 or so. Write to Walter. Am stopped in my dusting by Eddie, who wants his lessons before breakfast. Give him half an hour. Breakfast. I go to Walter's studio & stay till 12. Go to see Millie. Met Maria. Leave Millie Mrs. Carlyle's Letters. Ride back from Crawford st. (cars are off route just now.) Dine. Go to Roger W. Park with Eddie & row. Back by 6.40. Supper. Billiards with Eddie & Willie, & read to them.

Fri. Aug. 24th. 1883.

6.10. Mend chemiloon & shoe. Dust. Write to mother. Lessons. Arrange for packing all day nearly. Letter from Walter P.M. Read to Eddie & his hand out of Nonsense book. Write to Walter. Post it after tea. Read a little. Billiards with Eddie. Nearly beat him with much excitement. Jump a little. Bed by 9.55.

Sat. Aug. 25th. 1883—

6.3 or so. Wash certain "pieces." Letter from Walter. Lessons. Make muslin bags for Mrs. J[ackson]., 25 of 'em. Dine. Eddie & his mother go out. Finish letter to Cassie & put facing on old flannel dress. Supper. Go home with Susie

Phillips who is in for a moment. Read a piece of a fairy tale. Billiards with Eddie, & later with Willie Mauran & John Cutter. Bed by 10.10.

Sun. Aug. 26th. 1883.

6. Sew braid on old flannel dress. Dust parlor. Try on new shoes, brown cloth, given me by Mrs. Jackson. Too big for her. They don't fit well, but will be a "change". Play with and read to Eddie all day till 40.30 [*sic*] or so & then go for a walk; also accompanied by Gardy Cornett, a little boy. Back. Painted a little. Supped casually on fruit & cake. Walter till ten or a little after. Wrote a little to him. Bed by 10.45 I *think*, watch down stairs.

Mon. Aug. 27th. 1883.

About 6.15 or 20. Dust. Write to Walter. Breakfast. Letter from Kate. Sew and enjoy myself all the morning. Tie worsteds in the afternoon and evening. Susie P[hillips]. here to tea. See her home. Went down st. with E[ddie] I *think*.[8]

Tues. Aug. 28th. 1883.

7! Go down town & change worsteds for Mrs. J[ackson]. Stop and see Walter. Dine. Tie worsteds all P.M. Billiards with E., W. & John Cutler in the evening. Bed by 9.30.

Wed. Aug. 29th. 1883—

6.10–6.15. or less. Write to Walter. Breakfast. Read Mark Twain's "Prince & Pauper" during the day, and thoroughly *enjoy* it. Lessons late. Dine. Sew coat buttons on for Mrs. J. More or less billiards all day, and finally Eddie says to me "You lie!" over a disputed point. I leave immediately, tell his mother after a few moments reflection, and she forbids all games between us until Xmas! And seems to inwardly blame me for not attending to it by myself. A letter from Walter in the afternoon that made governessing a quick dream, and one from Mrs. Smith. E. & his father play billiards during the evening.

Thurs. Aug. 30th. 1883—

Ere 6.30 or 35. Dust a little. Pack. Look at Art Journals for an artists name Mrs. J[ackson]. wished to find out about. Knit. Read to Eddie & Willie Mauran. Knit & read. Sup. Call on Miss Phillips just to leave knit belt for her. Go & see mother, who is at home and very glad to see me. Read to Eddie & Willie again. Bed by 10.10 or 15.

[*Charlotte left with the Jackson family on Friday, August 31, 1883, for an extended stay at Moosehead Lake, Maine. She returned to Providence on Tuesday, October 2, 1883.*]

Fri. Aug. 31st. 1883—

6.11 or 12 Pack. Call on Miss Gladding, buy ½ cake madder brown [paint], a collar & four k'h'fs ($1.10), & stay with Walter from 10.15 till 11.25 or so. Then back, find mother waiting to lend me $2.00 that I may not be penniless, lunch, and are off at a little before 1—Mrs. J[ackson]., Norah, Eddie, & I. Dr. J[ackson]. meets us at station & we take 2.10 P.M. train for Boston. Dinner in the depot café—beautiful and good, that place, row with E. on the P.G. *lake*(!), loaf generally, go to B. & Me. depot, loaf more, Dr. J, is seized for a few minutes by that smoke-preventing-fire saving Mr. Sloper, and we are off to Maine at 7 P.M. Had stateroom in sleeping car! My first experience of berths.—Don't like em. Had upper one & open ventilators, but didn't sleep much. Reach Bangor at 5 A.M. & breakfast. Walk about in the chill fogginess and see Bangor a little. Loaf. 7.20 train for Blan[-]

Sat. Sept. 1st. 1883.

See last entry! -chard at 11.30 or so. Dinner. Drive to G.ville. Dust?*!!!!!!!!* Arrive here at 2.30 or 40. Eveleth House, Greenville, Moosehead Lake, Maine. Have room & things and *bathe*. Do memory sketch of forest-burned mountain, Eddie also painting. Begin letter to Walter. Supper. Write more. Bed!

Sun. Sept. 2nd. 1883—

5.50. Finish letter to Walter. Breakfast. Go out in boat with Eddie. Are subsequently joined by Mr. & Mrs. [Jackson] & we go up the lake a bit. Back in time to begin letter to mother. Read to Eddie. Dinner. Boat again till nearly five. Cut big sticks and trim them while I tell him stories. Supper. Play awhile with Eddie & a little bit of a boarder's boy. Bed by 9.5 or less.

Mon. Sept. 3rd. 1883.

5.50. As cold as yesterday was hot. Eddie digs worms & fishes and I read to him some, & read to myself as I can, beginning "Romola". Letter from Carrie Hazard, bless her. Bed a bit late as I write to Walter.

Tues. Sept. 4th. 1883.

6.30. Spend all day fishing at West Cove, I reading sketching and writing while they fish. Rowed 5 or 6 miles. A very happy day, thanks to wood & water, sky & wind. Wrote to Walter, & get letter from him.

[*Charlotte did not keep her journal up during her visit to Upper Wilson Pond. She resumed her writing on Sunday, September 9, the day after her return to Moosehead Lake.*]

Wed. Sept. 5th. 1883.

Went to Upper Wilson Pond, Mr. & Mrs. Jackson, a Mr. & Mrs. Hopkins of Prov[idence]., Eddie & I. Log cabin, cot beds, man cook, partridges in the door yard, lake for toothbrushing & wash in general, fishing & gunning; good time rather. I write to Walter, and got one letter from him. Painted certain berries, sketched a little, began "Felix Holt,"[9] Mr. Hopkin's book. Came home on Sat. 8th in rain & cloud. Bath & toilet.

Sun. Sept. 9th. 1883.

5.50 about, and write to Walter. (Found 4 letters from him, one from Kate & one from Miss Goslee; with "John Halifax"[10] & the Sept. Century sent by my love, on returning yesterday). Walk with Eddie, and otherwise amuse him, and we two begin a nonsense book of our own, I drawing & writing & he painting & helping occasionally on verses. Do two dozen, morning & afternoon. Mr. Lord, (an Englishman staying here, and who was in camp when we reached there and stayed till Fri.) thought the drawings very good. Eddie rather ruder than usual to me. Can I stand it all winter? 'M-m-m! Write to Walter.

Mon. Sept. 10th. 1883.

7.15–20 or so. Eddie goes hunting with his father in the morning. I read Romola, write a little to mother, talk to Mrs. Hopkins & knit. Mrs. H. is kind & sympathizes with me in this interesting situation of mine. Row with E[ddie]. P.M. & nonsense verses & pictures in the evening. Letter from Walter. Answer.

Tues. Sept. 11th. 1883.

All day in a little steamer; up to the head of the lake, dine, & back; nearly twelve hours. Read to self and Eddie and amuse him with the ballads, which he likes better & better. Bed early, but always a letter to Walter first. And one from him every day.

Wed. Sept. 12th. 1883.

All day in another little steamer, chartered by Dr. J. for fishing purposes. They catch 11 great beauties. I decide to eat no more fish; that are caught for "sport" at any rate. A few nonsense verses with Eddie till 8.30. Early release.

Thurs. Sept. 13th. 1883

All the morning row about with Eddy, beginning John Halifax, Gentleman. Romola finished yesterday. A little more fishing by Eddy P.M. & then he and his father go ahunting, and I am allowed the boat, and row out to a pretty little island and write and draw and am alone and happy. Forget my paints & never found it out till I was all ready & reached for them! "Powder, shot, caps,

& wads." Back by 6.25. E. fishes a bit more, (he had been waiting for me 25 minutes & was wroth.) supper, nonsense—releease at 8.50.

Fri. Sept 14th. 1883.

Two letters from Walter. E[ddie]. goes hunting with father & father's friend, and I tie worsted with Mrs. J[ackson]. & Mrs. H[opkins]. Eddie back, and we row till dinner time. Then more rowing, dig worms, row. Supper. Tell him stories for a hour nearly. Mrs. J. thinks he had better have school this winter. Hurrah!

Sat. Sept. 15th. 1883

Another on the steamer fishing. I finish John Halifax. A fine book. I will eat no more game fish, fish caught for the fun of it. *Fun!* Write to Walter as usual.

Sun. Sept. 16th. 1883

Out in a boat all the morning with Eddie & for a short time a certain Mr. Vinal—staying here, young, inoffensive. Change my dress. Dinner. Lounge about with E. for a while, and then we all go for a walk, much against his will. Home and write a bit. Tell stories to Eddie till supper. Read to him for nearly an hour. Write to Mrs. Smith & Martha.

Mon. Sept. 17th. 1883.

Wind worsted & go fishing & rowing with Eddie. He gets wet in the rain. I have begun Schillers Letters & Essays, Aesthetical & Philosophical. Read & tell stories P.M. Then jump & hop with E. & "play indian" after tea. Retire at 8.45. Two letters from Walter.

Tues. Sept. 18th. 1883.

Eddie goes hunting with his father & I go up the lake to paint, but find my water thing smashed. Enjoy the woods and write to Miss Gladding. Back & paint a little crescent. Dinner. Row & fish (E. does) awhile and then he goes hunting again & I come home and paint. A pretty good sketch, of a cloudy lake edge. Then play indian with E., "bear porridge", hide the thimble & other sports. Mr. Hopkins & Mr. Lord return. Letter from mother, Kate, & two from Walter.

Wed. Sept. 19th. 1883.

Out with steamer all day. I spend it on birch island, paint read & write. Very pleasant time too. Dinner on island. Stories to Eddie in the evening. Letter from Walter & one from Sam Simmons on business—.

Thurs. Sept. 20th. 1883.

Sent letters to Walter, Mother, Florrie, Sam Simmons & Miss Gladding. Boat with Eddie all the morning, reading Felix Holt, (of Mr. Hopkins lending) while he catches the useless but possibly sensitive chub. Afternoon the same. Evening of stories, I being driven to Bible ones for lack of lighter matter. *No letter!*

Fri. Sept. 21st. 1883.

Another day sketching on Birch Island while they fish. My letter was delayed by the Great Odd Fellows celebration probably. Came tonight & another one with it.

Sat. Sept. 22nd. 1883.

Morning in the boat with Eddie. Afternoon paint a little & then more boat with Eddie. A despicable boy. Short letter from Walter and card from Abbie Cooke.

Sun. Sept. 23rd. 1883.

Around with E. in the house & about it, games, painting, etc. Bathe & dress. Dine. Go to church with Mrs. Hopkins & Eddie. Write. Give E. a lot of stamps, old ones. Write to Walter & Carrie Hazard.

Mon. Sept. 24th. 1883—

Write. Boat & walk with Eddie, & read in Spenser's Faery Queen. Enjoy it. Dine. More boat. Letters from Walter & mother. Write a little. Play "Indian" & other games. Retire at 9 & write to Walter. Painted a very little during day.

Tues. Sept. 25th. 1883.

Boat and box trap; set the latter before dinner. Afterward "Indian" etc. Letter from Walter & one from Florrie, and note from Carrie Hazard sending me word of a handsome black silk dress she had sent me to be made over. Read "Bacon's Essays["] while Eddie fishes. Read Walter's letter. Games with E, supper, more games, and then he wants to go down in the parlor, where are two musically inclined youths. I attempt a sketch, we all talk somewhat, of gymnastic feats and arithmetical puzzles; and when I say goodnight they both rise and bow;. A refreshing piece of respect after all this while of daily ignominy.

Wed. Sept. 26th. 1883.

Go with E[ddie]. to look at his box-trap. No game. Stop and see the saw mill work. Fish a while on way up. Find the parlor empty & sitting therein am joined by one of the youths. Afterward E. & the other. Not wonderful young men, at least so far. Dinner. Go & read "Diseases of Modern Life" while Eddie fishes. Letter from Walter & one from Miss gladding. Play Indian &c. See the more robust of the youths, Samuel Smith by name, again; and he brings me down two books to see, Epictetus & a "Golden Treasury." [11] Sup. New game with E. in which my hands are beasts.

Thurs. Sept. 27th. 1883.

Boat all the morning, visit and reset the trap. Boat all the afternoon, off & on, & after the mail is in (letter from Walter.) I row from 3.30 to 6.10 about, with scarce an intermission, full 2½ hours row, beside all the morning! Am not unpleasantly tired after all; and find the reactionary effect, aided by a good supper, to be high good nature. Play "beast" with Eddie, and tell a story or two; beg off at 10 minutes of 9. No quarrel today. I am reading "Epictetus" lent by the Mr. Smith aforesaid. *Like* it; and put a pretty sketch on a blank page as a souvenir and "thankyou".

Fri. Sept. 28th. 1883.   *No letter!*

Up the lake to get the gentlemen at Lily Bay. Then back again as it was too rough to fish. I steered nearly all the time, and enjoyed being alone in the pilot house with the boat plunging like a horse. Am cold & tired in the afternoon; got wet in the morning going with E. after his trap, in a rowboat; combination of causes.

Sat. Sept. 29th. 1883.

Off in the Twilight again, fishing. None at Birch Island save one for Eddie. Then to Spencer Bay. None there. I have a sort of chill for an hour or so; am weak, cold, & querulous. Recover and steer as usual. Back to B[irch]. Island. There Eddie (he had a canoe & guide all to himself) caught three more, all there were by the whole party! He is triumphant. Letters from Walter & Martha.

Sunday. Sept. 30th. 1883.

A snow flurry yesterday & this morning an inch or two on the ground! Dismal, cold, cheerless. I am blue and unreasonable, don't even know what I want. Play with E[ddie]. reluctantly; have a chance to talk somewhat with Mr. Smith, but find little to attract. Dinner. Swathe myself in shawls and try to pack. Bah! I'd like to have a fierce racking pain shoot through & through and all over me for a few moments, so that it leave me clearer. Pack all I can; and "amuse Eddie." Grand musical in the parlor in the evening. Hymns.

Monday, Oct. 1st. 1883.

Finish packing. Off on the top of the stage at 11 or 12. Beautiful ride. Dine at Blanchard. Long trainride to Bangor. Good supper at that town. Then luxurious sleeping car to Boston. Pleasant night of it.

Tuesday, Oct. 2nd. 1883.

Breakfast at B. & P. station. Mrs. Jackson pays me $15.00 and off I set with the Hopkinses. Reach Prov[idence]. at 9.35 or so. See Miss Pratt in the depot. Leave bundles & go straight to Walter. A happy morning. Home to dinner. Talk to mother and Aunt C. Go to see Florrie about teaching her. Favorable.

Call on Lu for a few minutes, and hear of another place. Call on Mrs. Diman and, at her suggestion, fly around to get up a class in gymnastics. Favorable. Home and sup, and talk.

Wed. Oct. 3rd. 1883.

7.50. Breakfast. Write note to Sam. Call on Mrs. Blake, & the Slicer's, and Maria Brown. Post letter. Am weighed—127 lbs. Ask price of contemplated ad in Journal; 50 cts. first time & 15 afterward, 5 lines. Go to Walters and stay an hour or so. Show him sketches, leave one for A[rt]. C[lub]. ex[hibition]. Go to Gym, Dr. Brooks not in; go to express office to see about the silk dress Carrie Hazard said she sent. Not there. Pay Calder $10.00 on account—4.11 left to pay. Make inquiries at the Berlitz school of languages. Take car to Elmwood ([$]1.00 for tickets) to see a Mrs. Robert Knight about lessons; out, call at Mrs. Mason's, out. Walk down and stop to see Millie. Go to Miss Gladdings to dinner. Stop to see Dr. Brooks on the way down; a Miss Lane the teacher this year, a lady. Then home. Met grandma Anthony and her daughterinlaw and walked home with her, saw Carrie Richmond and walked a little way with her, saw Mrs. Blodgett (Minnie Torrey) at her window and stopped to speak with *her*. Take a bit nap, and write.

Thurs. Oct. 4th. 1883—

7. Finish gentian card for Sam, copy "King John & the Abbot of Canterbury" for Mr. Smith at Moosehead, & paint part of another card. Help mother about the drawing. Lunch. Phoebe Campbell came in the morning to join my gymn. class—there's the six! Call on her mother P.M. and then vibrate between the Dimans & the Congdons, all about the gym. Stopped at Florrie's too, and arranged to go there. Dine at Mrs. Diman's. Home. Write. Sam comes. Whist. Glad to see him.

Fri. Oct. 5th. 1883.

7. Spend the morning packing, (*three hours!*) at Mrs. Jackson's; box & trunk. Then home and paint another gentian card for Sam. Carry it down to his mother, and stay awhile. Then call on Grace Channing. Then on Annie Morse, out. Stop for Walter, but he was not there either. Go over to Anna's, stay to tea and till 8.45. Clarence's nephew Clarence there, and he goes home with me. Found at Mrs. J's her sister's wedding cards, Fanny Bogert's also, Sunday School notice, letters from Abbie Cooke, & Uncle Edward & Aunt Emily. Bed at 10. Black silk dress also at Mrs. J's, the one Carrie Hazard sent.

EIGHT

"In Duty, Bound"

October 6, 1883–December 30, 1883

THE DAY after Charlotte's return from Moosehead Lake, Walter revealed to her his growing anxiety over his lack of financial preparedness for marriage. He even briefly contemplated giving up his art for an occupation which would be more dependable and lucrative. Within a day or two, however, he had a change of heart, and he and Charlotte continued to plan their wedding.

Walter's precarious financial situation, however, continued to fuel his anxiety. When Charlotte visited his studio in late October and proposed that they marry before the year's end, Walter's frustration at the bleak reality of his economic condition was obvious. "It seemed almost wicked in me not to join in her enthusiasm, but I could not," he confided to his diary (*Endure*, p. 241). For her part, Charlotte coped with her growing unrest by immersing herself in a variety of activities: she worked out at the gymnasium, continued to teach painting, frequented the library, and enjoyed learning French. But while her days were full, Charlotte continued to be haunted by her own reservations about the drawbacks of marriage. On November 9 her misgivings were projected through her artistic expression, when she painted a "lugubrious picture of 'The Woman Against The Wall,'" which Walter described as "a literal transcript of her mind" (p. 244). In an attempt to confront some of her misgivings, Charlotte confided her fears to such friends as Retta Clarke and Jim and Sam Simmons, whom she found only marginally helpful. With Sam Simmons, for instance, she talked late into the night about women's rights, but to her utter disappointment she found him unsympathetic and narrow-minded.

As a form of catharsis, perhaps, for her growing uncertainty about the impending marriage, Charlotte composed a poem during this time, which significantly marked her first adult publication. "In Duty, Bound" was a lamentation on the loss of individualism in marriage (see Appendix B). The poem depicts the "wasting power," the death of "high ideals," and the broken spirit that Charlotte felt one must endure in marriage. If her painting of "The Woman Against The Wall" was a literal transcript of Charlotte's mind, "In Duty, Bound" was even more so. The metaphors of bondage and isolation are powerful; images of pain and despair are etched into every line.

When Charlotte learned that the *Woman's Journal* had accepted the poem for publication, she commented simply, "No pay, but it's a beginning." And it did mark the start of an incredibly prolific writing career which would span much of the next fifty-two years. But the poem also marked the beginning of the most difficult period of Charlotte's life, as her ill-fated marriage to Walter Stetson drew near.

After having "been miserable in divers ways for weeks," Charlotte left on December 26 for a visit to Martha and Charles Lane and their four-and-a-half-month-old son in Hingham, Massachusetts. Although she enjoyed seeing Martha again, the old pain of abandonment mercilessly resurfaced when the two young parents left Charlotte "sitting up in [a] lonely state" so that they could retire, alone, for the evening.

On December 29, 1883, Charlotte returned to Providence.

Sat. Oct. 6th. 1883

6. Write to Aunt E., Miss Goslee, & Carrie Hazard. Go to see Mrs. Diman but meet her and she stops here to wait a car. Go to Dr. Brooks & get figures for apparatus. Get placques etc. at Calders. Enquire price of Indian Clubs. Post letters in box. Call for Walter talk with him a little, & walk to Gilmore st. with him. He means to give up his Art! Because he cannot make it "pay", and because he must have money to marry, and he must marry. Well————. Car down, go to Clarence's and get more figures for apparatus. Stop at George's to see about dumbells. Go to the Browns to dinner and enjoy it. Home. Letter from Walter————. Henrietta Brown & Anna Comstock call, on Aunt C. who was out. Write address for my S. S. class. Go to Marys to tea.

Sun. Oct. 7th. 1883.

6.30 or so. Opening of Sunday School. All but two in my class, and all interested in my "address" and ready to begin. Church. Walk home with Florrie, who has her hair done up, a silk dress, and looks well. Sam called and brought me some knot-grass. Paint it, and other things. Anna & Clarence & Charlie & Mary call. Write to Charlotte Hedge somewhat. Walter from nearly 8 to 10.

Mon. Oct. 8th. 1883

6 or so. Begin with Florrie. Spend about an hour in planning gymnastic work for the winter for her. She is enthusiastic, and interested in all her studies. Call at Mrs. Dimans and make final arrangements about my gym. class. On Mrs. Congdon, who has a chestweight we can have. On Mrs. Moulton, &

Mrs. Fillinghast, and lunch there. Go to Hogg's & get 5 cts. worth of pansies, reading all the way in Blakie. Home & paint two pansies on placques. Mrs. H. Carpenter has concluded *not* to have me stay there; and so my big trunk & things have come home. Go with mother, Aunt C., & the Budlongs to see "Young Mrs. Winthrop" at the Opera House. Its success proves to be its truth, and its truth is its shame.

Tues. Oct. 9th. 1883.

6.30. Begin a brief article on last night's play. Florrie every day now, from 9 to 11. Paint pansie. Go with Florrie to see about the Berlitz. Stop with her at Walters to see about her portrait. Home and paint till I can't see. Downstairs and write. Write to Walter. Harry Manchester calls.

Wed. Oct. 10th. 1883.

6 to 7—forgotten. Write. Note from Carrie with Art Ex. ticket and order for $10.00 worth of cards. Letter from Walter. Nearly finish pansie placque. Go with Florrie to our first French lesson at the Berlitz. A delightful lady teacher, pretty and pleasant, sweetvoiced and kind. Enjoy it much. Stop and tell Walter I'll go to the A[rt]. C[lub]. Reception. Walk up with him and stop to sup at Miss Gladdings. But she wasn't there, and I run after him and go home with him instead. Sup there, welcomed by all of them; and then down again with Walter. My picture well mounted and placed, looks well. I'm as proud as the hen with one chicken. Home ere 9.30. John Willey here. Sketch his head.* Bed about 11.

Thurs. Oct. 11th. 1883.

7. Write. Paint wild rose placque. A hot day, so I wash my hair. read "Alpha" and nap.* Write, finishing critique of "Young Mrs. Winthrop". Write to Carrie Hazard & Charlotte Hedge. Bed before 11, I *think*.

Fri. Oct. 12th. 1883.

6.45. Write. [$]3.00 from Florrie. Send it to S. H. & write to Miss Alden, and to Retta Clarke. Call on Mrs. Diman about class. Go to French lesson with F. Order 10 pair of 2 lb. dumbbells. Get F. another P. L. card & Keary's "Dawn of History". Stop in at Waterman's with her. Home! Write to Walter (letter from him this morning). sup. Read a little. Sam calls & stays till 10.30 or so.

Sat. Oct. 13th. 1883—

7. Unpack, and arrange room for winter habitation. Room about 11 × 11, with low wall on one side; therein—1 bedstead, 1 bureau, 1 washstand, 2 chairs, 5 trunks, 1 chest, 1 box, 1 bookshelves. Letter from Walter morning & noon. Meet mother down st. & go to Art Ex. with her. Then call on Mr. Slicer and

have a talk with him; and borrow book for S. S. class. Then half an hour with Walter, then walk up with him to P. L., conclude not to go in; go through to Broad St., to ride, & rememember [*sic*] I took a postal card of Mr. S. to post, Walter walks to P. O. with me, & then home with me. I call at Lu's. Have some bread & butter & talk a while; and Lu plays to me. Home & now intend [to] read "Deterioration & Race Education," by Samuel Royce, Mr. Slicer's book.

Sun. Oct. 14th. 1883.

After 7. A wet Sunday, hence small school, hence I do not have regular lesson, but discourse on Jewish Hist. Church. Stop & speak to Mr. Slicer. Call on Mrs. Putnam, poor woman. Sidney died Aug. 3rd.'83. Home, dine. Begin letter to Cassie. Nap. Down & see Lizzie, Henrietta & Pardon. Dress in grandmother's muslin for Walter. 7.30. to 10 he is here. Bed ere 10.30.

Mon. Oct. 15th. 1883. Fire in Parlor Stove.

6.30. Write to Walter. Letter from Miss Alden with Greek course. Paint. Go down to see about dumbbells. Stamps, new 2's $.50. Inquire about gas stoves. Call at Mrs. Diman's. Home. Dine & read. Paint, write, read. First hour with gymnastic class. Great fun; they like it. Home. Sup & read, enjoying it much. Write to Walter, Cassie, & send "In Duty, Bound." [1] to the Century. Letters from Walter & Carrie Hazard.

Tues. Oct. 16th. 1883.

7. Go with Florrie for her first sitting to Walter. I rip Carrie's own silk dress. Pleasant time. Post letter to Walter & Century. Home. Dine. Florrie's lessons from 2 to 4 & then read her "Virginia". [2] She gets excited over it, a thing she never used to do. Home. Paint. Miss Murphy here to Supper. Write. Stop at Anna's. Leave sock and directions at Mrs. Jacksons, Eddie glad to see me. Call on Mrs. Mauran. Certain Misses Stockbridge walk home with me, on their way. Mr. Cranston, friend of the Mauran's, is to give me a gastove.

Wed. Oct. 17th. 1883.

6.40. Finish copying "Mrs. Winthrop" critique & send to Cassie. Begin Xmas card, lily in darkness, after preparing some sewing. Dine. Go with Florrie to buy shoes (her's), then to French lesson, then she changes her shoes, then home. Maria here. Letter from Walter P.M. Write & read a bit. Jim calls. Mother retires, and J. stays till 11.20 or so. A good talk.

Thurs. Oct. 18th. 1883.

7. Write to Walter. Call at Mrs. Diman's after lessons, to see about gym. Trot down on same errand, and stop at see [*sic*] Walter nearly an hour. Dumbells not done. Go to Clarence's. Other thing not done. Stop at Mrs. D[iman].'s again, lunch, & talk with her & John about lying. Go down and tell Phebe

Cambell the class is postponed. Stop at Florrie's to see that rose placque of theirs. Home. Paint till 5.25. Sup. Write.

Fri. Oct. 19th. 1883—

7.8. Letter from Walter. Read "Horatius" to Florrie. Finish wild rose placque. Write to Walter. Dine. Go with Florrie to sit. Walter has another letter for me. French lesson, a delightful one. Lend F[lorrie]. 18 cts. Home. Sup & read Odyssey. Write to Walter. Anna & Clarence call. Then Sam. I sew till there's no one left but Sam, and then we talk till 12.05 or 10. We are far apart.

Sat. Oct. 20th. 1883—

6.40 or so. Sweep my room. Finish pansie placque, & mother takes 'em in to Mrs. Budlong, who sends $5.00 which I repay mother. I sew, and fix my winter suit. It promises well. Also I read a little & nap a *little*. Sew, draw for mother in her infant's books & write. Letter from Walter A. M. & receipt from Miss Ticknor.

Sun. Oct. 21st. 1883.

7.20. Class full save George Mann. Begin lessons on the bad side of human life. Church. Teachers meeting. I am become one of a committee of three to nominate a new superintendent! Prescott Clarke walks nearly home with me, talking about it. I write him a letter on the subject. Dine. Wash two or three dishes. Mary & Alice in. Draw for Alice. Look over Century. Sup, peripatatically. Dress. Walter from 7.30 to 10.5–10. Copy for him a queer beast I drew for Alice.

Mon. Oct. 22nd. 1883.

6.40 or so. Florrie not back from Boston, so I paint all day, in oil. Letter from Kate. Answer. Call a moment at Mrs. Diman's to see about dumbbells. Miss Alden there. Stop for Walter, he goes to "George's" while I post letter, and get the advertised one; from Moosehead Mr. Smith, acknowledging mine. Then home with Walter to supper, & down again with him, he going to call on Mr. Grimshaw and I to Grace Channings. Candy and talk. She lends me "For Girls." Bed after 11.

Tues. Oct. 23rd. 1883.

7. Begin to read "For Girls" to Florrie, who likes it. Letter from Century returning poem. Not a printed form at any rate. Read some. Trim over that grey felt bonnet that was Ada's. Very pretty. Go to Mrs. Diman's, who is not very well, and have a nice talk with Miss Alden. Sew some. Bring work home, & get Odyssey for Miss A. Go to Mrs. Fillinghast's. Charlotte sick. Tell her stories. Dine. Talk to Annie & show her "For Girls." Advise her to buy it. Home by 9.40, in a rain. Sent "In Duty, Bound" to Harpers.

Wed. Oct. 24th. 1883—

6.40 or so. Mother dizzy so I help her before school. Read physiology "for girls" to Florrie till nearly 12. Home. Lunch. Sew. Put up chairs for mother. Leave hat and umbrella with Annie Aborn. Go to Walters & stay an hour & a half, good. Leave shoes to be tapped & mended at Pierces. French. Call on Millie. Home. Sup & finish Morrise's "Love is enough.["] Call for Nellie Peck & go to Mrs. Tibbetts as a committee of three. Little done.

Thurs. Oct. 25th. 1883.

7. Begin to be busy again. Write to Walter. Home at 11.30. Sew. Paint, finishing little card for mother, and lily-in-the wood Xmas card. Letter from Carrie Hazard A.M., offering me another Latin scholar, and arithmetic. Poor me with no Latin! Letter from Walter P.M. Emily & Louise Diman & Effie Rathbone in and out, about a kitten. Read "Juventus Mundi." Paint. Write to W. and mail. Sew, 10.30.

Fri. Oct. 26th. 1883

7.10. Letter from Walter & write to him.* Write more after school, paint red lily card and little lit woods one. Emily Diman in to say Dumbbells have come. Go to Walter's room returning "Love is Enough.["] Not in. Wait a while & then go to French lesson, stopping for shoes. Not ready. No one in class but "le monsieur" et moi. (Florrie not feeling very well.) Pleasant lesson. Get 2.40 cts. worth of cards at Calders. Get gas pipe, $1.50. Meet Walter. Get 2 lbs. paper, 70 cts, and a box of envelopes, .45 cts. Walter walks over to Anna's with me. Stay to supper. Home by 8.10. Write & sew.

Sat. Oct. 27th. 1883.

7.20. Send letter to Walter and get one, & circular of W. C. ex. Sew. Go to see Lu Manchester. Sew. Dine. Read J. M. Go to Mrs. Diman's, cover dumbbells & over see carpenter in erection of vaulting bar. Then gymnastics with much success. Home. Write to Walter. Sup & read "Lovers of Gudrun." Write to Martha & S. S. class. Bead [*sic*] after 11.

Sun. Oct. 28th. 1883—

7.30. Read sermon of last night to class. Well liked. Church. Teacher's meeting. P. O. Clarke refusing nomination as superintendant. Nominating committee is increased by two. Home. Sam here; and stays till 2.30, talking of S. school etc. Brought me three little tea roses, to paint. Mary comes, then Anna & Charlie, then Ray & Alice, then Clarence. I paint little green-trees card. Read J. M. Write. Walter from 7.40 to 10. Write a little more to him. Bed.

Mon. Oct. 29th. 1883—

7. Read & write. Carry dumbbells to Florrie. .20 cts. Home & paint tearose for Sam. Not a success. Carrie Hazard called. Order for screen. Dine & read "A Woman's Reason".³ Paint more. Call on Walter for a few moments, Mr. John Mason there. Go to the committee meeting. No great progress. Go to Miss Addie Brown to report of the same. Seems pleased with me. Call on Kate, dear Soul, and see Jessie Taylor & Miss George. Beg 6 cents of Kate to ride home with. Carry painted things to the Brown's, for the fair. Have some apple slump. Lizzie gives me a piece of illusion, & Uncle William & the boys car tickets, 2, 3, & 3. Ride home. Write.

Tues. Oct. 30th. 1883.

7.10. Letter from Retta Clarke & Charlotte Hedge. Paint tea rose card for Carrie Hazard leaves satin for screen. Letter from Walter. Paint. Go to gym. class. See Miss Alden again. They ask me to dinner but I stay not. Home. Sup. Write.

Wed. Oct. 31st. 1883.

7.30 almost. Letter from Walter & Harper's, returning poem, "In Duty, Bound." Nap on returning from Florrie's till 1.20. Arrange dress & go with her to Walter's. He does better with the portrait, and I try a charcoal study of her head. Then French, very pleasant. Then F. rides home & I go to our church fair. Find Lu Peck wanting a Herdic and trot back and get her a coupè, all the H.s being in business—rains hard. Ride back in it (10 cts.) and stay till 8.20 about. Go home with Nellie Peck. Supped with Kate & Miss Comstock. Told stories to little folks & bigger ones. Sam there & pays for three little folk's grabs. Home. Write & settle month's accts.

Thurs. Nov. 1st. 1883.

7.10. Letter from Walter. Florrie reads French. Finish lily card & paint one with m.gs. Gym. class. Home write sew. sup. sew. Read Centuries discontentedly.

Fri. Nov. 2nd. 1883.

7.30 or so. Good letter from Martha. Finish winter dress enough to wear it, and do so. Leave Florrie at Studio & dine with mother at Sutton's. She buys me some candy, good. A few minutes at stu. & then Florrie & I go to French lesson. Very interesting. Give the dear little lady teacher some "bon-bon". Get F[lorrie]. "Prince & Pauper" at Library. Go to studio again. Mr. Burleigh there. Walter walks up with me & leaves me at Miss Gladding's, where I sup. Walter comes for me, & we go to see Barrett⁴ in "Francisca de Riunini". Fine acting. Home. re-sup. Bed ere 12.

Sat. Nov. 3rd. 1883.

7.30–35. Paint begonia card, three hours work. *Very pretty.* Begin sermon. Write & draw in E. Diman's album. Write note to Charlotte Hedge. Read J. M. Gym. Class, all there, home with Phebe, who stops to look at Xmas cards. Home. Sup. Write "A Word to Myself".[5] & verse in L. Diman's A[utograph] album. Paint howling wolf on frozen lake at night.[6] Bed ere 12.

Sun. Nov. 4th. 1883.

8.30 almost. S. S. read in "Degeneration" book. Walk home with Grace Channing & call with her on Abbie Cooke. Search for Prof. Well's boarding house, in vain. Stop a moment to see Annie Aborn. Out. Home. Mend mother's dress. Dine. Put shorter binding on trained silk skirt Mrs. Fillinghast gave me, and fix neck & sleeves of camel's hair. Dress in hot haste. Walter from 7.30 to 10. He brings me a letter. Wishes me to be gentler.

Mon. Nov. 5th. 1883.

7.20 or so. Florrie begins to write French exercises. Write to Walter. Paint on Mrs. Mason's defaced tamborine & start two Sabbatia cards for Sam. Annie Aborn comes and stays some time; and Carrie Hazard calls, bless her heart, and gives me orders for some 16 dollars worth more cards, and wants to buy my moosehead sketch for $50.00! I won't have it; say $20.00. Undecided. Go to Children's Mission meeting, walking down with Annie, and home with her and to dinner. Gives me dark green winter suit. Home. Sam. Whist.

Tues. Nov. 6th. 1883—

7.15. Write to Walter. Paint 2 dollar lily card. Red lily. Gym. class. Poor little Charlotte Fillinghast drops the chestweight box, *fully*, on her toe! Little darling! She's the *sweetest* child I know. Carry her home in my arms. Run down with Phebe. Stay at Mrs. Diman's till 9 o'clock, waiting for carpenter. Don't come. Will Mauran called, twice. (they told him I'd be in). Sorry to miss him.

Wed. Nov. 7th. 1883.

? Two letters from Walter. Call at Mrs. Fillinghasts' to ask after Charlotte. She's all right. Go to Walter and stay about an hour. Take him a letter and some paper. Walk home with him. Call briefly on Millie; and wait for Mother at Tibbett's. More Sutton['s Restaurant] dinner, hurried. Then Florrie sits again. I read her the "Ancient Mariner", enjoy Noel Payton's illustrations thereof, and Percy's Reliques. Then French, very pleasant, counting clumsily. Make friends with the teacher and arrange to call on her, for mutual assistance, and because I like her. Buy toothbrush & paper with money I borrowed from mother. Home *via* Prof. Blake, where we stopped on a errand; but they were both asleep! No sooner home than John Diman comes for me to oversee the carpenter. Dine there. Home, and Will Mauran calls again! Are having a nice talk when Jim comes, late, and Will goes. Jim does retire before 10.30 though. *Bed*, late.

Thurs. Nov. 8th. 1883.

? Watch stopped. Paint on Sabbatias. Letter from Walter. Gym. Class. Home. Read Juventus Mundi. Write to Martha, and in Mabel Luther's album & draw also therein. Bed at *12*.

Fri. Nov. 9th. 1883—

? Left watch at Mrs. D[iman]'s last night. Emily brings it. Write F. ex. Cut, or rather tear out three new chemiloons. Dine. Walk down with Florrie in the rain and read Ovid & Percy's Reliques while she sits. French. I do enjoy learning a language. Buy buttons, 42 cts. for 1 ½ doz. Buy another big pad to write on, 25 cts. Ride home. Sup. Write. And paint lugubrious picture of "The Woman Against The Wall."[7]

Sat. Nov. 10th. 1883.

7.30. Drag around. Fix clothes & sweep room. Abbie Cooke calls and borrows pansies & things and leaves our novel. Gym class. Briefly and lively talk with Mrs. D. while dressing. Home. Sup. Write & draw in Charlotte's auto. album.

Sun. Nov. 11th. 1883—

7.30? Sermon on Proverbs in Class. All present but two and all go into church with me, as do the whole S. S. mostly, to sing Luther's hymn. Meeting afterwards. Mr. Stone is to be superintendant, Mr. Metcalf ass[istant]. super., & three ladies executive committee. Home. dine. Call on Madame Charbonnier. *Very* pleasant time. Call on Millie. Home. sup & read "Unknown to History", lent me by Annie Aborn without request. Am enjoying it. Dress. Walter. I'm happy again.

Mon. Nov. 12th. 1883.

7.20. Bright morning, feel frisky. Set Florrie to painting. Home & finish Sabbatia's, paint harebells & rosebud. Henrietta here & I help mother get supper. Read "Unknown" etc. at meals. Read Juventus Mundi over an hour. Write to Walter.

Tues. Nov. 13th. 1883

7.15. Paint card for Will Mauran, & sketch designs for screen. Go a bit early to Mrs. Dimans, & we cover the remaining dumbbells. Gym. Home. Mrs. D. gave me two Arion tickets & I left 'em at the Budlongs, who are always ready. Kate here. Get her som [*sic*] supper, Anna & Clarence call. Go home with Kate and stop and call on the Blakes. Whitney comes home with me. Show him cards. Write to Walter.

Wed. Nov. 14th. 1883—

7.33. Letter from Walter. Carry cards & picture & designs to the Hazards. See all the girls. More orders and encouragement, & check for $10.00 in advance. Took me down st. in the carriage, I cashed the check, home, dined, and down again with Florrie. Lend Walter five dollars. Read old ballads to self & Florrie. French. Florence gets discouraged, because we others are older, have studied it before somewhat, and get ahead faster. It is hard for her. Home. Sup. write. Bought two underwaists, and left Moosehead sketch at Watermans to be framed. Write on novel. Edward comes. Then Robert. Whist.

Thurs. Nov. 15th. 1883—

7.30. Paint gentians on gold disk & anemones on a little card. Dine. Sketch for Carrie's sonnets. She calls with them & the screen designs & Kane's Ex. for mother, & sabbatia card. Sketch more. Henrietta and Mrs. H. Carpenter call. Gym. Only three there. Home. Write. Harry Manchester calls.

Fri. Nov. 16th. 1883.

? Letter from Christian Register declining "In Duty Bound," only because they don't pay for poems unless ordered. Encouraging. Write on novel & doze. Paint *a little*. Go down with F[lorrie]. Walter late & not well: Weak & tired. French. F. rides home & I go to see Walter till 6. & then tea at the Slicer's. First meeting of a girl's club as yet nameless at the chapel. Younger girls of the S. S. 14 to 20 say, for reading & music etc. I am chosen president. Think it will be a good thing. See Mrs. Slicer home, then come myself & find Sam here. He stays till 11.45 nearly, talking Woman's Rights with me. A man far from broad. Bed bathless.

Sat. Nov. 17th. 1883.

8.30 about. Write my 7th chapter in the novel, & mend a bit. Sketch for Carrie. Lizzie Brown calls. Leave her here alone & go to Gym. class. All there. Home with Phebe. Run part way. Dine at the D's. Talk a bit, mostly on anatomy. Carry novel to Grace Channing's & stay till 9.30 or 40. Dr. C[hanning]. gives me a pretty napkinring of sumach wood. Home. Bath. Bed.

Sun. Nov. 18th. 1883.

8. S. S. Alfred Stone installed as Superintendant & Mr. Shaw reads a few closing remarks & departs gracefully. Mr. Manchester preaches. Walk home with Grace, & stop to call on Mrs. Wells. See Benjamin also a few moments. Home. Dine gorgeously on roast chicken. Go to Madame Charbonnier's & we "promenade" to Prospect Terrace and on the Reservoir & so home. She stops in to rest a few minutes & then I ride home with her & home again. Sup. Dress.

Walter. He is undecided on a question of right & wrong, but finally settles it. I wish we were well married—[8]

Mon. Nov. 19th. 1883.

7.30 about. Try more on Carrie's sketches, but can't do them—yet. Cannot paint, so take my things and go down to see Carry. Out. Go to Ath. & get "Hannah Thurston"[9] and address of magazines. Go to Blandings & look at directory. Back to Carrie's & wait for her, reading "Unknown to History". See Margie & then Helen & finally Carrie. Tell her I can't do what she wanted. She insists on my taking some quinine pills! I could not refuse her, but it was hard. See Helen some more & then home. Write poem headed "It needs must be that offenses come, but woe unto *her* / through whom the offense cometh." Sup. Finish "Unknown to history".

Tues. Nov. 20th. 1883.

7.30.(?) Go down to see Mrs. Cushing, who called yesterday to see if I would teach drawing in her school. Stop & see Walter. Go to Pierce's & order boots. Home. Dine. Paint. Write. Sew. Letter from Walter, & one from Carrie with $50.00.

Wed. Nov. 21st. 1883—

7.30.(?) Give first drawing lesson at Mrs. Cushing's. Leave waterproof & umbrella at Walters. Go to T. C. Greene, and ask him about the Hartford property. He cashes my check. Write letter there, to Uncle Charles Perkins. Go to Watermans. Lunch in Pub. Lib. on 2 graham rolls, 1 piece of new cheese & three apples; .10 reading Pop. Sci. the while with much enjoyment. Then hunt for plush for picture frame, unsuccessfully. Buy tuberose for Madame Charbonnier .05 {cents}. French lesson; Pleasant. Walk home with Madame. Go to Grace Channings to supper. Look at pictures & talk. Walter comes later. Nice time. Home by 10.15 or 20.

Thurs. Nov. 22nd. 1883

7.20. Read some J. M. ere 9. Paint till 4.30. Divers children call. Lend "Three Thousand Leagues Under the Sea" to Fred. Hines. Call on Lu Manchester, & have a nice talk with Fannie. Home & do three little ink cards. Write in jour[nal].

Fri. Nov. 23rd. 1883.

7.20. Paint gladiolus panel. A man is thrown from a buggy out here, and I go out and hold his head until he recovers. Seems not seriously hurt. Was drunk. buggy well smashed. Arranged sewing &, after lunching, go to Walter's with it. Stay until 3.40. French lesson. Get "Prince & Pauper" again for Florrie. Stop at Walter's again. Not in so I look at Mr. Burleigh's pictures, wait a bit longer for Walter and then home. Letter from Uncle Charles with account of property as desired. Write to Walter & Mr. Hazard.

Sat. Nov. 24th. 1883—

8. Paint red geranium on gold disc. Finish Gladiolus. Start arbutus. Finish Juventus Mundi & look at Raphael's pictures, (book Walter brought.) Dine. Copy "One Girl" poem and send it to the "Alpha".[10] Gym. class. Mrs. Fillinghast in. Home. Clarence in. Go home with him & eat some pears & bananas. Stop at Mrs. Diman's after my watch. Home. Write sermon on Proverbs.

Sun. Nov. 25th. 1883—

7! Bathe. Mend shoe. Breakfast. S. S. with Mrs. Rawson & Arney. George Mann rearrives. Walk home with Will Mauran. He stops in a moment & takes two cards—.75 cts. Dine. Sew lace in sleeves. Call on Madame Charbonnier. She shows me family photographs. Call on Millie. Home. Sup. Dress. Walter. I read him the letter I wrote Friday night. One of my turns of affectional paralysis.

Mon. Nov. 26th. 1883—

7. Paint Arbutus, unsuccessfully. Do yellow panel of screen. Sam in and orders cards. Pays me $4.00. in advance. Sup. Read "The Return of the Druses." [11] Write. Sew.

Tues. Nov. 27th. 1883—

7. Finish Arbutus, looks better. Do tiger lily panel of screen. Gorgeous. Letter from Walter with invitation to Art Club Concert. Lizzie calls. Gym. class. Retta there. Home with Phebe as usual, home. Kate here. Supper & talk. Kate & Lizzie go home together and I go & see Retta. Carry cards to show her & Mrs. D. Tell Retta "In Duty, Bound;" and read her "One girl out of many". Home. Write.

Wed. Nov. 28th. 1883

7(?) Lesson at Mrs. Cushman's. Call on Mrs. Williams, the colored woman our class are going to help. She is partially paralyzed, and has a little 9 year old boy. Lives in two little *holes* in an attic, & pays $4.00 a month for them! And there are four of these "suites" in that attic, $16.00. And our beautiful home with yard & fruit, is $15.00! Leave her 67 cts. of the class money. Stop to see Annie Aborn. Out. Call on Connie Pitman. Out. Change Hannah Thurston for Cox's "Tales of Anc. Greece" at the Ath. Buy 10 cts. worth of lunch and eat it in the studio. Half an hour with Walter before Florrie comes. She shops a little. French. Florrie renews her interest. She rides home & I go to the Browns to supper & arrange about the "Social Evening." Home. Jim. Sew.

Thurs. Nov. 29th. 1883.

8 about. Draw clematis design. Dress up in fine style & mother and I go to Anna's to dinner. Splendid dinner. Put elastic in my muff. Entertain young Clarence who in return entertains me with tales of Western life & adventures. He is a splendid specimen of that kind of a boy. Only just 21. Walks home with us and tells more stories. I was injudicious enough to wear my hair high; and it seems as if every hair ached. No bath.

Fri. Nov. 30th. 1883—

Ere 7. Help mother. Have a heavy swollen sort of feeling in head and throat, owing to cold air on my unprotected nape last night I suppose. That and the dinner. Gargle in salt-&-vinegar. Sew. Lizzie here. Dine lightly. Go down with Florrie. Sew. French, beginning over again. See F. to her car & then stop at Walter's. Not there. Go to the Slicer's to tea. He invites me to Mathew Arnold's lecture, Monday night. 2nd meeting of our club. Miss Ballou of the choir sings, & Miss Dexter. Cake & lemonade. Tudie Mauran takes Mrs. Slicer home & then me. Mother & Aunt C. gone to the theatre.

Sat. Dec. 1st. 1883.

8.30 nearly. Slept well & warm, in blanket. White spots on tonsils, little appetite, general debility. More salt-&-vinegar; and mother, little guessing the extent of my ailment, gives me some clear coffee. Finish clematis panel, and all Mrs. Augusta Hazard's cards. Bit of cracker at 4.30. gym class, Dimans away and Effie not there. Home. Sup quite well & feel better. Sew. Sam in for an hour or two, & orders more cards.

Sun. Dec. 2nd. 1883—

8 or after. S. S. with Mrs. R. & Arney. *Full* class. New regulations instituted. All the classes to study the same book—Life of Christ. General disaffection, and my class furious. See various people about various things, and home in the rain with Harry Manchester. Dine. Go and see Mr. Stone, the Superintendant, about the new rule. Compromise. Stop to see the Kelly girls & engaged them for café girls. Call on the Westcott's with similar intent; and stay a long time, waiting for their mother: prospect dubious. But made friends with the damsels & Carl. Home. Sup. Wash slates for mother. Dress. Walter from 7.30–45 to 10. He brought me Harper's for Dec. Mother spends the evening at Mary's, who has another little girl at 9 P.M. or thereabout.

Mon. Dec. 3rd. 1883.

7. or before. Mend carpet. After Florrie black boots & change dress, dine, and set forth. Return "Unknown to History" to Annie Aborn. Call on Mrs. Williams. Out. Leave card at Mrs. Binney's. $3.00. Have to decline Mr. B's order. Leave tickets for Miss Olmstead & Cousin, Café girls. Stop at Miss Brushe's

to see about tablecloths. Carry tickets to Lena Hill, and to the Misses Edgar. Meet Maria at the hall, (Am. Dram.) and arrange for the evening. Go home with her. Call on Carry Hazard, leave screen—check for $15.00. and show her aunt's cards. The Hartford hope extinguished. Go to Mrs. Tibbetts to see about tablecloths. Go to the Slicer's to tea & with them to hear Mathew Arnold lecture. Was measurably pleased. Home with Mrs. Tibbitts & then home. Mrs. Westcott & Carl here. Girls can't come. Jim here. Orders card. Oranges. bed about 12.

Tues. Dec. 4th. 1883.

7.20. Florrie has a headache and I don't go. Arrange for various things. Go to see about those tablecloths again. Then to see Maria. Then to Trust Company & cash my check, $15.00. Then to see Walter a little while. Then to P.O. Stamps 50, p. cards. 15. Then to get boots, not done. Buy little blocks for café girls 3–6[;] 35 cts. a doz. Allie gave me a lovely string of wax beads—amber. I *always* liked 'em! Then home. Met Junie Keach on George St. & she walked home with me and made a call. Dine. Paint about 40 cts. worth & doze over it. Gym. class, all there. Louise bumps her back. Home with Phebe, home, sup, write.

Wed. Dec. 5th. 1883.

7.40. Forget Mrs. Cushing—10 minutes late. Back, paint a little, dine; go down with Florrie. Read to her out of Harpers Mag. Buy dress protectors, 2 pair, 36 cts. Stop at Waterman's to see my picture, framed, & pay for it, $5.50. French. Monsieur le professeur is very suave with Miss Florrie. She is well steeled against his attractions however. Get cards at Calders. Home. Sup. Read Howells' little farce of "The Register" to mother. Mend muff. Write to Miss Alden with the briefest of articles on early Greece.

Thurs. Dec. 6th. 1883.

7.30 or after. Note from Mrs. Agusta [*sic*] Hazard with check for $15.00. Letter from Walter & Calder's bill [$]11.85 & another letter from Walter. Go to the hall & arrange tables. Home & arrange for dressing. Gym. class. Home. *Dress.* Go to the "Social Evening." Jim & Sam are there, and *do everything*. Jim home with me. bed by 1.45 A.M.

Fri. Dec. 7th. 1883—

7.30. Mrs. Blake calls to order cards, but I can't do 'em. Eat an apple & orange, and take a nap. A little brown bread & milk & then down st. with Florrie. Sew while she sits. French. Meet the Westcotts at the Pub. Lib. & see that they get cards. Show 'em all the workings; and they all get books. Home with Sarah & her friend, Miss Rogers, Carl having run for a fire. Note from Carrie with more Hartford hope. Lu Manchester comes in. Carl stops to say he's all right and posts my answer to Carrie. Sup. Sam in, wants more cards! Goes early. Read things to Lu. See her home. Write in journal.

Sat. Dec. 8th. 1883.

7.30 or so. Paint from 9 till 4, stopping for dinner. Do tea roses for Sam. & some of Carrie's little ones. Mrs. Blake stops to see if she left a jewelled pin here yesterday; and is rejoiced to find it. Letter from Martha. Gym. class, and stop a bit to talk with Mrs. D. Effie Rathbone *vaults*! at last. Home. Sup. Write. Prepare S. S. Lesson.

Sun. Dec. 9th. 1883.

8.20–30! S. S. My class is promoted to three seats & an arm chair, in a corner. Frank Cranston gives me his essay on slavery. A good one too. I'm pleased with him. Mr. Woodbury preaches. Home with Lu Man[chester]. & her mother. Dine. Call on Madame Charbonnier & Millie. Home. Sup. Dress. Walter.

Mon. Dec. 10th. 1883—

7 or so & help mother, who is not well. Finish Carrie's cards. Sam calls & takes one of 'em so I do two little funny ones in place of it. Jim comes, later, and stays till after 11; and I do three cards for him, monochrome.

Tues. Dec. 11th. 1883—

Ere 7. Do housework. Call on Mary & the baby. Carry cards to Carrie. Home. Paint anemone & hepatica for Sam. Too dark to paint at 4! Gym. class. Mrs. D. still indisposed; and Retta arrives radiant & most welcome. Dear girl! Home. Write herein. Draw cards for Sam. Write to Martha.

Wed. Dec. 12th. 1883

Ere 7. Housework. Florrie. Mrs. Cushing. Mrs. Williams & leave her a dollar. Leave little wooden plate for Miss Nightingale. Leave book at Ath. & get "Freeman's Hist. Geog. of Europe". Get lunch, 10 cts. Get two photograph cards 20 cts, & George Eliot's poems for Thomas, 80 cts. Get check cashed $15.00, met Annie Aborn who goes with me to the bank. Get lace fichu, Spanish, for Julia, $1.50. Go to the studio and see Walter awhile before Florrie comes. Eat lunch. Look at books with F. French, very nice. Pay bill at Calder's, $11.85. Look at more books with F. & get "Children's Garland" for Willie, $1.00 not paid yet. O & got new boots, dongola, beauties, $5.00 Home. Nap on chairs. Eat oranges. Write to Walter.

Thurs. Dec. 13th. 1883—

7.5 or so. Housework. Paint. Dine. Paint. Gym. A few words with Retta. Home. Write. Edward & Robert. Whist

Fri. Dec. 14th. 1883

7.30. nearly. Housework, some. Two letters from Walter & one from Woman's Journal accepting "In Duty Bound". The first step, the entering wedge. No pay, but it's a beginning. Retta called a moment while I was with Florrie. Paint. Dine. Stop at Walter's a few moments, meet F. at Tibbitt's where she buys "American Poets" for Mr. Howard. Tree calf, gilt-edge, very gorgeous; $6.00. She gets a card at Calder's, then French, then see her in car & go to Walter's again. Have some chocolate with him at Rausch's. Diminutive cup not full 15 cts! Girl's Literary Club—G.L.C. See Lily Randolph to the car & home. Write to Martha & Retta.

Sat. Dec. 15th. 1883—

8.35 about. Paint from 10 to 4.15, minus dinner. Miss Murphy here finishing mothers sealskin-cloth coat. Handsome & warm. Sam calls, takes what cards I have done, and pays me [$]2.50. Mother got me some cor. cards down st., 75 cts. Gym class. Home. Write.

Sun. Dec. 16th.

8 & after. S. S. Church. Home with Miss Nightingale, who has lost her sister. Home. dine. Paint. Bathe & dress. draw. Walter from 7.35 or 40 to 10. He brings me three pomegranates. I feel better; have been miserable in divers ways for weeks.

Mon. Dec. 17th. 1883.

7 or so. Carry Florrie half a pomegranate. Home & paint. lunch. paint. Go shopping at 4.30. Stop for Walter & he goes with me for an hour or so. And gets me pretty Canton china tea-cups & fings.[12] I spend $3.25 or so & get about 30 things. Great fun. Home. settle accts. & sup luxuriously. Read in English Ill. Mag. Walter brought last night. bed.

Tues. Dec. 18th. 1883—

7.10. Paint gladiolus & lily. Gym. class. Home with Phebe. Call on Anna to arrange for Aunt C.'s "Pear's Soap." Home & draw. Sam. Draw all his little cards & two others. Let him read the "Only a girl" poem. He takes it badly. I am afflicted with a foot. Rubbed by a seam in the new boots, and the rubber boots worn Monday on my shopping excursion drawing & inflaming it. Mother suggests calendula, & I do it up therein.

Wed. Dec. 19th. 1883.

7.45 about. Take car down st. & get my old boots. No charge. Put 'em on & walk home. Half hour late. Order for ribbon painted from Mrs. Hunt. Draw Xmas card for Florrie. Lesson at Mrs. Cushing's. Stop & tell Walter we shan't be down. Ride home. Paint two cor. cards & a little one. Fix Clarence's "Mormon Family".

Thurs. Dec. 20th. 1883.

7.20. Letter from Martha with ticket & photo of Chester.[13] Miss Alden sent a Hingham's & Boston ticket. Pleasant to be wanted. Florrie labors on her Xmas card for "Harry". Home & paint till after 4 P.M., only rising to "tend door" & fix fire. Gym. It is delightful, the affection those little girls have for me. Stay to dinner. Home. Sam here. Takes 9 cor. cards & goes. Paint. Jim later. I finish his cards & he takes 'em & pays me. $4.75.

Fri. Dec. 21st. 1883.

7.40 or so. A little while with F. then home & paint till too dark for it, stopping for dinner. Then take car down St. Stop for Walter. Mr. Hazeltine there. I get slippers for myself, & divers gifts for others. Walter goes home from Calders. I stopped at Millie's & left her a dollar I had over from the "party" money. Shop & meet Jim in Fillinghast's. He accompanies me around in the stores & home. Spend 4.33 cts. Arrange accts. Paint, draw, write, etc.

Sat. Dec. 22rd. 1883.

7.30? *Paint* all day. Finish all Sam's cards but one. No gym. class as Mrs. D. has sore throat. Jim comes for Sam's cards and pays me in full—$6.75. Do lovely little thermometer card for Walter. Things begin to be done.

Sun. Dec. 23rd. 1883.

7.50. *Awfully* cold, 10 below zero. Slept cold. My "foot" is chillblain. S. S. $3.00 over the regular contribution to get Xmas present for little Williams. Church. Home & finish Sam's gladiolus & work on m.g. card for Mrs. Diman. Anna in. Lizzie calls. dinner. fix things. dress. Walter. (Sam first. Brought me bottle of "Packers Cutaneous Charm" for my chillblain, Jim sent it after favorable trial.) Walter brought me George Eliot's Poems, a delightful fat little account book, and some sable w[ater]. color brushes. He has also purchased for me lots of old Canton blue china—teacup, bowls, etc. I gave him a bundle of paint rags, a bottle of violet extract, a little thermometer on a beribboned card, and a tiny wisp of my hair in a sheath pin box.

Mon. Dec. 24th. 1883.

7.30 or so. Paint. The Weeden twins call for me in their cutter and we call on Mrs. Williams to ascertain what her little boy needs most. Underclothes. Drive down town (*jam* of vehicles) and get 'em, two sets, 75 cts. apiece. Then a half dollar knife & a pound of 20 ct. candy. Carry it to his mother; and leave five cents over for him, and her rent money. Home & paint, finishing Mrs. Diman's great card at 3.30 or 4. Dine hurriedly. Take card to Mrs. D. & presents to Eliza Bailey's tree for Jim and Sam. Shop, spending about $1.25. Home. Ray over. Dress tree & fix presents. Card from Ada—postal note for $5.00.

Tues. Dec. 25th. 1883
Christmas Day.

7.30 or somewhere about there. Arrange presents & receive 'em from divers small pupils. Phebe Campbell brings me a pretty china box of finest bonbons and all the rest of the gym. class, cards. Kate Bucklin presents another silk umbrella & a book of Hawthorne. Mother gave me a photo. album, a Jap. nest of boxes, one cover & many boxes; a little black shopping bag, an ivory paper cutter, a little French set of finger nail beautifiers, an album for cards, & other things. Anna a black Spanish lace fichu. Aunt C. a new purse & a little Jap box. Lots of things. Lizzie six little silver pins. Henrietta a pretty box of candy. Aunt C. had her soap, Ray his stocking of small duds; & Clarence *his* stocking with the inimitable Mormon family. We had all the family to dinner, including Mary & the baby! The tree in Aunt C's parlor. Everybody more than satisfied, and Anna well tired of presents. A box from Thomas, with teaset of lovely *China*, frosted fruit cake, writing paper, h'k'f's, card, & bulb for mother, neckerchief & card for Aunt C., & card, box, h'k'f's, writing paper & Chinese baby for me. Jim came over between five & six & stayed till 10.30 or so. Brought me a little fishwife statuette, from him & Sam, more soap for Aunt C. & a tiny bust for mother. Tired.

Another snowstorm in the night.
Wed. Dec. 26th. 1883.

Rise unconernedly [*sic*] when I get ready, leisurely pack and prepare. Florrie calls. Take care down st. Leave bag & strap at Pierces. Go to Walter's. Out. Go in and write him note. Get rubber horse for Charles Chester Lane. 25 cts. Ape for Mr. L[ane]., 25, Jap. box for Martha, 35. bit of a basket for Miss Alden; 05. Chocolate & rolls at Café, 25 cts. Get boots and bundles & take train which was belated nearly half an hour. Read "The Mystery of Orcival" [14] on the train & enjoy it much. Post card to mother in the B. & P. station, & take Herdic to Old Colony. Train just ready. Ride serenely to Hingham. Met by Martha. All serene and cosy. Lovely baby. All glad to see me.

Thurs. Dec. 27th. 1883.

Go out with M. Letter from Walter. Sent him one by Mr. Lane. Meet Miss Alden and she takes me to their S. S. tree. Help dress it, very effectively. Go home with Miss Alden. Martha and I in the afternoon call on Mrs. Dr. Robbins and pop & string corn. It is consigned to the tree, but we return home. Enjoy being with Martha much. Write to Henry Townsend sending divers small verses. Read and enjoy myself, sitting up in lonely state after they go to bed. After 11 when I go.

Fri. Dec. 28th. 1883.

Write to Walter to say when I'm coming home. Get letter from him. Sweep and dust to help Martha who has a sickheadache, or did in the night, and whose present "girl" is———*obtuse*. Call on Miss Alden. Back to dinner. Sew, read to Martha, and help her diversely. Miss Alden, & Dr. & Mrs. Robbins to tea. A pleasant evening and I talk much with Mrs. R. who is a highly cultivated, intelligent woman, and who likes me. Says my profile and head are very much like the sitting Evangeline. So they said once of mother. Now to Packing.

Sat. Dec. 29th. 1883.

Ere seven, and finish packing. Go to 8.30 train. Call on Mrs. Smith, who talks vainly against my visiting Walter in his studio, and gives me two dollars. Back to station and buy ticket home, $1.00. Walk to Cambridge St. & take car to Dr. Hedge's. Mrs. H. gives me $5.00. I have some lunch, and wait for Miss Charlotte. She gives me two birthday presents—no[,] one her's & one her mother's. Go to the Hales and stay till 6. Arthur there, and puts me on the train when I go. See Nellie, dear girl; Aunt E. & Emily. Have some soup & crackers. 6.30 train home. Walter meets me, a bit late, & we walk up. Talk. Unpack.

Sunday. Dec. 30th; 1883—

8. S. S. See Conway Brown. Home. Paint glass panel for Mr. Briar. Clarence & Charlie up. Anna sick with diptheria. Aunt C. goes there. Ray & Alice in for a few moments. Henrietta calls. Supper for her. Dress. Draw gladiolus for Sam. He calls and says he's in no hurry. I'm much relieved. Walter. Happy evening.

NINE

"One does not die young who so desires it"

December 31, 1883–April 30, 1884

As 1883 drew to a close, Charlotte reflected on the year just passed. Her entry of December 31 is both prophetic and chilling.

The old, familiar feelings of loneliness and isolation resurfaced in full force. With her wedding just a few months away, Charlotte documented her increasingly frequent manic-depressive episodes, the "waves of misery" that were interspersed with brief and, to Charlotte's mind, inexplicable periods of happiness. In the final hours of that cold New Year's Eve, she perceived just how susceptible her relationship with Walter made her to the depression that was beginning to govern her life. "Let me not forget to be grateful for what I have" she wrote. "Some strength, some purpose, some design, . . . And some Love. Which I can neither feel nor believe in when the darkness comes," she wrote.

Chief among Charlotte's concerns that night was the growing fear—despite his reassurances to the contrary—that in marrying Walter she would be sacrificing her life's work, "to be of use to others." So profound was her pain as the new year approached that she was visited by a bold and defiant death wish, tempered only by her reluctance to hurt those who loved her. "I would gladly die than ever yet; saving for the bitter agony I should leave in the heart of him who loves me. And mother's pain," she wrote.

New Year's Day, 1884, however, brought the tragic news of the suicide of Conway Brown, a friend with whom Charlotte had spent considerable time during her previous summer's stay in Ogunquit, Maine. Charlotte understood Brown's suicide; she could sympathize with his "mental misery." His death, in fact, only reinforced her conviction that life could only have meaning when one has "enough real work" through which "to preserve one's self-respect."

Yet, despite her understanding of Conway Brown's suicide, the death of so many of Charlotte's friends in the three years before to her wedding to Walter Stetson had to have contributed to her growing unrest. The theme of loss—both actual and symbolic—was consistently reinforced. Since early 1881 Charlotte had attended the funerals of numerous people who had somehow shaped her life: Professor Lewis Diman, May Diman, Sidney Putnam, Isabel Jackson, Conway Brown. During that same period she had also accompanied her mother to numerous other funerals: a neighbor's young infant had died, as had a close family friend, Mr. Manchester, as well as two of Mary Perkins's friends, Mrs. Stimpson and Walter Smith. Their deaths forced Charlotte to reassess her own life. Her conclusions were grim. "One does not die young who so desires it," she wrote somberly.

Soon after Conway Brown's funeral, Charlotte tried to alleviate her despondency by immersing herself in her daily activities: painting, teaching, and exercising at the gym. At the same time she continued to write for publication. In early January her poem about a "fallen" woman, "One Girl of Many," was accepted for publication in *Alpha*. But even the triumph of publication was eclipsed by the shadow of ever-increasing doubts. Charlotte began to consciously suppress her misgivings: "Bed after 12, trying to forget personal misery in thought for others," she wrote just four months before her wedding. And on March 9: "Am lachrymose. Heaven send that my forebodings of future pain for both be untrue."

Still, however portentous her doubts, Charlotte seemed to enjoy decorating the rooms in which she and Walter would live. As the wedding day approached, they abandoned their plans to live with Mary Perkins in favor of renting a suite of rooms on the second floor of a house owned by a Dr. Wilcox: "Betake myself to the house, where I remain from 9 till 12, while gas men, stove men, other men and a boy bring divers things to our domicile. Walter arrives and remains with me. I sweep up the parlor. The stove is magnificent and color of paint and paper highly satisfactory. We exult in the prospect before us."

On May 2, 1884, Charlotte and Walter Stetson would enter their newly decorated quarters as husband and wife.

Monday. Dec. 31st. 1883.

8. Breakfast. Recommence with Florrie. Go to Kelly's and get flowers for Mrs. Stetson. 25 cts. Leave some of 'em for mother. Carry panel to Mr. Briar. $2.50. Take flowers to Mrs. S. She is very ill. See Walter a moment. Get some crackers & an orange. 10 cts. Call on Millie & eat lunch. Get some more of those lovely white beads, 25 cts. Get glass panel. 65 cts. Go to see Mr. Williams—Mr. Briars friend, out. Go to Tibbitt's and get Whittier calendar for mother. 75. journal paper 1.00, blank book .25 & box booklike cover for nothing. Go to gymnasium and join evening class pay him $10.00, and three to Miss Lane for shoes. Call on Mr. Williams again and he orders two more placques! Cash Ada's order. Call on Mrs. Blake & thank her for her Xmas card which came this morning, a note, a wee calendar, & a five dollar bill! Turkey

dinner at 5. or so. Write & settle accts. Harry Manchester calls, & brings me a Shakspeare calendar; wherewith I am well-pleased. Got at Pub. Lib. "Norse Tales" & "Prince & Page", last, Florrie's.

Almost Mid<u>night</u>

It is late. I am alone. The wind howls and sighs outside, the clock ticks loudly, and I sit waiting for the new year.

And this year gone?

Weakly begun, ill lived, little regarded.

Some things have I done and learned, but nothing to what I would have.

My clear life-governing will is dead or sleeping. I live on circumstances, and waves of misery sweep over me, resistless, unaccountable; or pale sunshine of happiness comes, as mysteriously.

I would more gladly die than ever yet; saving for the bitter agony I should leave in the heart of him who loves me. And mother's pain.

But O! God knows I am tired, tired, tired of life!

If I could only know that I was doing right————!

[1883———————1884]

Midnight————*Morning*—

The clocks ring 12.

With no pride, with little hope, with uncertain occasional happiness, with no glad energy and living power; with no faith or nearly none, but still, thank God! with firm belief in what is right and wrong; I begin the new year.

Let me recognize fully that I do not look forward to happiness; that I have no decided hope of success. So long must I live.

One does not die young who so desires it.

Perhaps it was not meant for me to work as I intended. Perhaps I am not to be of use to others.

I am weak.

I anticipate a future of failure and suffering. Children sickly and unhappy. Husband miserable because of my distress; and I————!

I think sometimes that it *may* be the other way; bright and happy; but this comes oftenest; holds longest. But this life is marked for me, I will not withdraw; and let me at least learn to be uncomplaining and unselfish. Let me do my work and not fling my pain on others.

Let me keep at least this ambition; to be a good and a pleasure to *some* one, to some others, no matter what I feel myself. Remembering always that the harder I work and more I bear and the better I bear it, sooner comes rest. Is it rest I wonder? I think if I woke, dead, and found myself unchanged——still adrift, still at the mercy of passing waves of feeling; I should go mad. Can the dead so lose themselves I wonder?

And now to bed.

And let me not forget to be grateful for what I have. Some strength, some purpose, some design, some progress, some esteem, respect and affection. And some Love. Which I can neither feel see nor believe in when the darkness comes.

I mean this year to try hard for somewhat of my former force and courage. As I remember it was got by practice.

January 1st. 1883—[sic]
Tuesday.

8. Brief breakfast, with "Prince and Page." Florrie finished "Bridal of Friermain" yesterday, and is now reading Ivanhoe. Mr. Howard gave her Scott's novels for a Christmas gift. Home and lunch, with Prince & Page. Paint on Sam's gladolus. More food at four, in same company. Gym. class. Mother goes with me and calls on Mrs. D. Home; find Kate here. Supper. Mrs. Springer also with us. Sew a little. Jim comes and plays casino with mother. Then Edward comes and we play whist; Kate waiting till 10.30, when all go. Write.

Conway Brown shot himself yesterday; at Mrs. Maurans. A bright-faced boy of 20 or 21, an only child, loved, cared for, the idol of his parents; with no known grief or trouble.

He told me last summer that he had times of horrible depression. And had often thought of shooting himself. What mental misery it must have been to make him forget his parents and all the other ties that bound him to earth! I can sympathize with him; mental misery is real; and in a season of physical depression might well grow unbearable.

How needful to live so that in such times there is enough real work to look back upon to preserve one's self-respect! The only safety is within.

Wed. Jan. 2nd. 1884.

8. or a trifle before. Begin a course of diet, by means of which, and other changes I trust to regain my old force and vigor. Kate calls at the Carpenter's for me. Mrs. Brown desired to see us—at the funeral. She waits me, I join her, and we go. Services at 12:30. The dear boy looked little like himself. His father seemed calm, his mother aged and worn already. Poor things! Poor things! Home and finish Sam's gladiolus card. Letter from Walter, (and one yesterday). His mother no better. Answer it. Wrote note to Mrs. Cushing excusing absence. Ride down to French lesson minus Florrie. Madame was much

pleased with her little Xmas box. Walk home with her. Call on Miss Gladding. First evening at the gymnasium. Delightful to be there again. Mr. Smith teaches, himself, and does it well. I have not lost so much strength as I feared, can still go up the rope and on the rings, &c. Off on vaulting of course. Hour from 6.45 to 8 or so. Walk home. Finish "Prince and Page." Have eaten today, an orange & cup of hulled corn & milk at 8.40 about, a cup of oatmeal and milk and two biscuit at 11.30 or so, two more biscuit with a cup of milk at 3., and two oranges at about 9.

Feel well and contented.

Thurs. Jan. 3rd. 1884.

7.30. Write a bit more to Walter. Light breakfast, then Florrie, then paint pansies in oil. Two boxes arrive, the contents of which prove on subsequent inquiry to be intended as follows. Black fichu for mother & white one for me from Mrs. Anthony; & ruching & gloves from Mrs. Fillinghast for mother. She gives me half the ruching. She goes out. I loaf a little, reading a red hot Irish newspaper Katie brought around clothes. Gym. class. Very Uproarious. Mother stops for me and we come home together. Colder. Sup. Go to see Mr. Brown to carry a sketch of Conway which I made last summer when we were together; and to tell him of certain things he told me. Glad I went. He says it seems to *prove* his insanity, and that is of course what they most want to do. Home. Write to Walter a little, copy a poem and then this. Am now going to sew and finish that so much needed chemiloon.

Fri. Jan. 4th. 1884.

7.20—Write a bit more to Walter. Some hot soup at 11.30, and go with Florrie to get her gymnastic suit. Get cartickets, $1.00. (Met Helen who said Carrie had posted a letter to me.) Get it at office, (Stamps, 50.) and read it in Pub. Lib. about the Hartford business. Read up concerning the bronze crabs about the base of the obelisk in Central Park. get life of Loyola for self and "Sensible Etiquette" for Florrie.

Get a few flowers for Mrs. Stetson (25 cts.) and go to see her. Walter walks down with me, both silent. He was hurt at the gaiety in one of my letters. I shouldn't have sent it. Late to my French. Walk down with Miss Ross, who was refreshingly glad to see me, and so to the Hazards. Carrie & Helen lying down, preparatory to the Arion Concert tonight; so chat with Margie in the parlor and lunch on bread & butter I'd carried in my little bag, and tea & cake of theirs. See Mr. Hazard & talk with him about the Hartford affair. Then to the club, knit, discourse on bronze crabs, read aloud, etc. Sing together and break up at about 9. Home. Write to Walter. Bed after 12, trying to forget personal misery in thought for others.

Sat. Jan. 5th. 1884.

8.15. Finish pansie placque. Two letters from Walter, and one from "Alpha"; accepting my poem with thanks, and saying they would be glad to hear from me again. Lunch or dine, & go down st. Stop at Ath. and get Freeman's Hist. Geog. of Europe again. Stop at T. C. Greens office. Out. Go to gym. Take delicious shower bath, and am measured. 5 ft. 5 in. barefooted,[1] & naked weight 118 lbs. Stop at Burgesses and do errands for mother. Stop at Mr. Greene's again & see him a few moments. Home. Eat a little graham bread & some milk. Go to gym. Home with Phebe. Home. Aunt returned. Write sermon for S. S. Write here. Alter buttons on chemiloon. Bed.

Sun. Jan. 6th. 1884.

8.15. or so. Breakfast. Dress and scuttle to school. All there. Church. A Mr. Grindal Reynolds Preaches on Unitarian missionary work till nearly 20 minutes past 12! Home with Lu Manchester. Dine. Nap and doze by the fire all P.M. Sup. Dress. Begin letter to Miss Charlotte. Walter after 8, and can only stay till 9.30. Glad, *glad* to see him. He brings me some thin paper. Write to him a little thereon & then here.

Mon. Jan. 7th. 1884.

7.30 Letter from Retta & note from Mrs. Cushing. Henry Townsend's paper also. Florrie. Put braid on skirt. Write to Mr. Hazard, empowering him to take steps to sell property. Finish letter to Miss C. Read Hist. geog. a little. Call at Mrs. Diman's for suit. She pays me for card, 3.00. Carry placque to Mr. Williams. $3.00. Leave suit at gym. Change collars Mrs. Springer gave me. Buy darning cotton. 10 cts. Stop at Waterman's, & Harry Manchester shows me artotypes. Call on Millie. Go to Pub. Lib. & get card and book for her, "Bricks without Straw"; Tourgee.[2] Read Pop. Sci. Begged paper & envelope of smiling lady at Lib. & wrote bit of note to Walter. Carry book to Millie. Post letters. Go to gym. Good time. Ride home. Jim here. Feast on oranges. Write a little to Walter. Jim goes. More supper. This.

Tues. Jan. 8th. 1884.

7.30. Over time with F. Home, listen to mother a few moments. Go to Mrs. Cushing's & give lesson. Leave S. S. dollar to Mrs. Williams. Take book sent by Mrs. Cushing to Charlotte Fillinghast, and Annie Aborn asks me to lunch. Stay, & then go home for work. Find letter from Walter; (one from Charlotte Hedge this morning.) read it; make bed, do up sewing & back to Annie's. Sew and talk till 4.40, & then gym class. Home with Phebe. Then home. sup. Write to Walter & post it. John Willey calls. Sew & talk. Goes early—9.30 or less. Write to Walter. Write this.

Wed. Jan. 9th. 1884.

7.40! A lashing southeast gale last night. Letter from Walter. Florrie. Read Freeman and dine. Sew. Join Florrie & go for her gym suit. Then to the French Prof. Larcher very polite and suave with Miss Florinda. Then up to see how Mrs. Stetson is; no better. Then to the gym., sup out of our baskets, dress, and enjoy ourselves. Florrie likes it intensely. Ride home. Lizzie here. See her to the car. Write to Walter and here.

Thurs. Jan. 10th. 1884

7.30. Florrie. Home & sew. Read Hist. Geog. & dine. Letter from Walter. Answer. Gym class. 30 times. Home. Write long letter to Charlotte Hedge. Arrange gym. class accts.

Fri. Jan. 11th. 1884

7.30. Arrange lunch etc. Florrie. Go to Kelly's & get flowers. Go to the studio and stay with Walter two hours. Happy & safe. Go home with him. Arrange flowers. Lunch with them, I out of my basket. French. Then to gym with Florrie. Feel *exceptionally hilarious* and cavort wildly. Pick up a 118 lb. girl, and *run* with her as easily as could be. Delightful shower bath afterwards. Ride home gaily. Write to Walter. Bed.

*Sun. Jan. 13th. 1884.**

12.12 *a.m.* Up at 8. Sew all day on chemiloon. Letter from Walter P.M. Bless him. Gym. Class. Home. Sew. Edward comes with oysters & crackers. I go and adorn myself; and later Sam & Jim arrive; and Edward & I play against them. They beat us 7 to 3; but our first & last games were "weasels" in our favor. Stew & coffee & nuts at 10.30 or so. Finish last game at 11.59! They go gaily home, and I write this Sunday morning.

Sun. Jan. 13th. 1884.

8 or less. Comfortable breakfast. S. S. & Children's Service in church. Mrs. Manchester walks home with me. Finish 2nd. chemiloon. Call on Madame Charbonnier. Draw in an autograph album for her. Ride home. Sup. Dress. Walter. A happy evening.

Mon. Jan. 14th. 1884.

Ere 7.30 I think. (Left watch down stairs.) Florrie. Read and dine. paint on pansy placque. Eat a bit at 4 or so. Call on Carrie Hazard. Out. Call on Kate Bucklin. Out. Then on Jennie & Mrs. Taylor. Then to gym, enjoying myself as usual. Florrie brings her mother & Mrs. Phillips, so I am free to bathe & dress leisurely; and walk home; running up College hill. Mrs. Westcott here to ask about my teaching Blanch. Darn stockings.

Tues. Jan. 15th. 1884.

7.40. Do housework, as mother has a head-ache. Letter from Mr. Brown, enclosing poem I gave Conway. Florrie. Home and have a "dejeuner a la four-chet." Lesson to Miss Cushing. She has winter cholera and don't look fit to sit up, so I stay a bit & hear a spelling class. Home. Carrie Hazard had called. Paint placque. Phebe Campbell calls for me. Gym. class. Home with Phebe. Home. Sup. Arrange work & call on the Manchesters. Glad to see me.

Wed. Jan. 16th. 1884.

7. Write to Walter. Letter from him. Marriage in May *almost* sure & safe. Florrie. Home & finish second pansy placque. Dine & read. Lesson in oil to Louise & Emily Diman, 1.00. French lesson. Call to see Carrie Hazard, but she was asleep. Saw Margie & Helen. Gym. class rather small & Miss Lane teacher. Walk home, running up College Hill. Florrie had a cold, & her mother wouldn't let her come. Oranges, read a little in—Ivanhoe! I'm so interested in it from Florrie's skipping chapters. Letter to Walter.

Thurs. Jan. 17th. 1884.

7.20. Florrie, half an hour over as is usual now. Help mother with her school. (She has a cold.) Dine. Mother goes with me to Mrs. S. Carpenters to look at some cheap blankets she bought, and then we go down street & *buy*: a pair of blankets, $6.00, Sheeting 24 yds., $8.40, hand towels, two nice damask, 1.20, two cheap rough ones, .25, 6 huckabuck, 1.50; piece of heavy crash (mother to take half) 3.13., 6 yds. of fine crash, 75; piece of diaper, $2.20. Total $23.48 cts. Rush home, (stopping to kiss Walter) get suit & go to the gym. class attended by Emily & Charlotte. Mrs. Fillinghast & Miss Sophy T. call on us. Home & cut up towels industriously. Read Ivanhoe(!) & sup. accts. & journal. Write to Walter till 10 or so & read Ivanhoe till nearly 11.30. Bed.

Fri. Jan. 18th. 1884.

7.15. Help mother some. A word to Walter. Note from Mrs. Slicer, saying she won't be at the club tonight, but I'm to take tea with Miss Nightingale instead of her. Florrie. Home & get lunch & things. Go down to studio. Walter not there. Go to Millies & lunch, (leaving new umbrella at Gilmore's to be mended). Henrietta there. Take Millie's book to Pub. Lib. & change it; renewing Loyola for myself & looking up St. Sebastian for the club. Get placque rest at Calder's & things for mother, carry placque to Mr. Williams, $3.15, get shoestrings, .10, go to Walter's again, out; take car up to his mother's, she is better. Stop & talk with the sister awhile. Car down again & call on Miss Gladding for a moment. French lesson. Go to Walters again, find him upstairs, stay till 6. Go to Miss Nightingale's to tea. She is very fond of me. Club, very few there. Read to 'em. Home with Miss Kelly. Write & sew.

Sat. Jan. 19th. 1884.

7.20. Letter from Henry Townsend with C. Cd.[3] & poem of mine in it. Sweep room. Sew a little, start "Letter Book;" and tear off my 4 pair sheets. Rip up black silk. Dine & read. Carry back Freeman to Ath, & get Thucidides, on suggestion of Prof. Wells whom I met there. His wife is sick. Go to gym to see about lectures, & have a small talk with Miss Lane. Go after umbrella. Not done. Get "Altiora Peto", for mother. Stop at Darling's music store to see a big painting. Meet Madam Charbonnier there. Call on Connie Pitman. Out. Home. Find "Woman's Journal" with "In Duty, Bound"[4] in it. Oranges. Carry two sheets to Mrs. Diman, who straightway begins to hem them. Gym. class. Stay to dinner, & talk a while afterwards. Walk down to the Ath. with John. Home. Read Sunday school lesson and write report of our private mission work. Do example in interest for Florrie. Write here. Darn somewhat.

Sun. Jan 20th. 1884.

7.30. Snow again. Carl Westcott joins the class in S. S. Walk home with Miss Wheeler, and she shows me her dear little house-studio from top to bottom. That's the way I meant to live! Home. Dine. Mend mittens & waterproof, copy poem & do other little jobs. Lizzie calls. Supper. She goes in 6.45 car. Walter at nearly 8. Show him towels & "works."

Mon. Jan. 21st. 1884.

7 to 7.30. Carry Raphael's pictures to show Florrie. Take work & go to see Carrie Hazard. Stop at Mabel Hill's, who is a little ill, & stay there to dinner. Find Carrie in at last, and not taking a nap. Stay most of the afternoon. Call to see Lu. Manchester on an errand of Mabel's. Stop for Florrie & go to the gymnasium. Nice time. Refreshing bath; and walk home with F. & a Miss Allen. 4 oranges, supper, and Thucydides.

Tues. Jan. 22nd. 1884.

7.20. Florrie. Home & get work, lunch, suit, & silk to make over. Leave suit at Mrs. Diman's. Go to studio. Empty. Lunch & read Josephus. Walter appears. Stop lunching thereat. Call on Mary Brown & have a bit of dinner there. See Mrs. Geer & leave stuff. Call on Millie. Take her book to Pub. Lib. & get her another, stopping to look at some old Punches and new Atlantics. Go to Mrs. D's. Gym. class, all but Effie. Home with Phebe. Home. Sup & read Thucydides. Start to write when Anna & Clarence call & then Harry Manchester & then Jim. Sleepy. Produce Jim's candy at 11 and he departs shortly.

Wed. Jan. 23rd. 1884.

7.30 Write card to Cassie Thurston. Florrie. Home late. Sew. Dine & read Loyola. Arrange things and plan valentine card. Call for F. and walk to French lesson & then gym. Make myself useful and friendly to divers damsels. Ride home with F. Oranges, & Thucydides. Drew & sign in Minnie Campbell's autograph album.

Thurs. Jan. 24th. 1884.

7.20. Florrie sends word not to come, as she has a headache, etc. Paint on valentine card. Lena Hill calls with note from May Bell, begging me to take part in her theatricals. I decline, but agree to go and ask Abbie Cooke to do it. Dine & read Loyola. Call on Abbie, who can't—can't act. Send card to M. to that affect, and names of other possible damsels. (Had letter from Grace Channing & answered it.) Gym. class. Home, darn stockings & change them, my feet being thoroughly wet. Sup with Loyola. Write.

Fri. Jan. 25th. 1884.

7.30? Florrie. Home and arrange to go out. Cassie Thurston arrives. Go out with her. Change "Thucidides" for "A Family Flight" for the club. Leave suit at gym. Get umbrella .25 cts. Go to Fillinghasts and back out on account of the crowd. Get lunch at Remington & Sessions (Cassie does) and try U. for C. W. reading room. Not open till 4 P.M. Then I take her to Walter's studio and we lunch in ease and quiet, she delighted with the place. Then she stops at a store to see her father and I see her to Music Hall and then go for my dressmaker. Forgot my pieces, and have to leave before she is through fitting. French class. Florrie not there. Walk down with Miss Ross. Go to gym. Sup, & sit alone, getting verse for the valentine I'm painting. Jolly time in class. Leisurely bath, and home.

Sat. Jan. 26th. 1884.

8! Buttonhole & button chemiloon no. 2. Ment [sic] coat pocket & sew button on. Set out with bag & baggage. Leave two more sheets with Mrs Diman and help Louise fix her skates. Leave a basket at little fruit store on S. Main St., borrowed it before Xmas. Go to Mrs. Geer's carrying pieces. Get the basque well under way, and agree to have her finish it. She offered to do it for $2.50! I called it $3.00. Lunch there while she bastes. Stop at Ladd's & get samples of black thin stuff for Mrs. Diman. Get tape in Boston Store; 6 cts. Go to the first of a series of "Emergency Lectures" given to the ladies of the gymnasium; and try a little book called "First Aid to the Injured", for 50 cts. Go to see Lizzie Brown who sent word she wanted me. not in. Stop at Claflins's & "Clarke's" for calendula plaster, vainly. A few moments with Walter; and to Mrs. D's again & have gym. class. Little talk on self conquest with the girls. Mrs. D. pleased with her dress samples & lends me Mahaffy's "Social Life in Greece." Home. Sup with Loyola. Write memory notes of lecture. Sam calls. Finish notes & then sew. Sam and mother play casino.

Sun. Jan. 27th. 1884.

7.40 S.S. Tell them about Loyola. Church. See Lizzie afterward, who wants me to design for embroidery a sofa cushion cover. Go home with the Slicers & leave a book I borrowed long since, "Deterioration & Race Education." Stop awhile and then home to dinner. Make mother's bed. Ride over to see Madame. Very nice time, she reading in English a little. Home. Sup and read. Dress. Walter. Make out list of necessities for our beginning. Finish Loyola.

Mon. Jan. 28th. 1884.

About 7. Do housework, as mother has "pinkeye" & headache and is unable. (She borrows $2.00 two dollars of me.) Florrie, lecture on general behavior. Home. Read Greek history, (Bonner's) & eat oranges. Dine with history. Paint on valentine. Write bills for gym girls. Read Rossetti. Sup. Go to Gym. A very jolly time. Walk home with Miss Allen. Sam here, came to show square for his quilt. Plays casino with mother. I eat more oranges & sew. Sleepy.

Tues. Jan. 29th. 1884.

7. Help in housework (Letters from Miss Alden and Martha. Mr. Lincoln has failed disgracefully and Mr. Lane is out of business.) Florrie. Home and settle various matters, lesson to Mrs. Cushing who pays me $9.00. Go and spend $1.58 for buttons, lace, edging, and insertion. Go to Waterman's & see "Scotland Forever" by Miss Thompson ("she that was".) Stop to see Walter. Pose for him to get the anatomy of some feminine shoulders in a picture he is finishing. Then stay awhile. Scurry up to the gym. class, & present bills. Mrs. Diman pays me with check. Home. Sup (& dine) very extensively. Accounts, etc. Write to Mary Chauncy Saunders (who has lately had & lost a little son) and note to Phebe Campbell with bill. Read Greek history.

Wed. Jan. 30th. 1884—

About 7. Do housework, breakfast with Greek history. Mrs. Slicer sends me two tickets for the entertainment tomorrow evening. Florrie. Home & dine, with G. hist., pack up & start off. Call on Mrs. Diman and leave her Loyola. Call on Mrs. Blodgett. Leave bulb for Sam, mother's gift. Call on grandma Anthony. Go and buy me 2nd French book—$1.00. Get some stuff for Sam's quilt, my square thereof, blk. satin, .38, red velvet .25, gold thread .25, em. silk, .05. Go to Pub. Lib; leave Mrs. Diman's book, and look at Punch for half an hour & over. Go and leave buttons with Mrs. Geer. Call on Millie & get her book. Take it to Lib, but get no more. Not back and tell her so & then to French lesson. Read in new book, very nice. Gym. with Florrie. Sup, read a little in "A Disquisition on the History of Ancient India" or some such title which I got at Lib. Exercise hilariously. Bath as usual. Ride home, with F. Accounts.

Thurs. Jan. 31st. 1884.

7.15. Do housework. Florrie. Home. Eat oranges and finish Bonner's Childs Hist. of Greece;" Wonderfully well done. Work on dragon. Fricassee chicken for dinner. Paint some, more dragon, gym. class. Charlotte pays me $7.20. Call on Mrs. Moulton to see if she'll let Effie Rathbone go to S. S. entertainment. After persuasion she agrees, providing we are home at 9. So I come home, sup, dress, & take her. Very nice what there was of it, we having to leave early (Mr. Moulton pays me also, $7.20) Home with E. & then home. Edward here. Accounts.

1st.

February. 1884.

7.20 or 24. Mother does most of the work. Card from Mrs. Cushing. Florrie. Call on Lu and borrow a book to read the club more on St. Sebastian. Home, dine, with Mahaffy's "Social Life in Greece". Draw pattern for Lizzie. Start off riding to Burrill St. Then to Mrs. Geer's; get dress, $3.00. Go to Pub. Lib., make out a list of books for Millie, & take her one. Lu Randolph there. Go to French Class. Leave Florrie in Mr. Phillips' store & get myself another spool of em. silk, .05; 3 pieces of tape 10; yd. of silk cord .02, & red silk kerchief .30. Go to Lizzie's to tea. Go to club. Read. Lu Manchester there, & plays for us. See her home. Sam here. Show him the dragon. Sew, darn, & write my nightly accts.

Sat. Feb. 2nd. 1884.

8. Our little handmaiden comes not, so I help mother a little. Finish dragon. Draw Fanny Manchester's sweeping costume as I saw it yesterday, as a peace-offering lest she be hurt at my laughing at her. Eat two oranges. Call for Florrie, leave suit at Mrs. D's and go to lecture. *Very* interesting, treatment of hemorrhage. Florrie goes on an errand, and I get ll cts. worth of lace & then stop a moment to see Walter. An old schoolfellow of his there, named Spring. Gym. class. Am forced to grieve Effie by refusing to admit her friend Emily Rogers. She goes home, Louise is not very well, so I have only two. Forget mother's yeastcake & go down to Allens after it. Home. Find Henry Townsend's paper. Accts. Sup & dine, with Mahaffy. Write mem. notes. Arrange lesson for S. S. Sew in lace, ruching, & dress protectors. Bed after 12.

Sun. Feb. 3rd. 1884.

7.55 or so. Light breakfast & get to school in good season; joined by Mrs. Rawson and Arney. Church; Lu Randolph sits with me. Home with Mrs. J. & Lu. Read, dine, ("proud" dinner). Anna, Clarence, & Charlie call. Pay Clarence for vaulting bar. Giving him an extra dollar because he couldn't change a two. Ride over to Madame's & have a nice time, she reading English. Ride back, Mahaffy both ways. Read more; sup, dress; Walter. Copy a bit valentine to send to Century.

Monday, Feb. 4th. 1884.

7.10. Breakfast with Mahaffy. Florrie. Then give my first hour's teaching to Blanche Westcott. Her mother stays & listens and is pleased. I stop and look at a tenement to let behind them, with glorious bay view. Like it much. Call on Mary & the baby. Home. Dine with Mahaffy. Go to see Walter about house. Stay till 5 and after. Post my & mother's letters & get stamps. Go to Pub. Lib. & read in Coulanger's Anc. City. Get a creamcake at café, .04. Go to gym, & am rather draggy; but on influx of visitors wake up and do well. Bath. Walk up with Miss Allen & Florrie. Bed. Read Mahaffy. Accts.

Tues. Feb. 5th. 1884.

7.20. Breakfast with Mahaffy. Florrie. Mrs. Cushing. Call on Annie Aborn and lunch there. She engages to make me some white skirts. 2nd lesson to Blanche. Go to see the little house again & like it still. Stop at home and get sewing & then go to Mrs. Diman's. Sew and talk awhile. Gym. class. Stay to dinner. Lively discussion with John on Political Economy & kindred subjects. Home by a little after nine. Dry stockings & feet, reading Mahaffy. Accts.

Wed. Feb. 6th. 1884.

Make fire. Get printed refusal from Century. Florrie. Blanche. She grows interested and likes it, and I delight to—*teach*! Home & dine, finishing Mahaffy. Mother and Aunt C. dine at the Budlong's, I don't though invited. Go to see Dr. Wilcox about his house. Meet his wife & walk a little way with her. Leave shoes to be soled. Get brooch, new-pinned, 10 cts. Return the library book I got for mother; 26 cts. Go to Dr. Wilcox office & after waiting & writing awhile, see him. I suggest alterations & improvements to his house, and he says he'll consider it. Call on Miss Gladding. French. Forgot my book again. Gym. with Florrie. Sup & talk. Not a good night for work, hot & wet. Ride home. Find Edward Jim & Sam here, and must needs play whist. Then write here. Letter from Walter P.M.

Feb. 7th. Thurs. 1884.

7 about. Wash dishes. Florrie. Blanche. Go & look at another house down there, a new tenement house, *very* new, and garishly modern & ugly in many

ways. Home. Dine, with Emerson (breakfasted with Bonner.) Sew, doze a very little, & write my report on G. History. Gym. class. Ellie pays his bill, and visits the class. Home. Kate here. Supper, & talk of my new home. Sew. Home with Kate. Back again. Accts. Write to Dr. Wilcox about tenement, and to Walter, bless him!

Fri. Feb. 8th. 1884.

7–10 Breakfast with Emerson. Florrie. Blanche. Home. Explain earth's rotation to mother, loaf a little, sew a little, ride to Millie's. Change her book, and mine on India, unread, for Baird's "Rise of the Huguenots in France." French. Go to Pub. Lib. with F. She renews "A Family Right". We look at Lon. Ill. News & Harper's Weekly. Gym. Supper. Exercise. Bathe in part. Ride home. Accts.

Sat. Feb. 9th. 1884.

9. Read "Altiora Peto." Go to lecture with Florrie. Get resoled shoes, $1.25. Leave Florrie there and stop a moment to see Walter. Then home at hot speed, literally, get suit, sheets, etc, and go to gym. class. Home, toast feet, and read Walter's letter of this afternoon. Sup on toast, chockolate, and stewed dried peaches; reading Altiora. Then finish her. Accts.

Sun. Feb. 10th. 1884.

8. 10 or so. S. S. Full class, 9! Church, sit with the Dunnells. Mr. Woodbury preaches. Home with Lu, Harry, & Mrs. M. Nap instead of dinner. Then try a little salt and water and regurgitate. Ray & Alice call. Also Mrs. & Miss Lewin in my absence, Julia Jastram, & Lizzie. Go to Madame's. She reads Casabianca, & part of a story. Then talk a little. Walk home. (Rode over reading Emerson). Lizzie to supper. Dress. Walter. Shortest evening we ever had, house discussion etc. Goes at a little after 10. Sit down and try to write my love and happiness but am to sleepy. Accts., after fixing chairs.

Mon. Feb. 11th. 1884.

7. 10 or 15. Help mother some. Florrie. Blanche. Call at Mary Phelon's a moment. Look at cottage on Benevolent St. *Horrid*! Home and dine. Take things and start to see Miss Nightingale. Find her going out. Go with her as far as Butler Exchange, leave gym. suit, & go to see Walter. Sit and sew demurely while he paints; with occasional kisses in between. He accompanies me to Ath. where I get Symonds "Essays on the Greek Poets". Then to gym, sup & read, exercise, crawl out on the roof again, bathe, and walk home with F. Will Mauran called, wanted to play chess. Sorry to miss him.

Tues. Feb. 12th. 1884.

7. Make fire. Florrie. Lesson to Mrs. C.'s infants. Call on Connie Pitman, talk Greek History (she's studying it) and stay to lunch. Blanche, and stay later than necessary, looking at a book. Home, eat two oranges, and doze a few minutes. Gym. class. Home. Toast feet, and pet Belinda. Sup, reading "Symond's etc." Write here, and valentine to Walter. Copy verses.

Wed. Feb. 13th. 1884.

ere 7.

(6.45) Mother not well, voice affected. Wash dishes. Florrie. Blanche. Home. lunch. Go to see the photographs of pictures at Miss Wheelers. Meet Will Mauran on the way. Meet Prescott Clarke there; and he walks down street with me. Stop and see Walter a little while; and tell him various plans of mine. Also leave valentine. Leave another Valentine at Journal office, to print. Try & get French book for Florrie. French. Am reprimanded by Madame for translating, and feel badly that I should need speaking to again. It's because of my mania for teaching. Gym. Sup. Exercise. A Miss Bartlett dislocates her elbow, and Mr. Smith sets it. Ride home. Mother worse. Write here & do arithmetic

Thurs. Feb. 14th. 1884.

St. Valentine's Day.

6.45 or so. Housework. Valentines during the day; from the children, 4. Florrie. Blanche. Home and help mother. Dine with Symonds. Go down street and get chloroform & Liebig's beef extract for mother. Vainly enquire for Calendula Plaster. Hunt for pearl clasps and silver fringe, unsatisfactorily. Stop to see Walter. He is not in so I leave him some verses and depart. Gym. class. Great fun over valentines. Home. Settle down comfortably to write. Do so, to Mrs. Smith, do some arithmetic also. Harry Manchester calls; and mother and aunt C. having retired we have a very pleasant evening, talking and discussing. Finish letter thereafter.

Fri. Feb. 15th. 1884.

Nearly 7. Housework. Florrie. Blanche. (Had some Liebig's Extract of beef for breakfast this morning. *Good*, and did me good.) Florrie gets a gorgeous valentine from Harry Howard. (I suppose). Home & read aloud for mother a little. Dine, pack up, and go with Florrie to her last sitting, *with* the blue silk waist. Then to French, and then gymnasium; stopping to look at some lovely photos in Tibbitts. Ride home. Feel particularly well. Sam here. Write to Walter.

Sat. Feb. 16th. 1884.

7.15 or so. Housework more or less. Then Mary comes & I go. Leave suit at Mrs. Diman's & take Loyola back for her. Stop to see Walter; out, leave a bit of a note. Shop for nearly two hours, get white beads .25; gilt buckle .10,

5 yds India Mull, 1¾ yds. wide (I *think*), 65 cts a yd.! 3.25.; & a pink & yellow striped Turkish towel, 1.00. Go to see Millie, & change her book again at Pub. Lib. Then to Walter's again for a few minutes. Then to the lecture; on insensibility and poisons. Another few moments with Walter, (Mr. Hazeltine there, sitting;) and then gym. class. Home and sup luxuriously on two cups of Liebig's tea, toast, bread, an orange, a fig & a sugar almond Walter gave me. Write here. Read Symonds. Sew, and talk "school" with mother.

Sun. Feb. 17th. 1884.

7.10 or 15 Find mother up, fire made and breakfast underway. S.S., walking down with our superintendant, Mr. Stone. .05 cts. as usual. Church. Home, part way with one of the Weedens. Gorgeous dinner, codfish, etc; splendid tomato, as good as fresh, charlotte russe, & oranges. Soft custards also if desired. Read a bit & begin letter to C. A. Hedge. Anna in after dinner. Charlie Baxter calls to return H. C. Andersen and bring letter from Walter saying he has a violent cold, and won't come to look at the house this afternoon. Answer, and lend Charlie "20 M. L. Under the Sea." Robert calls, wants another whale. Sup. dress. Walter, in the rain, and more than half sick with this cold. An evening all too short; me writing mostly instead of talking.

Mon. Feb. 18th. 1884

7. or so. Mother makes fires. Write bit of a note to Walter. Florrie. Blanche. Stop in at Mary's a moment to mend a loose pleat. Meet Sam on George St. & go home with him to see his bulb in bloom. Post letter. Go to Calders & get cardboard. Buy two T. towels for 37½ cts. apiece. Get some silk illusion for a veil, .75, and some satien for underwaists, 25. Also some lunch, crackers, & cheese, .05. Go to see Walter and lunch there. He is finishing Mr. Hazeltine "The Violinist." Call on Mrs. Wells. Then home. Mother out. Stop in at the Manchester's. Home again; and finally see mother approaching with Mr. Butcher the florist; who examines "the bulbs." Rest, read Symonds a little, and sup *luxuriously*. Charlotte Russe, Liebig's & bread & butter and an orange. Call for Florrie & go to the gym. *Very* jolly. Bathe, & walk home with F. & Miss Allen. Home. Two oranges and read a little. Accts. Arithmetic now.

Tues. Feb. 19th. 1884.

6.50. Down first & do work. More arithmetic. Florrie. Lesson at Mrs. Cushing's. Carry bulb to Mrs. Townsend. Home. Dine with Symond's. Blanche. Home. A little Symonds and a little doze. Gym. class. Call for mother at Mrs. Fillinghast's. Home. Sup with Symonds. Clean apron and red kerchief in honor of Henry Townsend; who arrives at about 7:30 and stays till 11 nearly. A good sort of fellow, steady and honest I should *think*, slow and not personally energetic.

Wed. Feb. 20th. 1884.

7. Homework. Symonds. Florrie. Blanche. Home & dine with Symonds. Go to see Walter some ¾ of an hour. Leave things at gym. See Dr. Wilcox about the house. Leave my Huguenot book (unread) at Lib. & get Mill's "Liberty".[5] Get Millie's book and change it. French. Prof. Berlitz himself in. Walk down with Miss Ross. Stop at Walters and eat supper. Walk up with him part way and then to gym. Small class but good time. Run 40 laps, vault 6, (on one side only) and lift three rungs on the ladder! Home alone, as Miss Allen had to stop for her sister. Oranges & Symonds. Piece of cake. This. Will cut out underwaists now.

Thurs. Feb. 21st. 1884.

7. Coal etc. Florrie. Blanche. Home & dine. Draw whale card. Abbie Cooke calls. Gym. class. Home, sup, and read J. S. Mills Liberty. Write to Charlotte Hedge. Sew.

Fri. Feb. 22nd. 1884.

7. Coal, etc. Letter from Walter and invitation to his reception.* Florrie. Blanche. Home. Lunch. Mrs. Blake calls. Stop & see Mrs. Slicer about a book. Carry whale to show Robert. Go to see Miss Gladding. French. No Flo. Stop and see Walter awhile. Gym. Home with Miss Allen and Fanny Manchester who visited the class. Discuss great questions with them. Home. Find Sam and Edward playing whist. Sup. Play. They go at 11.50 about. Accts.

Sat. Feb. 23rd. 1884.

8.40 or so. Mend dress. Finish 3rd chemiloon. Write essay on "Family Tyranny". Dine. Leave suit at Mrs. Diman's, stop and see Walter a moment, and go to the last of the Emergency lectures. Another moment with Walter, and then, gym. class. Ellen Clarke, who is visiting, exercises with us. Home with my last sheet. Sup on Liebig, bread & butter, spongecake crusts, and an orange; with Mill. Endeavor to modify my finger nails. Accts. Sew and write.

Sun. Feb. 24th. 1884.

7.15. or 20. S.S. Uncle Edward there. Ask him to dine, but he can't. Church. Good sermon. Home with Willie Weedens (I think.) & Lu a little way. Write. Set table, make bed etc. Dine. Read, finishing "Liberty" and beginning "On the Subjection of women". Walter comes and we go look at the house. He likes it but rather dampens my ardor by seeing drawbacks here and there. Home & warm toes, then walk as far as Annie Aborn's with him. Call on Annie. (He went home.) Am rapped to by all the Dimans in passing; and unanimously invited to tea. Decline, as I had just declined Annie. Home. Sup. Dress. Walter. Goes at 10.15 or so. Charlotte russe & 1 ½ oranges. Read scraps in paper & Century. Journal. Bed.

Mon. Feb. 25th. 1884.

6.45 Read Mill to Mother. Florrie. Blanche. Lecture on physiology with a pointed shoe for a pretext. Home. Dine, Mill to self & aloud. Work on whale card. Uncle Edward Hale calls. Walk down to the Hazard's with him. Home. Sup with Mill. Call for Florrie and go to gym. Lend "Phantasmagoria" to Miss Leavitt. Hour too short. Bath. Home with F. & Miss Allen. Home. Two oranges. Paint letters on card. Read a bit to mother. Write herein.

Tues. Feb. 26th. 1884.

6.55 about. A little soapine work, and darn mittens. Florrie. Lesson at Mrs. Cushings. Home. Dine. Read Mill. Blanche. Home. Soapine. Annie Westcott arrives. Gym. class. Only Louise & Emily. Home. Help set table. Supper. Whist. Clarence comes. They go at 9 or so. Soapine. Write note to Lizzie and letter to Walter and here.

Wed. Feb. 27th. 1884.

6.45 or less. Housework. Florrie. Blanche. Forget slippers again. Home. Dine. Work on soapine card. Call at Mrs. Slicer's to see about club. Go to Millie's. French. Pub. Lib. See the Doyle girls and talk with them. Read Punch. Carry Millie her book. Change my Mill for Robertson's "Human Race." Gym. Feel tired rather. Walk home alone. Lizzie here, and trys to get me more interested in the quilting party. In vain. Write here.

Thurs. Feb. 28. 1884.

6.35 or 40. Housework. Soapine card some. Leisurely breakfast with Symonds. Letter from Walter Go to Florrie's but she has gone somewhere. (Told me yesterday she'd go if 't was pleasant. Seems to go in a storm.) Heavy snowstorm till near noon and then sleet. Home & sew and revive so long since learned poetry of Longfellow's. Blanche. Home. Read Symonds a little, then work on card, dine with Symonds, more card, nap, gym. class, home, sup, write here. Write to Grace Channing, work a little on card, and on black silk skirt.

Fri. Feb. 29th. 1884.

7 nearly. Breakfast with Symonds. Letter from Walter, thick. Work on card. Blanche. Home & dine on Liebig & breadbutter, & a creamcake, with Symonds. Note from Walter, enclosing one from Dr. Wilcox, giving us the house from April 15. Go to see the dear boy and stay over an hour. Then French, 10 minutes late. Get shoestrings, .05. Call on Carrie Hazard and find a small afternoon tea—Meg Leslie, Mrs. Weeden, Miss Wheeler, Miss Robinson, & Mrs. Blodgett. Stop and partake; outstay them and have a little talk with Carrie and Helen, joying in my little house and plans in general. She is to give me table linen. Then to the Slicer's, where the Girl's Club meets. Sew & tell them the "Story of Maroof." Walk up with the Westcotts. Home, accts. Sew.

Sat. March. 1st. 1884.

8 Work on black silk skirt. Finish Soapine card. Gym. class. Stop and talk awhile. Home. Sup. Little excitement over a drunken man who walks around the house and tries to get in at the front door. Wants "the master", and "a bed for the night". Write for S.S. class. & sew. Bed late.

Sun. March 2nd. 1884.

7.30. S.S. Mr. Stone wants me to take sketch of Oakland Beach buildings. Give Soapine card to Robert. Leave message at Mrs. S. Carpenter's for Lizzie, and with Lu Manchester. Stop & see Lu. Home. Dine. Miss Murphy happens in. Anna, Clarence & Charlie. Go for Madame, and we walk over here. She comes in & has an orange & some cake. Put her in the car for home. Sup on oranges. Dress. No Walter. Read Symonds. Walter at last, at nearly 9.30. Stays till 10.45 or so. More supper.

Mon. March 3rd. 1884.

About 7. Florrie, who is sleepy after her Boston dissipation. Blanche. Home. Mend skirt. Dine. Fuss about with divers small things & set forth. Have to go back to Blanche's for Florrie's book which I had forgotten. Call on Mrs. Wells a moment. Stop and see Walters pictures beforehand. They look well. Buy gilt buckle, 10 cts, blk velvet ribbon, 2 yds. 24 cts., 8 yds. blue gingham. $1.20. Go to Pub. Lib. & read Pop. Sci. Gym. Walk home with Miss Allen. Am strangely tired. Home & sup, raw cracked-wheat, milk, crackers, bread butter & jelly. Write here.

Tues. March 4th. 1884.

about 7. Florrie. Mrs. Cushing. Home. Lunch. Study arithmetic for F. Blanche. Go to Kelly's for yellow flowers. Had none, so try Butcher and get some nice little ones, & a few violets. Home. More arithmetic & more lunch. Gym. class. Home & dress for Walters reception. Carrie's black silk, white Spanish tie, ruching, & lace in sleeves, yellow ribbon, yellow beads, gold comb, amber bracelet; yellow breast on bonnet, yellow flowers. Many people there, and all seemed pleased. Home with Lu & Mrs. Manchester in car. Ollinges. Bed.

Wed. March 5th. 1884.

ere 7. Begin "Greg's Enigmas." Florrie. Blanche. Home. Dine. Cut & try to fit a yoke of blue gingham. Go to see Walter. Has sold five pictures already. Mrs. Westcott, Sarah and Carl there. French. Back, & stay with Walter till 6.30 & over. Gym. Bath. Home in car, with Florrie & Miss Allen. Blancmange, a little, oranges 3, and a g. cracker,

Thurs. March 6th.

7. Fires etc. Florrie. Blanche. Home. Darn hose. Dine. Do felt table cover for Allie. Work on white underwaists. Henrietta calls. Gym. class. Miss Sophy there. Retta there. Stay to tea. Read 'em bits of Longfellow. Home by 8.30. Write here, and Greek report & note to Miss. Alden.

Fri. March 7th. 1884

7 or so. Housework. No Florrie as they were to have company, so I call for Retta & we go down and see the pictures. She likes 'em. Then she walks over with me and looks at our house. Go back with her a little and then go to Blanche. Home and dine, reading Greg's "Enigmas of Life". Splendid dinner; two cups of Liebig, unlimited bread & butter, & three oranges. Go to Millie's. Change books for her. (Bought 4 h'k'f's. on way up street $1.00) French. Take Madame Charbonnier to see the pictures. Henrietta there. Stay and see Walter awhile. Gym. Good time. Ride home. Florrie appeared not. Jim here, playing casino. Sew a bit & sup lightly.

Saturday. March 8th. 1884.

7.30 or so. Note from Mr. Stone saying we won't go in the storm, so I breakfast peaceably with Greg & letters & Alphas, and spend two or three hours and lots of blue gingham in learning to make a yoke. And I learn. Then dine, call on Annie Aborn, & go down to see Walter. Folks there inspite of the weather. Sold six last night. Then to the gym. class, a little subsequent lecture and home. Sup. Scald my left hand and enjoy it. Keep it in cold water at first, which is efficacious while it lasts, then put on plaster, which don't seem to be. Write to George Mann. Write here. Can think of nothing to say to my boys, so say nothing.

Sun. March 9th. 1884.

7.30 nearly. Luxurious breakfast, broiled codfish & cream, hot biscuit & butter, & chocolate. S.S. Talk promiscuously about divers religions. All go to church & sing, & Mr. Slicer gives a "children's sermon"! *He* talk to *children*! He can't. See Robert & get the $10.00. See Mr. Stone & tell him he'd better get some one else to do his little order, afraid I can't. Home. Dine. Make my last call on Madame. Ride both ways. Lizzie here, & stays to supper. Dress. Walter. Am lachrymose. Heaven send that my forebodings of future pain for both be untrue. Lent Walter $5.00 to get Irving[6] tickets.

Mon. March. 10th. 1884

7.15 or so. Write little note to Charlotte Hedge. Go to Florrie. Am affected emetic-wise. Blanche. Home. Sleep till 3 P.M. Dine lightly, (no breakfast) & set forth. Call on Mrs. Wells a few moments. Leave Symonds at Ath. I get 2nd Vol. of Felton's "Ancient & Modern Greece." Cash check at P. O. & post letters. Leave suit at gym. Get red cashmere for each, and buttons, beautiful both, $2.50. Darning cotton, 05, blk, lace .25, 2 bottles Packer's Cutaneous Charm, 50 cts. to mother, owed, 15 cts. Go to see Walter again. Has sold 16. See divers there. Gym. Am not lively, but do all but run. Have to run however to get car home. Accts.

Tues. March. 11th. 1884.

7.20 or so. Florrie. Lesson at Mrs. Cushings. Leave $2.00 with Mrs. Williams. Call on Miss Wheeler & walk up to Waterman & Hope with her. She warmly praises Walter's pictures. Which is a comfort to me. Home & dine. Blanche. Leave early as she wants to go out. Stop and see Mary's baby. Home & cut & sew. Feel happy. Louise & Charlotte call for me. Gym. class. Talk with Mrs. D. a little. Home. Mother dolorous. Sew. Grow dolorous myself. Write here. Am *miserable*. Write a piece of biography and some verses.

Wed. March 12. 1884

7.30 or so. Seven oranges for breakfast & nothing else. Florrie. Blanche. Home. Dine. Go out. Leave Miss Rathbone the verses she wanted. Get my scissors at Mrs. Slicers. Stop and see Walter. Am still miserable. Shop some, see acct. book. French. Shop some more. Meet Lu Manchester & shop some more. Sup with her at the café, she paying for mine, a quarter. Take her to the gym. My chocolate exhilerates me and I exercise delightedly and have a delicious bath thereafter. Home happy, arithmetic, talk, write to Walter and accts.

Thurs. March 13th. 1884

7.15 or so. Letter from Walter, bless him! Florrie. Blanche. Home. Dine. Set forth. Stop a moment and see Walter. Search more for my prospective brown plaid suit vainly. Buy pretty shaded brown and yellow ribbon for hat. Take red cashmere & blk. silicia to Mrs. Geer. Gym. class, (stopped again at Walter's but he wasn't there.) Ellie Congdon visits us & give me her tintype. Home. Devour 7 ½ oranges. Write here. Sew diligently on blue apron. Bed at 11 or so.

Fri. March 14th. 1884.

6.10 or 12. Sweep my room with great complacency. Good breakfast, omelette. Florrie. Blanche. Stop in and see my house, which is being painted & the stairs put on. Demand a door to the outside part. Home. Read a little in Felton, Dress, sewing new lace in sleeves, dine well on frizzled beef, breadandbutter and oranges, 4. Go to French. Walk home with Madame, get her address & leave her mine; with half a pound of "chocolats à la crème" and a bottle of Packers's Cutaneous Charm. Walk up to Walters and have supper there, good. Go with Walter (Bless him!) to see *Henry Irving*. The play was Louis 11th. Perfect throughout, in my untutored judgement; and Irving himself—a master. Walk home serenely in the wet, stopping at Greene's for soda & chocolate. Talk a little, write here, bed.

Sat. March 15th. 1884.

7.15 Mend a little, breakfast, and set forth. Run down and see about house, (those stairs), leave suit at Mrs. D's, & then to Walter, gaily. Stay there a couple of hours or more, lay out a list of china, and then we go and look at things. A Franklin stove costs $36.00! Go to Warren & Woods and order china & glass. Buy 6 graham rolls, Neufchatel cheese, and 6 bananas, I paying 10 cts. Return to the studio and eat it. Stay awhile longer, then go to gym. class. George Clarke being there Mrs. D. is very desirous that I should stay. Whisk home with yeastcake & change dress, then back to tea and talk with George & Mrs. D. He comes home with me, and we walk more than needful, talking. Write accts. Mend a bit now.

Sun. March 16th. 1884

7.15 or 20. S.S. Talk on miracles & suicide. Church. Home with Harry Manchester and his mother, & walk down to Red Bridge and back with H. Home & dine. Write some 5 pages of the novel, doze a while, Maria Brown calls, put upper drawer in order, supper, dress, Walter, write down tinware &c., in little book. He goes out to the car with Maria. Goes at 10.15 or so.

Mon. March. 17th. 1884

6.50 or 55. Make fire, etc. as mother overslept. Florrie. Blanche. Home. Read & dine & make list of tin & wooden things. Go to Walter's. Stay about an hour while he waited for an express man, and then go to Warren and woods and finish the glass & china business; for the present at least. Delightful but wearying in time. Then go to Mr. Lindsey's and get some wood and iron things. Then to Fillinghast's and have some chocolate and rolls. Then down to Brecks after letters, and up to the Gym. Mrs. Carpenter came down with Florrie, sole spectator of our maneuvers. Walk home. Write to Thomas, and accts. Bed.

March 18th. 1884

7. Mend dress. Florrie. She pays her bill, $30.00. Lesson at Mrs. Cushing's. Call on Connie Pitman, who was out. Home. Dine with Felton. Blanche. Home & sew. Emily & Charlotte stop for me and we go the gym class, finding Effie waiting at the head of the street. And Emily, (dear little chick!) actually gave up her side of me to Effie, and walked alone, hugging my suit to sweeten the exile! Genuine self sacrifice. Home. Cracker & milk. Dress. Julia and Pardon come. Walter comes and we go to see Annie Morse. She shows us many pictures. Home late, 11.10 or so, and feel tired. Accts.

Wed. March. 19th. 1884

7.15. Darn somewhat. Breakfast with Felton. Florrie. Blanche. Visit my house of course. Home. Dine with Felton. Set forth. Visit Walter. The aged Mr. Hazeltine enters with Walter (I got there first) and stay some twenty long minutes. I stay good two hours. Find that I've left my gym. suit at home. Walter goes to Pub. Lib. with me. I get Millies book but don't replace it. Walter goes to the car with me & I come home after suit. Sup, with Felton. Ride down to gym. Mrs. Keach & Junie called this P.M. & were in my car down. Only 6 at the gym, bad night, very. Run my mile, go up 14 rounds of the ladder, etc. etc. Ablutions, deliciously cold, & ride home. Accts. Sew. (changed Mdme. Remusats Letters,[7] which I hardly tasted, for Carlyle's Reminicences[8]

Thurs. March 20th. 1884.

7.15. Florrie. Blanche, Margie Hazard brings me a note from Carrie inviting me there to tea tomorrow night; also Walter and others. Rode to Blanche's with Margie & showed her "my house". Home & dine, with Felton. Sew all P.M. Gym. class. (Sent bit of note to Walter). Home & sup, an unusually fine repast, with Aunt C. to join us. Sew till 10.15 or so, finishing blue apron. Write here.

Fri. March 21st. 1884.

6.45. Write to Martha. Florrie. Blanche. Stop at house. Home. Dine & write more to Martha—Dress. Go with mother to the children's fair; an apparent success. Go to see Walter. Find Miss Jeffrey there. Like her. Comfort Walter who is a bit unhappy.* He gives me $10.—to keep for him—for us. My first trust of that sort. Go to French lesson. Only little M. Frost and Prof. Larcher. Pub. Lib for a little while, look at Punch & renew Florrie's book. Then to Carrie Hazard's. Mr. & Mrs. Mason, Mr. & Mrs. Burbank, and Grandfather Hazard. A fine "tea" Folk music & pictures. Go upstairs with Margie when she retires; and she shows me her attempts at art work. A dear girl. Walk home with the Masons.

Sat. March 22nd. 1884.

7 to 7.30. A fair clear warm beautiful Spring day. Wake early, lie happy and still, & sleep again conscience-free. Breakfast deliciously on eggs milk and fruit. A dear love-letter from my darling to add to the joyousness of the morning. Put on old spring suit, pretty felt hat that was Ada's, white tie, and some flowers mother got at the fair yesterday. Leave my suit at the Diman's, and go to see Walter. Stay with him a couple of hours, then he walks up with me to Martin's store & goes home. I look at dress goods, go to Pub. Lib. and get Millie's book & names of others for her; stop at Adam's to look at hats and buy some lovely old fashioned ribbons, 42 cts I *think* & hat lining $.10.

Then to Shepherd & Wilson's & get a brown "poplinet" dress, 8.25, 11 yds., some lovely yellowish ginghamy stuffs, 9 & 12 yds. $2.63, two pair of black stockings, $1.00, buttons, 2½ doz .63 and some lunch, 3 graham rolls, a little tinfoil cheese & a fig for 10 cts. Walter joins me as I go to get the lunch, and I go down to his room and eat it. Then he goes with me up to Mrs. Geer's, (I stopping to leave book at Millie's;) & have waist tried on, have dressgoods, rejoin Walter, and go back to his room for 10 minutes or so. Then to the gym. class; where Margie and Carrie Hazard look in on us for a few moments; then home to find Kate here with some oranges and bananas for us. She stays to supper and till 8.30, and I trim my new brown hat. A beauty when done, total cost less than 90 cts! Kate goes home alone, and I write sermon for my boys. Then a bath and bed deliciously. Found note from Eddie Jackson on reaching home.

> "March 20 1884
>
> Miss Pirkens
>
> i am verry sick and would like to have you make me sum funny rimes and pictures on square pieces of paper the way we did when we were down to Maine if you please
>
> There is a anser
>
> when can i
>
> have them
>
> Yours Truly
>
> Eddie Jackson 204
>
> Angell St."

Sun. March 23rd. 1884

About 7. Another spring morning. Wear grey suit to S.S. Don't like the appearance of Mr. Slicer's "exchange", so return home instead of going to church. Do divers small things, and make 8 "rimes and pictures on square pieces of paper" for Eddie. Darn a little. Read in Century. An orange or two, bit of cracker and sup of milk. Dress. Walter. Show him my "rimes" and he admires. A happy evening. Bed ere 11.

Mon. March 24. 1884.

About 7. Do most of the coal work. Darn some, dress, & breakfast with Felton. Florrie. Carry pictures to Eddie, and leave them at the door. Blanche. Find that they have put the door as I wished, shelf, nails, everything lovely. See the old Doctor there and thank him. Home. Get things and set out. Renew book at Ath., leave suit at gym. Get another doz. buttons. Go to Mrs. Geers and *stay*. Arrange about new dress, and try on red sack. Go to Miss Gladding's to dinner, and stay till time for French lesson. Only little

Frost. Mr. Fillion teaches, talking more than was necessary. Walk down with M. Frost, and stop to see if Walter was still down st. Wasn't. Then gym., enjoying it *intensely* and doing more than usual. Carried of a girl on *one arm* and hip—easily!* Delightful bath afterward, Miss Allen also taking one and liking it. Home with her, and then home, to find Will Mauran here. Nice talk. Accts.

Walter's Birthday
Tuesday. March 25th. 1884.

6.45 or so. Some housework; and write to Walter. Letter from, it is his birthday and I had forgotten it! It was not for lack of thought of him. Florrie. Lesson at Mrs. Cushings. Get 26 violets and some Jasmine for Walter, and a lovely glass bottle; and arrange them in his room. Leave letter also. Home and eat 3 oranges. (Felton with me all day.) Blanche. Home, write birthday poem for Walter & Emily posts it, sew & eat, waiting for Kate Bucklin who didn't come. Gym. class, Charlotte and Emily coming for me. A nice time there; Mrs. Diman and Mrs. De Wolf as spectators, and Ellie as visitor. Home and arrange dress. Go to Carrie Hazards to tea. Only she & Margie there. A youth calls later, name of Coleby, collegian as I gather. Carrie very thoughtfully wanted to send a messenger for Walter, and telephoned, but he didn't come, (the messenger boy,) and it got so sate [*sic*] I didn't care to send. Pleasant evening. Home in soft starlight. Am barked at by a dog, and assume the defensive, but am not attacked. Mr. Wells had called here. Glad I was out.

Wed. March. 26th 1884.

7 or so. Florrie. Begin to teach her chess in place of arithmetic. Blanche. Home and dine. Go to see Walter and stay till after 4. Leave suit at gym. and go to Waterman's with Walter. I concluded it was too wet to go to the dressmakers, too late to go home with Walter; so go to Pub. Lib. and read Pop. Sci. till time to go to gym. Only 4 of us—Miss Bartlett, the littlest Miss Gerald, Florrie & I. Pleasant time; especially the bath. Home ere 9.

Thur. March. 27th. 1884.

6. Do housework. All through with breakfast ere 7.30. Mark my sheets "C.A.P.S." Florrie. Blanche. Home; begin to dine, when mother says Emma Vaughn is coming to dinner. So we all have a feast together, the dear little girl getting "enough oranges" for once. Sew and cut. Emily & Char. after me. Go up with them. Call on Mrs. Fillinghast, who wanted to see me. Out. Then gym class, then Home, and sew and write to Ada. And here.

Fri. March. 28th. 1884.

6 or so. Sew. 2 dear letters from Walter and one from Mary Channing Saunders. Florrie. I have begun to teach her chess instead of arithmetic. Blanche. Home,

dine, write to Walter. Go to Mrs. Geer's & she cuts & fixes red sack. Stop and see Millie, sew talk and change her book. French lesson. Go to depot to try and meet Walter, but the train had come in earlier than he expected. Call at the Studio for him, out. Post letter to him, go to the Brown's to supper, Girl's club, then home to find Edward & the Simmonses playing whist with mother. Bed after 11.

Sat. March 29th. 1884.

7.45. Do little work; breakfast, Write on my chapter in the novel. Eat a banana and put three more in my bag. Go down to Walter's and eat them. He comes before long. My last visit there. The express men come and take his things. We are sorry to leave the dear room. Call on Abbie Cooke. Out. On Annie Morse. In New York. On Miss Wheeler and see a niece of hers and another little girl. Walk a bit of a way with Miss Wheeler who is going to a German conversation at Carrie Hazard's. Call on Miss Fillinghast and she inquires my preference for a wedding present. I suggest a willow rocking chair, which is acceded to. Stop and see Annie a few moments and walk a step or two with her as she goes out. Go to the Diman's, early for gym. Meet Mrs. D. outside and walk a little with *her*. Then gym. Home, chocolate, boiled eggs, shortcake, for supper, and I so sleepy thereafter that I doze on some chairs and then write in this and go to bed.

Sun. March. 30th. 1884.

7 or so. A howling hurricane in the night, and a cold snow & dusty day, real March, the first of the year. S. S. But do not stay to hear the Reverend Barrows. Home and write in Blanche's album (& paint), dine, write on novel, Lizzie over, dress, Walter. Not wellfilled day. Returned his $10.00; short trust!

Mon. March 31st. 1884.

7 or so. Do the work and let mother lie abed as long as she wants to. Florrie. Blanche. Home. Dine. Emma & Amy come up to see mother. Write to Walter, and a note to Grace to send with the novel. Go to Ath. & change Felton for Xenophon. See Mary Sharpe & Sophie Aborn there. Post letters. Leave suit at gym. Pub. Lib. Change Florrie's F. Hist. to my card; and get her stories of F. Hist. on her own. French lesson, two new scholars, a lady and child—demoiselle. Gym. A concourse of spectators. The Westcotts, mere et filles attend; and I walk home with them, nearly. Eat two bananas, read, and write accts.*

Tues. April 1st. 1884.

7 or so) Lazy and loafing. Florrie. Mrs. Cushing, pays me $9.00. Call on Mary Sharpe. Look at books in Tibbett's a few minutes and then go and meet Martha, 2 P.M. train. Walk to May Bell Hill's with her and stay awhile.

Blanche. Home and dine. Gym. class, all but Emily. Mrs. D. & E. are in Boston, John in New York, and Louise staying at the Packard's. Home. Am sleepy. Accts. Write to Mrs. Smith.

Wed. April 2nd. 1884.

7.14. *Snow!* Good breakfast, steak and griddle cakes. Florrie. Blanche. Take her album & am given Sarah's to do! Go to Mabel Hill's to dinner & see Martha. Go with her to Mrs. Crandall's, & then to see Walter (leaving suit at gym.) in his new place in Gould's Lane. Find him unsettled. He goes with me to Mrs. Geer's & then to wait me at Waterman's. Have my dress waist tried on and then join Walter. Go home with him, and have supper. Carrie there. Go to the gym and exercise moderately. Home in car with F. Snow & rain and various similar unpleasantries all day. Write to Eva Webster.

Thurs. April 3rd. 1884.

7.15 or so. A short and a long letter from my darling; and a note from Mrs. Crandall inviting me to spend the evening with Martha. Florrie. Blanche. Home and re-read my letters. Sew. Gym. class. Home & dress, ride to H.C. depot, meet Walter, and go to call on his sister Jane Gilmore on Mt. Pleasant. Like her. Home. A slight reresupper, and to bed.

Fri. April 4th. 1884.

7.30! Florrie. Blanche. Home, dine, (after writing a receipt for Mrs. Cushing & note, with verses, to Walter. Sew. Ride to French, reading "Enigma's of Life." Lesson, Pub. Lib. & look at Punch. Gym., careering gaily. Ride home, reading. Sup. Accts.

Sat. April 5th. 1884.

7. Sew a little. Breakfast & read B.C. Advocate & Greg. Set forth for the day. Purchase various articles, stamps, hose, "small wares," ribbons; total 4.17. Go to see Miss Gladding, sew, and have some lunch. Call on Millie. Go to dressmakers and *stay*. Stop to see Walter, stay a little while & then go awall-papering. Select some beautiful "terra-cotta" for the parlor. It gets late, so we postpone the rest till Monday. He comes to College St with me and then we go severally home. Cold & cloudy. A banquet for supper! Broiled steak, bread & butter, cheese, milk, poundcake, water. *Good.* Accts.

Sunday, April 6th. 1884.

7. Write to Charlotte Hedge. S.S. with Mrs. Rawson & Arney. Church. Unsatisfactory Sermon. Home with Lu, who stops in to see my salt & pepper. (Mrs. Luther's present.) Dine. Carrie Hazard and Margie stop and leave linen, Carrie an elegant white cloth and dozen napkins; Helen a heavy rich bedspread, Margie a lovely gold-and-silver fruit set, very lovely. Two Miss

Spencers of Pawtucket call, & a damsel with 'em. Walter comes for me and we go to measure house, and enjoy it. Home. Maria here, full of interest and curiosity about my wedding. Robert calls. Talk to 'em, supper, dress; in black silk skirt and Jersey, with white kerchief, and he likes it better than any yet he says. Guess he's forgotten grandma's muslin. R. goes. Maria goes later. Walter goes, (more's the pity,) at 10.10 or 15. Do tree in Arney's drawing book for mother. Write here. bed thereafter.

Mon. April 7th. 1884.

6.30. Help mother a little and eat leisurely breakfast. Florrie. Blanche. Home, change dress, dine, go to Mrs. Geer's and am more fitted. Stop for Walter and we go a-papering again & get 'em all, lovely ones. Then get some brass candlesticks and Sheldon's. Home with Walter to supper. He comes home with me. W. Present of 30 yds. Londale cambric from Mrs. Louisa Tibbetts.

Tues. April 8th. 1884.

6.15. Cut out chemiloon of my new cambric. Florrie. Home. Write on my Greek report. Dine and help mother a little. Write more. Letter from Walter my darling! Answer and post as I go to Blanche's at 3. Home, to find Maria & Josie Arnold here, the latter with a lovely salad dish for me. Go to my gym. class. Emilie's birthday. Home, to find Kate. Mother & Aunt C. go to "Aunt Polly Bassetts Singing Skewl" and Kate & I have supper and a nice time generally. Jim comes, I show 'em my presents, and he talks to me about politics at my request, and I learn *much*. Folks return, Jim retires with Kate, write here—bed.

Wed. April 9th. 1884.

6.40 or so. Do the work. Florrie. Blanche. Home. Sew. Dine, help mother a trifle. Go to see the Cooley's and change Millie's book. Get Walter, and we go to Humphrey's & get iron-ware and such, to the extent of $21.00 or so. Have chocolate with Walter at Café, gym, ride home, sew, write to my boy, this, bed.

Thurs. April 10th. 1884.

6.15. or so. Some housework & sewing. Florrie. Blanche. Home. Dine. Sew. Write to Walter. Gym. class. Write a little more to Walter & go post it. Lizzie here. Supper. Sew.

Fri. April 11th. 1884.

6. Housework, dishes, breakfast, darn.* Florrie. Blanch. Home. Darn. Dine. Go to Ath. & renew Xenophon. Get a pair of gloves & some buttons, & go to Walter's. Stay there an hour or more. Go with him to the furniture man's & see chairs, and to Sheldon's & get a kitchen table for a dollar & a quarter! Go

to the Slicer's to tea and then to the club. Sarah Westcott hems & gathers my apron. Home with Mrs. S, and then home. Accts. Write to Martha.

Sat. April 12th. 1884.

6.45. Sweep room. Breakfast. Sew & cut & plan. Dress. Dine. Go to Peirce's & order boots and shoes. Stop for dress at Mrs. Geer's. Not done but take waist. Stop a moment at Walter's and he walks to S. Main st. with me. Hurry home & get suit. Charlotte and Emily come for me. Gym. class. Home, sup. Mother & aunt C. return laden with presents. Robert sends his soapine to be sure; but also a magnificent brass fire-set; too lovely to use. I have set them on the centre table, in glory. Mother bestows a bread board and sells me the knife for a cent! Also an iron dishcloth. Kate had been here and left $30.00! Accts. Darn. Mrs. Geer arrives with my dress after 9! Try it on.

Easter Sun. April 13th. 1884.

6.15. Wake early and happy. Mother sick. Stay at home and do all the work. Sew, finishing little buff apron & hemming big one. Mary and baby stop at gate, Anna, Clarence & Charlie in P.M. Also Robert whom I do not see having gone up stairs to dress and had a nap there. Put on my new attire and go to the Children's Easter Service. Enjoy the singing much. Home with Harry Manchester, who stops in a minute to worship my brasses. Sup, dress, Walter. Show him things exultingly. Happy evening. Draw some things for mother to trace for her youngests.

Mon. April. 14th. 1884.

6.45. Help mother. Florrie. Blanche. Get a nearly new geography from Sarah, to give to little Blanche Arnold. Home, dine, dress, set forth. Call on Annie Aborn and Mrs. Fillinghast, who gives me $20.00 to buy our bookcase. Leave my monthly $2.00 with the worthy Mrs. Williams. Call on Mrs. Tibbits and thank her for the cambric. Leave suit at gym. Go and pay Mrs. Geer for suit, $10.45. Stop for Walter; and we go hunting for tablecloths and clocks. Supper at Café with him. Gym. Home. Lizzie here with fruit knives and market basket. Brings Allie's present too.

Tues. April 15th. 1884.

Ere 6. Do the work. Write to Walter. Letter from him. Florrie. Home and answer Walter's letter. Sew. Dine. Blanche. Home. Sew. Emily & Effie & Charlotte come to see me and escort me to the gym. Maria arrives and brings me a pretty syrup-cup. Gym. class. Louise likes to hear me sing! Home. Post letter. Loaf a little bit. Set table while mother gets supper for M. Sup. Sew, on 2nd waist.

Wed. April 16th. 1884.

Near 7. Help mother. Florrie. Blanche. (Stop and see house, painting done.) Home, dine. Dress and set out. Call on the Hazards and thank them. Stop for low shoes. Not done. Get some waists and nailbrushes and return for shoes. Not done. Leave suit and bundle at gym. Get a few violets & go to see Walter. Stop a little while, and then we go look at mattings. Then get the Ring. Inside "Walter" "Charlotte", the date, and "Ich liebe dich".[9] Then we go to Root's, and I get more hardware. Then a bit of bread & cheese at Burgesses and the gym. Ride home. Sam here. Accts. Bed.

Thurs. April 17th. 1884

6.15 Some work. Box from Grandma Perkins, with dish, spoonholder, 3 towels, $10.00 & a letter. Florrie. Blanche. Stop in to see about the paperers. Home. Sew. Dine. Run down to the house again. Home. Sew. Gym. class. Present bills, & Mrs. Diman pays hers with a check. Home. Sup on oranges. Write to Allie B. Elder, Thomas, & grandma. Sew now. Finish 2nd waist.

Fri. April 18th. 1884.

6.45 Dishes, a few. Letter from Walter. Florrie. Go to see the papering and then Blanche. Home, dress, dine, set forth. Leave note at the damsel at the Westcott's request; post divers other letters; stop to see about shoes at Pierce's, and call for Walter. Mr. Wall there. We go after a refrigerator with partial success, search for slop jars & clocks, order gas meter (funny time with the man) see about the pillows, look at the ring, &c. &c. Nice time. Go home with him and have some chocolate; go to Carrie's and have more supper, and stay till a little after 9. Walter comes in for a little while, as mother and Aunt C. had gone to the theatre. He goes. Take in milk, etc, accts. bed.

Sat. April 19th. 1884.

6.30. Sew, breakfast, and betake myself to the house, where I remain from 9 till 12, while gas men, stove men, other men and a boy bring divers things to our domicile. Walter arrives and remains with me. I sweep up the parlor. The stove is magnificent and color of paint and paper highly satisfactory. We exult in the prospect before us. Home. Sew, dine. Sew sew sew. Gym. class. Home. Sup. Accts & sermon. Sew.

Sun. April 20th. 1884.

6.45 or so. Help mother a little. Sew. S. S., Interesting discussion on "Business Honesty", with papers by self and Frank Cranston. Church. Call on Abbie Cooke. Home. Sew. Dine. Sew. Julia Jastrum calls, with Eddie & Tudie. Brings me a lovely amber "crackle" glass pitcher; and a dozen butter pats from the children. Amuse T. with books. Henrietta calls and brings me a beautiful Jap. silver basket and Shakespeare. Robert calls. All go but H. Some supper, dress, Walter. Show him things. Happy evening. Read a bit of "All's Well that ends Well" in my new book.

Mon. April 21st. 1884.

5.45) Fly around at home, and then trot down to our house bag & baggage, stopping to buy a pail. Mr. Bolan comes, he cleans and I scrub my bedroom floor. The man comes with the matting. I go to Florrie. Back again. Matting down and painters there. Blanche. Home. Dine. Dress. Set out. Cash both checks at Trust Company, 12 & 10. Go to Pierce's & pay for shoes. Leave suit in gym. Get pillow cases. Go to Irrepressible rooms & get address of sewing woman. Carry cases to her, way out on Olney St! Back. Get ring, my wedding ring! Pierce's again. Get rubbers, slippers, blacking, shoestrings. Gladdings again and get my wedding dress, and Walter's chiton. Also divers small wares. Look vainly for sash and skirt cloth. Go for Walter, (after much shopping) give him ring to keep till it is put on by him on our wedding night; & we trot about. Go to sup at Café; Kate comes in, and we have a nice time together. gym. Nice time. Bath with Miss Allen, and home with her as far as Ives. Find lovely little silver bound baking dish from Mary Sharpe! Write her a bit poem in answer.[10] Accts. *bed.* 10.35.

Tues. April 22nd. 1884.

6.25 or so). Some housework. Letter from Walter. Run down to the house with gold paper. Florrie. Mrs. Cushing. Home. Glorious day. Dine. Sew. Blanche. Home. Sew. Emily & Charlotte come for me with white violets. Gym. class. Home. Sew. Sup, with Charles Reade's stories. Sew. Edward calls. Three games of whist. Bed. My right arm ached dismally last night, and begins again now. Funny.

Wed. April 23rd. 1884.

5.45. Housework and baste hems. Letter from Ada with check for $50.00. Florrie. Blanche. Home. Dine, reading Reade. Go to Trust Company & cash check. Stop at Pierce's to see about white velvet slippers. Leave things at gym. Go to Bagley's. He can do slippers but not soon enough. Back to Pierces and get design I made and then to Teal's. They will make 'em. Go and pay Mrs. Geer for red waist and black silicia one. Stop for Walter and we go and get refrigerator and tub. Order gas fixtures. Get *lovely* curtain stuffs. Buy a beautiful black tall desk with Ada's money. Pay Mr. Bryan for my shoes, $5.00. Get the white sash I ordered at the Boston Store, $3.50, order little black kettle at Root's. Go home with Walter. Have a cup of chocolate and other refections. Walk briskly down to gym. (missed car.) Exercise mildly. Home partly with Miss Allen. We had some soda. Returned her book "Enigmas of life". Accts. Bed.

Thurs. April 24th. 1884.

6. Housework. sew. Florrie. Stop at house and find Walter there. Stay half and hour or so. Blanche. Back to house to see the refrigerator put in, and Walter. Finish Blanche. Home, dine with C. Reade. Sew. Last day of gym. Home. Sup with Reade. Write to Walter. Harry Manchester calls. Write more to Walter. Bed.

Friday. April 25th. 1884.

5.45 or thereabouts

Sew and housework. Letters from my darling. Last day with Florrie & Blanche. Stop in at the house and see my new desk in all its glory. Home. Sew. Dine. Sew. My gym. class sent their present today, Dana's household book of poetry; Mrs. & Mr. Blake a splendid atlas and W. Irving's works, Mrs. Diman the Cambridge edition of Longfellow. I feel rich. Make Walter's chiton. Dress and go the Slicers to tea; leaving Xenophon at the atheneaum. Girls Club, reading "In His Name".[11] Go home with Mrs. S., leave Lu Randolph at the depot, and take car home as it rains; borrowing ticket. Write note to Ada & accts.

Sat. April 26th. 1884.

6.30 Sew, till 8.45. Breakfast. Go down to the house and thence to the Hazard's where I see Carrie and Helen. Mr. & Mrs. Hazard present me with a dozen silver teaspoons, lovely ones. Go to Exhibition of Day Class at gym. Very enjoyable. See Kate there; and others. Shop a bit, then to Walter's, then with him after an expressman and a clock. He goes home and I to Miss Gladding's. Sew for an hour & a half or so. Go to the Studio and find Walter. Wait there till after three; no expressman. He goes to the house and I to Olney st. after Mrs. Burlingame and my pillowcases. That amiable dame had misunderstood me and made them *square*! Almost all used up and spoiled. I could have cried, but did not and comforted the poor woman; who was much distressed. Then home and leave my useless bundle, (the Diman crowd rushing out on me as I passed, Effie taking my things almost home, and Charlotte my umbrella nearly as far.) go down to the house and join Walter. We make a little fire in our stove. The hardware and china and wood comes. Bought the dearest little clock with $7.00 of Miss Nightingale's 10; yellow glass, in a plush case.* Home by 6.30 or so. Loaf a little, change shoes & waist, sup; and write to Uncle Edward (at Carrie & Helen's request) and to Mrs. Smith. Accts.

Sunday. April 27th. 1884.

6:30–35

Sew. Some housework. Sew. S. S. Home, with Westcott girls. Order $5.00 worth of flowers of John Kelly. Sew. Dine. Sew. Mary in. Sew. Robert in. Sew. Sup. Dress. Walter. The last Sunday here; for which I am truly thankful. And he. Wind my clock! Ascend the stair. Bed.

Mon. April 28th. 1884.

5.45 Do housework. Breakfast slightly. Mr. Bolan appears and we go down to the house & inventory dishes, tins, etc; wash china, scrub closet thoroughly, sweep up parlor, &c. &c. Have a little woodfire. Home, eat hurriedly, dress, back again. Walter there. Unpack his things, cut curtains, lay down rug, etc. Leave him putting down stair carpet, rush home, stopping at Mary's for mother & Aunt C, take a stitch in gym. suit, some bread & butter and some figs. Go to Gym. for the last time at present.[12] They see [*sic*] sorry to have me go. Walk home alone.

Tues. April 29th. 1884.

6.15. Pack, breakfast, pack. Go to Miss Cushing's. Go down st. & shop; getting more hardware, groceries, etc. Home and get some lunch. Go down to the house and eat it. Walter comes. Some of his things come. Hem curtains. Home. Lizzie calls with $10.00 from Fred Hedge; Kate comes, sew, supper, sew. Anna & Clarence call. Sew. Go up and pack dresses etc.

Wed. April 30th. 1884.

(May 3rd.)*

Omitted my journal on these last 3 days owing to much busy-ness. This and the next were occupied in fixing things at the house almost wholly. All my things brought over to the house. Big morning's work. Walter over. Wed P.M. I went down st. for some last shopping

TEN

~~~

"A crown of white roses"

May 1, 1884–August 17, 1884

IN THE EARLY evening hours of May 2, 1884, Charlotte and Walter Stetson were married. Charlotte's fears about wedlock were temporarily suspended as she reveled in the unfamiliar ecstasy of her wedding night. While Walter waited in another room, Charlotte joyfully decorated their bed with lace, silk, and flowers, made herself a crown of white roses, slipped into a sheer white gown, and emerged, seductively, to greet her new husband. Walter placed Charlotte's wedding ring upon her finger and then rapturously undressed his new bride. The thrill that Charlotte felt during the initiation of sexual intimacy is almost palpable in her simple description of the moment: "He lifts the crown, loosens the snood, unfastens the girdle, and then—and then," she wrote.

The next morning, Charlotte was still enthralled with what was ultimately just the illusion of wedded bliss: "Lie on the lounge in the soft spring sunshine and am happy. Happy. Happy. Walter stays quietly at home with me; and we rest and love each other." Predictably, however, the tranquillity was short-lived. Within a week, Charlotte was resisting her forced dependence on Walter: "I suggest that he pay me for my services; and he much dislikes the idea. I am grieved at offending him, mutual misery. Bed and cry." Whether the services for which Charlotte sought compensation included sexual as well as domestic duties is ambiguous, but in any event, the power struggle had begun.

During the next several weeks, both Charlotte and Walter tried to adjust to the new demands of marriage. There were, in fact, many happy hours spent reading together, drawing, and entertaining friends. There was also occasional heartache. Within weeks after the wedding, Charlotte reproached herself for being too "affectionately expressive," and Walter was forced to reaffirm his love whenever she grew insecure. In the early weeks of their marriage, however, the pleasure seemed to outweigh the pain.

By the end of July, Charlotte suspected that she might be pregnant. She apparently dismissed it, however, because a few days later, on August 5, she attributed her sickness to "inter-susception of the intestine." The symptoms, however, continued.

By the time Charlotte left Providence on August 18 for a visit to Martha Lane in Hingham, her pregnancy had been confirmed. During her two-week stay with Martha, Charlotte neglected her diary. When she resumed her writing on September 1, however, Charlotte made clear how annoyed she was by comments about her "condition."

Thurs. May 1st. 1884.

Down at the house as usual. Busy. Walter over P.M. Groceries come and other things. Home and sew. Reginald Brown and Mary call on us in the evening; he bringing me a lovely wastebasket and she a photo. of the three little girls in a hammered brass frame of Mr. Field's make; very pretty. Sew. Found Mary Phelon when I went home, and Blance [*sic*] Westcott came up and brought me a clothes pin basket, two dishclothes, and a towel. Miss Gladding's work basket came; a *beauty*, simply perfect; the handsomest one I ever saw.

Friday, May 2nd. 1884
My Wedding Day.

Am up betimes and finish my chemiloom. Down to the house betimes. Sew— Walter over. He goes between 2 & 3. I finish wedding dress; trim bonnet, arrange great stacks of flowers, and fly around generally. Home just after Mr. & Mrs. Stetson arrive. Bathe. Dress. Am ready at or near 6.30, and we are straightway wedded by Mr. S. Senior. Aunt C. hearty in her congratulations, his parents kind and affectionate, but mother declines to kiss me and merely says "goodbye". A splendid supper; for which I am well prepared; having forgotten to eat any lunch. Take many boxes, baskets, and bundles, and go— —H O M E ! Mary & Ray congratulate us out of the window.[1] Come in, drop our baggage, and I install Walter in the parlor & dining room while I retire to the bed chamber and finish it's decoration. The bed looks like a fairy bower with lace, white silk, and flowers. Make my self a crown of white roses. Wash again, and put on a thin drift of white mull fastened with a rosebud and velvet and pearl civeture. My little white velvet slippers* and a white snood. Go in to my husband. He meets me joyfully; we promise to be true to each other; and he puts on the ring and the crown. Then he lifts the crown, loosens the snood, unfastens the girdle, and then—and then.

> O my God! I thank thee
> for this heavenly happiness!
> O make me one with thy
> great life that I may best
> fulfill my duties to my love!

to my Husband!
    And if I am a mother
    ——let it be according
to thy will!
    O guide me! teach me,
help me to do right!

Sat. May 3rd. 1884.

Up at 8.20 or so. Get a nice little breakfast of omelette and chocolate. Lie on the lounge in the soft spring sunshine and am happy. Happy. Happy. Walter stays quietly at home with me; and we rest and love each other. Get johnny-cakes & frizzled beef for dinner; wash dishes, Walter wiping; and go down st. together. Get divers things, come home, have some supper; fix room, put my boy to bed, (he is well worn out with a long winter's work,) and essay to make bread; but can't find my yeastcake. Give it up in no ill humor; and write here.

O I am happy!
May I do right enough
to merit and deserve!

Thank God.

Sun. May 4th. 1884.

7.30 or so. Get breakfast hastily and hie me to S.S., overtaken and accompanied by Sarah Westcott. My boys seem generally unconscious. Stay to church. Home with the Manchesters and stop to see mother and aunt. Then *Home.* Walter in shortly, he having been to see his mother. Rest awhile. Get dinner. Katie comes for clothes. Wash dishes and mix bread while Walter reads to me; dear boy! Feel gently tired.

Mon. May 5th. 1884.

About 8 or less. Prodigious breakfast of oatmeal, chocolate, hot biscuit and salmon. Walter goes to work, and I go to sleep; and have a good three hour's nap with one wakeup. The young man returns at about 2; and I get him a little dinner. Then loaf a bit, wash dishes and fix bedroom. He feels dizzy; and I put him snugly to bed and then write. Am happy.

Tues. May 6th. 1884.

7.30 or so. Breakfast. Wash dishes, etc. and go to give lesson at Mrs. Cushings. (Stop at mothers to leave some things and am rapturously greeted by Emily and others.) Go down street and shop extensively. Call on Miss Gladding and Millie Cooley. Stop for Walter; and he comes home with me. Get a most delectable dinner of veal fried in batter and new potatoes. Very very delicious. Am tired later and am put tenderly to bed.

Wed. May 7th. 1884.

7.30 or so. Most excellent breakfast, oatmeal, frizzled beef and warmed up potato, all good. Am turning out a superior cook. Hem tablecloth, partly; and take nap. Rise and begin to work. Walter comes home unexpectedly. Glad to see him. He helps me lots. Get much in order; and make a good little soup for dinner. Then unpack box of letters, etc; knit, and read to each other.

Thurs. May. 8th. 1884.

7.10 or 15) Feel badly because Walter doesn't like the open windows; and because he casually drank the top of the milk that was to have been cream for him this morning; and because I broke the handle off a little Chinese tea cup. But he stays at home with me all day and I am consoled. Have a bit nap while he writes a reply to a Boston art critic who accused him of copying Monticelli. Get a most delectable dinner; including a dish of applesauce with egg top of peculiar deliciousness, which I bestow on the Arnold children after we've had some, as t'wouldn't keep. It was *good*! Clear the table, my dear boy helping as he did all day; light our new lamp; and sit down to sew and knit while he reads, aloud to me; out of Maclise and Dana. Quiet happiness. Write. Bed. O I am happy!

Fri. May 9th. 1884.

As usual.) Walter gone all day, and I do a good day's work; writing 7 notes of thanks, drawing some things for mother, arranging things in bureau drawers, etc. etc. Walter home a little after 6. He brings me an exquisite gauzy white Turkish scarf. Get a nice little dinner. I suggest that he pay me for my services; and he much dislikes the idea. I am grieved at offending him, mutual misery. Bed and cry.

Sat. May 10th. 1884.

7. Breakfast. Leave dishes and go to studio with Walter. Beautiful Spring morning. Call on Millie and change book for her. Look at Punch in Pub. Lib. Go about and shop. Take car for home, as it rains a little. Walter on it. Home. Rest a little. He brought me some lovely flowers. Get a lunch-dinner. Loaf and lie down. Mother and Aunt Caroline call. Three meal's dishes about, and much confusion. Wash dishes. Walter's father over with letter and pamphlet he thought were important. Stays a little. Make bread. Dress. Write for S.S. class.

Sun. May 11th. 1884.

5.50 or 55. Get breakfast. Go to Sunday school and stay to church. Incapable youth from Concord named "Bulkely" I believe, has the pulpit. Call on Mother & Aunt. Stop at Mary's after my key. Home. Find Walter hadn't been out. Work all P.M. He goes to his mother a little ere 2 and returns about 5 or 530.

Nice dinner. Katy comes for clothes. Dress and baste two pillowcases while Walter reads "Atalanta's Race" to me. Bed.

Mon. May 12th. 1884.

8. Rush about and get breakfast. Go to Florrie taking her Thackeray's "Chronicles of the Drum" to read. Home and fix the ice etc. Blanche. Home. Dine. Loaf and nap some 30 minutes. Do work. Walter home about 4.30. Get a most delectable dinner, soup, hash, and potato. Dress before dinner. Go to letter box with Walter. Back. Make bed. Accts. Read in poetry book.

Tues. May 13th. 1884.

7. Get breakfast and eat it, serenely. Florrie, carrying her Rip Van Winkle. Mrs. Cushing. Go down st. and "market". Go to see Walter. Not there. Call to see if Miss Jeffrey had gone; she had. Go to see Mary Brown and stay to dinner. Bessie accompanies me back to the studio. Walk to S. Main St. & then ride home, in *open car*. Do the work as usual. Walter home early, and we read and laugh at a "Fine Arts" from the Transcript Martha sent me. Dinner, vilely expensive; chops, 6 little chops, .50 cts! And canned peas, .25. Dress and sew on pillow case. Blanche, Sarah, and Carl Westcott in and out on a maybasket trick of Blanches. Walter reads me Maclise.

Wed. May 14th. 1884.

6.45. Wash dishes. Breakfast. Florrie, take her Maclise & read over sketch of Irving etc. Home and fix ice &c. Books come for Walter, Don Quixote, ill. by Tony Johannot, only $2.50! Blanche. Have her come in with me and read her divers war poems. She enjoys it. Show her atlas. Do work, doze, more work. Walter comes early, attended by Mr. Whittaker to see our view. He seems much pleased. Dinner. Write, sew, etc.

Thurs. May 15th. 1884.

6.30. Slept ill. Forgot to salt bread. Breakfast. Florrie. Home. Blanche. Helen & Carrie Hazard call while I'm there, and stop for me. So I go out and "call" in the carriage; Carrie having been ill and not caring to come in. Home. Hem curtains, mend Walter's clothes, read Naphey, etc. Mrs. Keach and Junie call. Walter home about 5. Brings me flowers, dear boy. Potatoes for dinner, egg-&-dried beef, herring. Finish bookcase while Walter draws me. He makes us some delicious iced lemonade. Loaf a bit. Bed.

Fri. May 16th. 1884.

8! Fly around. Florrie. Home. Blanche. Home. Work all P.M. washing vast accumulation of dishes, making little cakes, etc. Walter home about 5. Helps me. Omelette & griddle cakes for supper. Hem one end of tablecloth. Write to Uncle Edward, Aunt Emily, & Nellie, all in one. Have a tiny rere-supper, and bed.

Sat. May 17th. 1884.

Nearly 8. Breakfast. Go to Walters room with him. He doesn't feel like working so we return together, intending to go out in the woods but it is showery so we don't. I nap and he naps. A wild hail gust. Wash dishes and have a nice little supper. Write some Adolphus. Bed.

Sun. May 18th. 1884.

5.45. Write more Adolphus. Breakfast. S.S. Church. Call on mother (walked up with the Manchesters.) Home. Sweep parlor and dust. Walter fixes the rest of the parlor curtains and the front door. Dinner. Leave dishes. Bed at 8 or a little later.

Mon. May 19th. 1884.

6.45 or so. Wash dishes. Breakfast. Florrie. Blanche. (Stopped to see mother a moment, and leave her list of presents to send Julia. Children delighted to see me and Mabel Luther gives me some lovely apple blossoms.) Home and lunch. Carrie and Helen call and bring me canned peas, beans, and asparagus! They are delighted with the house &c. Work briskly. Get dinner, eat it, (Walter home at about 5) and actually wash the dishes! Sew, while Walter reads King John. Bed about 10.

Tues. May 20th. 1884.

8.45! Fly to Florrie, eating a lunch breakfast there. Miss Cushing. Shop. Ride home, as it showered. Walk down Pitman St. with Mr. Childs of Belowstairs. Home and get lunch & do chamberwork. Go to Blanche. Home. Make gingerbread original composition! Get dinner, steak, and some of Carrie's beans. Knit while Walter ends King John. Accts. Bed.

Wed. May 21st. 1884.

8.15? Florrie. Stopped at mother's and she gave me some lilies of the valley. Blanche. Home and fly around briskly, fixing things. Walters mother and sister Carrie, call. Seem to like it here. Bed early.

Thurs. May 22nd. 1884

? My first reception day. Florrie not well so I return for Walter and walk down with him. Get 8 pillowcases & a neckkerchief of Charlotte Hedges 10. 17 cts left. Ride home. Overtake Mary & Anna with their respective chicks. Anna, Alice, & Charlie come in to see "Cousin Charlotte's house." Fix things somewhat. Blanche. Home. Dress. Do work. Mrs. Blake and others with her called while I was at Blanche's; but no one else till after dinner when Mrs. Westcott calls. Then Mr. Dorrance, Robert Brown, and Blanche Westcott with Miss Dodge. (Lives in their house.) Stormy discussion between Robert and Mr. D. Rude and shallow. Go at 10.30 or so.

Fri. May 23rd. 1884.

9.15 or 20. Walter gets most of the breakfast. Letters for us both. He stays at home and draws me, in charcoal. Lunch, while a "Ploomber" fixes our sink, the pipe of which broke down yesterday[,]* no Wed. night. Blanche from 3 to 4. Home. Dishes, dinner, etc. Kate Bucklin comes and dines with us. Stays till 8.30 or 40. We walk home with her. *Home* then. Accts. bed.

Sat. May 24th. 1884.

9 or so. Breakfast. Aunt Caroline calls. Go down st. with Walter and shop. Ride home. Wash dishes and search top drawer for our small red friends. Annie Aborn calls. Read Longfellow to Walter. Make bread. Accts. Bed. Am disgusted with myself—numb—helpless. Tomorrow God helping me I will begin anew!

Sun. May. 25th. 1884.

7.30. Write. Adolphus, reading we stories from the Buffalo Christian Advocate to keep myself awake. Breakfast. S.S. Stop and thank Mrs. Anthony. Stop and see mother. Stop and speak to Mary & Alice & she gives me some pansies. Home. Walter here. Do some of the work and then————. Two of the Pawtucket Spencers call. Want us to come out there. Dr. Allen calls to see Walter. Emma Vaughn, Arney, & Alice Payton call but don't come in on account of the doctor. Dinner. Dishes, Walter reading to me. Bed.

Mon. May 26th. 1884.

8.45. Breakfast on one banana. Florrie. Home. Walter not gone. Blanche. Home. Get lunch. Walter goes. Do work. Accts. Mr. & Mrs. Burleigh send us a red rocking chair. Yesterday's little girls and another one call, and are much pleased herewith. Read 'em "The Cruise of The Rover." Walter home, with fish. Dinner. Dishes. Accts. Draw for mother. Bed.

Tues. May 27th. 1884.

7.30. Stop at mother's with drawings. Florrie. Mrs. Cushing. Shop. Get Uncle Edward's package at Earle & Prew's. Ride home. Open bundle with Walter as spectator. A set of his works, (not complete) elegantly bound. Eat. Blanche. While there am called suddenly home by Carl—Maude Arnold in a fit. I come in haste, get Walter, and we do what little we can; ice water to her head etc. Dr. Wilcox later says it's scarletina. Lu Manchester calls. Dinner. Dishes. Read "Rudder Grange" to Walter & knit. Accts. Answer uncle Edwards letter. Write invitation to gym class: & Mrs. Gilmore, to call.

Wed. May 28th. 1884.

6. Bed again. Florrie. Home and work a little. Blanche. Home. Dine & work. Wash kitchen floor, sweep bedroom, etc. Walter home P.M. & helps me. Also

fixes things in the house. Dinner. Dishes. Dress. He reads me an adulatory article sent by some Boston literary lady. Amusing. We don't *feel* famous in spite of the papers.

Thurs. May. 29th. 1884.

5.45 Dust, sweep, and wash parlor. Return to bed a little while, before dressing. Dress. Breakfast hastily. Florrie. Go to see Mrs. Tilling, Mrs. Moulton and Mrs. Diman about the children's coming here—scarletina. They all think not. Stop at mothers and leave word for Emily. Blanche. (Met Mrs. Putnam and she sent me some pansies.) Home. Dine. Clear up. Make rice pudding. Begin "Madame Thérèse" [2] over my dinner. Knit & read. Sophie Aborn calls. Mrs. Budlong calls, with Jessie. Mr. & Mrs. Richards call, but fear the scarletina and go away. Walter home. Sew. Dinner. Dishes. Knit & read. Mr. Burleigh calls. Accts. Bed.

Fri. May. 30th. 1884.

8.5, or so. Stay at home as it is Decoration Day. Finish "Madame Therese." Loaf, eat, rest, am lazy. So is Walter. Amuse ourselves in the evening with funny drawings.

Sat. May. 31st 1884.

5. Wash dishes & read "The Conscript." [3] Go down town with Walter. Shop. Call on Millie. Walk home. Express man brings my box, gasstove & desk from mother. Sew. Write Adolphus. Get good dinner, *roast beef* etc; *custard* & berries. Dishes. Finish Adolphus & write verse or two of "My Garden.["]

Sun. June 1st. 1884.

8.5 or 10. Breakfast. S.S. Singing service in church. The Channings have returned; walk a little ways with them; Grace, Mary & Mr. Saunders. Walk most way home with the Maurans, Mrs. & the three boys. Invite them to call. Stop and see mother a few moments. Home. Get lunch. Hurry about and go out to the Spencers in Pawtucket, 4 o'clock car. Tea, examine place, chat, and they bring us home in the carriage. Pleasant time. Glad to get home. Make hot cracker milk toast for Walter. Accts. Bed. Flowers & rhubarb.

Mon. June 2nd. 1884.

5.15 or so. Sweep kitchen, wash dishes, get Breakfast. Florrie. Home, work. Carry some rhubarb down stairs. Blanche comes up with some flowers from Maud, who is better. Comes up again P.M. and stays contentedly. Says she likes to come and see me. Lunched with "The Conscript". Made rhubarb sauce, & cake, *good*. Cost of loaf about 20 cts. Good dinner. (Sewed on pillowcases while Blanche was here.) Dishes. Accts. — — Bed.

Tuesday. June 3rd. 1884.

5.15 or 20. Scrub outhouse and stairs. Breakfast. Florrie. Mrs. Cushing. Shop. Meet Walter & have some cream at café. Home together. Rest awhile. Go over to mothers, darn stockings and talk. Home. —— Dine. Write.

Wed. June 4th. 1884.

5.10–20. Walter at 6.30 or so. Dishes. Breakfast. Dishes & "chores" in general. Go to mother's and say I'll leave Clarence's "poem" this afternoon. Florrie is to busy to want me. (It is the old folks golden wedding day, and to be celebrated at Henry's.) Home. Write poem & doze. Make bed. Finish poem. Carry it to mother. Home, lunch and work about, reading "Fair Maid of Perth"[4] at intervals. Expect Grace Channing but she cometh not. Walter. dinner. (fixed his charcoal drawings for him) Soup bad—soft custard too thick. Bread. dishes. accts. *Bed*.

Thurs. June 5th. 1884.

8.30–35 Florrie. Home. Work. Maria Brown calls. Asks questions. Walter goes off after I'm dressed. Draw Jim's card, doze, read. (Stopped at mother's and got note from Cousin Julia Seymour, with check for $10.00.) No callers P.M. Dine. Ben Wells calls. Mrs. & Mr. Slicer. Harry Manchester. Lemonade and talk. Leave dishes. Bed.

Fri. June 6th. 1884—

6.30 or so. Bed again. 8.30. Florrie. Home. Lunch. Finish "Fair Maid of Perth". Do chamberwork and wash dishes. Make blancmange. Paint gladiolus for Jim. Mend parasol. Walter. Get dinner, peas and popovers. Clear table. Accts. bed.

Sat. June 7th. 1884.

8.30. A long lazy day. Go down st. with Walter and shop. Get "Phantastes".[5] Ride home together. Read to him in Phan. He enjoys it. Lunch or dinner. More reading. A beautiful evening. Enjoyable operations in petty surgery. Supper. Talk earnestly on foreordination and free will. Does me good. Lie down alone awhile and think. Accts. Bed.

Sun. June 8th. 1884.

7. or so and wash dishes. Sweep kitchen. Bed again. Loaf all day. Go to see mother at 7.30. Henrietta there. Edward calls. Home by 8.35. Write.

Mon. June 9th. 1884.

7.15 or so. Florrie. Home. Housework, lunch, etc. reading "Waterloo." Found a note and package from Mary Bushnel Hazard,—a beautiful gold pin. Make gingerbread. (Washed refrigerator and gas stove). Read obstetrics diligently.

Abbie Cooke calls. Has a good time. Lemonade. Read more. Walter. dinner. Phantastes. Accts. bed.

Tues. June 10th 1884.

8.30–45. Florrie. Mrs. Cushing. Last day, pays me seven dollars and I'm to call for the other. Go and shop. Call on Millie and eat lunch. Read Century to her. Go to see Walter but he was out. Ride as it drizzles. Get dinner. Wash dishes. Bed, tired.

Wed. June 11th. 1884.

7.30 or so) Breakfast in peace. Florrie. Home. Do usual work, sweep & dust parlor & kitchen. Grace Channing arrives and stays some hour and a half. Walter. Dinner. Make bread. Go in and see the Westcotts, look at their books and enjoy ourselves. Home at 9.45 or so.

Thurs. June 12th. 1884.

8.30 or so. Go to Florrie's but return; the grandfather is no better. Stop and see mother. Home. Do the work. Put blanket & things in camphor. Read some. Dine. Dress. Paint on card for Mr. Brian. Do pansie in pen-&-ink. Nap. Walter. He gets supper himself & I eat none. Read Phantes. Bed.

Fri. June 13th. 1884

About 6. Feel sick and remain so all day. Walter stays at home and does every- thing for me. Bless him! Feel better late P.M. & get some mush & potatoes for dinner. Eat some myself. Walter fixes the letter box, & I make the lemon squeezer holes bigger. Read him a little "Rudder Grange" Draw and write.

Sat. June 14th. 1884

8.30 or so. Walter gets breakfast. (Canned chicken is very good sliced & fried in butter.) Go down st. with Walter. Shop. Home. Paint little cards for mother, three. Old Mr. Hazeltine calls and stays nearly 3 hours I guess. Gave him a plate of fruit and gingerbread which he seemed to enjoy. Talked widely and enjoyed it. Read, eat, wash dishes, get supper—Walter helps much. Good supper. Read & eat candy while Walter draws me in red. Am happy. Accts. Lemonade. Bed.

Sun. June 15th. 1884.

8 about. (Am sad: Last night & this morning. Because I find myself too—af- fectionately expressive. I must keep more to myself and be asked—not borne with.) Begin to make snowpudding. Little corncakes for breakfast. Sleep about three hours on mattress in garret. Come down and work till 8 or so. Gingerbread. Snow pudding. Dishes. Sweep kitchen. Chamberwork. Pillow- case. Bath. Dinner. etc. etc. Go and see mother a little while. Home. Show

Walter a little about perspective. Write note to Mary P. B. Hazard. Write here. Bed.

Mon. June 16th. 1884.

? Walter off late. Do up work & paint an hour about. Take things up to mother's and paint there, lunch, finish Mr. Brian's card and take it to him, $2.50. Trot about with mother a little. Go for Walter and walk home with him. Nice cool house and supper. Bed.

Tues. June 17th. 1884.

7 or so. Breakfast, dishes etc. Write note to Mrs. Smith. Walk over with Walter. Shop. Get a sponge for floors. Get my dollar of Mrs. Cushing and leave her receipt in full. Go to see Grace Channing & stay to lunch. Nice talk. Call on Mrs. Blake. Home. Walter here. Dinner. He clears up. Paint one little card and draw three funny little ink ones. Accts. Bed.

Wed. June 18th. 1884.

6.15—again 8.15 or so. Paint, paint, paint. Mrs. Smith sends the $2.00 she forgot last time. Blanche comes up with some daisies, and then Maude & Frank. They stay and stay. (Mrs. Luther called at 12.15. Glad to see her.) Paint 5 cards. Old Mr. Stetson calls and stays to tea. Walter home just after his father. It appears the old gentleman manufactures divers medicine & liniments for a living. Goes early. Walter & I talk a little.

Thurs. June 19th. 1884.

8.30 or so. Breakfast. Sweep parlor & kitchen. Bathe & dress. Wash dishes. Paint. Mother calls. Heavy storm. Walter home wet. Rest a bit. Mother took her 13 little cards. Dinner. Clear up. Harry Manchester calls, and later Mr. & Mrs. Lindsey & Charley Baxter. Hot. Lemonade.

20th.

? Not much of anything but go down and get a little lunch and some books and take the 12.10 car for Pawtucket. A long lovely happy afternoon on the river. I row mostly to my much content; we linger under shady trees, dip our feet in the cool water and are very happy. Home by 9.20 or so. Eat. Bed.

Sat. June 21st. 1884.

9 or thereabouts. Florrie calls. Go down town with Walter. Go to Market. Get raspberry phosphates. Go to Tibbetts & buy 5 little photo's, $1.15. Leave Phantastes at Perrins. Get groceries & fruit and dress & trimming, $1.88 & $1.40. We got books also, ice cream, etc. Ride home. Find the circular Mrs. Smith sent, a heavy woolen cloth, very rich and handsome. Eat, and drink of our raspberry syrup. I "sit" and Walter draws me. Supper. Accts. Bed. *Hot.*

Sun. June 22nd. 1884.

Late. Lazy. Read and am read to. Cut off breadths of new dress. Walter's brother and his wife call, and have a scrambling sort of lunch supper before going. Go up to mother's a while. Maria Brown there.

Mon. June 23rd. 1884

6.30 or so. Wash dishes. Write apologetic note to Mrs. J. A. Stetson, Jr. Florrie again. Home and work till 5 or so. Walter. Read a little. Dinner. Accts. Walter reads to me—bed.

Tues. June 24th. 1884.

8.15 or thereabouts. Florrie. Stop and see mother. Go a shopping. Call on Millie and get my bedspread. Ride home. Walter here. Don't do much of anything during the afternoon. Dress in black bye & bye and sew on dress while Walter reads "A Bold Stroke for a Wife" out of "The London Stage" I borrowed from mother today. Hamilton Macdougall calls. Stays till 11 or so. Bed.

Wed. June 25th. 1884.

8.30 or so. Florrie. Home. Breakfast. Housework, & accts. Sew. Walter home. Get miserable over my old woe—conviction* of being to outwardly expressive of affection. Draw. Sew. Bed.

Thurs. June 26th. 1884.

5.35 or so. Sweep parlor and living room. Breakfast. Florrie. Home. Eat. Work. Still miserable and feel tired. Write note to Mrs. Smith. Sew. Draw or begin to. Walter home. Am miserable some more but he persuades me to believe that he never tires of me. Mrs. Putman and Mrs. Poland call; Henrietta & Mrs. Dr. Wilcox. Later Kate Bucklin. Stays to dinner and enjoys her griddlecakes much. Dear girl! Sew and read (Walter reads) in the evening. Bed.

Fri. June 27th. 1884.

Last day with Florrie. Grace Ross calls & I stay to help Florrie refuse an invitation. Stop and see mother and lunch. Home. Work. Annie Morse calls. A dear girl. Sew. Walter. Finish fixing and put on a beautiful pink muslin dress that was mother's. Dinner. Mr. & Mrs. Westcott call. A *very* pleasant evening. Sew. Bed late.

Sat. June 28th. 1884.

Up late. Go down st. with Walter. Get groceries. See about photograph. Walter goes to work, and I to see his mother. Then to see Carrie. Ride down to studio. Walk home with Walter, eating cherries. Quick dinner. Loaf and read poetry & knit. Great excitement about hearing some one on the piazza roof directly under our windows. Discover nothing. I am as sure as one sense can make one that there *was* some person there. Bed late.

Sun. June 29th. 1884.

After 8. Do little in all day, but rest and read and get through what little housework must needs be done. Mean to work tomorrow. Accts. bed.

Mon. June 30th. 1884.

5.30. Clean and sweep and dust, wash kitchen, etc. Make blancmange. Carrie & Jennie call. Mrs. Diman & Louise & Emily call. (Walter here.) Read aloud. Dinner. Read. accts. bed.

Tuesday
July 1st. 1884

8 or 9 or so. Louise & Emily come and bring me a basket of beautiful cherries. Go down street with Walter, stopping at mother's & to leave bill at Florrie's. Ride down. Emma Vaughn in car, gives me pansies. Walter cashes check for $5.00 and pays all his debts but the little standing one at Calders. Gets me a new hat for 50 cts, and a pretty white kerchief. I have my photograph taken, at Hurds. We have a lunch, and raspberry phosphates. Ride home. *Tired*. Nap. Rise & eat cherries. Walter reads. Wash dishes. Trim Hat. Pretty. Bed.

Wed. July 2nd. 1884.

5.30 about. Cut baste and sew on waist to my new dress. Do housework. Go to see mother P.M. & stay nearly 2 hours. Call on Lu Manchester; out, but see her mother. Call on Mrs. Rawson. Too ill to see me, but I see Mrs. Payton & Pussy. Home. Stop a second at Maude's earnest request, but Walter comes home & I go up. Put on the potatos & then we two go out and get flowers, some magnificent elderflowers, and others. Arrange a lovely little dish of cherries and flowers for Walter. Dinner. *good*, am hungry. Carry money up to mother's to pay Robert for my soap. $1.87. Home. Harry Manchester here, wanted us to go on a 4th July excursion with them. We decline.

My 24th birthday.

Thurs. July 3rd. 1884.

5.15 or so. Empty, sweep, and scrub parlor and arrange work-basket. Breakfast. Chamberwork etc, dishes. Sweep kitchen, put up clothes, bathe, dress, mend clothes. Mouthful of lunch. Nap, brief & uncomfortable. Read "Alpha". Walter home. Brings proofs of photo. Like 'em all, some very much. Mrs. Tibbetts calls. Walter gets me some more elderflowers. Dinner. Rice griddlecakes and raspberries! Clear table, rearrange dress and sit down at our south window to contemplate the signs of tomorrow. Jim Simmons calls and brings me the money for his card—$1.50. Mercifully goes at a little after 10. Bed.

Fri. July 4th. 1884.

5–6 An unquiet night. Drunken laborers in the grove opposite, and, during the morning, preparations for a great Catholic picnic. Do the housework, sew, read, loaf, watch picnic. They leave at nightfall and it rains. Dress, dine, read Lucretius to Walter. "Lyddy" Westcott calls with the three dollars her father owed me for Blanche. Read Rudder Grange.

Sat. July 5th. 1884.

6. Wrote to Mrs. Smith. Read Lucretius. Breakfast. Walk down with Walter. Shop. Go to Pub. Lib. & read Punch & Pop. Sci. Ride home. Housework. Begin to write down my present creed and intentions. Walter comes. Dinner, good, *steak*, etc. Read Rudder Grange. Bed.

Sun. July 6th. 1884.

about 6. Mend striped skirt torn at Moosehead. Breakfast. Loaf all day, getting through the housework late and lazy. Made gingerbread; drew, and painted some. When shall I learn that the best way to get rid of work is to *do* it!

Mon. July 7th. 1884

ere 6. Sweep kitchen & backstairs &c. Breakfast. Letter from Thomas, very funny. Housework. Try on dress waist. Blanche up twice; brings autograph album. Had a nice nap, 1½ hour's. Wrote some little. Took sewing & went to mother's. Miss Murphy there. Freddy Guild took pictures of the house with us all outside, and Eddy Jastrum & Bessie Brown (who happened to go by) thrown in. Read Thomase's letter to mother & Miss M. & leave it for Aunt C. Mother gave me some flowers, mostly nasturtiums; some old muslins, and four little well worn gold studs. Meet Walter on Pitman St. and come home together. Happy. He brings a lot of paints and things to work on here; and a beautiful edition of Thomas A' Kempis. Dinner. Good little soup. Sew and Walter reads Rudder Grange & Thomas A'. Lemonade. Bed.

Tues. July 8th. 1884.

6., but being awake last night and feeling too sleepy to do anything, went to bed again and slept till 8.30. Breakfast. Carry "London Stage" back to mother, her eggbasket, mine, and her tin pail. She concludes not to go down st. Walk down with Walter. Shop. Go to Miss Gladding's and stay some two hours. Nice little lunch of potted herring & bread-&-butter. Go to see Mother Stetson and sew. Finish my two pillowcases. Gave her my ten cent fan & white crape kerchief.[6] Talk theology with Mr. Stetson. Walter comes. Supper. good. Then we two go up to Carrie's. More supper but I eat none, Charlie Baxter performs various tricks. A few puzzles. Leave at 9. Old Mrs. Lindsey there. Stop at Greene's and have some soda. "Catawba," bad.

Wed. July 9th. 1884

6, lazy.* bed again. Late breakfast. Loaf. Look over box upstairs with Walter. Mother returns Thoma's letter, and brings me 2 doz. eggs. Aunt C. calls. Paint some P.M. Children up. Get nice dinner of eggs & macaroni. Mend.

Thurs. July 10th. 1884

ere 6. Sweep and clean. Florrie calls. Walter home at noon with waterlilies. Bathe & dress. Paint. Doze. Mother & Mrs. Springer call. Sew a mite & paint. Get dinner. Blackberry pudding. Am *hungry*. Harry & Clarence Manchester call. Funny games &c. Rebuses.

Fri. July 11th. 1884.

Arose ere 6 and returned to bed. Arose again at 9 or thereabouts. Walter goes at about 10.30. Get my work done at 12 and then sew on white dress till 3 P.M. Have knives sharpened .25 cts. Go to see Lu Manchester as per appointment, but she must needs go down street on business. Stay to see Fanny. Her mother comes down and talks dolefully. Divers callers. They give me some currants, which I pick. Sew while there. Home. Walter here painting. Sit by him and sew. *Happy*. A good dinner. I much enjoy my present system of two meals a day—no lunch. We read each others early productions; Walter's being a tale called "Snorre Gustafson". A strange work. Bed.

Sat. July 12th. 1884.

ere 6. Finish white dress, very pretty. Put black velvet bows and gilt buckles on my shoes. Go down street with Walter. Stop to show dress & new hat to mother. Miss Murphy there. Shop. Subscribe for Century, Harper's Weekly, & Nation! Feel proud and happy therein. Take "The Lady & the Tiger"[7] and "Ben Hur" from Gregory's library. Walter rides home with me. Lunch, of which I unwisely partake, for it was good. Walter reads to me & I sew. I sleep 2 hours or so. Arise, wash dishes, and get dinner. Wisely eat none save a few raspberries. Make bed. More read and sew. Accts.

Sun. July 13th. 1884.

(ere 6.) Up early and write to Carrie Hazard & Lorne Smith. Read Ben-Hur. Get work done early and pose for Walter. He also for me. Go to see Lu again and get caught there in a shower. Home and get dinner. Old Mr. Stetson and Charlie Baxter stop in the morning on their way out to Rehoboth; and again at night as we are dining. They stop and have some, especially Charlie. Mrs. Diman, the girls, & Ellen Clarke call while I was out, and leave some raspberries. *Good*. Walter reads Don Quixote to me while I finish pillowcase. Fix clothes. bed.

Monday July 14th. 1884.

5.30 or so. Get up early by mistake; write to Annie Morse. Read Ben-Hur. Breakfast, work, make cake, Finish Ben-Hur. Painted a little. Louise, Emily & Ellen call again; and enjoy it. Lend Louise "Phantastes." Dinner. Tell & read Ben-Hur to Walter. Bed.

Tuesday. July 15th. 1884.

8. Go down st. with mother, who has 4 teeth out. Shop. Ride home with her. Do the housework, make some jelly, put up clothes, and go to sleep. Walter comes home at about three, & paints. I sleep till 5.30! Get good dinner; with good sweet corn. Walter finishes Rudder Grange, while I mend and sew. Accts. Bed.

Wed. July 16th. 1884.

8, I believe. Do housework. Stop and see how mother is. Walk down and have some soda. Take 11 o'clock boat for Silver Spring. Shoot at target, both of us. Dinner. good. Next boat home. I go to see Abbie Cooke & get novel. Call on Grace Channing, Sophie Aborn, Annie Aborn, Mrs. Diman. Borrow books of her. Stop at mothers and get nasturtiums. Home and put 'em in a bowl. Walk up to meet Walter. He comes not. Stop at Mary's and walk more, waiting till 7. Home & mop up refrigerator overflow and set table. Then Walter. Been hard at work. Read him my novel.

Thurs. July 17th. 1884.

8.30. Housework, note to Uncle Edward, sweep & dust. Paint grasshopper and some nasturtiums. My first Harper's Weekly comes! Read it. Paint. Walter. He helps get dinner. Dine. Sit down to accts. Harry Manchester calls. I am sleepy[,] goes early. Ice water. bed.

Fri. July 18th. 1884.

8.15 or so. Do housework. Paint in oils. Lizzie Brown and Fred Hedge call. Mother comes also, having descried them from afar. Paint more. The children come up. Attempt a sketch of Arty. Walter comes home with Mr. Cresson. I like him, and he me Walter says. Rip up brown skirt. Walter home. Talk together. Get dinner. Dr. Allen calls. Lie down awhile. Accts. Read novel to Walter. Bed.

Sat. July 19th. 1884.

? Begin to sweep bedroom before Walter is up. Do most of the work before starting. Go down street with Walter. Shop. Go up to see his mother and "Aunt Adeline." The latter however had gone. Stay awhile. Ride down to arcade. Get new shoes. Walk up to mother's & stay awhile. Home & cook busily. Blanche comes up and helps. Give her the wherewithal to make some huckleberry-griddlecakes and make some myself for dinner. Walter brings my photo's home. To our great disappointment they are not good. Dine. Bed.

Sun. July 20th. 1884

5. Wash dishes, sweep kitchen, etc. etc., breakfast, more dishes, bathe dress and go to church. Hear Uncle Edward and stop for him to come home to dinner with me. He can't, but will to supper. Stop and tell mother he's coming there. Home. Dine. Work more. Go up to mother's again to wait for Uncle E. Lizzie Brown calls. After a long time my uncle arriveth. Wait a little and then bring him home. He seems delighted with everything and talks voluminously about everything. Seems to like Walter. Walter likes him. A good supper. Goes soon after. Walter walks down with him. Put up clothes. Accts. Walter back.

Mon. 21st July. 1884.

? Feel tired and discouraged. Get work done after a while and go out to take a walk. Take the pistol in my bag. Go some five miles I should judge. Write a little, sketch a little more; bring home flowers. Nap. Walter home, half sick, has spoiled the Couture plate.[8] Too bad. Bed early.

Tues. July 22nd. 1884.

? Walter home all day—sick. About noon we take a little walk over Red Bridge. Eat lunch at noon and have some oatmeal gruel at night. Read aloud, with adjacent dictionary. Retta Clarke, Prescott, & John Diman call. Walter retires and lies down, not feeling well yet. Bed after a little.

Wed. July 23rd. 1884.

? Read to Walter while he shaves & makes a tracing for a new Couture. Get work done and try to paint[;] fail. Begin to write, when Charlie Baxter calls. Mend, chat, look at pictures with him, get dinner. Walter a little late. Good dinner; Charlie stays. Dress and go with Walter to call on Hamilton Macdougall and his mother. Icecream. Pleasant ride home after the rain. Hot and *tired*.

Thurs. July 24th. 1884.

8 or so. Mother in with flowers. Dear kind thoughtful little woman! Do the work. Read "Guenn" by Blanche Howard.[9] A fine book. Make apple sauce. Mother in again, with Allie Elder. Finish Guenn. (Walter home at about three.) Hasty pudding for dinner (*Hot.*) Accts. Bed—

Fri. July 25th. 1884.

? Leave dishes and go to mother's from 12 to 3. Home. Wash dishes. *The Century comes!* Blanche calls. Read & rest. Walter home. He has bought a Doré

Dante, "Inferno", for $2.00![10] And for me three Blank Books, bless him! Look at pictures. Read, both of us. Bed.

Sat. July 26. 1884

8 to 9. Happy. Breakfast. Read to Walter while he shaves. Go down st. with him. Shop. Ride home. Stop and see mother. Home. Put up things. Wash dishes. Blanche up. Show her Dante. Walter comes. Nap. Dinner, splendid.

Sun. July 27th. 1884.

Rise late and do nothing all day. Am not feeling thoroughly well. *Delicious* dinner, roast lamb & peas, peaches plums & raspberries. Look over anatomy & physiology. Bed.

Mon. July 28th. 1884.

8 or so. Nice breakfast of oatmeal, the little red plums & apples. Feel sick. Spend all the morning on the lounge. "The Nation" comes. Rise at 1.40 or so, wash dishes, etc. Read Nation & cut out Walter's silk neckties. Go down and make a long call on Mrs. Arnold; talking amicably & excitedly on matters of general importance. Return home and get dinner. Walter home. Brings peaches, corn, "tropical fruit laxative", benzine, etc. Another delicious dinner. Make necktie while Walter finishes the Story of a Peasant. Good. Accts. bed.

Tues. July 29th. 1884.

? Read. Housework. Make cake. Blanche up twice, beats eggs, show her Dante. Nap. Walter home early & paints a pink mallow from the yard while I sleep. Lamb hash on toast, warmed corn & fried potatoes. Fruit.

Wed. July 30th. 1884.

? Walter home all the morning owing to weather,—dark. Paints me. I do the work after he's gone and then go up to mother's. (Walter had his first encounter with "Topsy" and bids fair to banish her.) See mother awhile and then come down to Mary's. Anna there, & cousin Julia Jastrum. Wait for Walter who stops a moment. Home together. Dinner—lamb broth and rice—poor. Fruit. Evening with sewing & Rimmer's Anatomical plates.

Thurs. July 31st. 1884.

6. Sweep parlor. Walter gets breakfast. Eat the same—lose mine—eat another of fruit solely. Sweep kitchen, bathe & dress. Go up to mothers with Walter. He rides down town and I stay and get flowers and talk with mother. Tell her my expectation.[11] Home. Fix flowers. Bed. Dishes. Eat. Dress. Read. Make peculiar dish—cake (old) applesauce, lemonjuice and softcustard! Not very good as it turns out. Mother & Mrs. Simmons call. Enjoy it. Nap. Get dinner.

Walter. Dine. Johnny cakes & codfish "ala creme", *good*. He reads the last two chapters of our novel to me. Accts.

Fri. Aug. 1st. 1884.

5.30. Walter and I take a long delightful walk; via Red Bridge, E. Providence, India Bridge, & Gano St. Home at about 7. Do my work. Go up to mother's to borrow a teapot. Stop at Mary's to dinner. Clam cakes, good. Home. Make custard, and put up clothes. Bit of a nap. Mrs. Stetson comes. Later Carrie. Walter home early. They stay to tea. Not very good. Anna and Clarence in the evening.

Sat. Aug. 2nd. 1884.

Up late. Light breakfast. Go down down [*sic*] with Walter: feel weak; have nice little dinner at Hotel Dorrance restaurant. Enjoy it. More shopping. Ride home. Fix ice etc. Go up to Mother's and stay an hour or more. Bring home some things. Wash dishes, *ever so many*. Blanche up. Nap. Walter home. He reads me Felix Oswald after a milk cracker & berry supper. Bed.

Sun. Aug. 3rd. 1884.

5.30. Take another walk, over to the R.R. pond ice houses. Fog rises, disagreeable morning. Home, rest. Breakfast. Feel sick all day. Take "Golden Dew Drops", tamarind water, Sedlitz powder, figs, etc. etc. Steak & corn oysters for dinner. Loaf and read "Marie Antoinette & her Son." Accts.

Mon. Aug. 4th. 1884.

Do not feel well yet; but do the work and fix brown skirt. Go over to mothers in the afternoon. Get some relics, grandmother's needlework and such. Bring them home, start the dinner and go out to meet Walter. Succeed in meeting Cousin Ray first, my love in the next car. Home. Dine. to bed tired.

Tues. Aug. 5th. 1884.

A really sick day, the worst I remember for years. "Inter-susception of the intestine" we conclude. Walter tries hot cloths with success in relief, but I retain nothing in all day but a piece of watermelon and a fig. Mother and Aunt C. call in the afternoon. I was asleep while Walter had been down town to get some prunes, etc. Begin with "Sal Muscatelle" at bedtime.

Wednesday 6th. 1884.

Feel better! Oatmeal porridge and a fig. Read a little. We get ready and start for "down river". Stop at mothers a few moments. Take car, but are two [*sic*] late for 11 o'clock boat. Ride out to Oleneyville (almost) and back to 12 o'clock boat. Meet Harry Manchester by ticket office, (or are joined by him,) and he goes with us, to Bullocks Pt. Have some chowder and fish, which *I* enjoy much. Sit under trees and talk, scribble, and watch young damsels calmly undressing in what they seem to consider an impenetrable thicket. Very pleasant coming up in the steamer's bow. Get some peaches bananas and soda. Home in car. Guess Harry enjoyed himself. Read, finishing "Marie Antoinette and her Son". Interesting if true. Have a light supper. Make bed. Accts, and write.

Thurs. Aug. 7th 1884.

3.45 and wander disconsolate. Walter gets up too, but can do no good and slumbers again. Return to bed at about 6 and sleep till 9 or so. Mother calls while I'm dressing, and brings flowers. Eat two bananas. She goes soon, and Walter and I soon after.

Stop at Dr. Olive Herrick's.

a female physician, lately from New York. My first visit to a doctor, caused by real distress. I am ashamed. I tell her all the symptoms, and how we suspect "intersusception" etc. She makes digital examination and explains that the uterus is displaced, has fallen backwards. Not severe or dangerous. She fixes it with an instrument, inserts cotton, and gives me "bitter medesin". Walk to Rider's & wait for car. See Ray. Go to Walter's and tell him. He comes home with me. Afternoon of weariness and shame. Eat porridge. Write King and country allegory. Bed. Begin to take "enematas"

Fri. Aug. 8th. 1884.

Sick still. A small breakfast. Infest the lounge continuously. Walter goes off but returns early, bringing pears, peaches, etc; also much money. 25 for me, 25 for he, and 50 for *we*.* I eat, but Lo! it remaineth not within me but returneth to upper air. Mother and Aunt appear and I "spruce up" and appear amiable. Harry Manchester calls in the evening, but I must needs be excused. He'll tell his mother! And she—O woe is me!

Sat. Aug. 9th. 1884.

I have given in and take my medicine like a lamb. Have a little coffee also,* and feel a little better. Partake of iced milk in small quantity. Walter goes down town and does the "grocerying", also brings home grapes & oranges. Counting (3) preserves we have 13 kinds of fruit in the house! Walter cooks and washes dishes, dear boy.

Sun. Aug. 10th. 1884.

Eggs this morning, and coffee. *Dress*! Go over to Mother's with Walter. She is very glad to see me. We bring home silver tea set, barberries & porringer. Am not much tired. lie around as usual. Walter gets nice little supper. I hope *he* won't get sick, doing so much! Reads to me.

Mon. Aug. 11th. 1884.

Coffee. One egg. Walter goes to work—Letter from Martha. Doze and loaf. Arise at noon, take medicine, suck two olives. Eat 3 cold pears. Wait a while. Eat two eggs. Put potatoes in the ashes to bake. Eat big orange. Walter comes pretty late. Take some hot ginger. He brings nice peaches, salmon. Extract of Malt, etc. Cooks the salmon, which is nice; but I more enjoy a cup of weak breakfast tea and two toasted crackers which taste good all the way down. Bed shortly.

Tues. Aug. 12th. 1884.

Continue on eggs. Go to Mother's, Walter arriving soon. Stay a little and then take car. Go to Silver Spring and get dinner. *Good.* Home lively. Ride out and see Mrs. Stetson and Carry. Ride down. Walter gets in car. Home and have some hot ginger. Boiled salmon, potatoes & egg sauce. Good. Eat heartily. Bed early.

Wed. Aug. 13th. 1884

Not very vigorous. Walter goes to work. Mother come around and washes up all my dishes while I make buttonholes for her. Also sweeps kitchen. Goes about 4. Lizzie Brown calls with Arthur Perry from the West. I dislike him. Walter arrives, bringing peaches and grapes. In default of better dinner, make some poor fishballs and eat 6. Also some tea as usual. Harry Manchester calls in the evening. He thinks of going west, and I recommend it by all means. Bed.

Thurs. Aug. 14th. 1884.

Card from Dr. Keller and note from Martha. Ride down town with Walter. Feel sick. Have a little coffee soda at Greene's. Go to market and then walk home. Still sick. Arrange things and take nap, with the cat. She improves. Rise and begin to cook a small slice of tripe I got. Eva Webster calls, with Alice. Glad to see Eva, dear strong girl! Eat my dinner. They don't stay long. Sit around dolefully. Nation and Harper comes. Begin to look at them (letter from Kate, too,) when Walter comes. Sick all P.M. He gets nice dinner, corn steak and melon. Good, splendid corn. Eat well and feel better. Accts.

Fri. Aug. 15th. 1884

Wash my dishes! Take car and meet Walter down st. Go to Silver Spring. Was sick twice before leaving home, am sick on boat. We wait for the second dinner. Don't eat much. Watermelon good. We shoot, Walter with magnificent success, winning congratulations from an excitable onlooker. Meet Aunt C. and return on same boat. Excitable onlooker is late, and clambers and clambers [*sic*] on boat with his hat in his hand. Comes and offers us wild cherries, exclaiming to Walter, "That's for your shot!" Go to café and have cream, ice,

& cookies. Walter buys me Jean Ingelow's poems and I go and get weighed. Only 113![12] Home, stopping at mother's, both of us. Get supper mostly. Have tea and toast. Feel better thereafter and make bed etc. Dress up a bit. Read Jean while Walter sketches. Bed.

Sat. Aug. 16th. 1884.

Feel as well as ever on waking, but grow sick later and eat little breakfast. Walter goes off. Sleep till 1 or so, accompanied by the cat. Rise, am sick, eat some ice cream for dinner. Put the soup on. Lie down again. Mother and Aunt C. call, bringing various things, among them my linen travelling bag, all done but buttons & holes. I finish it. Mother has some cold corn cakes and cider. I have a cup of tea and some bread and butter & herring. Tastes better. Finish bag. Make bed and fix up. Mend. When Walter comes I send him out after tomatoes for the soup. Have some sweet potatoes also. Good dinner, eat and enjoy. Lie down. Accts.

Sun. Aug. 17th. 1884

Am sick before breakfast, but have recourse to my beloved tea and eat a good meal. Lie down awhile and Walter looks over my old letters to pick out the poetry for me to put in the pretty Russia leather book he gave me. Eat ginger-snaps. Baked sweet potatoes, baked apples, & tomatoes for dinner. *Good*. Rest a little. Wash the dishes. Rest some more. Comb and wash my hair, and am much wearied thereby. Rest & have some more tea. Carry and Henry call. We have supper, but they've had theirs. *Splendid* soup! They go early, and Walter goes up to mothers after paper with trains for Boston.[13] Back soon. Help make bed and get clothes ready. Bath and bed.

ELEVEN

"By reason of ill health"

September 1, 1884–March 14, 1885

As CHARLOTTE'S pregnancy progressed, she filled her days with housework, reading, and "trotting about" whenever she felt up to it. Some days found her decidedly testy when "impudent" inquiries were made about her weight gain. In mid-September, Mary Perkins left for an extended visit to Thomas, who was now in Utah, and since Charlotte frequently felt ill, Walter began assuming many of the household chores.

Occasionally Charlotte would feel "uncommonly well and brisk," but more often she felt "tired," "feeble," and "weak." Her susceptibility to sickness during her second trimester caused Charlotte to neglect her daily routines, including her diary writing, with increasing frequency. After a particularly rough period in mid-October, Charlotte stopped writing altogether, citing ill health as the primary factor. She resumed her diary again about ten weeks later, on January 1, 1885.

The entry of January 1 is a tangled mass of contradictions. "I am a happy wife," she wrote. "I bear a child. . . . Ambition sleeps. I make no motion but just live. And I am Happy? Every day almost finds me saying so, and truly. And yet—and yet—'call no man happy until he is dead.' "

Charlotte's ambivalence likely stemmed from her growing realization that despite all of her reservations, despite all of her misgivings, despite all of her various attempts to end her relationship with Walter because she "love[d] WORK better," she nevertheless found herself entrapped in a marriage that left her feeling suffocated and incomplete. The arrival of the baby would mark yet another setback in her long-stated desire to enter public service. All of the doubts and fears that she had expressed during her courtship were being realized, and Charlotte grew increasingly apprehensive as her due date approached. Five weeks before the baby was born, Charlotte reported becoming "so hysterical" that Walter felt compelled to stay home with her. And a couple of days later, on February 19, she reported a "wellnigh sleepless night. Hot, cold, hot; restless nervous hysterical. Walter is love and patience personified; gets up over and over, gets me warm winter-green, bromide, hot foot bath, more bromide—all to no purpose."

The unrest that Charlotte felt during her pregnancy was likely exacerbated by the dichotomy between the direction that her life was taking when compared to Walter's. After struggling against chronic poverty for years, Walter was at last enjoying at least a brief period of financial prosperity as he finally began to establish a reputation. He was, in fact, basking in the glory of newfound fame after a review in the September 1884 issue of *Art Amateur* offered highly favorable praise of his artistic talent. "The young man went home to Providence . . . and in a few days awoke famous, with the great guns of a fervor over his little things booming in the Boston newspapers," the review read (*Endure*, p. 265). "Young Stetson gave proof of a natural productive genius," it continued. Walter had finally established his career.

Charlotte, in the meantime, was still dealing with the loss of her independence and trying to fight off the attendant depression. "She is . . . easily fatigued both physically & mentally & at times despondent, especially when she has fears that all that dreamed of life of great usefulness, may be past or beyond her reach," Walter remarked in his diary in September (*Endure*, p. 264). But most of the time, Walter seemed to believe that Charlotte was content. In reality, Charlotte continued to wrestle with despondency throughout her pregnancy. Perhaps because he was finally gaining a sense of security in his own life, Walter tended to romanticize Charlotte's pregnancy. Perhaps it was easy for Walter to deny the severity of Charlotte's depression by simply attributing it to her "condition." Or, perhaps he was subconsciously avoiding a painful truth. Whatever the reason, he was able to deny that anything serious was wrong with their relationship. Again and again, in fact, Walter's diaries allude to Charlotte's utter happiness—and to his own. Only occasionally does Walter complain about having to do housework, which was "wasting [the] energy, power that should be applied to [his] art" (p. 276). Charlotte doubtless felt the same way about her own work, but for the most part she remained silent.

In early March, during the final weeks of Charlotte's pregnancy, the Stetsons hired one Mrs. Russell to serve as a temporary housekeeper for the young couple. The last two weeks before the baby was born were difficult ones. Charlotte felt "weak, draggy, [and] nervous," owing to the "unreasonable activity of the infant." All she could do now was wait.

Sept. 1st. 1884.
Monday—

near 8. Get breakfast. Am not actively sick. A glorious day. Write notes, to Alfred Stone and Martha. Stop at mothers (we) and leave my new dress there with Miss Murphy. Walk up to Matthewson St. with Walter, and he back with me to the Arcade, shopping a little. Meet Mother and Miss Bullock. Go with them a little and then wait for mother at Gregory's, reading "Dr. Zay".[1] Go with Mother to Sutton's, meet Aunt C. there, and dine. Accompany them to Root's and leave order for zinc and stove bringing. Walk down and meet S.P. car and ride out. Mother and Aunt stop at Mrs. Springer's daughter's, and I go and see Susie Stetson. They give me sapson apples & flowers. Stop for mother and play awhile. A fine place. Ride in, stopping in a wee shop and getting candy. Stop at Walters for fashion book and take Brook St. car to Miss Murphy's. See her about dress, and leave braid, silk, etc. Walk home, *angry*. Bessie Peck has been inquiring if I am growing large! Confound her impudence! Walter in soon. Good dinner. Haven't been sick today! Arrange photographs and Accts.* Bed.

Tues. Sept. 2nd. 1884.

6.20 but return to bed. & Again at near 8. Breakfast and arrange things for the stove men who appear at about 10 and set it up in fine style. Move the refrigerator into the outside entry. Walter goes. Put entry & kitchen in order, clothes on horse and teakettle on. Nap. Blanche up with Century. More nap. Rise. Lunch. Wash dishes and get dinner. Walter home by 4. (Made bed.) Dine. Mr. Rollins again, with pipe. Lie down awhile. Dress and go to mother's. Out. Home wearily. Bed presently.

Wed. Sept. 3rd. 1884.

6.10. Sick a little. Early breakfast & stop at mother's to see about expressage. Walter returns and shaves, for we settle to go shorewards. Mother & I take car down, get dinner tickets, meet Walter on wharf, and set off in a tremendous crowd. Good dinner. Walter returns and we stay till the 3.05 boat. Read "Noblesse Oblige,"[2] mother let me have it. Walter gets on the same car home. Feel sick, but eat some supper. Read. A Mr. Griffin calls, bringing some lady apples for Walter to paint! Funny old man.

Thurs. Sept. 4th. 1884.

Up ere dawn, back again, up at 8 or so. Clear up the attic, Walter helping. The things come from mother's. Finish "Noblesse Oblige". Read in Harper's. Fix parlor some, enema, chamberwork, bath. Make some white biscuit. Mother comes with flowers and pears. Lie and doze. Get mashed potatoes for dinner. Walter brings lobster home. Eat little, mostly biscuit. Read Nation. Walter deep in "A Perilous Secret."[3] Dismal evening, for I feel unable to do anything and am mortally tired of doing nothing. Get out on roof. Humbly ask if I can sleep there tonight and am told "No you cannot!" Serves me right for asking. Bed? I guess so.

Fri. Sept. 5th, 1884.

Another deathly hot day. Mend while Walter paints Lady-apples. Go up to mother's at noon. She gives me sherry with water, sugar, and nutmeg. Walter comes in. He goes down st. to work. Hot. Can't. Returns and has an egg-nog with sherry also. We feel enlivened thereby. All ride down town and get lunch at Café. Then go to Bullocks Pt, and back for coolness. Get little. Soda. All go home. Walter and I undress. He flourishes in two garments, I in one. Mrs. Westcott comes in with some white lilies & smilax, lovely.

Sat. Sept. 6th. 1884.

7.10. Expect mother, and Mary to clean. Mother comes and Mary doesn't. But we two do much, mostly mother. Get the closet all cleaned out and fixed beautifully. I arrange nice china, glass, etc. in—the bookcase! At nearly 4 we start for down town. Stop at mother's. See Walter coming home and stop him, but he prefers not to go down with us. We go. Aunt C. dines at the Café. We have soda & eat a bit of Aunt C.'s salad. Go to grocery and load up, all of us. Ride home in the same car we took down. Have nice little supper. Accts.

Sun. Sept. 7th 1884.

8.10. Breakfast. Loaf. Look over book boxes upstairs and screw 'em up. Read. Mend a little. Walter shaves, shampoos & bathes. Read to him. Dinner. More loafing. Wash dishes. The Dimans call. Later, Mr. Stetson Sen. He goes soon. Make some "Scotch Pancakes" (Royal Baking powder receipt) for our supper. Good, but very rich. Make bed. Write here.

[*A one-week gap in the diary entries appears at this point.*]

Sun. Sept. 14th. 1884.

8.45. Fire in parlor and breakfast before it. Don't do much all day. Dinner at noon. Nap, long one. Grace Channing, Mary, & Mr. Saunders call. Hot biscuit and baked apples for supper. I go up to mother's and Walter comes after me later. Lizzie, Henrietta, Edward, Clarence, Anna, Mrs. Springer, and Aunt Caroline. Home with silver trunk.

Mon. Sept. 15th. 1884.

8 or less. Get breakfast and eat heartily. Sew tucks in Walter's shirt sleeves. Mother sends Mary over and I thankfully set her to dishwashing. Prepare meat for croquettes. Things come from mothers. Get croquettes all ready, dress and go to mother's with Mary. Go down st. and get Walter. Dinner at Sutton's. *Good.* He goes down to Riders with me, and I wait for Mother, reading. We shop. Order coal and wood. Get "Art Amateur" for notice of Walter. Ride home. Get dinner and fix things. Walter comes. Croquettes delicious. Accts.

———

Tues. Sept. 16th. 1884.

8 to 9. Great time putting out fire when we start. Go to mother's. Walter departs. I stay a bit, and then call on Mrs. Diman and Annie Aborn. Get her version of the continually growing Dorrance-Aborn story. Back to Mother's; lunch. She gets no letter. Go down st. with her, and trot about to P.O., Depot, etc. She goes to see Grandma Anthony, I wait at Riders, make last call for letter, don't get it, and wait for mother at Claflin's. See Walter in car and get him. All home together. Stop at mothers and get flowers, pears, and bread. Home. Telegram *here* for mother, with money order. Walter takes it up. Get supper. Eat some. Nap thereafter. Rise. Bathe. Am sick. Seidlitz powder. Bed.

Wed. Sept. 17th. 1884.

6:30 or so. Hurry off, stop for mother, Walter comes after. Go to Miss Murphy's. Walter stops there and goes off with Mother while I stay and am fitted. Then go and join mother and she gets her ticket, her boots, and divers sundries.[4] I get more cloth for sash. Mother goes to Julia Jastrums to dinner and I home. Read "Tom Fiddler's Ground". Pick up things. Prepare dinner. Start letter to mother. Miss Alden calls, attended by the Diman children, who, after brief stay, wait without. Walter. Supper. Mrs. Westcott in. Go up and see mother. Miss Allen & another, Lizzie and Edward, & Mrs. Vaughn call. Home. Ice Water. Accts. Bed.

Thurs. Sept. 18th. 1884.

6–7. Get breakfast (?). Coal comes, and wood. Mary comes and washes dishes. I go up to Mother's for the last time. Walter says goodbye to her. Anna, Mary and the little ones come. Mrs. Guild calls. Julia Jastrum brings down some oysters. I help her pick up last things and get ready. Eat a lunch there. Leave at 12.30 or so. Stop and leave her picture for Mrs. Sayles. Home. Do various things. Mrs. Payton calls, and Abbie Cooke. Scalloped oysters for supper— *good.* A delicious rain in the evening, the first this month. No calls.

Fri. September 19th. 1884.

8 Get breakfast. *Delicious* omelette! Walter brings up our first hod of coal. I have a nat [*sic*] ere noon, but otherwise spend the day getting my kitchen in order. Have seven baskets in the back entry! Grace Channing calls and Aunt C. Get everything well arranged. Hasty pudding for dinner. Good. Teach Walter Everlasting and Gobang in the evening. He likes it

Sat. Sept. 20th. 1884.

8 or so. Get breakfast and eat thereof. Mary comes and washes dishes. Mrs. Arnold calls! She sends me up a dish of hot soup. Good. I stop at Mary's and leave letter. Go to Miss Murphy's. Am faint & dizzy and have to lie down.

Frisk down st. Meet Mr. Slicer. Do my marketing, exulting in a chicken! Get sundries beside, and a bite and sup at Café. Ride home. Aunt C. stops me at Mary's; she has had a card from mother. Home. Walter here. Get good supper. Make bread. Blanche in. Spends the evening. Carl comes for her. *A fine family*! Feel tired and sickish.

Sun. Sept. 21st. 1884.

6.15. Arise betimes. Make fire for first time. Does not "draw" very well. Get breakfast ready, hot biscuit, baked sweet potatoes, oatmeal, coffee—fine. (and cold bluefish!) Take bath and dress. Sick twice. Had Great Expectations of much work today, baking of bread and cake, dinner (no joke, with my first chicken) dishwashing, etc. etc. Give out completely at breakfast! Try hot ginger. Lose it. Try claret. Lose that. Do nothing all day, and am sicker than I've been since the worst part of it. Walter gets the dinner, dear boy, and does everything. Faith Stetson and two New Hampshire cousins call. Later Carl comes in to show book, and leaves Swiss F[amily]. R[obinson]. for Walter to read. Still later Blanche with bread. We exchange. I tried iced milk P.M. and lost that. Kept however some "dewdrops", which seemed beneficial. Eat about an ounce or 2 of dinner. To bed, still prone.

Monday, Sept. 22nd. 1884.

7–8. Walter gets breakfast and makes a wee fire. Are late in the morning, but finally start off together. Get flowers for his mother's birthday. Stop at Warren & Woods & get her some other things. Ride up there and stay till nearly 5. Walter goes to work after dinner. Carry comes in during afternoon. I ride down and meet Walter and so home. Mrs. Diman and Emily in a moment with letter from Miss Alden. Cold chicken for dinner. Walter reads to me. Bed.

Tues. Sept. 23rd. 1884.

8.10 about. Feel better. Get breakfast. Put soup on, read, write, do some housework. Miss Murphy comes, much to my delight. So does Aunt C. still later, and we all revel in chicken soup. *Good*! As good as mother's, Aunt C. said so! Miss M. stays till 4. Go out with her, meaning to go see Lu Manchester, but meet Walter and return. Nice little fire, more soup, accts, and now what I like till bedtime.

Wed. Sept. 24th. 1884.

Aunt C. comes down to see Mary the Handmaid, who cometh not till late. Anna is sick, sciatic rheumatism. Mary washeth many dishes. Ray calls with telegram from mother. Arrived safe. Work helping Mary. Am very tired when Walter comes. Omelette for supper.

Thurs. Sept. 25th. 1884.

Do little all day. Eat little and lose most of that. Crack walnuts and eat therof. Blanche brings me some green apples, and stays a good while. I make some jumbles. Not very good. Thunder shower, mostly rain. Carl comes in later, with some grapes. I teach him gobang. Walter rather late. Brings fruit and oysters, and makes a savory stew. I eat somewhat, and keep it. John Willey calls. Doze. Bed.

Fri. Sept. 26th. 1884.

We wait impatiently a check from Noyes. *I* don't mind. Start out with Walter. Meet Mary. Walk along with her to Lu Manchester's & call. Out. Go to see Mrs. Diman. Out. Call on Mrs. Carpenter Sen. Out. Call on Florrie and her mother to get Pub. Lib. card. Lost. Stop awhile. Home. Nap. Eat walnut & then imbibe salt. Make bed etc. Write to Kate. Walter. Hasty pudding for dinner. Finish letter while Walter fixes lock. Then I sketch for "Robin Hood & Allin a Dale" scheme and he mails letter. Write here. Bed.

Sat. Sept. 27th. 1884.

? Make fire. Eat good breakfast with cup of weak coffee. *Make a pie*! A apple pie! And it was good. Make some farina and some gingerbread. Mary doesn't come so I wash most of the dishes at great speed, after a light lunch. Car down st. and stop at P.O. for Noyes' expected check. Not there. Go to market. Get gorgeous apples and dried beef at R & S. Go to Pub. Lib. and give notice for new card. Read Punch. Go to Walter's and wait for him. Both to Suttons and eat. Stop for letter at P.O. Not there yet. Forsworn Art dealer! Get some smoked salmon & ginger ale, and home. Rest awhile, then make cakes and omelette for supper. Good pie. Darn socks. Bath and bed. Mr. Hazeltine fiddles down stairs.

Sun. Sept. 28th. 1884.

About 8. Good breakfast, salmon, biscuit, & coffee. Eat 5 biscuit. Write long letter to mother. Corn beef dinner, good. Aunt C. calls. Nap P.M. Pick up dishes. Finish letter. Write here. Sup.

Mon. Sept. 29th. 1884.

7–8. Rained tremendously in the night and Perfect day thereafter. I *long* for the country, but we are short of money and can't go. Wash dishes. Lu Manchester calls. Glad to see her. Dine copiously. Gradually finish dishes and read in Century. Paint some, a card of small green birds. Get dinner. Very tired thereafter. Walter reads to me.

Tues. Sept. 30th. 1884.

after 8. Am enjoying café au lait breakfasts very much. We fix the clock. Note from Miss Pease accepting full engagement at $12.00 a week. Glad. Walter goes off. (He had letter about the recreant Tewksberry—Dunn's Agency— says he's a square man.) Feel uncommonly well and brisk. Put clothes on horse, do chamberwork, make bed, etc. etc. quite as of old. How nice it seems! Wrote to Miss Pease and Dr. Keller with photo. Lunch.

Wed. Oct. 1st. 1884.

Do up work, prepare hash for dinner, etc. Ride gaily over to Mother Stetson's, dine there and stay till near five. Walter comes for me, tired. Home together. Eat little. Bed early.

Thurs. Oct. 2nd. 1884.

Wash innumerable dishes. Dress in aged green serge thing. Looks fine. Lizzie Brown calls. In the evening Sam Simmons, and, later Mary Peck and Mr. Dorrance. The latter tries to conciliate me. Get them to talking business and politics and enjoy it. Go late. Excited and tired.

Fri. Oct. 3rd. 1884.

The long hoped for letter from Mr. Tewksberry arrives, with check for $85.00 Bless him! Walter has to go down st. to meet Dorrance, but I follow as soon as the work's done, and we shop. Get morning dress and fixings. Home. Tired. Bed early.

Sat. Oct. 4th. 1884.

We walk down together. Stop at Miss Murphy's. Out. Meet and pay her $9.25. Walter goes to work and I do marketing and get bonnet materials. Salad at Café with "Dr. Zay". Call on Milly Cooley. Stop for Walter but he's not ready to come. Fix things a little and lie down. Walter home. Small supper. He reads to me a little. Bed.

Sun. Oct. 5th. 1884.

Lazy and comfortable. Good breakfast. Accts. Start to trim bonnet. Get tired, and cry bitterly for shame at my feebleness. Get up fiercely and go to work. Mary and Alice call and ask me to go to ride. I decline on plea of work. Have lunch. Am unable to wash dishes so Walter does it. Bless him! Good dinner, fricasseed chicken, potatoes both, and spinach all of which I eat. Write to mother. Bed.

Mon. Oct. 6th. 1884.

More bonnet. Miss Murphy calls with dress, but forgot part. Stays to dinner. Finish bonnet trimming. A *beauty*. Piece of gold bracelet on in front for a clasp—looks like a beetle. Walter home early and feels sick, "wind colic". He has to go down st. again after cake etc. I go to the Westcott's to beg some vine leaves, and they give me a lot of flowers and leaves beside. Home and get supper hot. Walter comes. After supper we both dress in our best; and, very late, Hamilton McDougal and his mother call. Later still Dr. Allen and Miss Barnard. We have a "banquet" of cake and fruit. Good. Go late, naturally. Ti-i-*ired*![5]

Tues. Oct. 7th.

Start my new green morning dress. Get it all cut out. Am tired when Walter comes home, but enjoyed the good day's work. Walter brings home my dress from Miss Murphy's.

Wed. Oct. 8th. 1884

Still the green dress. Launch out bravely on the machine and get all the long seams stitched. Katy comes to clean, attended by her youthful son; and *does* clean, most satisfactorily. Mrs. Stetson, Carrie, and Mrs. Lindsey call. I receive them in confusion, but cordially. Walter rather early. Steak for supper. He reads Shakespeare to me while I continue to work on dress. Carrie helped me also.

Thurs. Oct. 9th. 1884.

Green dress prospering finely. Feel well. Sew diligently. Lunch, dress, sew on. Mrs. Springer calls. Afterward Mrs. Daniels. Walter brings oysters. Scallop 'em. Sup, dress, no calls.

Fri. Oct. 10th. 1884.

Glorious weather now. I have coffee in bed mornings while Walter briskly makes the fires and gets breakfast. O dear! That I should come to this! Another letter from Mr. Tewksbury, (To Walter), with draft for $25.00. Surely a practical admirer. Accts. Call on Lu Manchester. Go shopping. Stop for Walter and home with him.

Sat. Oct. 11th.'84

Katy to clean. Sew, sew, sew. Get most done. Nice letter from mother— Answer in part.

Sun. Oct. 12th.'84

Remodel Walter's new hat with great success. Finish wrapper. Lu calls. Shakespeare in the evening.

Mon. Oct. 13th.'84

Up early and fly around. Make little plush turban with yellow breast.

[1885.]

January. 1st. Thurs.

My journal has been long neglected, by reason of ill health. I am now better, and hope to keep it regularly and to some purpose. This day has not been a successful one, as I was sicker than for some weeks. Walter also was not very well, and stayed at home; primarily on my account. He has worked for me and for us both, waited on me in every tenderest way, played to me, read to me, done all for me as he always does. God be thanked for my husband! I have done nothing today in way of work. Have slept and idled and read a little. No one has been here but Carl to wish us A Happy New Year.

This last year has been short. I have done little, read little, written little, felt and thought——little to what I should have.

I am a happy wife. I bear a child. I have been far from well. I do not know that I am better in any way. Unless it be better to be wider in sensation and experience, and, perhaps, humbler. Ambition sleeps. I make no motion but just live.

And I am Happy? Every day almost finds me saying so, and truly. And yet—and yet—"call no man happy until he is dead." I will see what my life counts when I am old. I do harm to no one that I know of; and one soul at least is much the happier by me. Another soul is coming. Much depends on that. If it and possible others are world helpers then indeed I shall hope.

God knows. I should not be afraid to die now; but should hate to leave my own happiness and cause fierce pain.

Yes. I am happy.

Fri. Jan. 2nd. 1885.

9 or so. Good breakfast, got by my dear boy. A beautiful cold day. Wash dishes. Clear kitchen and Katy comes and scrubs. Dine and read Nation. Fix Walter's undershirt sleeves and finish petticoat. (or nearly.) He comes at about 5 and brings frost fish. Good dinner. He reads "Titus Andronicus"[6] to me. Nearly through. Poor stuff. Accts. bed.

Sat. Jan. 3rd. 1885—

8–8.20. Make popovers for breakfast. Eat rather unsatisfactorily. Feel sick. Leave dishes and dress. Aunt C. calls. Read her letters of mothers and show her baby things. Postman brings Walter an admonitory letter from a friend of his at which he is much incensed.[7] Reads it to Aunt C. & I, *sans* signature. Answers. Aunt departing presently we walk down st. together. He goes to see his careful friend and I go marketing & shopping. Lunch at Fillinghasts. Junie Keach comes in and has a cup of coffee at my table. Sensible girl I guess in most ways. Buy almost $30.00 worth of baby things. Dress goods, etc. Call for Walter and find him reeking in horrible odors. Gus[8] there serene. Depart and make brief call on Millie. Rejoin Walter, get creamcakes & biscuit, and ride home together. Find letter from mother. Rest and read it, with creamcakes, while fires rekindle. Get supper. Walter dresses and goes to see John Mason. Accts., make bread, more accts. Now write to mother.

Sun. Jan. 4th. 1885.

9.30 about. Good breakfast. Walter and I clean and rearrange the parlor in great shape. Lunch. I wash some dishes and give out. Walter finishes. I lie down awhile and sleep some. Bathe & dress. Broiled chicken & tomato for supper. Dress. Mr. Purrington calls. Pleasant evening. He seems to be an intelligent man, but biassed

Mon. Jan. 5th. 1885.

8 or so. Help get breakfast. Finish letter to mother. Wash dishes and prepare chicken for soup. Dine, reading Alpha and Century. Write to Miss Gladding & Carrie Hazard. Sew, mendind [sic] Walter's under-drawers, hose, my hose, and finishing white waist. Fix fire, put soup on, and go to walk. Go to Red Bridge & back, up to post letters, in to see Mary a few moments and back. See to supper and regale myself with the harmonica. Walter. Show him all my pretty baby things which arrived at noon. Cut two aprons. Sup. Feel— unpleasantly, owing to some peanuts. Cut nine diapers; and make one. Accts.

Tues. Jan. 6th. 1885.

8.30 or so. A dreary warm rainstorm. Miss Dodge comes in to see if Walter will do an errand for her at Reid the Printers, which he does. We get a letter from Mr. Purinton, most astonishing. Also I get a paper with poem marked therein from the same. Walter answers his letter and writes others before he starts. I answer later, forcibly. Sew on aprons, dine & read Century, wash dishes. Write note to Miss Alden and begin one to Mrs. Smith. Sarah Westcott calls. Sew more; and talk to her about Marie Stuart and the stage generally. Supper. Then I sew more and Walter reads Hamerton's "Human Intercourse" to me. Also a little of Sartor Resartus. Accts.

Wed. Jan. 7th. 1885.

8.31 Help get breakfast. Stitch on machine, finishing on apron, part another. Finish note to Mrs. Smith and send it with Miss Alden's and Mr. Purintons. Get dishes ready to wash. Cut and plan scarlet sack. Dine. Blanche W. in. Wash dishes. She borrows my light sunshade for Sarah in her play. Write to

Mrs. Cresson, long letter. Walter comes, and goes out again to get food. Expressman brings up gorgeous rug he bought for $10.00 at auction! Supper. He reads a little more Hamerton and I parody it quite successfully in a brief essay "On Rubber Overshoes". Then we make nonsense pictures, fine ones.[9] Fix them to go to Mrs. Cresson, with note. Accts. Fix rugs. Bed late.

Thursday. Jan. 8th. 1885—

9. Make biscuit and cook steak. Another letter from Mr. Purinton, very feeble. One from Carrie Hazard. Blanche W. comes in to borrow my yellow necklace for Miss Dodge in "the play." I read her Mr. P's letter and we have some lively talk not altogether complimentary to that gentlemen. Do chamber work fix dishes, change dress and clear and rearrange my desk. Great satisfaction, but considerable work. Dine, reading Century. Wash dishes. (Found in drawer of desk my last letter to mother! Gave it to post man P.M., and sent her another note by evening mail.) Lie down awhile. Finish letter to Retta enclosing nonsense poem. Fix fire. Walter comes. Oyster stew and talk about tabulating human misery etc. Jim Simmons calls. Cuttlefish! Eel! Waterbug!

1885. Friday. Jan. 9th.

8.30. Good breakfast. Arrange things generally, dress and go down with Walter. Shop, changing Jennie's Keats for two books of Poe's tales, .30, Thackeray's Ballads, .15; and 12 of Emerson's Essays, 20. Good exchange. Get "Rome & Carthage["] out of Pub. Lib. Car up to mother S[tetson]'s. Dinner. Go up to Carrie's, but stay little, as she was just going out. Return with her to her mothers, sew on diapers. Read Mother S. "The Black Cat".[10] Walk down to Chestnut St. Meet Walter. Get candy and ride home. Nice supper of milk-toast, omelette, and fried bananas (for him). Then he reads me Emerson's "Compensation". We do not think much of it.

Sat. Jan. 10th. 1885.

9. A poor day. Walter does not feel very well and stays at home. Same with me. Succeed in washing the dishes, sewing and reading some. Walter planes off one of our our [*sic*] perverse doors. Broiled chick for supper. Sew a bit more, accts., write.

Sun. Jan. 11th. 1885.

10. Good breakfast. Read in "Danbury News" book. Fix Walter's undershirt sleeves. Bathe & dress. We go out to Jennie's to Dinner. Carrie Henry & Charlie there. Good dinner.'Twas to christen her dishes. Dr. Knapp in during the evening. The four men lift Carrie by breathing etc; with just their fingers. Home at 10.30, tired.

Mon. Jan. 12th. 1885.

8–8.30. Was sick last night, owing to dinner and weariness. My darling cared for me with ineffable tenderness. A stormy night but slept well after I did sleep. He was up rather earlier than usual to carry Gus'es picture down as agreed; but didn't as it rained hard. We neither of us feel very well. Sew some on red sack; and he reads to me, Poe, & Keats. He goes down st. on errands, taking picture; and I take a nap. Then lunch and wash most of the dishes. He returns and I sew a little more. Then he dresses; we have a sad little supper, and he very reluctantly goes to New York. It is to see the Watts Exhibition; Mr. Whitaker goes with him. Says he never will leave me again unless he *has* to! Dear dear love. I am now going in to the Westcott's, to spend the night.

Tues. Jan. 13th. 1885—

7.50 or so. Pleasant evening at the W's. Read aloud, sewed, and played three games of chess with Mr. W., beating the last two. Bed late. Slept well. Good breakfast. Sit around a while, talk to Mr. & make a buttonhole for Mrs. Home about 10.30. Black stove start fire, sweep kitchen, empty slops, wash dishes, clean lam [*sic*]. Rest some and write to Martha. Back to the W's to dinner. Then home again and write more. Blanche in a minute with milk can I carried over. Write till I'm too tired, lie down awhile; fix things, write little poem for my darling to find tomorrow, accts. & off again next door.

Wed. Jan 14th. 1885.

7.40. Went serenely in to play chess with Mr. Westcott last night; and were well in the first game; when lo! Walter! He went home and awoke the fires while I stayed and was beaten—not ignominiously. Then home, and glad to be there. We had a little supper and a little talk and so to bed. This morning *I* got up while he slept on; and did all the work but coal & ashes! (and bed). Finished letter to Martha, and then walked down st. with Walter. Shopped a little. Walked nearly to Snow St. then took car and rode to the Brown's, where I dined. On rabbit pie. Hemmed two diapers. Rode home. Stopped at Butcher's and got two or three flowers—to paint tomorrow if I can. Mr. Westcott & Carl there. Walk home with them. Meet Mr. & Mrs. Wells, who had just left a card. They return with me; but stay not long. Am tired. Walter comes, and gets supper. Blanche W. in. Feel better. Cut 2nd piece of diaper while Walter writes. Bed.

Thurs. Jan. 15th. 1885.

9.15–20. Not very well. Walter does things. I just make some buckwheats (Hecker's) and after breakfast collapse. A bad wet dreary day. I get so tremulous and teary that my boy stays with me. A long nap does me good. He gets some oysters and milk, I make milk-toast, and we have a good little dinner. I put the tongue to boil and clear things up generally. Then he paints an hour or two, and I sew. Then he reads some, supper. I write a note to Annie Morse, and now this.

Fri. Jan. 16th. 1885—

7.50. Rise first, make fires, get breakfast, and wash some dishes before breakfast. Then sew on red sack. Then write "The Sin of Sickness" for Henry Townsend and note to him. Walter home ere three. Lunch, buckwheats. Then wash dishes again. Then sew more while Walter reads me some of his poetry of past years. Then supper. Then make funny pictures. Only one good. Accts. bed.*

Sat. Jan. 17th. 1885.

8.30. Walter does things. I sew some, nap some, arrange bureau drawers, eat what little I can find, reading Century the whilst; sew more, wash dishes, sew, read in new Harpers. Louise Diman calls. Read her "Sister Helen." Finish red sack. Read more. Walter comes. He cooks steak for supper. Hem half diaper. Bed. Made three little poems last night while awake.

Jan. Sun. 18th. 1885.

About 10. Slept cold. Do dishes etc. Read some. Bathe & dress. Fanny Manchester calls. Nice talk. Dinner. Write to mother.

Mon. Jan. 19th. 1885.

8.25 or so. Are aroused from our morning lingering by an express-man. Lovely blue and white blanket for baby from Carrie Hazard. Note later. We both fly around and Walter actually starts by 9.35 or 40! I wash dishes, sweep kitchen, arrange drawers, etc. etc. Florrie calls and we have a nice talk. Carrie Lindsey calls. The rent man comes. Blanche W. brings me some hot pudding. Walter comes, gets oysters and we have 'em fried. Eat good supper. Read some in Rome & Carthage, & Harper's. Sew on diapers. Walter reads Arabian nights.

Tues. Jan. 20th. 1885

9.20. Breakfast leisurely. Clear up dishes, do chamberwork, walk down st. with Walter. Market. Stop at Ladd's. Car to Carrie's. Dine there, stay awhile and go with her to her mothers. Sew on pillowcase and talk of sickness. Ride down and call for Walter. Ride home. Sup on grouse. Blanche W. in for a moment to ask about "Last days of Pompeii"—whether I think she'd enjoy reading it! I don't. Sew some, Walter reads me Hamerton, and we talk forcibly about "Manners."

Wed. Jan. 21st. 1885.

9.30 or so. Not very well. Injections. My darling gets me a delicious breakfast all himself. Not lively thereafter. Lie down. Sleep some. Blanche W. calls for stamps and to weigh book. Sleep more. Get to work about 1.45. Fire out in kitchen. Black stove some, make fire, do chamberwork, wash dishes, get good dinner. Retta Clarke's mother calls for a few moments. Walter home. Can't eat but little dinner. No lunch but two grouse legs. This won't do! Walter reads the Century to me, and I sew a little. Accts. *Bed.*

Thurs. Jan. 22nd. 1885—

About 9. Not well yet. Lie around all day. Very cold weather. Walter stays at home with me. I manage to get a little dinner, and wash some of the dishes. Injection with unsatisfying result. Walter makes Parchesi board on paper and beats me *seven* games! A swallow of tea, slice of toast & cup of prune juice for supper.

Fri. Jan. 23rd. 1885.

9. Spend the morning after Walter goes in making a parchesi board. *Good one.* Then dine very comfortably, reading Rome and Carthage. Wash dishes, get things ready for dinner and do various little chores. Play parchesi when Walter comes. Get dinner and eat thereof. Play & sew. Walter reluctantly makes a long promised call on Mr. Hoyt.

Sat. Jan. 24th. 1885.

? Not at all well. Walter has a headache and feels about as bad. I send note to Lizzie saying we can't come tonight. Finish little napping blanket. Read a little in R. & C. Walter goes out to the store. Sago for dinner. Take more of his mild laxative powder tea. Gradual effect. Good supper. Play Parchesi at intervals. Walter reads me two of his old stories.

Sun. Jan. 25th. 1885—

11. Accomplish little save the devouring of a good breakfast and supper. Mary and Alice call, and Mary overlooks my store of infant apparel actual and potential and commends the same. Mrs. Westcott calls. I wash some dishes. Walter gets supper. He writes my letter to mother. Bath and bed.

Mon. Jan. 26th. 1885.

8.30. Arise while the husband man sleepeth and make fire. Fanny Manchester drops in for a bit of call, being near. Wash dishes, etc. Dine. Ride down to Luther's and get size of Walter's watchkey which he inadvertently left out. Car to Dr. T's and get laxative pills. Walk briskly down to bridge with him, posting calico to mother. Ride home—he walks. Sup on jarred huckleberries & bread & butter. Overcast towels while he reads to me. Parchesi. Beat the rubber! Accts. Bed.

Tues. Jan. 27th. 1885—

About 9. Eat little; do not feel well. Sleep some between 11 & 12. Mrs. West-cott calls—can't stay any time—can't take her things off—stays 3 hours! An enjoyable talk. Show her box of baby clothes which arrive from Mrs. Cresson. Lovely sensible and numerous. Lunch after she goes on bread & butter & tea, huckleberries & figs and read R. & C. Do chamberwork and wash dishes. Watch for Walter and make little verses. Katy with clothes. Pay her for this & last week. Walter. Supper. Read, darn hose, parchesi, bed.

Wed. Jan. 28th. 1885—

? Not well yet. Manage after a two hours sleep to do my usual housework, but hardly. A cold driving snowstorm. Finish "Rome & Carthage". Walter home early. He reads to me while I wash the dishes. After supper we each write to Mrs. Cresson. Accts. Bed.

Thurs. Jan. 29th. 1885.

8.45 or so. Worse. Miserable night. Do nothing whatever but clean up the parlor somewhat, and put clothes on horse. My boy gets home early, and goes straight out again to get me things—oranges—oysters—medicine. I eat some raw oysters & an orange. Very hot and nervous evening. He gives me a hot footbath, hot "Dew-drops", and puts me to bed in a blanket.

Friday. Jan. 30th. 1885—

? Slept warm—dripping, and well. Much better this morning. Wash dishes during the day and cook some rice for supper. Worse in afternoon and evening, but not so bad as yesterday. Bed in blanket. Get frantically hot and nervous and kick out of it. Bad night, lame all over.

Sat. Jan. 31st. 1885.

9 or so. Eat a little steak, some weak tea & bread for breakfast. Sweep kitchen. Collapse for a while, but mean to go out now. Call on Miss Harris and leave word about washwoman. Stop at Mary's and eat some mashed potato and milk. Call on Mrs. Briggs and leave directions for telephone. Stop in at the Westcott's and stay. Feel better there. Copy letter in play for Sarah. Hem diaper. Eat a little weak rice pudding with some quince juice thereon. Walter comes there for me—was dizzy and had to come home. He goes home, I follow in a few moments and do what I can for him. He gets better, goes out to the store. I manage to get the bread mixed. Don't sleep well—*Hot*. Have to get up and get water. *Wasn't* it good!

Sunday, February 1st. 1885—

? Walter gets breakfast, even to rolling out the bread, which he does very well. Eat somewhat. Lie around. Get some dishes washed in course of the day. Father Stetson calls and seems concerned. Leaves me some bromide of potassium for an opiate. Eat some supper, and write 7 *pages* to mother! And then nearly two days journal!

Monday, Feb. 2nd. 1885.

About 9. Took my bromide last night and slept much better; quieter in nerves even when awake and uneasy. Still weak today. Sew the least bit; read a very little. Feel so downcast that I take out my comforter, Walter's journal, and get new strength and courage thence, learning how good and brave he is. I *must* be strong and not hinder him. Eat good breakfast, dinner, lunch & supper. Have beef-tea again. That and sleep will fix me I know. Walter home well welcome. He settles all my monthly accounts. Dear dear love! I cleaned up somewhat, but did not wash dishes. Weak yet.

Tues. Feb. 3rd. 1885.

9 or so. Downhearted and woebegone. A poor night and feel no better; that is, no stronger. Letter from Martha, and brief note from Uncle Edward, asking Thomas' address. Go into the Westcott's to keep from lonely dolor. Lizzie Brown calls while I'm out; and leaves present from Mrs. Anthony, nice piece of diaper, and note from Mrs. Townsend, who wants to make a flannel skirt. Come home and have some beeftea and bread & milk. Back again. Sew a very little; mend glove for Carl. Miss Dodge arrives from somewhere, and plays to me. Carrie Lindsey calls for me, and I come home with her and show her Mrs. Cresson's box of pretty things. Talk. Walter, rather late. He makes me some lemonade, and gets supper; Steak & peas. Eat quite well. Parchesi. Try hop tea but can't drink it—stomach won't have it. Bromide. Bed.

Wed. Feb. 4th. 1885.

? Slept pretty well; and feel *lots* better. Eat real good breakfast. Write note to Mrs. Townsend. Manage during day to wash nearly all the dishes, lying down between whiles. Miss Harris calls to tell me of a little girl who could wash my dishes. Postman with Punch and Alpha. Make beef stew or soup. Am very very tired and lame at night; which displeaseth and grieveth my Walter. "I didn't *mean* to!"

Thurs. Feb. 5th. 1885.

8.30 or so. Am well. Help get breakfast. Write "sentiment" for the Envelope party of the W. E. & I. Society and note to Mrs. Cresson. Sit on warm tin roof in the sun! Work some. Go to Mary's to dinner. Anna there. Home. Write first of a review on Rome & Carthage. Read in Aurora Leigh.[11] Sleep some. Make over soup. Am well after supper, write to mother & read more.

Friday Feb. 6th. 1885.

9 or so. Not so well after breakfast, for some unknown reason. Loaf and doze all the morning & read Aurora—finish it. Sarah Westcott calls and borrows my beloved circular to wear in a play. Brings it back at night. Wash dishes and empty slops in the afternoon. Nice supper, peas, tomatoes, potatoes, white & sweet, fried fresh salmon. Walter reads papers, and Nonsense Book to me.

Sat. Feb. 7th. 1885.

8.25 or so. Arise briskly and help get breakfast. Clear up dishes &c. Then feel badly awhile. Dress & go out with Walter. ("Advocate" with my "The Sin of Sickness".) Stop at Mary's a few minutes. Walter walks. Take car. Go to Market. Ride up to Mother Stetson's to dinner. Got out and walk down a little to meet Walter whom I saw from the car window at Mrs. Dr. Wilcox instigation. Lie down awhile after dinner, rest and talk. Then ride down st. again and shop. Get lovely little seal and key for Walter's birthday, and leave to be marked. Home. Stop at Mary's, store, & the Westcott's. Fix fires, orange, read Babyhood. Good magazine, we'll take it. Oysters for supper and two little Charlotte Russes I got.

Sun. Feb. 8th. 1885

9.30 almost. Good breakfast. Make graham bread. Make new necktie for Walter, two watchguards, and darn hose. Lunch. Sit & lie around all P. M. Get dinner, good dinner, roast beef. And eat it too, heartily. Write to mother. Feel well. (Sudden weariness later, didn't bathe.)

Mon. Feb. 9th. 1885.

9 or so. A long day, very bright and warm in the morning. Sit out on the roof in the sun. Wash the dishes. Make a little custard and have nice dinner ready. Nap in the afternoon. Sew on diapers in the evening. Bathe by parlor fire. Bed.

Tues. Feb. 10th. 1885—

Near 9. Am eating pretty well now. Clear up dishes to wash after breakfast. Wood comes. Kitchen fire goes out; remake it. A howling southerly storm last night, sleep ill, both of us. Walter stays at home it is so dark and foggy and paints me, in green wrapper, yellowish lace and camelian pin. Good. Lunch. Mrs. Cresson's baby basket arrives. Very lovely and complete. Walter helps me get closet and chest in order; with old sheets, rags, etc. all handy. Tired. Cut up diapers. Horning for dinner. Write to Mrs. Cresson.

Wed. Feb. 11th. 1885—

after 9. Feel pretty well, save for the usual after breakfast abasement. Wash dishes, all of 'em; empty slops, take 2 o'clock car down st. Stop at Tilden's.

Seal not done yet. Get 6 yds. olive green double faced canton flannel for kitchen curtains. Have some tomato soup at Fillinghast's. Get Plutarch's Lives at Pub. Lib. Call on Miss Gladding. Stop for Walter, call on Aunt Caroline who has been ill, back for Walter, and home together. Get nice little supper. Make curtain while he reads me "Coriolanus" & part of "Alcibiades." [12]

Thurs. Feb. 12th. 1885.

9.30 or so. Have got to eating oatmeal again, and enjoy it. Lie down when Walter goes; but boy comes with his corduroys & then Sarah Westcott comes to stay; so I don't sleep. Sew and talk. Boiled eggs, toast & milk for dinner. Wash dishes. Lie down from 4 till Walter comes. He brings oysters & we have 'em stewed and raw for supper. Read "Nation". Sew while he reads "Alcibiades."

Fri. February 13th. 1885.

About 8. Get dishes & chamberwork done and set out with Walter near 10.30! Go to cousin Julia Jastram's & stay till 3.30 or so. Bit of lunch at 12, dinner at 2. Lots of talk—mostly Julia's. I hem two diapers & she one for me. Gives me two tablecloths, & a sheet all made up in little d.s. I take car to the Brown's. Out. Ride up to Walter's. Call on Millie a few moments. Maria calls while I'm there. Meet Walter, get creamcakes, home. Get steak. Am very tired.

Sat. Feb. 14th. 1885.

Near 9. Rise and find a lovely Valentine from my darling; who sat up, tired, till late last night to write it. A sonnet, beautiful. Lie down awhile after breakfast. Spend most of the day painting and writing to make a Valentine for him. He likes it as much as I could wish. (Letters from Grace & Mary Channing this morning, with package containing blanket, sack, and hood. Real pretty. Also bundle from Mrs. Smith with three dresses, two skirts & a shirt. Not very nice, but useful.) Wash dishes. Horning for supper. Make inventory of all my baby things (Walter doing the writing) for mother; and write to her. Accts. Bed.

Sun. Feb. 15th. 1885.

8.15 or so. Good breakfast. Wash dishes. Sew rings on curtain. Feel faint and lie down awhile. Rise, lunch, make soft custard and gingerbread. Write to mother. Walter paints. Get dinner. Walter reads to me some. Write to Grace & Mary in the evening.

Monday. Feb. 16th. 1885.

? Pretty poor day. Couldn't eat my breakfast. Managed to live however on installments of beeftea, milk, etc. during the day. Mrs. Westcott & Mrs. Russell call. I show 'em all my things to their great admiration. Make arrangements about Mrs. R's staying with me through March till Miss Pease comes. Finish another curtain. Darn hose. Lie around feebly. Another screaming storm in the evening. Take some bromide as a precautionary measure, and sleep pretty well.

Tues. Feb. 17th. 1885.

? Not well in the morning; so hysterical indeed that Walter decides to stay with me; but after having a slight chill, some sherry, beeftea & toast, I feel better; and he goes later. Sew on curtain, loaf about; and bye and bye wash a few dishes. Belle and Sarah make me a call about 5, much to my relief. Walter brings oysters and icecream for supper; and a volume of DeKay's poems. We don't think much of most of them—small thought or feeling and weak workmanship. Supper. Walter goes to see some Rembrandt reproductions at Mr. Mason's. I finish curtain & look at the magazine of Art.

Wed. Feb. 18th. 1885.

? Lie around all the morning, reading in Harper's. Am hungry. Wash dishes late. Get nice dinner, (Walter brings steak,) baked potatoes, tomato, cornstarch pudding. Enjoy it immensely.

Thurs. Feb. 19th. 1885.

9.25. A wellnigh sleepless night. Hot, cold, hot; restless nervous hysterical. Walter is love and patience personified; gets up over and over, gets me warm winter-green, bromide, hot foot bath, more bromide—all to no purpose. About 2 or 3 I get up despairing, and go into the parlor. Fix fire and sleep some after a while, on lounge. Back to bed towards morning & sleep more. We rise late. Expressman of course—afghan & "Handicraftsman" from Retta. Good breakfast. Loaf & read. Wash dishes, do chamberwork. Carl in, nice talk, mostly on French Rev. Walter. Supper. Look over "ballads". Tired.

Fri. Feb. 20th. 1885.

9 or near it. Breakfast, dress, set out with Walter. Go to his mothers to dinner. Nice time. Charlie Baxter in wild with chillblains. Give him a quarter & send him forth after Packer's Cutaneous charm; which seems to do some good. Carrie in, and walks out with me to the car. Go to Root's and get sundry hardwares. To Tildens and get Walter's birthday present—a little onyx & gold watch-key and seal. Get box of wax and tapers too. Stop at Riders & warm feet. Funny little woman in. Mr. Rider jokes her unmercifully—good as a play. Home. Stop at the Westcott's & talk to Mr. W. Walter comes for me. Home. Fix fires and have supper—late. Rest awhile. Bed.

Sat. Feb. 21st. 1885.

about 8. Sarah comes at 10, and does a fine day's cleaning. Front entry, parlor, bedroom, a little in the kitchen & a lot of dishes. Carrie & Jennie call in the afternoon; and look at all the baby things. Leave me very nervous & excited. Carrie brought a mince pie. Walter late. light supper. Walter reads. Bed.

Sun. Feb. 22nd. 1885.

10 or so. Good breakfast. Do little or nothing all day, and keep pretty well. Baked beans. Mrs. Springer calls in the evening. Baby things again. Then Walter writes to mother for me.

Mon. Feb. 23rd. 1885.

8.30 or so. Mother's letter. Mrs. Springer comes & makes "anise brodt" to show me how. I wash a lot of dishes & get dinner. Walter home in the afternoon; brings me some lovely roses and smilax, bless him. Henrietta Brown calls and stays tiresomely. Supper. Mrs. Springer again to read me mother's letter to her. Get ready to go to bed at 8, but Sam Simmons calls. Goes at 9.20 or so.

Tues. Feb. 24th. 1885.

About 9. Good breakfast. Good day generally. Read some. Sew some. Get & eat good dinner. Wash dishes. Empty pail. Susie & Mrs. McKenna call. Show them the baby things; enjoy their friendliness and admiration of the pretty things. Lie down awhile. Walter pretty late. Get dinner. Eat it too. Lie down some more. Write to Mrs. Smith, Miss Pease, & Dr. Keller.

Wed. Feb. 25th. 1885—

9.15 or 20. Don't feel *very* well; but sew, write to mother, get and eat dinner, and wash dishes. Walter home at 5.15. Carl in, much pleased with the Postman's Benefit, for which we gave them tickets. Supper. Sew while Walter writes. Accts. Note to Retta.

Thurs. February 26th. 1885.

? Do not feel very well before breakfast; but am better afterward than for long. Aunt Caroline calls. I work about in general. Fix the poor Madeira vines and set 'em out in the sun. Abbie Cooke calls. Talk. Show baby clothes. Wash dishes. Dine on brownbread and milk—hot. (Sarah Westcott was in before Abbie; and borrows things for another play or something.) Belle comes and cleans. Outhouse, stove, kitchen, lots and lots. That Mrs. Brown who lived below us in Mr. Sayles house calls! I never asked her. Says she's coming again! Hasty pudding. Pleasant evening with "Two Gentlemen of Verona". Sew.

Fri. Feb. 27th. 1885.

Ere 8. Feel very well and strong. Walter not seeming so—I was restless again last night & he up with me, cooked me an egg—I rise and make the fires and get breakfast. He doesn't have one thing to do, for Sarah comes at 9.30 and gets coal, wood, etc. Cleans kitchen closet, puts garret in order, & does ever so many things, while I cut up sheet and make diapers. Eat very hearty dinner. Walter home early. Good supper. He reads "The Earthly Paradise." [13] Very warm night—

Sat. Feb. 28th. 1885.

? Not very lively. Sarah comes and cleans windows, dishes, etc. etc. Bell in the afternoon, irons & cleans silver etc. I hem bedroom curtains, make diapers, mend clothes. I help clean the silver. Another good supper. Walter's two studio rugs come. Very pretty. Earthly Paradise in the evening

MARCH

Sunday. March 1st. 1885.

? Up late. Have caught cold again, a bad one. Big rug turns out lamentably threadbare. I mend on it for two hours and then we conclude to make a fuss about it. Wash dishes. Lunch. Mary Phelon calls, glad to see her. Show her the things she hadn't seen. Fix chicken for dinner. Walter makes dressing. Lie down awhile! Sew rings on bedroom curtains & Walter puts them up. Chicken not a success. Accts. Walter writes to mother for me.

Mon. March 2nd. 1885.

About 8. Breakfast and loaf about awhile. Walter goes, postmanless. Get ready to wash dishes. Mrs. Russel arrives, with small baggage. She sits about and I work. Work considerable. She helps some. After lunch I go out in state, and call on the Manchester's. Stop and see Sarah a minute. Home. Sew. Get dinner. Mrs. R. stays till 8.30 or so.

Tuesday. March 3rd. 1885.

About 8. Mrs. Russell arrives early, much to our disgust, especially Walter's. She came because the Westcotts were in great confusion, owing to Blanche's return from N. Y. and divers similar occurrences. I am not very well. Do not go out. Blanche comes in. Mrs. R. makes pies, squash.

Wed. March 4th. 1885.

About 8. Mrs. R. after 9. She washes the breakfast dishes & I go out. Call on Mary. Get "Babyhood" which she has read enjoyed & profited by. Call on Mrs. Diman. She was very glad to see me. Stop and see Mrs. Westcott a moment. Home. Mrs. R. had made some cake—good. Get dinner after resting a bit. Eat well. Lie down awhile and sleep some. Get up and wash dishes. Carrie

Lindsey calls. Mrs. Russell, adorned in my circular(!) goes out to call on some wealthy friends. I was glad to see her so pleased, and *intensely* amused at the effect. Dr. Tomlinson calls, prescribes for cold, insomnia, and night sweats. I like her much. Walter rather late. Oyster stew. Show photographs to Mrs. R. Accts. Bed.

Thurs. March. 5th. 1885.

7.50. A little better than yesterday. Wash dishes & clean lamp. Make some cornbread for dinner, good. Mrs. R. washes dishes & cooks a pickerel for supper. Mrs. Burleigh calls. Tires me. Lizzie Brown, May and little May call. Show them the baby things. Walter a little late.

Fri. March 6th. 1885.

8.15 Had my alcohol and alum sponge bath last night, and bromide. Slept well, for a wonder. Feel much better this morning. Cold better. Wash breakfast dishes. Sew some. Mrs. R. sews for me. Lie down some. Good dinner of chops and things. Miss Harris calls with some apples and a piece of sponge cake. Mrs. Manchester calls. Belle comes with the wash and cleans some paint and silver. I have a half nap. Show Mrs. R. Dante's Inferno—Doré. She is much impressed, remarks very amusing. Rice for supper. I write card to mother. Accts.

Sat. March 7th. 1885.

8.15 Feel well. Slept well again. Sweep parlor. Sew some. Get dinner & wash dishes. Annie Townsend calls and brings a flannel skirt for the baby. Mrs. R. makes more squash pies. Blanche comes in. Walter, supper. Teach Mrs. R. "Parchesi" which she plays with avidity. Accts. baths & bed.

Sunday. March 8th. 1885.

9.20 or so. Slept well and long. Eat a tremendous breakfast. Wash the dishes briskly. Write a long letter to mother finishing in the evening—28 pages. Have a lunch, and roast beef dinner at night. Doze somewhat in the afternoon. Mrs. Russel reads quietly in the kitchen all day. I show her a lot of pictures in the evening. She improves on acquaintance.

Mon. March 9th. 1885.

8.30. Winter again. Aunt C. comes just as I was going out. Let her rest a bit and then go out with her. Mrs. R. washes her clothes and the dishes. I go to Mary's but don't stay long. Home tired. Nap, broken by peddling pinopolmine mattress man. Lunch. Sew. Feel tired and lame. Walter. Supper. Lie down. Note to Miss Alden. Card to mother. accts.

Tues. March 10th. 1885.

8.15 or so. Not a good day. Do next to nothing. Lu calls and reads me a letter from Martha. We look at Punch and enjoy ourselves. Sarah W. calls too, but don't come in. Get lunch and wash dishes. Sew a little. Play parchesi with Mrs. R. in the evening at her suggestion.

Wed. March 11th. 1885.

8.30. Another feeble day. Kate Bucklin calls, stays some three hours, has a lunch and good time generally. Mrs. R. makes brown bread & bread pudding. I wash dinner dishes. Tired, very. Just about asleep, when aroused as I expected. Maria Brown. About an hour. Nearly asleep again when Walter comes. Get supper, and eat thereof. Mrs. R. washes dishes. Read "Babyhood,["] & doze. She goes at 8.30. Accts.

Thurs. March 12th. 1885.

8.35. Can't stand or walk much on account of the muscular force and unreasonable activity of the infant. Do breakfast dishes, which were but few. Lie down mostly. Look over piece bag and give Mrs. R. some bits of silk for "crazy quilts". Mrs. Westcott calls. Miss Murphy also, but don't stay long. Steamed brown bread and milk for dinner. Lie down more. Jennie Bucklin & Julia Mauran call. Glad to see 'em. Feel better towards night & sew on pillowcase. Walter. Codfish dinner. He goes to the first meeting of the new club—art talk and sandwiches. Mrs. R. leaves at 8.20 or so. Card to Mother & this. Edward Brown calls.

Friday March 13th. 1885.

8.30 or so. Cold morning. Not very well. Wash dishes. Receive from mother two pair of little knit leggings. Have a nap but feel rather the worse for it. Mrs. R. gets lunch and washes the dishes. I sew some. She sews for me, and boils out and irons all the last diapers. Kate calls in the afternoon, and stays to dinner. Walter home late. Brings me Mr. Mason's Rembrandt Etchings— reproductions—to look at. A very merry dinner. Young Mrs. R. Hazard sends me another blanket! Very pretty, white flannel bound with satin ribbon and worked a little. Kate and Mrs. R. depart about 8.30. Accts. Tired.

Sat. March 14th. 1885.

8.35 or so. Good breakfast. Feel pretty well. Anna calls and brings "pilch". Mrs. Russel washes all the morning dishes! A lot. I get letter from mother and one from Dr. T[omlinson]. enclosing powder and full of directions. Prepare medicine accordingly and snuffle and swale. Get dinner and wash dishes. Cut up napkins, and unbaste diapers. Get supper. Write to mother.

TWELVE

"Motherhood means——Giving."

March 15, 1885–August 5, 1885

ON MARCH 20, 1885, a young nurse, Maria Pease, arrived at the Stetson household to relieve Mrs. Russell, the housekeeper, of her responsibilities. She and Charlotte fast became friends, and Charlotte seemed calmer under her care. They spent the final days before the baby's arrival engaged in long and "delightful" conversations.

Just before 9:00 A.M. on the morning of March 23, 1885, Charlotte gave birth to a daughter, Katharine Beecher Stetson. Her diary comments reporting the birth of her child are sparse but telling:

> Brief ecstasy. Long pain.
> Then years of joy again.
>
> Motherhood means——Giving.

The weeks following Katharine's birth were difficult ones, particularly after Maria Pease departed in late April, when her month-long contract was up. For the first time Charlotte was left alone to care for the baby. Her diary entries for May reveal the extent of her anxiety as she tried to cope with the demands of new motherhood. "I wonder what people do who know even less than we about babies! And what women do whose husbands are less—sufficient," she dubiously remarked.

Many years later in her autobiography, Charlotte described in detail the misery she experienced following the birth of Katharine. "I, the ceaselessly industrious, could do no work of any kind. I was so weak that the knife and fork sank from my hands—too tired to eat. I could not read nor write nor paint nor sew nor talk nor listen to talking, nor anything. I lay on that lounge and wept all day. The tears ran down into my ears on either side. I went to bed crying, woke in the night crying, sat on the edge of the bed in the morning and cried—from sheer continuous pain"

(*Living*, p. 91). That pain, "a constant dragging weariness" (p. 91), would eventually lead to a nervous breakdown. As the days passed into months, the depression began to consume her.

May 2, the first anniversary of Charlotte and Walter's wedding, was a monumental letdown. "I am tired with long sleeplessness and disappointed at being unable to celebrate the day. So I cry," Charlotte wrote plaintively. Certainly both Charlotte and Walter must have been struck by the difference that a year had made in their relationship. Gone was the thrill of their newfound intimacy. Gone, too, was the innocence of their youthful illusions.

Within a few weeks after Maria Pease's departure, fatigue and depression had taken their toll on Charlotte's nerves. On May 8 she recorded just the latest in a series of adversities: "A fine scare with Miss Baby. She slips off my hand and gets her face under water a moment. Frightens her and me too. Hard day in consequence, she restless and cryful, I tired." The next day Charlotte awoke very tired and depressed. To her utter relief Mary Perkins arrived back from her long trip to Utah in the afternoon. Her return, however, was a mixed blessing.

Charlotte welcomed her mother's help with Katharine, but at the same time the old wounds of never feeling loved by Mary must have resurfaced in full force. The pattern from her own childhood, and the unresolved conflicts, seemed to be mercilessly repeating: "I would hold her close—that lovely child—and instead of love and happiness, feel only pain. The tears ran down on my breast. . . . Nothing was more utterly bitter than this, that even motherhood brought no joy" (*Living*, pp. 91–92).

Mary's apparent ease with the baby also seemed to exacerbate Charlotte's fears of maternal incompetence. "Mother over early," she wrote on May 10. "She takes all the care of the baby day times; washes her today with infinite delight. I fear I shall forget how to take care of the baby." Two days later Charlotte inscribed the date, "Tues. May 12th," but she never wrote the entry that she had apparently intended.

Tuesday, May 12, in fact, marked the beginning of another significant break of nearly three months in Charlotte's diary writing. She attempted again on August 5 to resume her writing, but it wasn't until the end of August that she was able to do so with some regularity. Charlotte had become increasingly depressed during the summer months. Her frustration at not being able to write is evident on August 5 when she lamented that she had "long been ill; weak, nerveless, forced to be idle and let things drift." But as bad as things were, the worst was yet to come.

Sun. March 15th. 1885.

8.30 or 40. Bad night, miserable morning. Weak, draggy, nervous. Lie around. Write some to Mother. Get bed made up with the mattress from upstairs. Mrs. R. does about all the work. Better in the evening. Write note to Mrs. Hazard, and finish mothers letter.

Mon. March 16th. 1885.

7–7.30. Up early on account of Mrs. Sullivan. Partially clean head with fine comb. Get all ready for her. She doesn't come—was to be here at 9—finally arrives to excuse herself and say she'll be here at 1. Attend to my nose, which improves. Julia Jastram calls with little Julia. Brings me some sweet oranges. Kate comes. Julia talks to her till I get faint with the rattle and ask her to stop. Kate stays to dinner. Nice, eat "a much". Then cometh Mrs. S. and I have a nice shampoo. Tires me though. Little nap, broken as usual by Postman. Get up and flourish round a bit. Pick up clothes for Belle, etc. Walter. Supper— griddlecakes. Fold hem of napkins and hold forth to Mrs. R. on the Mormon question. Start her to reading "The Fate of Madame La Tour." Walter looks at Rembrandts.

Tues. March. 17th. 1885.

8.35 or so. Bad night with little sleep, but feel pretty well in the morning. Get a nice nap. Mrs. Manchester calls to inquire for me but does not enter. Eat good dinner. Aunt Caroline calls. I read a story in Don Quixote & paint wild rose in Sarah Westcott's album. Walter. Supper. He sketches.

Wed. March 18th. 1885.

8.30 or so. Cold. Feel well. Eat big breakfast. Pick up dishes. Have delicious nap. Mrs. Slicer calls. Dine. Do my usual heavy housework. Sew on necktie for Walter and read in new Harpers. Kate calls. Walter. Supper. Read, Accts.

Thurs. March 19th. 1885.

8.25. Another good day. Nap as usual. Dine. *Wash dishes*! Make another necktie. Read Harpers and Nation. Sing and feel jolly. Louise Diman calls to see how I am. Walter. Supper. Read a little. Write here.

Fri. March 20th. 1885

8.35 or so Up gaily and get good breakfast—chocolate, codfish à la crème, hot biscuit. Get Mrs. Russell over to partake. Eat heartily. Try to sleep afterward but can't, expecting Miss Pease. Blanche W. in about noon. Miss P. at somewhere near 1. Talk much and get dinner. Good. Mrs. R. washes dishes while I show all my things to Miss P. Try to sleep again but can't. Mrs. R. departs in peace at about 4. Have a real good talk with Miss P. and enjoy it. Like her *very* much. Mrs. Westcott calls. Walter. Supper. Good. She writes. So do I—here.

Sat. March 21st. 1885.

6.30 or so. Belle comes and begins her duties. Does well. Miss Pease continues delightful. Read and talk to her and show her things. Fanny Manchester calls.

Miss. P. shows her baby things. Afterward I have a nap I'm thankful to say, and feel weak and sleepy again. Belle between two and five, cleaning up etc. Walter, supper, quiet evening. Miss P. gives me my bath. Bed.

Sun. March 22nd. 1885.

7. 10 or so. A pleasant day. Enjoy Miss Pease more and more. Sleep some. Read to her. Pale dinner of veal and things. Read some of my things to Miss Pease. Feel weak and sleepy. Write to mother.

March 23rd. 1885.

This day, at about five minuts
to nine in the morning, was born
my child, Katharine.

Brief ecstasy. Long pain.
Then years of joy again.

Motherhood means———Giving.

[*After the birth of Katharine, Charlotte neglected her diary for three weeks.*]

Sunday. April 12th. 1885.

First entry in three weeks. Am "up" but not vigorous. Retta Clarke called. Wrote to Mother.

Mon. April 13th. 1885.

Very bright and well, having had good night. Susie and her sister called, bringing me three photos of the children, and one of herself. She was very sweet and nice with the baby. I like her. Miss P. showed pretty baby things to Jennie. Jennie Bucklin called later. Retta came.

Tues. April 14th. 1885.

Still better day, with two or three hour's nap at noon. Mrs. Frank Sheldon & Hattie call. They tire me exceedingly. Retta.

Wed. April 15th. 1885.

Bad night, poor day. Don't sleep much at noon. Blanche W. in. Kate comes. Aunt Caroline. Retta. Kate brought a lovely silver cup for little K., and takes it away to be marked

Thurs. April 16th. 1885.

Go to ride with Walter—does me *good*. Horrify Miss P. by jumping from the buggy step. Lunch. Nurse baby. Sleep. Get up. Blanche W. in. Dinner, good appetite.

Friday, April 17th. 1885.

Get up while they breakfast. Read and sit around. Two Miss Manchesters call on Miss Pease. I see 'em. Miss P. goes off with them in fine style, to have her photograph taken. Blanche W. comes in and stays with me. I prepare to sleep but the baby wakes. Blanche "changes" her and I nurse her. Then she sleeps again. Belle comes. I dine. Then I have a nice nap and wake lively. Talk to Belle. Miss P. returns with Walter; had a splendid time. Glad she went. Dinner. Nurse baby. Walter draws Miss P. I write rhymes for her sister's knives.

Sat. April 18th. 1885.

Get up and take a bath. Breakfast. Baby for nearly two hours. Then a long nap. Then dinner. Then Baby. Then supper.

[*Another break occurs in the diaries between April 19 and May 1, 1885.*]

May 1885.
Fri. May 1st.

Am pretty well used up by loss of sleep. Walter stays at home in the morning and lets me have a nap. We begin to take ice. Katharine is better; sleeps from 11 till 3, is asleep again before 5 without pain and crying and now remains so at about 7. She has been troubled with indigestion and "wind"; I took some ginger today and think that helped. Mean to leave off cocoa for a while; as we fear it is too rich. She also has a cold. I wonder what people do who know even less than we about babies! And what women do whose husbands are less— sufficient.

Sat. May 2nd. 1885.

The first anniversary of my wedding day. I am tired with long sleeplessness and disappointed at being unable to celebrate the day. So I cry. Walter stays till 12. Belle comes and cleans up for me as usual. I send her for flowers to beautify our little house, and dress myself in black silk, jersey, and yellow crape kerchief. Haven't been "dressed" before in months. Belle is astonished. Walter brings me lovely roses.

Sunday. May 3rd. 1885.

A clear bright lovely day. Go out between 1 & 2, calling on Cousin Mary and Mrs. Diman. Cousin Mary also calls on me; then Mr. & Mrs. Burleigh call, and afterward Guss. Miss Katharine is duly exhibited and behaves well. Get to bed about 9 I think.

Mon. May. 4th. 1885.

A good night; baby slept till 3. Get her washed before Walter goes; and after she is asleep proceed to lunch and do housework. Seems good to be at it again.

Miss Murphy comes, has a bite, washes part of the dishes, looks over my wardrobe actual and potential, and rehangs my black silk skirt. I tend baby and do a little on bonnet. Telegram from mother. She starts today. O I shall be glad to see her![1]

Tues. May. 5th. 1885.

Good night again. Good day; baby sleeps well and I sew, write, and dine at ease. Neither does she cry at all, evidently ginger agrees with her via mama. And we gave her chamomille also last night. Lu Manchester calls. Walter, supper, accts, bed.

Wed. May. 6th. 1885.

Katharine developes an unseemly inclination to wake and rise at two o'clock at night or so and remain awake for some hour and a half or two hours. She has a hard day, with considerable cry, very little sleep, and bad "diaper". I am very tired, very. Am starving for fear of giving her the colic. Guess I'd better eat more freely, as she has it anyway.

Thurs. May. 7th. 1885.

Night same as last, only I sleep better while I do sleep. Tired day too; but the baby is well. Eat a banana defiantly with no perceptible ill effect on K. Eat canned peaches; fish (cod) potato, tomato, farina & peaches for dinner. Blanche in.

Fri. May. 8th. 1885.

A fine scare with Miss Baby. She slips off my hand and gets her face under water a moment. Frightens her and me too. Hard day in consequence, she restless and cryful, I tired. Mrs. Westcott comes in at nightfall and revives me much.

Sat. May 9th. 1885.

Another good* night—but am very tired and depressed in the morning. Walter shakes me up, sets me to eating, sends me out. I call on Mary and get flowers at Butcher's for mother. Come home with them and then take them up into her room. Home and get things ready to wash baby. At about noon mother comes, bless her, and thereafter all goes well. She worships the baby of course; and to my great relief and joy declares her perfectly well. We have a happy afternoon. Mary Chafee calls. Walter comes, but goes out again after dinner to post letters and get some old rum for mother, who has a heavy cold. I go over to her room with her.

Sun. May. 10th. 1885.

Not very good night. Mother over early. She takes all the care of the baby day times; washes her today with infinite delight. I fear I shall forget how to take care of the baby. Alice comes to see Aunt Mary in the morning; and later with her mother. Jennie and her husband call. I get dinner, and Walter and I go to walk afterward. Mother goes to bed early. Mrs. Westcott calls.

Mon. May. 11th. 1885.

Fair night's sleep. Good day. So nice to have mother here. I wash dishes again. Anna comes, would have been surprised but for Mary. She brings Clarence in the evening, and he *is* surprised. Another blanket comes—from Miss Alden.

Tuesday {August} 4th.

[*Charlotte apparently intended to write an entry but did not.*]

August. 5th. 1885——

5.30 Yesterday I arranged my books once more; hoping to be able to keep account of my life and expenses again. I have long been ill; weak, nerveless, forced to be idle and let things drift. Perhaps now I can pick up the broken threads again and make out some kind of a career after all. Arose this morning at 5.30 and nursed the baby. Took my Mellin's Food as usual and got breakfast. Mine consisted of cocoa and a little bread. Nurse again at 8.45. Then write.

THIRTEEN

"How irrevocably bound I am"

August 28, 1885–April 3, 1886

O VER THE next several months, Charlotte's depression continued to deepen. On August 28 she reported feeling "highly excited, hysterical; seeming to myself wellnigh insane." The extent of Charlotte's "hysteria" on that August day is apparent in her misspelling of young Katharine's name, an error that she repeated numerous times over the next several weeks. On other days her entries were disjointed or incoherent (see September 2, for example). By August 30, 1885, Charlotte faced "every morning [with] the same hopeless waking." The depth of her despair is stark and haunting: "Retreat impossible, escape impossible. . . . [Walter] offers to let me go free, . . . but he cannot see how irrevocably bound I am, for life, for life. No, unless he die and the baby die, or he change or I change there is no way out."

Even Martha Lane, to whom Charlotte confided her pain, seemed unusually unsympathetic. Complained Charlotte to her diary, "I wrote her my heart and she answers with not overwise head."

During these months Charlotte's depression became so acute that she occasionally shirked even her maternal responsibilities, perhaps as a way to avoid yet another failed relationship. Her preference to "go down street and do errands . . . to staying at home alone with [the] care of [the] baby" seems to have been a futile attempt to reclaim at least some of the independence that she had surrendered. Most of the days she was left alone with Katharine were passed miserably. On September 14, for example, Charlotte's depression was considerable. After a particularly difficult morning, she reported feeling "an oppressive pain that sees no outlet." As she came closer to the edge of emotional collapse, her rejection of domestic responsibilities became more pronounced. On September 17, while preparing dinner, Charlotte reported "giv[ing] out," so "Walter makes the bread." That same evening, however, she mustered the energy to play whist, an activity that she enjoyed immensely during the independent years before her marriage.

By late September, Charlotte was close to the breaking point. Even the arrival of Katharine's new nursemaid, Elisa Gärtner, did little to alleviate Charlotte's pain. "Dreary days these," she wrote. "Only feel well about half an hour in all day." In early October, Charlotte, Walter, and Mary finally concluded that Charlotte should journey west to rest her frazzled nerves. Her diary entry reflecting the decision is unusually optimistic. "We propound discuss and decide the question of shall I travel? Yes, I shall. I contemplate wintering in California. Hope dawns. To come back *well*!"

In late October, Charlotte left Mary and the new nursemaid in care of Katharine and headed west, first to visit her brother Thomas in Utah, next to see her father briefly in San Francisco, and then to her final destination: Pasadena, California, where she would spend the winter with her friends the Channings.

Although Charlotte suspended her journal writing during her visit west, her autobiography reflects the dramatic transformation that took place in her spirits when she was out of reach of the demands of matrimony and motherhood. "From the moment the wheels began to turn, the train to move, I felt better," she wrote (*Living*, p. 94). In California, Charlotte thrived. "This place . . . was paradise. Kind and congenial friends, pleasant society, amusement, out-door sports, the blessed mountains, the long, unbroken sweep of the valley, with snow-peaks at the far eastern end—with such surroundings I recovered so fast, to outward appearance at least, that I was taken for a vigorous young girl" (p. 94).

Almost immediately after Charlotte returned home in the spring of 1886, however, she experienced a major relapse. Her autobiography depicts her loss of hope: "I reached home with a heavy bronchial cold, which hung on long, the dark fog rose again in my mind, the miserable weakness—within a month I was as low as before leaving. . . ." (p. 95).

In addition to having to confront the severity of her emotional illness, Charlotte also had to cope with the reality of her entrapment. "Am trying to get accustomed to life here," she wrote upon her return. "It will take some time." But no amount of time would prepare Charlotte for the pain that was still ahead.

Fri. Aug. 28th. 1885.

It is vain to expect regularity at present. Any entry is better than nothing. On *Wed. the 26th* Katherine first put on short clothes. We have a girl. Daffney Lynch by name. She came *Mon. the 17th.* I paid her last Sat. She is eminently satisfactory. I am having a doctor. Dr. Knight. He came first I think on *Fri. the 14th.* Again, having considered the case on Sun. 16th. I had had one of my bad times when he was first sent for. The next day was bad too; highly excited, hysterical; seeming to myself wellnigh insane. Sun. when he came some better. Mon. (17th.) much better, walking down street with Walter, well all day. Tues. rode down, growing ill feelings in afternoon; ill turn at night, with pain and vomiting. Bad Wed. morning, better in afternoon when he came. *Very* well *Thurs.* 20th. Painted a little, wrote verses for long neglected albums, tended baby while mother went out; began article on "The Inutility of Sporadic Reform". Felt clear headed and strong. Fri. not so well, but worked hard getting backroom in order; "baby's room". Very much used up Sat. when he came again; but read essay for him and talked glibly. Sun. felt pretty well and "dressed up". Put desk in order in the morning. Began to write P.M. but guests arrived. Mon. 24th. *miserable,* but so far better than I have been that I was able to write it down. Tues. Walter came home at noon and we took the baby to ride. Heavy showers. Wed. I rode down about noon, met Mr. Stetson Sen. and went home with him to dinner. Walter joined me there and so home. *Cold* The weather is *very* cold just now. Nurse baby, ginger tea, long nap. Thurs. still cold. Darn and mend pretty much all day. Mary, Anna, Aunt C., Alice, Charlie, Anna & Henrietta call. Today have embroidered some on Katherines flannel petticoat, and now write. We began to read "Hard Times" last night.

Sat. Aug. 29th. 1885.

Another quarter of the petticoat done. Went down street with mother after yeast and fruit. Home. Dress. Dr. Knight comes. He thinks I am getting better.

Sun. Aug. 30th. 1885—

Every morning the same hopeless waking. Every day the same weary drag. To die mere cowardice. Retreat impossible, escape impossible. I let Walter read a letter to Martha in which I tell my grief as strongly as I can. He offers to let me go free, he would do everything in the world for me; but he cannot see how irrevocably bound I am, for life, for life. No, unless he die and the baby die, or he change or I change there is no way out. Well.

Mon. Aug. 31st. 1885—

Robert Brown last night. This morning Mr. Stetson & two country cousins. I walk down street with them, to the Terrace etc. Rest at Walter's and home. Lunch. Tend baby. Mother goes up to see Clarence, who is better. Nap.

1885. Tues. September 1st.

The first reasonably happy day for a long time. Looked out trimming. Arranged workbasket. Embroidered. Mary, Alice & Anna in. Went down town, did a bit of shopping, stopped for Walter and rode home with him. Dinner. Read and sew. *Babyhood* and *Century* came. Began James' "The Bostonians".[1]

Wed. Sept. 2nd. 1885.

The eventful day on which we earnestly Mr. Tewkbury's uncle and other relatives will Buy.[2] As we are low in funds. I still feel pretty well.

Thurs. Sept. 3rd.'85.

Kept well all day. Sewed and read. Rode down and walked home with Walter.
Colonel Johnson, wife and sister, called as arranged. Bought $45.00 worth and
intend to buy more. Good dinner, read in the evening, bed. Feel well today.
Settle accts. and pay milk bill. Start at 11.45 and go to Danforth St. Smiths
Hill after a "girl", and then to Waverly St. for a reference. So home. Tired.
Lunch & rest. Dr. comes. Is pleased to find me better. Walter. Supper. *Mutual
Friend*. Bed. Alpha came with my article on "Advertising for Marriage.["]

Fri. Sept. 4th. 1885—

Not a very good day. Manage to sew in the morning. Aunt Caroline spends
the day. Lizzie Brown comes to invite us all down to supper. I have a nap in
the afternoon, but do not feel very well thereafter. I am much displeased with
"The Bostonians."

Sat. Sept. 5th. 1885.

Not very well yet. Sew and mend. Letter from Martha. I wrote her my heart
and she answers with not overwise head. We all go to the Brown's for supper
and have a game of whist afterward. Baked beans the "piece de resistance". I
enjoy it until after the baby wakes up and cries. They sing and play, and the
poor little baby is well nigh crazed. Leave at 9. "Daphne" in the car. We hate
to lose her.[3] Home tired. Sit up and talk and cry till near 12. Better so than
in bed.

Sun. Sept. 6th. 1885—

Sleep till 8.10 when mother wakes me. Daffney goes to early church—
9 o'clock. We breakfast, watch baby's bath. We all go to see Mr. Bolan, his
wife and place. Very pleasant time. Bit of lunch on returning. Rest. Dinner.
Clarence calls. I begin Mrs. Cressons note paper. Pardon Jastram & Eddie call.
Daffney goes, more's the pity. Miss Katy Tighe calls to say Annie wont come
till Tuesday.

Mon. Sept. 7th. 1885.

No girl! Walter makes the fire and gets breakfast, bless him. Dawdle about
the work. Annie Vaughn, baby and nurse come, and stay. Sew. They go. I do
chamberwork. Do another sheet of notepaper. Finish letter to Mrs. Cresson.
Write here. Mrs. Springer called this morning and brought some splendid
pears. Mother and I give Walter his first lesson in whist. Tired.

Tues. Sept. 8th. 1885.

Cold bath. Breakfast. Sew a little. Clear table. Do chamberwork. Tend baby.
Lunch. Emily & Charlotte call. I go out with baby and stop to say goodbye
to Mrs. Diman. Miss Sophie Fillinghast there. I walk up to Mrs. F's with
her. They admire the baby. Go up through the new street; and inquire for

Mrs. Blodgett, is she sick? has her nurse come"? Home tired. Aunt C. here; and Mrs. Gallup. The new girl arrives; mother likes her. Show her about the table etc. Write here.

Wed. Sept. 9th. 1885

Up early and show new damsel about breakfast. Do two sheets of paper. Sew a wee bit. Go to dine with Aunt C., stopping to send up plumber. She rides back with me. Write to Ada. Warm. Wore grandma's muslin in the evening. Very tired. Mother Stetson sends some knit lace for Kathie's nightgowns.

Thurs. Sept. 10th. 1885—

Don't feel very well. Go down street and do errands preferably to staying at home alone with care of baby, Belle, and Annie. Very tired. Twitching and nervous. Dummy whist. Walter home early.

Fri. Sept. 11th. 1885—

A dear letter from Martha. Mother goes out & I tend baby. Dr. comes. More phosphorous & prescribes elixer coca. Show him my paintings. Read a little in the evening. Walter tired and we get into a quarrel over the windows, open vs. shut. I have a bad time; get out of bed and come down stairs in the dark.

Sat. 12th. 1885. Sept.

Better but still cross. Dressed in pongee and walked down with Walter. Looked at "Westminster Stove." Splendid. Rode up to Mother Stetson's and dined, lightly. Jennie there. Rode home. Tired. Took elixir, no noticable results. Unhappy afternoon.

Sept. Sun. 13th. 1885

Mother and Mrs. Springer go out to Mr. Bolan's. Clarence and Anna with Charlie come in the afternoon. So does Fraulein Gärtner and her friend. Make bread

Mon. Sept. 14th. 1885.

Go down and roll out bread. Back to bed a few moments. 8 o'clock! No time for bath! Cry and whimper, all upset. Feel badly. Cry more after breakfast. An oppressive pain that sees no outlet. Bathe and feel better. Letter from Julia with crocheted lace for K's petticoats. Answer. Write a very little. Get flies out and set paper for 'em. I hate flies. Whist in the evening. Westcott girls called. Man stained the rest of the diningroom floor.

Tues. Sept. 15th. 1885

Feel a little better. Yesterday the worst day in some time. Mother goes to Cousin Ray's with the baby carriage, to get apples. Write. Begin to arrange back room. Tend baby. Mother takes her out and I dress in grandmothers gown. Lu and a Miss Tingley call. Feel well and glad to see them. Talk. Walter has a bad cold.

Wed. Sept. 16th. 1885—

Busy in the morning. Walk down st. Stop at Creamery & have some lunch, graham bread and cream. Hunt about for stuff to put over the front doors. Get it. Home rather tired. Tend baby. Sew on curtains. Walter. Supper. Whist.

Thurs. Sept. 17th. 1885.

Feel well. Baby slept *all* night. Go down and sell old brown dress for $1.25. Leave it for Walter to get theatre tickets. Tomato soup at Fillinghast's. *Excellent*. Pub. Lib. and get books. Home. Mary, Alice & Anna here. Lu calls. Mrs. Rounds and daughter call. We get supper. I give out and Walter makes the bread. Whist. We weasel mother.

Friday. Sept. 18th. 1885—

Baby slept all night again. Delicious bread. Aunt Caroline comes and stays all day. Good dinner. I go down street at 3.20 and get new hat. Meet Carrie & go about with her. Soda. Go to Walter's. Dr. Allen and wife there. Home. Want some more soda so much that I go down on Governor St. after it. Buy beer too. Anna & Clarence come and do up their jelly. Tired.*

Sat. Sept. 19th. 1885

Feel poorly but manage to sew some. Walter home early owing to indisposition. We put up front door curtains and take 'em down again. Early dinner. Annie departs with good wishes. Whist.

Sun. Sept. 20th. 1885

Walter makes fire. Our new girl, Elisa Gärtner and her father arrive about 9.30. Nice old gentleman. Takes snuff! Seems to think his daughter well situated. She sets to work in fine style. I help her a good while and then Will Mauran calls. Brings (and leaves[)] Dick's book on Palmistry. I talk to him as I always do. Lunch, dress, and go over to Mother Stetson's with Katherine and Walter. Soup. Home before dark. Mrs. Springer had been here and talked to Elisa. Supper and Palmistry.

Mon. Sept. 21st. 1885.

Up at 5 with baby and small sleep after. Show Elisa about breakfast and set table. Clear it, and wash dishes as mother feels sick. Dead tired and lie down till afternoon. Then finish Kate's nightdress, make watch guards and white tie for Walter, sup, dress, nurse baby, and off to the theater. "RHEA" in Sardon's "A Dangerous Game." Opera House all renovated. Bad bad bad. Bad color, bad pattern, bad curtain, bad smell of paint. Globes crack and fall till they have to lower the gas. Terrible draft where we sit. Miserably poor play, and only middling acting. Felt pretty well however. Coffee and Soda at Green's thereafter. Walter got cold and headache. Hope we'll do better next time.

Mrs. Tewksbury called on Walter today and bought "A Fool's Errand"[4] & "Morning Measure"—$650.00.

Tues. Sept. 22nd. 1885.

Feel pretty well at first but give out after breakfast. A Poor day, and general breakdown about night. The new table comes. Splendid, old San Domingo Mahogany, beautiful legs,—only ten dollars! Will Mauran comes and we play whist.

Wed. Sept. 23rd. 1885—

Bad day. Sleep in the morning. Cut pattern for baby's shoes. Finish front door curtains. Dummy whist

Thurs. Sept. 24th. 1885—

Don't feel well. Walk down st. with Walter and get measured for shoes. Used up in the afternoon. Mary, Anna, etc. call. Dr. comes. Says I must wean her. Leaves "yellow jessamine" to alternate with phos. Walter reads some and we play. Beat dummy gloriously, 13 tricks!

Fri. Sept. 25th. 1885.

Dreary days these. Only feel well about half an hour in all day. Give Lisa a reading lesson and quite enjoy it. Jim & Sam call. Whist. Tired.

Sat. Sept. 26rd. {sic}* 1885

Down street with Walter; rather late. Shop. Call on Milly. Julia & Julie there. Ride home. Miss Murphy here. Gives me cloth. I eat wine jelly and feel it. Nap. Mother's "air tight" up. Dummy whist.

Sun. Sept. 27th. 1885—

Go to walk with Walter and baby. Good time. Hot and hazy. Mary, Ray, Mother, and young ones go to Mr. Bolan's. The Spencer's call with grapes and apples. Mary brought grapes and pears. We had bought grapes. Mr. Bolan brought grapes. Mr. Cole calls. Supper. Read. Bed.

Mon. Sept. 28th. 1885

Arise and go to Boston; or rather to Jamaica Plain, and see Dr. Keller. Carry on the whole journey in a peculiarly lame and injudicious way—showing my illness. Am examined and speculumed and told that I am all right. Great is my satisfaction and relief. Home late but not very tired. Feel as if I should get well.

Tues. Sept. 29th. 1885.

Go down and have Katherine's picture taken. Home. Mother goes down to the Brown's & stays to tea. I tend baby, call on Miss Pease and bring her home, and keep her to dinner. Walter glad to see her. Mother comes home with Edward. Whist.

Wed. Sept. 30th. 1885—

Mother goes with Lizzie and has *her* picture taken. I tend baby, and go out in the afternoon, shopping, and coming home with Walter. Tired. He reads to me. (I am reading the Mill on the Floss⁵ with much enjoyment.)

October. Thurs. 1st. 1885.

We are beginning to feed the baby once or twice a day, on Mellin's food. I don't mind since it's better for her. Go out again, to Pub. Lib., call on Miss Gladding and have a good talk, soup at Fillinghast's, not very good, get moss agate for breastpin for Miss Pease, and home. Call on Mrs. Vaughn. Dr. comes. Hyla Tingley calls. Leaves me Austin Dobson's Vignettes in Rhyme & takes Shelley. Returns Morris. Walter reads in the evening.

Fri. Oct. 2nd. 1885—

Write note to Lu about place with Miss Gladding. Accounts. Bad weather; so I loaf about all day, reading mostly. Finish chamois shoes—failure. Have a good nap. Call from Dame Slicer. Daffney comes to see us. I guess she would come back if we wanted her.* Benny Gallup calls with flowers and stays to dinner. Funny little boy. Walter reads.

Sat. Oct. 3rd. 1885—

Another dismal day. Go down town in the afternoon, market, studio, and get shoes, paying the remaining $2.50. thereon. Home. Miss Pease here. Walter and I go to the theatre. See Mrs. Barry and Mr. Redmund in "A Midnight Marriage". Fair to middling. Soda. Home. Dick Aldrich in the car.

Sun. Oct. 4th. 1885.

Walter and I go to Carrie's to dinner and then call on his parents. Home by 7. Baby cried for us for the first time. Mother very tired. Read.

Monday. Oct. 5th. 1885.

Letters from Lu, Grace, & Helen. Go down with Walter. Call on Miss Gladding about Lu. Not in. Get another patern for baby's coat, lining, etc. Try bouillon at Fill's. Bad. Home. Nap. Miss Pease again. Stays to dinner. Walter goes home with her and then reads. Feel badly.

Tuesday Oct. 6th. 1885—

Up about 8.30. Miss Pease here to breakfast and see the baby bathe. Does so with great enjoyment. Goes. Accts. Mother cuts out baby's coat. Whist, cry.

Wed. Oct. 7th. 1885.

Take the baby to see the Westcott's, and further. Tired. Can't get nap. Sew some on baby's coat. Am very much discouraged at getting no better. Julia & Julie call. Soup, good. Whist, we beat.

Thurs. Oct. 8th. 1885—

We propound discuss and decide the question of shall I travel? Yes, I shall. I contemplate wintering in California. Hope dawns. To come back *well*! Sew on coat. No nap again. Whist?

Fri. Oct. 9th. 1885.

Call on Annie Vaughn, and on Mrs. William Phelon, who wasn't there. Then ride over to Carrie's. Nobody at home. Go to mothers and dine. Talk with father. Get to discussing myself and feel badly. Go shopping. Get dress goods and fixings. Home with Mrs. Vaughn. Miss Pease here. Show her her breastpin, but must have it altered—sheathed. Bed.

Sat. Oct. 10th. 1885—

Take coca and work. Plan, & cut, two and baste one breast-supporter waist. Also cut out dress. Anna & Mrs. Carpenter call, with Charlie. Miss Harris calls. Walter brings me $320.00 to travel with. John Mason's mother lent it. Also brings "Ramona"[6] and begins to read it.*

Sun. Oct. 11th. 1885.

Went to walk with Walter and the baby. Walter bathes me at night as I am much exhausted and my breasts trouble me some. They have to resort to the baby before morning. I had bound them up in accordance with Miss Pease's theory and practice. But disapprove of the effects and let 'em down.

Mon. Oct. 12th. 1885.

I don't remember this day—

Tues. Oct. 13th. 1885.

Go to Dr. Gay's and have a tooth filled. Used up thereby.

Wed. Oct. 14th. 1885.

Go to Carrie's with my new dress and dine there. She takes hold obligingly and makes a good start. Home tired.

Thurs. Oct. 15th. 1885—

Off early and have more teeth filled. Read "An Old Maid's Paradise"[7] the while. Good, and funny. Soup at Sutton's, get breastpins and home. Aunt Caroline here. Josie Arnold & her boy Harold call. Josiah Westcott's wife calls. Abbie Cook calls. The doctor calls. Mrs. Springer calls. Mrs. Russell and Blanche Westcott call but sew some. Mrs. S. stays to supper. Tired.

Fri. Oct. 16th. 1885.

Finish hemming pleating for new suit. Mother goes down town. Western cousin calls. Nice sort of boy—of his sort. Walk out with him and the baby. Meet Carrie Hazard in carraige. Leave cousin and go back. Stop to see Miss Pease and remember that cousin has gone off with her pin in his pocket. Home in haste. Miss Gladding calls. Don't come in—too many steps and too little time. Carrie reappears and makes a nice call. Lisa having got the baby asleep, I write here.

[Charlotte suspended her journal writing during her months in California.]

April. {1} 1886.
Thurs.

1st. Went down town with mother and Julia. Visited Reim's exhibition and Walter's Studio—"An Fleur de Lys." A beautiful place. His father's birthday. Went over there in the evening.

Fri. April 2nd.

Tended baby in the morning. Aunt C. called, Kate Bucklin, Julia Jastram & little Julia. Mother & Julie went to the Museè P.M. I took baby out in her carriage. Walked to meet Walter. Looked at "Lauria."

Sat. April 3rd.

Up betimes. Ordered things to eat. Breakfast late. Am trying to get accustomed to life here. It will take some time. I must systematize things some how.

FOURTEEN

"O sick and miserable heart be still!"

August 27, 1886–October 31, 1886

CHARLOTTE resumed her journal writing on August 27, 1886. She did experience some good days during that autumn; her spirits soared during periods of productivity. Whether it be the reward of payment for her first publication, the pleasure of designing hand-painted stationery for friends, or the exhilaration of rowing Walter home from a moonlight visit to Pawtucket, Charlotte's "good days" followed a distinct and predictable pattern. When she was confined to the house or unable to work, the likelihood of her "great misery" returning rose significantly. Increasingly, Walter was called upon to intervene when Charlotte's depression became acute. The entry for September 19 describes a typical scene: "Get hysterical in the evening while putting K. to sleep. Walter finishes the undertaking and sleeps with her."

The autumn of 1886 also saw a dramatic rise in Charlotte's activism on behalf of women's rights. She began to write a series of articles and poems including "Why Women Do Not Reform Their Dress" and "The Answer" for publication in the *Woman's Journal*, and she was incensed by an article written by English writer Ouida on female suffrage. "A *contemptible* piece of writing, bad in aim and execution," she complained in her diary. More significantly, Charlotte attended her first Women's Suffrage Convention in October and became friends with women's right activist Alice Stone Blackwell. As Charlotte expanded her awareness of women's issues, she also became more assertive in her views. On October 9, for example, Charlotte stopped by Walter's studio and criticized one of his paintings. She judged it "so harshly from a moral point of view that he smashes & burns it. I feel badly; and after some tears he comes home with me." At the same time tensions outside of the household also escalated with a new intensity. On October 22 Charlotte noted an encounter with her cousin Robert Brown. "Robert makes an ass of himself by his loudmouthed contempt of women's rights and other justice. It is hard to be despised by such men as that."

Along with her increasing activism, another event that affected Charlotte during this period was the unexpected death of Thomas's young wife, Julia, who died very suddenly from complications associated with heart disease. Charlotte had stayed with them during her trip out west the previous winter, and the news of Julia's tragic death was a shock. Charlotte always became more reflective about her own life following the deaths of relatives, friends, and acquaintances. For the moment, Julia's death seemed to draw Charlotte and Walter closer together, if only briefly. They collaborated together on writing a play—a comedy—which they tried to sell to American actor William Gillette. While Gillette was "favorably impressed" by the play, he was not inclined to buy it.

Undeterred by Gillette's rejection, however, Charlotte was determined to continue to write. For the first time in her marriage, she was managing, however precariously, to balance the demands of marriage and motherhood with her desire to work.

Fri. August. 27th. 1886.

Begin to feel myself again. Am taking Buckland's Essence of Oats, with infinite good effect. Katharine and all are well. Am doing some note paper for Mrs. C. in pen and ink. Ate a good dinner today. Baby exasperating about her nap. Have just finished a letter to Julia. Have just received a letter from Atlantic Monthly actually praising my [poem] "Nevada"! But not accepting.

Sat. Aug. 28th. 1886.

A good day. Work more on Mrs. C's note paper. Go rowing with Eliza and baby later, and enjoy it. Paint in the evening—

Sun. Aug. 29th. 1886.

Finish paper. Go to see Gus & Susie. Dine there. The children greatly pleased with the baby. Draw in the evening.

Mon. Aug. 30th. 1886.

Up with baby. Don't feel very brilliant. Wash dishes. Wash baby, put her to sleep and set her porridge boiling. Read and loaf and accomplish little.

Tues. 31st.

Poor day again. Manage to paint two sheets of note paper, under great disadvantages from Miss Katharine.

September 1886.

Up at 8, early for us. Feel well. Write note to Mrs. C. Paint two sheets of paper. Walk down st. Cash Mrs. C's check. Go to gym. Mr. Smith not in. Shop. Change "Gesta Christ" for "The Chain of life" & "The Quincy Methods.["] Go to gym. again. Am horrified to find that Mr. S. don't mean to have a ladies class till the new building is open! I reason with him. Go to Walter's. We go to Mr. Chas. Smith the broker & auctioneer; and I talk to him about my "property." He says I can't do anything but wait. A mere business man, patronizing and contemptuous to a "woman". Ride home. Walter reads Century.

Thurs. Sept. 2nd.

Baby burns her hand on the stove. Not very badly, just the fingers ends; but enough to keep her away in the future I guess. Walter comes home at noon, goes out after a pine branch sketch, returns, dresses, and starts for Seaconnet. Some work for the Art Workers Guild. Is to return Mon. I go to see Mrs. Wells with baby; but they are away. Home, read, sup heartily on succotash and watermelon; sew till ten. To bed content.

Fri. Sept. 3rd. 1886.

Up at 7.30. Baby slept well thanks to the coolness. Feel well. Paint *eight* sheets of note paper. Boiled dinner and scallops. Mother over to dinner. Go home with her and stay an hour. Read. Bed.

Sat. Sept. 4th. 1886.

Baby did not sleep well so I slept late. Walter returns about eleven! Recieve three dollars from the Journal for my poem "On the Pawtuxet."[1] My first payment for Mss! May it not be the last! Go to Mrs. Lamb's and get flowers to paint. She is very kind. Do but two however. Maria Brown calls and eats peaches. Cut out undergarment and baste & fit it in the evening.

Sun. Sept. 5th. 1886.

10! Bad night again. Sew some. Paint one & a half flowers. Walter goes out with the baby. Write "An Allegory" about the man and his brother in the evening.

Mon. Sept. 6th. 1886.

8. Not overmuch sleep. Up earlier as its washing day. Wash dishes and baby and paint one sheet of paper paper [*sic*] poorly. Also finish another begun yesterday. Nap after four P.M. Begin Aurora Leigh in the evening, to Walter. Dear Walter.

Tues. Sept. 7th. 1886.

About 7. Walter slept with the baby to rest me; so I took her when she woke. A poor day. Accomplish nothing to speak of; only read a little in the geology book. Mother over to supper. Nice letter from Grace, which I answer immediately. Note from Mr. Smith of the gym. There are to be no ladies admitted till the new building is opened. I am much disappointed.

Wed. Sept. 8th. 1886.

Near 9. Feel miserably. Go down street at noon. Shop, spending my three dollars, all but 30 cents. Stop at Walter's. Ride home. Dine and read. Feel better.

Thurs. Sept. 9th. 1886.

about 9. Feel better. Paint two & a part sheets of note. Emily Diman and Charlotte Fillinghast come and spend the morning. I invite them to a row and moonlight supper on the water. But it rains and we don't go. Read again in the evening.

Fri. Sept. 10th. 1886.

Feel better. Paint all day. Call on Mrs. Lamb to show her paper. She is not in. Finish it. Letter from Mrs. C. with three dollars for her paper and orders for more. Walter and I ride down town and mail the paper to her after supper. Then I draw a head with stars on.

Sat. Sept. 11th. 1886.

Near 9. Feel dismal. Cut and baste, and take work over to mother's. She stitches for me. Home and fix lunch. Walter and I go rowing on the See-Konk. A splendid night. Full moon, no wind, warm. Go up to Pawtucket. Call on the Spencers. I row home, in fifty minutes, Four minutes. Enjoyed it very much, and it did me good. Bath, bed, and good sleep.

Sun. Sept. 12th. 1886

9. Fix my garters—harness, rather. Get dinner. Clean my hair and head. Mr. Purinton was expected in the evening but didn't come as it rained heavily. I finish Aurora Leigh to Walter. It brings up my grief. Anything does.
My four mile row did not tire or lame me *at all*, did me good. Washing my hair today utterly exhausted me! Tired back and brain. Write poem "O sick and miserable heart be still!"

Mon. Sept. 13th. 1886.

Near 8. Sew all day. Make one small waist for Katharine. Begin to fix bonnet. Walter sends me one of the new Postal Sheets, just to show it me and say "I love you". Dear tender heart! Write letter to Billah. Send him some of my watercolors to copy. Write to Mrs. Masters in the evening. A fairly good day. But always the pain underneath.

Tues. Sept. 14th. 1886.

9. Finish bonnet, curling the feathers quite successfully. Pretty. Expect Mrs. Stetson, but she doesn't come. Sew on baby clothes. Walter home early. Dress and go to Mrs. Grimshaw's to tea. A Miss. Crompton there, alias Adelaide Fairbrother, actess [*sic*], the one the Westcotts think so much of. Funny

that we should meet. I like her. She recites "A Railway Station" *admirably*. I recite "Rivers & Lakes of Maine." Villetta, the daughter, plays the piano for our delectation, beautifully. A rere-supper later, cake and wine. Home late. Near 12 now, but had a good time.

Wed. Sept. 15th. 1886.

9. Slept well. Feel well. Cut out brown dress. Bill sends me a note with sketch of a peach. Pretty good. Letter from Mrs. Cresson with more orders. I begin to feel like living. Call a few moments on Mrs. Diman. Then down street. Shop. Stop for Walter. Car home. Write to William Gillette.[2]

Thurs. Sept. 16th. 1886.

Paint on dinner cards, woodbine & long white flower. Mrs. & Mr. Stetson Sen. come & stay for dinner. Katharine in high feather. Don't enjoy it much. We have little in common. Sew after they go.

Fri. Sept. 17th. 1886.

8. Paint four cards; Jap. apple, yellow lily, gentian, & cardinal. Kate Bucklin comes and spends the morning. Glad to see her. So was little Kate. Go out to meet Walter for exercise. Hasty pudding supper. Mother, Miss Murphy, & Mrs. Kate Tilden call. Sew afterwards. Woman here today about machines. Three weeks on trial, I mean to try one, and do up a lot of sewing.

Sat. Sept. 18th. 1886.

9. Sew, cut & baste. Give my first lesson to Villetta Grimshaw, half an hour late. I like her. Stop to see Walter. Dr. Knight there, and a young Frost. I shop somewhat. Call for Walter. Wait till 7 for him. Ride home. Mr. Stetson comes over with a kitten for us, or rather a young cat. A beauty. Looks just like Belinda. The tamest sweetest little puss I ever saw.

Sun. Sept. 19th. 1886.

9. Do not feel well during the day. Sew some on dress. Cold and windy. Good dinner. Get hysterical in the evening while putting K. to sleep. Walter finishes the undertaking, and sleeps with her. When I am nervous she never does sleep easily—what wonder.

Mon. Sept. 20th.

6.30. Work on dress. "Nevada" back from the "Argonaut", Cal. Dress all day. Walk down st. with Walter and Katharine towards night. He came home early, tired with getting off his pictures to Pittsfield. Sewing machine comes. Wilcox & Gibbs' Automatic. Make waist for K. in the evening. Tired.

Tues. Sept. 21st. 1886.

8.30? Don't feel well yet. Take Katharine over to see mother before bath. Miss Murphy there. Letter from Thomas. Julia is going to have a baby in May '87. Home. Work on dress. Walk out to meet Walter with K. Read Sunday Journal in the evening.

Wed. Sept. 22nd. 1886

7.30. Feel better. Do but little in the morning, for Elise goes out. Lesson to Villetta at 2. Two hours. Mostly talk with Mrs. Grimshaw. Stop at Studio. Shop a little, getting some things for Villetta. Stop for Walter and walk home. (Miss Chapin went up street with me). Dutch apple cake for supper. Good. Mother and Miss Murphy call. Lecture on shoes, feet, etc. with illustration.

Thurs. Sept. 23rd. 1886.

Work on dress all day. Draw in the evening, while Walter cleans Mr. Bates' etchings.

Friday. Sept. 24th. 1886.

Sew some. Help Eliza move our furniture into the back room, where mother was. So as to share the advantages of the air-tight, and that I need sleep no longer on a lounge cushion and a cot bed. Aunt C. in for a moment. Go over to see mother for the last time this season, she going to Mrs. Budlongs on Sunday. Aunt Caroline, Anna, & Charley call there to my much weariness; by reason of their contention with Charlie. Home tired. Eliza puts the baby to sleep. Sew. Go to bed at 10.30, and lo! the babe awakes in her new surroundings and doesn't go to sleep till about 2.30! Naturally I don't, nor Walter. Didn't seem to be sick, only nervous.

Sat. Sept. 25th. 1886.

Baby wakes at 7.30, and I can't sleep after, though, I lie miserably trying till 10. Sew a little. Put baby to sleep. Try new dress again, most done. Then dress and go out. Call on Annie Aborn Fillinghast who is just on for a visit with husband and baby. Lesson to Villetta. They pay me for three lessons, and the materials I got her. She walks up street with me. I pay Calder the $2.93 for her things. Then shop a little; stop for Walter, and home. Talk with Mrs. Austin, our neighbor across the way, in car. The Womans Journal comes. Bed early. Write to Alice Stone Blackwell,[3] & write "A Use of Memory." Get *my new watch*! *Hurrah*! Pay $3.00 on it—price $11.00. Just like the lost jewel.

Sun. Sept. 26th. 1886.

8.30 or so. Sunday is usually a hard day for us both; Walter tries to do nothing but help me, and I get dinner and get tired. Today we both industriously bathed before breakfast. Then I cut his hair.[4] Tried to paint, but couldn't.

Sketched designs for salt & pepper set, dancing elves. Go elaborate fricasee dinner. Good. Then I succumbed utterly; but aroused myself and took Kate up to Mrs. Diman's. Saw them all, and a Harry Gardiner. Walter met me, and home on the run, as it sprinkled. He is now putting K. to sleep. Write long letter to Martha.

Mon. Sept. 27th. 1886.

7. Not a very good night, very hot and awake often. Do not feel well in the morning. Walter stays till I have washed the dishes. Paint. Sketch baby a little. Do three more cards, rose, m. glory & the purple flowers Mr. S. sen. brought me. Mrs. Allen and little Leah call, and Katharine does *her* best to entertain at least. Go out and meet Walter with K. Mrs. Fillinghast comes out to speak to K. from Mrs. Diman's. Home. Sup. Eliza puts K. to sleep. Sew all the evening while Walter reads Burton's Anatomy of Melancholy. Funny book enough.

Tues. Sept. 28th. 1886.

8. Cut and baste and sew all day. The machine damsel comes P.M. and explains the hemmers, etc. Letter from Mrs. Cresson enclosing Miss Dunham's $5.00 for the painted paper. Another order too, $3.00 one, dozen pen-&-ink cards. That's good. Feel pretty well all day. Kate is too good to believe. She plays about all day, with me or Eliza, with little rags and pins and divers toys; busy, sweet, and patient. Bless her little heart! I love her. Good dinner. Read to Walter in the evening, while he cleans etchings.

Wed. Sept. 29th. 1886.

7.30. Sew some. Paint a little. Emily and Charlotte come in. I love to have them. Lunch on a bowl of bread and milk and set forth, walking up with them. But I meet Mr. Grimshaw, and he tells me Villetta is out. Stop at Walter's and we go to the Public Library and read Ouida's article on Female Suffrage.[5] A *contemptible* piece of writing, bad in aim and execution. Read more after he goes. Then leave watch at Mr. Luthers' (I stopped it somehow) and to Walter's again. A little talk with Miss Chapin. All up the hill together. Home. Rice, potatoes, and pudding for supper: eke a fried egg for Walter. Was going to write, but Edward Brown calls. Pleasant evening.

Thurs. Sept. 30th. 1886.

Paint all day. Go out with K. to meet "papa" at eve. Mrs. Diman and Emily call, and arrange about lessons for E. Read to Walter in the evening while he fixes etchings, try to write on our comedy, sew some. Feel well.

Fri. October 1st. 1886

7.30. Well and lively. Up at 7.30. Sew and cut a little. Emily at 9.30. Nice lesson. Then wash K. and put her to sleep. Then paint. Aunt Caroline calls. Emily comes down again, with Charlotte. Lizzie Brown calls. Century comes, ghost story from Frank Leslie's, and bill from Dr. Keller. Walter reads to me out of Century in the evening and I sew. Went to meet him with K. at dusk as usual.

Sat. Oct. 2nd. 1886.

7. Walter goes out and gets me some lingering wildflowers before breakfast. Paint "butter 'n' eggs" and a thistle. The first poor, second good. Dine in haste, dress and out. (Woman's Journal comes with my poem in the *first* place.) Go to Villettas, give first lesson in color. Get dollar. Get Miss Abbott's address, and call there to see about pupils. Stop at Walters. Stop at Mr. Luther's for watch. Not done. Pay him $5.00. Meet the Misses Spencer there and walk up with them. Get Miss Chace's address, and Miss Fielden's. Go to them, but neither is at home. Leave books at Pub. Lib; but forget cards, so get none. On way down call on Miss Gladding. She looks old and ill. Miss Hoppin calls while I am there. I speak about pupils to them. Stop for Walter again. He buys stamps for me and I get 10 cts. worth of gum drops. I must have walked a good six miles. Am not tired nor discouraged. Sew in the evening, finishing chemiloon. Bed.

Sun. Oct. 3rd. 1886.*

9.15. Write up herein since Wed. last. Do not feel very well and accomplish little. Walter takes the baby out, and I start a little article—"Why Women do not Reform Their Dress." A telegram comes here for mother. Send it up to her unopened. Presently she comes back with it—"Julia died this morning". From Mr. Farrel. O my poor brother!

I send telegram and letter, and Walter goes with them. Takes mother down to Anna's also. Poor Eliza feels as badly as any of us.

Mon. Oct. 4th. 1886.

7.30 or so. Try to paint, but do little. My heart is heavy. Walter and I go out to call on the Smythes in the evening. I stop a few minutes at mother's and leave her my cards to look at. Walk down to the bridge and then ride out to Johnston. 9 when we get there. Stay about an hour. Have to run for the car in the dark and I strike a hitching post and go down like a nine pin. Doesn't hurt me at all! I must be made of whalebone. Ride to bridge, and walk home.

Tues. Oct. 5th. 1886.

Work all day, though not easily, and finish Mrs. Dunn's cards. Go up to see mother, but she was out. Don't see Walter, so come home. Sew in the evening, on chemiloon while Walter reads "King Victor and King Charles."

Wed. Oct. 6th. 1886.

About 8. Sew on that endless and unsatisfactory brown dress. Get K. to sleep and then out. Stop at Mother's. She was drearily washing dishes. She got a letter from Julia yesterday! Written last Wednesday. It is a dreadful blow to mother. Mrs. Budlong invites me to dinner, but I only take a plate of soup, and a biscuit. Call on Mrs. Blake. Out. Stop for watch. Not done. Go to Mrs. C. & F's school. See them both and do my errand. Nice little talk with Miss Chace. Then to my first Woman Suffrage Convention. A good audience. Mrs. Stone was the first speaker, then her husband, Mr. Blackwell, then Miss Haggart of Indiana. I left during her address, as her voice, high and monotonous, affected my nerves painfully. Mrs. E. B. Chace conducted the meeting. Mrs. Stone is a lovely motherly sweet little woman with a soft quiet voice. Mr. B. spoke well and briefly. Miss H.s speech was good enough in itself, though somewhat over rhetorical. After to the Pub. Lib. and read "A Bachelor's Blunder" in Lippincott's. Get Montaigne and Spencer. Stop at Walter's and eat a few graham crackers as I famish. Call again on Mrs. Blake, show her cards and tell her my desires in the pupil line. Walter stops for me. Home. Good dinner.

Thurs. Oct. 7th. 1886.

Near 9. Sew a little and paint one card. Carry Lindsey, Mrs. Ripley & Mrs. Spaulding call. Afterwards I call on Mrs. Lamb, and show her cards. She admires them much, as does her sister also, who means to take lessons. Good. Walter goes to his club. I sew, and Eliza reads aloud. Walter returns at eleven, and surprises us. He is elate over his prowess in opening beer bottles when all the others failed.

Fri. Oct. 8th. 1886.

8.5 Do not feel over lively. Very nice lesson to Emily Diman. Charlotte F. comes down for her. Then draw two cards ready to paint. Walter comes home to lunch. Cut out another night dress. Take Katharine to see mother, and travel about after her (m.) and with her. Eliza comes and takes K. home and I go to Mrs. Diman's to tea. Take sewing, read Morris and Browning, and talk theology with John, who arrives late. Enjoy it much. Home. Bill for Calder today. $13.98. Write to Thomas, and copy "A Transparency" for Woman's Journal. Walter home late.* bed.

Sat. Oct. 9th. 1886.

Do but little in the morning, as I expect Mrs. Lamb & sister who don't come. Read Woman's Journal, and draw & paint a little. Walter home to lunch. Dress and walk down with him. Lesson to Villetta, one dollar. Stop at Walter's. Criticize his pictures, one so harshly from a moral point of view that he smashes & burns it. I feel badly; and after some tears he comes home with me. Find a letter from Mrs. Dun with check for twenty dollars, and two orders! Rejoice thereat. Draw and sew.

Sun. Oct. 10th. 1886.

Write to Bill. Sketch baby in tub and asleep. Walter takes her out thereafter, and I paint pansy. Mrs. Springer calls, and mother. Mrs. S. stays to dinner. Design for fans in evening, while Walter reads Swinburne and Longfellow.

Mon. Oct. 11th. 1886.

8. Write to Mrs. Farrell. (after washing dishes.) Run hem of overskirt. Bathe Miss K. and put her to sleep as usual. Paint a little. Feed K. Dine self, lightly. Take K. and go to mother's. She had had a letter from Bill, telling how Julia died. Heart disease. Only sick four hours. I am glad it was that instead of what we thought. Go to studio and leave K. while I cash check and do a few errands. Take her again and call on Mrs. Alden in her pretty school house, and Mrs. Chapin. Also Miss Wheeler, who was out. Get some wildflowers on way home. Feed K; Oysters for supper. Try to write poem, "The City Vines" but fail. Eliza has gone to the Pub. Lib.

Tues. Oct. 12th. 1886.

8. Paint my bee twice, and two cards. Mrs. Diman and Miss Alden make me a very pleasant call in the morning; and Henrietta comes later stays a long time. Baby rather worrisome, teeth I suppose. A letter comes from Thomas to mother. I send it up by Eliza.

I get ready to go up to her when Julia Jastram and little Julie call. They go up with me, and mother reads the letter aloud. My poor poor brother! He was not with her; but gone hunting as we all feared. He has taken the great sorrow in a noble way; and means to live well for his orphan boy's sake.————— Letter from Alice Stone Blackwell today, very kind, says "The Answer" covers a year's subscription. The Boston Sunday Herald copied it! Letter from Carrie Hazard. Wants 30 dinner cards, at $1.00 apiece! She shall have them. Write in the evening. Have a cold.

Wed. Oct. 13th. 1886.

6. Write two notes, and copy play for an hour before breakfast. Paint two cards and finish another. A nice call from Miss Wheeler. Eliza was out with the

baby. We go to see mother a little while, and then call on Dr. Allen and wife. Don't get on very well talking with Mrs. A. Home. Bed.

Thurs. Oct. 14th. 1886.

8. Paint one card, woodbine. Kate Bucklin here, stays to lunch. Glad to see her. We go out P.M. with K. See about washwoman, call on mother. Aunt C. comes there. Kate and I bring K. home, and then go to Walter's. She lends me $10.00. Letters from Mrs. Cresson & Carrie Hazard. Sewing machine retaken.

Fri. Oct. 15th. 1886.

9. A very hard night with baby; who has a head cold. Two hours sleep after she's up. Walter very much objects to going, (16th.), says he has a prejudice against the Hazards. Natheless we take the 12.50 train for Peace Dale, and spend the night at Oakwoods. A very very pleasant time. Annie Morse is there. Little Roy comes up also for the night; a delightful little boy. We go with Carrie and Annie to call on the Janviers in the afternoon, and enjoy meeting them exceedingly. Look at Carrie & Annie's sketches in the evening and Margie sings. A rich soft contralto voice. She is radiantly lovely.

Sat. Oct. 16th. 1886.

But O the "billowy bed" they gave us! What is called a "wire mattrass." Too soft is as bad as too hard. But we sleep happily, and wake refreshed. Start at ten for Mrs. Cresson's, and stay there till 4 o'clock; when I return solus, leaving Walter for over Sunday. Safe home, walk up, and find all well and flourishing. Mother here, and the dining room fire made. Time too, it is real cold. Write note to Walter and to landlord; and put Kate to sleep. Tired, but not unpleasantly so.

Sun. Oct. 17th. 1886.

Up late, and do nothing all day but read "What's Mine's Mine"[6] by Macdonald. Take baby up to Mrs. Diman's in the afternoon. Mother came while I was there, also a Mrs. Hinckley. Home. Feed baby. Eliza comes while I am trying to put K. to sleep, and gets me a nice little supper. She is a comfort. Finish book. Bed at eleven.*

Mon. Oct. 18th. 1886.

8.20 or so. Bathe. Breakfast. Write here. Paint all day on begonias. Get used up about 4, as it is dull and cloudy; and walk down to meet Walter at train. He doesn't come—I wasn't sure he would. Walk briskly home. Miss Chapin stops me and walks part way. Mrs. Springer calls. A long letter from Thomas today, with my linen travelling bag, and a pretty pink worsted hood Julia was making for my baby the last thing before she died! It is not done. Write to him in the evening.

Tues. Oct. 19th. 1886.

Paint all day, begonia and neurophila[?]. Walter home about three. Mother in for a few moments, bad cold, wretched. Brought cough syrup for Eliza, who wont take it. So glad to see Walter! Mrs. Cresson sent flowers and Littell's.

Wed. Oct. 20th. 1886.

8 or so. Paint all the morning. Lesson to Valletta at 2. One dollar. She begins to paint flowers, and likes it. I discorse at large on laws of beauty and similar topics. Call on Ada Hazard. Out, but see Mrs. Blake. Stop some time at mother's. Home and play with baby till Walter comes. Put her to sleep, and get so sleepy in consequence that I do nothing in the evening.

Thurs. Oct. 21st. 1886.

8.30. Paint three cards before 2 o'clock. Letter from Bill with further particulars of Julia's death. Four cards done and a fifth started. Sew in the evening, and talk to Lisa, on natural history etc. Baby wakes when I undress and stays so till 1 or 2 o'clock. Walter went to his club.

Fri. Oct. 22nd. 1886.

8.30. Accomplish little. Good lesson to Emily in the morning. Eliza sweeps up stairs. Mary comes with little Anna in the afternoon. Finish one card and do most of another. Sew a little. Go down to the Browns in the evening. Pleasant games of cards. All there, and a Mrs. Wilkinson also. Robert makes an ass of himself by his loudmouthed contempt of women's rights and other justice. It is hard to be despised by such men as that.

Sat. Oct. 23rd. 1886.

9.15. Up till 1 again last night with K. Not sick but awake. Paint one card and finish another. Mrs. Brinnell here cleaning. Get a full mail, three copies of W[oman's]. J[ournal]. with my article "Why women do not reform their dress" in it, box of barberries from Carrie H., letter from Bill, and one from Mary B. Hazard, ordering miniature of her little Betty. Lesson to Villetta, last one. Talk with Mrs. Grimshaw, not successfully. Stop at Walters & leave Rimmer's anatomy. Shop a little, and call on Milly, leaving her some checkerberries. Nice call. Stop for Walter and home. Read W. J. and finish little dress for K. Sleeve made wrong, must alter. Begin Ode to a Fool.

Sunday, Oct. 24th. 1886.

9 or so. Poor night again. Feel rather used up. Drag around generally, but manage to start out with K. and Walter and go to his mother's and then to Jennie's to dinner. Katharine enjoys herself, and so do her relatives. Mrs. Knapp called there. Home by 7.15 or so. Get K. to bed about 8.30. Sleeps pretty well however. Read Littells a little while. Bed.

Mon. Oct. 25th. 1886.

8. Paint five cards by three o'clock—from 9 to 3. Then eyes give out, so stop painting and write 10 pages of fools cap, copying play. Then bathe and dress. Supper. Go to call on Prof. Liscomb and wife. A very wearisome evening to me; spent in looking at photograps of statues.

Tues. Oct. 26th. 1886.

Finish cards. Go down street and get materials for tomorrow's supper. Walk up with Walter. Eliza goes to Library & I put K. to sleep. Copy play.

Wed. Oct. 27th. 1886.

The great day. Succeed in getting everything well arranged and myself dressed by three o'clock. Shortly after Mr. Gillette appears. A very pleasant afternoon with him. Mother comes over to supper, radiant in her best black silk. A good supper. Read play thereafter. He is favorably impressed, but does not stop to give a full opinion, having to catch train. But he liked it. Gave us pass for three to his play now being given here.

Thurs. Oct. 28th. 1886.

A good week since I've had full sleep, K's *doings* of course. She will crawl over into our bed. Rise late and do little. Write a couple of notes, one to Miss Dunham, to whom I also send her cards. One to Charles Saunders. Sleep in the afternoon. Retta Clarke calls, and asks us up to tea at Mrs. Diman's. I go with her and Walter comes later. The satin arrived from Mrs. Dun in the morning, and a note. Also one from Alice Stone Blackwell and a letter from Mrs. Farrell to mother and I.

Fri. Oct. 29th. 1886.

9.30. Good sleep, as I constrain the infant to remain in her own bed. Lesson to Emily. Letter from Mary Bushnell. Sew a little, and make up accts. Go to see "Held by the Enemy" on Mr. Gillette's pass. Take Mary Phelon. Start early and call on mother. Mrs. Springer there. Enjoyed the play very much. A very *dramatic* play; cleverly working on sentiments common to or at least understood by all; and meeting a deserved success. Only one bad actor—Rufus the old darky.

Sat. Oct. 30th. 1886.

8 or so. Good sleep. Feel well. Darn Hose. Stop at Mrs. Diman's and get 12.00, in advance. Go and buy coal. Take N. H. Review to Milly and read Ouida's article to them. Much excitment. Stop and read it to Mrs. Diman and Retta. Bring home "Man's Knowledge of God["] from Mrs. D.'s and read it. Good.

Sun. Oct. 31st. 1886.

Am played a scurry trick by my watch, which lost an hour in the night and yet went on; so after getting all dressed to go with Retta and hear Dr. Hedge, I find myself an hour late. Fairly cry over it. Carry book back to Mrs. Diman's however, and dine there. Retta home with me, but doesn't stay. Nice long call from Sam Simmons.

FIFTEEN

"Traitor to my cause"

November 1, 1886–December 31, 1886

As 1886 drew to a close, Charlotte was finally beginning to gain a sense of accomplishment from her writing. "Get a paper from Walton, N.Y. with [my poem] 'The Answer' in it," she wrote on November 1. "Getting famous! . . . Read Women's Journal and Century in the evening, the latter to Walter. I am very happy."

As Charlotte and Walter immersed themselves into the frenzy of the holiday season, they did, indeed, seem to be very happy. Ultimately, however, they were avoiding, rather than confronting, the issues that would eventually end their marriage. Even though Charlotte continued to experience fatigue, disappointment, and "gloomy days," the two were somehow lulled into a false sense of security. They peacefully coexisted over the next several weeks, with Walter often attending Art Club meetings in the evenings while Charlotte stole whatever quiet moments she could to write or to paint—or to express her growing contempt for domesticity. "Dress and go to Annie Rawson Vaughns tea," Charlotte wrote on December 8. "Very gorgeous indeed, wish I hadn't gone. I despise the whole business," she wrote derisively.

If afternoon teas were not to her taste, neither was any other activity that wasted precious time. "Accomplish nothing in all day, owing to late rising; baby tending, and putting her to sleep in the evening," she protested on December 12. But the next evening was spent more productively and, consequently, more happily. "Do ink dinner cards in the evening—Walter and I are very happy together." Christmas Day was also spent happily with Walter: "Mother puts the baby to sleep; and Walter goes home with her. Then he and I have a little more chocolate and sandwich, and go happily to bed." And on December 26: "Up late, and pass a lazy happy day." But in her New Year's Eve retrospective of the year just past, Charlotte was considerably more ambivalent in her views of both her relationship with Walter and the status of her "world's work."

I have become a person more in harmony with my surroundings; better fitted to live peacefully among my friends; and yet have not lost a keen interest in the world's work. . . .

But I certainly have lost much of my self abandoning enthusiasm and fierce determination in the cause of right. . . . I feel in some ways lowered—degraded—traitor to my cause. But I am not sure, it may be a lingering trace of the disordered period just passed. Within a few weeks, Charlotte would be sure; "the disordered period just passed" would be minor compared to the misery that lay ahead. Indeed, Charlotte was about to confront the most difficult trial of her life.

Mon. November 1st

Paint two cards for Carrie Hazard. Mr. Burleigh here to lunch, and Walter. Get a paper from Walter. Get a paper from Walton N.Y. with "The Answer" in it. Getting famous! Go over and see the house Walter is decorating, call on Mrs. Kimball, go to see mother for a few moments. Read Women's Journal and Century in the evening, the latter to Walter. I am very happy.*

Tues. Nov. 2nd. 1886.

8.35. Paint three cards, good ones. Jennie Bucklin & Tudie Mauran call. I send "Nevada" to the Journal. Walter goes to his Art Club; and I go and call on Dr. Mary Walker. Like her; but am not converted. She has no feeling for beauty in costume; thinks it beneath intelligent beings. She wears heels; and was put to it for a reason when I attacked them. Her costume was old-fashioned, very. Short hair of course.

Wed. Nov. 3rd. 1886.

Don't feel very well. Start sofa cushion. Read all the afternoon. Evening too.

Thurs. Nov. 4th. 1886.

Sew. Finish guimpe and pink dress for Katharine. Mother spends the afternoon and evening. Walter goes to club. Bed late.

Fri. Nov. 5th. 1886.

Letter from Mr. Saunders, announcing his coming. Eliza makes cake and custard and I go down street and get oysters steak and apples. Wait for him at the studio, but he doesn't come. Dr. Knight does though; some talk. Walk up with Walter, and Mr. S. arrives immediately thereafter. Nice talk and nice supper. He writes a letter home, and talked house decoration with Walter afterwards. We walk down and see him off.

Sat. Nov. 6th. 1886.

Feel badly. do little all day. Paint a bit on cushion, and sew a few stitches. Woman's Journal; admiring comment on my Dress Reform article by Celia B. Whitehead. Sleep all P.M. Wash K. and put her to sleep for once. "Nevada" in todays Journal.

Sun. Nov. 7th. 1886.

8.05. Go out with Walter after material for dinner cards. Nice time, but very cold & windy. Return. Put K. to sleep. Arrange trophies of search. Make custard apple-pie, with Horsford crust. Feed K, and self. Paint some, and so does Walter for me. Dine lightly. Sew. Put K. to bed—a work of time. Write to Bill & Thomas.

Mon. Nov. 8th. 1886.

8. Paint on cushion all the morning; Telegram saying Mr. Tewksbury is coming, comes with wife. To lunch and dinner. He and Walter go off together; and I try to get acquainted with Mrs. T. but don't get far. She is shy. A large woman with a fearfully small waist, an absolute deformity. Have great difficulty in not talking to her about it. Mr. T. brought me a great basket of fruit, very nice. Also a box of good candy in the afternoon. Two good meals anyway I gave 'em. Pleasant time.

Tues. Nov. 9th. 1886.

8 or so. Guests depart about 10. Begin to paint at eleven. Finish cushion. Mother and Miss Murphy come in towards night, and admire. Walter likes it much. Try to design a little for the doylies; but dont accomplish much.

Wed. Nov. 10th. 1886.

9. My eyes are troubling me with this fine work. Paint three cards, well. Call on Mrs. Cotton. Go down with Walter and carry linen for doylies over to Carrie's to fringe for me. They were out, so I left stuff with Charlie and went up to Mother S's. Pleasant evening with them. Walter comes for me. Ride home.

Thurs. Nov. 11th. 1886.

7.50. Write letter to Grace. Carry N. A. Review to Dr. Mary Walker. Go to studio & meet Mr. Saunders there. He gets a buggy, and we drive around and look at pretty houses. I take a sketch or two and the addresses. Bring him to lunch. Good one. Walter in later, and they ride down together. Doze an hour and then paint till dark. Put K. to sleep, or at least work two hours at it; and let Lisa go out.

Fri. Nov. 12th. 1886.

8. Lesson to Emily, fruit Study. Paint two cards. Mrs. Cotton brings her mother-in-law down to see my work. Mother S. and Carrie call. Rather used up in the evening.

Sat. Nov. 13th 1886.

7 or so. Paint four cards before two o'clock. One, oak-apple, very good. Try a doyley in the afternoon, just the cutting and edging. Read Womans Journal. Walter goes to the Art Club Jury and I write an article and a half in the evening: "Necessary Steps" & "The Dress of Women etc."

Sun. Nov. 14th. 1886.

Paint one card and finish cotton-flannel dress for K. Walter reads to me.

Mon. Nov. 15. 1886.

10. Paint two cards, nearly three. Bathe & dress. Stop at mothers a little while and then make a very pleasant call on Rev. Mr. Richards & wife. Nice people, and very lovely rooms.

Tues. Nov. 16th. 1886.

ere 7. Paint four cards & finish yesterdays 3rd. Anna, Charlie, and Aunt C. call; and Mrs. Willey. Card show. I go down street. Get some things at Calder's & pay for them. Change books and read "A Bachelors Blunder"[1] at Library. Home with Walter. He paints a landscape for me in the evening, on panel card. Tired. Mother over to supper, and puts K. to sleep.

Wed. Nov. 17th. 1886.

7. Paint five cards, almost six. Mother calls with a little Mrs. Allen, who is to fix the doylies for me. Sleep an hour before supper. Do nothing afterward. Walter paints another panel. John Willey in to see cards.

Thurs. Nov. 18th. 1886.

9. Very tired. Another gloomy day. Paint nothing but a beginning of large card for Mr. Cresson. Call on Mrs. Babcock in the afternoon. Mother there. Show her cards. Call on Prof. Bailey with same intent, but they were engaged. Call on Mrs. Simmons, but she was at Eliza's, and neither of the boys in. Call on the Slicers. Out. Call on Ada. In, and stay to supper. Very pleasant time. Home by 8.30 or so. Read. Bed. Annie & Will Fillinghast call.

Fri. Nov. 19th. 1886. *

8. Put silver lettering on cards. Take them to Tilden's, calling on Mrs. Diman, Annie & Mrs. Fillinghast, Miss Wheeler, & Miss Nightingale on the way, all out. Get some sheath pins & meet Walter at Art Club. My little water color looks very well there. Home in car. Ada had called, too bad. Sew a little. Take a Tamar Indien.[2]

Sat. Nov. 20th. 1886.

8–9 Paint three cards. Mother calls. Woman's Journal. Read it. The ponderous African who is doing our outside work overweens. I must ship her. Read in evening.

Sun. Nov. 21st. 1886.

8.45. Go to with [*sic*] Walter to Hunt's Mills & thereabouts. Get, to my surprise and joy, witch-hazel & cranberry, also little hemlock boughs and fern and tansy. Home. Feed baby and eat a bit of lunch. Paint witch-hazel & part of cranberry. Lizzie calls, with little Marian Elder; radiant in scarlet coat and black velvet hood. Then Robert arrives with some queer pattern of vase he wants me to draw for him. Then Mr. and Mrs. Smythe and their baby. The poor little tot is better, but O so thin & weak. Katharine looked like a great pink peony side of him. Then Mr. & Mrs. Westcott call; not staying long. She is going to travel with the girls this winter! The Smythes stay to dinner, and seem to enjoy themselves. Tired of course.

Mon. Nov. 22nd. 1886.

7.15. Finish all cards by 1.30. Do them up and take down to studio. Send by mail, with note to Carry. Read at Pub. Lib. an hour. Go to see Anna and Clarence in the evening, and C. gives me a very clear talk on politics.

Tues. Nov. 23rd. 1886.

9 or later. Finish large m.g. card for Mr. Cresson Sen. Mother in for a few minutes. Put K to sleep and let Elise go out for a call. Fall asleep in my chair.

Wed. Nov. 24th. 1886.

Paint large gentian card for Mr. Cresson Sen. Letter from Carry with check for $36.00. Begin pink satin fan. Walk out and meet Walter.

Thurs. Nov. 25th. 1886.

THANKSGIVING DAY. An extremely disappointing day. Prepare to have dinner at two, and get everything well underway when Walter arrives and says they wont come till late. Eat a lunch, and have dinner at five, but don't enjoy it. Mother S. brought me over a huckleberry pie and a jar of quince. Pleasant time. Sew some

Fri. Nov. 26th. 1886.

Paint some on fan. Go down to cask [*sic*] check and order coal. Go to Pub. Lib. to read. Thomas Hope accosts me there, and is so conversational that I take him out and he walks home with me, stopping at studio. Mother and Mrs. Springer come over and mother puts the baby to sleep. Miss Oldfield and Dr. Mary Walker call, and we have a lively evening.

Sat. Nov. 27th. 1886

Paint on fan, but don't feel well, so go and get mother to call on Mrs. Smythe with me, which she does, gladly. Says she thinks the child will be a cripple. Home to good turkey soup, in a very contentend [*sic*] frame of mind. Put K. to sleep. And go to sleep myself thereafter.

Sun. Nov. 28th. 1886.

Cut Walters hair. Sew some; sewed in both sleeves of K's nightgown wrong!

Mon. Nov. 29th. 1886

Paint on fan; like it better. John Willey calls with reciept for the $30.00. The fifteen arrives from Mrs. Dun. Take it down and cash it. Pub. Lib. awhile and read "This Man's Wife."[3] Leave early. Call on Ada, out; on Annie Fillinghast; out, Mrs. Diman, in. Then home, and sup. Run around and pay John the 15.00$. Stop and see mother a few minutes. Mrs. Springer there.

Tues. Nov. 30th.

Finish fan. Note from Mrs. Cresson; her father-in-law wants 12 cards, flowers. Do six sheets note paper. Go to see Mr. Smythe about his baby. Call on Ada. On Annie Fil: out. on Mrs. Allen & get some of the doylies. Walter does seven sheets of paper for me in the evening.

DECEMBER.
1886—
Wed. 1st.

Paint wildroses and appleblossoms. Sew a little. Mother in about noon. Century comes. Walter does nine sheets of paper in the evening, and I read to him. Stockton is too tiresome to read aloud. Send off fan to Mrs. Dun with note.

*Thurs. Dec. 2nd. 1886.**

Work on appleblossoms and nasturtiums. Walter goes to his club, and I call on Mrs. Buffum opposite, and about spend the evening.

Fri. Dec. 3rd. 1886.

Emily as usual. Paint till dusk, then dress up and go with Mrs. Buffam to call on Annie Vaughn, née Rawson. Then on mother, who is blue. It's a cold spell, very. Go to the Slicers in the evening, and spend a pleasant evening while Walter is at an Art Club Meeting. He stops for me.

Sat. Dec. 4th. 1886.

Kate Bucklin comes at about 10, and stays till four. I go with her to see mother, and we two help Aunt Caroline bring around some bed clothing from Mary's. Then down street with Kate. Stop at Walter's, out. Kate gets some apples. Back to Walter's & wait awhile. He doesn't arrive, so Kate comes back as far as Hope St. with me. Nice girl. Finish cotton flannel dress for baby.

*Sun. Dec. 5th. 1886.**

Paint a little and so does Walter. Eliza doesn't go home as the snow is deep and driving. Make little snow scene in the evening.

Mon. Dec. 6th. 1886.

Paint on passion flowers. Eliza goes home. Get dinner. Walter does more of the note paper while I paint two more snow scenes.

Tues. Dec. 7th. 1886.

Snows again, heavily. Paint water lilies and draw little dancing figurines in the evening while Walter finishes the note paper. Note to Mrs. Grimshaw.

Wed. Dec. 8th. 1886.

Paint blue flowers in vase. Clear and bright. Dress and go to Annie Rawson Vaughns tea. Very gorgeous indeed, wish I hadn't gone. I despise the whole business. Stop at mother's. Only Aunt Caroline there. Paint a nice little bird in the snow and Walter does some pretty cards.

Thurs. Dec. 9th. 1886.

With much ado in preparation succeed in inking five of the little doylies. Go to see mother again towards dusk. Miss Murphy there. Some good Indian pudding. Get the last two doyleys. Finish drawing them in the evening. Walter paints a most ludicrous ape in a tree, doleful to the last extreme.

Fri. Dec. 10th. 1886.

Finish doyleys. Check comes for Walter and I go down with it. Cash it. Pay Calder $10.00 and get some more things. Meet Hattie Salisbury and she goes about with me: get some roses to paint. Stop at Walter's with her. Dr. Knight there. Miss Wheeler calls there too. She didn't show much sense in her remarks. We all admire Walter's portrait of Mayor Doyle, just begun. Home together. Eliza goes to the Library and I put Kate to sleep. Then try my new cards, write here, etc.

Sat. Dec. 11th. 1886.

Sleep very ill and rise very late in consequence. Paint till dusk on roses, Walter says the best I have done yet. Mother in. Do little salt and pepper in the evening. Pretty.

Sun. Dec. 12th. 1886.

Accomplish nothing in all day, owing to late rising; baby tending, and putting her to sleep in the evening—

Mon. Dec. 13th. 1886.

Draw and paint Gladiolus. Emily Diman and Charlotte T. down for an hour, E's lesson. Do ink dinner cards in the evening—Walter and I are very happy together.

Tues. Dec. 14th. 1886.

Walter home to lunch and then goes off to Sakonnet. Paint gladiolus and part of white lilies. Go to Pub. Lib. and change books. Get two blocks and two salt & pepper sets at Calders. Go to mothers to supper. 8 now.

Wed. Dec. 15th. 1886.

7.50 or so. Slept well though Walterless. Up and at work early. Finish white lilies and start pansies. Mother over P.M. with little Mrs. Allen to see the doyleys. I go down town and get three pansies. Meet Mr. Slicer and walk up to Transit St. with him. Home. Sup, talk, and to work again. Finish cards. Eliza goes home with mother.

Thurs. Dec. 16th. 1886.

Paint seven hours straight; Pansies. Snowstorm.

Fri. Dec. 17th. 1886.

Paint daisies in tumbler. Walter gets home ere noon, much to our mutual satisfaction. He looks the paintings all over and adds a few touches. Go up to Mrs. Diman's and show her the lot. She was pleased. Draw sweet peas in the evening.

Sat. Dec. 18th. 1886.

Paint sweet peas, and finally touch and sign all of them. Emily diman comes for her lesson. Carry them round to show mother, and then down to Walter, who sends them off. *Horrid slush.* Eliza goes down street, and I put K. to sleep.

Sun. Dec. 19th. 1886

Wash out doyleys and send off, with bill. Get up some invitations for relatives. Charlie Baxter comes to dinner. Put K. to sleep and fall asleep myself.

Mon. Dec. 20th. 1886.

Pretty well used up. Nap after breakfast. Mother comes over and tends baby, and Eliza and I go down street and do some Xmas shopping. She carries a bag and basket; and we fill them both. Enjoy it, especially taking her into the rich stores. Stop for Walter and ride home. *Tired.* Dine. He goes down to Art Club building to do a frieze for them. I write more invitations and finish letter to Grace. I learn from Mrs. Cresson that "Nevada" has been copied by a Philadelphia paper. Write here.

Tues. Dec. 21st. 1886.

Walter not home till after 12 last night, and I don't get up till 12 today. Emily comes for lesson at that time. Then Mrs. Diman calls with Edward Hale. I carry invitations to Anna & Mary. Stop to see mother, who wasn't in. Go down st. Stop at Walters. Edward calls there with Miss Caroline Richmond. Try to change Walter's slippers and home with him. Edward there already, in amicable relations with baby. I put on silk dress and red slippers, and we have a good dinner. Give him the grig card. He has to go somewhere else so departs; Bed early.

Wed. Dec. 22nd. 1886.

Stay at home all day, waiting for Ada and painting. Mother calls P.M. Ada calls later, with a lovely white coat for Kate. Walter of in the evening, and I fix presents and write verses. Check from Mrs. Dun.

Thurs. Dec. 23rd.*

Emily for lesson. Paint salt for Ada. Go down st. Cash check and spend it, giving Kate her ten and leaving eight at mothers for Mrs. Allen. Home & paint more, finishing paper. Dr. Knight calls. Says baby has bronchitis. Walter. Supper. Mrs. Cresson's box arrives; full. Walter, silk hdkfs, under flannels, candy. Me, red Jersey, hdkfs, bonnet, trimming, ruching; Kate, cloak & cap; & picture book. I write to her, and paint some.

Fri. Dec. 24th. 1886.*

Down st. again, meeting Emily. Cast [*sic*] $57.00 check. Give Walter five and get a few more things. Home. Meet Kate Bucklin; who had left gifts here. Find Emily, and she finishes calendar for her mother. Fix tree in the evening. Tired. Got violets for Walter.

Christmas Day. 1886.

Up first and give Walter his violets and a bit of a verse.[4] Finish fixing tree and presents in the morning while Walter goes down town. Bathe and dress in good season. Anna, etc. first arrivals; then Mary etc. Walter has to go at the last moment and borrow mother's teaspoons. Clarence dessicates the turkey carcase. Stetsons, en masse at a little before five; all but Mr. Gilmore, who comes later. Get the repast ready about 5.15, the two families fraternizing meanwhile. A delightful supper, which I enjoy as much as anybody. Chopped turkey sandwiches, delicate, small, and crustless, hot coffee and chocolate, some of mothers nice rusk and Eliza's sponge cake and cookies, fruit and candy. Enough and *good*. I ate for six myself. Then our tree, gorgeous with candles. An immensity of presents, the floor and table full. Universal satisfaction. Our folks go first on account of children; all of whom behaved admirably. All depart by about eight. Mother puts the baby to sleep; and Walter goes home with her. Then he and I have a little more chocolate and sandwich, and go happily to bed.

Sun. Dec. 26th. 1886.*

Up late, and pass a lazy happy day. Walter has to go to studio and do some plates. While he is gone I rearrange tree as well as I can, and recandle it. Also finish large card for Sophie while Katharine plays about with her new toys. Ada and Mr. Hazard, with Whitney, Ellery, and Sophie, arrive, and we have a re-illumination. Manage to give something to them all. They have scarce gone when Louise and Emily Diman & Ellen Clarke appear; cake and candy for both parties. Walter home. Sup on the remains of the feast.

Monday. Dec. 27th. 1886.

Eliza up at five with her new alarm clock; and gets her washing done in great shape. Mother over P.M. I wash breakfast dishes, and baby, and make beds while Eliza feeds her. Get letter from Lucy Anderson & cards from the children. Cards from Carrie Hazard Xmas day; and Dr. Channing. These last lovely photograps, most welcome to me.

Tues. Dec. 28th. 1886.

Ironing day. I wash dishes again. Annie Aborn calls P.M. with Charlotte Fill., finding Kate dressless save for her little cotton flannel underdress.

Wed. Dec. 29th. 1886.

Got a chill putting Kate to sleep Monday; and didn't improve it last night by a weary nap on a chair and two beds. Feel quite ill, weak and cold. Lie down at about ten, and sleep till 1.20. Then rise and dress. Note from Ada, saying she cannot meet me as appointed. Go to see mother. Out. Call on Mary Phelon and get warm. Then start out again, and meet mother. Back home with her and have some friccasseed chicken; my first meal today. Henrietta Brown calls. Mrs. Springer later. She brought me some of her queer German confectionery. Home. Start with Walter to Julia Jastram's. All out but Eddy. Go down to the Browns and spend evening. Home. Eat a little. bed.

Thurs. Dec. 30th. 1886.

Up late. Now 12.30 and have done nothing but tend baby and write up here. Write letters to Dr. Channing, Lucy Anderson, Mrs. Lynch, Mrs. Geer, (note) and Miss Pease. Sew some. Feel pretty well. Century came, with two numbers of The Critic as advertisement, and letter for Walter from Mr. Saunders. Read and sew in the evening, winding up between ten and eleven with temperance.

Fri. Dec. 31st. 1886.

Up about 8. Sew some, tend baby, read a little in "Century". Arrange Mss. and Journal's in the evening.

I leave behind me tonight a year of much happiness, growth, and progress; also of great misery. But the happiness and progress are real and well founded; and the misery was owing mainly to a diseased condition of the nervous system. It is past, I hope forever.

I have become a person more in harmony with my surroundings; better fitted to live peacefully among my friends; and yet have not lost a keen interest in the world's work. I can write and paint better than before; and think as well when I am strong enough.

But I certainly have lost much of my self abandoning enthusiasm and fierce determination in the cause of right. Perhaps it is as well for the ultimate work done. I do not feel so. I feel in some ways lowered—degraded—traitor to my cause. But I am not sure, it may be a lingering trace of the disordered period just passed. When I know myself to be *well* in all ways I can better judge.

I have written half a play this year and a little good poetry. Also some painting and drawing which has been very profitable to me as work. This is an immense gain on last year and that before. At any rate, I feel happy and contented with my home and family; and have hope and courage for the New Year.

May it be fruitful of good!

SIXTEEN

"Very sick with nervous prostration"

January 1, 1887–April 19, 1887

CHARLOTTE began 1887 with a mission: "Have started on a course of reading about women," she asserted on January 5. Some of the reading she dismissed as too "scriptural and solemn"; the works she preferred were those which allowed "duties to Society as well as husband and child." As had always been the case with Charlotte, self-education through reading would inform her life's philosophy; it would help to shape her plan of "serving humanity." Conversely, however, it would also amplify her discontent over her limited roles of wife and mother. On January 6 Charlotte began to draft an article "on the distinction between the sexes," a theme which would influence most of her writing from that point onward. Walter attempted to be supportive, reading aloud to her Margaret Fuller's book, *Woman in the Nineteenth Century*, but he was clearly threatened by Charlotte's intellectual growth. He quickly imposed a two-week moratorium on her reading anything about "the woman question." She nevertheless continued to write, sending off an article titled "A Protest against Petticoats" because, she insisted, "it is well to keep the ball rolling."

Charlotte did, however, try to maintain a balance between indulging her own needs for intellectual stimulation and fulfilling her domestic responsibilities. She wasn't always successful. Sunday, January 9: "A wearying day. . . . Fall with K[atharine]. in my arms; bumping her head and lamming my knees. Then she tires me out in the sleepgoing; and I get real nervous and shaky. Walter gives me a warm bath and puts me to bed." Although Walter tried to console Charlotte when she became weepy, his patience began to wane, and subconsciously, perhaps, he began to retaliate. Undermining her confidence where she was most vulnerable, Walter criticized her maternal competence: "Begin to give Kate her bath before breakfast, but get discouraged by Walter, who thinks eating directly afterward is injudicious. Accomplish little all day."

Walter's insecurity about Charlotte's renewed interest in women's issues was undoubtedly exacerbated by their latest financial setback—after a period of brief prosperity from the sale of some artwork—which reached a crisis in mid-February. "No coal, no money," Charlotte reported succinctly. "I tell Walter he *must* get it, or I will; and he does." Just four days later Alice Stone Blackwell asked Charlotte to manage a women's suffrage column in the Providence newspaper, which Charlotte agreed to do. She also resumed her reading about women's issues with renewed vigor and commiserated with "another victim" whose husband used his "'marital rights' at her vital expense." Significantly, a few days later, Charlotte reported feeling "desperately out of place among a lot of young mothers" at a birthday party which she attended with Katharine. Charlotte was, perhaps unwittingly, beginning to more clearly articulate her growing conviction: the conventional roles of wife and mother made her feel desperately ill at ease and "out of place." This sense of displacement was at the center of her conflict. Her first priority was, and would always remain, her commitment to helping humanity.

A visit to Martha Lane and her newborn daughter, Margaret, in late February likely contributed to Charlotte's growing unrest. While she was buoyed by the appearance of her women's suffrage column in the *People*, she seems to have never fully recovered from the exhaustion that resulted from a cold she suffered during her visit to Martha and which she passed to Katharine. By March 9, Charlotte was feeling the effects of Katharine's illness: "I give out completely in the morning, crying with weariness." But even when Katharine seemed to recover, Charlotte did not completely regain her strength. March 11: "When [Walter] gets back I am asleep on the bed, exhausted." And on March 13: "I have a crying fit while trying to make Kate go to sleep, and am all used up. . . . I put the baby to bed and collapse therein myself." Charlotte's depression had reached a dangerous new stage. The months of physical exhaustion and constant worry over their most recent financial troubles, added to the years of unresolved conflicts and resentment toward Walter, took their toll. "Get chilly and have a crying fit. Sleep ill, and am utterly useless the next day." Even Maria Pease, the nurse who had offered Charlotte kindness and sympathy just before and after Katharine's birth, seemed not to understand the extent of Charlotte's depression. "I love her, but she doesn't sooth me at all," Charlotte complained. Charlotte was still seeking to be soothed, supported, loved; she was a conflicted young mother still desperately in need of mothering herself.

During the spring months Charlotte had resumed her exercise regimen at the Providence Ladies Gymnasium. Although the workouts provided stress reduction and time away from Walter and Katharine, she soon started skipping time at the gymnasium in favor of her writing. When Charlotte initially resumed her routine in mid-January, she could barely contain her joy. "Find myself happy to the verge of idiocy at being there again," she confessed. "Am as light apparently but not as strong as of old." By March 18, however, Charlotte simply could not accommodate both activities in her schedule. Something had to go. Exercising was dispensable; writing was not: "I dont' go to gym., because I want to write some paragraphs for 'The Amendment.'" Within a couple of days, however, Charlotte was once again in the throes of despair: "Getting back to the edge of insanity again," she wrote somberly. "Write my 'column' though."

Over the next several weeks, Charlotte reported feeling increasingly anxious and on the verge of insanity. The combination of Katharine's frequent illnesses, Charlotte's subsequent exhaustion, increasing friction between her and Walter, and the defeat of the amendment supporting women's suffrage, which was a profound disappointment to Charlotte, all contributed to her "hysteria." On April 5 she was saved from a "hysterical" fit by the timely arrival of her longtime friend Jim Simmons, who managed to calm her. Walter, however, unable to cope with Charlotte's mood swing or to accept Simmons's ability to soothe Charlotte, stormed out of the house. When Walter returned, he broke down, and Charlotte had to suppress her own misery in order to attend to his.

During the following week Charlotte's depression deepened, and she began to make inquiries of her physician, Dr. Knight, about treatment in a sanitarium. On April 13 Charlotte began a week's "rest" at her mother's house, while Walter slept alone in the home that they had shared for nearly three years. By April 18 a decision had been made to send Charlotte to Philadelphia to seek the rest cure from Dr. Silas Weir Mitchell. Her longtime friend Mrs. J. Lewis Diman generously donated the $100 that would cover the cost of the treatment. Charlotte wanted to get well, but she also wanted Walter to accept at least some blame for her condition. Her unrestrained hostility toward him peppers the pages of her April 18 entry. In a rare departure from her usual practice, she used the diary entry to damn Walter directly, accusing him of broken promises, holding him accountable for her pain, and insisting that he bear sole responsibility for his misguided and destructive judgment, "before it seeks to mould another life as it has mine."

The next day, Tuesday, April 19, was Charlotte's last diary entry before she left to seek treatment from Mitchell. The entry is an ironic and chilling metaphorical depiction of Charlotte's condition as she describes being "locked out" of her home and "struggling" to find her way back in "with much effort." Her final words for 1887 are stark and ominous: "Begin to write an account of myself for the doctor."

January 1st. 1887

8 and after. Sew on Kate's dress and tend that damsel till three o'clock, when I dress in waterproof attire, and ride over to Calder's. Restock my paint box and get some other supplies. Go to Pub. Lib. and get new card. Fill it with books on Women. Read article in the Forum on Woman Suffrage by Higginson. Buy some hose and lace for Jersey sleeves. Stop at Walter's and he gives me his

Xmas present as a New Year's gift; an exquisite Calendar on parchment; full of his sweetest thoughts in color and verse.[1] A dainty lovely thing. Bless his dear heart! Home together in the awful slop and slush and ice. Dine well on roast chicken. Then I christen my new sketch book and pencils. Then here.

*Sun. Jan 1st. 1887.**

8 and after. A far better Sunday than usual. I am busy all day; mending, writing, arranging. Good dinner. I find I get tired and cross—i.e. used up, at about 5 P.M. Put Kate to sleep and then finish "Ode to A Fool." Mother came over at dusk, in spite of the terrible icyness just to see how I was. Dear mother!

Monday. Jan. 3rd. 1887.

8.10. Do not feel well; but improve as the day passess [sic]. Wash dishes, read Sun. Journal, loaf rather. Take Kate and call on Annie Aborn and the others. Wagon wheel out of order, and Mrs. T. brings me home in sleigh. Photograph of Chester Lane and note from Mrs. Geer, with W. Journal. Read it, and read to K. Walter. Supper. Write part of article "Ought Wealthy Women to Work."

Tues. Jan. 4th. 1887.

8.20. Iron an hour in hopes of getting out in the afternoon. Sew some. Anna, Aunt C. and Charlie come and stay an hour or two, much to Kate's delight. "Alpha" comes. Walter goes to show Mayor Doyles portrait to "relatives & friends". Write. Our refractory student lamp takes fire, and Eliza and I have a lively time. Scorch the rugs and the table, ruin the lamp, spill the ink, and Eliza cuts her hand and breaks a pane of glass trying to open a window. I put the fire out with rugs, and don't get burnt at all.

Wed. Jan. 5th. 1887.

10.30. Sleep ill, owing to Kate's waking, and the night's being warmer. Up very late, 10.30. Have cup of coffee and some bread and butter. Sew some, write some; and ride down town. See dentist and make appointment. Get cloth for gym. suit. Get raw sienna at Calder's. Carry cloth to Mrs. Geer on Maple St. Call on Hattie Salisbury, out. See her mother though. Call on May Brown. Out. Call on Milly. Go to Pub. Lib. and read Howell's "Mouse trap". Rather poor for him; too exaggerated to be funny.[2] Get "Women of France" by Julia Kavanagh. Have started on a course of reading about women. 1st Monod's "Life & Mission of Women". Very scriptural and solemn, the rib theory at its utmost. 2nd. "Women in America." A little better than Monod; allowing duties to Society as well as husband and child. This third is historical and promises well. Stop for Walter. Out. Ride home. Good supper. Alter one of K's night dresses again, making it a big bag this time. Walter goes down to have his exhibition of Mayor Doyle's portrait.

Thurs. Jan. 6th. 1887.

9.20 or so. Make buttonholes in Katharine's skirt. Bathe that bewitching damsel and put her to sleep. Begin article on the distinction of the sexes. Read with my dinner. Mend some. Go to see mother between 5 & 6. Home. Supper. Go up to Mrs. Diman's with Walter, and stay there till 9.30 or near it. Home. Write here. Presently he will come from the studio, dear boy!

Fri. Jan. 7th. 1887.

8.45. Emily Diman for first lesson of new term. After K. is asleep I paint my hand.[3] Sew some buttons on and go to Mrs. Geer to try on gym. suit. Stop for Walter and walk up together. He goes down again. I draw in charcoal, an ideal head and a sketch of Eliza.

Sat. Jan. 8th. 1887.

Mend all day. Walter calls on a prospective sitter, Miss Smith, in the evening; and I go to see mother. Sew. Walter stops for me. Cold.

Sun. Jan. 9th. 1887.

9 or so. A wearying day. Mend some. Get supper as usual. Fall with K. in my arms; bumping her head and lamming my knees. Then she tires me out in the sleepgoing; and I get real nervous and shaky. Walter gives me a warm bath and puts me to bed.

Mon. Jan. 10th. 1887.

8.15. Bring K. down and feed her. Breakfast. Wash dishes. Sew some. Put K. to sleep and draw skulls, studying the bones. Dine on pie. Go down and sit for Walter as Eve. Shop a little. Stop for Walter again and home together. Good dinner. Hem two dishclothes. Look over Ballads to decide on one for our Xmas picture book. Choose "The Dragon of Waultey".

Tues. Jan. 11th. 1887.

late. Sew some. Take Kate over to see Mrs. Buffum's little girls in the afternoon. Very pleasant call. Draw dragons in the evening with Walter.

Wed. Jan. 12th. 1887.

8. or so. Start down in the morning with Walter, meaning to call on Miss Chapin; but she has a model; so I go to see Susie Stetson instead. Very pleasant time there. Walk back, and have two teeth filled at Gay's. Then go to library to get book for Susie. Then walk up to Mrs. Geer's for gym. suit. Not done. Walk back, stopping at gym. to see about hours. Then to Walter's, and walk home. 5 miles I guess. Read in the evening.

Thurs. Jan. 13th. 1886. {sic}

8.45. Sew some. Ada comes at 11 and takes me sleighing for an hour. Baby makes an uncommon todo over her nap. Take her over to mother's in the afternoon. Thomas has lost his position as Clerk of Court, or is to lose it soon. Hope he'll come east. Home. Begin to seat chair for Eliza. Walter goes to his club in the evening and I call on the Wells'. Pleasant evening; very. Home. Write here.

Fri. Jan. 14th, 1887.

8.20. Lesson to Emily. Bathe & bed sweet Kate. Draw an hour. Feed K. & self. Finish "Women of France." A profitable book in some ways. Read "A Tale of Two Cities" to Walter in the evening, and sew some while he reads

Sat. Jan. 15th. 1887.

8.40. Sew some. Kate as usual. Do up bottle of Avena for Lucy Anderson. Write to Thomas & Martha. Take car down street in snowstorm. Carry books to Pub. Lib. Go to P. O. Stop for Walter and walk home together. Good roast beef dinner. Read my story book while he reads W. Journal & looks at his big volume of sculpture. Then we read Tale of Two Cities.

Sun. Jan. 16th. 1887.

Very tired and miserable. Do nothing to speak of. Mother over in the afternoon. Cut Walter's hair, well. Walter puts baby to sleep, supplemented by Eliza when she comes. Read some.

Mon. Jan. 17th. 1887.

Still feel poorly. Arrange items of dress, and depart at 6 for the gymnasium. Speedily make friends; and resume my old position. Find myself happy to the verge of idiocy at being there again. Am as light apparently but not as strong as of old. Miss a car in returning and have to wait half an hour on the bridge, but there are several of us so we do not mind. Home happy. Chocolate and bread and butter.

Tues. Jan. 18th. 1887.

9.30! Feel well. Sew some. The Briggs girls call, wanting some painting done. Retta Clarke calls. Sit up late and finish Tale of Two Cities. It is a poem.

Wed. Jan. 19th. 1887.

Start down early and have two more teeth filled. To be six dollars. Go up to mother Stetson's with Walter for dinner and stay there most of the afternoon. Shop a little and stop for Walter. Home. Feel very tired. He reads to me, "Women of the 19th Century," by Margaret Fuller.[4]

Thurs. Jan. 20th. 1887.

8.20. Sew some. Kate Bucklin comes, and stays till four or so. Susie and the children come about three. Pleasant afternoon, very; Guss comes up with Walter. Good dinner. They take 8.30 car. Write.

Fri. Jan 21st. 1887.

Lesson to Emily. Sew some, and read. Go over in the afternoon and get Mrs. Buffum to bring the chicks over. We have a nice talk. Emily Briggs calls with the satin for me to paint. Walter home early and dresses for Mr. Pegram's dinner. I go down with him and go to the gym. Feel very tired and draggy. Talk with Mr. Smith about new gym. Call at Miss Oldfield's for my North American. See her and Dr. Walker. Home. Sup.

Sat. Jan. 22nd. 1887.

8. Feel very mean, but gradually recover. Woman's Journal comes, always welcome. Write part of "A Protest Against Petticoats," answering a plea for them. It is well to keep the ball rolling. Go over to see mother a few moments. Mrs. Springer there. Home. Sup. Write.

Sun. Jan. 23rd. 1887.

9.5. Finish letter to Martha and article against petticoats. Also dress for Kate. A warm thaw. Mother over to dinner and stays to put K. to sleep. Walter was to go out; but didn't. Read Sun. Journal. Finish Margaret Fuller's book; Fine! Bed 10.30.

Mon. Jan. 24th. 1887.

7.40. Feel very draggy and appetiteless. Southerly storm; rain coming. See to Kate and wash dishes. Formulate resolutions on health. Go to gym in evening. Walk up with Miss Davis. Stop to see how Louise is and find Retta there. Talk awhile. Bath.*

Tues. Jan. 25th. 1887.

Paint white satin square for Miss Briggs. Call on Retta again in the evening. Nice letter from Grace.

Wed. Jan. 26th. 1887.

8.20 Out in the morning with Walter. Call on Miss Chapin till 1. Lunch at Creamery. Go to Pub. Lib. and look up books for Susie. Tiresome, very. Snow storm to come home in. Mrs. Buffum called and brought Macey's catalogue for me. Begin Carlyle's French Revolution to Walter.

Thurs. Jan. 27th. 1887.

Paint on passion flowers for Ada. Make design for valentine card. Go out to find picture of mountain ash and find tree itself on Waterman St. which does as well. Meet Annie Fillinghast and she invites herself to go down to Walter's studio. We go, and she manifests rather less artistic spirit and receptivity than I gave her credit for. Then we go to a market for her to rebuke the man, and then home. I stop with her a few moments to warm my feet—she had to walk slow. Walter goes to his club; and I read some of Uncle Edwards books.

Fri. Jan. 28th. 1887

Paint mountain ash on satin. Go to see mother. Eddie Jastram comes to play chess with her, and plays a game and a half with me—both in his favor. Then I leave satin at Miss Briggs's and get the $4.00 therefor. Home in the wet, sup, and go to gym. Very few there. Don't have a very good time. Ride home. Have chocolate and bread.

Sat. Jan. 29th. 1887.

By mistake Walter shut the window and I sleep very ill. Feel dolorous therefor. Mabel Luther & Alice Peyton call—Emily comes for her lesson and pays for the term. The glass in our cracked window falls out and I send for a glazier, vide Eliza and Walter. He comes, two of him and set the light, much to Katharine's entertainment. Paint some on passion flowers. My new drawing-table arrives; a bargain and I utilize it straitway. Price only $3.00! Nice letter from Martha.

Sun. Jan. 30th. 1887.

As usual a doleful day. Mrs. Diman & Emily call for a moment or two, and I lend her two of Uncle Edward's books to read to Louise. Write to Martha. Walter puts K. to sleep.

Mon. Jan. 31st.

7.20. Do dishes, wash K. and start out with her in 11.20 car to spend day at Grandma Stetsons. Pleasant time. Home to supper. Then gym. Also pleasant time. Walk up.

Tues. February 1st.

7.20. Paint on passion flowers and design for Valentine. Mother in. Call on Anna between 5 & 6. Draw for Valentine in the evening.

Wed. February 2nd.

9.30 Down street with Walter in snowstorm. Send two poems to John Boyle O'Reilly. Try to get work of Reid, Printer, but fail. Order coal. Go to Pub. Lib. and get book for Eliza. Write article "Appeal for the Gymnasium". Go to Young Women's tea room & get good lunch, big cup chocolate, two biscuit & butter, two fishballs, 14 cts. Back to library & finish article. Call on Milly. Pay Carl Westcott for the necktie he let me have, 50 cts. Stop for Walter and walk home. Read article to Walter. He likes it very much. Copy it in the evening. Good day.

Thurs. Feb. 3rd. 1887.

Go down with Walter. Stop to see Art Club building. Leave article with the unpropitious Williams, Ed. of Journal. Ride home. Bathe Kate. Nap in chair. Lunch. Read gym. book brought from the Library. Sew some. Call on Mrs. Bradford, and Mrs. Blodgett. Home. Sew. sup. sew. Talk. Write this.

Fri. Feb. 4th. 1887.

Lesson to Emily. Officiate with Kate. Paint head of infant. lunch. See to Kate again. Paint on Valentine. Kate Bucklin calls. Sup hastily & ride down town. Gym. Good time. Ride home with Miss Allen.

Sat. Feb. 5th. 1887.

Paint all day and go over to see mother towards night. Walter brings home "The History of Womankind in Western Europe". I had left off my course of reading for two weeks, to oblige him. This is a very useful book.

Sun. Feb. 6th. 1887.

Walter paints on Valentine for me. Write to Martha. Roast beef for dinner. Read some.

Mon. Feb. 7th. 1887.

Begin to give Kate her bath before breakfast, but get discouraged by Walter, who thinks eating directly afterward is injudicious. Accomplish little all day, but have a very jolly time at the gym. in the evening. I seem to slip into my old position of inspirer very easily. And the girls like it. Walk up with Miss Bailey; an attractive earnest little woman. Chocolate & bed.

Tues. Feb. 8th. 1887.

9. Accomplish little again; some small sewing and reading only. We spend the evening with Mother. Mrs. Springer there. Did write some too; short paragraphs on the suffrage question for Mrs. Stone Blackwell, with letter to her.

Wed. Feb. 9th. 1887.

Stay in in the morning, and see to Kate, as Eliza had ironing left over and a cold. Make calls P.M: Mrs. Hopkins, out, Mrs. Vaughn, in. Mrs. Kendall, out, Mrs. Blodgett, unable to see me, Mrs. Diman the same, Mrs. Chamberlain, out. An unsatisfactory time too, though some good talk with Mrs. V. Read in evening.

Thurs. Feb. 10th. 1887.

Feel badly again; but lie late and rise fresher at 10. Finish "Chaplet of Pearls",[5] borrowed of Mrs. Diman yesterday. Sew a little. Walter goes to club, and I go and call on Rev. Frederic Hinckley. Mixed sensations.

Fri. Feb. 11th. 1887.

Very poor day. accomplish very little. Walter brings Max Kilvert home to supper. A very nice boy indeed, I like him. All walk down together, but I don't go to gym; having left my black hose at home. Walter goes to an Art Club Committee meeting; and I stay in his studio and read Ruskin.[6] Feel much better for it.

Sat. Feb. 12th. 1887.

Feel well. Finish passion flowers. Emily Diman, long lesson. Walk up with her; stop and see Louise a moment, walk up and down with Mrs. D. a few moments; then down to Mrs. Blake's; leave my picture and collect—$6.00. Stop to see if Emma Vaughn was coming to see me, find she was, go to mother's— out, to Mary Phelon's & get some lunch, then back for Emma. She comes home with me and we spend a pleasant afternoon; I talking much. Mother here some two hours—goes after I come. Mend in the evening.

Sun. Feb. 13th. 1887.

10! Get Kate attended to and go over to Carrie's to dinner. Start in 3 o'clock car. Nice time. Home ere 8. Katharine very good indeed, as usual.[7] Eliza comes and puts her to sleep.

Mon. Feb. 14th. 1887.[8]

A dreary and useless day. Attend to Kate and wash dishes. Dr. Knight comes to see about K: says her liver is not working right, and to give her meat. Leaves medicine. Mother in a little while. Carry up to see Mrs. Cotton; and she (K.) makes herself disagreeable as usual. But the children are angelic and get on with her very well. Home tired out. Eat no supper. Gym. Good time there. Walk home with Miss Bailey, stopping at the Browns to leave invitation. Home. Sup. Bed.

Tues. Feb. 15th. 1887.

A Financial Crisis. No coal, no money. I tell Walter he *must* get it, or I will; and he does. Sit doleful a little, then manage to eat something, and get to work. Finish of Valentine; doctoring Walter's part a good deal. Then go up stairs; and write another verse of "The Sea." After supper Walter writes letter of Opphacher Bros. and fixes Valentine to send off. Then I try to make him design another card; but he don't work.

Wed. Feb. 16th. 1887.

Design Xmas card, attend to Kate, dine, tuck a small skirt, dress self & infant and go to mother's. Out. Call on Mrs. Allen next door. Out. Go to Anna's & spend the afternoon. Kate and Charlie have a fine time. Home. Meet Annie Fillinghast. She stops a while, and orders picture. Walter. Supper. Rest awhile. Write here. Sent off Valentine and poem "The Rock" & "The Sea" to Atlantic Monthly. Pleasant day.

Thurs. Feb. 17th. 1887—

Another Spring day. Begin picture "The Hot-House Wall." Get roses at Butcher's but they wilt and I back and paint in the hot house. And very warm work it is. Stop and see mother and play game of chess with her and Eddie Jastram. Beat both. Home. Sup. Write to Martha.

Fri. Feb. 18th. 1887.

Emily. Paint very little. Feel dismal. Kate kept me awake last night too. Gym. in the evening. Does me good.

Sat. Feb. 19th. 1887. *

Feel better. Paint. See to Kate. Dine. Go out bill paying; Mrs. Phillips. 9.26, Mrs. Geer, 5.27. Stop at Calder's. Change books at library. Buy some jelly-cake pans, a sink-scraper, some cotton duck for floor cloths, rubbers for baby. Stop for Walter. Get some oranges & bananas, he paying. Ride home. Mend clothes and read Charlotte Yonge's "Womankind". A weak book.

Sun. Feb. 20th. 1887.

Read. S. Journal while Walter sleeps; loaf till 11.30, wash Kate and nap her, write to Alice Stone Blackwell, accepting offer; feed K, dress, read some poetry, cry some over our incompatibility. Mr. & Mrs. Smythe call, and we get them to stay to some dinner. Have a good talk with Mrs. S. She is "another victim". Young, girlish, inexperienced, sickly; with a sickly child, and no servant; and now very sick herself. Ignorant both, and he using his "marital rights" at her vital expense. Ah well!

Mon. Feb. 21st. 1887.

Work on roses, rather perfunctorily. Anna, Charlie, and Aunt C. make a long call. Miss Bailey calls later, and invites me to go with her to Y.M.C. Gym. Ex., which I do, and enjoy it very much. Think I'll try teaching gymnastics next winter, if Mr. S. will have me. Walk home between 10 & 11, unmolested save by a barking dog, whom I quell with threatening umbrella.

Tues. Feb. 22nd. 1887.

Finish roses, not to perfection. Take Kate to Nannie Cotton's birthday party. She enjoys herself in a stately and solemn fashion. I feel desperately out of place among a lot of young mothers. Home, sup, carry picture up to Annie and leave it to her to consider over night. Home and read "Sordello"⁹ to Walter; the first book. See *some* light in it. Bed late.

Wed. Feb. 23rd. 1887.

Up very late. The little Cotton's bring down some flowers & cake to Katharine. Mrs. Diman and Retta call. Kate Bucklin later. We go to see mother. Baby has a fine time there. Tea at Mrs. Diman's. Gym. Miss Bailey.

Thurs. Feb. 24th. 1887.

8.30. train to Boston. Rain & snow. Go to see Alice Stone Blackwell. Out. Start for Miss Allens Gym. but stop instead to see Mrs. Kilvert. See "Max" also, and her mother. She is very kind and pleasant. Go to Mrs. Smiths, get nice lunch & talk. 2.35 train to Hingham; meet Mr. Lane at station. He is not enthusiastic; Chester being sick. But I go out, meaning to return. Stay however; and make myself agreeable to Chester & the baby.

Fri. Feb. 25th. 1887.

Awake a good deal in the night, owing to Miss. Margaret. Amuse Chester & read some. Nice nap after dinner, and then go to walk with Martha. Good talk with her. Bed early.

Sat. Feb. 26th. 1887.

In town with Mr. Lane, 8.35 train. Go to Cambridge first seeing dear Miss Charlotte and her mother. lunch too, much needed. Then go to the gymnasium and see Dr. Sargent. Then to W. J. office and see A[lice]. S[tone]. B[lackwell]. Nice talk. Then to Miss A.'s gym. again. No one there Sat. P.M. Then to Roxbury, and find only grandma and Rob. at home. Have a long talk with her and a short one with him, and more lunch. Then back to Boston and home, driving snow, rain in Prov. Talk with Walter. Supper. Bed.

Sun. Feb. 27th. 1887

Wake up with sore throat. Feel pretty bad by afternoon, but Mrs. Smythe arrives, and later Kate, and we have a nice time. Hurried supper, Mr. Smythe and Walter arriving just in time. Then we women ride down in the 6.30 car to the gym. stopping to wait at Miss. Brown's on Gano St. whose warmhearted hospitality I shall not soon forget. We have a very gay time, thanks to Kate, who keeps little Mrs. S. in "a gale". She also does great feats at the gym. in spite of her skirts. Mr. S. calls for his wife at the door, and I go home with Kate.

Tues. March. 1st. 1887.

A miserable day. Cold worse of course. Go to see Anna & Aunt C. in the morning, then mother, & at her suggestion Julia Jastram, about my whist party.

Mother comes over early and puts Kate to sleep. Julia and Pardon come first, and we have a game. Get letter from Robert Grieve, ed. of "The People", and finish notes and cuttings for my column. Then Edward & Lizzie and the Simmons boys. I play a rubber with Edward, against Walter & Lizzie. Julia and Sam, Pardon & Jim. Chocolate, sandwiches, and cookies. But O my cold! It waxeth. Bed late and can't sleep then till I get four pillows and am fairly tired out.

Wed. March. 2nd. 1887.

Start down with Walter. Stop to see Art Club House. Carry papers to Mr. Grieve and have some talk with him. Then go to Gregory's and buy paper & envelopes. Then to Pub. Lib. and get books, Madame D'Hericourt's, Philosophie of Woman, and Sir Joshua Reynolds works for Walter. Then to Jennie's, rest and lunch. Then to see Mother S. a few moments, to Dr. Knight & get medicine to Plainfield St. car, and Mrs. Smythe. Talk to her like a mother. Ride down with her, meet her husband and bring them to Walters Studio. They soon depart and we ride home. Walter reads D'Hericourt to me.

Thurs. March. 3rd. 1887.

Not down till after 11. Do nothing till 4, when I go to see if Miss Pease has come, she has not, and call on Mrs. Diman. Nice talk, Home. sup. Write here.

Fri. March. 4th. 1887.

Emily for lesson. A good one, drawing freehand with charcoal. Wash Kate. Take her over to Mrs. Buffum's, much to her delight. (Bound her little shoes with black velvet.) Gym. in the evening, and feel ever so much better for it. Talk a little too.*

Sat. March 5th. 1887.

First day of improvement. Really do a little mending! Read Woman's Journal, Alpha, and Prov. Journal mother brings over. She worries over me of course. Go to see Mrs. Bailey about Painting lessons. See Mr. B. the longest, she being out until I was ready to go almost. Stop for Walter but don't find him and walk home alone. He brings my "exchanges" when he comes, and I spend the evenening [*sic*] reading and writing.

Sun. March. 6th. 1887.

Manage to write to Mrs. Smith & Charlotte Hedge. Katharine has taken my cold. I hope she will not have it as badly. Emily Diman and Ellen Clarke call. Roast beef dinner. Put Kate to sleep. Write here. Write to Grandma.

Mon. March. 7th. 1887.

A very hard night. Katharine down with my cold, way down. Walter sends for doctor and tells mother, who arrives speedily. But it don't do me much good, for Kate will go to no one but me. I hold her all day, as I did about all night. My cold getting better. Dr. comes about noon.

Tues. March. 8th. 1887.

Mother again, Dr. again. But yesterday's medicine was effective, and she had a very much better night. I get out towards night, go up to meet Walter and stop at Mrs. Dimans a few moments. Effie Rathbone called with her Egyptian story for me to read. Bed.

Wed. March. 9th. 1887.

Bad night again, (colder room,) and baby worse in the morning. Diarrhoea sets in. I give out completely in the morning, crying with weariness. But Kate seems better in the afternoon, we both getting some noon sleep; and I start out. Call at Mrs. Buffum's, leaving diapers; ride down town, stop at Walter's, go to see the Bayeux Tapestry copy at the Art Club, and then shop a little. Ride home, very tired. Mrs. Lockwood Bradford had called. Walter home early, and tries his "eggs en coquille" for supper. Then rides down and gets me some coca, & some calendula.

Thurs. March. 10th. 1887.

No better. Mother again and doctor again. He says it is only the "cold" that makes the diarrhoea. A dismal rain and snow. I take coca, but do not feel brilliant. Note from Mrs. Bailey. The change in medicine seems to benefit Kate, and also some of mother's milk porridge; so that she is quite bright in the evening, and when I put her to sleep seems really herself. I am glad.

Fri. March. 11th. 1887.

Baby better. Mother again. I give my first lesson to Eliza Bailey. Walk up with Walter. Put K. to sleep while Walter goes out to his Eggs "en coquille" supper. When he gets back I am asleep on the bed, exhausted. He gets me some bread and milk and I feel better.

Sat. March. 12th. 1887.

Feel pretty well. Mend some clothes. Ride down street, change book and get "A Woman's Thoughts About Women" by Mulock-Craik. Shop a little. Stop and see Dr. Brooks about gym. Stop for Walter. Walk up. Eliza puts baby to sleep and I read and write for "column."

Sun. March. 13th. 1887.

A very hard day. I have a crying fit while trying to make Kate go to sleep, and am all used up. Miss Pease comes in the afternoon, and cheers us somewhat.

Stays to dinner. Clarence drops in for a few moments. Then I put the baby to bed and collapse therein myself.

Mon. March. 14th. 1887.

A fair spring day. Up very late. Take K. out all the morning, give her a long nap and share it with her, and go to the gymnasium as merry as a grig. Lots of spectators and several new members. Home with the Allens.

Tues. March. 15th. 1887.

Bad day. A cold snow storm. I rose early and felt pretty well, but got tired of couse [sic] later. Lesson to Eliza Bailey in the afternoon. Home with Walter. Put K. to sleep and sleep in the rocking chair myself. Get chilly and have a crying fit. Sleep ill, and am utterly useless the next day, Wed. March 16th.* Call on Mrs. Buffum and stay to dinner, getting much help. A Mrs. Batty there, a Friend, nice woman. Then I go to see Miss Pease, long talk, then meet Walter on Angell St; and go to the Slicer's to tea. Pleasant evening. Home by 10.30 to lonesome Walter.

Thurs. March. 17th.

Sleep miserably and then lie in bed till noon. Feel better. Paint some. Take Kate to Mrs. Buffums while I consult that lady about K's clothes. Home. Supper. Finish book. Miss Pease calls. I love her, but she doesn't soothe me at all.

Fri. March. 18th. 1887.

Feel pretty well. Write note to Ellen Clarke, thanking her for Miss Allen's gym. circulars. Copy "The Rock & The Sea" for Scribners. Bathe Kate and put to sleep. Dress and dine. Mrs. Buffum stops for me and we go shopping, she helping my ignorance with her skill and taste. Get Kate's summer things. She has errands too, and then we go to Walter's studio for a few moments. Ride home. I dont' go to gym., because I want to write some paragraphs for "The Amendment". Walter goes to Club, and takes the key as usual. I take off polonaise, and put on jersey to be comfortable. Settle down to write, when lo! the Bell! John Diman and Prescott Clarke! I have to send them around to the back door. But we have a very pleasant evening, at least I did, and I guess they too, for they stayed till 10.40. Write here.

Sat. March. 19th. 1887.

Up early and write paragraphs for "The Amendment". Mend clothes a bit. Wash K. Paint some. Take K. to see the little Cottons in the afternoon, and pay milk bill, $1.92. Too tired to work, sleep all the evening.

Sun. March. 20th. 1887.

Bathe. Bad day. Getting back to the edge of insanity again. Anna and Aunt C. call. Put K. to sleep and feel desperate. Write my "column" though

Monday. March. 21st. 1887.

Slept in the spare room last night, and feel much better. Take K. out in the morning, revoking my party invitations and stopping to see mother. Call for Effie Rathbone and she walks with me to Miss Austin's on Congdon St, wheeling baby by special request on her part. But Miss Kate weeps and wails when we get there, and makes me carry her back to Effie's gate in my arms. Wheel her home from there, feed her a little, eat a bit myself, and start out in 2 o'clock car. Go to Calder's and get paints for Eliza Bailey. Change Kate's shoes, get hose for self, stop at W[omen's]. S[uffrage]. A[ssociation]. and get more "Amendments" to circulate, stop at "People" office and leave copy, Mr. Grieve showing me the type etc. I invite him to call. Stop at Walters a few minutes. Then lesson to Eliza. Mrs. Simmons there, and Sam. Sam invites me there to supper, and I go gladly. They have a lot of fine books. Sam lends me one vol. of Poe's works. Jim looks amazed when he comes in. Then rush down to the gym, and find Mrs. Buffum waiting for me, alone, as Mrs. Cotton couldn't come. But she seemed to enjoy herself, and liked the costumes immensely. Ride home with her. Find a very nice letter from Dr. Channing and one from Martha. (A fine one from father in the morning, a little cat book from Thomas and a card from Miss Austin.) Also one from Mother by a boy, with petticoat for Kate.

Tues. March 22nd. 1887.

Try the spare room again, but Miss Kate howls for me in the night, won't let her father touch her. Up late, but feel pretty well. Write accts. finish picture for Annie Fillinghast. Carry little chessboard over to mother. Write a little historical criticism on a "piece" in Monday's Journal. Cut out a lot of suffrage articles. Miss Brown on Gano St. sends me some leaflets. So does father Stetson.

Wed. March. 23rd. 1887.

Baby's birthday. Mother gave her a dress & petticoat, mother Stetson a wee napkin & bib, Jennie a bib. Kate Bucklin gave me ten dollars for her. I finish Will Fillinghast's picture and take it up there. See Mrs. T. She is to have a parlor meeting and discuss W[omen's]. S[uffrage]. Call to see if Ada has gone. Went yesterday. Call on Miss Bailey to get her to go to the meeting. Out. Go to Mrs. Diman's to dinner. Call for Mrs. Kendall, Mrs. Vaughn, Mrs. Tompkins, to go. In vain. Get mother however, and stop for Mrs. Diman & Miss Sophie Fillinghast. A very pleasant occasion. Mrs. Zerelda Wallace & Miss

Eastman spoke. Also another lady a few words. Various of the audience made a few remarks. Home, sup, and write a little.

Thurs. March. 24th. 1887

Yesterday we tried an experiment on Kate. No nap at noon. Bed by 7.30. Good nights sleep. Woke at 6. this morning. We got up early too, and I felt better than I have in a long time. Put my workbasket in order and get sewing material, ready for next week. Write to Mrs. Masters. Spend afternoon at Mrs. Buffum's with Kate, and later take her to ride while Mrs. B. makes some calls. Mother here, met her as I returned. Walter goes to club and I to bed.

Fri. March. 25th. 1887.*

Baby sick. Wakeful night for us both, but don't seem sick till she gets up. Goes to sleep in my arms, and won't leave me in all day. Mother over, and doctor comes. Says it may be measles. Left medicine. Administer it, and she recovers with great speed, eating supper, and seeming as well as ever.

Sat. March. 26th. 1887.

Some sleep last night. Baby seems all right this morning. Write an answer to Journal article, begun last night. Bathe Kate, nap and feed her. W. J. comes, the People & father's weekly Star. Take 2.40 car to Pub. Lib. Shop a little. Stop at W.S. headquarters and get some new Amendments. Stay and help them put a ballot in a tract parcel, and the tracts in an "Amendment". Lots of work going on there. Three hundred dollars just for postage. Stop for Walter and ride home. Write some in the evening, and mend Walters clothes—one of 'em.

Sun. March. 27th. 1887.

Dismal of course, being Sunday. But we get up very late, so there is less of it; and I muster up strength enough to travel over to Mother S.'s with Kate and Walter. They enjoy seeing her. Very good dinner. Home by six. Give Kate a bath and some milk and put her to bed. Write

Mon. March. 28th. 1887.

Miss Brown arrives and begins sewing. I like her very much. She has had nervous prostration too. Take her to the gym. in the evening. Am very tired and low.

Tues. March. 29. 1887.

Miss Brown sews and I read to her and talk a lot. Borrow news-papers of Mrs. Buffum, and read suffrage articles aloud. She comes over with the children and we all enjoy it. Jim Simmons calls in the evening. Talk about politics & W. suffrage.

Wed. March. 30th.

Borrow Mrs. Buffum's hand attachment for Miss Brown to sew with. A box arrives from Mrs. Cresson full of nice clothes for us all. I get Mrs. Buffum to come and see them. Sew some myself. Read in the evening, Walter goes to see mother.

Thurs. March 31st. 1887.

Borrow a pair of infant drawers of Mrs. Buffum, and Miss B. cuts pairs innumerable therefrom. Carry Kate over to mother's for a morning call. Feel miserable. Eat a copious dinner however. Read papers and cut out W.S. article. Take Miss Brown down to see Walter's studio. Then shop some. Ride home. Got book "Women in the Civil War". Supper. Read the Light of Asia to Miss B. Sam Simmons calls. Good solid satisfactory talk.

April 1st.
1887.   *Friday.*

Some snow as an "April Fool." Emily for her lesson. "People" P.M. Feel too miserable to go to the gym. Walter goes to his club and I have a deep talk with Miss Brown, more to my satisfaction than hers I fancy.

Sat. April. 2nd. 1887.

A violent snow storm, as bad as any we have had this winter. Go out nevertheless, meet Clarence & ride down with him, cash check for $8.00, give lesson to Eliza Bailey, get $6.00 from her, for paints, ride home with Walter, an hours trip. Deep snow.

Sun. April 3rd. 1887.

Miss Brown stays over, on account of storm. Miserable day, as usual. Go to see mother for a few moments. Write for Woman's Column in the evening.

Mon. April 4th. 1887.

A lovely day. Make buttonholes & sew on buttons. Take baby out. Stop to see Miss Browne a moment, (my Miss Brown left before breakfast this morning;) call on Miss Pease and Mrs. Diman. Home. Eat and read Woman's Journal. Nap till 4. eat a little more about 5, and go for the Miss Allens. Meet Mrs. MaKinney and go in with her to see her house. Then walk down with the Allens. Meet Miss Browne who says forty women are ready to go to the polls Wed. to distribute ballots and influence votes. I don't see my way clear to do that, and am not able now, either. Overtake Kate and Jenny Bucklin. Kate was at the mass meeting this afternoon. Do not exercise much, but talk a good deal. Tell some of the girls things about our laws that they didn't know before. Stay late talking and walk home, very tired.

Tues. April 5th. 1887.

A miserable night and day. Take Kate to see the "tiddly", but Mrs. Buffum is going out. Call on Mrs. Kimball, but she is housecleaning. Home and sew. Mrs. Buffums again P.M. but am too far gone to have her help me any. Evening approaching to frenzy, but Jim Simmons arrives just as I get hysterical and calms me down finely. Walter rushes out for a walk and Jim drawls and talks and is as pleasant as can be. After he goes Walter breaks down, and I soothe him and love him and get him to sleep.

Wed. April 6th. 1887.

Good night. Good day. Take baby out to Susie's. Have a nice time. Mother over to supper, and Miss Brown calls. We all ride down town to get the election returns. *Woman suffrage defeated* as I expected. Miss Brown stays all night.

Thurs. April 7th. 1887.

Bad again. Take Kate up to see Mrs. Wells, and stay to dinner. Talk with the Professor. Get tired and nervous and come home. They lent me "She" and I read it in the evening. Rather enjoyable.

Fri. April 8th. 1887.

Bad again. Emily as usual. Go to mother Stetsons to dinner, quahaug pie. Don't like it overmuch. Lesson to Eliza Bailey from 3 to 4, and then we and her mother go to Walter's studio. Take tea with Eliza and Jim comes later, and escorts me home. His old aggravating self again.

Sat. April 9th. 1887.

Worse. Take Kate over to mothers and leave her there, while I go see Dr. Knight. Explain my condition and he gives me two medicines. Wearily return, bring Kate back, and lie down. More physical exhaustion than I've felt yet.

Sun. April 10th. 1887.

Don't feel so much active misery, but am in a pitiful condition nervously. The least irritation upsets me quite. Walter takes baby out. I call on Mrs. Diman. Have some dinner there. She and E. walk down with me. Then I take the "tiddly" for a little walk. Lie down a little. Walter, baby, mother, supper. bed finally.

Mon. April 11th. 1887.

Emily comes down for me and I dine there again. Mrs. Diman proposes to give me a hundred dollars! That is to send me away to get well. I ride over to Hattie Salisbury's and inquire about Clifton Springs. Come back exhausted.

Tues. April 12th. 1887

Ride over to Dr. Knights to inquire about sanitarium, sea voyages etc. Find it hard to walk. Come back to Mrs. Diman's, rest, dine, come home. Call on Mrs. Buffum a few minutes. Guss comes to supper and spends the evening, and I talk California to him.

Wed. April 13th. 1887.

Paint daffodils for Mrs. Buffum, on linen "splasher", with tapestry dyes. Kate Bucklin comes & stays. Go out together with little Kate, dine, carry things over to mothers, take Kate 2nd and call on Miss Pease. Begin my week at mother's to rest Eliza. Walter sups with us and sleeps & breakfasts alone in the house.

Thurs. April 14th. 1887.

Find it pretty hard at mothers, but I am so weak now I don't mind much. Come over to the house and make bed for Walter, etc. Call on Mrs. D, Miss Pease, Mrs. Fillinghast, Mrs. J. Willey.

Friday. April 15th. 1887.

Take baby to Mary Phelon's as yesterday, during school. Lesson to Eliza Bailey at 4. *Get $6.00.* Go home to tea with Mrs. Simmons. Sam lends me a lot of books. Jim comes home with me.

Sat. April 16th 1887.

Lesson to Emily. Walk down St. Shop, getting shoes, $3.00 down, 3 more due; bonnet 75 cts., elastic & lining, 13, Cambric and Silesia for new dress 73. car fare 6. Home. Mother goes down St.

Sun. April 17th. 1887.

Walter take baby to ride and I come over here and clean up as I have managed to every day. Then he comes here. Send him off with bag for mother. Follow. Meet Anna & Aunt C. and find Julia Jastram and little Julia. Edward Brown, and Miss Pease. All go. dinner. Mend Walter's overcoat lining. Mrs. Allen in to see about dress.

Mon. April 18th. 1887.

Take baby to Mrs. Vaughn's during school. Back very tired. Egg nogg. doze. dine. Come over home, and am here now. Have made bed, made fire, washed dishes, write two notes. Am very tired.

I have kept a journal since I was fifteen, the only blanks being in these last years of sickness and pain. I have done it because it was useful. Now I am to go away for my health, and shall not try to take any responsibilites [*sic*] with me, even this old friend.

I am very sick with nervous prostration, and I think with some brain disease as well. No one can ever know what I have suffered in these last five years. Pain pain pain, till my mind has given way.

O blind and cruel! Can *Love* hurt like this?

You found me—you remember what.

I leave you—O remember what, and learn to doubt your judgement before it seeks to mould another life as it has mine.

I asked you a few days only before our marriage if you would take the responsibility entirely on yourself. You said yes. Bear it then.

Tues. April 19th. 1887.

Snowed yesterday. Cold night. Wintry this morning. Another letter from Mrs. Cresson. Take baby to Mary's. Back and lunch. Come over home. Doors locked. No key to be found. Struggle in at bay window with much effort. Clear up and write here. Begin to write an account of myself for the doctor.

[*This entry was Charlotte's last before she went to seek treatment from Dr. S. Weir Mitchell. She abandoned her diary writing until 1890.*]

Explanatory Notes to Volume 1

PROLOGUE: *"Gentle reader, wouldst know me?"*

1. While many scholars tend to use the terms *diary* and *journal* interchangeably, for Charlotte the distinction between the two was important. Diaries were commercially prepared books in which daily entries were recorded. Their typically small size, however, restricted the length of the entry that was made. Charlotte's journals, on the other hand, were loose-leaf notebooks that offered her the flexibility to write entires of unlimited length.

2. It was Sidney Putnam who introduced Charlotte to Walter Stetson early in 1882.

3. Aunt Caroline was Caroline Robbins, Mary Perkins's widowed half sister who resided with Charlotte and Mary off and on for many years.

4. Caroline "Carrie" Hazard (1856–1945) was the daughter of Rowland Hazard II, a wealthy philanthropist and manager of the Peacedale Woolen Mills of Rhode Island. Carrie Hazard published books of verse and educational theory and served as president of Wellesley College from 1899 to 1910. Throughout her life Hazard demonstrated enormous generosity toward Charlotte, often sending money during some of Charlotte's worst financial crises.

5. "House and Brain" seems likely to have been a magazine article.

6. Charles A. Fecter (1824–79) was a British actor.

7. Charlotte referred to the youth as simply "W." in her entry for March 28, 1879, as well. It is likely that she was referring to Walter Smith, one of her friends at Harvard University.

8. Kellup: a nickname for Charlotte's friend Caleb Burbank.

9. This allusion to Martha Luther is Charlotte's first. Her diary references to Martha span forty-four years, although most are concentrated between early 1880 and Oct. 5, 1882, the date of Martha's wedding to Charles Lane. Charlotte referred to Martha by a number of nicknames: Marthar, Pussie, Chick, etc.

10. During her youth Charlotte's second cousin Robert Brown made known his attraction to her. Charlotte cited impropriety, on the basis of their kinship, in her refusal to return Robert's affection. (She later overcame this concern when she married first cousin Houghton Gilman in 1900). Robert was persistent, however, and Charlotte often struggled with the question of propriety and with her own ambivalence. See, for example, her entries dated Aug. 24, 1879, March 4, 1880, and Jan. 30 and Feb. 17, 1881. Over the years her feelings toward Robert ranged from quiet tolerance (particularly when they

formed a brief business partnership) to mild annoyance (see, for example, April 2, 1881) to unbridled contempt (see her entry dated Oct. 22, 1886).

11. Grace Channing, who married Walter Stetson after Charlotte's 1894 divorce, remained a lifelong friend of Charlotte's. See the chapter entitled "Grace" in Ann J. Lane's biography of Gilman, *To Herland and Beyond*, for an account of their friendship.

12. Although she survived this mishap, Charlotte's friend May Diman was killed less than two years later in a similar accident. See Charlotte's entries for April 29 and 30, May 1 and 2, and July 7, 1881.

13. Charlotte went to visit her aunt Katie Gilman (and her cousins Houghton and Francis) on Nov. 17. On Dec. 2, just twelve days after returning to Providence, Charlotte learned that her aunt had died. During the fall of 1879 she began exchanging frequent letters with Houghton Gilman.

14. Charlotte may be alluding to Emily Jolly's novel *My Son's Wife*, published in 1877.

15. See Appendix B for the text of "To D—— G——." which was Charlotte's first published poem.

16. The Walter referred to here was Walter Smith, one of Charlotte's Harvard friends.

17. Charlotte's second cousin Robert Brown designed advertising cards for Soapine, a household cleaning product manufactured by the Kendall Manufacturing Company of Providence, R.I. Brown commissioned Charlotte to draw the concepts that he envisioned. Several of her sketches survive in the Gilman collection at the Schlesinger Library. Soapine advertising cards designed by Charlotte and Robert Brown can still be found at flea markets and antique shows throughout the northeast United States.

ONE: *"As lonely a heart as ever cried"*

1. Black stove: The process of applying blacking to a cast-iron stove.

2. *The Confessions of a Frivolous Girl*, by American lawyer and novelist Robert Grant (1852–1940), was first published in 1880.

3. Charlotte is referring to the Governor Street streetcar.

4. Charlotte occasionally used pins to keep herself awake. See *Living*, pp. 10–11.

5. Ada Blake was a friend of Charlotte's. A newspaper account of Blake's Feb. 24, 1881, wedding to her "swain" spelled her first name "Ehda."

6. *A Chance Acquaintance*, by American author and editor William Dean Howells (1837–1920), was first published in 1873.

7. Peut-être-pas: [Fr.] perhaps not.

8. *A Fair Barbarian*, by American writer Frances E. Burnett (1849–1924), was first published in 1877.

9. *The Hunting of the Snark*, by English writer Lewis Carroll (1832–98), was published in 1876.

10. *Crusoe in New York*, by American author Edward Everett Hale (1822–1909), was published in 1880.

11. *Sevenoaks: A Story of To-Day*, by American author Josiah G. Holland (1819–81), was first published in 1875.

12. Brown University history professor J. Lewis Diman was the father of Charlotte's close friend May Diman, who died less than three months later.

13. *The Guardian Angel*, by American writer Oliver Wendell Holmes (1809–94), was first published in 1867.

14. *My Wayward Partner*, by American writer Marietta Holley (1836–1926), was published in 1878.

15. Oui mon ami, il est. Quelquefois: [Fr.] Yes, my friend, it is. Sometimes.

16. *Samantha at the Centennial* (1877) was written by Marietta Holley.

17. Charlotte is probably alluding to the absence of Jim's brother, Sam Simmons, from their recent activities.

18. The bride's father was Eli Whitney Blake, a professor of physics at Brown University.

19. *Hudibras*, by English satirical poet Samuel Butler (1612–80), was first published in three parts between 1663 and 1678.

20. Charlotte's second cousin Robert Brown devised a variety of business "enterprises" to help Charlotte and her mother make ends meet in their financially impoverished household. The pie business was short-lived.

21. Uncle Edward was Edward Everett Hale, prominent Unitarian clergyman and author and a descendant of Revolutionary War hero Nathan Hale (1755–76).

22. *Children's Garland*, by English writer Charlotte M. Tucker (1821–93), was published in 1876.

23. *Phantasmagoria* (1869) was written by Lewis Carroll.

24. Charlotte maintained racist views throughout her life. See, for example, her acocunt of a visit to a "Negro Lunatic Asylum" in *Living*, where she writes: "I was told that insanity had increased greatly among the Negroes since they were freed, probably owing to the strain of having to look out for themselves in a civilization far beyond them" (p. 245). Also of interest is Susan A. Lanser's essay, "Feminist Criticism, 'The Yellow Wallpaper,' and the Politics of Color in America," *Feminist Studies* 15, no. 3 (1989): 415–41.

25. See Appendix B for a sample of one of Charlotte's numerous valentine poems to May Diman.

26. *Light of Asia*, by English poet and journalist Sir Edwin Arnold (1832–1904), was published in 1879.

27. *The Story of Avis*, by American writer Elizabeth Stuart Phelps (1844–1911), was first published in 1877.

Two: *"The damsel Martha"*

1. Charlotte is alluding here to a $100 loan that she was attempting to secure from businessman George Bissell at her brother Thomas's request.

2. See Appendix B for the text of a poem that Charlotte wrote commemorating her invitation to Class Day.

3. *Billy Taylor* was a play by English comedian and playwright John B. Buckstone (1802–79).

4. After nearly completing her drawings of the whale for the Soapine cards, Charlotte had been commissioned next to draw the horse that appeared on the advertising cards. Her original sketch of the Soapine horse is still among her papers at the Schlesinger Library.

5. *Rudder Grange*, by American fiction writer Frank R. Stockton (1834–1902), was first published in 1879.

6. James Abram Garfield (1831–81), twentieth president of the United States, was shot in the Washington, D.C., railroad station on July 2, 1881. He died Sept. 19, 1881.

7. *Evangeline: A Tale of Acadie*, by American poet Henry Wadsworth Longfellow (1807–82), was first published in 1847.

8. Roger Williams Park in Providence, R.I.

9. M.g.s: Either marigolds or morning glories.

10. *Lady of Shalott*, by English poet Alfred, Lord Tennyson (1809–92), was first published in 1832.

11. Charlotte was ordering tickets for a fair to be held on Sept. 8, 1881, in which she participated.

12. Charlotte was apparently unhappy that she had no lamp by which to study Latin.

13. Charlotte was instrumental in seeing that the Providence Ladies Gymnasium became a reality (*Living*, pp. 67–68; note, however, that the date on p. 67 should be 1881, rather than 1891).

14. *Warlock, O' Glenwarlock*, by Scottish novelist and poet George Macdonald (1824–1905), was published in 1881.

THREE: *"She hath a ring. I have a pain"*

1. Martha Luther married Charles Lane on October 5, 1882.

2. Probably Charlotte's friend Walter Paine.

3. *Robert Falconer* (1881) was written by George Macdonald.

4. Charlotte sketched at the bottom of this entry a mountain peak surrounded by clouds. Just three days later, on Nov. 1, Charlotte learned of Martha's engagement to Lane.

5. Charlotte designed a stencil for the gymnasium's wall border.

6. Charlotte modeled occasionally for artist Sydney Burleigh and was accompanied at times by her mother or her Aunt Caroline. See, for example, her entry dated Nov. 23, 1881.

7. Charlotte's Nov. 14, 1881, letter to Sam Simmons has survived. See Appendix B.

8. Charlotte probably either meant "younkers," which simply means "youths," or she coined her own term, as she often did, to mean "young kids."

9. *Cape Cod Folks*, by American author Sarah Pratt McLean Greene (1856–1935), was published in 1881.

10. Charlotte is referring to orders for personalized greeting cards, name cards, invitations, dinner cards, etc., that she hand painted.

11. Charlotte is probably alluding to her poem dated Dec. 13, 1881, titled "Unsent." See Appendix B for the text of the poem.

12. *Little Men*, by American author Louisa May Alcott (1832–88), was first published in 1871.

13. I am indebted to Eva S. Moseley, curator of manuscripts at the Schlesinger Library,

for offering an interpretation of this somewhat awkward passage. Moseley suggested that taking "a bite" was suggestive of devouring or "taking in" the aesthetic qualities of the painting that Charlotte was viewing. (Waterman's store occasionally displayed Charlotte's own artwork in their window.) Although the passage is unusual, Charlotte sometimes used oral metaphors to describe various experiences. See, for example, her Nov. 14, 1881, letter to Sam Simmons in Appendix B, where she mentions having "feasted on costume" (i.e., she looked at some women's suits) at Waterman's earlier in the day. Similarly, on Feb. 26, 1883, Charlotte wrote: "Feast eyes in Tildens window while waiting for cars."

14. Edwin Thomas Booth (1833–93) was an American actor and brother of John Wilkes Booth, who had assassinated President Lincoln in 1865.

15. This is Charlotte's first reference to Charles Walter Stetson.

FOUR: *"A twighlight tête-a-tête with Charles Walt"*

1. Charlotte composed a poem this date (the day after being introduced to Charles Walter Stetson) titled "The Suicides Burial." See Appendix B for the text.

2. Herodotus was one of Charlotte's nicknames for Charles Walter Stetson. She had been reading a book about Herodotus, the Greek 5th century B.C. historian, when she was introduced to Stetson. She sometimes abbreviated Herodotus as "He."

3. Although Stetson includes a lengthy paraphrase of their discussion that evening in his own diary, which included the subject of marriage (*Endure*, pp. 30–36), he does not specifically say that he asked Charlotte to marry him.

4. On Jan. 31, 1882, Charlotte composed "An Anchor to Windward." See Appendix B for the text.

5. Jean Ingelow (1820–97) was an English poet and fiction writer.

6. American actress Maggie Mitchell (1837–1918) played the part of Fanchon in George Sand's *Fanchon the Cricket*.

7. John Stuart Mill (1806–73), English philosopher and economist, was an advocate of women's suffrage. Among his many books was *The Subjection of Women*, published in 1869.

8. Charlotte made the trip in twelve minutes. She was apparently proud of the fitness, strength, and agility that she had gained since beginning an exercise regimen at the Providence Ladies Gymnasium.

9. Hamilton MacDougall was a close friend of Stetson's.

10. *Romance of the 19th Century*, by English writer William H. Mallock (1849–1923), was published in 1881.

11. *The Fate of Madame La Tour*, by writer Cornelia Paddock, was published in 1881.

12. *The Emperor*, by German novelist Georg Ebers (1837–98), was published in 1881.

13. *A Strange Disappearance*, by American writer of detective fiction Anna K. Green (1846–1935), was published in 1879.

14. *Stillwater Tragedy*, by American author and editor Thomas B. Aldrich (1863–1937), was published in 1880.

FIVE: *"Even Heaven looks misty & grey"*

1. *Sartor Resartus*, a discussion of philosophical creeds, was written by Scottish essayist and historian Thomas Carlyle (1795–1881). It was first published in *Fraser's Magazine* in 1833–34.

2. *Adam Bede*, a novel by English writer George Eliot (1819–80) about a misguided romance in Georgian England, was first published in 1859.

3. Charlotte's reference isn't clear, but it appears that she was alluding to some kind of flower, since she gathered and painted several during her stay at the shore.

4. *Moondyne: Story from the Underworld*, by British-born American writer John B. O'Reilly (1844–90), was published in 1879.

5. Charlotte variously referred to Charles Walter Stetson as Love, Herodotus, He., Charles Walt, C. W., Mr. Stetson, and later as "my boy."

6. Charlotte was reading Herbert Spencer's *Data of Ethics* (1879) and *An Echo of Passion* (1882) by American writer George P. Lathrop (1851–98), husband of Nathaniel Hawthorne's daughter, Rose.

7. Charlotte, her mother, and Aunt Caroline left for Martha's Vineyard, off the coast of Massachusetts, the following morning.

8. *Bella* may have been *Bella Trelawney; or Time Works Wonders*, by J. F. Smith, published in 1882.

9. *Mosses from an Old Manse*, by American writer Nathaniel Hawthorne (1804–64), was first published in 1846. *Sesame and Lilies*, by English sociological writer John Ruskin (1819–1900), was published in 1865. *Littells Living Age* was a reprint series of primarily British works.

10. According to Walter Stetson's diaries (*Endure*, p. 98), Charlotte had asked him to purchase a peninsula at Malagawatch, Nova Scotia, where they could build a log cabin and lead a simple life.

11. Charlotte hosted a garden party on this date; her need for a carpenter, however, isn't clear.

12. Charlotte's inclusion of a poem in her diary entry of this date seems to have been inspired by Walter's poem to her, "The Painting of the Portrait," also dated Sept. 23, 1882. See Appendix B for the text of Walter's poem.

13. *Judas Maccabeus*, by English bookseller and writer Claude R. Conder (1848–1910), was published in 1879.

SIX: *"Hot tears and self-abasement"*

1. Charlotte wrote Thomas and his bride, Julia, a poem for their wedding. See Appendix B for the text.

2. See *Endure*, pp. 110–13, for Walter's account of Mary Perkins's visit to his studio.

3. Charlotte wrote a poem for Walter dated Oct. 20, 1882. See Appendix B for the text of the poem.

4. *Through One Administration* (1883) was written by Frances H. Burnett.

5. *Hereward the Wake*, by English clergyman and writer Charles Kingsley (1819–75), was published in 1866.

6. Charlotte wrote "Reserved" for her friend Retta Clarke, to whom she delivered the poem the following day. Clarke, whom Charlotte described as "a strong good woman soul," had, according to Charlotte, loved her and wished for Charlotte to kiss her (see *Endure*, p. 179). The subject of the poem, however, is Walter Stetson. See Appendix B for the text of the poem.

7. *A Blot in the 'Scutcheon* was a play by English writer Robert Browning (1812–89).

8. *The Man in the Iron Mask*, a drama by French writer Alexandre Dumas (1802–70), was written in 1848.

9. *Vice Versa; or A Lesson to Fathers*, a novel by English writer Thomas A. Guthrie (1856–1934), was published in 1882.

10. Possibly an allusion to Tennyson's *Harold* (1876).

11. *A Double Story* (1871) was written by George Macdonald. *Little Pilgrim*, by Scottish novelist Margaret O. W. Oliphant (1828–97), was published in 1882.

12. Charlotte is referring to her first cousin and second husband, Houghton Gilman, and his brother Francis.

13. *Happy Thoughts*, by English playwright and *Punch* editor Francis C. Burnand (1836–1917), was published in 1866.

14. *The Princess and Curdie* (1882?) was written by George Macdonald.

15. *Romola* (1881) was written by George Eliot.

16. *The Princess and the Goblin* (1871) was written by George Macdonald.

17. See Appendix B for the text of Walter's sonnet, dated Jan. 27, 1883.

18. *The Talisman*, by Scottish writer Sir Walter Scott (1771–1832), was published in 1825.

19. Charlotte wrote a poem to Walter dated March 1, 1883. See Appendix B for the text of the poem.

20. Walter Stetson reported in his journal that Charlotte confessed that evening to having a "relapse"; i.e., her affection for him was waning as she felt an increasing desire to pursue her life's ambition to work (*Endure*, p. 143).

21. *Uncivilized Races* was written by English writer John G. Wood (1827–89).

22. The actual title was *Mary Stuart*, a play about Mary, Queen of Scots. Fanny Janauschek (1830–1904) was a Bohemian actress.

23. Charlotte and Walter, although corresponding frequently, remained apart until May 14, 1883.

24. See Appendix B for the text of the poem to Mrs. Jackson.

25. Belinda was the family cat.

26. Charlotte "murdered" a number of cats over the years, beginning with "Brinnle," when she was seventeen. On July 18, 1877, she wrote: "I try to chloroform Brinnle. Brinnle wont. He dances over that fence. What shall I do with him?" Two days later, on July 20, she reported, "Brinnle is drowned! No tears are shed. Nevertheless I mourn slightly." The last mention of putting a cat to death is in the diary entry for July 29, 1925, when Charlotte was sixty-five years old. "To save myself continuous suffering, humiliation and anger I chloroformed my darling pussy cat. She died in my arms, peacefully." See also the entry for Aug. 11, 1883.

27. *Pearls of the Faith* (1879) was written by Sir Edwin Arnold.

SEVEN: *"A despicable boy"*

1. *Daughters of an Egyptian King* (1878?) was written by Georg Ebers.

2. *How to Do It* (1877) was written by Edward Everett Hale.

3. *Wenderholme*, by English writer Philip G. Hamerton (1834–94), was published in 1876.

4. *John Ploughman's Talks*, by English Baptist preacher Charles H. Spurgeon (1834–92), was first published in 1869.

5. Jane Baillie Carlyle (1801–66) was the long-suffering wife of Scottish essayist and historian Thomas Carlyle (1795–1881).

6. Marcus Aurelius Antoninus (121–180 A.D.) was a Roman emperor and author of *Meditations*, a collection of precepts of practical morality.

7. It was Sidney Putnam who introduced Charlotte to Charles Walter Stetson on Jan. 11, 1882. Stetson appears to have been somewhat more grieved over Putnam's death than Charlotte was and surmised that his drowning death might have been a suicide (*Endure*, pp. 221–22).

8. Occasionally, Charlotte got behind on her journal writing by a day or two; apparently in this instance there was some confusion as she tried to reconstruct the day's events.

9. *Felix Holt the Radical* (1866) was written by George Eliot.

10. *John Halifax, Gentleman*, by English writer Dinah M. Craik (1826–87), was first published in 1857.

11. *The Golden Treasury* was a selection of prayers primarily from the works of St. Alphonsus Liguori.

EIGHT: *"In Duty, Bound"*

1. Although it was rejected by *Century*, Charlotte's poem "In Duty, Bound" was accepted a few weeks later for publication in the *Woman's Journal*.

2. There were several works in print at the time with the title *Virginia*; it is not clear which Charlotte was reading.

3. *A Woman's Reason* (1883) was a novel by William Dean Howells.

4. Lawrence Barrett (1838–91) was an American actor particularly renowned for his Shakespearean roles.

5. See Appendix A for the complete text of "A Word to Myself."

6. Charlotte's painting of a howling wolf on a frozen lake at night is housed with the Gilman Papers at the Schlesinger Library.

7. Charlotte looked in vain for this picture many years later for inclusion in her autobiography. Walter Stetson described the picture in his diary as depicting "a wan creature who had traversed a desert and came, worn out, to an insurmountable wall which extended around the earth. . . . It *was* powerful. . . . I know it was a literal transcript of her mind" (*Endure*, p. 244).

8. Stetson reported in his diary that he and Charlotte had spent a "painful evening" because of a remark he had made about "harlotry" leading her to believe that he might

resort to enlisting the services of a prostitute as a result of the long wait before consummating their relationship. Charlotte apparently convinced Stetson that in his case such a recourse would be unjustifiable (*Endure*, p. 245).

9. *Hannah Thurston: A Story of American Life*, by American writer Bayard Taylor (1825–78), was published in 1863.

10. "One Girl of Many," a poem in defense of the "fallen" woman, was published in the Feb. 1, 1884, edition of *Alpha*. Charlotte cites "One Girl of Many" as her first published poem in *Living* (p. 62). Her memory, however, is faulty. "In Duty, Bound" was published just over two weeks earlier in the Jan. 12, 1884, issue of the *Woman's Journal*, followed by "My View" in the Buffalo *Christian Advocate* a few days later. Moreover, her poem, "To D—— G—— ," was published in the May 20, 1880, issue of the *New-England Journal of Education* when Charlotte was only nineteen. See Appendix B for the text of "To D—— G——" and "In Duty, Bound."

11. The play *Return of the Druses* was written by Robert Browning.

12. Fings: probably fingans, small coffee cups without handles, made of thin porcelain and supported by ornamental metal holders.

13. Chester was Martha Luther Lane's infant son, born Aug. 6, 1883.

14. *The Mystery of Orcival* was a work by French writer of detective fiction Emile Gaboriau (1835–73).

NINE: *"One does not die young who so desires it"*

1. Biographers' assertions that Charlotte was 5 feet 6½ inches tall are likely based on her journal entry of Jan. 1, 1879. That entry, however, reports her height with shoes, making her an inch and a half taller than she actually was.

2. *Bricks without Straw*, by American politician and writer Albion Tourgée (1838–1905), was published in 1880.

3. C. Cd.: probably "Christmas Card."

4. See Appendix B for the text of "In Duty, Bound."

5. *On Liberty* (1859) was written by John Stuart Mill.

6. Henry Irving (1838–1905) was a popular English actor whose first tour of America was in 1883–84. He was the first actor to be knighted (in 1895) and is buried in Westminster Abbey.

7. Claire Elisabeth Gravier de Vergennes, comtesse de Remusat (1780–1821), was a French writer and lady in waiting to the empress Josephine. Her letters, for which she is best known, were published by her grandson in 1881.

8. Thomas Carlyle's *Reminiscences* were published, unedited, in 1881.

9. Ich liebe dich: [G.] I love you.

10. See Appendix B for the text of the poem.

11. *In His Name* (1873) was written by Edward Everett Hale.

12. Charlotte had previously reported that Thursday, April 24, had been her last day at the gym.

TEN: *"A crown of white roses"*

1. Mary and Ray Phelon were friends and neighbors of Charlotte and Mary Perkins.

2. *Madame Thérèse*, a novel by French writers Emile Erckmann (1822–99) and Alexandre Chatrain (1826–90), was published in 1863.

3. *The Conscript* (1864) was also written by Erckmann and Chatrain.

4. *Fair Maid of Perth* (1828) was written by Sir Walter Scott.

5. *Phantastes* (n.d.) was published by George Macdonald.

6. Walter had bought the kerchief for Charlotte just one week earlier.

7. *The Lady or the Tiger?* (1882) was written by Frank R. Stockton.

8. Walter had been commissioned to make etchings of paintings by various European master artists, including one by French painter Thomas Couture (1815–79).

9. Blanche Willis Howard (1847–98) was an American novelist and author of such works as *One Summer* (1875), *Aunt Serena* (1881), *Guenn* (1883), and *The Open Door* (1889).

10. Paul Gustave Doré (1833–83) was a French illustrator and painter. Dante's *Divine Comedy* was among the books he illustrated.

11. This is the first allusion to Charlotte's possible suspicion that the sickness she was experiencing might be the result of her being pregnant. A few days later, however, on Aug. 5, she attributed her sickness to "intersusception of the intestine."

12. In January, Charlotte weighed 118 pounds; her inability to keep food down during the early stages of her pregnancy most likely caused her weight loss.

13. Charlotte left the next morning for a two-week visit to Martha Luther Lane.

ELEVEN: *"By reason of ill health"*

1. *Dr. Zay* (1882) was written by Elizabeth Stuart Phelps.

2. *Noblesse Oblige*, by writer Margaret Roberts, was published in 1876.

3. *A Perilous Secret*, a novel by Charles Reade (1814–84), was published posthumously in 1884.

4. Charlotte's mother, Mary Perkins, left the next day for an extended trip west to visit her son, Thomas, and his family.

5. Charlotte's "ire" apparently was raised by the late departure of her guests.

6. Shakespeare wrote his play *Titus Andronicus* in 1593.

7. The letter was probably from Frank Purinton, a friend, who accused Walter of slighting his work, being uncommunicative, etc. (*Endure*, p. 272).

8. Gus Stetson was Walter's brother.

9. Several of the "nonsense" or double pictures that Charlotte and Walter drew together have been preserved, including those sent to Mrs. Cresson, mentioned in this entry. They are part of collection no. 177, ser. 6, box 25, folder 317, of the Charlotte Perkins Gilman Papers at the Schlesinger Library. See also *Living*, p. 87.

10. "The Black Cat" is a short story by American author Edgar Allan Poe (1809–49).

11. *Aurora Leigh*, by English poet Elizabeth Barrett Browning (1806–61), was published in 1856.

12. Shakespeare wrote his play *Coriolanus* in 1608–9. *Alcibiades* (1675) was written by English dramatist Thomas Otway (1652–85).

13. *The Earthly Paradise*, a volume of poetry by English writer and artist William Morris (1834–96), was first published in 1868.

TWELVE: *"Motherhood means——Giving"*

1. Mary Perkins was en route from Utah, where she had been visiting Charlotte's brother, Thomas, and his wife for several months.

THIRTEEN: *"How irrevocably bound I am"*

1. *The Bostonians*, by American author Henry James (1843–1916), was first published separately in 1886.
2. Walter was hoping to sell some of his paintings to collector George Tewksbury and to others.
3. Daphne Lynch, the Stetsons' recently hired maid, had announced her resignation.
4. Mary A. Hill, in *Endure*, lists the title of this painting as *Fool's Sermon* (p. 292).
5. *Mill on the Floss* (1860) was written by George Eliot.
6. *Ramona*, a novel by American writer Helen Maria Hunt Jackson (1830–85), was published in 1884.
7. *An Old Maid's Paradise* (1885) was written by Elizabeth Stuart Phelps.

FOURTEEN: *"O sick & miserable heart be still!"*

1. "On the Paxtuxet," the work for which Charlotte received her first payment, originally appeared in the *Providence Journal* on Aug. 1, 1886. It was later reprinted in *In This Our World*.
2. William Gillette (1855–1937) was an American actor to whom Charlotte was attempting to sell a comedy that she had written with Walter.
3. Alice Stone Blackwell (1857–1950) was an American advocate of woman's suffrage and assistant editor of *Woman's Journal*. She and Charlotte met a few weeks later; their friendship lasted for many years.
4. Charlotte kept a lock of Walter's hair tucked away in a little envelope. One of his golden curls is among the collection of Gilman memorabilia at the Schlesinger Library.
5. Ouida was the pseudonym of English novelist Marie Louise de la Ramée (1839–1908).
6. *What's Mine's Mine*, a novel by George Macdonald, was published in 1886.

FIFTEEN: *"Traitor to my cause"*

1. *A Bachelor's Blunder*, by English novelist William E. Norris (1847–1925), was published in 1886.
2. Possibly Charlotte's shorthand abbreviation for tamarind enema, since the seedpod of the tamarind was used for medicinal purposes and Charlotte occasionally experimented with various laxatives and enemas.

3. *This Man's Wife*, by English novelist George Manville Fenn (1831–1909), was published in 1886.

4. See Appendix B for the text of Charlotte's Christmas verse to Walter.

SIXTEEN: *"Very sick with nervous prostration"*

1. A description of this calendar, as well as some excerpts from it, is included in Appendix B.

2. Charlotte eventually became friends with William Dean Howells after corresponding with him in 1890 and finally meeting him on March 20, 1897, after he attended one of her public lectures.

3. The painting of Charlotte's hand is included in the Gilman Papers at the Schlesinger Library.

4. *Woman in the Nineteenth Century*, by American critic and social reformer Margaret Fuller (1810–50), was published in 1845.

5. *Chaplet of Pearls*, by English novelist and historical writer Charlotte M. Yonge (1823–1901), was published in 1886.

6. John Ruskin (1819–1900), English art critic and writer, urged social and economic reform in his writings.

7. The next day Charlotte contradicted herself by writing that Katharine "makes herself disagreeable as usual."

8. Although Charlotte reported Feb. 14 as being "a dreary and useless day," she did receive from Walter a loving Valentine's poem, which is inserted in the diary for 1887. See Appendix B for the text of the poem.

9. *Sordello* (1840) was a long dramatic narrative poem by Robert Browning.

Textual Notes to Volume 1

The purpose of these Textual Notes is to provide to the reader additional information about the diaries which does not appear in the transcribed entries. Scattered throughout the diaries, for example, are sketches and illustrations that Charlotte included which have been impossible to reproduce in the text. The inclusion of these illustrations in her original entries, however, helps to elucidate her activities, her experiences, and, occasionally, her emotional state. Therefore, a note has been provided to cite the existence of such illustrations. Other information that is documented in this section includes the charting of Charlotte's menstrual cycles (which she began tracking in her diaries in 1890 at the age of twenty-nine), her method of denoting in her diaries the death of friends and loved ones, and various editorial emendations she made, including corrected text, insertions or deletions, transpositions, and the like. A physical description of each journal or diary is also included.

[1879]

The journal for January 1, 1879–October 10, 1879, is a commercial copybook with a gilt-bordered black leather cover, measuring approximately 6½ by 7⅞ inches. The journal for October 11, 1879–December 31, 1879, continues in a commercial notebook which was used originally by Charlotte for studying German. She made the transition from notebook to journal by writing, "Abandoning German perforce, I hereby utilize the remaining sheets as a second edition of my '79 diary, which has given out at this date."

February 17, 1879   Charlotte included in this entry a drawing of teardrops as an illustration of her distress.

June 3, 1879   Charlotte included in this entry two exaggerated sketches of her cold sore.

November 17, 1879   Charlotte included in this entry a sketch of the clothing she had been given: a long dress, a coat, and a hat.

[1880–81]

The journal for January 1, 1880–December 31, 1881, is missing from the Gilman Papers at the Schlesinger Library. According to Curator of Manuscripts Eva S.

Moseley, the journal has been missing for several years. As a result, transcriptions in this edition have been taken directly from, and verified against, a microfiched copy of the original journal.

February 9, 1880   Just over a year later, Charlotte appended the following note to this entry: "Feb. 20th.'81. He [Jim Simmons] amounts to a great deal, but is hardly a caller.   CAP."

September 23, 1880   Charlotte later appended to this entry: "Sam called! Mother doesn't speak to him!!"

February 13, 1881   Charlotte included in this entry a diminutive sketch of Robert seated next to her on a sofa.

February 18, 1881   Charlotte included in this entry a sketch of the bonnet she had made.

April 3, 1881   Charlotte wrote *"Cold"* over this entry and the next in big bold letters.

May 14, 1881   Charlotte skipped this date in her diary; she wrote the entry on a separate sheet of paper and inserted it in the diary with "Omitted!" written above the date.

May 20, 1881   Charlotte included at the end of this entry a sketch of a handshake that she presumably shared with Sam Simmons.

July 4, 1881   Charlotte included in the middle of this entry a drawing of a marble-sized hailstone followed by an exclamation point.

August 25, 1881   Charlotte included in this entry sketches of the letterhead and monogram that she had designed.

September 14, 1881   The correct date for Thursday was September 15.

September 24, 1881   Charlotte scrawled "HOT" in large bold letters over this entry and the next three, as a record of the late September heat wave that had hit Providence.

October 7, 1881   Charlotte wrote "Sleepy" at the end of this entry, but she subsequently crossed it out.

October 16, 1881   Charlotte wrote "escorts me home," but she subsequently changed "escorts" to "sees."

December 25, 1881   Charlotte wrote two separate entries for Sunday, December 25, 1881, Christmas Day. She did not write an entry, however, for Monday, December 26.

[1882–83]

The journal for January 1, 1882–December 31, 1883, is a black and marble leather-bound book with gilt inlay and white, lined pages, measuring approximately 6¾ by 8⅜ inches.

January 22, 1882   Charlotte included in this entry a drawing of large bold stars on each side of the date.

August 23, 1882   Charlotte inserted in the margin of this entry "Letters from Mother & Miss Gladding."

September 3, 1882   Charlotte included in this entry a side-profile sketch of herself featuring the ruffled neckline she described.

September 28, 1882   Charlotte included in this entry a sketch of her hair style, which featured four separate chignons formed at the nape of her neck.

January 9, 1883   Charlotte wrote "He.", one of her many nicknames for Charles Walter Stetson, but crossed it out in favor of "Walter."

February 15, 1883   Charlotte added "write to Martha," but she subsequently crossed it out.

April 10, 1883   Charlotte wrote "don't think about it," but she subsequently changed "don't" to "wont".

October 10, 1883   Charlotte included in this entry a minute sketch of Willey's head.

October 11, 1883   This sentence originally read "Nap and read 'Alpha.' " Charlotte subsequently edited the sentence with a transposition symbol.

October 26, 1883   This line originally read "Write to Walter & letter from him." Charlotte subsequently edited the sentence with a transposition symbol.

[1884–86]

The journal for January 1, 1884–December 31, 1886, consists of a set of single white, lined leaves loosely bound with white string along the left edge. The journal has a paper cover measuring approximately 5 ⅝ by 9 inches.

January 13, 1884   Charlotte wrote "Sat. Jan. 12th. 1884.," but because she actually wrote the entry after midnight, she subsequently crossed it out and replaced it with "Sun. Jan. 13th. 1884."; hence, there are two entries dated Sunday, January 13.

February 22, 1884   This line originally read "Letter from Walter and reception to his invitation." Charlotte subsequently edited the sentence with a transposition symbol.

March 21, 1884   Charlotte wrote "doleful" but subsequently changed it to "unhappy."

March 24, 1884   Charlotte included in this entry a sketch of herself carrying a girl on one arm and hip.

March 31, 1884   This sentence originally read "Eat two bananas, write accts, and read." Charlotte edited the sentence with a transposition symbol.

April 11, 1884   This sentence originally read "Housework, dishes, darn, breakfast." Charlotte subsequently edited the sentence with a transposition symbol.

April 26, 1884   Charlotte inserted into this entry a small sketch of the clock case.

April 30, 1884   Charlotte inserted "May 3rd." in parentheses presumably to indicate that she was reconstructing the events of the previous three days on May 3, rather than writing the entries as they occurred. She began an entry listing the date for Thursday, May 1, but subsequently crossed it out. Her original entry for Friday, May 2 (which was subsequently replaced by another entry for that date), was crossed out. Originally, it read: "Down at the house all day, sewing mostly. Groceries come, etc. Finish wedding dress. Walter over P.M. A lot of flowers come; and I fix them. Trim bonnet. Get home at about 5.45." These events apparently took place on Thursday, May 1, instead of Friday, May 2, which was Charlotte's wedding day.

May 2, 1884   Charlotte inserted into this entry a sketch of her velvet wedding-night slippers.

May 8, 1884   Charlotte added "hem tablecloth" in the margin of this entry.

May 23, 1884   Charlotte subsequently crossed out "yesterday."

June 25, 1884   Charlotte wrote "suspicion," but she crossed it out and substituted "conviction."

July 9, 1884   Charlotte wrote "6, but am so weary and was up so late." She crossed it out, however, and substituted "6, lazy" instead.

August 8, 1884   Charlotte wrote "50 for '*weeeee*,'" but crossed it out and replaced it with "*we*."

August 9, 1884   Charlotte originally followed "coffee also" with "and eat two eggs," but she subsequently crossed it out.

September 1, 1884   This sentence originally read "Accts, and arrange photographs." Charlotte subsequently edited it with a transposition symbol.

January 16, 1885   Charlotte inserted in the margin of this entry "Blanche W. called."

May 9, 1885   Charlotte originally wrote "hard" instead of "good."

September 18, 1885   Charlotte added in the margin of this entry "Henrietta called & Anna & Charlie."

September 26, 1885   Charlotte recorded the day as September 23 and then changed the "3" to a "6." She neglected, however, to change "rd" to "th."

October 2, 1885   Charlotte followed this sentence with "Miss Pease calls," but she subsequently crossed it out.

October 10, 1885   Charlotte inserted into the margin of this entry "Annie Vaughn calls."

October 3, 1886   Charlotte drew dark, heavy borders around the entry for October 3, 1886, to denote the death of her sister-in-law, Julia.

October 8, 1886   Charlotte wrote "Nice talk" here, but she subsequently crossed it out.

October 17, 1886   Charlotte inserted in the margin of this entry "Mrs. Merrifield called to bring me some beautiful begonias."

November 1, 1886   Charlotte inserted in the margin of this entry "Century, Woman's Journal and letter from Grace."

November 19, 1886   Charlotte inserted in the margin of this entry "Julia Jastram called, with Julie & Marian Elder."

December 2, 1886   Charlotte inserted "*Cold*" in the margin between this entry and the entry for Friday, December 3, 1886.

December 5, 1886   Charlotte inserted in the margin of this entry the word "*Snow*."

December 23, 1886   Charlotte inserted in the margin of this entry: "Ada with little Sophy and stuff for tree. Walk down with her."

December 24, 1886   Charlotte inserted in the margin of this entry "Mother over to help with Kate & doctor here again."

December 26, 1886   Charlotte inserted in the margin of this entry: "Dr. Knight in the morning. Kate better, much."

[1887]

The journal for January 1, 1887–April 19, 1887, consists of a set of single white, lined leaves loosely bound with white string along the left edge. The journal has a paper cover measuring approximately 5 ⅝ by 9 inches.

January 1, 1887   The date, in fact, was January 2.

January 24, 1887   Charlotte inserted in the margin of this entry "Send off [article on] 'Petticoats.'"

February 19, 1887   Charlotte inserted in the margin of this entry "Letter from Miss Stone Blackwell asking me to manage a W[omen's]. Suffrage Colum in Prov[idence]. paper."

March 4, 1887   Charlotte inserted in the margin of this entry "The People comes with my "Womans Column" in it."

March 15, 1887   Charlotte did not write a separate entry for Wednesday, March 16, 1887; she included it instead under Tuesday, March 15.

March 25, 1887   Charlotte inserted in the margin of this entry "Walter goes to club and I write some."